CONTENTS

Acknowledgements	*viii*
Note on editor	*x*
List of contributors	*xi*
1 Introduction: a decade of critical terrorism studies Richard Jackson	1

PART I
Critical approaches to the study of terrorism — 15

2 The emergence of terrorism studies as a field Lisa Stampnitzky	17
3 Critical terrorism studies after 9/11 Lee Jarvis	28
4 The real and the bluff: on the ontology of terrorism Joseba Zulaika	39
5 Critical epistemologies of terrorism James Fitzgerald	49
6 Post-structuralism and constructivism Charlotte Heath-Kelly	60
7 Critical theory and terrorism studies: ethics and emancipation Harmonie Toros	70

| 8 | The historical materialist approach to critical terrorism studies
Douglas Porpora | 80 |
| 9 | Methodology and the critical study of terrorism
Jacob L. Stump | 90 |

PART II
The nature and causes of terrorism — 101

10	The definition of terrorism *Timothy Shanahan*	103
11	The narrative of terrorism as an existential threat *Jessica Wolfendale*	114
12	New versus old terrorism *Alexander Spencer*	124
13	Religion and terrorism *Ioannis Tellidis*	134
14	Female terrorism and militancy *Caron Gentry and Laura Sjoberg*	145

PART III
State terrorism — 157

15	Understanding Western state terrorism *Ruth Blakeley and Sam Raphael*	159
16	Torture *Bob Brecher*	170
17	Rendition in the "war on terror" *Sam Raphael and Ruth Blakeley*	181
18	Targeted killing and drone warfare *Laurie Calhoun*	190

PART IV
Contemporary responses to terrorism — 201

| 19 | The language of counterterrorism
Jack Holland | 203 |

20	Critical evaluation of counterterrorism *Sondre Lindahl*	214
21	A critical perspective on the global war on terror *Paul Rogers*	225
22	The governmentality of terrorism: uncertainty, risk management, and surveillance *Luca Mavelli*	237
23	Radicalization, de-radicalization, and counter-radicalization *Lasse Lindekilde*	248

PART V
Emerging debates — 261

24	Ecoterrorism and expansionary counterterrorism *John Sorenson*	263
25	Media coverage of terrorism *Ben O'Loughlin*	276
26	Collective memory and terrorism *Charlotte Heath-Kelly*	287
27	Terrorism and peace studies *Ioannis Tellidis*	298

Index — *309*

ACKNOWLEDGEMENTS

The critical terrorism studies (CTS) project is a community effort. It would never have gotten off the ground without a great many people who freely gave their time and energy to its core activities and ongoing development. In the beginning, wonderful scholars like Jeroen Gunning, Marie Breen Smyth, Joseba Zulaika, George Kassimeris, Piers Robinson, Paul Rogers, John Mueller, Matt McDonald, David Miller, and many others from the original editorial board of the journal *Critical Studies on Terrorism* came together to give encouragement, suggestions, and creative energy to the initiative. They all worked hard in different ways to ensure the success of the new project, and I thank them for their efforts. Today, a new generation of gifted young scholars, many of whom were influenced by the ideas articulated by the first generation of CTS, and several of whom are contributors to this volume, is taking responsibility for consolidating the field and moving it forward in new and exciting ways. I am always impressed and grateful to the enthusiastic, talented young scholars in the British International Studies Association (BISA) Critical Studies on Terrorism Working Group (CSTWG) for their efforts to put on an annual conference where the latest research is presented, organise a special journal issue, maintain the online network, arrange workshops and seminars, and offer panels for the International Studies Association (ISA) and BISA annual conferences. Going into its second decade, the project is in good hands, for which I am deeply grateful.

Similarly, this volume, which examines the achievements of CTS in its first decade, is a community effort that would not have been possible without the generosity of a great many people. I am deeply grateful to all the contributors who agreed to write for it, in particular those generous individuals who came in at the last moment to fill unexpected gaps. It is extremely gratifying and humbling to see the tremendous achievements made by the wider CTS community over the past decade of research and to have so many outstanding scholars represented in this volume.

I could not have completed this volume without the studious hard work of Sondre Lindahl, the editorial assistant on the project. A talented young scholar in his own right (see his chapter in the volume), he worked steadily and patiently in the near-impossible task of herding 27 academics towards a common goal, and in preparing the chapters for publication. I am sure he will be one of the leading lights in the next generation of CTS scholars.

I am also grateful to the National Centre for Peace and Conflict Studies at the University of Otago, which provides a highly supportive and collegial environment in which to complete a volume like this. My colleagues Kevin Clements, Heather Devere, Charles Butcher, Katerina

ROUTLEDGE HANDBOOK OF CRITICAL TERRORISM STUDIES

This new handbook is a comprehensive collection of cutting-edge essays that investigate the contribution of critical terrorism studies to our understanding of contemporary terrorism and counterterrorism.

Terrorism remains one of the most important security and political issues of our time. After 9/11, critical terrorism studies (CTS) emerged as an alternative approach to the mainstream study of terrorism and counterterrorism, one which combined innovative methods with a searching critique of the abuses of the war on terror. This volume explores the unique contribution of CTS to our understanding of contemporary non-state violence and the state's response to it. It draws together contributions from key thinkers in the field who explore critical questions around the nature and study of terrorism, the causes of terrorism, state terrorism, responses to terrorism, the war on terror, and emerging issues in terrorism research. Covering a wide range of topics, including key debates in the field and emerging issues, the *Routledge Handbook of Critical Terrorism Studies* will set a benchmark for future research on terrorism and the response to it.

This handbook will be of great interest to students of terrorism studies, political violence, critical security studies, and IR in general.

Richard Jackson is Professor of Peace Studies and Director of the National Centre for Peace and Conflict Studies, University of Otago, New Zealand. He is the Editor-in-Chief of the journal *Critical Studies on Terrorism* and author of numerous titles, including most recently *Confessions of a Terrorist* (2014), *Contemporary Debates on Terrorism* (co-edited, Routledge, 2012) and *Terrorism: A Critical Introduction* (co-authored, 2011).

ROUTLEDGE HANDBOOK OF CRITICAL TERRORISM STUDIES

Edited by Richard Jackson

LONDON AND NEW YORK

First published 2016
by Routledge
2 Park Square, Milton Park, Abingdon, Oxon OX14 4RN

and by Routledge
711 Third Avenue, New York, NY 10017

First issued in paperback 2018

Routledge is an imprint of the Taylor & Francis Group, an informa business

© 2016 selection and editorial material, Richard Jackson; individual chapters, the contributors

The right of the editor to be identified as the author of the editorial material, and of the authors for their individual chapters, has been asserted in accordance with sections 77 and 78 of the Copyright, Designs and Patents Act 1988.

All rights reserved. No part of this book may be reprinted or reproduced or utilised in any form or by any electronic, mechanical, or other means, now known or hereafter invented, including photocopying and recording, or in any information storage or retrieval system, without permission in writing from the publishers.

Trademark notice: Product or corporate names may be trademarks or registered trademarks, and are used only for identification and explanation without intent to infringe.

British Library Cataloguing-in-Publication Data
A catalogue record for this book is available from the British Library

Library of Congress Cataloging-in-Publication Data
Names: Jackson, Richard, 1966– editor.
Title: Routledge handbook of critical terrorism studies / edited by Richard Jackson.
Other titles: Critical terrorism studies
Description: New York : Routledge, 2016. | Includes bibliographical references and index.
Identifiers: LCCN 2015041527 | ISBN 9780415743761 (hardback) | ISBN 9781315813462 (ebook)
Subjects: LCSH: Terrorism—Research. | Terrorism—Political aspects—Research.
Classification: LCC HV6431 .R68 2016 | DDC 363.325—dc23
LC record available at http://lccn.loc.gov/2015041527

ISBN 13: 978-1-138-60114-7 (pbk)
ISBN 13: 978-0-415-74376-1 (hbk)

Typeset in Bembo
by Apex CoVantage, LLC

Acknowledgements

Standish, Sung Yong Lee, and Patrik Johansson and the Centre's erstwhile administrator, Rosemary McBryde, all have my deep thanks for their friendship, forbearance, and support. I am also thankful to my always-enthusiastic students, especially those in my critical terrorism studies course, who have asked questions and intelligently discussed the issues covered in this volume, thereby shaping and sharpening it in a multitude of ways over the past few years.

The professional team at Routledge, especially the advice and support of Andrew Humphrys, has, as always, been crucial to the success of this project. I am especially grateful for their patience while I tried to finish the volume while juggling the many balls thrown up by being Centre Director.

Finally, as always, I am eternally grateful to Michelle Jackson for her unfailing support of my work and her deep belief in what I am trying to do. All this effort would be meaningless without her.

NOTE ON EDITOR

Richard Jackson is Professor of Peace Studies and acting Director of The National Centre for Peace and Conflict Studies, University of Otago, New Zealand. He held previous academic positions at the University of Manchester and Aberystwyth University. He is the founding editor and current Editor-in-Chief of the journal *Critical Studies on Terrorism*, the editor of the Routledge Critical Terrorism Studies Book Series, and the author or editor of, among others, the following books: *Contemporary Debates on Terrorism* (Routledge, 2012; co-edited with Justin Sinclair); *Terrorism: A Critical Introduction* (Palgrave-Macmillan, 2011; co-authored with Lee Jarvis, Jeroen Gunning, and Marie Breen Smyth); *Contemporary State Terrorism: Theory and Cases* (2010, Routledge; co-edited with Eamon Murphy and Scott Poynting); *Critical Terrorism Studies: A New Research Agenda* (2009, Routledge; co-edited with Marie Breen Smyth and Jeroen Gunning); and *Writing the War on Terrorism: Language, Politics and Counterterrorism* (2005, Manchester University Press). His most recent book is a research-based novel entitled *Confessions of a Terrorist* (2014, Zed).

CONTRIBUTORS

Ruth Blakeley is Professor in International Relations at the University of Kent and Co-Director of The Rendition Project (www.therenditionproject.org.uk). Her research focuses on the use of state violence, particularly by liberal democratic states. She is the author of *State Terrorism and Neoliberalism* (Routledge, 2009), and she has published widely on torture, state violence, and human rights. As Co-Director of The Rendition Project, she has worked closely with a range of NGOs and legal teams to investigate and understand the contours of the CIA's torture programme. She was an academic advisor to John Pilger for his documentary film, *War on Democracy*.

Bob Brecher is Professor of Moral Philosophy at the University of Brighton, UK; Director of its Centre for Applied Philosophy, Politics & Ethics; and Co-Director of its violent conflict research cluster. He has published on moral theory, applied ethics and politics, health care and medical ethics, sexual politics, terror, and the politics of higher education. A past president of the Association for Legal & Social Philosophy, he is also on the board of a number of academic journals, as well as a contributor to popular publications. He rejects any clear divide between academic work and activism: the purpose of the academy is to make the world a better place.

Laurie Calhoun is the author of *We Kill Because We Can: From Soldiering to Assassination in the Drone Age* (Zed Books, 2015) and *War and Delusion: A Critical Examination* (Palgrave Macmillan, 2013). She has also published a book of metaphilosophy and dozens of essays, including book chapters. Calhoun participated in a multi-year international project group on Human Security and Peacebuilding (sponsored by the Japan Foundation) and has given presentations and served on panels at International Studies Association conferences. She is currently exploring the topic of tyranny in an experimental work of creative nonfiction, "The Tyrant's Secret."

James Fitzgerald is Lecturer in Terrorism Studies at the School of Law and Government, Dublin City University, and the co-convenor of the Critical Studies on Terrorism Working Group (CSTWG). His current research interests include everyday resistances to (counter) terrorism, discourse analysis of the primary statements of al Qaeda and the Islamic State (IS), post-foundational politics, and exploring (in)orthodoxies of "academic writing" and the types of knowledge produced thereof.

Contributors

Caron Gentry is a Lecturer within the School of International Relations at the University of St. Andrews. Her work has focused on gender and terrorism for over a decade, and her current book, *Offering Hospitality: Questioning Christian Approaches to War* (Notre Dame, 2013), is a feminist political theology on war. Drawing upon both feminist theory and gender studies, as well as political theory, Caron is currently pursuing a research agenda that examines women's everyday insecurities in the West and how these impact and are impacted by international security.

Charlotte Heath-Kelly is Assistant Professor of Politics and International Studies at the University of Warwick. She currently holds an ESRC Future Research Leaders fellowship to investigate the reconstruction of post-terrorist space. Her research has appeared in journals including *Security Dialogue*, *Politics*, *The British Journal of Politics and IR*, and *Critical Studies on Terrorism*. She has also published a monograph which was shortlisted for the 2014 Susan Strange Book Prize, titled *Politics of Violence: Militancy, International Politics, Killing in the Name* (Routledge, 2013). Together with Lee Jarvis and Christopher Baker-Beall, she has edited two books (*Counter-Radicalisation: Critical Perspectives*, Routledge, 2014; *Neoliberalism and Terror: Critical Engagements*, Routledge, 2015) and two special issues of the journal *Critical Studies on Terrorism*.

Jack Holland is Associate Professor in International Security at University of Leeds. He is the author of *Selling the War on Terror* (Routledge, 2013), co-author of *Security: A Critical Introduction* (Palgrave, 2014), and co-editor of *Obama's Foreign Policy* (Routledge, 2013). His work critically analyses US, UK, and Australian foreign and security policy. He has recently published in *European Journal of International Relations*, *International Political Sociology*, *Millennium Journal of International Studies*, *British Journal of Politics and International Relations*, *Intervention and Statebuilding*, *Australian Journal of Political Science*, *Critical Studies on Security*, and *Critical Studies on Terrorism*.

Lee Jarvis is a Reader in International Security at the University of East Anglia, UK. His work on the politics of terrorism, counterterrorism, and security has been published in journals, including *Millennium: Journal of International Studies*, *Security Dialogue*, *Political Studies*, *Terrorism & Political Violence*, and *Critical Studies on Terrorism*. His recent books include *Security: A Critical Introduction* (Palgrave, 2015, with Jack Holland), *Counter-Radicalisation: Critical Perspectives* (Routledge, 2015, edited with Christopher Baker-Beall and Charlotte Heath-Kelly), and *Critical Perspectives on Counter-terrorism* (Routledge, 2015, edited with Michael Lister), *Anti-terrorism, Citizenship and Security* (Manchester University Press, 2015, with Michael Lister) and *Terrorism Online: Politics, Law and Technology* (Routledge, 2015, co-edited with Stuart Macdonald and Tom Chen). He is co-director of the multidisciplinary Cyberterrorism Project and runs the critical global politics research group at the University of East Anglia.

Sondre Lindahl is a PhD Candidate at the National Centre for Peace and Conflict Studies at the University of Otago, New Zealand. His main research interests are terrorism, counterterrorism, and critical security studies. His doctoral project focuses on an analysis of Norway's approach to counterterrorism following the Breivik attack. He is a regular commentator in the Norwegian media on issues of security and terrorism and is the assistant editor of this handbook.

Lasse Lindekilde is Associate Professor in the Department of Political Science, Aarhus University, where he teaches political sociology and methodology. Lasse received his PhD from the European University Institute, Florence (2008), for a dissertation on the mobilization and claims-making of Danish Muslims in reaction to the publication of the Muhammad cartoons. His recent research has focused on violent radicalization and the design, implementation, and effects of counter-radicalization policies in northwestern Europe. He has conducted field-based research on mechanisms of radicalization and the impact of counter-radicalization policies on target group perceptions and identity formation, assessing the risk of negative, unintended consequences of policy implementation. Between August 2014 and August 2015 he was a Visiting Fellow at the Department of Communication, University of California Santa Barbara, where he conducted experimental research on the effects of small-group deliberation on the radicalization of attitudes and action preparedness. Dr. Lindekilde has published several international journal articles which have appeared in, for example, *International Journal of Conflict and Violence, Journal of Ethnic and Migration Studies, European Journal of Criminal Policy and Research*, and *Critical Studies on Terrorism*.

Luca Mavelli is Senior Lecturer in Politics and International Relations at the University of Kent, UK. His research lies at the intersection of biopolitics, security and secularism. He is the author of *Europe's Encounter with Islam: The Secular and the Postsecular* (Routledge, 2012), and has co-edited *The Postsecular in International Relations* (2012 Special Issue of the *Review of International Studies*), *Towards a Postsecular International Politics: New Forms of Community, Identity, and Power* (Palgrave, 2014), and *The Refugee Crisis and Religion: Secularism, Security and Hospitality in Question* (Rowman and Littlefield, forthcoming 2016). His articles have appeared in the *European Journal of International Relations, Review of International Studies, Security Dialogue, Millennium, International Politics, Critical Studies on Terrorism, Journal of Religion in Europe*, and *Teaching in Higher Education*.

Ben O'Loughlin is Professor of International Relations and Co-Director of the New Political Communication Unit at Royal Holloway, University of London. He is Co-Editor of the journal *Media, War & Conflict*. His latest book is *Forging the World: Strategic Narratives and International Relations* (University of Michigan Press, 2016, with Alister Miskimmon and Laura Roselle).

Douglas Porpora is a Professor of Sociology at Drexel University, USA. In addition to working on social theory and terrorism, he writes on other macro-moral issues like war, genocide, torture, and human trafficking. Among his books on these topics are *How Holocausts Happen: The United States in Central America* (Temple, 1992) and *Post-Ethical Society: The Iraq War, Abu Ghraib, and the Moral Failure of the Secular* (Chicago, 2013). Despite the dismal issues that seem to draw him, Porpora is reported to have a positive disposition. His newest book is *Reconstructing Sociology: The Critical Realist Approach* (Cambridge, 2015).

Sam Raphael is Senior Lecturer in International Relations at the University of Westminster and Co-Director of The Rendition Project (www.therenditionproject.org.uk). His research focuses on the intersection between US foreign policy, human rights, and counterterrorism. He has published in the field of critical terrorism studies on the topics of terrorism "expertise," Colombian state terror, and torture in the "war on terror." As Co-Director of The Rendition Project, he has worked closely with a range of NGOs and legal teams to investigate and understand the contours of the CIA's torture programme. He has also published work focusing on the intersections between US energy security, global oil supplies, and human rights, and he is co-author of *Global Energy Security and American Hegemony* (Johns Hopkins University Press, 2010).

Paul Rogers worked originally in the biological and environmental sciences, including lecturing at Imperial College and working in East Africa, but he has worked for the past 35 years on international security. He is Professor of Peace Studies at Bradford University and a Consultant to the Oxford Research Group, an independent UK think tank, writes on international security issues for www.opendemocracy.net, and is a frequent broadcaster. His forthcoming book, *Irregular War*, will be published by I. B. Taurus early in 2016.

Timothy Shanahan is Professor of Philosophy at Loyola Marymount University, Los Angeles, California, USA. He is the author of *Reason and Insight: Western and Eastern Perspectives on the Pursuit of Moral Wisdom* (Wadsworth, 2003), *The Evolution of Darwinism: Selection, Adaptation, and Progress in Evolutionary Biology* (Cambridge University Press, 2004), *Philosophy 9/11: Thinking About the War on Terrorism* (Open Court, 2005), *The Provisional Irish Republican Army and the Morality of Terrorism* (Edinburgh University Press, 2009), and *Philosophy and Blade Runner* (Palgrave Macmillan, 2014).

Laura Sjoberg is Associate Professor of Political Science with a courtesy affiliation in Women's Studies and Gender Research at the University of Florida, USA. Her research on gender and international security has been published in more than three dozen journals in political science, international relations, and gender studies. She is the author or editor of nine books, most recently, *Gendering Global Conflict: Toward a Feminist Theory of War* (Columbia University Press, 2013) and *Gender, War and Conflict* (Polity Press, 2014). Dr. Sjoberg is the home-base editor of the *International Feminist Journal of Politics* and the 2015–2015 Vice President of the International Studies Association.

John Sorenson is Professor of Sociology at Brock University, St. Catharine's, Canada. He teaches courses on nonhuman animals and human society and corporate globalization. His past research focused on war, nationalism, and refugees, and he was active in Third World solidarity groups and in relief work in the Horn of Africa with the Eritrean Relief Association. Recent books include *Critical Animal Studies: Thinking the Unthinkable* and *Defining Critical Animal Studies: An Intersectional Social Justice Approach for Liberation*. His current projects include a book about ecoterrorism and the repression of dissent, a book about canid-human relations, an edited volume on critical animal studies, and research on wildlife in Asia.

Alexander Spencer is Associate Professor at the Ludwig-Maximilians-University in Munich, Germany. His research centres on the potential of constructivist international relations theory for the field of terrorism research. His work has been published in journals such as *Foreign Policy Analysis, Security Dialogue, International Studies Perspectives*, and *Critical Studies on Terrorism*. He has published a book titled *The Tabloid Terrorist* (Palgrave, 2010) and co-edited a volume with Judith Renner, *Reconciliation after Terrorism* (Routledge, 2012).

Lisa Stampnitzky is Lecturer in Social Studies at Harvard University, and she earned her PhD in Sociology at the University of California, Berkeley, USA. She is the author of *Disciplining Terror: How Experts Invented "Terrorism"* (Cambridge University Press, 2013), which has been awarded the Social Science History Association's President's Book Award, the Francesco Guicciardini Prize for Best Book in Historical International Relations, and the International Political Sociology Book Award from the International Studies Association. Her current book project, *How Torture Became Speakable,* analyses the public justification of human rights violations in the war on terror.

Jacob L. Stump is Assistant Professor of Political Science at Shepherd University. His primary research focus is on stories about terrorism and how those stories shape peoples' conduct. Most recently, he is co-editor with Priya Dixit of the book *Critical Studies on Terrorism* (Routledge, 2015).

Contributors

Ioannis Tellidis is Assistant Professor of International Relations at the College of International Studies, Kyung Hee University, South Korea, and Associate Editor of the journal *Peacebuilding*. His interests include terrorism and political violence, peace and conflict studies, technology and peacebuilding, and the effects of the emergence of new international actors. He is co-editor of *Researching Terrorism, Peace and Conflict: Interaction, Synthesis and Opposition* (Routledge, 2015) and *Terrorism, Peace and Conflict Studies: Investigating the Crossroad* (Routledge, 2014, both with Harmonie Toros), and his research has been published in *Critical Studies on Terrorism, Global Governance, International Studies Review, Peace Review*, and *Terrorism and Political Violence*.

Harmonie Toros is Senior Lecturer in International Conflict Analysis at the University of Kent, UK. Her research lies at the crossroads between conflict resolution and terrorism studies. She has published works developing a critical theory-based approach to terrorism and examining the transformation of conflicts marked by terrorist violence. Following a BA in Contemporary History (Sussex) and a Maîtrise in History (Paris IV-Sorbonne), she worked as reporter and editor for major international news agencies (The Associated Press and Agence France-Presse) for eight years in Turkey, Italy, France, and the United States before returning to academia in 2003. She completed her PhD at the Department of International Politics of Aberystwyth University in 2010. She is the author of *Terrorism, Talking and Transformation: A Critical Approach* (Routledge, 2012) and an Associate Editor of the journal *Critical Studies on Terrorism*.

Jessica Wolfendale is Associate Professor of Philosophy at West Virginia University, USA. She is the author of *Torture and the Military Profession* (Palgrave-Macmillan, 2007) and co-editor of *New Wars and New Soldiers: Military Ethics in the Contemporary World* (Ashgate, 2012). She has written extensively on terrorism, military ethics, and the ethics of torture, and her research has been published in *Studies in Conflict and Terrorism, Ethics and International Affairs, Social Theory and Practice,* and *The Journal of Military Ethics*.

Joseba Zulaika is an anthropologist (Princeton, 1982) working at the Center for Basque Studies, University of Nevada, Reno, US. He is the author of *Basque Violence: Metaphor and Sacrament* (University of Nevada Press, 1984), *Terror and Taboo: The Follies, Fables, and Faces of Terrorism* (Routledge, 1996, with William Douglass), and *Terrorism: The Self-Fulfilling Prophecy* (University of Chicago Press, 2009).

1
INTRODUCTION
A decade of critical terrorism studies

Richard Jackson

A series of high-profile terrorism attacks, as well as international concern about the military successes and social media activities of Islamic State (IS) in Syria and Iraq, means that fourteen years after the beginning of the global "war on terror," academic, media, and political interest in terrorism and counterterrorism remain as high as they have ever been. Since that momentous day in September 2001, terrorism – and the global response to it – has taken on a prominent role in foreign and security policy, policing, intelligence gathering, lawmaking, immigration, banking, homeland security, the news media, art, literature and movies, international relations, and academic research, among a multitude of other aspects of social, economic, political, and cultural life. In fact, in many respects, terrorism – or more accurately, the response to it – has become the fulcrum for a series of deep and profound transformations in the processes of international relations, the conduct of the state, culture and society, and the subjectivity of the citizen-subject. The rise and consolidation of the new academic field of critical terrorism studies (CTS) have been parts of this social history since 2001.

As I have analysed elsewhere (Jackson 2015a), serious discussions about developing an explicitly "critical" academic approach to terrorism research similar to what occurred in critical security studies (CSS) began in late 2004. Motivated in part by deep dismay at the Abu Ghraib scandal in April 2004 and what it revealed about the nature of the war on terror and counterterrorism more generally, and based on an earlier literature critical of the so-called terrorism industry (see Chomsky 1979; Herman 1982; Herman and O'Sullivan 1989; George 1991) which seemed particularly relevant in the post-9/11 context, discussions between myself, Marie Breen Smyth, Jeroen Gunning, and others led to the organisation of a small conference at the University of Manchester in 2006 titled "Is it time for a critical terrorism studies?" From this humble beginning, an expanding group of scholars went on to establish the BISA Critical Studies on Terrorism Working Group (CSTWG); a new peer-reviewed academic journal titled *Critical Studies on Terrorism*; a series of publications outlining what we thought the CTS approach was and what it ought to focus on (see Jackson 2007; Gunning 2007a; Jackson, Breen Smyth, and Gunning 2009); a dedicated CTS book series published by Routledge; numerous conference panels, papers, seminars, and workshops; the establishment of an annual CSTWG conference; and eventually, a CTS textbook for teaching purposes (Jackson, Jarvis, Gunning, and Breen Smyth 2011), among other related activities.

In the first decade of its existence as an identifiable subfield, CTS has chalked up a number of quite important achievements, a few of which I will mention here. First, building on a number of other previous and contemporaneous assessments (see Stohl 1979; Schmid and Jongman 1988; Zulaika and Douglass 1996; Reid 1997; Silke 2004; Ranstorp 2006), the CTS project has witnessed an expanded and deepened discussion about terrorism studies as a field of research, teaching, and public engagement – including discussions about its conditions of possibility, its ontology and epistemology, its knowledge-production and disciplinary practices, its relationship to political power, its experts and expertise, and so on. In this respect, it can be argued that CTS has strengthened the wider field's reflexivity and heightened its self-consciousness about the labels, definitions, categories, assumptions, values, theories, approaches, institutional relationships, and media biases which are central to its knowledge practices and institutions.

Second, CTS has succeeded in opening up, and in other cases widening and deepening, key debates in the field about the nature and definition of terrorism, the use of the "terrorist" label and the language of terrorism, the terrorism taboo and the need for more primary research, the silence on state terrorism, the exaggeration of the terrorism threat, the evaluation of counter-terrorism and the war on terror, the normative dimension of terrorism research, the gendered aspect of terrorism research, and other key issues (see Jackson and Sinclair 2012). It is reasonable to suggest that many of these subjects would have remained relatively unacknowledged or underdiscussed in the field's journals, publications, and meetings without their highlighting by CTS scholars and activities.

Third, CTS scholarship has played an important role in bringing the kinds of social theory and foundational debates which international relations and other social science fields engaged in much earlier into the terrorism studies field. Before the emergence of CTS, with only a few exceptions (see, for example, Zulaika and Douglass 1996), it was nearly impossible to find within terrorism studies journals, publications, or conferences any serious discussion of ontology, epistemology, methodology, and praxis, and the vast majority of terrorism scholars did not engage with, or utilise in any systematic way, any alternative theoretical approaches such as constructivism, critical theory, post-structuralism, feminist theory, post-colonialism, and the like. It is in part due to CTS that increasing numbers of publications within the field now engage seriously with social theory and exhibit a pluralisation of methodological and epistemological approaches in their research (see Jackson 2012).

Fourth, CTS has succeeded in establishing itself as a unique and recognisable approach within the broader security and terrorism studies fields. That is, CTS is now recognised for its particular critical theory-influenced ontology, its epistemological concerns, its methodological pluralism, its scepticism towards official counterterrorism culture and practice, and its sustained normative critique of the war on terror and Western counterterrorism practices. This distinctive approach has provided a vocabulary and a set of theoretical tools and assumptions for scholars wanting to study terrorism and counterterrorism from a post-positivist, normatively inspired perspective. It has proved to be particularly inspirational for many young scholars who have come to terrorism studies in the years after 9/11 when the war on terror had already been embedded and normalised in politics, academia, and society.

Fifth, CTS has played a not unsubstantial role in reinvigorating the serious academic study of state terrorism (see Blakeley 2007, 2009; Jackson, Murphy, and Poynting 2010; Jarvis and Lister 2014). Prior to the emergence of CTS, with only a few notable exceptions that were in any case largely ignored by the orthodox terrorism studies field (see Stohl and Lopez 1984, 1986; George 1991; Oliverio 1998), state terrorism was notable by its absence in the field's journals, publications, and conferences (see Silke 2004; Jackson 2008; Raphael 2009, 2010). As a consequence, it was generally taken for granted that any discussion of "terrorism" referred exclusively to non-state actors. Today, partly as a result of CTS, it is normal to specify whether one is referring to state or non-state terrorism and to refer to the growing literature on state terrorism.

Finally, as it has been institutionalised and established through the BISA working group, the journal, book series, textbook, and so on, CTS has provided a recognised and legitimate intellectual "home" for critically oriented scholars who wish to engage in terrorism-related research but who perhaps feel uncomfortable being associated with what they perceive as the orthodox, state-centric, and state-supportive "terrorism industry." The word *critical* in front of *terrorism studies* therefore provides a psychologically reassuring and professionally legitimate identity with an identifiable community of scholars and an accompanying set of activities. It also provides a set of resources for both teaching and research and a pathway for professional development and advancement.

The aim of this volume is to provide an overview and assessment of some of the main areas of interest and concern to CTS and scholars associated with the CTS project and to outline some of the key findings and issues identified thus far in research on these topics. In addition to providing a kind of state-of-the-art snapshot, the volume highlights some key areas and topics for research in the coming decades of CTS.

Outline of the volume

Critical approaches to the study of terrorism

The number and scope of the issues examined in this volume preclude a comprehensive description of each chapter in this brief introduction. Instead, I will seek to provide a general overview and discussion of the main themes, issues, approaches, findings, and lines of debate in each main section. Part I of the volume examines some of the central themes and issues raised within CTS over the past ten years about how we study terrorism. Rooted in the critical theory-inspired axiom that all theory is from somewhere and for someone (see Cox 1986), and that we ought to therefore be reflexive about both the context in which our research emerges and the impact that it can have on people and society, this section first of all explores where terrorism studies – and later, critical terrorism studies – came from and how this has affected its subsequent development. These early chapters reveal that the material and discursive origins of terrorism studies in cold war counter-insurgency research, as well as the impact of 9/11, continue to influence the focus and direction of the broader field, particularly in terms of its state centricity and its thorny relationship to state security, its struggle to create a bounded academic field with accepted professional standards for expertise, and its ongoing crisis of knowledge (see Zulaika 2012; Stampnitzky 2013; Frank 2014; Jackson 2015b).

The other chapters in this section focus on some of the perennial concerns of CTS about ontology, epistemology, methodology, and approach within terrorism studies. They reveal first of all that, building on important earlier literature (see, for example, Gold-Biss 1994; Zulaika and Douglass 1996), CTS scholars have made some significant interventions in clearly articulating the different ways in which *terrorism* is a socially constructed category or signifier without any essential ontological content and some of the implications this has for gathering knowledge about it and for responding to acts of violence which have been labelled as *terrorism*. They also reveal that a much clearer picture is starting to emerge about the value and advantages of employing different methodological approaches based on different ontologies and epistemologies – such as neo-positivist, reflexivist, relational, and critical realist approaches – in terrorism-related research (see Dixit and Stump 2016; Stump, this volume). These chapters also explain why it is so important to pay close attention to issues of ontology, epistemology, and methodology, namely because different approaches determine what can be known about terrorism and how we can know them.

Importantly, the chapters in this section highlight some of the ways in which there are useful complementarities in the knowledge produced by different approaches, deep differences in ontology notwithstanding. For example, constructivist and post-structuralist-based studies on the discourse of the war on terror have revealed a great deal about the ideational and discursive structures and mechanisms of contemporary counterterrorism. These studies, far from being antithetical to, are complemented by critical theory-inspired and historical-materialist analyses of the geo-political and economic interests and processes which are evident in the war on terror. Putting these different critical analyses together reveals the war on terror to be a historical phase of neoliberal capitalist expansion led by the hegemonic geostrategic impulses of the United States which, in a dialectical process, both reflects and co-constructs a broader legitimising discourse of counterterrorism based on notions of Western exceptionalism, civilisational struggle, and risk management. In this way, positivist and post-positivist critical approaches work together to paint a rich picture of the historical epoch we inhabit and provide us with something of a "history of the present."

However, in addition to the achievements of CTS thus far, the chapters in this section also remind us that there remains a great deal left for critically oriented scholars to do. For example, much of the discourse analytic research in CTS has focused on Western states – their leaders, media, public, experts, and so on – while much less research has focused on the discourses of the "terrorist" groups and their supporters. In terms of methodology, this speaks to the frequently noted need for more research directly with terrorists and militants, in order to better understand their subjectivity and worldviews. Although extremely challenging, particularly in the current global context, such research is eminently possible, as some notable studies demonstrate (see, for example, Mahmood 1996; Gunning 2007b). Similarly, from a normative perspective, while critical theory-inspired research has focused on the critique of counterterrorism and the state's responses to terrorism, much less effort has been put into exploring how ethics and emancipation apply to the actions and intentions of terrorist groups.

The nature and causes of terrorism

Part II on the nature and causes of terrorism includes chapters on the perennial question of how to define *terrorism,* the reality and assessment of the terrorist threat, the question of whether there is a "new" kind of terrorism, the related question of whether religion is a cause of contemporary forms of terrorism, and the perennially underexamined gender dimension to terrorism and how we understand it. On these issues, CTS has made a number of important interventions in the field, not least in relentlessly critiquing the way in which political leaders and the media have described and exaggerated the threat of terrorism in Western societies and, more importantly, how they have manipulated public fear for political (and material) gain (see Mueller and Stewart 2011, 2012; Jackson 2013). There is little question any more that as a threat to the individual safety of citizens, the Western way of life, or the integrity of the state as an institution, the danger posed by terrorism has been vastly overexaggerated. As a consequence, the response to the threat of terrorism since 9/11 has been one of unnecessary and counterproductive overreaction (Mueller 2006; Zulaika 2009). CTS has been at the forefront of detailing the nature, extent, and consequences of this exaggeration and overreaction, providing important analysis of how it has been leveraged for much more profound and invasive processes of surveillance, securitisation, border management, social control, democratic constriction, neoliberalisation, legal transformation, and exceptional politics.

These chapters also highlight the contribution made by CTS to exposing not only the fallacies of the "new terrorism" thesis, but also the way in which this particular narrative functions to legitimise new, more violent counterterrorism practices such as torture, extrajudicial killings, rendition, and the like, as well as new and more intrusive approaches to policing, militarism, risk management, surveillance, and so on. The chapters also disturb common-sense understandings of the role of religion in contemporary terrorism, again highlighting both the fallacies at the heart of a great deal of academic and political discourse about terrorism, as well as the discursive functions of the religion-terrorism association. For example, one of the main functions of the "religious terrorism" narrative is to de-politicise, as well as de-legitimise and demonise, actors who violently resist Western foreign policy in the Middle East (see Gunning and Jackson 2011).

A very important strand of critical research on terrorism has highlighted both the hidden (or ignored) role of women in militant and counterterrorist groups and the gendered ways in which such involvement is studied and understood. More recently, it has begun to expose the way in which dominant gendered understandings of terrorism function to hide from view and exclude the daily, intimate terror that millions of women face from a violent patriarchal order and the way this undoubtedly *political* violence disempowers its victims further by rendering it as a private sphere violence (see Ortbals and Poloni-Staudinger 2014; Sjoberg and Gentry 2015). Once again, this kind of research is helpful for exposing the way in which the terrorism discourse functions to maintain much broader patriarchal gender relations and discourses in academia and society, to de-politicise the agency and motives of politically violent women, and to prevent the coalescing of a broader emancipatory movement.

On the other hand, and as before, these chapters also draw attention to how much research has yet to be undertaken by critical scholars on issues such as intimate terrorism and the role of religion in resistance movements (see Dunning 2015). In particular, one of the noticeable gaps here is a richer set of CTS-inspired or influenced accounts of the "causes" of terrorism, whether state or non-state, public or private. In part, this failure may be due to the current focus on official responses to terrorism rather than terrorism itself. More likely, it is due to the current predominance of post-positivist approaches in CTS which tend to shy away from making claims about "causes" and causality in social processes. However, this need not be an obstacle, as there are well-developed ways of investigating the antecedents and conditions of social processes which utilise post-positivist ontologies and approaches and which do not go as far as making claims about "causal mechanisms" but nonetheless tell a kind of "causal story" or make a set of contingent "causal inferences" (see Yee 1996; Sandberg 2005; Banta 2012).

For example, there is no reason at all why more critical accounts of the causes of terrorism cannot be made which focus on the structural (ideational, discursive, and material) constitution of group subjectivity and action; or on the dynamic interaction between states, oppressed groups, and violent resistance; or on providing thick descriptions of the history, context, culture, and political dynamics of particular cases, as Joseba Zulaika (1984) has done for Basque terrorism – among others. Similarly, there is a need for more research on the relational interactions between state and non-state actors and, in particular, on the impact of foreign policy in provoking violent resistance in some localities. It is common within CTS to assert a link between coercive and oppressive Western foreign policy and the violent resistance of armed groups, including terrorists; however, there is a pressing need for more systematic empirically based research which demonstrates these kinds of relationships and action-reaction cycles.

State terrorism

Part III of this volume looks at state terrorism, a widely acknowledged gap within the broader security and terrorism fields. The general failure of terrorism studies to study state terrorism is due to a number of factors, including the historical practice of states to exclude their own actions from the definition of terrorism, a practice which many orthodox scholars have chosen to adopt; the origins of the terrorism studies field in counter-insurgency studies and the consequent construction of non-state terrorism as a security "problem" in need of solving through coordinated academic research and counterterrorist practice; the state's funding of much terrorism research; the broader role of the university as a system-maintaining institution; academic socialisation and training practices in the field; the values of terrorism scholars; and the like. As a consequence, orthodox terrorism scholars tend to either reject the notion of state terrorism altogether or to argue that its inclusion would be too inflationary and would distort the present study of non-state terrorism. Critical scholars, on the other hand, tend to accept that states can be terrorists, too, and assume that there are both analytical and normative reasons for documenting, studying, and better understanding how states use terror-directed violence for political purposes. At the very least, critical scholars suggest that many acts of non-state terrorism can be best understood in relation to, and as a reaction to, state terrorism.

The chapters in this section focus on the long history of Western state terrorism and the practices of torture, rendition, and targeted killing which have become prominent in the counterterrorism practices of many states in the war on terror period. The critical research highlighted in these chapters has been extremely important for detailing and explicating the deeply unethical and immoral nature of these practices, as well as their dubious legality, their ineffectiveness in reducing terrorism and their counterproductivity, their deleterious effects on accepted norms and the legal order, their regional instability-generating effects, and so on. At the very least, research such as that done by The Rendition Project (see Raphael and Blakeley, this volume) has provided a strong evidentiary base for knowing about activities that states have tried to hide and deny the existence of. This has enabled human rights activists, lawyers, and the victims of abuses to pursue justice and discover the truth, as well as scholars and journalists to better understand the processes, causes, and consequences of state terrorism. Similarly, critical research has played an important analytical and normative role in debunking justificatory narratives, such as the "ticking bomb scenario," which are used by state officials and their academic apologists to justify torture practices.

At the same time, these chapters reveal that there is still a great deal to do in this area; notwithstanding an earlier generation of outstanding research on Western state terrorism during the Cold War (see Chomsky 1979; Stohl and Lopez 1984, 1986; George 1991), we have really only begun to scratch the surface in terms of excavating the nature, types, causes, and consequences of contemporary state terrorism, and there are, in my view, too few scholars currently working on the topic. This may in part be due to the considerable, but not insurmountable, challenges involved in researching state terrorism, which include the secrecy often involved in such actions and the efforts states put into concealing their violent activities, the complexity of state structures and processes (see Jarvis and Lister 2014), the lack of research support for projects into the terroristic activities of Western states and their allies, and the sheer volume of state violence which may need to be included.

As I have argued before (see Jackson, Murphy, and Poynting 2010), there are analytical and normative reasons to dedicate research efforts to the study of state terrorism. In the first place, our understanding of terrorism as a mode of contentious politics and a political phenomenon is enhanced through understanding the way in which terrorism was first employed by states, the way in which non-state actors sought to (and continue to seek to) imitate state practices of violence, and the way in which non-state terrorism is in many localities directly linked to state terrorism. Second, there is a clear normative value in scrutinising state violence to determine if it is terroristic, because terroristic state violence will most certainly be illegitimate, illegal under international law, and unethical. Moreover, the "terrorism" label now has the legal and normative power to induce behavioural change. If, through careful academic research and its public dissemination, states could be forced to limit their violence to practices that do not cross over into terrorism, this would be a positive step forward for many victims, although it would of course still leave other forms of state violence in need of addressing.

To this end, it is my belief that there is a need for, along with more detailed case studies of both contemporary and historic state terrorism, the construction of a public multidimensional database on state terrorism, perhaps starting with the war on terror period. I have outlined elsewhere how this project might be realised (Jackson 2010), and Blakeley and Raphael's Rendition Project provides an exemplary example of how it could be done. There is also more research to be done on the causes of state terrorism and the conditions under which democratic states, in particular, choose to engage in terrorism and how they convince their publics to tolerate it. We also do not yet understand how and why states end their use of terrorism and the most effective ways of forcing them to do so. Finally, there are one or two cases where research into state terrorism remains taboo. Israeli state terrorism, for example, despite it clearly falling under the definition of *state terrorism* and there being a wealth of cases and instances to examine, remains with only a few exceptions (see, for example, Nasr 2010) scandalously underresearched. Notwithstanding the documented risks to scholars of publishing research critical of Israel, there are strong analytical and normative reasons for systematic research into the causes, nature, effects, and efforts to counter Israeli state terrorism. Such a study would tell us a great deal about why and how states employ terrorism, as well as why Palestinian resistance has also employed terrorist tactics.

Contemporary responses to terrorism

Part IV turns attention to the analysis of counterterrorism and the war on terror. It includes chapters on the counterterrorism approach of Western states, the military dimension of the global war on terror, mass surveillance, and the increasingly prominent issue of de-radicalisation. A key finding here, one most strongly articulated by CTS, is that Western counterterrorism approaches and practices are constituted in and through the discourses of counterterrorism that are employed to explain and justify them. That is, the language of terrorism and counterterrorism employed, particularly by elites after 9/11, has both legitimised the approach taken to domestic and international audiences and shaped the approach itself by determining its internal logic and acceptable limits. Moreover, this has occurred in contingent and contextual ways in different localities: the way in which US elites have constructed, explained, and enacted their counterterrorism practices has differed in culturally and politically expedient ways from the approaches taken by elites in the UK, Australia, and elsewhere (see, for example, Holland 2012).

In addition, critical research in this area has greatly helped us to better understand how domestic counterterrorism practices have been grafted onto, or have had grafted onto them, techniques of neoliberal governmentality through mass surveillance and public monitoring, biopolitical controls and practices, risk management, securitisation practices, urban architecture and design, and counter-radicalisation and de-radicalisation programmes, among others. In particular, a sophisticated literature has emerged detailing the centrality of counterterrorism (or employing counterterrorism as the primary justification) to population control measures which are intended to police risky subjects and bodies, maintain borders, control and direct political dissent, protect the consumer culture, and construct particular types of neoliberal subjectivity. This literature demonstrates that counterterrorism and the war on terror are now deeply entwined with the state and neoliberal capitalism. It may even be the case that the counterterrorism and security sector has staved off the worst effects of the 2008 global financial crisis (see Boukalas 2015).

One of the most vibrant and expansive areas of critical research in recent years has focused on the analysis and evaluation of state-led de-radicalisation approaches. There is now a rich literature, much of it from CTS scholars, which has critically deconstructed the diagnostic framework of "radicalisation" and the often flawed policies it has resulted in. Rooted in systematic empirical research, as well as careful case study and discourse analytic work, this literature reveals how the radicalisation approach frequently misdiagnoses the reasons for violent acts, fails to prevent acts of terrorism, constructs "suspect communities" and risky subjects, produces false positives and violates human rights, feeds grievances, fuels fear and misperception, attempts to construct a particular neoliberal subjectivity among targeted groups, and may even be a source of violent radicalisation itself. Given how counter-radicalisation has expanded to become one of the central processes of domestic counterterrorism, the resources poured into it, and its spread into more and more areas of social life, this literature provides a crucial foundation for further research, critique, and resistance.

The global war on terror has also been the focus of a great deal of critical analysis in CTS. This literature has been important for revealing the origins of the war on terror and its continuities with earlier military-based responses to terrorism and for documenting and assessing the depth, breadth, and profound impacts it has had over the past fourteen years on international relations, international law, human rights, regional stability, peace processes, international development, military cooperation, development, and many more.

More importantly, this literature has clearly demonstrated that by every reasonable measure, the war on terror has been a complete failure and a colossal waste of lives and resources (see Buckley and Singh 2006; Cole 2007). Resulting in more than a million casualties in two major wars and numerous other smaller military interventions, it has multiplied al Qaeda spin-offs, spawned new groups such as Islamic State, destabilised regions like the Middle East, undermined a number of ongoing peace processes, increased levels of militarisation, undermined the global human rights regime, elevated levels of anti-Americanism, and increased levels of terrorist activity in some areas, among others. It has, in fact, become a self-fulfilling prophesy (Zulaika 2009). Sadly, the war on terror shows little sign of ending; in fact, like the Cold War before it, it is now deeply embedded in US and world politics and is a self-sustaining structure (Jackson 2011, 2014a).

On the other hand, these chapters highlight some of the areas where more in-depth research on the war on terror and counterterrorism is still required. For example, it is clear that while the discursive construction and basis of post-9/11 counterterrorism has been very well researched (see Jackson 2016), with some notable exceptions, there is a dearth of research inspired by historical-materialist approaches which could tell us about the material and geo-strategic interests that have driven contemporary counterterrorism and the war on terror. It seems clear that the war on terror and many aspects of contemporary counterterrorism policy directly benefit Western nations, help to sustain the existing international hierarchical order, and reinforce US and Western hegemony, but more research is needed to flesh out these aspects and processes.

Similarly, there is clearly a need for more research on the effectiveness and legitimacy of non-violent, peaceful forms of counterterrorism, such as dialogue and negotiations, political reforms and concessions, dealing with grievances, and the like. While there is a small but important literature on the effectiveness of dialogue in reducing terrorism (see Goertzig 2010; Toros 2012) and a very large literature on negotiation and mediation in armed conflict, there is nonetheless a need for more systematic analyses of when and how negotiations with groups that employ terrorist strategies can be legitimate and effective. In turn, this gap is related to the need for CTS as a whole to go beyond the critique of existing approaches to counterterrorism to a normatively and empirically grounded counterterrorism paradigm of its own – one based on strong ethical, theoretical, and empirical foundations.

Somewhat related to this, there is a clear need for more research into the ways in which counterterrorism and the war on terror – and their effects on human rights, privacy, freedom of movement, and the like – are being resisted, contested, and deconstructed. We know that such resistance is occurring in a variety of social and political sites, from film and humour to protest and activism, but with only a few exceptions (see Heath-Kelly 2012) we lack systematic research into the possibilities, forms, effectiveness, and impacts of such resistance. Such research is needed for both analytical and normative reasons. At the very least, we need it in order to more effectively organise resistance to the many destructive and harmful processes of the ongoing war on terror. Finally, with only a few exceptions to date (see, for example, Smith 2010), there is a real need for more research from the perspective of the global south, particularly those countries that have borne the brunt of the war on terror and who experience deeply intrusive Western counterterrorism measures.

Emerging debates

The final section of the volume focuses on a number of topics which are emerging as increasingly important new areas of inquiry within CTS. The chapters in this section focus on the ways in which the broader counterterrorism discourse is expanding to take in wider forms of political protest and activism, most notably environmental activism, as well as how the media studies field is being forced to find new ways of studying the impact and response to terrorist attacks within the new media ecology, how processes of collective memory about terrorist attacks are emerging and the important role they play in national politics, and how critical movements within peace studies and terrorism studies are finding ways to engage with questions of political violence in more holistic ways.

Obviously, there is a real need for much more sustained research on each of these topics, and many more besides. As counterterrorism becomes ever more deeply embedded in our society and our world, there will inevitably be more and more areas and issues in need of rigorous critical research. For example, among many other potential topics, there is clearly a need for more systematic research on the ever-expanding role of private security companies in counterterrorism and the war on terror; the militarisation of the police as a response to counterterrorism imperatives; and following the so-called vernacular turn in international relations (IR), the ways in which counterterrorism impacts, and is reflected in, the "everyday" discourses of ordinary people (see Jackson and Hall 2016). As noted at the beginning of this chapter, terrorism and counterterrorism have emerged since 9/11 as fulcrums on which a great many other developments and evolutions hinge. It is our task as critical scholars to document, assess, critique, and struggle for alternatives in all these areas.

Conclusion: the next phase of critical terrorism studies

When CTS first emerged as an organised effort to intervene in the field of terrorism studies, we laid out a research agenda for taking the field forward (see Breen Smyth, Gunning, and Jackson 2008; Jackson, Gunning, and Breen Smyth 2009). This included outlining some of the key topics and questions for research and investigation that we felt were crucial for the broader field. As I have attempted to show here, while some of these topics have since been the subject of important and enlightening research, a number of them remain underresearched. While it cannot be expected that all the important topics we highlighted could be thoroughly researched in the initial years of CTS, this introductory chapter should nonetheless be taken as a clarion call for more sustained engagement with some of the neglected issues and topics highlighted here.

In addition to issues of pure research, our original discussions about the future of CTS focused on some deeper questions surrounding the role of the researcher in the academy and society and the current sociology of terrorism research. We noted, for example, that the field was state- and Eurocentric and that there was something of a trans-Atlantic divide: CTS scholars for the most part came from Europe and Australasia, and scholarly engagement with terrorism scholars from the United States was minimal. Sadly, this situation continues to characterise the field, although there is a gradual broadening of scholars from different parts of the world in CTS activities.

Another issue highlighted early on was the question of how critically oriented scholars could – or should – engage with the structures of power in society, in particular, policymakers. This question has taken on even greater significance in the intervening years, not least because counterterrorism and counter-radicalisation programmes have expanded across the academy and society in unforeseeable ways. At a CSTWG workshop in June 2015, the question was hotly debated. Some participants argued that scholars ought to take every opportunity to have input into policymaking or to advise and evaluate actual programmes. On the other side, it was argued that the war on terror and contemporary counterterrorism are now so intrusive, so misguided, and so destructive that direct opposition and resistance are the most ethical positions to take, as any kind of official involvement could be viewed as legitimising for the actions of the authorities. It was suggested that CTS scholars ought to ally themselves with community activists and work openly against state counterterrorism practices.

In other words, the questions of whether and how critically oriented scholars ought to engage with existing power structures and practices, and what the real merits of "outsider theorising" and choosing the side of resistance to the state are, remain contested. Much more debate and investigation on this crucial issue will be needed in the coming years. At the very least, there is no question that ethics, praxis, and emancipatory practice are central concerns of CTS. As such, there is a need for continual wider and deeper discussions about what it means to be a critical scholar in the present war on terror context.

A final issue worth raising here is the need for CTS to widen its modes of critical engagement. As I have noted elsewhere (Jackson 2015a), the CTS project has thus far been primarily aimed at the academic field. While this is crucially important and reflects our roles as scholars, it will also be important to broaden our modes and methods of inquiry and research dissemination so that there is a deeper engagement with the public sphere and with political debate, popular culture, and all those elements of society that do not necessarily come into direct contact with the academy. This is the "collective intellectual" model of academic engagement. It is with this in mind that I published a research-based novel (Jackson 2014b; see also Jackson 2015c) which attempts to communicate much of what CTS has attempted to say but in a more accessible narrative form designed for popular consumption. In short, this is a call for CTS scholars to consider how they might communicate their expertise and research findings to a broader audience through forms of artistic and aesthetic engagement; that is, there is a need for more CTS-inspired novels, films, theatre, art installations, comic books, music, and the like.

In conclusion, it is important to note that in addition to all the challenges, there are also genuine reasons to be optimistic about the future of CTS. Apart from the undoubted achievements of CTS and the solid foundations upon which it can continue to grow, the structural conditions under which we are working are, to my mind, conducive to the kind of critical engagement we are presently engaged in. In the first place, the broader field of study and research has matured and pluralised (Jackson 2012), providing an opportunity for building stronger and broader research and practice coalitions. In addition, at the public level, there is not only a palpable sense of war-weariness induced by fourteen years of the failure of the war on terror to reduce violence or create a greater sense of security, but also a greater consciousness of the interlinked crises of insecurity brought about by climate change, inequality, and militarism. This provides a discursive opening for articulating criticism of current policies, as well as more ethical and effective alternatives to dealing with political violence. In this space, there is genuine potential for the emergence of broad-based coalitions capable of reconfiguring current approaches to, and cultures of, security. To effect such change, this opportune moment must be seized by critical scholars of terrorism.

References

Banta, B., 2012. "Analysing Discourse as a Causal Mechanism", *European Journal of International Relations*, 19(2): 379–402.
Blakeley, R., 2007. "Bringing the State Back into Terrorism Studies", *European Political Science*, 6(3): 228–253.
Blakeley, R., 2009. *State Terrorism and Neoliberalism: The North in the South*, Abingdon: Routledge.
Boukalas, C., 2015. "Class War-on-Terror: Counterterrorism, Accumulation, Crisis", *Critical Studies on Terrorism*, 8(1): 55–71.
Breen Smyth, M., Gunning, J., and Jackson, R., 2008. "Symposium: Critical Terrorism Studies – An Introduction", *Critical Studies on Terrorism*, 1(1): 1–4.
Buckley, M., and Singh, R., eds., 2006. *The Bush Doctrine and the War on Terrorism: Global Responses, Global Consequences*, London: Routledge.
Chomsky, N., 1979. *The Washington Connection and Third World Fascism*, New York: South End Press.
Cole, D., 2007. *Less Safe, Less Free: Why We Are Losing the War on Terror*, New York and London: The New Press.
Cox, R., 1986. "Social Forces, States and World Orders: Beyond International Relations Theory", in Keohane, R., ed., *Neorealism and Its Critics*, New York: Columbia University Press, pp. 204–254.
Dixit, P., and Stump, J., eds., 2016. *Critical Methods in Terrorism Studies*, Abingdon: Routledge.
Dunning, T., 2015. "Islam and Resistance: Hamas, Ideology and Islamic Values in Palestine", *Critical Studies on Terrorism*, 8(2): 284–305.
Frank, M., 2014. *Narrating Terror: The Cultural Imaginary of Terrorism in Public Discourse, Literature, and Film*. Habilitation Thesis, University of Constance, Germany.
George, A., ed., 1991. *Western State Terrorism*, Cambridge: Polity Press.
Goertzig, C., 2010. *Talking to Terrorists: Concessions and the Renunciation of Violence*, Abingdon: Routledge.
Gold-Biss, M., 1994. *The Discourse on Terrorism: Political Violence and Subcommittee on Security and Terrorism 1981–1986*, New York: Peter Lang.
Gunning, J., 2007a. "A Case for Critical Terrorism Studies?", *Government and Opposition*, 42(3): 363–393.
Gunning, J., 2007b. *Hamas in Politics: Democracy, Religion, Violence*, London: Hurst.
Gunning, J., and Jackson, R., 2011. "What's so 'Religious' about 'Religious Terrorism'?", *Critical Studies on Terrorism*, 4(3): 369–388.
Heath-Kelly, C., 2012. "Can We Laugh Yet? Reading Post-9/11 Counterterrorism Policy as Magical Realism and Opening a Third-Space of Resistance," *European Journal on Criminal Policy and Research*, 18: 343–360.
Herman, E., 1982. *The Real Terror Network: Terrorism in Fact and Propaganda*, New York: South End Press.
Herman, E., and O'Sullivan, G., 1989. *The "Terrorism" Industry: The Experts and Institutions that Shape our View of Terror*, New York: Pantheon Books.
Holland, J., 2012. *Selling the War on Terror: Foreign Policy Discourses after 9/11*, Abingdon: Routledge.
Jackson, R., 2007. "The Core Commitments of Critical Terrorism Studies", *European Political Science*, 6(3): 244–251.
Jackson, R., 2008. "The Ghosts of State Terror: Knowledge, Politics and Terrorism Studies", *Critical Studies on Terrorism*, 1(3): 377–392.
Jackson, R., 2010. "Conclusion: Contemporary State Terrorism: Towards a New Research Agenda", in Jackson, R., Poynting, S., and Murphy, E., eds., *Contemporary State Terrorism: Theory and Cases*, Abingdon: Routledge, pp. 228–239.
Jackson, R., 2011. "Culture, Identity and Hegemony: Continuity and (the Lack of) Change in US Counter-terrorism Policy from Bush to Obama", *International Politics*, 48(2/3): 390–411.
Jackson, R., 2012. "The Study of Terrorism 10 Years After 9/11: Successes, Issues, Challenges", *Uluslararası İlişkiler*, (*Journal of International Relations – Turkey*), 8(32): 1–16.
Jackson, R., 2013. "The Politics of Terrorism Fear", in Sinclair, S., ed., *The Political Psychology of Terrorism Fears*, Cambridge: Cambridge University Press, pp. 267–282.
Jackson, R., 2014a. "Bush, Obama, Bush, Obama, Bush, Obama . . . : The War on Terror as a Durable Social Structure", in Bentley, M., and Holland, J., eds., *Obama's Foreign Policy: Ending the War on Terror*, Abingdon: Routledge, pp. 76–90.

Jackson, R., 2014b. *Confessions of a Terrorist: A Novel*, London: Zed.
Jackson, R., 2015a. "On how to be a Collective Intellectual – Critical Terrorism Studies (CTS) and the Countering of Hegemonic Discourse", in Bueger, C., and Villumsen Berling, T., eds., *Capturing Security Expertise: Concepts, Power, Practice*, London: Routledge, pp. 186–203.
Jackson, R., 2015b. "The Epistemological Crisis of Counterterrorism", *Critical Studies on Terrorism*, 8(1): 33–54.
Jackson, R., 2015c. "Terrorism, Taboo and Discursive Resistance: The Agonistic Potential of the Terrorism Novel", *International Studies Review*, 17: 396–413.
Jackson, R., 2016. "Critical Discourse Analysis", in Dixit, P., and Stump, J., eds., *Critical Methods in Terrorism Studies*, Abingdon: Routledge, pp. 77–90.
Jackson, R., Breen Smyth, M., and Gunning, J., eds., 2009. *Critical Terrorism Studies: A New Research Agenda*, Abingdon: Routledge.
Jackson, R., Gunning, J., and Breen Smyth, M., 2009. "Critical Terrorism Studies: Framing a New Research Agenda", in Jackson, R., Breen Smyth, M., and Gunning, J., eds., 2009. *Critical Terrorism Studies: A New Research Agenda*, Abingdon: Routledge, pp. 216–236.
Jackson, R., and Hall, G., 2016. "Talking about Terrorism: A Study of Vernacular Discourse", *Politics*, 36(2).
Jackson, R., Jarvis, L., Gunning, J., and Breen Smyth, M., 2011. *Terrorism: A Critical Introduction*, Basingstoke: Palgrave-Macmillan.
Jackson, R., Murphy, E., and Poynting, S., eds., 2010. *Contemporary State Terrorism: Theory and Cases*, Abingdon: Routledge.
Jackson, R., and Sinclair, S., eds., 2012. *Contemporary Debates on Terrorism*, Abingdon: Routledge.
Jarvis, L., and Lister, M., 2014. "State Terrorism Research and Critical Terrorism Studies: An Assessment", *Critical Studies on Terrorism*, 7(1): 43–61.
Mahmood, C., 1996. *Fighting for Faith and Nation: Dialogues with Sikh Militants*, Philadelphia: University of Pennsylvania Press.
Mueller, J., 2006. *Overblown: How Politicians and the Terrorism Industry Inflate National Security Threats and Why We Believe Them*, New York: The Free Press.
Mueller, J., and Stewart, M., 2011. *Terrorism, Security, and Money: Balancing the Risks, Benefits, and Costs of Homeland Security*, Oxford: Oxford University Press.
Mueller, J., and Stewart, M., 2012. "The Terrorism Delusion: America's Overwrought Response to September 11", *International Security*, 37(1): 81–110.
Nasr, S., 2010. "Israel's Other Terrorism Challenge", in Jackson, R., Poynting, S., and Murphy, E., eds., *Contemporary State Terrorism: Theory and Cases*, Abingdon: Routledge, pp. 68–85.
Oliverio, A., 1998. *The State of Terror*, New York: State University of New York Press.
Ortbals, C., and Poloni-Staudinger, L., 2014. "Women Defining Terrorism: Ethnonationalist, State, and Machista Terrorism", *Critical Studies on Terrorism*, 7(3): 336–356.
Ranstorp, M., ed., 2006. *Mapping Terrorism Research: State of the Art, Gaps and Future Direction*, London: Routledge.
Raphael, S., 2009. "In the Service of Power: Terrorism Studies and US Intervention in the Global South", in Jackson, R., Breen Smyth, M., and Gunning, J., eds., *Critical Terrorism Studies: A New Research Agenda*, Abingdon: Routledge, pp. 49–65.
Raphael, S., 2010. *Terrorism Studies, the United States and Terrorist Violence in the Global South*, PhD Thesis, King's College, University of London, January 2010.
Reid, E., 1997. "Evolution of a Body of Knowledge: An Analysis of Terrorism Research", *Information Processing and Management*, 33(1): 91–106.
Sandberg, J., 2005. "How Do We Justify Knowledge Produced Within Interpretive Approaches?", *Organizational Research Methods*, 8(1): 41–68.
Schmid, A., and A. Jongman, 1988. *Political Terrorism: A New Guide to Actors, Authors, Concepts, Databases, Theories and Literature*, Oxford: North Holland.
Silke, A., ed., 2004. *Research on Terrorism: Trends, Achievements and Failures*, London: Frank Cass.
Sjoberg, L., and Gentry, C., 2015. "Introduction: Gender and Everyday/Intimate Terrorism", *Critical Studies on Terrorism*, 8(3): 358–361.
Smith, M., eds., 2010. *Securing Africa: Post-9/11 Discourses on Terrorism*, Farnham: Ashgate.
Stampnitzky, L., 2013. *Disciplining Terror: How Experts and Others Invented Terrorism*, Cambridge: Cambridge University Press.
Stohl, M., 1979. "Myths and Realities of Political Terrorism", in Stohl, M., ed., *The Politics of Terrorism*, New York: Marcel Dekker, pp. 1–19.

Stohl, M., and Lopez, G., eds., 1984. *The State as Terrorist: The Dynamics of Governmental Violence and Repression*, Westport, CT: Greenwood Press.

Stohl, M., and Lopez, eds., 1986. *Government Violence and Repression: An Agenda for Research*, Westport, CT: Greenwood Press.

Toros, H., 2012. *Terrorism, Talking and Transformation: A Critical Approach*, Abingdon: Routledge.

Yee, A., 1996. "The Causal Effects of Ideas on Policies", *International Organization*, 50(1): 69–108.

Zulaika, J., 1984. *Basque Violence: Metaphor and Sacrament*, Reno, NA: University of Nevada Press.

Zulaika, J., 2009. *Terrorism: The Self-Fulfilling Prophesy*, Chicago: University of Chicago Press.

Zulaika, J., 2012. "Drones, Witches and Other Flying Objects: The Force of Fantasy in US Counterterrorism", *Critical Studies on Terrorism*, 5(1): 51–68.

Zulaika, J., and Douglass, W., 1996. *Terror and Taboo: The Follies, Fables, and Faces of Terrorism*. London: Routledge.

PART I

Critical approaches to the study of terrorism

2
THE EMERGENCE OF TERRORISM STUDIES AS A FIELD

Lisa Stampnitzky

Introduction: the co-construction of "terrorism" and "terrorism studies"

Why is it important to study the history of terrorism expertise? This chapter begins with the assertion that *terrorism* is not a natural category, but one with a history, and that the field of terrorism expertise came into existence together with the contemporary conceptualization of terrorism. This does not mean that terrorism is not "real," merely that both the events that comprise terrorism and the ways that we understand the problem have been shaped by social and political forces. This history can denaturalize popular assumptions about the problem and the field of knowledge to show that both understandings of the problem and the construction of expert knowledge about it have changed over time and should therefore be understood as both contingent (rather than necessary or natural) and potentially subject to further change. In other words, the expert field and the terrorism discourse have been co-produced, and therefore, if we wish to understand the terrorism discourse (along with its limitations and possibilities), we must understand the structuring of the expert field. A key question in studies of terrorism expertise is whether experts have autonomy or whether they primarily mirror the interests of states and other powerful actors. If it is the case, as some have suggested (see, for example, Bartosiewicz 2008; Burnett and Whyte 2005; Herman and O'Sullivan 1989), that terrorism expertise is primarily a smokescreen for reproducing the views of states, then it makes little sense to devote further attention to the expert field rather than the field of state power itself. If, on the other hand, as I have argued elsewhere (Stampnitzky 2011, 2013a), experts do have (limited) autonomy, then the question of how and when expertise is shaped becomes ever more crucial.

What do we know about the history of terrorism studies?

There is a small but growing literature on the history of terrorism and terrorism expertise, with a number of useful overviews (see Ranstorp 2007; Schmid 2011; Silke 2004). Some of the core questions under debate include the following: is "terrorism studies" properly a field or discipline at all; to what extent are terrorism experts and terrorism studies autonomous from the state and other centers of power; and what constraints or taboos do terrorism researchers face?

Some of the earliest research on the emergence and development of terrorism studies comes from Edna Ferguson Reid, whose 1983 doctoral dissertation concluded that the field "seems to be developing into a heterogeneous body of knowledge with ill-defined boundaries . . . blurred by the large number of authors, few specialists, a proliferation of title, and an embryonic nucleus of journals and few identifiable institutions" (Reid 1983:107), but which also asserted that by the late 1970s/early 1980s there was an "invisible college" of terrorism researchers in place. More recently, Reid has argued that terrorism research in the United States has been highly influenced by the media and the government, leading to "invisible colleges of pro-Western terrorism researchers and a generation of many terrorism studies from a one-sided perspective of terrorism from below" (Reid 1997:91). Similarly, Avishag Gordon has published a number of studies addressing the question of why terrorism studies has not developed into a mature scientific field, and whether it is likely to become one (Gordon 2005), with her most recent work arguing that it is in the process of becoming an autonomous discipline (Gordon 2010).

On the question of the relative autonomy of terrorism expertise, the strongest negative view comes from Herman and O'Sullivan (1989), who seek to debunk what they call the "terrorism industry." Terrorism "expertise," they suggest, is merely a cover for the interests of the state, in which "these institutions and associated experts meet a 'demand' for intellectual-ideological service by states and other powerful interests, analogous to the demand for tanks by the army or advertising copy by the producers of soap" (Herman and O'Sullivan 1989:7). Other early critiques of the field also came from the work of Christopher Hitchens (1986) and Edward Said, who, writing in 1988, suggested that, "Its gurus . . . are journalists with obscure, even ambiguous, backgrounds. Most writing about terrorism is brief, pithy, totally devoid of the scholarly armature of evidence, proof, argument" (Said 2001 [1988]:150). More recently, Miller and Mills have focused on documenting the dominance of what they term "orthodox" terrorism experts in the mainstream media, arguing that "what has been called an 'invisible college' of experts operates as a nexus of interests connecting academia with military, intelligence and government agencies, with the security industry and the media" (Miller and Mills 2009:414).

Others, rather than aiming to document the exclusion of "dissenting" researchers or attributing the shaping of terrorism discourse to a complete lack of autonomy in the field, have focused on the particular social and historical constraints that have shaped the production of knowledge. For example, Remi Brulin has traced the history of terrorism discourse in the UN and American political and media sites (Brulin 2011), with a particular focus on how the discourse of terrorism came to exclude violence by states (Brulin 2013). Anthropologists Zulaika and Douglass have argued that the terrorism discourse is shaped by "taboos" that prevent serious analysis of terrorism (Zulaika and Douglass 1996), and others (see Ilardi 2004) have analyzed why terrorism researchers have tended to avoid firsthand contact with terrorists, a phenomenon that I have elsewhere labeled "anti-knowledge" (Stampnitzky 2013a). Thus, in addition to tracing the origins of terrorism expertise, this chapter will reflect on these core questions of whether terrorism studies has become a field, to what extent terrorism experts are autonomous, and the various other constraints shaping the discourse and the field.

How terrorism became an object of expertise

How and why did the discourse on terrorism and the field of expertise emerge? The answer lies in a combination of new sorts of events, new sorts of state responses, and new sorts of experts (Stampnitzky 2013a). A first crucial turning point dates to the late 1960s and early 1970s. This period witnessed the rise of an innovative form of political-theatrical violence, exemplified by the media-centric hijackings and hostage takings perpetrated by Palestinian nationalists in the years after the 1967 war. While political violence by sub-state actors against civilians was, of course, not new, what was new here was that nationalist and anti-colonial violence transgressed geopolitical boundaries in new ways. Whereas previous political violence had generally been fairly locally contained, targeting sites within the territories under contention, this new form of political-theatrical violence began to target Americans and other "Westerners," both as direct victims and as the intended media audience. It did so by striking at transnational sites such as international air travel and, in an incident that came to be seen a seminal trigger for the US concern with terrorism, the Olympic Games.

On September 5, 1972, eight members of the Palestinian national group Black September entered the dormitory of the Israeli athletes at the Munich Olympics, killing two and taking nine others hostage. The subsequent crisis reverberated around the world, broadcast live to an audience estimated at 900 million television viewers worldwide by the global media that had gathered for the Olympic Games.[1] While this event was an important turning point, events alone do not immediately or transparently lead to changes in discourse. Rather, transformations occur through a combination of events and the subsequent struggles over how they should be defined and over who has the authority to do this defining.

While some called the attacks "terrorism" right away, it was not yet clear what exactly this entailed or whether terrorism was indeed the proper framework for making sense of these events. The *New York Times* wrote that, "yesterday's murderous assault in Munich plumbed new depths of criminality" ("Murder in Munich" 1972a), while world leaders condemned the attacks as "insane terror," an "insane assault," "an abhorrent crime," and the work of "sick minds who do not belong to humanity." US President Nixon condemned them as "outlaws who will stop at nothing to accomplish goals" ("World Leaders . . ." 1972b).

The Olympic attacks spurred the American government to take action in ways that earlier hijackings and hostage-takings had not. One significant form that this action would take was the calling into being of a new field of expertise. Shortly after the events at Munich, President Nixon established a Cabinet Committee to Combat Terrorism, the first US government body specifically devoted to terrorism. The State Department and the Cabinet Committee to Combat Terrorism commissioned studies, organized conferences, and consulted internal and external researchers, all in the name of developing an understanding of this "new" problem of terrorism. By 1976, the State Department's Office of External Research was managing a "quarter-million-dollar program of research and analysis on the subject" (US Department of State 1976).

One result of this activity was that within the space of a few years, terrorism was transformed from a topic with almost nothing written on it to a problem around which entire institutes, journals, and conferences were organized. Figure 2.1 illustrates the rise of "terrorism" and its surpassing of *insurgency* (and related terms) in 1972 and the years just after. By 1977, at least eleven bibliographic catalogues had been compiled to keep track of an ever-increasing number of publications, and a few years later it would be observed that "authors have spilled almost as much ink as the actors of terrorism have spilled blood" (Schmid and Jongman 1988:xiii).

The first American conference on terrorism was held in 1972; by 1978, twenty-nine such conferences had been held, with presentations from over 400 distinct individuals (Stampnitzky 2013a). And this was not simply a quantitative increase, but also the growth of a set of relationships among those who were taking on a new identity, that of the "terrorism expert." By the late 1970s, a networked group of terrorism scholars had emerged, sometimes calling themselves, not

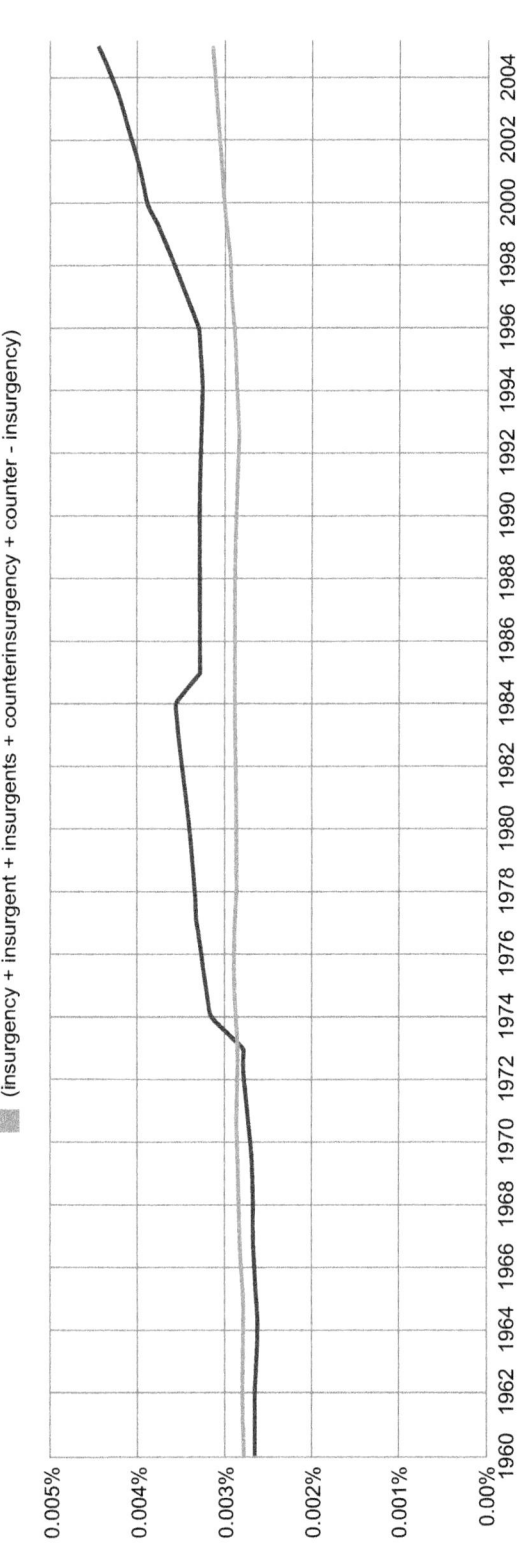

Figure 2.1 Insurgency versus terrorism
Source: Google Books Ngram Viewer http://books.google.com/ngram

without a touch of irony, the "terrorism mafia." The editors of a book collecting papers from two conferences held in 1976 and 1977 proclaimed that

> The study of terrorism has now "arrived" internationally, as evidenced by the birth of a new international multidisciplinary journal, *Terrorism*; the proliferation of scientific conferences and papers; and the growth of university research and teaching on the subject.
> (Alexander, Carlton, and Wilkinson 1979:ix)

However, to understand the emergence of terrorism expertise, we need to understand not only how there came to be terrorism experts, but also how terrorism came to be a distinct object of knowledge. This occurred through a process by which *terrorism* was differentiated from *insurgency*, which had previously been the primary discourse through which political violence was understood. The earliest expert discourses on terrorism grew directly out of the discourse on insurgency, but it would take several additional years for terrorism to become fully differentiated from insurgency and take the key features that characterize the discourse today.

From counterinsurgency to counterterrorism

Although the events they deal with – bombings, hijackings, and assassinations – may appear similar, the discourses of counterinsurgency and counterterrorism differed significantly in their conceptualizations of the problem, its causes, and the potential responses they tended to suggest. While the counterinsurgency discourse tended to conceptualize insurgents and counterinsurgents as parallel roles, the discourse on terrorism would be characterized by an ongoing tension over whether terrorists were necessarily evil, pathological, irrational individuals and organizations that were fundamentally different from normal actors.

Within the discourse of insurgency, violent actors were portrayed as rational actors with coherent goals that we may or may not condemn. In the discourse of terrorism, on the other hand, violent actors were understood as evil and irrational, both in their methods and their ultimate goals. Integrally tied to this shift was the move from understanding "terror" as a tactic that any sort of group might employ to thinking of "terrorist" as an identity. This identity would come to almost contain its own explanation: terrorists are evil, irrational actors whose actions are driven not by normal interests or political motives but by their very nature. Within the insurgency framework, however, it was possible, and even common, to separate an evaluation of the tactics a group used from an evaluation of their goals. With the rise of the terrorism framework, evaluations of goals and tactics would come to be inextricably intertwined.

Counterinsurgent writers frequently expressed a degree of respect for their opponents that would be quite unusual in the terrorism literature. As the Preface to one of the classic works of modern counterinsurgency, Roger Trinquier's (1964) *Modern Warfare*, would put it, the author approached the insurgents with "the cold respect of a professional warrior. He describes an enemy who is deeply committed to his cause, and ingenious in its pursuit" (Trinquier 2006 (1964):xii). Within the counterinsurgency discourse, "terror" was viewed as but one stage in a broader process of insurgency or revolution – a stage through which groups could pass without permanently tainting their reputations.

Typical of this approach were the participants at a 1962 counterinsurgency symposium at the US government-funded think tank, RAND. Analysts at this conference did not reflexively condemn terrorism, but instead they spoke of the possibility of "using terror wisely and selectively." The report from this conference starts out by discussing structural problems that may lead to guerrilla movements in different parts of the world, such as unemployment, inequality, and colonialism. An acknowledgment of the importance of a "cause" to insurgents and guerrillas was almost universal in this literature, and it imposed on counterinsurgency experts the importance of understanding insurgents' "minds, their mentality and their motives" (Paget 1967:162). A similar approach was evidenced at a 1962 symposium on "limited war" (another term for counterinsurgency) held at SORO (the Department of Defense sponsored special operations research office). The report from this conference illustrates both the perceived need for understanding insurgents and the social causes of insurgency and the articulated goal of mobilizing these knowledges in counterinsurgency strategies. As the Preface to the symposium report asserted,

> Whether one is concerned with programs to alleviate political, social, or economic sources of discontent, with techniques of indirect influence, with the social environment in which actions occur, or with the social and political factors which are targets of action, the kind of underlying knowledge required is the understanding and prediction of human behavior at the individual, political and social group, and society levels.
> *(Lybrand 1962:x)*

Aspects of this insurgency framework, in which terror was seen as more a tactic than a defining act, carried over into the earliest expert analyses of terrorism. These continuities between the insurgency discourse and the early expert discourse on terrorism can be seen in the scope of the debate on terrorism in the first years after it was identified as a problem. At the very first American conference on terrorism, held in 1972 at the US State Department, there was a general consensus that "nearly every variety of political and ethnic group is likely under certain (generally desperate) circumstances to resort to terrorism;" that terrorism "is a tool not confined to opposition forces; it can also be applied by established regimes;" and that "terrorism was the product of frustration induced by unresolved grievances" (Perenyi 1972). Similarly, a 1974 US government memo on "Guidelines for dealing with terrorism with international ramifications" noted that "the US Government recognizes the merit of elimination of causes of terrorism, including legitimate grievances which motivate potential terrorists" (Stampnitzky 2013b).

By the mid-1970s, however, discussions of terrorism had begun to move away from the counterinsurgency framework and toward a reconceptualization of terrorism as a practice that defined a certain type of actor: the terrorist. Speakers at a 1976 State Department conference agreed that terrorism was the activity of sub-state actors, "doubted that the direct causes of terrorism could be discovered in political or socioeconomic conditions," and "were sceptical of the argument that the way to stop terrorism was to 'remove its causes'" (Johnson 1976:18). At this conference, the question of whether terrorists could ever be "freedom fighters" was hotly debated, with the majority of presenters arguing that the categories were mutually exclusive. This very opposition between "terrorists" and "freedom fighters," which may seem almost obvious today, would have been relatively nonsensical within the earlier counterinsurgency discourse that did not pose them as mutually exclusive categories.

The contrast between the discussion at this second State Department conference held in 1976 and the first one held just four years prior is striking. At the 1972 conference, there had been a general consensus that a variety of different types of actors, even including states, might commit terrorism; that terrorism was generally caused by concrete grievances; and that these grievances might even sometimes be legitimate. In other words, while at the 1972 conference "terrorism" was understood very similarly to how political violence had been conceptualized within the prior "counterinsurgency" framework, by the 1976 conference almost all of the major assumptions of that discourse had been overturned. Terrorism, by the mid-1970s, was assumed to be a particular type of action, committed by particular types of actors, with a particular moral and political valence.

Is terrorism studies a "field"?

By the end of the 1970s, both terrorism experts and "terrorism" as a distinct object of knowledge had emerged. But what was the social structure of this field of terrorism expertise? What forces shaped the production and regulation of experts and expertise? Although the study of terrorism was, and is, a booming field, whether measured in terms of funding, publications, or numbers of aspiring experts, it has defied sociological expectations of what a scientific field, discipline, or profession ought to look like. As I have argued elsewhere, terrorism studies is best understood as an "interstitial space of knowledge production" interacting with multiple social fields, most significantly, academia, the media, and the state. Further, this space of terrorism studies is characterized by an ongoing struggle between those who would institutionalize it as a "science" and forces that tend to pull it back into the political field (Stampnitzky 2011:3).

The sociological literature on expertise has tended to focus on fairly bounded arenas such as academic disciplines and professions, tracing processes such as institutionalization, professionalization, and boundary maintenance (see, for example, Abbott 1988; Bourdieu 1993, 1996, 2005; Gieryn 1983; Larson 1977). However, these conceptualizations do not adequately describe the field of terrorism studies. Unlike archetypal examples of professions or disciplines such as medicine, physics, or economics, terrorism studies has neither been able to establish control over both the definition of the particular problem nor the production and certification of legitimate experts. In fact, one of the most consistent features of the field since its formation is that almost anyone can become a terrorism expert. Those occupying the role range from scholars to journalists, to the self-taught or self-proclaimed.

Whether one looks at television, print media, or government consultants, experts come from a wide variety of backgrounds, many with little background that would seem to qualify them for the role of expert on terrorism. More surprisingly, large numbers of those publishing in scholarly journals and presenting at conferences on the subject have relatively limited training. The first terrorism experts emerged, for the most part, not out of academia, but from think tanks, journalism, and the state. This continued as the field developed, with large proportions of those presenting at terrorism conferences and publishing in terrorism studies journals being "one-timers" with no background in the field and often no future engagement.[2] This pattern would lead many of those more consistently engaged in the field to decry that the lack of barriers to entry into terrorism studies occasioned an opportunistic approach to the field, with outsiders seeing it as an easy way to get publications with little sustained engagement necessary. This continues to be true today, with large numbers of new experts emerging after the events of 9/11, in particular, many of whom have no prior training or experience in the subject.

This matters because it means that those who study terrorism lack the ability to regulate who may speak or what will count as expertise. While this is also a challenge faced by other, more "disciplined" areas of study ranging from sociology to economics, the difference here is between fields in which there are certified or recognized experts who can attempt to draw on their authority (more or less successfully) to intervene in public debate, as opposed to a situation in terrorism studies in which not only are there no certified experts, but also no group of experts has been able to fully establish disciplinary authority to impose a definition of what it is they are talking about.

Attempts to stabilize the definition of terrorism have been a constant feature of terrorism studies. However, these attempts at purification have consistently been resisted. Three main strands or justifications for these movements can be identified. First are those who aim to stabilize the definition of terrorism so as to form the basis for a more scientific study of the topic. This first strand of purifiers generally emerged from the more academic corners of the field, aiming to stabilize terrorism by implementing a "neutral" or "de-politicized" definition. The problem for this first strand was understood as the intrusion of political definitions into what (they thought) ought to be an apolitical scientific arena.

A second strand also viewed discussions of terrorism as polluted by politicized definitions and manipulated by the US and other Western countries to further their geopolitical interests and draw attention away from their own uses of political violence. But rather than *removing* politics from the discourse, these critics either aimed to *redirect* terrorism as a term of approbation onto those they saw as the greater perpetrators of wrongdoing – that is, the US and other Western states, rather sub-state actors (see Chomsky 1986; Herman 1982; Herman and O'Sullivan 1989) – while others sought to discredit the term altogether, seeing it as irredeemably compromised (Hitchens 1986). The post-9/11 school of "critical terrorism studies" (as represented in this volume) can be seen in some ways as a successor to all of these efforts. What all of these projects share, however, is that they pick up on, and attempt to resolve, in differing ways, existing tensions within the field.

Even though terrorism studies does not control or dominate the production of discourse about terrorism in society at large, understanding the field and its emergence remains important for those who wish to understand the problem of terrorism and the discourses around it. First, the emergence of a specialized arena itself devoted to the problem of terrorism is an important historical development, indicating the distinction of terrorism from other forms of violence as something specific and needing of separate inquiry. Second, to the extent to which terrorism studies has been able to establish itself as a legitimate arena, it can exert significant impact on the discourse throughout society. (As I will discuss, however, the extent to which this is the case is debatable.) Third, even if terrorism studies does not *control* discourse, it is still a key site to look to if we wish to understand the larger terrorism discourse, because this is a locus where many of the key conflicts over what terrorism is and who may speak about it play out.

Lasting effects of the emergence of terrorism as an object of knowledge

This history of how terrorism took shape as an object of knowledge has had significant effects on the production of experts and expertise about the subject. A first, and often unarticulated, effect is that the key question about violent incidents becomes "is this terrorism?" This encourages us to ask, after every incident, whether it is terrorism, and the answer to that question determines our subsequent response. Thus, we can ask why the Boston Marathon bombing was considered terrorism, but the Sandy Hook, Connecticut, school shootings were not. And while there is much discussion of *how* this question gets answered – that is, whether or not this or that event *really* ought to be classified as terrorism – there is somewhat less consideration of the reason why *this* question is the one that frames the debate. Further, the framings of terrorism as an essentially unacceptable act and of "terrorist" as an identity have the effect of making these struggles proxies for debates over which acts and actors are acceptable and unacceptable, funneling energies into debates over classification that could potentially be better spent elsewhere.

Second, the framing of political violence as terrorism affects how we speak about violence and who is authorized to speak. I have argued elsewhere (Stampnitzky 2013a) that both expert and popular discourse on terrorism have come to be characterized by what I call a politics of "anti-knowledge" – an active refusal of explanation itself, in which rational and scientific forms of explanation became opposed to a discourse of terrorism as caused by inexplicable evil. In the situation of anti-knowledge, knowing the terrorist is proscribed. It is as though the language of evil creates a "black box" around the terrorist, which creates its own explanation: terrorists commit terrorism because they are evil. And if terrorists are evil and irrational, then one cannot – and, indeed, *should not* – seek to know anything more about them. Like James Ferguson's (1994) concept of "anti-politics," the concept of anti-knowledge suggests that the problem has been removed from the realm of (some types of) political debate. In this case, though, the mechanism is not the capture of a problem by experts professing technological solutions; in fact, it is quite the opposite, as the most frequent complaint of terrorism experts after 9/11 was that their views were marginalized and ignored.

As terrorism took shape as a way of understanding political violence, experts began to face increasing difficulty presenting themselves and their work as legitimate. In order to be a credible expert on terrorism, one must not get too close to actual terrorists or to understanding their worldviews, lest one be deemed sympathetic and thus tainted. In order to maintain their credibility and authority, experts needed to maintain a certain distance from their very object of expertise. Experts on terrorism who sought explanations for the attacks and highlighted the need to understand the motivations of terrorists were viewed with suspicion. Political scientist Martha Crenshaw recalled that "people [in the government] would feel mostly indignant, they would get upset when we said you have to understand the motivations of terrorists" (quoted in Easton 2001).

The paucity of studies based on firsthand contact with those labelled terrorists is a common critique of the field (Schmid 2011; Silke 2004). Brian Jenkins, one of the founders of the field, once compared terrorism analysts to Africa's Victorian cartographers:

> Just as the cartographers a century ago mapped from a distance a vast and impenetrable continent few of them had ever seen, most contemporary terrorism research is conducted far removed from, and therefore with little direct knowledge of, the actual terrorists themselves.
>
> (Quoted in Hoffman 2004:xviii)

In conclusion, as terrorism solidified as an object of expert knowledge, it did not become "purified" of its political or moral character; rather, the expert discourse came to be characterized by an intertwining of moral, political, and scientific/analytical concerns, leading to persistent difficulties for those who would treat political violence as an object of rational knowledge. It has been difficult for experts to carve out a position from which to produce expertise that is rational, apolitical, and value-neutral, and experts who seem to get too close to terrorists may be tagged as sympathetic and thus lose their credibility. This history also has direct implications for the sorts of policies and practices that are enabled. If one thinks of one's enemies as rational actors with coherent goals, one may try to simply eliminate them, but one might also try to prevent violence in other ways, such as removing grievances, convincing them to change their goals, or altering incentives such that violence no longer seems like a fruitful way to achieve such goals. But the dominant logic of the war on terror has been to find and kill the "bad guys."

Conclusions and questions for further research

As I noted in the opening to this chapter, some of the current points of contention about the emergence and development of the field are as follows: first, whether terrorism studies is institutionalizing or becoming a "field" (Gordon 2010)[3] and whether the meaning of *terrorism* will stabilize or whether it will remain an "essentially contested concept." Another live question is the extent to which terrorism experts have autonomy from the state and how this connects to the conditions under which the field emerged. Finally, we have the questions of how and why various taboos in terrorism studies – from the study of state terrorism to firsthand research with those deemed terrorists – originated and continue to structure the field. Additional areas that demand further investigation include the linkages, both past and future, between anti-terrorism knowledge, counterinsurgency, and colonialism. Research might look into earlier discourses on terrorism and political violence, for example, in Europe in the 1960s, in the US in the early twentieth century, and in the nineteenth century colonial context. A final area for research is the question of comparative analysis. Terrorism and terrorism expertise are both transnational phenomena. Are there distinctly national fields of expertise? And if so, how might the differing histories of political violence and terrorism in different countries have shaped the production of knowledge? All of these questions suggest the topic of the origins of "terrorism" is one still ripe for inquiry.

Notes

1 These events have been dramatized in films (Macdonald 1999; Spielberg 2005) and books (Reeve 2001). See also Stampnitzky (2013a) for a more in-depth analysis of these events and the responses they precipitated.
2 Of almost 2,000 individuals presenting at conferences on terrorism between 1972 and 2001, 84% of these were "one-timers" who made only one appearance (Stampnitzky 2011). Similarly, a study by Silke (2004:69) found that more than 80% of journal articles on terrorism were written by one-time authors.
3 The status of terrorism studies is also itself a key site of contention for experts *within* the field; see, for example, the recent debate between Sageman and respondents in *Terrorism and Political Violence* (Sageman 2014).

References

1972a. "Murder in Munich." *New York Times*, Sept. 6, p. 44.
1972b. "World leaders voice horror, condemnation." *Los Angeles Times*, Sept. 6, p. A11.
Abbott, A., 1988. *The system of professions: An essay on the division of expert labor.* Chicago: University of Chicago Press.
Alexander, Y., Carlton, D., and Wilkinson, P., 1979. *Terrorism: Theory and practice.* Boulder, CO: Westview.
Bartosiewicz, P., 2008. "Experts in terror." *The Nation*, 02/04/2008, pp. 18–22.
Bourdieu, P., 1993. *The field of cultural production: Essays on art and literature.* New York: Columbia University Press.
Bourdieu, P., 1996. *The rules of art: Genesis and structure of the literary field.* Cambridge: Polity Press.
Bourdieu, P., 2005. "The political field, the social science field, and the journalistic field" in *Bourdieu and the journalistic field*, edited by R. Benson and E. Neveu. Cambridge: Polity.
Brulin, R., 2011. "Le discours americain sur le terrorisme: Constitution, évolution et contextes d'énonciation (1972–1992)." Anglais (Civilisation américaine), L'Université de la Sorbonne Nouvelle – Paris 3, Paris, France.
Brulin, R., 2013. "Defining 'Terrorism': The 1972 General Assembly Debates on 'International Terrorism' and Their Coverage by the New York Times." *NYTimes eXaminer*. Available online at: www.nytexaminer.com/2013/09/defining-terrorism/
Burnett, J., and Whyte, D., 2005. "Embedded expertise and the new terrorism." *Journal for Crime, Conflict and the Media* 1:1–18.
Chomsky, N., 1986. *Pirates and emperors: International terrorism in the real world.* New York: Claremont Research and Publications.
Easton, N. J., 2001. "Putting theory into practice: Those once-obscure terrorism experts are now trying to answer the tough questions – as the world watches." *Los Angeles Times*, Nov. 18, p. E1.
Ferguson, J., 1994. *The anti-politics machine: 'Development', depoliticization, and bureaucratic power in Lesotho.* Minneapolis: University of Minnesota Press.
Gieryn, T., 1983. "Boundary work and the demarcation of science from non-science: Strains and interests in professional ideologies of scientists." *American Sociological Review* 48:781–795.
Gordon, A., 2005. "Terrorism as an academic subject after 9/11: Searching the Internet reveals a Stockholm Syndrome trend." *Studies in Conflict and Terrorism* 28:45–49.
Gordon, A., 2010. "Can terrorism become a scientific discipline? A diagnostic study." *Critical Studies on Terrorism* 3:437–458.

Herman, E. S., 1982. *The real terror network: Terrorism in fact and propaganda.* Boston: South End Press.

Herman, E. S., and O'Sullivan, G., 1989. *The "terrorism" industry: The experts and institutions that shape our view of terror.* New York: Pantheon Books.

Hitchens, C., 1986. "Wanton acts of usage. Terrorism: A cliche in search of meaning." *Harper's,* 09/2008, pp. 66–70.

Hoffman, B., 2004. "Foreword" in *Research on terrorism: Trends, achievements and failures,* edited by A. Silke. London: Frank Cass.

Ilardi, G. J., 2004. "Redefining the issues: The future of terrorism research and the search for empathy" in *Research on terrorism: Trends, achievements, and failures,* edited by A. Silke. New York: Frank Cass.

Johnson, C., 1976. "Perspectives on terrorism" in *Terrorism: Special studies 1975–1985 (microfilm collection, published 1986),* edited by M. Davis. Frederick, MD: University Publications of America.

Larson, M. S., 1977. *The rise of professionalism: A sociological analysis.* Berkeley: University of California Press.

Lybrand, W. (ed.), 1962. "Symposium proceedings: The U.S. Army's limited war mission and social science research." Washington DC, SORO, June 1962.

Macdonald, K., 1999. *One Day in September* (film). Sony Pictures.

Miller, D., and Mills, T., 2009. "The terror experts and the mainstream media: The expert nexus and its dominance in the news media." *Critical Studies on Terrorism* 2:414–437.

Paget, J., 1967. *Counter-insurgency operations: Techniques of guerrilla warfare.* New York: Walker and Co.

Perenyi, P., 1972. "State Department conference on terrorism: Summary of conference sponsored by the Bureau of Intelligence and Research and the Planning and Coordination Staff (XR/RNAS-21)." US Department of State, Washington, DC.

Ranstorp, M., 2007. *Mapping terrorism research: State of the art, gaps and future direction.* London: Routledge.

Reeve, S., 2001. *One day in September: The full story of the 1972 Munich Olympic massacre and the Israeli operation 'Wrath of God.'* New York: Arcade Publishing.

Reid, E. F., 1983. "An analysis of terrorism literature: A bibliometric and content analysis study." Ph.D. Thesis, Library Science, University of Southern California, Los Angeles.

Reid, E.O.F., 1997. "Evolution of a body of knowledge: An analysis of terrorism research." *Information Processing and Management* 33:91–106.

Sageman, M., 2014. "The stagnation in terrorism research." *Terrorism and Political Violence* 26(4):565–580.

Said, E., 2001 (1988). "The essential terrorist" in *Blaming the victims: Spurious scholarship and the Palestinian question,* edited by E. Said and C. Hitchens. New York: Verso.

Schmid, A. P., 2011. *The Routledge handbook of terrorism research.* London: Routledge.

Schmid, A. P., and Jongman, A. J., 1988. *Political terrorism: A new guide to actors, authors, concepts, data bases, theories and literature.* New Brunswick, NJ: Transaction Books.

Silke, A., 2004. *Research on terrorism: Trends, achievements, and failures.* New York: Frank Cass.

Spielberg, S., 2005. *Munich* (film). Universal.

Stampnitzky, L., 2011. "Disciplining an unruly field: Terrorism studies and theories of scientific/intellectual production." *Qualitative Sociology* 34:1–19.

Stampnitzky, L., 2013a. *Disciplining terror: How experts invented terrorism.* Cambridge, UK: Cambridge University Press.

Stampnitzky, L., 2013b. U.S. government memo on "Guidelines for dealing with terrorism with international ramification, 1974."

Trinquier, R., 2006 (1964). *Modern warfare: A French view of counterinsurgency.* Translated by D. Lee. Westport, CT: Praeger Security International.

US Department of State. 1976. "International Terrorism." *Far Horizons (Department of State Newsletter),* p. 3.

Zulaika, J., and Douglass, W. A., 1996. *Terror and taboo: The follies, fables and faces of terrorism.* New York: Routledge.

3
CRITICAL TERRORISM STUDIES AFTER 9/11

Lee Jarvis

Introduction

Although terrorism research has tended toward problem-solving and policy-relevant analysis (Jarvis 2009a), a number of alternative, critical interventions took place during and immediately after the Cold War period (see Jackson et al. 2011: 31–33). Despite its importance – in its own right and for subsequent developments – this work comprised a set of heterogeneous and disconnected studies situated in disciplines such as anthropology, sociology, and political economy. As such, it did not offer – or seek to offer – anything approaching an alternative paradigm for the study of terrorism. And, perhaps because of this, it had limited impact on the field of terrorism research itself (Gunning 2007a: 237). Something similar happened in the immediate aftermath of the 9/11 attacks where a further body of research emerged exploring the framing and consequences of George W. Bush's "war on terror[ism]". Although, again, this was not specifically directed at debates within "terrorism studies", this work was also important for subsequent developments because it included sustained explorations of the rhetoric used to describe and to justify this new security paradigm (Collins and Glover 2002; Silberstein 2002).

In this chapter, I focus on a body of more contemporary scholarship that has often self-consciously and explicitly portrayed itself as a "critical" alternative to what is variously described as orthodox, conventional, traditional or mainstream terrorism studies. The profile of this work – referred to here as *critical terrorism studies* (CTS) – has grown rapidly from 2006 onwards, gaining momentum with initiatives such as the establishment of a new academic journal, *Critical Studies on Terrorism*; the formation of a professional working group of the same name within the British International Studies Association (BISA); and the regular holding of academic events such as conferences on this theme (see Jackson et al. 2009b: 1–3). Although there remains considerable theoretical, methodological, and normative diversity across the various work identifying as or associated with CTS (compare Jarvis 2009a; Herring and Stokes 2011; Prixit and Stump 2011), the landscape of terrorism research has undeniably been affected by it. To explore how this has been so, this chapter begins by elucidating five major contributions of this work, namely: criticisms of "traditional" terrorism research; elaborating an alternative critical paradigm or set of commitments for the study of terrorism; excavating and unpacking the discursive construction of terrorism across sites including mainstream politics, the news media, popular culture, and everyday life; directing attention to the continuing importance of state terrorism; and outlining the diverse impacts of counterterrorism practices and technologies.

The chapter's second section then focuses on five criticisms or limitations of critical terrorism studies in which it is seen as predicated on a "straw person" account of "orthodox terrorism studies"; lacking in originality; too interested in political point-scoring; internally fractured; and reliant on an unpersuasive understanding of political discourse and its centrality within the politics of terror. The chapter concludes by pointing to future trajectories of CTS. While optimistic about those futures, it argues that all labels – terrorism, orthodox terrorism studies, critical terrorism studies – should be approached as unstable and porous short-hands which are unable to capture the fluid and complex reality they purport to describe.

Core themes and contributions

Perhaps the most prominent theme connecting research associated with critical terrorism studies has been a shared attempt to highlight a number of potentially serious problems within "mainstream" terrorism research. Four types of criticism have been particularly significant here. First is a series of conceptual and definitional criticisms of this work, including accusations of a theoretical lacuna within much terrorism scholarship (Ranstorp 2009: 33–34) and the presentism therein, which has led to a widespread neglect of historical contexts and cases (Silke 2009: 45–46). Especially important here is the argument that terrorism studies has tended to treat terrorism as an objective reality rather than a social construction – as a form of violence or tactic whose meaning is self-evident rather than an outcome of representation (Jackson et al. 2011: 15). A subsidiary criticism is that in doing so, terrorism research has also tended to reduce terrorism to a very narrow and specific set of violences, namely those conducted by non-state actors against civilians. As we shall see later, this is often seen to preclude discussion of state terrorism: a form of violence that is, for many, of far greater historical and contemporary significance.

Second are the perceived methodological limitations of much traditional work on terrorism. Several authors have pointed to a lack of primary empirical research in this field and the recycling of assumptions and truisms that this encourages. Part of the problem here is the continuing existence of a taboo that encourages researchers to not speak directly to those designated as terrorists in order to protect their scholarly independence (see Zulaika and Douglass 1996; Zulaika 2012: 52–53). Concerns about the researcher's personal safety also play into this problem, as do perceived difficulties of access with clandestine violent organisations. Although there is some excellent terrorism research which draws directly on interviews and other forms of encounter with current or former terrorists (see, for example, Horgan 2009), such projects were, until recently, relatively rare. This is problematic because it leads to a partial – incomplete and biased – understanding of the motivations leading people to join, participate in, and leave such groups. As the anthropologist Jeffrey Sluka (2008: 168) put it:

> The most obvious and fatal failure in the objectivity of pro-state terrorism experts is their refusal to look at the question from the point of view of those defined as "terrorists" or from the perspective of the people living in communities where "terrorists" originate and find their popular support.

A third criticism elaborated within CTS focuses on the politics of terrorism research. In this criticism, terrorism researchers are seen to lack critical distance from the interests and agendas of governments or think tanks with whom there are often close professional or financial ties – for instance, via research funding. Although such networks are neither unique to terrorism research nor in themselves evidence of a lack of scholarly integrity, critics argue that these relationships have been fundamental in shaping the evolution of terrorism research (see, for example, Burnett and Whyte 2005). These criticisms build on earlier and contemporary accounts of a "terrorism industry" (see Herman and O'Sullivan 1989; George 1991a), understood as a loose network of journalists, politicians, researchers, bureaucrats, security entrepreneurs and others who contribute to "the costly stoking of fear and the often even more costly encouragement of overreaction [to terrorism]" (Mueller 2006: 33; see also Mueller 2005). These criticisms are important because they encourage us to think more carefully about the nature and foundations of terrorism "expertise" (see Stampnitzky 2011, this volume), as well as the question of what may or may not be said by those claiming this moniker (Jackson 2012).

A fourth – and arguably the most important – criticism refers to the *purposes* of terrorism research. Here, traditional terrorism research is seen as unduly limited by a very narrow conception of scholarly responsibility that amounts to the production of "policy-relevant, problem-solving research" (Jarvis 2009a: 15). This is unfortunate for critics because it tends toward simplistic and conservative understandings of the world:

> The problem-solving approach is positivist and objectivist, and seeks to explain the "terrorist other" from within state-centric paradigms rather than to understand the "other" inter-subjectively using interpretative or ethnographic methods. It divides the world sharply into dichotomies (for instance, between the legitimate and "good" state, and the illegitimate and "evil" "terrorists"). It posits assumptions based on these dichotomies, often without adequately exploring whether these assumptions are borne out in practice.
> *(Gunning 2007b: 371–372)*

Although this characterisation is a little caricatured, as Gunning (2007b: 371) himself notes, terrorism research has, in the main, tended to try to stand back from terrorist violence, in an attempt to explain and prevent it, without reflecting on the prior questions of why, how and which violences become designated *terrorist*. As a result, those engaging in this research have been accused of seeing themselves as little more than an "adjunct to the various Western counterterrorism agencies" (Brannan et al. cited in Breen Smyth 2009: 196).

As this suggests, CTS has devoted considerable attention to unpacking and exploring the ways in which terrorism research has traditionally been conducted. In the remainder of this section, I turn to four areas of substantive research which have been particularly productive in recent work. Although there are potential tensions between some of these research areas – a point to which I return in the following section – they together contribute to a vital and growing research agenda with real potential to fundamentally shape the direction of terrorism research more broadly.

A first contribution has been the elaboration of an alternative framework – or, less strongly, a set of commitments – through which to study terrorism. The original pioneers of CTS – Richard Jackson, Marie Breen Smyth and Jeroen Gunning – have written most fully on this, arguing in an early position statement:

> CTS has a particular approach and orientation that marks it out from much of the orthodox terrorism studies literature in terms of its ontological position, its epistemology, its methodological orientation, its research ethics and praxis, its normative commitment, particularly in regards to emancipation, its reflexivity, and its expanded research foci and priorities.
> *(Jackson et al. 2009a: 227)*

As they elaborate, this involves approaching terrorism as a social rather than a brute fact; prioritising human rather than national security as the referent for terrorism research; a normative commitment to ending the human suffering caused by terrorism and counterterrorism alike; a continuous and critical reflexivity toward terrorism knowledge; and a commitment to methodological pluralism and responsible research ethics (Jackson et al. 2009a: 221–226). Subsequent contributions to the literature have worked both to develop this alternative research framework – for example, via fuller discussion of methodological issues (Stump and Dixit 2013) – as well as to render it accessible for newcomers to terrorism research in the form of introductory textbooks (Jackson et al. 2011). The most important contribution of this elaboration of a new set of research commitments has been its emphasis on, and sensitivity toward, the politics of labelling and a movement from definition to description in the analysis of "terrorism" (Jackson et al. 2011: 115–116).

A second major contribution of CTS has been its encouragement of a large body of work unpacking the construction and consequences of discourses on terrorism and counterterrorism. Despite the early contributions noted in this chapter's introduction, Jackson's (2005) *Writing the War on Terrorism* was pivotal in setting this research agenda, providing what remains the fullest excavation of the political discourse surrounding the war on terrorism (see also Jackson 2007b), including how the American self and terrorist other were constructed in this paradigm. In his subsequent work, Jackson (2007c) turned his attention to the role of this discourse in normalising torture in Abu Ghraib and beyond, as well as its continuity into the presidency of Barack Obama (Jackson 2011; also Bentley and Holland 2013; Jarvis and Holland 2014). Related research has interrogated the "radicalisation" discourse which has been so prominent in debates around the causes of terrorism (see Kundnani 2012; Heath-Kelly 2013; Baker-Beall et al. 2015); the gendered nature of terrorism discourse and assumptions therein about the perpetrators and victims of violence (see Shepherd 2006; Sjoberg and Gentry 2007; Sjoberg 2009; Sylvester and Parashar 2009); the role of claims about time and history within the war on terror discourse (see Holland 2009; Jarvis 2009b; Fisher 2015); and the (re)production of terrorism discourse within popular culture (see Puar and Rai 2002; Croft 2006; Wild 2014). More recently, other studies have broadened the emphasis on Western elites within much of this discursive work by looking at the ways in which actors outside of the global south (Bartolucci 2010), as well as "ordinary" or non-elite actors (O'Loughlin and Gillespie 2012; Jarvis and Lister 2015) understand and articulate (counter)terrorism. Although clearly diverse, this work has been invaluable in demonstrating the contingency of specific representations of terrorism, the importance of exclusions and absences within terrorism discourse and how such representations "travel" across time, space and domain.

A third area in which CTS has been particularly productive is in explorations of the significance and role of state terrorism within national, regional and global politics. Although important precedents for this work may again be identified (see, for example, Stohl and Lopez 1984, 1988; George 1991b), contemporary critical scholars have been vital in working to "bring the state back in" to terrorism research (Blakeley 2007, 2008). Ruth Blakeley (2009: 4) has been at the forefront of these efforts, arguing in her monograph on the topic that "Northern liberal democratic states have frequently used state terrorism, along with other forms of repression, in pursuit of their foreign policy objectives", including, but not limited to, the war on terrorism (Blakeley 2010a; see also Aksan and Bailes 2013). Related work has confronted common objections to the very concept of state terrorism (see Blakeley 2010b; Jackson et al. 2010), explored reasons for the concept's limited historical presence in terrorism research (see Jackson 2008) and highlighted the importance of such violences for power relations in the global political economy more broadly (see Herring and Stokes

2011; McKeown 2011). Other scholars have developed detailed analyses of the operation of state terrorism in specific national or regional contexts, including in Colombia (Stokes 2005), the Philippines (Holden 2011), Pakistan (Murphy 2013) and beyond (Byman 2005). This work is significant not only because it encourages a rethinking of the status and significance of terrorism within the global system, but because it also unsettles broader assumptions within international relations (IR) and terrorism research, including assumptions around the legitimacy of various violences and their protagonists (Jarvis and Lister 2014).

A further significant research area concerns the subjection of counterterrorism practices, policies and techniques to critical scrutiny. Widespread concern around the conduct of the war on terrorism across the world has underpinned much of this work, with its enormous death and injury tolls, immense financial costs, abuses of prisoners, various scandals and trampling over human rights. Blakeley and Raphael's (n.d.) *Rendition Project* is a good example of this work. It documents in painstaking detail the global rendition and detention system drawing on public information, including flight data. Aslam (2011) has similarly questioned the less secretive, but no less controversial, usage of "drone strikes" as a counterterrorism tool by the Bush and Obama administrations (see also Calhoun, this volume).

At the domestic level, much attention has focused on the production and treatment of Muslim populations as "suspect" after 9/11 (see Breen Smyth 2009, 2015; Ali 2015; Ragazzi 2015), while other work has charted the impact of counterterrorism policies on everyday life and citizenship more broadly (see Jarvis and Lister 2013; Lister and Jarvis 2013). This research not only calls the efficacy, legality and legitimacy of dominant counterterrorism practices into question – a task given added urgency with the war on terrorism's movement from the exceptional to the normal (Heath-Kelly et al. 2014; Sylvester 2014). It also points to potentially significant historical precedents and continuities with earlier counterterrorism campaigns, especially by the British state in Northern Ireland.

Criticisms and limitations of CTS

Given the ambition and scope of the above-mentioned research, it is perhaps unsurprising that CTS has in turn been subject to criticism of varying degrees of hostility. Amongst the most significant of these criticisms has been the "straw person" argument that the very existence of a mainstream or orthodox terrorism studies is itself questionable – an accusation that works to question the need for and validity of any form of CTS research agenda. Horgan and Boyle (2008: 57), for instance, highlight considerable heterogeneity within "traditional" terrorism literature, arguing:

> A cursory review of the terrorism literature reveals that attempts to generalize about something called Orthodox Terrorism Studies are deeply problematic. . . . Among terrorism scholars, there are wide disagreements about, among others, the definition of terrorism, the causes of terrorism, the role and value of the concept of "radicalization" and "extremism", the role of state terror, the role that foreign policy plays in motivating or facilitating terrorism, the ethics of terrorism, and the proper way to conduct "counter-terrorism".
>
> *(Horgan and Boyle: 57)*

A related criticism is that the perceived methodological and conceptual limitations of traditional terrorism research – such as its state-centrism or lack of primary research – had already been widely recognised and, at times, addressed before the arrival of CTS (Horgan and Boyle 2008; Weinberg and Eubank 2008: 190–191; Jones and Smith 2009: 295; Hayward 2011: 57–58).

Lutz (2010), for example, argues that the neglect of state violences within terrorism research had been well-documented prior to the recent critical turn and, in addition, that there had been some engagement with state terror practices in spite of this neglect (see also Michel and Richards 2009). Lutz's (2010: 36–38) broader argument here is that CTS should be cautious in using "state terrorism" as a label, given that even the most reprehensible or "evil" of state violences may not always be accurately described this way.

A third criticism – perhaps an extension of the previous two – is that CTS, at least in its earliest conceptions, was overenthusiastic in its attempts to differentiate itself from orthodox or traditional terrorism research. Viewed thus, CTS had been distracted by an attempt to demarcate a simplistic, unnecessary and potentially counterproductive traditional/critical distinction in a move more reminiscent of political point-scoring than serious academic research. For Egerton (2009: 58), for example, "the case of the existence of a coherent orthodoxy has been overstated in the pursuit of a uniform point of contrast". He goes on to say that this "exceeds the construction of a straw man. It leads to those advocating a 'critical' approach standing on the outside and critiquing an orthodoxy of their own making rather than also developing a normatively driven, substantive, critical approach" (Egerton 2009: 59; see also Stokes 2009: 87–88). It is important here to remember that traditional terrorism studies have been notoriously self-critical of their own research record (Stampnitzky 2011). One of the most famous overviews of the field – first published in 1988 – argued, for example, that "there are probably few areas in the social science literature on which so much is written on the basis of so little research" (Schmid and Jongman 1988: 179; also Schmid 2011: 462–470).

A fourth issue concerns the identity of CTS and whether it represents a single coherent framework or an umbrella term for a variety of non-traditional approaches to terrorism research. Statements of "core commitments" and the like imply the former: that critical terrorism studies possesses an identifiable collection of meta-theoretical and normative assumptions and values (Jackson 2007a; Jackson et al 2011: 34–42). Prominent within these are discussions of the importance of "emancipation" as a goal of such research; discussions which connect CTS to Frankfurt School Critical Theory in particular (compare McDonald 2009; Toros and Gunning 2009; Heath-Kelly 2010). Other contributions to this literature, however, have depicted CTS as a more diverse research orientation cohered around a shared impulse to intervene in the politics of (counter)terrorism (Gunning 2007b; Jarvis 2009a; Stump and Dixit 2013). As Burke (2008: 38) put it in an early contribution:

> the greatest possible pluralism and engagement consistent with the critical enterprise should be encouraged – one that can encompass works that are, in their concerns and conception, profoundly challenging to elites and policy practitioners, works much closer in style and focus to theirs, and everything in between.

This tension between the desire to forge a distinct academic/political identity and a willingness to encourage pluralism and inclusivity is one that continues to confront critical security studies, an important forerunner of CTS in many respects (compare Krause and Williams 1997 with Booth 2007).

A final set of charges centres on the importance and understanding of discourse within CTS. Stump and Dixit (2012: 211), for instance, posit a methodological inconsistency within CTS such that "terrorism is treated as a discursive construction and an independently existing state of affairs". Their response is to argue for a thicker, interpretivist approach to terrorism discourse in which "whether or not terrorism exists is less important than *how* terrorism and terrorists are constructed in practice" (Stump and Dixit 2012: 212; see also Hülsse and Spencer 2008). Others draw the opposite conclusion, arguing that CTS attributes *too great* an importance to the role of discourse within the politics of counterterrorism. Stokes (2009: 88), for example, suggests that:

> wars launched in the name of counter-terrorism are not purely driven by certain hegemonic discourses, but are also part of the West's economic interests in oil, strategic interests in military bases in the Middle East, and the desire to maintain American hegemony into the twenty-first century by controlling one of the crucial resource-rich regions for global capitalism.

Against this backdrop of extradiscursive interests and contexts, Joseph (2009: 97) argues that critical terrorism studies needs to engage in critical analysis of "the real structures of power and oppression that have an objective basis and that give meaning to the [terrorism] discourse just as the discourse might give meaning to them". More recently still, Herring and Stokes (2011) have similarly suggested that historical materialism and critical realism provide useful but as yet underemployed insights for CTS.

Conclusion

It would be premature to assess the likely legacy of CTS, given that much of the literature discussed in this chapter is, at most, ten years old and often far younger. It is clear, however, that this work has already had a significant impact on the field of terrorism research. As Tables 3.1 and 3.2 demonstrate, the main CTS journal – *Critical Studies on Terrorism* – had published work by authors located in over twenty different countries within its first seven volumes alone. Importantly for an explicitly "critical" outlet, this included considerable contributions by female scholars. As indicated, the value of this and related work has been considerable, including establishing major new research projects and priorities (for example, around terrorism discourse) and encouraging a revisiting of previously axiomatic assumptions and conventions (for example, around the terrorism/non-state connection). Moreover, however valid one believes the criticisms of this work to be, scholars associated with CTS research have addressed many of these at length, often either before or coterminous with the identification of such criticisms by others (see, for example, Jackson et al. 2009a: 232–236).

Looking ahead, future work in CTS is likely to benefit, in my view, from still greater effort toward genuinely multidisciplinary initiatives, including with researchers in disciplines such as

Table 3.1 Geographical residence of lead author in items published in *Critical Studies on Terrorism* (Volumes 1–7)[1]

Country	Number
United Kingdom	93
United States of America	44
Australia, Canada, Denmark, Germany	5
Finland, Republic of Ireland	4
New Zealand, the Netherlands, Norway	3
Pakistan, Portugal	2
Belgium, Bosnia-Herzegovina, Czech Republic Ghana, Israel, the Philippines, Sweden, Turkey, United Arab Emirates	1
None listed	1

Table 3.2 Gender balance of items published in *Critical Studies on Terrorism* (Volumes 1–7)

Gender	Number
Male, single-authored	89
Female, single-authored	53
Male only, co-authored	24
Female only, co-authored	5
Mixed, co-authored	19

the physical sciences, linguistics, law, psychology and media studies. The distinction with "traditional" terrorism studies is also likely to become less prominent within attempts to contextualise and justify new research projects now that significant and high profile trajectories of "critical" terrorism research have been established. While far less Western-centric than earlier traditions of terrorism research, there is also scope for further work still on the politics of (counter)terrorism beyond the global north. The increasing visibility of militant groups such as the Lord's Resistance Army, Boko Haram and al Shabaab, amongst others, means that African regions in particular are likely to attract increasing attention amongst terrorism researchers of various stripes.

However CTS does develop in the future, it is likely to undergo considerable change from its earliest imaginations and instantiations. That, for me, is a desirable outcome of the vibrancy and internal debate associated with any serious and living research programme. What this will mean for the identity of CTS will be up for debate, especially given its successes in attracting early career researchers to this project (if it is such a thing). This, again, is as it should be: just as "terrorism" is a political label, so too is "critical terrorism studies" and indeed "traditional terrorism studies" or any of its synonyms. Such labels constitute the thing they purport to describe, rather than reflect its essence or reality. Thus, if CTS continues to be seen as a relevant way of identifying and differentiating particular types of terrorism research from others (by virtue of theoretical or normative commitments), then the term will remain both useful and in use. Experience thus far suggests that this will be the case.

Note

1 Data was collected by the author from a manual search of the relevant contents pages listed on the Taylor & Francis *Critical Studies on Terrorism* website.

References

Aksan, C. and Bailes, J., eds. 2013. *Weapon of the Strong: Conversations on US State Terrorism*, London: Pluto.
Ali, N., 2015. "Mapping the Muslim Community: The Politics of Counter-radicalisation in Britain", in C. Baker-Beall, C. Heath-Kelly and L. Jarvis, eds., *Counter-Radicalisation: Critical Perspectives*, Abingdon: Routledge, pp.139–155.
Aslam, M., 2011. "A Critical Evaluation of American Drone Strikes in Pakistan: Legality, Legitimacy and Prudence", *Critical Studies on Terrorism* 4(3): 313–329.
Baker-Beall, C., Heath-Kelly, C. and Jarvis, L., 2015. *Counter-Radicalisation: Critical Perspectives*, Abingdon: Routledge.
Bartolucci, V., 2010. "Analysing Elite Discourse on Terrorism and its Implications: The Case of Morocco", *Critical Studies on Terrorism* 3(1): 119–135.
Bentley, M. and Holland, J., eds. 2013. *Obama's Foreign Policy: Ending the War on Terror*, Abingdon: Routledge.
Blakeley, R., 2007. "Bringing the State Back into Terrorism Studies", *European Political Science* 6(3): 228–235.

Blakeley, R., 2008. "The Elephant in the Room: A Response to John Horgan and Michael J. Boyle", *Critical Studies on Terrorism* 1(2): 151–165.
Blakeley, R., 2009. *State Terrorism and Neoliberalism: The North in the South*, Abingdon: Routledge.
Blakeley, R., 2010a. "Liberal Democracies and the Globalisation of State Terrorism in the 21st Century", *Critical Studies on Terrorism* 3(2): 169–172.
Blakeley, R., 2010b. "State Terrorism in the Social Sciences: Theories, Methods and Concepts", in R. Jackson, E. Murphy and S. Poynting, eds., *Contemporary State Terrorism: Theory and Practice*, Abingdon: Routledge, pp. 12–27.
Blakeley, R. and Raphael, S., n.d. *The Rendition Project*. Available online at: www.therenditionproject.org.uk/ Last accessed 31 October 2014.
Booth, K., 2007. *Theory of World Security*, Cambridge: Cambridge University Press.
Breen Smyth, M., 2009. "Subjectivities, 'Suspect Communities', Governments, and the Ethics of Research on 'Terrorism'", in R. Jackson, M. Breen Smyth and J. Gunning, eds., *Critical Terrorism Studies: A New Research Agenda*, Abingdon: Routledge, pp. 194–215.
Breen Smyth, M., 2015. "Theorising the 'Suspect Community': Counterterrorism, Security Practices and the Public Imagination", *Critical Studies on Terrorism* 7(2): 223–240.
Burke, A., 2008. "The End of Terrorism Studies", *Critical Studies on Terrorism* 1(1): 37–49.
Burnett, J. and Whyte, D., 2005. "Embedded Expertise and the New Terrorism", *Journal for Crime, Conflict and the Media* 1(4): 1–18.
Byman, D., 2005. *Deadly Connections: States that Sponsor Terrorism*, Cambridge: Cambridge University Press.
Collins, J. and Glover, R., eds. 2002. *Collateral Language: A User's Guide to America's New War*, New York, NY: New York University Press.
Croft, S., 2006. *Culture, Crisis and America's War on Terrorism*, Cambridge: Cambridge University Press.
Egerton, F., 2009. "A Case for a Critical Approach to Terrorism", *European Political Science* 8(1): 57–67.
Fisher, K., 2015. "Spatial and Temporal Imaginaries in the Securitisation of Terrorism", in L. Jarvis and M. Lister, eds., *Critical Perspectives on Counter-terrorism*, Abingdon: Routledge, pp. 56–76.
George, A., 1991a. "The Discipline of Terrorology", in A. George, ed., *Western State Terrorism*. Cambridge: Polity, pp. 76–101.
George, A., ed. 1991b. *Western State Terrorism*, Cambridge: Polity.
Gunning, J., 2007a. "Babies and Bathwaters: Reflecting on the Pitfalls of Critical Terrorism Studies", *European Political Science* 6(3): 236–243.
Gunning, J., 2007b. "A Case for Critical Terrorism Studies", *Government and Opposition* 42(3): 363–393.
Hayward, K., 2011. "The Critical Terrorism Studies–Cultural Criminology Nexus: Some Thoughts on how to 'toughen up' the Critical Studies Approach", *Critical Studies on Terrorism* 4(1): 57–73.
Heath-Kelly, C., 2010. "Critical Terrorism Studies, Critical Theory and the Naturalistic Fallacy", *Security Dialogue* 41(3): 235–254.
Heath-Kelly, C., 2013. "Counter-Terrorism and the Counterfactual: Producing the 'Radicalisation' Discourse and the UK PREVENT Strategy", *The British Journal of Politics & International Relations* 15(3): 394–415.
Heath-Kelly, C., Jarvis, L. and Baker-Beall, C., 2014. "Editors' Introduction: Critical Terrorism Studies: Practice, Limits and Experience", *Critical Studies on Terrorism* 7(1): 1–10.
Herman, E. and O'Sullivan, G., 1989. *The Terrorism Industry: The Experts and Institutions that Shape Our View of Terror*, New York, NY: Pantheon.
Herring, E. and Stokes, D., 2011. "Critical Realism and Historical Materialism as Resources for Critical Terrorism Studies", *Critical Studies on Terrorism* 4(1): 5–21.
Holden, W., 2011. "Neoliberalism and State Terrorism in the Philippines: The Fingerprints of Phoenix", *Critical Studies on Terrorism* 4(3): 331–350.
Holland, J., 2009. "From September 11th, 2001 to 9-11: From Void to Crisis", *International Political Sociology* 3(3): 275–292.
Horgan, J., 2009. *Walking Away from Terrorism: Accounts of Disengagement from Radical and Extremist Movements*, Abingdon: Routledge.
Horgan, J. and Boyle, M., 2008. "A Case Against 'Critical Terrorism Studies'", *Critical Studies on Terrorism* 1(1): 51–64.
Hülsse, R. and Spencer, A., 2008. "The Metaphor of Terror: Terrorism Studies and the Constructivist Turn", *Security Dialogue* 39(6): 571–592.
Jackson, R., 2005. *Writing the War on Terrorism: Language, Politics and Counter-Terrorism*, Manchester: Manchester University Press.

Jackson, R., 2007a. "The Core Commitments of Critical Terrorism Studies", *European Political Science* 6(3): 244–251.

Jackson, R., 2007b. "Constructing Enemies: 'Islamic Terrorism' in Political and Academic Discourse", *Government and Opposition* 42(3): 394–426.

Jackson, R., 2007c. "Language, Policy and the Construction of a Torture Culture in the War on Terrorism", *Review of International Studies* 33(3): 353–371.

Jackson, R., 2008. "The Ghosts of State Terror: Knowledge, Politics and Terrorism Studies", *Critical Studies on Terrorism* 1(3): 377–392.

Jackson, R., 2011. "Culture, Identity and Hegemony: Continuity and (the lack of) Change in US Counter-terrorism Policy from Bush to Obama", *International Politics* 48(2): 390–411.

Jackson, R., 2012. "Unknown Knowns: The Subjugated Knowledge of Terrorism Studies", *Critical Studies on Terrorism* 5(1): 11–29.

Jackson, R., Breen Smyth, M. and Gunning, J., 2009a. "Critical Terrorism Studies: Framing a New Research Agenda", in R. Jackson, M. Breen Smyth and J. Gunning, eds., *Critical Terrorism Studies: A New Research Agenda*, Abingdon: Routledge, pp. 216–236.

Jackson, R., Breen Smyth, M. and Gunning, J., 2009b. "Introduction: The Case for Critical Terrorism Studies", in R. Jackson, M. Breen Smyth and J. Gunning, eds., *Critical Terrorism Studies: A New Research Agenda*. Abingdon: Routledge, pp. 1–9.

Jackson, R., Jarvis, L., Gunning, J. and Breen Smyth, M., 2011. *Terrorism: A Critical Introduction*, Basingstoke: Palgrave.

Jackson, R., Murphy, E. and Poynting, S., 2010. "Introduction: Terrorism, the State and the Study of Political Terror", in R. Jackson, E. Murphy and S. Poynting, eds., *Contemporary State Terrorism: Theory and Practice*, Abingdon: Routledge, pp. 1–11.

Jarvis, L., 2009a. "The Spaces and Faces of Critical Terrorism Studies", *Security Dialogue* 40(1): 5–27.

Jarvis, L., 2009b. *Times of Terror: Discourse, Temporality and the War on Terror*, Basingstoke: Palgrave.

Jarvis, L. and Holland, J., 2014. "'We [for]got him': Remembering and Forgetting in the Narration of bin Laden's Death", *Millennium: Journal of International Studies* 42(2): 425–447.

Jarvis, L. and Lister, M., 2013. "Disconnected Citizenship? The Impacts of Anti-terrorism Policy on Citizenship in the UK", *Political Studies* 61(3): 656–675.

Jarvis, L. and Lister, M., 2014. "State Terrorism Research and Critical Terrorism Studies: An Assessment", *Critical Studies on Terrorism* 7(1): 43–61.

Jarvis, L. and Lister, M., 2015. "'I read it in the FT': 'Everyday' Knowledge of Counter-terrorism and its Construction", in L. Jarvis and M. Lister, eds., *Critical Perspectives on Counter-terrorism*, Abingdon: Routledge, pp. 109–129.

Jones, M. and Smith, M., 2009. "We're All Terrorists Now: Critical – or Hypocritical – Studies 'on' Terrorism?", *Studies in Conflict & Terrorism* 32(4): 292–302.

Joseph, J., 2009. "Critical of What? Terrorism and its Study", *International Relations* 23(1): 93–98.

Krause, K. and Williams, M. J., eds. 1997. *Critical Security Studies: Concepts and Cases*, Minneapolis: University of Minnesota Press.

Kundnani, A., 2012. "Radicalisation: The Journey of a Concept", *Race & Class* 54(2): 3–25.

Lister, M. and Jarvis, L., 2013. "Disconnection and Resistance: Anti-Terrorism and Citizenship in the UK", *Citizenship Studies* 17(6–7): 727–740.

Lutz, J., 2010. "A Critical View of Critical Terrorism Studies", *Perspectives on Terrorism* 4(6): 31–40.

McDonald, M., 2009. "Emancipation and Critical Terrorism Studies", in R. Jackson, M. Breen Smyth and J. Gunning, eds., *Critical Terrorism Studies: A New Research Agenda*, Abingdon: Routledge, pp. 109–123.

McKeown, A., 2011. "The Structural Production of State Terrorism: Capitalism, Imperialism and International Class Dynamics", *Critical Studies on Terrorism* 4(1): 75–93.

Michel, T. and Richards, A., 2009. "False Dawns or New Horizons? Further Issues and Challenges for Critical Terrorism Studies", *Critical Studies on Terrorism* 2(3): 399–413.

Mueller, J., 2005. "Six Rather Unusual Propositions About Terrorism", *Terrorism and Political Violence* 17(4): 487–505.

Mueller, J., 2006. *Overblown: How Politicians and the Terrorism Industry Inflate National Security Threats, and Why We Believe Them*, New York, NY: Free Press.

Murphy, E., 2013. "Class Conflict, State Terrorism and the Pakistani Military: The Okara Military Farms Dispute", *Critical Studies on Terrorism*, 6(2): 299–311.

O'Loughlin, B. and Gillespie, M., 2012. "Dissenting Citizenship? Young People and Political Participation in the Media-security Nexus", *Parliamentary Affairs* 65(1): 115–137.

Prixit, D. and Stump, J., 2011. "Response to Jones and Smith: It's Not as Bad as It Seems; Or, Five Ways to Move Critical Terrorism Studies Forward", *Studies in Conflict and Terrorism* 34(6): 501–511.

Puar, J. and Rai, S., 2002. "Monster, Terrorist, Fag: The War on Terrorism and the Production of Docile Patriots", *Social Text* 20(3): 117–148.

Ragazzi, F., 2015. "Policed Multiculturalism? The Impact of Counter-terrorism and Counter-Radicalization and the 'End' of Multiculturalism", in C. Baker-Beall, C. Heath-Kelly and L. Jarvis, eds., *Counter-Radicalisation: Critical Perspectives*, Abingdon: Routledge, pp. 156–174.

Ranstorp, M., 2009. 'Mapping Terrorism Studies After 9/11: An Academic Field of Old Problems and New Prospects", in R. Jackson, M. Breen Smyth and J. Gunning, eds., *Critical Terrorism Studies: A New Research Agenda*, Abingdon: Routledge, pp. 13–33.

Schmid, A., 2011. "The Literature on Terrorism", in A. Schmid, ed., *The Routledge Handbook of Terrorism Research*, Abingdon: Routledge, pp. 457–474.

Schmid, A. and Jongman, A., 1988. *Political Terrorism: A New Guide to Actors, Authors, Concepts, Data Bases, Theories and Literature*, New York, NY: Transaction.

Shepherd, L. J., 2006. "Veiled References: Constructions of Gender in the Bush Administration Discourse on the Attacks on Afghanistan Post-9/11", *International Feminist Journal of Politics* 8(1): 19–41.

Silberstein, S., 2002. *War of Words: Language, Politics and 9/11*, Abingdon: Routledge.

Silke, A., 2009. "Contemporary Terrorism Studies: Issues in Research", in R. Jackson, M. Breen Smyth and J. Gunning, eds., *Critical Terrorism Studies: A New Research Agenda*, Abingdon: Routledge, pp. 34–48.

Sjoberg, L., 2009. "Feminist Interrogations of Terrorism/Terrorism Studies", *International Relations* 23(1): 69–74.

Sjoberg, L. and Gentry, C. E., 2007. *Mothers, Monsters, Whores: Women's Violence in Global Politics*, London: Zed Books.

Sluka, J., 2008. "Terrorism and Taboo: An Anthropological Perspective on Political Violence against Civilians", *Critical Studies on Terrorism* 1(2): 167–183.

Stampnitzky, L., 2011. "Disciplining an Unruly Field: Terrorism Experts and Theories of Scientific/Intellectual Production", *Qualitative Sociology* 34(1): 1–19.

Stohl, M. and Lopez, G., eds. 1984. *The State as Terrorist: The Dynamics of Governmental Violence and Repression*, Westport, CT: Greenwood Press.

Stohl, M. and Lopez, G., eds. 1988. *Terrible Beyond Endurance? The Foreign Policy of State Terrorism*, New York, NY: Greenwood Press.

Stokes, D., 2005. *America's Other War: Terrorizing Colombia*, London: Zed.

Stokes, D., 2009. "Ideas and Avocados: Ontologising Critical Terrorism Studies", *International Relations* 23(1): 85–92.

Stump, J. L. and Dixit, P., 2012. "Toward a Completely Constructivist Critical Terrorism Studies", *International Relations* 26(2): 199–217.

Stump, J. and Dixit, P., 2013. *Critical Terrorism Studies: An Introduction to Research Methods*, Abingdon: Routledge.

Sylvester, C., 2014. "TerrorWars: Boston, Iraq", *Critical Studies on Terrorism* 7(1): 11–23.

Sylvester, C. and Parashar, S., 2009. "The Contemporary 'Mahabharata' and the many 'Draupadis': Bringing Gender to Critical Terrorism Studies", in R. Jackson, M. Breen Smyth and J. Gunning, eds., *Critical Terrorism Studies: A New Research Agenda*, Abingdon: Routledge, pp. 178–193.

Toros, H. and Gunning, J., 2009. "Exploring a Critical Theory Approach to Terrorism Studies", in R. Jackson, M. Breen Smyth and J. Gunning, eds., *Critical Terrorism Studies: A New Research Agenda*, Abingdon: Routledge, pp. 87–108.

Weinberg, L. and Eubank, W., 2008. "Problems with the Critical Studies Approach to the Study of Terrorism", *Critical Studies on Terrorism* 1(2): 185–195.

Wild, P., 2014. "Sam Fisher and the 'War on Terror': An Analysis of Splinter Cell in a post-9/11 Context", *Critical Studies on Terrorism* 7(3): 434–445.

Zulaika, J., 2012. "Drones, Witches and Other Flying Objects: The Force of Fantasy in US Counterterrorism", *Critical Studies on Terrorism* 5(1): 51–68.

Zulaika, J. and Douglass, W., 1996. *Terror and Taboo: The Follies, Fables and Faces of Terrorism*, Abingdon: Routledge.

4
THE REAL AND THE BLUFF
On the ontology of terrorism

Joseba Zulaika

Introduction: the real and the bluff

An event from my own biography, which I placed at the beginning of an ethnography of violence in a Basque village, can serve as a small illustration of vividly experienced terror: the killing of an alleged police informer from my own village by *Euskadi Ta Askatasuna* (ETA) in the bus he was driving and in front of the terrified women who were riding in it, my mother included. The women were taken to the village, still crying and sobbing, by drivers passing by. As I went out into the street, several of them surrounded me in a daze, asking, "But how can that be?" I couldn't say a word (Zulaika 1988: 74–75). It was real terror.

Still, the villagers did not refer to what happened that Saturday morning as "terror*ism*," but only as "killing." Were they wrong in not calling it terrorism? A parallel question would be: was it wrong that the killing of President Kennedy was not labeled terrorism? In 1963, there was no public discourse of terrorism used by the media to cover such events as assassinations, kidnappings or threats of violence; it was mostly after 1972 that such events began to be reported as terrorism (Zulaika and Douglass 1996: 45–46). Thus, discourse itself, the writing of it (Jackson 2005), becomes a decisive difference, a fundamental aspect of what turns a killing or a threat into a terrorist killing or a terrorist threat. The *naming* is the essence of the entire phenomenon. The act of assassination is not in itself more terrible for calling it *terrorist*, but it has now been subjected to a process of *classification* by which it belongs to the class of phenomena named terrorist. If the facts on the ground can be described as killing, kidnapping, threat, and so on, one may ask: apart from the naming, does the discourse of terrorism itself add anything essential, ontologically real, to the violent event itself?

The Basque case was only a regional violent insurgency at the periphery. We live now in the post-9/11 era in which the murder of 3,000 people in New York confronted the United States with the reality of suicidal terrorism. It provoked the US-led global "war on terror." The most consequential chapter in this war was the invasion of Iraq, which was legitimized by faulty intelligence: the belief that Saddam Hussein did have or was about to have weapons of mass destruction (WMD), weapons that could fall into the hands of terrorists. The dreaded weapons were never found, but after the removal of Hussein there was declassified information, based on FBI interviews with him, and all the major media outlets reported on July 2, 2009, that he had in fact been *bluffing* as to his possession of weapons of mass destruction so as to keep in check regional enemies such as Iran. "Why did most countries (including those who opposed the Iraq war) believe in 2002 that Saddam Hussein had WMDs?" asked David Kilcullen. "Because they were intercepting the regime's communications, and many senior Iraqi regime members believed Iraq had them" (2009: 293). In short, the US went to war with Iraq, and with the support of the public opinion, in good part because counterterrorism was unable to sort out the misinformation planted by Hussein. Bluffing was the true *reality* behind Hussein's threat.

The problem is primarily epistemological, that is, it concerns the type of knowledge needed to sort out fakery from actual threat. But false or true, once a given intelligence is believed, it becomes reality. Counterterrorism is a prime example of what Robert Merton labeled "the Thomas theorem," namely: "If men define situations as real, they are real in their consequences" (1968: 475). In ontological terms, the questions we must address have to do with what is bluffing and what is real terrorism, and how they constitute each other.

An event, a news story

Terrorism is initially an event and a news story. A typical, alarming case of terrorism news is when the afternoon cable news opens up with some thwarted terrorist plot. According to a Heritage Foundation report, the US has foiled sixty terrorist plots since 9/11 (see Zuckerman, Bucci and Carafano 2013). Theresa May, the British Home Secretary, claimed in November 2014 that British security services had foiled forty terror plots since the 2005 London attacks (Travis 2014). There is a frightening reality behind these news stories. But not all of the reality is revealed to the shocked viewer. It will take time to find out that plots that were known as the Washington Metro bombing plot, the New York subway plot, the plot to blow up the Sears Tower, the plot to bomb a Portland Christmas tree lighting ceremony, and dozens more across the nation were in fact organized and led by the FBI.

Mother Jones (Aaronson 2011: 30–43), having examined the prosecutions of 508 defendants in terrorism-related cases, found that all the high-profile terrorism plots of the last decade, with the exception of three,[1] were in fact FBI stings. This makes the "reality" of terrorism and counterterrorism far more complicated than the initial alarm might suggest.[2] As one defense lawyer put it, "They're creating crimes to solve crimes so they can claim a victory in the war on terror" (quoted in Aaronson 2011: 33). Attorney Eric Holder argued that sting operations have "proven to be an essential law enforcement tool in uncovering and preventing potential terror attacks" (quoted in Aaronson 2011: 33). What this view doesn't take into account is the extent to which the sting operation might actually create terrorism. In March 2009, a report by a national coalition of Islamic organizations expanded on "several high-profile cases in which informers have infiltrated mosques and have helped promote plots" (Vitello and Semple 2009: A1–A33).

As an event and a news story, terrorism is an action with a plot and a narrative sequence, a discursive and political construct in which "the event is that which can be narrated" (Feldman 1991: 14). As in the case of any storyteller or historian, the terrorism writer has to select a narrative form; no matter how "real" the facts he or she is describing, the writer cannot escape the shadow of the "tropes" of narration (metaphor, metonym, synecdoche, irony) – that is, "the process by which all discourse *constitutes* the objects which it pretends only to describe realistically and to analyze objectively" (White 1978: 2). This raises the question of the extent to which the discourse on terrorism borrows from rhetoric and from forms of fictionalization –not that the information provided is feigned, but that the crafting of the story shapes and molds a given discourse. Rhetoric thus becomes pivotal to the phenomenon; that is, it becomes efficient depending on how the public interprets and reacts to the terrorist strategy, for "it is the response which becomes the primary persuasive vehicle for the terrorists" (Palmerton 1988: 107).

But attention to discourse doesn't mean that there is a shortage of actual violent events, including gruesomely barbaric ones such as the beheadings by ISIS. As I write this chapter, the airwaves are filled with the news of three gunmen attacking the satirical newspaper *Charlie Hebdo* in Paris, which had in the past lampooned the Prophet Muhammad, killing twelve people (there would be five more in subsequent days). Satire and comedy belong to the frame "this is play;" for the attackers, it was "this is war." Play is real, but its reality consists in distorting the literal meaning of words and contexts, turning reality into the unreal by manipulating semantics. What is the *real* of such a fateful interaction between satire and terrorism?

Playing terrorist

Terrorism is by definition deadly serious, even when provoked by comedy and satire. Still, an ontological analysis of terrorism has to focus on the extent to which much of what passes for terrorism can simply be pretending and bluffing. This includes threats, a staple of the entire phenomenon. Consider Ted Kaczynski, known as the Unabomber, the former Berkeley mathematician turned terrorist trickster who in June of 1995 brought California's airports to a standstill with a letter he sent to the *San Francisco Chronicler* stating that he was going to down an airliner within a week. Simultaneously, he sent another letter to the *New York Times* declaring the threat to be a "prank." The Unabomber was front-page news for weeks. Was he being a real terrorist when he was simply pretending? What was the reality of his terrorist threat?

The Unabomber, we might say, was "playing terrorist" (Aretxaga 2005: 215–229). And so were the counterterrorist FBI agents and informants who posed as radical Islamists trying to snare potential terrorists. But can a frame of behavior such as "this is play" – ruled by the premise "all the statements in this frame are untrue" (Bateson 1972: 184) – be applied to deadly terrorism? The prank was surely a terrorist act that brought fear and disrupted California transportation for days. But what type of reality did it have?

Ritual is a related field in which the meanings of certain kinds of actions do not denote what they stand for. A bite means aggression, but a playful bite among two dogs does not mean aggression. Ritual is efficient in terms of the cultural conventions of the believers and not in terms of strictly rational means. Students of animal behavior distinguish between functional types of action (eating, flying, mating, walking) and ritual types of behavior (bee dances, bird songs, displays, courtship, simulated aggression). Anthropologists studying primitive forms of warfare in premodern societies have insisted on their "ritualism" (Vayda 1968: 470). Many terrorist acts could be typified as ritual bluff within a highly symbolic discourse rather than as strictly rational means-ends causality in military terms. Terrorism has a lot to do with personal initiation, a play with chance, ritual sacrifice, the logic of all-or-nothing. Ritual simulation compensates in terrorism for its disadvantages in actual military terms. The terrorists' fight is a very economical war in that they convey their message of total antagonism by producing only a randomly chosen few symbolic casualties.

In a threat, there is a difference between what the threatening action denotes and what actually happens. One thing is bluff and another is combat, yet military strategy is notorious for the use of bluff and stratagem. An army ready to strike means real combat; with an underground terrorist group's threat of violence, you never know with certainty if it is for real until it happens. Still, threats are terrorist incidents, since intentionality is in itself a criterion for terrorism, as summed up by Schmid: "The nature of terrorism is not inherent in the violent act itself. One and the same act . . . can be terrorist or not, depending on intention and circumstance" (1983: 101). Intention is subject to interpretation. Whether you become "terrorized" by the threat, its very reality will depend on the extent of your reaction to it.

John Mueller appropriately has asked the question: "Which is the greater threat: terrorism, or our reaction to it?" (2006: 1).

The ontology of terrorism has to look at the dynamics between form and formlessness intrinsic to the metaphysical powers and dangers of ritual, magic, pollution, taboo, and the like studied by anthropologists. A key idea is that "ritual recognizes the potency of disorder" (Douglas 1966: 94). Terrorism makes good use of similar premises, for everything touched by terrorism becomes irregular, informal, contagious, explosive – a political taboo in the strict sense of the term (Zulaika and Douglass 1996: 151–52). Contrary to the explicit formality and strict rule-based culture of regular military and political organizations, "formlessness" affects the structures and tactics of terrorist groups. Given the invisible and illegal nature of revolutionary/terrorist action, abrogation of form expresses its logic of chance, its disregard for any stable rule, the bluff of ritual threat, the contagiousness of taboo, the elimination of geographical boundaries, the charismatic nature of the activist who is at once "a priest and a murderer" (Frazer 1963: 1). One crucial dimension of such abrogation of form is the difficulty in *ending* a terrorist type of war, as there are no established protocols for such unstructured types of action and organization to come face-to-face with its constituency, much less negotiate with its sworn enemies. Its lack of formal structures make "the war on terror" essentially unwinnable.

Thus, chess is not the best model to track the moves in terrorism (see Sick 1985: 82). Rather, poker is a much better one, as it combines the elements of reality and bluff. In chess, the moves can be predicted in advance; in poker, as in terrorism, the cards are unpredictable. Critical for poker thinking are "cheating and thwarting cheaters, leveraging uncertainty, bluffing and sussing out bluffers, managing risk and reward" (McManus 2009: 18). Chance or bluff in poker are not elements that deny its systemic nature; their admission is only a realization that we are dealing with a system that simply has more complex statistics (see Von Neuman and Morgenstern 1944).

Terrorism as military strategy is close to the concept of stratagem – a class of ploys that implies trickery, disinformation, betrayal, deception, ambush, surprise, feigned attacks and retreats, sophistic treaties, and the like. Such forms of bluffing are inherent to all modern warfare, nuclear deterrence in particular. These are not performances of actual battle, but rather "as if" forms of engagement. Again, what type of reality is this? Terrorism discourse, if anything, is one of stark factuality and apocalyptic imagery. Yet, if we take account of the frames discussed previously, is also one that may easily confuse sign and context, map and territory, reality and make believe. As shown by the violent reactions to comedy and satire, terrorism thrives in situations in which the meta-statement "this is *only* play" is ruled out. The triumph of the discourse consists in imposing a context of "this *is* real war" – when much of it is "as if" kind of war.

"Like sheer fantasy"

The *New York Times* reported that the informer Emad Salem "began his testimony by admitting that he had lied to just about everybody he ever met," that Salem was "always ready with another believe-or-not exploit," and that his testimony sounded "like sheer fantasy" (MacFarquhar 1995: A9). The report was about the trial of Omar Abdul Rahman, known also as the "Blind Sheikh," in the context of the historically pivotal case of the first attack on the Twin Towers. A fatwa by the sheikh would later follow, and is considered a key event in the making of 9/11. An editorial added that the indictment of the sheikh "only required to prove *the intention* to wage a terror campaign" and concluded that "only the sketchiest connections [were] established between Sheikh Omar Abdul-Rahman and the alleged mastermind of that crime, Ramzi Ahmed Yousef" (MacFarquhar 1995: A14).

What is the reality of this "sheer fantasy" on the basis of which the Blind Sheikh was condemned to life in prison? Many Muslims considered him their supreme spiritual leader and legal authority, including the man who had been supporting his stay in the US, Osama bin Laden, and the one who had been tortured with him in an Egyptian prison, Ayman al-Zawahiri.

But Salem's "fantasy" was not just his. The counterterrorism industry had recruited Salem and was monitoring his every step. And soon, according to John Miller and Michael Stone, the infiltrated "Salem was offering to restart the paramilitary training that had lapsed in the year since Nosair's [Al Khifa's former leader] arrest" (2002: 74). Salem was the one who secured for his few fellow plotters "a warehouse in which to build bombs" (Miller and Stone 2002: 74). That is, nothing was going on in the Blind Sheikh's circle, so the FBI actually planted someone in order to activate illegal paramilitary activities, including renting a warehouse for them to start making bombs. Not surprisingly, there was concern within the FBI that "the Bureau was training potential terrorists, holy warriors who may not be breaking the law now, but who might one day turn the skills they were acquiring against the U.S." (2002: 88). The premise here was to preemptively push potential terrorists into action in order to find out how far they were willing to go.

This was not the end of Salem's successes. In April 1993, two months after the first World Trade Center attacks (and before Abdul Rahman and others had been arrested), Salem warned the FBI that the Blind Sheikh's circle was planning a simultaneous bombing of the Lincoln and Holland tunnels, the United Nations, and the New York offices of the FBI. And once again, according to Miller and Stone, since the plotters allegedly needed a safe house in which to build bombs, "Salem offered to find one," and then the co-conspirators "accepted the offer" (2002: 114). If the informant "offered" to find a place to build bombs and the terrorists "accepted" the offer, who took the initiative again? The counterterrorist was clearly *playing terrorist* in order to catch the real terrorists. But what is real about such *deep play* in which both terrorist and counterterrorist are taking part, opposed yet inextricably intertwined?

The infiltrated Salem had tried unsuccessfully for months to have on tape Rahman's fatwa for the plotters to act on. Soon after Rahman's life sentence, his sons were plotting hijacking planes and distributing plastic-laminated cards containing their father's picture and his written "will" for a fatwa calling for the destruction of America. In the opinion of journalist Peter Bergen, who interviewed bin Laden and many other al Qaeda jihadists, that card "is a key to understanding why some 3,000 Americans lost their lives on the morning of September 11, 2001" (2006: 204).

In conclusion: what is *real* about this chain of events that lead to 9/11? What we have here is a circle of jihadists who had fought the anti-Soviet crusade in Afghanistan hand-in-hand with the CIA – the agency that issued repeated visas for the Blind Sheikh to come to the United States. As Robert Friedman found out, the CIA's involvement with the first attack on the World Trade Center was, through setting up jihad offices such as Al Khifa across the country, "far greater" than was known to the general public (1995: 46). The potential terrorists were people whom the counterterrorists knew as their associates in the past, who had been under their surveillance, and who could be infiltrated by paid informers. The final result was that the Blind Sheikh, who was for millions of Islamists what the Pope is for Catholics, was sent to life in prison. The unasked question remains: was this a triumph of counterterrorism to be celebrated, or was sending such a man to life in prison on the basis of a paid informant's "sheer fantasy" the height of judicial and political blindness – the very prelude to 9/11?

The latest in counterterrorism – "the only game in town," according to Leon Panetta – is drones. The drone war, conceptualized largely as a *game,* has been described as "sheer fantasy, if not literally science fiction" (Sluka 2011: 72). The assumption is that underground terrorists all over the world will be eliminated by the Hellfire missiles launched from these pilotless drones flying in the sky at 10,000 feet. Many of them are operated by agents 7,500 miles away at Nellis Air Force Base near Las Vegas, Nevada, close to the famously secretive Area 51, the setting for a lot of science fiction with more than sixty movies, TV shows, and video games (Singer 2009: 138). The killings by drones are justified as "this is war," but for the drone operator, they are "like playing the computer game Civilization" (Martin and Sasser 2010: 31); that is, they also belong to "this is play." The *killings* of the remote victims by the drone operator are far removed from any real context of reciprocity, which legally justifies the right to kill in warfare, and they belong rather to the domain of hunting (see Chamayou 2013). No wonder the drone pilots have a problem recognizing what they are engaged in and that "it would take some time for the reality of what happened so far away to sink in, for 'real' to become *real*" (Martin and Sasser 2010: 31).

These facts lead us to question the ontological ambivalence of what is the reality of terrorism and the extent to which sheer fantasy is complicit in the entire phenomenon (see Zulaika 2012). Following psychoanalysis, a valid theory of fantasy is one that does not render it into the "not-real," but rather considers that fantasy "constitutes a dimension of the real" (Butler 1990: 108). A positivist view uses the representational realism of the media to reproduce and consolidate the real by excluding phantasmatically what is absent from ordinary politics. Terrorism is that exclusion that returns to the system as anomaly and which, by creating a state of exception, serves to give ground to the politically real. In the end, fantasy becomes the mask of the real when that phantasmatic exclusion, by counterterrorism producing and legitimizing the "sheer fantasy" of people like Salem, "assumes the status of the real, that is, when the two become compellingly conflated" (Butler 1990: 107). Just consider the stark fact that, on the basis of the figure of the terrorist, the US defense budget has almost doubled since the Cold War when it emerged as the only superpower. What can be real, and what fantasy, behind the figure of the terrorist that justifies such military buildup by which the US defense budget surpasses the combined budgets of most other countries combined (Kilcullen 2009: 22)?

The waiting for terror

Time is what distinguishes fantasy from historic reality. The ontology of terrorism has to address situations in which time is manipulated and the waiting for terror becomes the true reality. Threats, for example, play with the representation of yet future events. In such a context of waiting, what *could* happen may weigh as much as what *is* actually the case. The axis of time becomes intrinsic to the threat. Time is the difference between mythical and factual narratives. Unlike dreams or fantasy, terrorism takes place in real time; yet, there is a clear distortion of temporality in the self-fulfilling quality (Zulaika 2009) of the "waiting for terror" and the implications of the doctrine of preemption when actual historical temporality becomes subservient to the feared future. The logic of preemption operated in the US during the post-9/11 targeting of Arabs and Muslims as suspect terrorists when the administration incarcerated thousands of them in secret, while the courts did nothing. As Merton put it,

> The self-fulfilling prophecy is, in the beginning, a *false* definition of the situation evoking a new behavior which makes the original false conception come *true*. This specious validity of the self-fulfilling prophecy perpetuates a reign of terror. For the prophet will cite the actual course of events as proof that he was right from the very beginning . . . such are the perversities of social logic.
>
> *(1968: 477)*

More than one analyst has observed such a self-fulfilling quality in the drone campaign, which has not only ignited anti-American sentiment in the Arab world,[3] but scores of countries are also currently developing drone technology to be used as military robots, and their use by terrorists "is not far away" (Caryl 2011: 58).

The self-fulfilling manipulations of temporality typical of the counterterrorist waiting for terror are reminiscent of phenomena studied by anthropologists in premodern societies within cultural contexts such as the belief in divination and witchcraft. The discussion of the primitive notions of causality and temporality that prevail in such social phenomena have led anthropologists to study issues of ontology and epistemology. It is the distortions of time that are most revealing of the manipulations of associative magic, as shown in divination. Terrorism discourse's mantra that the likelihood of future terrorism acts, including nuclear terrorism, is "not if, but when" is reminiscent of the oracular revelations studied by anthropologists, which "are not treated as hypotheses. . . . They are not a matter of intellectual interest but the main way in which Azande decide how they should act. . . . We might say that the revelation has the logical status of an unfulfilled hypothetical" (Winch 1977: 88). The senses perceive the events, yet magical thinking provides the explanation. The hidden knowledge provided by a secret source reveals the evil of witchcraft – or terrorism. The feared future dominates the explanation of the current state of events.

The Bush administration's doctrine of preemptive war in the nuclear era testifies to the radical subversion of self-fulfilling temporality adopted by the war on terror. By definition, "the logic of pre-emption entails action *before* the event, and relies upon an imaginary of extreme threats, which justify otherwise unthinkable actions" (Stampnitzky 2013: 168). Thus, much of counterterrorism operates before the crimes have been committed; that is, against the *non*actions of potential terrorists. The doctrine of preemption continues to justify the imposition of a state of exception on American politics, which includes indefinite detention and extrajudicial killings by drones – a situation described by Agamben as one in which "it is impossible to distinguish transgression of the law from the execution of the law, such that what violates a rule and what conforms to it coincide without any reminder" (1998: 57). The Dantesque reality of this exceptional state is vividly described in Mohamedou Ould Slahi's *Guantánamo Diary* (2005).

It is worth noticing what happens to the axis of time in the expectations of the drones' robotic technology as well. An army colonel observed, "as the loop gets shorter and shorter, there won't be any time in it for humans" (quoted in Singer 2009: 64). As the speed of the decision cycle gets reduced from minutes to microseconds, the direction of the new robotic technology is to simply eliminate altogether human time.

Conclusion

The mutually opposed yet mutually constitutive antagonisms of the terrorist and counterterrorist are like two surfaces that display the qualities of what the Lacanian psychoanalysts label "the edge" – a feature that is intrinsic to the reality of the unconscious; namely,

> a duality that has nothing to do with the dichotomies between complementary oppositional terms . . . the edge is the thing whose only substantiality consists in its simultaneously separating and linking two surfaces. This specific duality aims at the Real, and makes it take place through the very split that gives structure to this duality. It is a duality that simultaneously constitutes the cause, the advent, and the consequences of the Real.
>
> *(Zupancic 2003: 19)*

Such an edge may force that nonterror becomes a terrorism problem, or that real terror goes undetected. There is a *nonrelationship* between the two surfaces, yet the very impossibility constitutes the edge. How to conceptualize such a dynamic should be critical to terrorism studies.

Jacques Derrida's notion of *autoimmunity* provides another key to grasping this dynamic, a process he defines as "that strange behavior where a living being, in quasi-*suicidal* fashion, 'itself' works to destroy its own protection, to immunize itself *against* its 'own' immunity" (Borradori 2003: 94). Derrida compares the perverse effects of this process to those of a repression, in either psychoanalytic or political senses, which "ends up producing, reproducing, and regenerating the very thing it seeks to disarm" (Borradori 2003: 99). The self-generating nature of the two antagonistic fronts of terrorism and counterterrorism is what escapes public debate, and this is what must be grasped in its radicalness and lead to the decision to change its coordinates. What counterterrorism is unable to see is that it often becomes terrorism's best ally for perpetuating an unending struggle.

The inability to sort out real from feigned threats, bluffing from actual combat, is primarily an epistemological problem. It is similar to the kind of situation an ethnographer faces in an alien culture, or a writer such as Capote faces when dealing with the narration of a multiple murderer, or a police detective faces when solving a crime. Terrorist subjectivity is obviously the core of the taboo. The last thing the counterterrorist wants to "understand" is the suicidal desire of an actor that seems to have gone mad; it is much easier to proclaim it as an unchanging "identity" or "personality type." Yet, it is the will of the terrorist subject that the confusion of acts and non-acts will create havoc, as shown by the Unabomber's prank or Hussein's bluff. Thus, *terrorism* is not only the actual deed but also the intentional subjectivity of the plotters, including their "death instinct," their humiliations and desires, and their potential for madness.

It is counterterrorism's unwillingness to engage with the terrorist's political subjectivity that makes it unable not only to detect the elements of bluff in the terrorist agenda, but also to be paralyzed by the fatalistic fear of the element of chance employed by the enemy. This is best expressed in the "Cheney doctrine" of the one percent: "Even if there's just a one percent chance of the unimaginable coming true, act as if it is a certainty" (Suskind 2006: 62). The art of poker consists in minimizing the element of chance, yet it is based on the knowledge that not only can it never be completely eliminated from the game, but luck becomes a key strategic component to use to one's advantage and prevail. Otherwise, one surrenders to a traumatized mindset unwilling to face any risk and ready to justify an "asymmetric warfare" in which the United States was spending in one hour in Iraq, for years at a time, the equivalent of the total of al Qaeda financial resources (Singer 2009: 271).

In the final analysis, the true reality of terrorism consists in having become a catalyst for confusing various semantic levels of linguistic, ritual, and military actions – the real and the bluff. The categorical confusions between the frames of war, threat, play, and ritual – frames which contain internal paradoxes of the type "I'm lying" and in which the actions do not denote literally what they are meant to denote – are intrinsic to the terrorism/counterterrorism dynamic. Actions embedded in "this is war" and "this is play" are categorically different – as in the map/territory categorical principle (Bateson 1979), a difference that is clear from the rational point of view but gets lost in the types of behavior ruled by the symbolic and the affective when the flag *is* identical with the country. A valid ontology of terrorism should keep in check the basic principle of map/territory relations (for which a valid theory of play and fantasy might be as relevant as theories of war) and should investigate the dynamic of the terrorism/counterterrorism feedback as the very thing that is constitutive of the entire phenomenon.

Notes

1 The three exceptions were Najibulla Zazi, who attempted to bomb the New York City subway in September 2009; Hesham Nohamed Hadayet, who fired a gun at the Los Angeles airport's El-Al ticket counter; and the Times Square failed bomber, Faisal Shahzad.
2 In his article "The Informants," Trevor Aaronson describes the various steps by which potential terrorists are entrapped by FBI agents (2011: 33).
3 In Pakistan, for instance, the number of terrorist attacks went up sharply in a wave of anti-Americanism, for Pakistanis "overwhelmingly believe that most of those who die in the attacks are civilians" (Caryl 2011: 56.)

References

Aaronson, T., 2011. "The Informants", *Mother Jones*, Sept.–Oct. 2011, 30–43.
Agamben, G., 1998. *Homo Sacer: Sovereign Power and Bare Life*. Stanford: Stanford University Press.
Aretxaga, B., 2005. "Playing Terrorist." In Begoña Aretxaga, ed., *States of Terror*. Reno: Center for Basque Studies, 215–29.
Bateson, G., 1972. *Steps to an Ecology of Mind*. New York: Ballantine Books.
Bateson, G., 1979. *Mind and Nature: A Necessary Unity*. New York: E.P. Dutton.
Bergen, P., 2006. *The Osama Bin Laden I Know: An Oral History of Al Qaeda's Leader*. New York: Free Press.
Borradori, G., 2003. *Philosophy in a Time of Terror: Dialogues with Jurgen Habermas and Jacques Derrida*. Chicago: The University of Chicago Press.
Butler, J., 1990. "The Force of Fantasy: Feminism, Mapplethorpe, and Discursive Excess", *Difference: A Journal of Feminist Cultural Studies* 2(2):105–125.
Caryl, C., 2011. "Predators and Robots at War", *The New York Review of Books*, September 29, 55–57.
Chamayou, G., 2013. *A Theory of the Drone*. Translated by Janet Lloyd. New York and London: The New Press.
Douglas, M., 1966. *Purity and Danger*. London: Routledge and Kegan.
Feldman, A., 1991. *Formations of Violence: The Narrative of the Body and Political Terror in Northern Ireland*. Chicago: University of Chicago Press.
Frazer, J., 1963. *The Golden Bough: A Study in Magic and Religion*. New York: Macmillan.
Friedman, R., 1995. "The CIA's Jihad", *New York Magazine*, March 27, 36–47.
Jackson, R., 2005. *Writing the War on Terrorism: Language, Politics, and Counter-Terrorism*. Manchester: Manchester University Press.
Kilcullen, D., 2009. *The Accidental Guerrilla: Fighting Small Wars in the Midst of a Big One*. Oxford: Oxford University Press.
MacFarquhar, N., 1995. "In Bombing, A Deluge of Details", *New York Times*, March 19, A9.
Martin, M., and Sasser, C., 2010. *Predator: The Remote-Control Air War over Iraq and Afghanistan: A Pilot's Story*. Minneapolis: Zenith Press.
McManus, J., 2009. *Cowboys Full: The Story of Poker*. New York: Farrar, Straus and Giroux.
Merton, R., 1968. *Social Theory and Social Structure*. New York: Free Press.
Miller, J., and Stone, M., 2002. *The Cell: Inside the 9/11 Plot*. New York: Hyperion.
Mueller, J., 2006. *Overblown: How Politicians and the Terrorism Industry Inflate National Security Threats, and Why We Believe Them*. New York: Free Press.
Palmerton, P., 1988. "The Rhetoric of Terrorism and the Media Responses to the 'Crisis of Iran'", *Western Journal of Speech Communication* 52(2):105–121.
Schmid, A., 1983. *Political Terrorism: A Research Guide to Concepts, Theories, Data Bases and Literature*. New Brunswick, NJ: Transaction Books.
Sick, G., 1985. *All Fall Down: America's Tragic Encounter with Iran*. New York: Random House.
Singer, P., 2009. *Wired for War: The Robotics Revolution and Conflict in the 21st Century*. New York: Penguin Books.
Slahi, M., 2015. *Guantánamo Diary*. Edited by Larry Siems. New York: Little, Brown and Company.
Sluka, J., 2011. "Death from Above: UAVs and Losing Hearts and Minds", *Military Review* 91(3, May–June): 70–76.
Suskind, R., 2006. *The One Percent Doctrine: Deep Inside America's Pursuit of Its Enemies Since 9/11*. New York: Simon & Schuster.
Stampnitzky, L., 2013. *Disciplining Terror: How Experts Invented "Terrorism."* Cambridge: Cambridge University Press.

Travis, A., 2014. "UK Counter-Terrorism Bill to Include Campus Ban on Extremists", *The Guardian*, November 24. Available online at: www.theguardian.com/politics/2014/nov/24/uk-terrorism-measures-campus-ban-extremists-theresa-may.

Vayda, A., 1968. "Primitive Warfare." In D. L. Sills, ed., *International Encyclopedia of the Social Sciences,* vol. 16. New York: Macmillan and Free Press, 468–71.

Vitello, P., and Semple, K., 2009. "Muslims Say F.B.I. Tactics Sow Anger and Fear", *New York Times,* December 18, 2009.

Von Neumann, J., and Morgenstern, O., 1944. *Theory of Games and Economic Behavior.* Princeton: Princeton University Press.

White, H., 1978. *Tropics of Terror: Essays in Cultural Criticism.* Baltimore: John Hopkins University Press.

Winch, P., 1977. "Understanding a Primitive Society." In B. R. Wilson, ed., *Rationality.* Oxford: Basil Blackwell.

Zuckerman, J., Bucci, S., and Carafano, J., 2013. "60 Terrorist Plots Since 9/11: Continued Lessons in Domestic Counterterrorism", Special Report from the Douglas and Sarah Allison Center for Foreign Policy Studies, The Heritage Foundation.

Zulaika, J., 1988. *Basque Violence: Metaphor and Sacrament.* Reno: University of Nevada Press.

Zulaika, J., 2009. *Terrorism: The Self-Fulfilling Prophecy.* Chicago: The University of Chicago Press.

Zulaika, J., 2012. "Drones, Witches and Other Flying Objects: The Force of Fantasy in US Counterterrorism", *Critical Studies in Terrorism* 5(1, April):51–68.

Zulaika, J., and Douglass, W., 1996. *Terror and Taboo: On the Follies, Fables, and Faces of Terrorism.* New York: Routledge.

Zupancic, A., 2003. *The Shortest Shadow: Nietzsche's Philosophy of the Two.* Cambridge: The MIY Press.

5
CRITICAL EPISTEMOLOGIES OF TERRORISM

James Fitzgerald

Introduction

"There is . . . no such thing as theory in itself, divorced from a standpoint in time and space. When any theory so represents itself, it is more important to examine it as ideology, and to lay bare its concealed perspective" (Cox 1981: 128). Thus lies the logic behind Robert Cox's seminal argument that "theory is always *for* someone and *for* some purpose" (Cox 1981: 128), a reflexive standpoint on the nature of knowledge production that critical terrorism studies (CTS) has internalised from the very beginning. A cursory look at CTS's earliest – and perhaps most formative – works is indicative. Jeroen Gunning makes a case for Critical Terrorism Studies by immediately criticising the "methodological and conceptual shortcomings of [existing] terrorism research" (2007: 363–364); Richard Jackson submits that CTS is "founded on a series of powerful critiques of the current state of orthodox terrorism studies" (2007: 225); while Marie Breen Smyth cites the "troublesome features" of recent terrorism literature as that which CTS must both avoid and address as part of its critical research agenda (2007: 260). This approach is replicated in subsequent key texts – such as the inaugural issue of CTS's dedicated journal, *Critical Studies on Terrorism* (2008); the edited volume *Critical Terrorism Studies: A New Research Agenda* (2009); and the textbook *Terrorism: A Critical Introduction* (2011) – suggesting that CTS's foundational identity is born of the ills of what has become retroactively labelled as "orthodox" or "traditional" terrorism studies.

This is not to suggest, however, that CTS automatically rejects all knowledge(s) produced in orthodox terrorism studies; to the contrary, CTS scholars have consistently highlighted the existence of accomplished scholarship produced thereof and have argued that CTS should build upon and supplement these insights (see, for example, Jackson and Sinclair 2013). It is important to emphasise, therefore, that the target of CTS's formative critique is not orthodox terrorism studies per se, but an orthodoxy produced both within and beyond terrorism studies that tends to treat particular knowledge(s) on terrorism as essentially knowable and self-evidently true.[1] CTS scholars (see Gunning 2007; Jarvis 2009) have often denoted this orthodoxy in terms of *problem-solving* theory, which "takes the world as it finds it, with the prevailing social and power relationships and the institutions into which they are organised, as the given framework for action" (Cox 1981: 128). CTS offers a highly visible platform for *critical* perspectives on terrorism – which typically eschew notions of objective "truth" and therefore constitute a collective challenge to this problem-solving orthodoxy – to flourish, thus significantly enriching contemporary debates on terrorism.

In charting this dynamic, one is essentially speaking of myriad ways of *knowing* terrorism, each of which bear its own assumptions with regard to how we perceive reality (*ontology*) and "how we know what we know" within this reality, that is, *epistemology* (see Zulaika, this volume). The purpose of this chapter is not to simply provide a descriptive sketch of the various *types* of epistemological approaches that have been presented under a CTS umbrella (see Stump, this volume); rather, references to diverse epistemologies of terrorism are interspersed across a broader investigation of (i) the (onto-)epistemological commitments of mainstream terrorism knowledges; (ii) the (onto-)epistemological commitments of CTS as an inclusive space for intellectual and disciplinary pluralism; and (iii) the onto-epistemological commitments of CTS as a programme for emancipatory progress. The chapter will conclude by posing an initial inquiry into the belongingness of "poststructuralism" within a CTS framework (see Heath-Kelly, this volume), an area of inquiry which might be developed in future research.

Orthodox knowledges on terrorism

Though the academic study of low-intensity political violence had been prevalent long before the 1970s, the popular emergence and consolidation of "terrorism" during this decade saw a marked increase in sustained investigation into this seemingly new phenomenon. Much of this early scholarship was concerned with empirical fact-finding and providing an informed rebuttal to the simplistic media-driven narratives that most often construed terrorists as apolitical and irrational actors (see Bell 1977; Laqueur 1977). As the discipline of terrorism studies developed through the 1980s and 1990s, social scientific methodologies were increasingly applied to large-n studies in order to derive generalisable truths about terrorism, such as the (welcome) perspectives that terrorists are rational decision-makers, that terrorism is driven by *political* motivations, and that poverty does not directly cause terrorism. With its close proximity to policy-making institutions – and particularly in the US (see Burnett and Whyte 2005; Stampnitzky 2013, this volume) – terrorism studies began to crystalise as a field clearly dedicated to a problem-solving ideal of understanding terrorism as a means of ultimately eradicating it.

As outlined by Lisa Stampnitzky (2011), however, the production of (orthodox) terrorism expertise over time could never *quite* match terrorism studies' overarching ideals of policy relevance and scientific significance. Contestations over the nature and meanings of terrorism continued to affect the field, with wholesale agreement on core concepts – such as a "neutral" definition of terrorism – proving particularly difficult. With the object of study (terrorism) existing in a state of continuous flux, terrorism studies failed to develop into what would be typically denoted as a scientific field, operating instead as an *interstitial space* "characterized by a constant dialectic between attempts to institutionalize it as a 'science' and forces that pull it back into relation with other fields (largely the state)" (Stampnitzky 2011: 3). While such conceptual flux (which effectively forecloses the possibility of uncovering objective truths about terrorism) is typically embraced by more critically oriented scholars (see later), the continuing lament among core terrorism studies scholars with regard to the "definitional problem" is emblematic of terrorism studies' internal dilemma with regard to the *types* of knowledge it can produce. A close reading of noted terrorism studies scholar Alex P. Schmid's (2011) recent and authoritative overview of the "definition of terrorism" helps us to further contextualise this dynamic.

Building on the seminal work of Schmid and Jongman (1988), Schmid immediately recalls that the very concept of a *definition* is derived from science; hence, the entrenched practice of listing prominent features of terrorism as an elucidatory device is wholly insufficient.[2] The essentially contestable nature of terrorism – as a concept mediated by language – is thereby characterised as problematic,[3] with associated conceptual "relativism" being something that "academics in pursuit of logic and truth cannot accept" (Schmid and Jongman 1988: 40). Schimd's conclusion ultimately seals an analysis deeply concerned with the *epistemological* basis of how terrorism may be legitimately defined and, therefore, (further) stabilised as an object of inquiry:

> The social sciences and the humanities do not have mathematics as their common language, as do the natural sciences. They are constantly *under assault from both popular and political discourses* as they share a common language with these forces that express social preferences and political power. While the rise of universities in the past thousand years and the rise of the exact sciences within them have led to technical discoveries that have changed the face of the world and our understanding of it, the academic contributions of the social sciences have been much more modest. It can be argued that this is partly due to a certain *deficit in precision in the social sciences which has caused our academic knowledge to be much less cumulative than it could have been were there greater consensus on its objects under investigation*. In that sense, striving for academic consensus does matter, and our search for an academic consensus definition of terrorism has not been a useless exercise.
>
> *(2011: 87; emphasis added)*

The prioritisation of "scientific" knowledge (and a related progressive consensus) on social phenomena is not, of course, limited to terrorism studies; rather, it is representative of a deeper orthodoxy of epistemological *naturalism* that is evident across the social sciences and in cognate fields such as international relations (see P. T. Jackson 2011) and security studies (see Buzan and Hansen 2009). Here, naturalism is defined as "most generally, a sympathy with the view that ultimately nothing resists explanation by the methods characteristic of the natural sciences" (Blackburn 2008). Much like in the case of international relations, however, calls to make terrorism studies more scientific are premised not on rigorous evaluations of what exactly constitutes the scientific quality of knowledge, but "a vague and general sensibility" (P. T. Jackson 2011: 3), for to invoke science is to "call to mind a panoply of notions connected with truth, progress, reason . . . and, perhaps more importantly, to implicitly reference a record of demonstrated empirical success" (P. T. Jackson 2011: 3). Hence, in the case of Silke (2007), the increase in the proportion of statistical analyses published in post-9/11 terrorism studies represents one of the few positives to be taken from the "explosion" of academic interest that followed the events. Similarly, for Senechal de la Roche (2004), progression towards a "scientific theory of terrorism" is not only desirable, but patently achievable, provided that such analyses deliver "one or more simple, falsifiable, and new propositions *applicable across all times and places that successfully predict and explain the known facts*" (de la Roche 2004: 4; emphasis added).

Studies from Sinai (2007), Gordon (2010), and Young and Findley (2011) provide a sobering rebuttal to the hopes of Schimd et al., however. Gordon (2010) finds that early fragmentation of research on terrorism has prevented – and will most likely continue to prevent – the development of a truly scientific discipline. Similarly, for Sinai (2007), terrorism studies has yet to achieve the status of a hard science due to continuing difficulties in "problem areas", such as reaching a consensus definition of terrorism and a lack of uniform coding and counting rules across a range of terrorism incident databases. For Young and Findley (2011), the problems run much deeper, as their study finds that quantitative analyses on terrorism are typically beset by (often basic) conceptual, definitional, and research design problems, entailing that the associated functions of explaining and thus *preventing* terrorism – logics imbued in the very formation of terrorism studies[4] – continue to be hampered by bad science:

> Since [the quantitative study of terrorism] is inherently policy relevant, it is important that we produce models that generate accurate predictions. . . . Before [our] suggestions are offered to policy makers as ways to reduce terrorism, the results should be robust and should apply to the appropriate domain. The consequences when implementing foreign policies can be monumental.
>
> *(Young and Findley 2011: 428)*

The findings of Young and Findley mark a quite precarious state of affairs with regard to the orthodox study of terrorism. If the very (problem-solving) logic underpinning such scholarship is intrinsically tied to questions of policy relevance – and related understandings of terrorism are (de)legitimised by the degrees to which they can explain and predict its happenings (see Fitzgerald 2014: 18–49) – does the internally recognised failure of this orthodoxy to either constitute itself as a science or offer highly actionable insight to state policy (see Sageman 2014; Sánchez-Cuenca 2014) represent a failure of terrorism studies itself? Marc Sageman's (2014) recent polemic strikes at the heart of this issue.

A scholar who, by his own admission, has "had a foot in the academic and intelligence communities" over a long and hybrid career, Sageman uses his authority to argue that a stagnation in terrorism research exists *precisely* on account of the pronounced gap between the academic and policy worlds. The reasons are relatively straightforward: terrorism studies has been replete with poor scholarship (especially in the post-9/11 era), while those scholars adequately trained in the tradition of (positivist) social sciences lack sufficient data which is being withheld by intelligence agencies. On the other hand, those in the intelligence communities have access to essential primary data, but lack the requisite social scientific training to adequately process this data towards answering what Sageman decrees as the ultimate question for all terrorism research: What leads people to turn to political violence? Sageman's panacea – like so many arguments for effective change within terrorism studies – is nonetheless bound to the very same (onto-)epistemological framework(s) from which said "crises" have arisen: to proscribe progressive solutions on the basis of *more* science and *more* direct intertwinement with state policy is to reinforce the very basis of a problem-solving orthodoxy in terrorism research. There must be another way.

A space for critique: critical terrorism studies

Formulaically conceived between 2005 and 2007 (see Jackson 2007), critical terrorism studies has rapidly developed through numerous books, articles, conferences, research projects, and the establishment of a dedicated journal, *Critical Studies on Terrorism*. Much akin to critical security studies (see Booth 2005; Brincat et al. 2012), it operates a *dual identity* of sorts, offering an accommodating space for a wide range of contending perspectives on terrorism, on the one hand, while embracing a normative commitment to emancipatory progress on the other (see Jackson et al. 2009a). As noted in the introduction, CTS's early literature is intently focused on critiquing the orthodoxy of terrorism studies and knowledges produced thereof, the primary purpose of which is to provide the requisite space(s) within which a range of critical analyses of terrorism can be presented. Jarvis (this volume) provides a useful synopsis of these critiques, which I relate here to a broader discussion on critical epistemologies of terrorism.

The first critique posits that terrorism studies tends to treat terrorism as an objectively knowable phenomenon amenable to essential capture. The epistemological orthodoxy of naturalism – as seen previously– thrives under this (ontological) assumption, with the attendant effect that critical approaches which treat terrorism as a discursively mediated phenomenon are actively silenced within mainstream spaces. As a result, important critiques on terrorism and associated knowledges have been typically dispersed across a range of intellectual and disciplinary spaces, and while this diversity does not constitute a de facto problem for the study of terrorism, the atomised nature of these analyses arguably dilutes their potential impact as a collective counterpoint to mainstream terrorism knowledges. In providing an accommodating space for a range of contending perspectives on terrorism, CTS explicitly seeks to address this issue.

The second critique relates to the perceived methodological limitations of much research associated with terrorism studies, which are exacerbated by factors such as a distinct lack of primary research, the significant growth of a poor standard of research on terrorism following 9/11, and the reactive prioritisation of studies inquiring into Jihadist/Islamist terrorism (see Ranstorp 2009; Silke 2009) at the expense of other important topics, though this has changed in recent years. The gravity of this methodological deficit is explicated by Dixit and Stump (2011) who, having reviewed over forty syllabi on terrorism across the United States, found that the most popularly assigned course texts tend not to address the "ontological and epistemological underpinnings of their research" (Yanow and Schwartz-Shea 2006: xxxi, cited in Dixit and Stump 2011: 502). The embedded assumption that "terrorism is an existential threat whose identity is not open to question (and states, usually, are the defenders of such threats)" (Dixit and Stump 2011: 502) thereby goes (relatively) unchallenged and is arguably ingrained in how terrorism continues to be taught to new generations of scholars/policymakers (Dixit and Stump 2011: 504).

The third critique posits that "traditional" terrorism researchers often lack "critical distance" from the interests of governments or think tanks, whose specific research agendas are bound to "the costly stoking of fear and the often even more costly encouragement of overreaction [to terrorism]" (Mueller 2006: 33, quoted in Jarvis, this volume).[5] This dynamic is perhaps most apparent with regard to the influential "new terrorism" thesis (see Burnett and Whyte 2005; Spencer, this volume), which argues that contemporary "religious" terrorism is catastrophic in nature, thereby requiring a fundamental shift in counterterrorism practice(s). This, amongst other effects, forecloses the progressive possibility of talking to/negotiating with "irrational" terrorist actors and may also help to entrench repressive state policies enacted in the name of countering and preventing terrorism (see Gunning and Jackson 2011; Toros 2012; Mac Ginty 2013).

The fourth – and directly related – critique concerns the prioritisation of policy-relevant knowledge as the basis of legitimate academic output on terrorism. As scholars such as Lisa Anderson (2003), Steve Smith (2000), and Stanley Hoffman (1977) have outlined with reference to international relations, the suitability of academic output for policy consumption is bound up in an epistemological expediency (Fitzgerald 2014: 166) largely associated with positivist-orientated, quantitative, and large-n studies. Thus conceived, the quest to orientate terrorism studies towards a science (see earlier) further entrenches already-dominant (problem-solving) perspectives on terrorism, which hold, amongst other assumptions, that terrorism is violence limited to non-state actors against civilian/noncombatant targets. Read in this context, Sageman's (2014) call to more actively unite academy and policy towards a collective uncovering of the supposed *sine qua non* of all terrorism research – "what leads people to turn to political violence?" – represents *anything but* a neutral call for progress.

Critical epistemologies of terrorism: orthodoxy, emancipation, poststructuralism

While CTS's main identity is that of a "broad church" for intellectual pluralism (Jackson et al. 2009b, p. 222), it is simultaneously defined by a programmatic dedication to the concept of emancipatory progress (see Lindahl, this volume). In a key text outlining CTS's lineage in critical theory, Toros and Gunning (2009) situate emancipation as that which helps to (further) define CTS away from the embedded orthodoxy of terrorism studies, while also defining a particular horizon of possibilities for future CTS research:

> [the] *sine qua non* of Critical Theory is emancipation. . . . Emancipation within a Critical Theory framework, however, is not about utopian goals out of humanity's reach, but must rather be grounded in feasible alternatives that grow out of the here and now – that is, the immanent. . . . It achieves this through **immanent critique**, by seeking within society the sources of emancipation and change rather than trying to find them in an extraneous utopia. Thus, contradictions are sought in the existing order, in the fissures through which the possibility of transformation transpires.
> *(Toros and Gunning 2009: 99–100; bold emphasis added)*

Immanent critique entails seeking sources of emancipation within society (examples might include investigating individuals' existing experiences of terrorism or explicitly supporting an activist cause), rather than seeking emancipation via extraneous utopias that may be seen as patently unrealistic (see McDonald 2009: 113–114; Heath-Kelly 2010). For Matt McDonald, effective immanent critique can be performed by accentuating – and thereby desubjugating (see also Jackson 2012) – those marginalised voices which articulate marked alternatives to the dominant orthodoxy of how terrorism is popularly known. One can argue that CTS has been particularly active in this regard.

For example, *Critical Studies on Terrorism* has accommodated interviews with ex-combatants (see, for example, Toros and Tellidis 2013), there has been a clear focus on the negative impacts of counterterrorism legislation in creating and perpetuating suspect communities (see Breen Smyth 2014; Martin 2014), and, more recently, a number of scholars have called for the use of storytelling/narrative approaches to desubjugate the voices of "ordinary citizens" as a means of challenging dominant discourses of (counter)terrorism (see Jarvis and Lister 2013; Fitzgerald 2015; Furtado 2015). The potential contributions of alternative literatures and theoretical approaches have also been welcomed; thus, for instance, a basic compatibility between Middle East studies and CTS has been identified (see Dalacoura 2009; Jackson 2012; Fitzgerald 2014), the contributions of social movement theory (SMT) and anthropology to alternative understandings of terrorism have been championed (see Gunning 2007, 2009; Sluka 2009), and a number of retrospective book reviews have sought to highlight and reorientate existing critical contributions to the study of terrorism that have been traditionally marginalised in orthodox spaces (see Jackson 2009; Zulaika 2009).

While it could be argued that these works align with McDonald's (and others') basic conception of immanent critique, issues become a little more complex when one considers that, as Charlotte Heath-Kelly outlines, a CTS commitment to immanent critique operates in tandem with an onto-epistemological dedication to *minimal foundationalism*, defined as:

> [The] critical doctrine that, through mutually constitutive relationships, both subject and object can be said to exist. Their constitution does not collapse into intersubjective

meanings and objective regularities, so objective regularities can be said to exist within socio-historical epochs.

(2010: 240, n. 3)

From this perspective, although using discursive approaches to inquire terrorism (for example, investigating the discursive construction of the war on terror) is to be positively embraced, such analyses should be grounded and explicitly related to matters of real-world significance (for example, how particular foreign and domestic policies enacted as a means to combat terrorism have been justified in political discourse). As Richard Jackson clarifies:

> Accepting . . . a "minimal foundationalism" in which the ontological distinction between subject and object is preserved, and discourse and materiality are conceptualized as shaping each other in a dialectical, never ceasing dynamic (rather than the one being solely constituted by the other), allows for research on both instances of "real world" political violence like terrorism, as well as the discursive processes by which such violence is given meaning.
>
> *(2011: 118)*

This commitment to minimal foundationalism can be found in the work of various scholars who have published under the auspices of CTS. Joseba Zulaika, for example, combines discourse analysis with anthropological and ethnographic approaches to challenge the (onto-epistemic) boundaries of how terrorism may be conceived as essentially "real" (or not), thereby informing a nuanced vision of how counterterrorist knowledge and practice may be suitably adjusted (see Zulaika 2012, this volume). The scholarship of Ruth Blakeley – which focuses on the discursive silencing of "state terrorism" (2007) and the materiality of associated practices, such as torture and rendition (see Blakeley 2011; Blakeley and Raphael 2012) – can also be categorised in this vein.

In these cases – and in myriad others – discourse is recognised as playing a *constitutive* role (that is, language actively *creates* "reality"), but one that nonetheless relates to something real that exists *beyond* discourse. Tellingly, a survey from Herring and Stokes (2011) found that the vast majority of articles published in *Critical Studies on Terrorism* (2008–2010) adhere to a minimal foundationalist approach (66%). Despite this, some scholars have argued that CTS has too often neglected the necessary anchorage of real-world significance, favouring instead analyses which depict terrorism as an all *too* discursive phenomenon:

> Because terrorism is not a clearly identifiable "thing", we immediately find ourselves involved in disputes when we try to identify it. Unfortunately, this has led CTS scholars to move too far in a constructivist or post-structuralist direction and say instead that terrorism is a discursive "construction".
>
> *(Joseph 2011: 34)*

Here, as elsewhere in international relations and security studies, *poststructuralism* is characterised as a potentially dangerous harbinger of ontological instability and epistemological irrelevance. Indeed, one finds that the implicit dangers of poststructuralism have been written into the very foundations of critical terrorism studies itself:

> Applying insights from the Welsh School and other Critical Theory sources . . . to the study of terrorism can offer an important alternative to *both traditional and post-structuralist*

approaches to terrorism. It offers a powerful tool for the investigation and critique of the dominant approach. But it also offers a rich, theoretically-grounded framework through which an alternative conceptualisation of terrorism and a concrete research agenda emerges – *thus marking a crucial difference from post-structuralist work* which has critiqued traditional studies but has largely failed to move beyond deconstructing existing discourses.

(Toros and Gunning 2009: 88–89; emphasis added)

There is a danger that critical scholarship, with its understandable concern for interrogating the discursive foundations upon which the study of terrorism is founded, will become so self-conscious that it becomes simply the study of its own (and other) discourses and progressively disengages from the empirical study of political violence and its foundations in the "real" world. . . . *A related danger is that CTS will come to be viewed as a largely post-structuralist or constructivist project with theory associated ontological and epistemological positions*, and other approaches . . . will be discouraged from participating in CTS' activities and debates.

(Jackson et al. 2009b: 233)

For scholars such as Michel and Richards, to significantly dilute CTS's programmatic commitment to minimal foundationalism would be to risk a disastrous "plunge into epistemological relativism" (2009: 404), a dangerous scenario that could "easily lead to the exoneration and legitimisation of specific violent practices by claiming their rootedness in a specific historical environment that cannot be judged by standards outside itself" (2009: 404). This may indeed be the case; yet, such an eventuality is hardly presented by poststructuralist analyses that, although they may reject the notion that reality can be interpreted outside of discourse (thus offering a de facto challenge to the analytical separation between subject and object that underpins a CTS commitment minimal foundationalism), have very real things to say about terrorism and political violence – just as poststructuralist scholars have had very real things to say about topics such as surveillance and population control in the context of critical security studies (see, for example, Dillon and Neal 2008; Debrix and Barder 2009).

Future research

Examining the history of CTS, there is enough evidence to suggest that it has remained dedicated to its primary identity as a broad church open to a variety of critical and orthodox perspectives alike. There is, undoubtedly, sufficient space for productive engagement with poststructuralist approaches to (counter)terrorism, and Heath-Kelly's (this volume) examination of the contributions of poststructuralism analyses to date is both timely and encouraging. Further questions need to be asked with regard to why so few poststructuralist analyses have been submitted under a CTS umbrella: perhaps it is because CTS is seen to wed itself to a minimal foundationalist position; perhaps it is because poststructuralists writing on matters of security already publish in spaces such as those provided by *Security Dialogue* and *Millennium*; perhaps there is simply a dearth of scholars specifically writing on matters of terrorism from a poststructuralist perspective.

Whatever the answer, we cannot lose sight of the reason *why* the encouragement of such intellectual and disciplinary pluralism is so important. Nearly ten years since the inception of critical terrorism studies, we remain faced with all-too-familiar narratives of threat: "Islamic terrorism" – and its most barbaric incarnation of the Islamic State (IS) – remains front and centre of today's security milieu and has played a major role in states' implementation (and justification) of domestic and foreign policy agendas. In 2015 alone, France passed sweeping surveillance measures in the aftermath of the *Charlie Hebdo* attacks, while in the UK, facets of the much-maligned PREVENT strategy have become enshrined in law through the Counter-Terrorism and Security (CTS) Act.

Under the CTS Act, it is now a *statutory* duty for certain public servants in the UK – such as schoolteachers and university lecturers – to report individuals who they believe to be at risk of radicalisation. For this task, the UK government explicitly expects "appropriate members of staff to have an understanding of the factors that make people vulnerable to being drawn into terrorism and to challenge extremist ideas which are used by terrorist groups and can purport to legitimise terrorist activity" (Home Office 2015: 18–19). With over forty years of scholarship on terrorism across orthodox and critical perspectives alike, a checklist understanding of the factors that draw individuals to terrorism remains elusive – whether one conceives of terrorism as an objectively knowable phenomenon or a slippery signifier that exists only in perpetual flux.

As the UK government increasingly attempts to mould the definitional parameters for *extremism* and *terrorism*, academic spaces are faced with a very real threat of constriction, and it is in this environment that critical epistemologies of (counter)terrorism themselves may come under threat. Does exposing students to the possibility of Western state terrorism or arguing that even terrorists of the Islamic State are driven by political grievances contribute to a risk of radicalisation? If scholars are to be silenced on this basis, what of the lecturers' responsibilities to enrich the learning experiences of their students to the fullest extent possible? Hopefully, such outcomes will never come to pass; yet, whatever happens, CTS must not be afraid to facilitate the speaking of truth to power – by whatever epistemology it is articulated.

Notes

1. This perspective is, thus, anathema to the CTS approach: "[a] CTS approach to terrorism research begins with the acceptance that wholly objective or neutral knowledge – any kind of absolute or real 'truth'– about terrorism is impossible and that there is always an ideological, ethical and political dimension to the research process" (Jackson et al. 2011: 37).
2. As Schmid argues, "[the] listing of frequent and similar elements of terrorism is in itself not a definition. In science, a definition is basically an equation: a new, unknown or ill-understood term (the definiendum) is described (defined) by a combination of at least two known, understandable terms (the definiens)" (Schmid 2011: 39–40).
3. As Schmid says, "unlike a mathematical equation, a definition is a conceptualisation not with numbers and algebraic symbols but using mostly everyday language. A definition says what a word is meant to mean. Usually, users of new words achieve some agreement as to the meaning soon after their introduction. (However, this meaning is not fixed for all time)" (Schmid 2011: 40).
4. Here, one notes the development of terrorism studies as a subfield of counterinsurgency studies (see Jackson et al. 2011; Stampnitzky 2013).
5. Although this is an important point of critique for various CTS scholars, it should be noted that proximity to state funding is not *necessarily* evidence of epistemic co-option. While individual cases may, of course, vary, CTS is more intently focused on the systemic nature of this problem and how it governs the production of certain "truths" on terrorism.

References

Anderson, L., 2003. *Pursuing Truth, Exercising Power: Social Science and Public Policy in the Twenty-First Century*. New York: Columbia University Press.
Bell, J. B., 1977. "Trends on terror: the analysis of political violence", *World Politics*, 29(3): 476–488.
Blackburn, S., ed., 2008. *The Oxford Dictionary of Philosophy (2nd revised ed.)*. Oxford: Oxford University Press.
Blakeley, R., 2007. "Bringing the state back into terrorism studies", *European Political Science*, 6(3): 228–235.

Blakeley, R., 2011. "Dirty hands, clean conscience? The CIA inspector general's investigation of "enhanced interrogation techniques" in the war on terror and the torture debate", *Journal of Human Rights*, 10(4): 544–561.

Blakeley, R., and Raphael, S., 2012. *The Rendition Project*. Available online at: www.therenditionproject.org.uk.

Booth, K., ed., 2005. *Critical Security Studies and World Politics*. London: Lynne Rienner Publishers.

Breen Smyth, M., 2007. "A critical research agenda for the study of political terror", *European Political Science*, 6(3): 260–267.

Breen Smyth, M., 2014. "Theorising the 'suspect community': counterterrorism, security practices and the public imagination", *Critical Studies on Terrorism*, 7(2): 223–240.

Brincat, S., Lima, L., and Nunes, J., eds., 2012. *Critical Theory in International Relations and Security Studies: Interviews and Reflections*. London: Routledge.

Burnett, J., and Whyte, D., 2005. "Embedded expertise and the new terrorism", *Journal for Crime, Conflict and the Media*, 1(4): 1–18.

Buzan, B., and Hansen, L., 2009. *The Evolution of International Security Studies*. Cambridge: Cambridge University Press.

Cox, R. W., 1981. "Social forces, states and world orders: beyond international relations theory", *Millennium: Journal of International Studies*, 10(2): 126–155.

Dalacoura, K., 2009. "Middle East area studies and terrorism studies: establishing links via a critical approach", in Jackson, R., Gunning, J., and Breen Smyth, M., eds., *Critical Terrorism Studies: A New Research Agenda*. Abingdon: Routledge.

Debrix, F., and Barder, A. D., 2009. "Nothing to fear but fear: governmentality and the biopolitical production of terror", *International Political Sociology*, 3(4): 398–413.

Dillon, M., and Neal, A. W., eds., 2008. *Foucault on Politics, Security and War*. Hampshire: Palgrave Macmillan.

Dixit, P., and Stump, J. L., 2011. "A response to Jones and Smith: it's not as bad as it seems; or, five ways to move critical terrorism studies forward", *Studies in Conflict & Terrorism*, 34(6): 501–511.

Fitzgerald, J., 2014. *Between the Lines: 'al Qaeda', 'Islamic Extremism' and the Authorship of Critique*. PhD dissertation held at Dublin City University. Available online at: http://doras.dcu.ie/20238/1/James_Fitzgerald_PhD_Dissertation_Hard_Bound_Final.pdf.

Fitzgerald, J., 2015. "Why me? An autoethnographic account of the bizarre logic of counterterrorism", *Critical Studies on Terrorism*, 8(1): 163–180.

Furtado, H. T., 2015. "Against state terror: lessons on memory, counterterrorism and resistance from the Global South", *Critical Studies on Terrorism*, 8(1): 72–89.

Gordon, A., 2010. "Can terrorism become a scientific discipline? A diagnostic study", *Critical Studies on Terrorism*, 3(3): 437–458.

Gunning, J., 2007. "The case for critical terrorism studies?", *Government and Opposition*, 42(3): 363–393.

Gunning, J., 2009. "Social movement theory and the study of terrorism", in Jackson, R., Gunning, J., and Breen Smyth, M., eds., *Critical Terrorism Studies: A New Research Agenda*. Abingdon: Routledge.

Gunning, J., and Jackson, R., 2011. "What's so 'religious' about 'religious terrorism'?", *Critical Studies on Terrorism*, 4(3): 369–388.

Heath-Kelly, C., 2010. "Critical terrorism studies, critical theory and the 'naturalistic fallacy'". *Security Dialogue*, 41(3): 235–254.

Herring, E., and Stokes, D., 2011. "Critical realism and historical materialism as resources for critical terrorism studies", *Critical Studies on Terrorism*, 4(1): 5–21.

Hoffmann, S., 1977. "An American social science: international relations", *Daedalus*, 106(3): 41–60.

Home Office, 2015. *Prevent Duty Guidance*. HM Government. Available online at: www.legislation.gov.uk/ukdsi/2015/9780111133309/pdfs/ukdsiod_9780111133309_en.pdf.

Jackson, P. T., 2011. *The Conduct of Inquiry in International Relations: Philosophy of Science and its Implications for the Study of World Politics*. London: Routledge.

Jackson, R., 2007. "The core commitments of critical terrorism studies", *European Political Science*, 6(3): 244–251.

Jackson, R., 2009. "Commentary on Joseba Zulaika, Basque violence: metaphor and sacrament", *Critical Studies on Terrorism*, 2(2): 341–343.

Jackson, R., 2011. "In defence of 'terrorism': finding a way through a forest of misconceptions". *Behavioral Sciences of Terrorism and Political Aggression*, 3(2): 116–130.

Jackson, R., 2012. "Unknown knowns: the subjugated knowledge of terrorism studies", *Critical Studies on Terrorism*, 5(1): 11–29.

Jackson, R., Breen Smyth, M., and Gunning, J., eds., 2009a. *Critical Terrorism Studies: A New Research Agenda*. London: Routledge.

Jackson, R., Breen Smyth, M., and Gunning, J., 2009b. "Critical terrorism studies: framing a new research agenda", in Jackson, R., Gunning, J., and Breen Smyth, M., eds., *Critical Terrorism Studies: A New Research Agenda*. Abingdon: Routledge.

Jackson, R., Jarvis, L., Gunning, J., and Breen Smyth, M., 2011. *Terrorism: A Critical Introduction*. London: Palgrave Macmillan.

Jackson, R., and Sinclair, J., eds., 2013. *Contemporary Debates on Terrorism*. London: Routledge.

Jarvis, L., 2009. "The spaces and faces of critical terrorism studies", *Security Dialogue*, 40(1): 5–27.

Jarvis, L., and Lister, M., 2013. "Vernacular securities and their study: a qualitative analysis and research agenda", *International Relations*, 27(2): 158–179.

Joseph, J., 2011. "Terrorism as a social relation within capitalism: theoretical and emancipatory implications", *Critical Studies on Terrorism*, 4(1): 23–37.

Laqueur, W., 1977. *Terrorism*. London: Weidenfeld and Nicholson.

Mac Ginty, R., 2013. "Looks who's talking: terrorism, dialogue and conflict transformation", *Critical Studies on Terrorism*, 6(1): 216–223.

Martin, T., 2014. "Governing an unknowable future: the politics of Britain's Prevent policy", *Critical Studies on Terrorism*, 7(1): 62–78.

McDonald, M., 2009. "Emancipation and critical terrorism studies", in Jackson, R., Gunning, J., and Breen Smyth, M., eds., *Critical Terrorism Studies: A New Research Agenda*. London: Routledge.

Michel, T., and Richards, A., 2009. "False dawns or new horizons? Further issues and challenges for critical terrorism studies", *Critical Studies on Terrorism*, 2(3): 399–413.

Mueller, J. E., 2006. *Overblown: How Politicians and the Terrorism Industry Inflate National Security Threats, and Why We Believe Them*. New York: Simon and Schuster.

Ranstorp, M., 2009. "Mapping terrorism studies after 9/11: an academic field of old problems and new prospects", in Jackson, R., Gunning, J., and Breen Smyth, M., eds., *Critical Terrorism Studies: A New Research Agenda*. London: Routledge.

Sageman, M., 2014. "The stagnation in terrorism research", *Terrorism and Political Violence*, 26(4): 565–580.

Sánchez-Cuenca, I., 2014. "Why do we know so little about terrorism?", *International Interactions*, 40(4): 590–601.

Schmid, A., and Jongman, A., 1988. *Political Terrorism: A New Guide to Actors, Authors, Concepts, Data Bases, Theories and Literature*. New Brunswick, NJ: Transaction Publishers.

Schmid, A. P., 2011. "The definition of terrorism", in Schimd, A., ed., *The Routledge Handbook of Terrorism Research*. London: Routledge.

Senechal de la Roche, R., 2004. "Toward a scientific theory of terrorism", *Sociological Theory*, 22(1): 1–4.

Silke, A., 2007. "The impact on 9/11 on research on terrorism", in Ranstorp, M., ed., *Mapping Terrorism Research: State of the Art, Gaps and Future Direction*. London: Routledge.

Silke, A., 2009. "Contemporary terrorism studies: issues in research", in Jackson, R., Gunning, J., and Breen Smyth, M., eds., *Critical Terrorism Studies: A New Research Agenda*. Abingdon: Routledge.

Sinai, J., 2007. "New trends in terrorism studies: strengths and weaknesses", in Ranstorp, M., ed., *Mapping Terrorism Research: State of the Art, Gaps and Future Direction*. London: Routledge.

Sluka, J. A., 2009. "The contribution of anthropology to critical terrorism studies", in Jackson, R., Gunning, J., and Breen Smyth, M., eds., *Critical Terrorism Studies: A New Research Agenda*. Abingdon: Routledge.

Smith, S., 2000. "The discipline of international relations: still an American social science?", *The British Journal of Politics and International Relations*, 2(3): 374–402.

Stampnitzky, L., 2011. "Disciplining an unruly field: Terrorism experts and theories of scientific/intellectual production", *Qualitative Sociology*, 34(1): 1–19.

Stampnitzky, L., 2013. *Disciplining Terror: How Experts Invented 'Terrorism'*. Cambridge: Cambridge University Press.

Toros, H., 2012. *Terrorism, Talking and Transformation: A Critical Approach*. London: Routledge.

Toros, H., and Gunning, J., 2009. "Exploring a critical theory approach to terrorism studies", in Jackson, R., Gunning, J., and Breen Smyth, M., eds., *Critical Terrorism Studies: A New Research Agenda*. Abingdon: Routledge.

Toros, H., and Tellidis, I., 2013. "From paramilitarism to peacebuilding in Northern Ireland: an interview with Noel Large", *Critical Studies on Terrorism*, 6(1): 209–215.

Yanow, D., and Schwartz-Shea, P., eds., 2006. *Interpretation and Method*. Armonk, NY: M. E. Sharpe.

Young, J. K., and Findley, M. G., 2011. "Promise and pitfalls of terrorism research", *International Studies Review*, 13(3): 411–431.

Zulaika, J., 2009. "Response to Richard Jackson", *Critical Studies on Terrorism*, 2(2): 345–347.

Zulaika, J., 2012. "Drones, witches and other flying objects: the force of fantasy in US counterterrorism", *Critical Studies on Terrorism*, 5(1): 51–68.

6
POST-STRUCTURALISM AND CONSTRUCTIVISM

Charlotte Heath-Kelly

Introduction: cats, constructivists and critical terrorism studies

The particular contributions of post-structuralism and constructivism to critical terrorism studies stem from their refusal to accept "terrorist" and "terrorism" as objective categories which exist in the world. In doing so, these approaches do not step away from engagement with the "real world", as criticisms can often suggest; rather, they become able to engage with the politics of terrorism. They become able to explore the creation of a discursive reality where the concept of terrorism is used to delegitimise certain actors, achieve policy goals and conceal the ambiguities at work in the international system. In short, post-structuralist and constructivist approaches to terrorism get at what really matters – the politics of violence.

To begin this assessment of their contributions to critical terrorism studies, we must first understand why terrorism is not an objective, unquestionable "thing in the world". To explain this, I am going to explore the roots of critical thinking in linguistic theory, rather than rehearse debates about the deceptive labelling of some violence as legitimate (interventions, the use of air power, self-defence by sovereign actors) and other violence as illegitimate. However, this is equally important and interested readers might find it useful to consult literature which unpicks this binary (Bhatia 2005; Blakeley 2007; Sluka 2009).

Post-structuralism and constructivism both have their intellectual heritage in twentieth century linguistic philosophy, particularly the early twentieth century structuralist movement which questioned the relationship between the world and systems of language. Ferdinand De Saussure was integral to the development of structuralism in the study of linguistics (Sanders 2004). He argued that there is no direct relationship between words and the objects they represent in the world. For example, the same object is known by different words across different languages. A cat is a chat, is a katze, is a macska, is a felis and so on. Given this realisation (and one might also think of the changing meaning of words over time, such as *gay* shifting from "happy" to "homosexual"), it becomes clear that words don't have timeless connections to the objects they represent. Words change, and there are multiple words for each object. So what is the relationship between language and the world? The premise of structuralism rests upon the division of linguistics into categories of "signified" and "signifier" to explore this, emphasising the lack of a direct, natural, objective relationship between the two. We have signs to represent the world, but these signs are not directly connected to the objects they signify: they change, they are plural, they mutate.

A cat could be called anything. Really, it could. And yet, interestingly, you know what I mean when I say *cat* and you know what George Bush meant when he said *terrorist*. But how do you know, if there is no connection between the word and the object it signifies? This is an epistemological question (see Fitzgerald, this volume) to which the structuralist school responded that a hidden structure of language renders it functional. You know what any given word represents because it is situated within a structure of other words, and it obtains its meaning through contrast and juxtaposition. Simply put, you know what *cat* is because it isn't *dog*. While the word *cat* has no intrinsic relationship to the referent animal, it is situated in relationships with a potentially infinite number of other words within the structure of language. As such, a word has no "objective" meaning (no timeless connection to the object it represents); instead, words give meaning to each other through their relationships in a structure. Cat is not dog, is not terrorist, is not president.

If you understand this, then you understand the intellectual heritage of the post-structuralist and constructivist schools of international relations (IR). Constructivist IR theory is based upon the argument that the identities of states are not pre-given, but instead developed through comparison and contrast with other members of the international community. Identities and the "international" are constituted through discursive performance. Essentially, this is the cornerstone of Alexander Wendt's argument in "Anarchy is What States Make of It" (1992), a key work within constructivism.[1] Writing against the dominant neorealist conception of anarchy as determining the behaviour of states within the international community, Wendt argued that anarchy does not have a timeless objective status. It isn't an objective thing. It is a social construction. Essentially, states constitute the meaning of the international arena through their actions. If the international is anarchic, then this is what states have made of it. But it is possible to change it over time.

Meaning is a social product, not an objective truth. Constructivist scholars of terrorism took this approach and began to explore very different questions to their strategic studies counterparts. For example, traditional terrorism studies does not question that a category of "terrorist" exists; rather, it accepts it as a neutral reflection of reality. As such, traditional terrorism studies dedicates its attention to measuring terrorist phenomena and applying scientific method to understand which variables increase, or decrease, terrorist violence (Bjorgo 2005; Horgan 2005; Pape 2006; Piazza 2007). But constructivist scholars are interested in the attributions of terrorism made by political elites, among others, and how these processes of labelling function. Terrorism, here, is not an objective reality, but the application of a label and the performance of meaning. The effect of labelling juxtaposes the identities of evil-doer and legitimate power, functioning to emphasise the labeller's position within legitimate politics and his or her identity as respectable.

The arguments within the most prominent constructivist research on terrorism rest upon the interconnection of war and words. Both Stuart Croft's *Culture, Crisis and America's War on Terror* (2006) and Richard Jackson's *Writing the War on Terrorism* (2005) explore the multidirectional relationship between words and the practice of the war on terror, namely that: (1) words make war possible. Threats and crises are socially constructed, not objective realities. The practice of the war on terror would not have been possible without the discursive construction of terrorism as the most salient and terrible global threat; and (2) war in turn makes meanings. The violence perpetrated by the coalition during the war on terror has been functional, securing "Western" state identities as righteous and legitimate against the threat of the barbarous other.

The first point might be summarised as "terrorism is what states make of it", to paraphrase Wendt. Constructivist research into the war on terror emphasises that while America was struck by attacks on September 11, 2001, there was nothing objective, obvious or natural about their response (Croft 2006: 2). The US could, for example, have treated the matter as a criminal act, pursuing the prosecution of those responsible in courts of law. Yet, the rhetoric of the aftermath began the discursive construction of 9/11 as an act of war and as evidence of an international security crisis, legitimating the era of the war on terror. Jackson describes this process as follows:

> The words chosen to describe these events were not simply a neutral reflection of what had happened, but actually worked to enforce a particular interpretation and meaning, most significantly that they were an "act of war". This politically constructed understanding of the events normalised the administration's response; because it was an "act of war", a "war on terrorism" appeared reasonable and logical. This war-based approach was reinforced by embedding the narrative of September 11, 2001 within larger meta-narratives about Pearl Harbour and World War II, the Cold War, civilisation versus barbarism and the advance of globalisation. In large part the purpose of the language was to prevent any interpretation that implicated American foreign policy.
>
> *(Jackson 2005: 5)*

Stuart Croft (2006) similarly describes this process as the social construction of 9/11 as a security crisis. Multiple phases of social construction are implicated in this: first, a phase whereby "we" are identified and solidified, against which "they" are identified and demonised, and this oppositional fixing is then used to present a situation of crisis requiring a firm response. Crises are made, they are not objective.[2] And they are extremely productive for political elites, enabling new potential within law-making, war-making and power consolidation.

On the second point, once the response to crisis is initiated, it serves the consolidation of identity and meaning. Put simply, it is very useful for the practice of statecraft to identify an external bad guy. Given that constructivism broadly follows the tenets of structuralist linguistic theory, the existence of a bad guy creates your own state as the good guy through linguistic and performative juxtaposition. It reaffirms your identity as legitimate, rational and civilised. Exploring the discursive construction of "Islamic terrorism" across political and academic media, Jackson finds that:

> One of the most important functions of the discourse of "Islamic terrorism" is to construct and maintain national identity, primarily through the articulation of a contrasting, negative "other" who defines the Western "self" through negation . . . as David Campbell has convincingly demonstrated, the elaboration of an external threat such as that posed by "Islamic terrorism" is crucial to maintaining internal/external, self/other boundaries and the "writing" of national identity. In fact, some have argued that Western identity is dependent on the appropriation of a backward, illiberal, violent Islamic "other" against which the West can organize a collective liberal, civilized "self" and consolidate its cultural and political norms.
>
> *(Jackson 2007: 420)*

States "write" themselves through their conflicts with others: they perform themselves as defenders of just causes and legitimate standard bearers of civilisation against the barbarous other. This is the functionality of generational crises such as the Cold War (Campbell 1992) and the war on terror (Croft 2006; Jackson 2005) – they form a matrix of understanding whereby states can assert themselves as legitimate actors and find their purpose on the world stage. Authority and legitimacy are performances that rely upon the discursive construction of threatening others.

Post-structuralism

There is not a firm dividing line between the schools of constructivism and post-structuralism, especially regarding the study of terrorism, but post-structuralism made a definite break with the linguistic school of structuralism, as one might guess from the name. In this regard, its heritage pertains to more radical features of analysis which can be absent from constructivist research. Structuralism provides a secure, closed system where we can apply rational scientific method to trace the interplay of signifiers: we know things through their opposites and their relationship synonyms. We *can know*. Jacques Derrida issued a pertinent critique of this method in *Of Grammatology* (1976), asserting that while structuralism claims a "truth" and objectivity, it is actually reliant upon Western cultural and rationalist norms and is a reflection of its historical and geographical context, rather than a method which produces truth. Derrida argued that the structuralist reliance on oppositions and binaries reflects a Western metaphysics of "presence", whereby one term is always dominant through its juxtaposition with its opposite. For example, consider the juxtaposition of *man* and *woman,* where one category is defined through what it lacks and has not. There is a hidden power structure behind the structuralist system which belies its origins in Western rationalism, and, as such, its claims to truth cannot be extended from the method's historical, cultural and geographic origins.

Claims to the particularity and cultural constitution of "truth" are a key aspect of post-structuralism: there is no such thing as a truth that is true for all times. Instead, we witness paradigms of truth which shift – even in science (Kuhn 1962). Thomas Kuhn coined the term *paradigm shift* to refer to the paradox within science, whereby the method supposed to obtain timeless truth actually produces periods of stable truth and then revolution. A truth holds for a while, as objective fact, until its operational deficiencies overcome it and it is replaced with another "timeless" truth. For example, think of the Copernican Revolution in astrophysics where, suddenly, truth changed and the Earth no longer occupied the centre of the universe as it supposedly had for hundreds of years of scientific research.

There are multiple methods in IR which deploy post-structuralist insights. Arguably, the most famous are Derrida's method of deconstruction and Foucault's genealogy. Derrida's deconstruction works by exploring and exposing the hidden power structures which constitute the hierarchy of binary terms, such as inside/outside, man/woman, activity/passivity. Foucauldian genealogy, on the other hand, takes a historical approach to the constitution of supposedly stable truths and epochs, exposing the shifts in practice whereby meanings attained their composition. One of Foucault's most famous texts, *Discipline and Punish* (1978), uses genealogy to explore the shifting regimes of punishment from the Middle Ages to the contemporary era of Western European civilisation, exposing how changing understandings of subjectivity and freedom informed a shift towards imprisonment and surveillance rather than violently hurting the body. The rise of liberalism informed a transition from "sovereign power", where bodies were executed as a demonstration of state power, to disciplinary technologies which aim to produce certain forms of conduct from subjects. Things did not become "more humane" with the advent of liberalism and humanitarian reform, as such; rather, power became subtler and more insidious.

To summarise the post-structuralist approach to meaning, there is a radical destabilisation of the relationship between signifier and signified. No longer can meaning be securely established through the structure of binary opposites, qua structuralism. Instead, invisible structures of political, racial and sexual power combine to produce the world as we know it. Importantly, the lack of foundation for objective truth and stable meaning have profound effects upon politics. The claim to authority has to be repeatedly invoked and performed by states, because the foundation of sovereignty is but a fiction: nothing less than the entire edifice of meaning and legitimate power depends upon the maintenance of the illusion. With regards to maintaining the illusion of state sovereignty founded upon the sturdy ground of legitimacy and historical precedence, terrorism plays an important role (Heath-Kelly 2014). It provides the "constitutive outside" which gives meaning to the inside through its performance. This chapter now turns to examine three post-structuralist approaches to the politics of terrorism.

Post-structuralism on terror #1: state of the exception

Given the predominance of identity politics in constructivist approaches to terrorism, whereby states perform their legitimacy through contrast with a barbarous other, one might argue that the "state of exception" thesis is the post-structuralist variant. In its original formulation, Carl Schmitt made the profound statement in *Political Theology* that "sovereign is he who decides on the exception", meaning the exception to legal norms (1985: 5). Sovereignty is identifiable through the ability to suspend law and kill without legal sanction. This decisionist understanding of political sovereignty highlights the slumber of the sovereign authority in times of normalcy and the sudden awakening of the sovereign when stability is threatened by a crisis (Schwab 1989: 50), when action must be taken. Unavoidably then, the essence of political sovereignty (which we normally associate with stable control) is actually connected to its juxtaposition with crisis and emergency.

Giorgio Agamben picked up on this point for the cornerstone of his state of exception thesis. While drawing a historical trajectory from ancient Rome, Agamben focuses on the war on terror and the US Patriot Act as the clearest contemporary examples of sovereignty acting through the definition of spaces and persons as "beyond the law". Just like the Nazi concentration camps, the United States created the space of Guantanamo Bay where inmates were placed beyond normal law, stripped of their names and rights and made into things (Agamben 2005: 3–4). Having constituted the terrorist threat as an international crisis through discourse, the US was then able to suspend the rule of law regarding the treatment of detainees (and the invasion of Iraq) by invoking the exception.

While there are many threads of this Agambenian analysis which have generated productive engagement within IR, the most pertinent for this current text concerns exceptionality and "bare life".[3] What is really important about this post-structuralist take on the war on terror is how Agamben explores the functionality of exceptional rule and the resultant rendering of people as less than human: as bare life (consider the jump-suited, nameless and stateless detainees of Guantanamo). In a compelling, complicated and debated thesis, Agamben makes the startling argument that political rule performs itself through deployment of the exception. Its claim to legal authority would mean nothing without the space-beyond-law of the evil barbarous other. Sovereignty functions through the suspension of the law and the creation of extra-legal spaces.

This looks quite like structuralism at first: knowing things through their opposites. However, Agamben's thesis focuses the coupling between sovereignty and exception around the foundationlessness of law and authority. Law has no solid ground upon which to rest, a claim also made by Walter Benjamin and Jacques Derrida, given that legal regimes are always the result of violent seizures of sovereignty (democratic revolutions, coup d'etat). Politics makes the pretence that law is the foundation for society, but it rests on nothing but a hidden history of violent conquest. Proof of this is evident every time a crisis intercedes – the suspension of law is declared because force, not jurists, must make the decision. Law is radically absent and the performance of the exception – such as Guantanamo Bay, the invasions of the war on terror and the abuse of detainees in Bagram airbase and other prisons – constitutes it. Law and authority are constituted, paradoxically, through their suspension. Looking at the treatment of exceptional figures, such as the terrorist, confirms this.

Post-structuralism on terror #2: technologies of anticipation

While Agamben makes contextual reference to the war on terror in his thesis, post-structuralist literatures on risk and anticipation have centralised counterterrorism. Building upon literatures in health and social policy which have explored the turn towards statistics and risk management in governing populations through the encouragement of "good" choices, security scholars have explored the conducting of populations through risk analysis. The preemption deployed within contemporary counterterrorism has been a fruitful topic for post-structuralist analyses which explore the production of "knowledge" about who might launch a terrorist attack, and when. These approaches look at the production of "truth" by the state within the realm of the unknown.

The introduction of the new traveller screening programmes, such as Automated Targeting System (ATS), by the Department of Homeland Security and others has attracted particular attention from scholars of risk. Such programmes collect varieties of data about each traveller, such as their addresses, method of ticket payment, financial records, "no show" history, motor vehicle records, and/or past one-way travel. Each piece of data suggests nothing about a passenger's propensity towards terrorism on its own. However, ATS collates this seemingly unconnected data into a matrix and then accords each traveller a risk score (Amoore & De Goede 2008). It *invents* knowledge within the domain of the unknown.

The screening of passenger records and the assessment of international financial flows (Amoore & De Goede 2005) are technologies which reveal the quest for preemption through mathematical modelling in the war on terror. These technologies suggest that security now attempts to anticipate and disrupt terrorists before they become terrorist, using predictive tools. This is important because it represents a shift in how the neoliberal state constitutes its citizens: while they are still individuals moulded by governmental tools, the war on terror (and broader changes in the penal system) points to an increasing tendency towards treating citizens as compilations of abstract risk factors (Valverde & Mopas 2004: 240).

The implications of this speak to the way we understand statecraft and security. Amoore and De Goede (2005) point to the increasingly evident two-tier system created by the turn towards preemptive security, where governmentality and the potential for sovereign action sit side-by-side. Citizens are still trained to take responsibility for their own risk – in line with Foucault's description of neoliberal governmentality as governing through the inducement of positive behaviours. We can see this in the repeated injunctions upon transport systems that we report suspicious behaviour to an officer or that we make disaster readiness plans. The "good" citizen is still trained, produced and educated to be responsible for risk aversion.

However, the development of preemptive technologies of security constitutes a simultaneous system whereby security services might at any moment strike upon the subject determined to be risky. One might consider the juxtaposition of everyday Londoners, travelling to work on the tube, being suddenly confronted with the brutal assassination of Jean Charles de Menezes at Stockwell station in 2005. De Menezes, a Brazilian electrician, had been mistaken for Hussein Osman – a failed suicide bomber from the previous day – even through their racial profiles were different. Despite having no connections to terrorism, the matrixes of probability which constitute preemptive security flagged him as risky – necessitating that he be followed by police officers and then executed as he boarded a train (Heath-Kelly 2012).

Brian Massumi's arguments about "lightning flashes" of sovereign power can be used to connect false positives, like the mistaken rendering of a Brazilian electrician as Hussein Osman, to logics of preemption. By the time you see a lightning strike it has already gone, just like the flash of sovereign power that sidesteps the need for judicial processes in favour of a perceived need to act on the future without delay (Massumi 2005). As such, behind the neoliberal governmentality which teaches us to go to work, make healthy choices and take responsibility for our own risk, we are simultaneously constituted as abstracted compositions of data which, if deemed suspect, could unleash the full weight of sovereign power upon us.

Post-structuralism on terror #3: counter-radicalisation

Yet the quest to preempt terrorism through the production of anticipatory "knowledge" has extended well beyond attempts to discover risky travellers and the international preparation of terrorist plots. The murder of Theo Van Gogh in Amsterdam in 2004 and the London bombings of 2005 confronted European policymakers and security services with the involvement of their own citizens in "homegrown" terrorism. In response, European counterterrorism policy shifted its focus from the airport to domestic Muslim populations, constructing a matrix whereby the risk posed by individuals could be quantified through the assessment of "radicalisation" indicators. These indicators, like the data analysed by ATS, indicate nothing by themselves; yet they are woven together to produce pre-terrorism knowledge through a matrix of suspicion. Such indicators that individuals have a tendency towards terrorism have included, at various stages in the life of the UK's PREVENT policy, the following:

- A focus on scripture as an exclusive moral source
- A conspiratorial mindset
- Expressions of political ideology such as support for the Islamic political system
- Seeing the West as a source of evil

(Quilliam Foundation, cited in Kundnani 2009)

Leaving aside that these indicators are so broad that they could make almost anybody liable to prosecution or intervention for having radicalised, the critical literature on counter-radicalisation has focused on the application of counter-radicalisation to Muslim communities largely to the exclusion of other groups. If the creation of thought-crime within preemptive policing were not debatable enough, the application of counter-radicalisation suggests that this offence can apparently only be committed by Muslims.[4] As Thomas Martin has argued, the quest to stop terrorism before it even becomes crystallised in a potential perpetrator's mind relies, in the case of UK PREVENT, upon indicators of disassociation from Britishness (Martin 2014). The individual who is vulnerable to radicalisation, according to Home Office documentation, supposedly experiences immigration-related crises of identity and belonging which preface their exploration of radical ideology. According to the Home Office, it is apparently common sense to assume that Britishness and belonging might not easily extend to Islamic communities – and that this makes them "vulnerable" to producing terrorists. Given the policy heritage of the PREVENT policy in previous problematisation of integration, the community cohesion strategy and media controversies which "othered" British Muslims (Heath-Kelly 2013), there is more than enough evidence to suspect that British counter-radicalisation is accompanied by a particularly obnoxious colonialist smell wafting up from history.

But what I would like to focus on here is the post-structuralist critique of counter-radicalisation as relevant to the production of knowledge and the making-governable of the future through actionable matrixes of risk. Before 2004, a "radicalisation process" did not exist. *Radicalisation* had previously been a little-used term which suggested, in a nonquantified manner, a drift towards more radical politics of any sort, and without any necessary connection to violence. Yet, the attacks upon Theo Van Gogh and Londoners were interpreted by policymakers, given the recent introduction of passenger screening and the development of biometric security tools, as necessitating the introduction of preemptive systems to stop citizens from becoming terrorists. This required a narrative about how people turn towards violence. Radicalisation was thus invented, constituted through the discursive environment of the early war on terror whereby "root causes" (poverty, foreign policy, failure of protest) for violence were silenced by policymakers and academics while, conversely, the ideological narratives of groups were highlighted (Kundnani 2014; Sedgwick 2010). Ideas and beliefs had become the "truth" about the causation of terrorism, contra decades of social movement theory research by established terrorism scholars (Crenshaw 1992; della Porta 1995). Simultaneously, the term radicalisation became a prominently studied "process" within strategic studies and security literatures.

The "fit" between the radicalisation narrative and the security discourse of preemption ensured its success. It enabled policymakers to extend preemptive governance to their own communities and not only air travel, financial flows and communications data. Counter-radicalisation policy has maintained the pretence of acting upon "truth" concerning an ideological process that leads to terrorism, despite the sudden invention of this knowledge in 2004–2005 and its discredited status in the academic literature. Both critical and more traditional scholars have highlighted the confusion surrounding the radicalisation concept, its lack of empirical basis and its lack of predictive power (Githens-Mazer & Lambert 2010; Richards 2011). Instead of *responding to* knowledge about transitions to terrorism, then, policy is *creating and performing* that "knowledge" – creating circular justification for its own subsequent interventions. The use of "risk" in security policy thus no longer refers to the measuring of objectively evident dangers. Instead, risk has become performative – producing the foundations for the interventions of security services. The radicalisation discourse has produced a narrative about a process of ideological brainwashing to enable the pretence that security can identify terrorists and extend its actions into the sphere of the unknown (Heath-Kelly 2013).

At this point, we can clearly see the difference between post-structuralism and structuralism through the instability of language and knowledge in their relationship to the world. Risks are no longer identifiable as being distinct from the unthreatening; instead, the preemptive politics of counter-radicalisation (and indeed passenger screening technologies) takes innocuous data and processes it through a matrix which produces "danger" – the danger which then legitimates an anticipatory remit for security and consolidates the pretence that security services can prevent terrorism before it even starts.

Conclusions and deer

In this brief exploration of the contributions of constructivist and post-structuralist approaches to terrorism, I have highlighted the common heritage of both in linguistic theory and shown how they interrogate the politics of terrorism through the denial of its objective existence as a thing in the world. By using a methodology which highlights the social construction of terrorism, rather than its natural existence as an unproblematic category, constructivist and post-structuralist research is able to thoroughly interrogate the functionality of "the dangerous terrorist other" for politics. These schools are able to explain the paradox of terrorism – whereby it kills less people per year than "accident causing deer" (Mueller 2006: 13), and yet simultaneously generates a global war on terror and the expenditure of trillions of dollars. Terrorism is extremely productive for politics, despite its low casualty figures. It is not a thing in the world, but a functional discourse. The framing of exceptional terrorist threat enables the passing of new laws, the constitution of one's state identity as legitimate and civilised, the extension of surveillance technologies, and the legitimation of a preemptive sphere of action. At no point does it seem to matter that terrorist violence kills surprisingly few people.

In conclusion then, while constructivist and post-structuralist approaches are often accused by positivists of dodging the real world in favour of a study of discourse, they actually enable researchers to engage with the politics and functionality of terrorism and violence. Indeed, without these critical reflections upon terrorism, we would be left with the question of deer, and why security policy finds fascination in one cause of death and not another.

In terms of a future research agenda, there remain issues which critical approaches to terrorism have not fully engaged with. Security policy constantly evolves and academia is often left to catch up. The most pressing development for constructivist and post-structuralist approaches to terrorism to explore is the transformation of security policies around resilience. We have yet to account for state practices of counterterrorism in this era. It is important that this be done, given the radical shift in the constitution of security made by the resilience agenda. Resilience has taken steps away from the preventative approach to terrorism, admitting that not all attacks can be stopped; security, as such, no longer promises to keep populations safe. Instead, it invents the prospect of resilient recovery from disaster whereby consequences of emergencies are planned for and supposedly mediated.

How has this changed the governance of terrorism? Can constructivist insights still be applied to contemporary resilience policy, even though security policy appears to have ditched identity politics in favour of abstracted "crisis events" (rather than enemies) and the protection of infrastructure (rather than populations framed as "us")? These are questions which require answers, lest policy outpace critique.

Notes

1 For post-structuralist critique of this piece, see Zehfuss 2001.
2 For further literature on the social construction of crisis, see the Copenhagen School of Security Studies (Buzan et al. 1998; McDonald 2008), constructivist work in political science (Hay 1996) and post-structuralist work on the performativity of emergency and crisis (Brassett & Vaughan-Williams 2012).
3 "Bare life" signifies the life which has been reduced to biological function, losing all of its human attributes. The most frequently invoked example is the subjectivity of concentration camp detainees.
4 See Bentley (2014) for a discussion of the unconvincing attempt by UK policymakers to demonstrate that counter-radicalisation does not solely target Islamic communities by extending the coverage of PREVENT to right-wing extremism.

References

Agamben, G., 2005. *State of Exception*, Chicago: University of Chicago Press.
Amoore, L. & De Goede, M., 2005. "Governance, Risk and Dataveillance in the War on Terror", *Crime, Law and Social Change* 43(2–3): 149–73.
Amoore, L. & De Goede, M., 2008. "Introduction", in Amoore, L., and De Goede, M., eds., *Risk and the War on Terror*, Abingdon: Routledge, pp. 5–19.
Bentley, M., 2014. "Recognition Masking Response: Preventing Far-Right Extremism and Radicalisation", in Baker-Beall, C., Heath-Kelly, C., and Jarvis, L., eds., *Counter-Radicalisation: Critical Perspectives*, Abingdon: Routledge, pp. 106–22.
Bhatia, M., 2005. "Fighting Words: Naming Terrorists, Bandits, Rebels and Other Violent Actors", *Third World Quarterly* 26(1): 5–22.
Bjorgo, T., ed. 2005. *The Root Causes of Terrorism*, Abingdon: Routledge.
Blakeley, R., 2007. "Bringing the State Back Into Terrorism Studies", *European Political Science* 6(3): 228–35.
Brassett, J. & Vaughan-Williams, N., 2012. "Governing Traumatic Events", *Alternatives: Global, Local, Political* 37(3): 183–7.
Buzan, B., Waever, O. & de Wilde, J., 1998. *Security: A New Framework for Analysis,* London: Lynne Reinner.
Campbell, D., 1992. *Writing Security: United States Foreign Policy and the Politics of Identity,* Minneapolis: University of Minnesota Press.

Crenshaw, M., 1992. "Decisions to use Terrorism: Psychological Constraints on Instrumental Reasoning", in della Porta, D., ed., *Social Movements and Violence: Participation in Underground Organisations*, London: JAI, pp.29–42.

Croft, S., 2006. *Culture, Crisis and America's War on Terror*, Cambridge: Cambridge University Press.

della Porta, D., 1995. *Social Movements, Political Violence and the State: A Comparative Analysis of Italy and Germany*, Cambridge: Cambridge University Press.

Derrida, J., 1976. *Of Grammatology*, Baltimore: Johns Hopkins University Press.

Foucault, M., 1978. *Discipline and Punish: The Birth of the Prison*, New York: Pantheon.

Githens-Mazer, J. & Lambert, R., 2010. "Why Conventional Wisdom on Radicalization Fails: The Persistence of a Failed Discourse", *International Affairs* 86(4): 889–901.

Hay, C., 1996. "Narrating Crisis: The Discursive Construction of the 'Winter of Discontent'", *Sociology* 30(2): 253–77.

Heath-Kelly, C., 2012. "Reinventing Prevention or Exposing the Gap? False Positives in UK Terrorism Governance and the Quest for Pre-Emption", *Critical Studies on Terrorism* 5(1): 69–87.

Heath-Kelly, C., 2013. "Counter-Terrorism and the Counterfactual: Producing the 'Radicalisation' Discourse and the UK PREVENT strategy", *British Journal of Politics and International Relations* 15(3): 394–415.

Heath-Kelly, C., 2014. "Counter-Terrorism: The Ends of a Secular Ministry", in Jarvis, L., and Lister, M., eds., *Critical Perspectives on Counter-Terrorism*, Abingdon: Routledge, pp.41–55.

Horgan, J., 2005. *The Psychology of Terrorism*, Abingdon: Routledge.

Jackson, R., 2005. *Writing the War on Terrorism: Language, Politics and Counter-Terrorism*, Manchester: Manchester University Press.

Jackson, R., 2007. "Constructing Enemies: 'Islamic Terrorism' in Political and Academic Discourse", *Government and Opposition* 42(3): 394–426.

Kuhn, T., 1962. *The Structure of Scientific Revolutions*, Chicago: University of Chicago Press.

Kundnani, A., 2009. *Spooked: How Not to Prevent Violent Extremism*, London: Institute of Race Relations.

Kundnani, A., 2014. "Radicalisation: The Journey of a Concept", in Baker-Beall, C., Heath-Kelly, C., and Jarvis, L., eds., *Counter-Radicalisation: Critical Perspectives*, Abingdon: Routledge, pp.14–35.

Martin, T., 2014. "Challenging the Separation of Counter-Terrorism and Community Cohesion in Prevent: The Potential Threat of the Radicalised Subject", in Baker-Beall, C., Heath-Kelly, C., and Jarvis, L., eds., *Counter-Radicalisation: Critical Perspectives*, Abingdon: Routledge, pp.190–205.

Massumi, B., 2005. "The Future Birth of the Affective Fact", in *Conference Proceedings: Genealogies of Biopolitics*, available online at: http://browse.reticular.info/text/collected/massumi.pdf (accessed 10/09/2014).

McDonald, M., 2008. "Securitisation and the Construction of Security", *European Journal of International Relations* 14(4): 563–87.

Mueller, J., 2006. *Overblown: How Politicians and the Terrorism Industry Inflate National Security Threats, and Why We Believe Them*, New York: Free Press.

Pape, R., 2006. *Dying to Win: The Strategic Logic of Suicide Terrorism*, New York: Random House.

Piazza, J., 2007. "Draining the Swamp: Democracy Promotion, State Failure, and Terrorism in 19 Middle Eastern Countries", *Studies in Conflict and Terrorism* 30(6): 521–39.

Richards, A., 2011. "The Problem with 'Radicalization': The Remit of 'Prevent' and the Need to Refocus on Terrorism in the UK", *International Affairs* 87(1): 143–52.

Sanders, C., ed. 2004. *The Cambridge Companion to Saussure*, Cambridge: Cambridge University Press.

Schmitt, C., 1985. *Political Theology*, Cambridge, MA: MIT Press.

Schwab, G., 1989. *The Challenge of the Exception: An Introduction to the Political Ideas of Carl Schmitt Between 1921 and 1936*, Westport: Greenwood.

Sedgwick, M., 2010. "The Concept of Radicalization as a Source of Confusion", *Terrorism and Political Violence* 22(4): 479–94.

Sluka, J., 2009. "The Contribution of Anthropology to Critical Terrorism Studies", in Jackson, R., Breen-Smyth, M., & Gunning, J., eds., *Critical Terrorism Studies: A New Research Agenda*, Abingdon: Routledge, pp.138–55.

Valverde, M. & Mopas, M., 2004. "Insecurity and the Dream of Targeted Governance", in Larner, W., and Walters, W., eds., *Global Governmentality: Governing International Spaces*, Abingdon: Routledge, pp.233–50.

Wendt, A., 1992. "Anarchy is What States Make of It: The Social Construction of Power Politics", *International Organisation* 46(2): 391–425.

Zehfuss, M., 2001. "Constructivism and Identity: A Dangerous Liaison", *European Journal of International Relations* 7(3): 315–48.

7
CRITICAL THEORY AND TERRORISM STUDIES
Ethics and emancipation

Harmonie Toros

Introduction

Why do we study terrorism? How do we study terrorism? To what end do we study terrorism? Answering these questions is at the heart of critical terrorism studies (CTS) and, in particular, of the work of those CTS scholars who draw on Frankfurt School Critical Theory. This chapter focuses on this latter critical theory-based approach, highlighting the principal contributions it has made to the study of terrorism and examining some of the key areas in which it has yet to realize its full potential. It will be argued here that critical theory pushed CTS to focus on two key themes: ethics and emancipation. Thus, the first section of this chapter will examine questions such as: What are the ethics surrounding the study of terrorism? How has terrorism been studied so far and what are the principal problems surrounding its study? As we shall see, a critical theory-based approach leads to a trenchant critique of mainstream approaches to terrorism, exposing its dangerous statism and ahistoricism.

However, simply critiquing mainstream approaches is not sufficient for a critical theory-based approach, which also requires scholars to find better ways to understand and engage with social practices – in this case, terrorist violence. This is where the concept of emancipation comes in. The second section will examine what an emancipatory approach to terrorism looks like and the difficulties faced by scholars adopting such an approach. The final section will point at some of the omissions and ellipses (Wibben 2011) that can be identified in critical theory-based work so far: What commitments have we failed to live up to? What have we failed to investigate? What are some of the most important research paths that remain unexplored?

The ethics of studying terrorism: Who are we? Who are they?

In 1937, Max Horkheimer published "Traditional and Critical Theory," a text that would impact upon generations of scholars studying the social world. In it, he distinguished between scholars dedicated to traditional theory, who saw the world "as a sum-total of facts: it is there and must be accepted" (Horkheimer 1982a: 199) and those dedicated to critical theory who believe the established order and its assumptions need to be questioned and challenged. For Horkheimer (1982b: 178), traditional theory "relinquishes its claim to exercise criticism." Its aim is to improve the system or order, not challenge it. In the study of terrorism, this has principally meant investigating what forms of counterterrorism are most effective: military strategies, police-led strategies, special legislation, and so forth. The deans of terrorism studies – from the late Paul Wilkinson to Bruce Hoffman – have indeed published volumes examining how to effectively counter terrorism. Just examining a few recent issues of the mainstream terrorism journal, *Terrorism and Political Violence*, one can find numerous examples of such research, from whether and when it may be effective to kill terrorist leaders (Freeman 2014) to whether US "hearts and minds" campaigns in Africa can be effective to prevent terrorist recruitment (Aldrich 2014). Although such scholars have produced interesting research, they all accept the established order as given. As such, states become legitimate actors that need to defend themselves – and us – from terrorists.

What critical theory argues is that "society [is] in need of radical transformation and not simply reform" (Hoffman 1987: 232). This means "challenging the very categories of better, useful, appropriate, productive, and valuable . . . and refus[ing] to take them as nonscientific presuppositions about which one can do nothing" (Horkheimer 1982a: 207). Engaging with terrorism studies, this means investigating what categories, practices, and orders traditional terrorism scholarship is taking for granted and the effects that these assumptions have on its understanding of terrorism. Broadly, one can identify three central assumptions put forward by mainstream terrorism scholars. First, they base their research on positivist assumptions. This means that they believe research should adopt an objective standpoint from which to carry out a neutral analysis of data leading to the establishment of orderly, causal narratives. Second, they broadly view politics through a realist lens. The state is central to their narrative as the protector of all that is "good" and anything directly challenging the state is presented as undermining the wellbeing of the collectivity. Finally, and based on the realist position, traditional terrorism scholarship largely advocates that terrorism needs to be countered, most likely through violence, for it to be eradicated.

Before examining each of these arguments in turn, it is important to note that "traditional terrorism scholarship" is not a monolithic undertaking that speaks with one voice. Traditional terrorism scholars routinely disagree with each other, including on fundamental questions such as whether states can engage in terrorist violence, as with the disagreement between Bruce Hoffman (1998) and Paul Wilkinson (2001). However, traditional scholars overall tend to follow the three assumptions to be examined in this section: positivism, realism, and the need to use force to respond to terrorism. Furthermore, due to a striking poverty in primary research, particularly in the pre-9/11 era, "researchers tended to create closed and circular research systems where they relied on each other's work which was synthesized and functioned in a constantly reinforcing feedback loop" (Ranstorp 2009: 20; see also Raphael 2009; Reid and Chen 2007; Silke, 2004, 2009). Thus, it seems possible to make generalizations on traditional terrorism scholarship, while recognizing that it is varied and has made original contributions to the field. Similarly, although scholars developing a critical theory-based approach to terrorism have diverged in various questions – from the importance of discourse in the construction of "terrorism" to how emancipation should be understood in the context of terrorism – they can be associated with the approach by their common inspiration in the Frankfurt School of Critical Theory and the Aberystwyth School of Critical Security Studies. Indeed, the arguments put forward in this chapter are in part drawn from works written by scholars working in or linked to Aberystwyth, including Booth (2008), Jackson (2005), Toros and Gunning (2009), McDonald (2009), and Toros (2012).

"Seeking eternal answers to eternal questions"

As argued by Ken Booth (2008: 67), terrorism, like security, is "a derivative field of study, with people bringing to it ideas based on their most basic assumptions about politics." The first aim of a critical theory-based approach is thus to unearth the basic assumptions about politics, but also about social sciences more broadly, that lie beneath terrorism scholarship. Traditional terrorism studies is based on the assumption, possibly best exemplified by Wilkinson (2006: 1), that there are "independent objective verifiable criteria to enable us to distinguish terrorism from other forms of activity." There is an order of things and it is up to the social scientist to reveal this order. To cite Pierre Bourdieu (cited in Acciaioli 1981: 40), such scholars are "seeking eternal answers to eternal questions."

This search is particularly problematic as it directly leads to one of the principle weaknesses of traditional terrorism studies: its ahistoricism. Seeking eternal answers to eternal questions leads to research that seeks to "transcend history" (Cox 1986: 247), that is, research that ignores fundamental social, political, economic, and historical contexts in which terrorist violence occurs. This becomes clear in the numerous typologies that fill traditional terrorism articles and books. Groups emerging in starkly different contexts – from the Front for the Liberation of Quebec (FLQ) to the LTTE in Sri Lanka – become examples of a single category of terrorist groups ("nationalist-separatist terrorism"), and "revolutionary terrorism" includes groups ranging from the Weather Underground in the United States to Dev Sol (Revolutionary Left) in Turkey (Weinberg and Davis 1989: 48–69). Such an approach constitutes a "homogenization and trivialization of vastly different social realities under the buzzword 'terrorism'" (Zulaika and Douglass 1996: 23).

This homogenization leads to a dangerous disconnect between the analysis of the violence and the context of each conflict. Thus, terrorism is understood as an aberration rather than as part of an ecology of violence perpetrated by states, non-state actors and international actors. Terrorism is understood as a dysfunction in the social order rather than as a symptom of a dysfunctional social order. Thus, the central question being asked is, "how can the social order be rectified to end terrorist violence?" – a traditional theory approach – rather than, "what power inequalities does it reflect or what functions does the violence serve in the social order?" – a critical theory approach. The response to terrorism becomes a technical one – how do we technically stop it – ignoring its essential political challenge to the system. Terrorism is thus politically disarmed; it is de-politicized and turned into an "apolitical monstrosity" (Gold-Biss 1994: 6).

Thus, the positivist position of traditional terrorism scholarship has important political repercussions: it stands squarely in support of the status quo of the liberal international regime of states. Its position is far from neutral or objective, but rather as all theory, it is "*from* somewhere, *for* someone, and *for* some purpose" (Booth 2007: 150). Indeed, the position of traditional terrorism scholars reflects their underlying realist position that sees terrorism as an aberration to the normal, and most of all, legitimate functioning of the state. It is to the realist assumptions of traditional terrorism scholarship that we now turn.

In defense of the state

For Annemarie Oliverio, traditional terrorism scholarship should be understood as an "active part of statecraft" standing in defense of the nation-state against dangerous popular uprisings. Indeed, the term took on its negative connotation in its English usage to denote dangers such as the French revolutionary *terreur* or terror. More importantly, "what has remained constant is the construct's reference as acts undermining the state and its representative institutions and organizations in society as terrorism" (Oliverio 1998: 31). As such, terrorists come to represent everything that is dangerous and bad, and the opposing "we" represent everything that is good and orderly (Said 1988: 53). Indeed, many traditional terrorism scholars reject the possibility of state terrorism, and those who do recognize that states too can engage in terrorist violence see it as the work of a "bad" state and not a reflection of state behavior more broadly (see also Oliverio 1998: 34–35).

Alex Schmid (2004: 203) compares terrorism to war crimes and states that "terrorism distinguishes itself from combat through disregard for principles of chivalry and humanity." Thus, states fight with chivalry and humanity while terrorists are understood as those who disregard these principles. This moral contrast is transferred to the international stage where terrorism "is framed according to a definite world view that opposes countries and cultures within a hierarchy of values in which 'we' are at the top and the practitioners of terrorism are at the bottom" (Zulaika and Douglass 1996: 13). Consequently, numerous scholars will examine how states can work together to defeat terrorism, most notably in the international coalition that joined the US-led "war on terror."

The combination of positivism and realism makes for a particularly powerful basis for traditional terrorism scholars, as the statism of realism becomes the only possible approach to take once one accepts a positivist epistemology. Indeed, since traditional terrorism scholarship claims to be neutrally and objectively examining the "real world," their arguments in defense of the state and presenting this stark dichotomy between a chivalrous and human state and dastardly and conniving terrorists become a reflection of "reality" and thus the only possible interpretation.

Counterterrorism

If the only possible approach to terrorism is one that stands in defense of the status quo and the legitimacy of states, then naturally the prime policy goal of traditional terrorism scholarship is to find the best means to defend states from terrorists. What is almost exclusively put forward as the appropriate response is *counterterrorism* – a term that from a critical theory perspective needs to be examined. Indeed, the term itself is problematic as it establishes a timeline in which state violence (usually counterterrorism involves the use of some form of police or military force) comes *as a response to* non-state violence, the "terrorism." This automatically poses the state in a legitimate position of self-defense while situating "terrorists" as the aggressors (see Toros forthcoming).

Furthermore, increasing research has shown that policies labeled as counterterrorism often preceded the terrorist violence and are given the new label to award them renewed legitimacy (see the interesting work of Doug Stokes [2005] on Colombia in this regard). In other cases, terrorist attacks become the trigger to undertake policies that states want to carry out for other political, economic, or ideological goals. An excellent example of this is the war in Iraq, presented as part of the war on terror using false and inflated intelligence to establish links between the regime of Saddam Hussein and al Qaeda. Thus, simply by accepting the term counterterrorism uncritically, traditional terrorism scholarship legitimizes state violence in response to terrorist attacks.

Indeed, counterterrorism often involving large-scale violence is presented as the self-evident response to terrorism (Hocking 1993; Jackson 2005, 2009). Order must be restored for states to keep functioning. Wilkinson (2001: x), for example, argues that terrorism such as al Qaeda's "must be suppressed by criminal law enforcement and armed force because of the danger [it] pose[s] to peace, security, and the rule of law." The restoration of order becomes *sine qua non* for traditional terrorism scholars, without any questioning of the very order that is being restored. Traditional terrorism studies thus "functions ideologically to reinforce and reify existing structures of power in society, particularly that of the state" (Jackson 2009: 67), structures that led to groups turning to terrorist violence in the first place.

Furthermore, it is not uncommon for scholars to use particularly aggressive language in justifying the restoration of order. Realist Colin Gray (2002: 229) argued shortly after September 11 that a hegemon like the United States must "hunt down [these] irregular forces to the last man and to the ends of the earth." Others have reached surprising extremes: Jan Narveson (1991: 163) argued in an academic publication that to end a hostage taking, states should "begin shooting the presently imprisoned terrorists, one by one" unless hostages are released, and if terrorists kill any hostages, "there is a question whether the terrorist's friends, family, or close associates might not also be eligible" for retaliatory violence.

This focus on a violent counterterrorist response also undermines the potential for other responses to terrorist violence. For example, conflict prevention responses continue to take the liberal democratic state and the international system of states as their referent objects to be protected. Thus, long-term policies or "hearts and minds" strategies are taken into account only if they uphold the legitimacy of the state and international system of states. Meanwhile, conflict resolution responses – such as negotiation with terrorist groups – are entirely shunned. As Richard Jackson (2005: 9) argues, by constructing these stark dichotomies between the legitimate "good" state and the illegitimate "evil" terrorists, "eradicating [the terrorists] appears opposite while negotiating with them appears absurd." Indeed, traditional terrorism scholarship has overall positioned itself against the possibility of negotiations and dialogue with terrorist groups arguing that such talks would: (a) undermine the legitimacy of the state; (b) incite more violence; and (c) be doomed to fail as terrorists cannot be trusted to stand by agreements reached (for further discussion of this issue, see Toros 2012).

As we have seen, by urging scholars to examine the basic assumptions behind scholarship, a critical theory-based approach leads to a powerful critique of traditional terrorism studies, revealing its positivism, its statism, and its overwhelming support for violent counterterrorist responses. This in itself makes an important contribution to the study of terrorism. But, for a critical theory-based approach to be true to the ideas of the Frankfurt School, it is not sufficient to simply critique the current system and scholarship. As argued by Richard Wyn Jones (2005: 219), to "challenge and question the status quo it is necessary to have some notion of what would constitute an improvement upon it; it is precisely what provides critical purchase on the object of inquiry"; or, to follow Karl Marx's injunction, theory that does not aim to "change the world" is not critical, but falls back into traditional theory. The next section will therefore examine how critical theory provides a framework upon which to reconceptualize terrorism.

Terrorism and emancipation

Reflecting the work advocated by Booth (1991, 2007) in developing a critical theory-based approach to security – which became the Aberystwyth School of Critical Security Studies (CSS) – a critical theory-based approach to terrorism engages in the two fundamental moves of *deepening* and *broadening* our understanding of terrorism. Indeed, terrorism can be viewed as the tip of an iceberg formed of layers of social, political, economic, and human conflict (see Toros and Gunning [2009] for a lengthier discussion). Of the two moves, the deepening is arguably the most important one, as it allows for scholars to discover the breadth that lies beneath the sea level. I shall thus begin by examining how to deepen our understanding of terrorism studies before outlining what constitutes a broadened understanding. What will become clear is that in both moves, the concept of emancipation is key to a critical theory-based engagement with terrorism.

The depth and breath of emancipation

Just as it is important to uncover the assumptions of traditional terrorism scholars, critical theory-based scholars need to be reflexive about their basic assumptions about how the social world can be understood (a question of research) and how it is to be engaged with (a question of politics). To begin with the former, critical theory takes on a minimal foundationalist position with regard to the "world out there." This means that it believes there *is* a world out there, but that we can only access it from within our social, political, economic, and historical context. For terrorism, this means that critical theory-based scholars accept that there is a category of violence that can be understood as terrorism – broadly understood as political violence aimed at impacting a larger audience than its immediate target – but that this understanding changes and evolves along with the context in which it occurs and the context from which it is studied. Thus, unlike post-structuralist scholars who focus entirely on the social construction of the discourses of terrorism (see Heath-Kelly, this volume), critical theory-based scholars engage with both material acts of terrorist violence and their social construction and reconstruction in competing discourses.

Answering the second question – how is the world to be engaged with? – the deepening move reveals that the Frankfurt School is explicitly normative, another aspect that distinguishes it markedly from other critical theories such as post-structuralism and constructivism, and its normative goal is emancipation. Indeed, Wyn Jones (1999: 56) states that critical theory "stands and falls by the possibility that emancipatory potential exists," that is, the potential for humanity's emancipation from slavery (Horkheimer 1982a: 246). Booth (2007: 181) elaborates: emancipation is the "theory and practice of inventing humanity, with a view of freeing people, as individuals and collectivities, from contingent and structural oppressions." Thus, the goal of any research in terrorism should be not to sustain the statist status quo, but rather to support progress toward the greater emancipation of all. But what does this actually mean? How do these words not remain empty promises for a very distant better future?

One way of giving substance to emancipation is to link it to violence. Emancipation from violence is thus a first way of understanding this relationship. This means emancipation from terrorist violence but also, in a broadening move, emancipation from counterterrorist violence. It means trying to support nonviolent responses in conflicts marked by terrorist violence, such as negotiations between the parties, nonviolent engagement with the root causes of conflict, and supporting nonviolent factions within both the state and opposition movements. Indeed, considerable critical theory-based work has examined the potential for negotiations in contexts of terrorism (Gunning 2004, 2009; Toros 2008, 2012) or how to support grassroots organizations that have been linked to armed factions (the work of Victoria Fontan [2015] on Occupy Fallujah movement is particularly interesting).

An emancipatory approach can also mean studying contexts of terrorist violence to identify those nonviolent voices that are being drowned out by the violence. Indeed, Matt McDonald (2009: 216), in his work on how to apply the concept of emancipation to critical terrorism studies, argues that

> An emancipatory approach would entail locating solidarist, non-violent, and inclusive approaches to problems of political violence precisely within the voices marginalised and silenced in reactionary mainstream and elite accounts. Such an approach would also be relevant to the ways in which moderate voices on all sides of violent conflict can become marginalised, and a broader conflict captured by those militant voices engaged in "terrorist" violence claiming to speak for a particular community.

Thus, it would mean engaging in research that highlights such solidarist nonviolent voices and thus sustains them in their actions.

Although such a strategy is likely to lead to supporting many worthy emancipatory initiatives, theoretically the argument is problematic. Indeed, supporting nonviolent initiatives, such as dialogue, and nonviolent factions focuses primarily on direct violence or physical violence – a problem that arguably mars many critical scholars when engaging with terrorist violence. Their position seems to be that those who use nonviolent means (that is, emancipatory means) are solidarist and inclusive (that is, seeking emancipatory ends), while those using violence (counter-emancipatory means) are militant or reactionary (having counter-emancipatory ends). What I argue here is that although it may be generally true that means and ends are true to each other, it is not necessarily the case.

The best means to unravel this assumed relationship is to distinguish between different types of violence, in particular, direct violence and structural violence. Johan Galtung (1969: 170–171) distinguishes between different forms of violence as follows:

> where there is an actor that commits the violence as *personal* or *direct*, and to the violence where there is no such actor as *structural* or *indirect*. In both cases individuals may be killed or mutilated, hit or hurt in both senses of these words, and manipulated by means of stick or carrot strategies. But whereas in the first case these consequences can be traced to concrete persons as actors, in the second case this is no longer meaningful. There may not be any person who directly harms another person in the structure. The violence is built into the structure and shows up as unequal power and consequently as unequal life chances.

Based on this distinction, the argument I make here is that some actors use direct violence to fight structural violence – thus using counter-emancipatory means to fight an emancipatory battle – while others may refrain from using direct violence but their goals may be sustaining structural violence, thus using emancipatory means but working toward a counter-emancipatory goal. Although linking emancipation to violence allows critical theory-based scholars to give emancipation a more concrete basis and avoid the danger of abstract utopianism, when one unpacks the concept of violence, it becomes clear that the relationship between terrorism and emancipation is extremely complex.

Emancipatory terrorism: a contradiction in terms?

In his engagement with terrorism, Ken Booth is very clear regarding the use of violence for emancipatory ends. Although he understands how those faced with unbearable structural violence may turn toward direct violence, he nonetheless argues that "good guys should behave as if they are . . . [and] the warning against employing means that are contrary to ends must be honoured as far as possible. Emancipatory terrorism is a contradiction in terms" (Booth 2008: 77). Drawing on Mahatma Gandhi's nondualistic position that means and ends have "to be true to each other," Booth (2007: 255) argues that if "those who want to create a radically new world attempt to do it through the employment of traditional strategic action (violence), then success will tend to confirm the lesson that violence is indispensable." Thus, perpetrating terrorist violence with the aim of ending human slavery cannot be understood as emancipatory, for authors such as Booth, for it enslaves by its very use of violence.

Such a position is certainly tenable, and if one is a pacifist, terrorism aimed at emancipation is indeed a contradiction in terms. One must be careful, however, as it could be argued that there are conditions under which such a blanket rejection of violent means may condemn populations to live under regimes of extreme structural violence with no hope of ever extracting themselves. What happens to those living in contexts in which nonviolent opposition is impossible? Are they condemned to wait for a dialogical opening to engage nonviolently with a regime? And are we speaking of a rejection of both structural *and* direct violence? If so, many emancipatory projects, even if they are not brought forward through direct violence, involve some structural violence against some groups within society. Indeed, one can argue that any campaign aimed at radical change involves some degree of violence against some sections of society, even if only against those who have reaped the benefits of structural violence in the past.

Thus, the relationship between emancipation and terrorism remains a particularly difficult one to conceptualize for critical theory-based scholars. It is a relationship that can only be addressed on a case-by-case basis, taking into account the violences on all sides. There is no doubt that adopting such a case-by-case approach that allows the possibility that violence can be a legitimate means toward emancipation is a slippery slope, one on which it is very difficult to draw a line. Lines, of course, need to be drawn to avoid a blanket "the end justifies the means" approach that has led to endless death and destruction, exemplified by the French *terreur*.

Conclusion: where from here?

Thus, one of the central questions that needs further investigation is that of the relationship between terrorism and emancipation. Importantly, if one accepts that means and ends are not necessarily always aligned – although they should be as much as possible – this has a considerable impact on future research avenues. Indeed, this means that all actors are capable of emancipatory *and* counter-emancipatory means and of working toward emancipatory *and* counter-emancipatory ends, and that all such combinations need to be examined. This argument challenges the CTS focus so far on state violence on the one side and on factions within non-state groups willing to engage in dialogue and end violence on the other. Indeed, because CTS was born in contrast to traditional terrorism studies and its focus on state legitimacy and non-state illegitimacy, it chose to examine the very state terrorism and counterterrorism that was being ignored and sustained by traditional scholarship.

However, such a focus has arguably left some other important areas underexamined. The argument here is that by focusing on the social, political, economic, and historical contexts surrounding acts of non-state terrorist violence, CTS has turned its attention largely to state violence, be it in the form of state terrorism or counterterrorism. When non-state terrorism is examined, it tends to be through a discursive framework examining state discourses (for example, through its politics of labeling, such as in the work of Haspeslagh [2013], or more broadly on the discursive construction of non-state terrorism, such as Jackson [2005], among others). Ten years after the start of the CTS project, it is time, however, to expand our focus beyond state violence. This should push research in two directions.

First, we need to find a way to offer a critical engagement with non-state terrorism. So far, much research in CTS has avoided a direct investigation of non-state terrorist attacks, although work such as Gunning (2009) on Hamas, Zulaika and Douglass (1990) on ETA, and Devji (2005) on al Qaeda has offered an investigation and analysis of non-state violence. One reason is that traditional scholarship used their descriptions of the extreme violence and gore of such attacks to justify violent counterterrorism practices, and CTS scholars did not want to participate in sustaining state counterterrorist violence.

There are, however, considerable drawbacks in this omission. To begin with, it provides ammunition for traditional terrorism scholars who accuse CTS scholars of ignoring non-state terrorist violence, indeed of willfully overlooking it, if not of justifying it (see for example, Jones and Smith 2009). It also leaves the analysis of such acts by traditional scholars uncontested, granting them the monopoly of interpretation of such acts. Maybe most importantly though, it leaves an entire aspect of terrorist violence largely sidelined in our investigations. For those of us who accept "terrorism" also as a category of violence (interpreted through and rendered meaningful by discursive constructions), it leaves a hole in the absolute heart of our research. Critical theory-based research thus needs to investigate non-state violence while placing it in its social, political, economic, and historical contexts. It means finding a way to engage with such attacks and giving them a meaning that goes beyond that of the "apolitical monstrosity." It means repoliticizing non-state terrorism, rather than ignoring it.

The second avenue that needs to be investigated is what elements of the state are open to and engaging in emancipatory means and ends. Which elements of the state are attempting to open dialogue with non-state armed groups? Which elements are resisting the violent logics of counter-terrorism? Who is working toward radical change? There are of course dangers of cooptation involved in engaging with state actors. In speaking with state actors, particularly military and police actors, one may feel the need to "use their language" – a statist language that is often gendered and orientalized in problematic ways. In empathizing with state actors, one may come to accept logics of extreme violence and eventually, if this happens often enough, normalize them. The danger of "going native" exists just as much with state actors as it does with non-state actors.

Unlike research with non-state armed groups that may involve the danger of romanticizing clandestinity and resistance, research with state actors can be dangerous through its capacity to confer legitimacy and prestige. It often involves perks such as comfortable travel and wining and dining. Most of all, it is often recognized by funders and university managers as prestigious and as having the potential for "impact" – a term used within the university system to describe engagement with the wider "real" world. All these pitfalls notwithstanding, however, it remains important to engage with all parties to terrorist and (counter)terrorist violence in our work toward emancipatory change. Thus, a next step for a critical theory-based approach to terrorism and for CTS more broadly is to accept that emancipatory and counter-emancipatory logics and practices exist on all sides and require that we investigate all such logics and practices. It is by finding paths toward emancipation for all actors and by demanding that all actors aspire to emancipation both in their means and ends that CTS can truly come of age.

References

Acciaioli, G., 1981. "Knowing What You're Doing: A Review of Pierre Bourdieu's Outline of a Theory of Practice," *Canberra Anthropology*, 4(1): 23–51.
Aldrich, D., 2014. "First Steps Towards Hearts and Minds? USAID's Countering Violent Extremism Policies in Africa," *Terrorism and Political Violence*, 26(3): 523–546.
Booth, K., 1991. "Security and Emancipation," *Review of International Studies*, 17(4): 313–326.
Booth, K., 2007. *Theory of World Security*, Cambridge: Cambridge University Press.
Booth, K., 2008. "The Human Faces of Terror: Reflections in a Cracked Looking-Glass," *Critical Studies on Terrorism*, 1(1): 65–79.
Cox, R., 1986. "Social Forces, States and World Orders: Beyond International Relations Theory," in Keohane, R., ed., *Neorealism and Its Critics*, New York: Columbia University Press, pp. 204–254.
Devji, F., 2005. *Landscapes of Jihad: Militancy, Morality, and Modernity*, Ithaca, NY: Cornell University Press.
Fontan, V., 2015. "Out Beyond Occupy Fallujah and the Islamic State in Iraq and Sham, There is a Field. . . ," in Tellidis, I. & Toros, H., eds., *Researching Terrorism, Peace and Conflict Studies: Interaction, Synthesis and Opposition*, Abingdon: Routledge, pp. 165–186.
Freeman, M., 2014. "A Theory of Terrorism Leadership and its Consequences for Leadership Targeting," *Terrorism and Political Violence*, 26(4): 666–687.
Galtung, J., 1969. "Violence, Peace and Peace Research," *Journal of Peace Research*, 6(3): 167–191.
Gold-Biss, M., 1994. *The Discourse on Terrorism: Political Violence and the Subcommittee on Security and Terrorism 1981–1986*, New York: Peter Lang.
Gray, C., 2002. "World Politics as Usual after September 11: Realism Vindicated," in Booth, K. & Dunne, T., eds., *Worlds in Collision: Terror and the Future of Global Order*, Basingstoke: Blackwell, pp. 226–234.
Gunning, J., 2004. "Peace with Hamas? The Transforming Potential of Political Participation," *International Affairs*, 80(2): 233–255.

Gunning, J., 2009. *Hamas in Politics: Democracy, Religion and Violence*, New York: Columbia University Press.
Haspeslagh, S., 2013. "'Listing Terrorists': The Impact of Proscription on Third-Party Efforts to Engage Armed Groups in Peace Processes – A Practioner's Perspective," *Critical Studies on Terrorism*, 6(1): 189–208.
Hocking, J., 1993. *Beyond Terrorism: The Development of the Australian Security State*, St Leonards, NSW, Australia: Allen and Unwin.
Hoffman, B., 1998. *Inside Terrorism*, London: Gollancz.
Hoffman, M., 1987. "Critical Theory and the Inter-Paradigm Debate," *Millennium: Journal of International Studies*, 16(2): 231–249.
Horkheimer, M., 1982a. "Traditional and Critical Theory," in Horkheimer, M., ed., *Critical Theory: Selected Essays*, New York: Continuum, pp. 188–252.
Horkheimer, M., 1982b. "The Latest Attack on Metaphysics," in Horkheimer, M., ed., *Critical Theory: Selected Essays*, New York: Continuum, pp. 132–187.
Jackson, R., 2005. *Writing the War on Terrorism: Language, Politics and Counter-Terrorism*, Manchester: Manchester University Press.
Jackson, R., 2009. "Knowledge, Power and Politics in the Study of Political Terrorism," in Jackson, R., Breen Smyth, M. & Gunning, J., eds., *Critical Terrorism Studies: A New Research Agenda*, London: Routledge, pp. 66–83.
Jones, D. M. and Smith, M.L.R., 2009. "We're All Terrorists Now: Critical – or Hypocritical – Studies 'on' Terrorism," *Studies in Conflict and Terrorism*, 32(4): 292–302.
McDonald, M., 2009. "Emancipation and Critical Terrorism Studies," in Jackson, R., Breen Smyth, M. & Gunning, J., eds., *Critical Terrorism Studies: A New Research Agenda*, London: Routledge, pp. 109–123.
Narveson, J., 1991. "Terrorism and Morality," in Frey, R. G. & Morris, C., eds., *Violence, Terrorism and Justice*, Cambridge: Cambridge University Press, pp. 116–169.
Oliverio, A., 1998. *The State of Terror*, Albany: SUNY Press.
Ranstorp, M., 2009. "Mapping Terrorism Studies after 9/11: An Academic Field of Old Problems and New Prospects," in Jackson, R., Breen Smyth, M. & Gunning, J., eds., *Critical Terrorism Studies: A New Research Agenda*, London: Routledge, pp. 13–33.
Raphael, S., 2009. "In the Service of Power: Terrorism Studies and US Intervention in the Global South," in Jackson, R., Breen Smyth, M. & Gunning, J., eds., *Critical Terrorism Studies: A New Research Agenda*, London: Routledge, pp. 49–65.
Reid, E. and Chen, H., 2007. "Mapping the Contemporary Terrorist Research Domain," *International Journal of Human-Computer Skills*, 65(1): 42–56.
Said, E., 1988. "Identity, Negation and Violence," *New Left Review*, 171: 46–60.
Schmid, A., 2004. "Frameworks for Conceptualising Terrorism," *Terrorism and Political Violence*, 16(2): 197–221.
Silke, A., 2004. *Research on Terrorism: Trends, Achievements and Failures*, London: Frank Cass.
Silke, A., 2009. "Contemporary Terrorism Studies: Issues in Research," in Jackson, R., Breen Smyth, M. & Gunning, J., eds., *Critical Terrorism Studies: A New Research Agenda*, London: Routledge, pp. 34–48.
Stokes, D., 2005. *America's Other War: Terrorizing Colombia*, London: Zed Books.
Toros, H., 2008. "'We Don't Negotiate with Terrorists!': Legitimacy and Complexity in Terrorist Conflicts," *Security Dialogue* 39(4): 407–426.
Toros, H., 2012. *Terrorism, Talking and Transformation: A Critical Approach*, Abingdon: Routledge.
Toros, H., forthcoming. "Enraptured by the Drama? Terrorism, Structural Violence and CSS," in Dunne, T. & Stullerova, K., eds., *Security and Emancipation*.
Toros, H. and Gunning, J., 2009. "Exploring a Critical Theory Approach to Terrorism Studies," in Jackson, R., Breen Smyth, M. & Gunning, J., eds., *Critical Terrorism Studies: A New Research Agenda*, London: Routledge, pp. 87–108.
Weinberg, L. and Davis, P., 1989. *Introduction to Political Terrorism*, New York: McGraw-Hill.
Wibben, A., 2011. *Feminist Security Studies: A Narrative Approach*, Abingdon: Routledge.
Wilkinson, P., 2001. *Terrorism Versus Democracy: The Liberal State Response*, London: Frank Cass.
Wilkinson, P., 2006. *Terrorism Versus Democracy: The Liberal State Response*, London: Frank Cass, 2nd Edition.
Wyn Jones, R., 1999. *Security, Strategy, and Critical Theory*, Boulder, CO: Lynne Rienner.
Wyn Jones, R., 2005. "On Emancipation: Necessity, Capacity and Concrete Utopias," in Booth, K., ed., *Critical Security Studies and World Politics*, Boulder, CO: Lynne Rienner, pp. 215–236.
Zulaika, J. and Douglass, W., 1990. "On the Interpretation of Terrorist Violence: ETA and the Basque Political Process," *Comparative Studies in Society and History* 32(2): 238–257.
Zulaika, J. and Douglass, W., 1996. *Terror and Taboo: The Follies, Fables and Faces of Terrorism*, New York: Routledge.

8
THE HISTORICAL MATERIALIST APPROACH TO CRITICAL TERRORISM STUDIES

Douglas Porpora

Introduction

Although it sounds paradoxical, historical materialism might be said to be one of the earliest approaches to critical terrorism studies (CTS) and yet simultaneously a relative newcomer to it. The reason is that historical materialism is one of the designations Marx gave his distinct approach to social theory, and Marx and materialism both went out of academic favor for a while in the late 1970s. Thus, there is something of a hiatus between early work done on terrorism from this perspective, which concerned mostly state terrorism and even state terrorism within the Communist bloc, and the contemporary emphasis on terrorism perpetrated by non-state actors.

As Marx and materialism both make something of a return, the contribution of historical materialism to CTS has been, aside from a continued focus on state terrorism, mostly to offer a critical corrective to what it perceives as overly discursive approaches to CTS (see, for example, Joseph 2009; Stokes 2009). That contribution was most concentrated in the special 2011 issue of *Critical Studies of Terrorism* (CST), guest edited by Eric Herring and Doug Stokes, called "Bringing Critical Realism and Historical Materialism into Critical Terrorism Studies."

As a contemporary perspective, historical materialism is certainly no longer tied to any form of Communist orthodoxy, but rather, as the title of the special issue of CST suggests, is now closely allied with the post-positivist philosophy of science called critical realism (CR). Thus, to understand the contemporary historical materialist approach to CTS, some understanding of CR will need to be provided, and, because of both its past associations and its long eclipse within the academy, some broader outline of contemporary historical materialism is needed as well. This chapter will provide both.

The very designation historical materialism needs clarification. As indicated, it was one of the ways Marx referred to his general social theory. As the designation suggests, Marx's social theory was historical in nature, meaning that human society could not be understood in a positivist manner from a static set of laws presumed to be historically universal. Instead, each historical epoch had its own internal logic that needed to be understood, and the contradictions within it were what led from one social formation to another in a way that had to be grasped through the analysis of specifically narrative history. Given that today the prevailing social formation globally is capitalist, historical materialist accounts of terrorism are characteristically tied in some way to that global context.

So much for the historical aspect of historical materialism. The material aspect is twofold. In the first place, it refers to a realist epistemology and ontology (see also Stump, this volume) that is now strongly upheld by CR. What CR calls *ontological realism* means that there is a real world "out there," independent of the thought of human observers. *Epistemic realism* holds that that independent reality can reliably be known by us, even if not in the straightforward manner depicted by positivism. Thus, historical materialism responds to Richard Jackson's (2007: 246–247) paradigm-setting call for CTS to "destabilize the dominant interpretations . . . to reveal the politics behind seemingly neutral knowledge," not by denying that there is a real truth to terrorism but, through the force of argument, by showing the real truth to be counterhegemonic. As will be seen, historical materialism's philosophical affirmation of a continued role for truth distinguishes it from certain post-structuralist and social constructionist tendencies. Specifically, historical materialism understands itself to be advancing the pursuit of actual truth rather than a position of "no truth."

The second materialist aspect of historical materialism follows from the philosophical aspect but is sociological in nature. It is the affirmation of both an extradiscursive dimension to social reality – something "outside the text" – and its importance. In other words, for historical materialism, not everything consequential in social life is discourse or even solely discourse combined with practice. For one thing, in addition to discourses and human practices, historical materialism considers causally consequential as well the circumstances under which people act. The insight goes back to Marx (1959: 320) that people make their own history but not under circumstances of their own making. And, the circumstances under which people make their own history are not just discourses but also physical conditions and objective or material relations.

Let us begin, however, with people. Along with circumstances, the historical materialist approach believes in human agency. History ultimately is made not by impersonal structures and forces but by people – concrete agents. Concrete agents act in ways that are not all discursive. Human agents also do things like hijack planes and operate assassin drones that are not speech acts. In all they do, human agents are ever creative and novel, and so their actions cannot be captured by abstract laws nor invariably predicted from social positions. Yet, although motivations are varied and do not arise deterministically, historical materialism considers it analytically important to consider the objective interests from which fundamental motivations often stem.

Accordingly, in the case of state terrorism (see Blakeley and Raphael, this volume), a key part of historical materialist analysis has been to link that terrorism to the objective interests of the actors perpetrating it. We see this connection in the work on state terrorism by Blakeley (2011) and Stokes (2005). Both show how the objective interests served by state terrorism varied historically. Blakeley takes us back to how imperial powers employed terrorism to maintain order among subjugated colonies and how that practice came to serve new interests, first in the Cold War and subsequently with the advent of neoliberalism. It is the latter shift in national interests on which Stokes (2005) focuses. Both Blakeley and Stokes – and Gateau (2010) as well – document how as objective interests and circumstances changed, so did hegemonic discourses. In such a way, for example, displacing an obsolete Cold War discourse of communist containment, there emerged the new discourse of a "war on terror." Behind that last discursive change, Blakeley and Stokes argue, there has lain an abiding capitalist interest in markets, resources, and cheap labor.

From the standpoint of historical materialism, objective interests are not reducible to actors' discourses about them. Objective interests instead reflect the imperatives of a social positionality that incumbents of those positions neglect only at personal cost. No matter, for example, how capitalists may speak of their interests, if they cease their attempts to maximize profit, they will not remain capitalists for long. Profit maximization is in this sense, an objective or material interest and, as such, extradiscursive.

Given that profit maximization requires access to markets, natural resources, and cheap labor, it is in the interest of capitalists worldwide to secure them. It is that interest, in turn, historical materialists argue, that fosters not just state terrorism but simultaneously the discourses surrounding non-state terrorism that direct attention away from the much larger-scale terrorism initiated by states. If interests are built into social positions, positions only make sense as the relata of relations. In other words, there are no social positions without social relations. Like interests themselves, at least some important social relations are extradiscursive; that is, some are material. Power relations, for example, where they exist, may derive from discursive constructions like constitutive rules, but a power relation is not itself a constitutive rule nor even anything discursive. Where, for example, constitutive rules – or other factors – endow a certain social position with power, that power exists objectively, independent of how actors further speak of it or, indeed, if they speak of it at all. The global power of the United States, for example, is not made to disappear by just not talking about it or talking about it differently.

It is not just power relations that have this extradiscursive nature. The same is true of inequality; or dependency – whether national, international, or individual; or of the kind of capitalist competition referenced above. Going back to Marx, a hallmark of the historical materialist approach is this distinction between how actors may speak of themselves or their situation and the way – from the historical materialist analyst's perspective – things actually or materially are.

This very distinction between what is and what is not said by a hegemonic discourse is also important to certain discourse theorists within CTS, most notably Jackson (2007, 2008) and his colleagues (see Gunning 2007; Toros and Gunning 2009). The issue between such discourse analysts and the historical materialists is a meta-theoretical rather than theoretical one: how that distinction is best conceptualized. To review, the materialism of the historical materialist perspective involves not only an affirmation of objective truths but also the consequentiality of certain extradiscursive features of the social world: actors themselves and their consciousness; their material circumstances such as oil resources or their lack; the relations in which actors find themselves and their positions within them; and, finally, the interests, powers, privileges, and liabilities that ensue from those social positions.

The approach is perhaps well expressed by Blakeley (2011). Citing the words of Mark Rupert, Blakeley (2011: 17) denies any kind of "economistic reductionist Marxism," and instead affirms "an approach which contends that 'states and systems of interstate power relations are embedded in and (to a significant degree) produced through a system of relations which encompass (among other things) the social organization of production.'" Thus, social relations and their effects are a particular focus of historical materialism.

Critical realism

In distinguishing historical materialism from what is called *discourse theory* or *social constructionism*, reference was made in the previous section to meta-theory. Meta-theory refers to the implicit philosophical assumptions underlying a theory. Meta-theory is thus the philosophy of science on which a theory relies. As noted, the meta-theoretical foundation of historical materialism is CR. CR, in fact, is a philosophy of science abstracted from historical materialism itself (for more, see Porpora 2011). The adjective *critical* in CR is meant to distinguish CR from what might be called *naïve* realism, according to which reality invariably speaks to us clearly and simply in a transparent manner. Instead, like other post-positivist views, CR denies that there is any uninterpreted apprehension of reality. CR thus denies the distinctions positivism makes between facts and theories and between facts and values.

At the same time, CR insists nevertheless that there still are objective apprehensions of reality, even of reality as it is in itself. In other words, according to CR, it is perfectly possible for our interpretations to match reality as it actually is. Thus, CR stands in opposition to the reductive constructionism of Hülsse and Spencer (2008), who admonish Jackson and his colleagues for their hermeneutic efforts to understand terrorist motivations. According to Hülsse and Spencer, "if terrorism is a social construction, the terrorist itself can no longer be the primary source for terrorism scholars. The terrorist is a consequence of discourse rather than vice versa" (575–576).

From the CR perspective, reducing inquiry just to discourse is analytically debilitating. If terrorism is not something "out there," what then can we make of the suggestion of Chalmers Johnson (2004) that terrorist attacks on Western powers are often "blowback" responses by units that Western powers – for their own purposes – had previously mobilized in the first place? Because it presumes a reality "out there," such a compelling idea lies entirely outside the reach of Hülsse and Spencer's discursive reductionism. If, similarly, we follow Stump and Dixit (2012: 212) in denying in principle even the possibility that terrorist threats could be ontologically real, our analysis even of discourse is crippled; we thereby lose discursive distinctions otherwise available between pretext, paranoid fantasy, and valid assessment. Discursive reductionism does not seem a great bargain.

Although it is thus firmly in opposition to what it considers the idealist reductionism of post-structuralism, Foucaldian discourse analysis, and extreme social constructionism, CR is broadly consistent with the "minimal foundationalism" upheld by the discourse analysis of Richard Jackson (2008) and his colleagues (Toros and Gunning 2009):

> Of course, at the more interpretivist and poststructuralist end of the CTS spectrum, it may be ontologically problematic to talk of "actual violence". However, Toros and Gunning (2009) have put forward the case for adopting a more Frankfurt School-inspired ontology which maintains a "minimal foundationalism" in which the ontological distinction between subject and object is preserved and discourse and materiality are conceptualised as shaping each other in a dialectical, never-ceasing dynamic (rather than the one being solely constituted by the other).
>
> *(Jackson 2008: 5)*

Again, in contrast with the more interpretivist and poststructuralist end of the CTS spectrum that Jackson mentions, CR has no problem with talk of "actual violence" or, indeed, with anything actual. It certainly agrees with the distinctions Jackson makes between subject and object and between discourse and materiality and with the dialectical dynamic between them that Jackson also cites.

Yet, while CR thus converges with the spirit of Jackson's position, it arrives at the same place from a different perspective. It may seem paradoxical given CR's realist ontology, but CR declines any affiliation with a foundationalist epistemology, even a minimal one. Foundationalist epistemologies – and postmodern antifoundationalist ones as well – derive from what has been termed an epistemic view of truth (see Alston 1997). According to epistemic accounts, truth is equated with the *epistemic* certainty reached by following some foundational methodology. Positivism believes there are such foundational methodologies, making certainty possible, whereas denying any such methodological road to certainty, postmodernist perspectives deny, therefore, the possibility of truth.

In contrast with such epistemic conception of truth, it is an alethic conception of truth that is upheld by CR – or at least by the strain of CR involved in CTS. Precisely because the alethic view detaches truth from both certainty and method, it is said to offer a non-epistemic account of truth. Rather than an epistemic account of truth, the alethic account is ontological insofar as it is the world rather than our methods or certainty that determines what is true.

According to the alethic view, what truth means is that what we say or believe about the world corresponds to the way the world actually is (Alston 1997). Put otherwise, there may be no uninterpreted grasp of the world, but some of our interpretations can and do correspond with the way the world is. The way the world actually is, moreover, is the way it *objectively* is, independent of the observer's conceptions. The alethic conception of truth thus resecures a place for ontological objectivity. In these terms, it is precisely because the hegemonic accounts of terrorism fail to accord with the way the world actually is that CTS contests them.

CR's alethic account of truth is fallibilist. In the absence of epistemic algorithms invariably producing certainty, all we can do is rely on the best argument. Being fallible, that reliance is ever open to renegotiation. Often we do not arrive at certainty, but since truth has now been severed from certainty, that failure does not necessarily signify the absence of truth. Instead, what is true can be apprehended at epistemic levels short of certainty as when we make a judgment "beyond a reasonable doubt" or assess there to be a preponderance of evidence one way or the other. In all cases, contrary to the epistemic account, the best argument does not actually create the truth, which remains something independent of our judgment. The best argument is instead merely our guide to what the truth actually is, a guide that can also often steer us wrong so that we think we have arrived at truth when we have not. There is no relativism here but only a humility about truth.

Historical materialist work: from state to non-state terrorism

Although it is perhaps startling, not to say unnerving, to observe, the historical materialist approach to CTS actually began its life debating the merits of terrorism. Yet, in that debate were important lessons and insights for the present. Is an element of terror inherent in even progressive or just revolutions? That was the question debated by two early Marxists, Karl Kautsky (1919) and Leon Trotsky (1920), with continued reflection up through historian Arno Mayer (2002) and philosopher Slavoj Žižek (2007). In what little he wrote on the topic, Marx himself seemed to be of two minds about it (see Herring and Stokes 2011: 19).

If terrorism is characteristic even of revolutions with which we might otherwise be sympathetic, what should we expect of revolutions more generally? Is it true, as Kautsky and Trotsky debated the proposition, that "he who desires revolution must put up with terrorism" (Trotsky 1920)? The debate, Mayer (2002: 99) tells us, goes back to Machiavelli, who "considered terrorism the essential stratagem for rulers seeking to establish a new political regime." The terrorism associated with revolutionary governments has been relatively neglected today by emphasis on the terrorism of non-state actors, but as revolutions are not entirely behind us, attention to this sort of terrorism remains important. It is important as well to the broadest understanding of terrorism.

At issue between Kautsky and Trotsky was the Bolshevik terrorism of the new Soviet state. As Mayer (2002: 229) put it, "Nicholas II was executed in mid-July 1918, and mass terror was decreed in early September." From the first, Soviet terror was defended by analogy with the French revolution, which, championing *liberté, égalité,* and *faternité,* became, despite its own Reign of Terror, what Žižek (2007: vii) calls "the founding event of modern democracy." It was the comparison between the Russian and French revolutions that Kautsky specifically attacked and Trotsky sought to uphold. Although the exchange was passionate on both sides, the argument already exhibited the features that would come to characterize the nonreductive historical materialist approach. The materialism was evident in explanatory appeal by both disputants to positional class interests and objective circumstances such as internal and external threats. The volitional agency of human actors was nevertheless also acknowledged by the narrative form of argument that portrayed actors responding in nondeterministic ways to their concrete situations.

Whether or not terrorism is an ineluctable feature of revolution – whether in particular it was avoidable in the French and Russian revolutions – continues to be debated today, as in the historical work of Mayer (2002) or by Žižek, who reflecting on Robespierre, admonishes the left: "first, the terrorist past has to be accepted as *ours*, even – or precisely because – it is critically rejected" (Žižek 2007: ix). As Herring and Stokes (2011: 16–17) note, the historical materialism that contributes to CTS continues to contribute normative arguments for the rejection of all terrorism.

Perhaps proving that terrorism need not accompany even violent revolution, terror was definitively rejected in 1980 by the triumphant and Christian-affiliated Sandinista National Liberation Front (SNFL) in Nicaragua. In the famous words of Tomás Borge, the Sandinistas declaimed, "our vengeance is forgiveness" (see Janz 1998: 90).

The Sandinistas were soon to pay for that benevolence. The counter-revolutionaries they forgave, the so-called *Contras*, were subsequently mobilized by the United States to oppose the new regime via the kind of non-state terrorism with which we are now familiar. By this time, historical materialist attention to terrorism had shifted from what in theory might be expected of revolutionary socialist governments to the ongoing terrorism that actually was being perpetrated by the liberal, democratic United States. State terrorism in which the US was complicit was attendant either on CIA-sponsored coups, such as the one that occurred on the original September 11, 1973, that saw Chilean President Salvador Allende overthrown, or prevalent in the practice of the right-wing dictatorships the US was actively supporting – from military juntas in Guatemala and El Salvador to Ferdinand Marcos in the Philippines.

Although there have been newer historical materialist analyses, up through and including the work of Blakeley (2011), Stokes (2005), and Gateau (2010) previously mentioned, perhaps still most prominent are those produced by Noam Chomsky (1999) and Edward Herman (1990, 1999). Certainly, among the most influential distinctions to emerge from this literature, which has found its way outside the historical materialist tradition (see, for example, Goodwin 2006) is that between *wholesale* and *retail* terrorism. Whereas, it is observed, non-state actors generally – although not always – produce small-scale, episodic, or *retail*-level terrorism, despotic states directly – and their US backer indirectly – produce terrorism on a more ongoing and therefore more massive scale. They are the *wholesalers* of the terrorism industry.

True to the nonreductive character of this form of historical materialism, much of the previously mentioned literature has been directed at discourse. In particular, the analysis aims at showing how American propaganda shifted public attention away from the more massive wholesale terrorism that Americans themselves were helping to perpetrate to the smaller, retail-scale, non-state terrorism practiced by America's designated enemies. Herman and his collaborators further showed that it was not only government propaganda that functioned this way. They also showed how the American news media colluded in this effort, as if American news organizations were state-run as opposed to the free press they proudly profess themselves to be.

This perspective was pursued further in Herman and Chomsky's *Manufacturing Consent* (2002), which became a classic in the field of communication as the *propaganda model* of the US press. A more nuanced understanding of the press was elaborated independently by Porpora (1990) and Bennett (1990), which, following Bennett, has come to be called the *indexing model*. According to this model, the problem is less that the press follows only the government line on foreign affairs, but rather that it remains exclusively within the confines of acceptable opinion represented by the interpretive frames of American elites. Thus, as Porpora put it, a kind of echo chamber is established in which a political frame arises from debate exclusively within American elite circles with the press following up exclusively within that frame of argument and effectively confirming it.

Powerful examples of this process are adduced in Edward Herman and Frank Brodhead's (1984) *Demonstration Elections,* which documents how the American press can become focused on the conduct and outcome of "staged" elections in a way that ignores the prevailing terrorism that contextualizes such events. Porpora (1990) pursued that line of analysis further by examining the political, economic, and social-psychological structures that make the American public morally indifferent to the distant terrorism in which their own government is complicit. Goodwin (2006) carries that analysis further still by arguing that it is such complacent complicity in oppression on the part of a democratic public that certain terrorist groups seek to unsettle by their terrorist acts.

This work on American state terrorism is characterized by a number of salient features. First, it is neither reductively materialist nor reductively idealist. Discourse is examined, but always within a larger context of material circumstances and relations. For all its materialism, the analytical framework avoids determinism. Generally following a form of historical narrative, actors are depicted making choices occasioned by their circumstances that nonetheless are creative rather that predetermined. Significantly, too, as in the title of Herman's (1999) *The Real Terror Network*, there is no hesitation to speak of what is real rather than false. Ontologically, the overall perspective is realist. Throughout the whole, there is a strong normative cast with empirical interest in how all forms of terrorism come to be accepted and even justified.

Characteristically as well, historical materialist work seeks to relate terrorism to capitalism. This characteristic is also evident in two of the pieces (Maher and Thomson 2011; McKeown 2011) in the CST special issue on historical materialism that are meant to exemplify empirical historical materialist analyses. Both pieces address continued state and right-wing paramilitary violence in Colombia, although the McKeown (2011) piece also addresses Brazil.

Both studies see top-down state and allied paramilitary terrorism as arising out of class conflict as weak states attempt to manage disruptive social change. For McKeown (2011), the social change involves a general, neoliberal agenda of recommodification and restructuring that inspires resistance from the lower classes most affected by it. In such cases, state terrorism or condoned terrorism by allied paramilitary units are a last resort effort at pacification. For their part, Maher and Thomson (2011) argue that paramilitary violence in Colombia serves a pacification need for American investments in that country. Thus, although to secure passage by the US Congress of a bilateral trade agreement Colombia has had to present a better human rights record, it has done so by trying to distance itself from paramilitary violence without actually suppressing it.

The other side of the coin in Colombia is terrorism by the Revolutionary Armed Forces of Colombia (FARC), an originally Marxist guerrilla group. FARC terrorism is considered a "political involution" because it is directed at the civilian population that was formerly FARC's base of support. This lamentable development has been subject to at least two historical materialist analyses. On the one hand, it has been explained in terms of what is called "the political economy of war" as a result of changed priorities – from ideals to greed – that resulted from tactical alliances with narco-traffickers (see Hough 2011: 38–381). Hough, however, offers a rival historical materialist account: that the increasing militarization and paramilitarization of the region "pressured the FARC to extract resources from the local population in a way that no longer served that population's legitimate protection needs" (Hough 2011: 379).

Analyses of FARC aside, empirical historical materialist attention to current non-state violence has been sparse. That assessment applies not only to the historical materialist tradition more narrowly, but also to the broader sociological literature influenced by it on social movements.

Reviews of the social movements literature themselves complain that terrorism has been a neglected topic (Beck 2008; della Porta 2008) but suggest general ways that the social movements approach might contribute. Along the lines pursued by Hough, the social movements literature tends to focus on resource mobilization potentials and the opportunity structures available to social movements. It likewise is inclined to consider terrorist groups themselves as social movements and terrorism as a movement tactic. Searching for a larger theoretical context, that literature would like to see terrorism assimilated as an extreme within the broader category of political violence.

More direct help comes from the world systems perspective in sociology, also broadly historical materialist in orientation. In particular, Alan Bergesen and Omar Lizardo (2004: 47) argue that non-state terrorism is tied to "cyclical rhythms of the global system and characterized by a set of common international conditions: (1) hegemonic decline; (2) globalization; (3) empire/colonial competition; and (4) terrorist origination in autocratic semiperipheral world-system zones." There is much in these conditions to unpack. Building on them, Boyns and Ballard (2004: 11) observe that "terrorism is often a powerful response to powerlessness." They concur with Bergesen and Lizardo that (non-state) terrorism is "a defensive reaction to modernization, industrialization, and globalization," reflecting shifts in geopolitical power (Boyns and Ballard 2004: 13). Thus, they aver, "terrorists groups . . . are always characteristically reactionary countermovements" (2004: 12).

The theoretical framework articulated above is potentially of great value, especially as it combines both discursive and extradiscursive elements. Given its emphasis on shifting relations of global power, themselves grounded in shifting military, economic, and political potentials, the framework is oriented around a strong material base. The concept of hegemony, however, goes back to the nonreductive, Italian Marxism of Antonio Gramsci and refers to contesting discourses. Thus, as Boyns and Ballard (2004) make clear, what ultimately matters are actor perceptions of powerlessness and lost hegemony, as played out in cultural dynamics. So, discursive and emotional dimensions are featured as well. In the end, however, the proof of the pudding is in the eating. So it remains to be seen how this conceptual framework gets empirically fleshed out.

Conclusion: moving forward

Moving forward, the historical materialist framework requires greater filling out empirically. It has done much to explore state terrorism but needs to do more to account empirically for non-state terrorism, perhaps along the theoretical lines suggested by Bergesen and Lizardo (2004). Historical materialists have also begun to look at developments within religion (Langman and Morris 2002), but here too more is needed to reach a better understanding of how religion can express a loss of hegemony.

The empirical research agenda of historical materialism is now considerably advanced with a new book by Colin Wight (2015), *Rethinking Terrorism: Terrorism, Violence, and the State*. In the most sustained way so far, Wight carries historical materialism beyond the state terrorism on which it has almost exclusively focused to the violence of non-state actors more usually associated with terrorism. In fact, one of the most controversial arguments Wight makes is that we go wrong analytically even speaking of state terrorism as we have other, better designations for such illegitimate state violence.

Still, Wight believes that the terrorism of non-state actors is intimately bound up with the modern nation state. Wight makes the point that we cannot rest with the hundred or so different definitions of terrorism now in existence, as they reflect the strong interests governments have to define terrorism. Against those definitions, Wight defines terrorism as a strike against state legitimacy by non-state actors that indiscriminately targets not only state actors but also non-state actors.

In keeping with CR's realist ontology, Wight thus affirms that non-state terrorism is something out there despite its susceptibility to multiple interpretations. One provocative suggestion Wight makes both in this book and elsewhere (Wight 2009) is that terrorism be conceptualized as a kind of political communication – that, in other words, terrorists be understood as trying to say something by way of their terrorism. This line has also been pursued by Patwell et al. (2015), who argue that for a variety of reasons, terrorism usually fails as a form of communication. Terrorists, for example, may be trying to impress on target populations their complicity in the putative crimes of their government, but the target populations will generally fail to interpret the violence perpetrated against them as such instruction. The treatment, however, of terrorism as a form of political communication is one that deserves more research.

Wight also initiates an investigation of non-state terrorism "as a context-bound and structurally induced practice" that therefore changes form historically. Like Langman, Wight takes seriously the new role that religion plays in terrorism's development. Wight goes further, however, in examining the extent to which terrorist networks can be conceptualized as self-organizing systems. This idea as well is worth further empirical pursuit.

In the end, Breen Smyth (2007) and others call for CTS to examine terrorism in its larger historical trajectory. To the extent that history involves more than just talk, it must be something like historical materialism rather than any purely discursive approach that can address that task. All in all, an historical materialism grounded in critical realism is a philosophically and sociologically strong approach that remains in need of more laborers. Hopefully, as scholarship now seems starting to shift in a realist direction, the laborers will come.

References

Alston, W., 1997. *A Realist Conception of Truth*, Ithaca: Cornell University Press.
Beck, C. J., 2008. "The Contribution of Social Movement Theory to Understanding Terrorism", *Sociology Compass*, 2(5): 1565–1581.
Bennett, W., 1990. "Toward a Theory of Press-State Relations in the United States", *Journal of Communication*, 40(2): 103–127.
Bergesen, A., and Lizardo, O., 2004. "International Terrorism and the World System", *Sociological Theory*, 22(1): 38–52.
Blakeley, R., 2011. *State Terrorism and Neoliberalism: The North in the South*, New York: Routledge.
Boyns, D., and Ballard, J., 2004. "Developing a Sociological Theory for the Empirical Understanding of Terrorism", *American Sociologist*, 35(2): 5–25.
Breen Smyth, M., 2007. "A Critical Research Agenda for the Study of Political Terror", *European Political Science*, 6(3): 260–267.
Chomsky, N., 1999. *The Culture of Terrorism*, Boston: South End Press.
della Porta, D., 2008. "Research on Social Movements and Political Violence", *Qualitative Sociology*, 31: 221–230.
Gateau, F., 2010. *State Terrorism and the United States: From Counterinsurgency to the War on Terrorism*, New York: Clarity Press.
Goodwin, J., 2006. "A Theory of Categorical Terrorism", *Social Forces*, 84(4): 2027–2046.
Gunning, J., 2007. "A Case for Critical Terrorism Studies", *Government and Opposition*, 43(3): 363–393.
Herman, E., 1999. *The Real Terror Network: Terrorism in Fact and Propaganda*, Boston: South End Press.
Herman, E., and Brodhead, F., 1984. *Demonstration Elections: U.S.-Staged Elections in the Dominican Republic, Vietnam, and El Salvador*, Boston: South End Press.
Herman, E., and Chomsky, N., 2002. *Manufacturing Consent: The Political Economy of the Mass Media*, New York: Pantheon.

Herman, G., 1990. *The Terrorism Industry: The Experts and Institutions that Shape Our View of Terror*, New York: Pantheon.

Herring, E., and Stokes, D., 2011. "Critical Realism and Historical Materialism as Resources for Critical Terrorism Studies", *Critical Studies on Terrorism*, 4(1): 5–22.

Hough, P., 2011. "Guerrilla Insurgency as Organized Crime: Explaining the So-Called 'Political Involution', of the Revolutionary Armed Forces of Colombia", *Politics & Society*, 39: 379–414.

Hülsse, R., and Spencer, A., 2008. "The Metaphor of Terror: Terrorism Studies and the Constructivist Turn", *Security Dialogue*, 39(6): 571–592.

Jackson, R., 2007. "The Core Commitments of Critical Terrorism Studies", *European Political Science*, 6(3): 244–251.

Jackson, R., 2008. "Critical Terrorism Studies: An Explanation, a Defence and a Way Forward", British International Studies Association Conference, Leicester, UK.

Janz, D., 1998. *World Christianity and Marxism*, New York: Oxford University Press.

Johnson, C., 2004. *Blowback: The Costs and Consequences of American Empire*, New York: American Empire Project.

Joseph, J., 2009. "Critical of What? Terrorism and Its Study", *International Relations*, 23(1): 93–98.

Kautsky, K., 1919. *Terrorism and Communism*, available online at: www.marxists.org/archive/kautsky/1919/terrcomm/ [Accessed September 14, 2014.]

Langman, L., and Morris, D., 2002. "Islamic Terrorism: From Retrenchment to Ressentiment and Beyond", in H. Kushner, ed., *Essential Readings of Political Terrorism: Analyses of Problems and Prospects for the 21st Century*, Lincoln, NE: Gordian Knot Books, pp. 130–184.

Maher, D., and Thomson, A., 2011. "The Terror that Underpins the 'Peace': The Political Economy of Colombia's Paramilitary Demobilization Process", *Critical Studies in Terrorism*, 4(1): 95–114.

Marx, K., 1959. "Extracts from the 18th Brumaire of Louis Bonaparte", in L. Feuer, ed., *Marx and Engels*, New York: Anchor, pp. 318–348.

Mayer, A., 2002. *The Furies: Violence and Terror in the French and Russian Revolutions*, Princeton: Princeton University Press.

McKeown, A., 2011. "The Structural Production of State Terrorism: Capitalism, Imperialism, and International Class Dynamics", *Critical Studies in Terrorism*, 4(1): 75–94.

Patwell, A., Mitman, T., and Porpora, D., 2015. "Terrorism as a Communicative Act", *International Journal of Communication*, 9: 1120–1139.

Porpora, D., 1990. *How Holocausts Happen: The U.S. in Central America*, Philadelphia: Temple University Press.

Porpora, D., 2011. "Critical Terrorism Studies: A Political Economic Approach Grounded in Critical Realism", *Critical Studies in Terrorism*, 4(1): 39–56.

Stokes, D., 2005. *America's Other War: Terrorizing Colombia*, New York: Zed.

Stokes, D., 2009. "Ideas and Avocados: Ontologizing Critical Terrorism Studies", *International Relations*, 23(1): 86–92.

Stump, J., and Dixit, P., 2012. "Toward a Completely Constructive Critical Terrorism Studies", *International Relations*, 26: 199–217.

Toros, H., and Gunning, J., 2009. "Exploring a Critical Theory Approach to Terrorism Studies", in R. Jackson, M. B. Smyth, and J. Gunning, eds., *Critical Terrorism Studies: A New Research Agenda*, New York: Routledge, pp. 87–108.

Trotsky, L., 1920. *Terrorism and Communism*, available online at: www.marxists.org/archive/trotsky/1920/terrcomm/ [Accessed September 14, 2014.]

Wight, C., 2009. "Theorizing Terrorism: The State, Structure, and History", *International Relations*, 23(1): 99–106.

Wight, C., 2015. *Rethinking Terrorism: Terrorism, Violence and the State*, New York: Palgrave Macmillan.

Žižek, S., 2007. "Introduction", in M. Robespierre, ed., *Virtue and Terror*, New York: Verso, pp. vii–L.

9
METHODOLOGY AND THE CRITICAL STUDY OF TERRORISM

Jacob L. Stump

Introduction: methodological prudence

Methodology has been a primary site of debate in the discussion growing around the critical study of terrorism. Before the institutionalization of critical terrorism studies (CTS) in the mid-2000s, there was a comparative silence among more traditional and strategic studies of terrorism on the matter of methodology. This silence was read as an incitement to write, reflect, and debate methodology among a number of researchers working in a critical vein, including many authors in this volume.

The renewed emphasis on methodology is important for the study of terrorism (critical or otherwise) for at least a couple of reasons. One reason is philosophical and definitional robustness (Yanow 2006: 72). To be more precise, a consistent perspective applied consistently to a particular puzzle or problem related to terrorism is more logical and plausible than its alternative. Another reason is political. The methodological position that a researcher adopts, as well as the methods applied from that perspective, are politically consequential, advancing some projects and undermining others.

Perhaps in the most general sense, methodology can be thought of as "applied philosophy" (Schwartz-Shea and Dvora Yanow 2012: 4). If philosophy is the explicit and rational discussion of matters on which humans cannot help but have commitments (Pettit 2006: 35), then methodology connects that explicit and rational discussion with particular combinations of methods (of data gathering and data analysis) and substantive conclusions. Methodological discussion, to phrase it differently, marks a starting point or logically consistent perspective through which world politics are constituted, inquired into, understood, explained, and critiqued.

Cutting to the heart of the methodology debate is the concept of *ontology* (see Zulaika, this volume; Porpora, this volume). There are two basic notions of ontology. One is *scientific* ontology, which is a claim about what exists in the world. Terrorists, seen as a coherent class of actors that engage in violence against states and citizens, for example, are with little dissent widely recognized as an important feature of contemporary world politics. But, logically preceding any particular scientific ontology are the presuppositions that make it possible for such a claim to be made in the first instance. This is *philosophical* ontology, or the "necessarily conceptual basis" for making particular kinds of claims about terrorists and terrorism (Jackson 2008: 151). Philosophical ontologies are, in a sense, *value commitments* or bets about the relationship between knower and known, subject and object, agent and structure. They "are presented as necessary conditions for knowledge *and yet are beyond proof*" (Monteiro and Ruby 2009: 26).

Thus, rather than making a partisan case for one or another methodological stance and attempting to subsume CTS under that warrant, I suggest a thoughtful and "prudent attitude" toward the adoption of a particular philosophical foundation (Monteiro and Ruby 2009: 36). Put differently, CTS would benefit from the recognition that genuine methodological pluralism entails at least three significant points: first, researchers must make genuine choices about what value commitments they are adopting; second, there are no *a priori* bases on which to recommend one stance over another; and third, each bet and its subsequent methodological stance implies a politics, which should be more clearly spelled out in our research.

Looking at those value commitments more closely, there are two logically distinct starting points: *dualism* and *monism* (Jackson 2008; Stump and Dixit 2011). Dualism is a commitment to classical objectivity or a bet that the "world is composed . . . of two orders of being": objective, mind-independent material things, on one hand, and, on the other, subjective thoughts, ideas, knowledge, and discourse about those things (Jackson 2008: 103). Monism is the logically opposite position. It wagers that there is no such divide. Rather, monism holds that there is "a fundamental continuity of knowledge with the world" and thus "at the most basic logical level it is quite impossible to disentangle that world from the practical knowledge activities that we use" to study it (Jackson 2008: 133, 147). So, depending on which value commitment one bets on, the researcher moves down a different path toward the generation of social scientific knowledge.

That initial bet takes us to epistemology (see Fitzgerald, this volume), or how we produce worldly knowledge. Dualism and monism, as distinctly different logical starting points, unsurprisingly give rise to different modes of knowledge production. Each mode depends on the relationship between knowledge and observation *presumed* by the researcher: "The key issue here is whether knowledge is purely related to things that can be experienced and empirically observed, or whether it is possible to generate knowledge of in-principle unobservable objects" (P. T. Jackson 2011: 36). Depending on the combination of ontological and epistemological wagers that a researcher makes (for example, dualism or monism; empirical-experiential or unobservable), then different methodological perspectives are yielded.

Varieties of methodologies in critical terrorism studies

This section explicates four distinct methodological stances: neo-positivism, critical realism, relationalism, and reflexivism. For each of these methodological stances, my concern is to compare and contrast their similarities and differences, as well as to highlight their implications and limitations in producing knowledge. To help concentrate the analysis, I look at five points within the context of each methodology: the value commitments adopted by that stance, the way that stance treats data, the methods of data analysis commonly employed from within that stance, how language and discourse are claimed to function by that stance, and conceptualizations of terrorism appropriate to that stance.

Neo-positivist methodology

A sizable chunk of articles published in the flagship journal for CTS work from a neo-positivist methodological perspective (Herring and Stokes 2011: 7). Since the behavioral revolution in the social science more generally and political science more specifically, neo-positivism has sat atop the "established power hierarchy." Research in this vein presumes that social "scientific" political knowledge is "immune from politics, values, and subjective bias" (Hawkesworth 2006: 28). It effectively "drowned out all other" methodologies and remains dismissive of the "human dimension" in the study of politics, especially in terms of the "context-free, universalizing quantitative reasoning and modeling" that one often sees in political science (Yanow and Schwartz-Shea 2006: 387–388). Those concerns remain and deserve increased scrutiny and critique, even as neo-positivism finds a place among CTS.

A neo-positivist methodology arises from a commitment to philosophical dualism and a commitment to knowledge as experiential-empirical. Such a stance assumes that an objective world of observable things, namely terrorists and terrorism, can be known by subjective researchers employing specific methods of analysis.

The commitment to the objective character of the world entails that neo-positivist research design treats data, in some sense, as if it were lying about waiting to be collected by the researcher (Schwartz-Shea and Yanow 2012: 79), which contrasts in more or less sharp ways with the other three methodological stances that I discuss in this chapter. Consequentially, this stance toward data means that, for example, institutional stratification along racial and gendered lines was overlooked by neo-positivists for decades. In other words, the consequences of methodological choices are overlooked. The situation of the researcher and the framing of the research question; the role of gender, race, and class; and the significance of institutionalized power relations are ignored or treated as obstacles to be overcome with proper data gathering methods and controls and a rigid adherence to sets of procedures – such as random data selection, neutral survey questions, and clearly defined terms. A robust reflexivist methodology is the antidote to this commitment to the objective world and the stance it takes toward data.

A neo-positivist methodology approaches language as a mirror, as Rorty argued (1979). Language is assumed to mirror the world of things more or less accurately. The words *terrorism* and *terrorists* are assumed to be *not* politically and socially significant labels that constitute the world and impact human life. Rather, they are viewed through a neo-positivist lens as neutral categories that more or less accurately reflect features of world politics. Terrorists and terrorism are things in the world existing independently of the minds of researchers, sort of like rocks or plants exist in the world for natural scientists. It should be noted that all three other methodologies that I cover in this chapter find this neo-positivist position problematic.

From a neo-positivist perspective, methods of data analysis focus on clearly defining and measuring variables, testing hypothetical relations of correlation and linear causation between variables, and falsifying conjectures through experimentation, statistical regression, and case studies. For instance, Michael Stohl (2008) has falsified a number of "old myths" and "new fantasies" about terrorism – such as the claims that terrorists are insane non-state actors and that states always oppose non-state terrorist violence – by subjecting their veracity to empirical tests. Along similar lines, Woods (2011) conducted an experimental study by testing the framing of communicative texts about terrorism. He found that framing texts around radical Islam and nuclear terrorism correlated with a rise in the audiences' perception of terrorism and negative emotions toward Muslims. Rykka, Laegreid, and Fimreite (2011) use survey data to measure Norwegian citizens' attitudes toward counterterrorist policies. They find that public opinion in Norway is fairly permissive toward more invasive counterterrorist measures.

Consistent with the neo-positivist methodology but notable nonetheless, these studies are wholly unreflexive. They fail to consider the situation of the researcher and how peculiar contexts, histories, and biographies shaped the research or its conclusions. Nor do they consider how adopting a neo-positivist methodology implicitly reinforces particular logics of distinction along national, gender, racial, or religious lines.

Critical realist methodology

Critical realism (CR) is a methodological position that also adopts a dualist philosophical ontology (see Porpora, this volume). CR and neo-positivism both give rise to attempts to (re)claim reality, but how that is done varies. The variance emerges around the different assumptions that neo-positivists and CR make in regards to *how* knowledge can be generated. Knowledge for neo-positivists is made by reference to empirical observation and experience. CR takes a different stance: that it is possible to generate knowledge of in-principle unobservable structures or relations. In other words, for CR "there is more to reality than direct causal relations between events – there are unrealized causal powers . . . [and] realized causal powers" that are operating "even if we are not aware of [their] patterns of operation or why those patterns exist" (Herring and Stokes 2011:11). In terms of CTS, this means that a CR project must criticize the discourse of terrorism, such as that generated by state security agencies and the media. It also means that researchers must criticize "extra-discursive structures that produce and interact with this discourse" of terrorism, like the very exclusions and alienated identities that the enactment of a counterterrorist policy creates (Joseph 2009: 93).

Epistemologically, then, the aim of CR is geared toward getting approximately close to the world of things and disclosing the dispositional properties that compose that world (P. Jackson 2011: 198). This disclosing is fulfilled largely through a "dialectical oscillation" (P. Jackson 2011: 103) between empirical observations and transcendental arguments.

There are two ways this oscillation occurs in CR arguments about terrorism. One is that an observation about people acting violently toward one another is made. Then a claim is made about particular kinds of violence having some (historically contingent but nonetheless relatively stable) distinguishing material characteristics. These materials are interpreted by researchers as indispensable to their explanations of terrorism (R. Jackson 2011). Another way that CR oscillates between empirical and transcendental claims is this: an observation about the sociality of knowledge of terrorism is made. Then a claim follows that social knowledge of terrorism can only be understood and explained because of "antecedent material" structures that interact with and make that changing social knowledge possible in the first instance (Joseph 2011: 26). Moving between visible and invisible, between empirical observation and conceptual refinement, "CR argues that numerous and changing social mechanisms interact [with discursive and material features] to generate causal tendencies" (Herring and Stokes 2011: 10). These causal tendencies are deep material structures that, with the help of a CR methodology, can be approximated. This opens the door to emancipatory politics and the possibility of circumstantially dependent political transition from an oppressive state of affairs to a more empowering state of affairs.

A number of methods of data analysis are used by those working from a CR perspective. Critical discourse analysis (CDA) is one common method. The point of these analyses is to examine how discourse is constrained and enabled by the materiality of persons, other social relations, and the physical world of things (Herring and Stokes 2011: 10). Joseph (2015; see also Bartolucci 2010; Jackson 2015), for instance, looked at the UK anti-terrorism policy document *CONTEST: The United Kingdom's Strategy for Countering Terrorism* and its implementation. Joseph argues that this document discursively constructed "subjectivity in a certain way" and its material implementation had negative consequences on Muslims in the UK, such as limiting the availability of public subjectivities for Muslims and framing Muslims as instrumentally valuable to government security operations. Another method is process tracing, especially when combined with a theoretical resource like historical materialism (HM) (Herring and Stokes 2011: 12). Such a perspective might, for instance, focus on terrorism as an instrument of capitalist class rule, which is how Maher and Thomson (2015) used the approach. They closely examine a single case study in the context of Colombia by conducting a detailed process-tracing that provides a class-based explanation of violent attempts to contest and stabilize political and economic structures. Detailing interconnections between terrorism and capitalism, they show how state terrorism targeting the poor and working class has created opportunities for both domestic and foreign capital to expand.

Whereas neo-positivist methodology assumes that language and discourse function as mirrors, CR insists that discourse and language have potentially multiple possible functions: as more or less accurate mirrors of the world, as politically useful tools for elites to justify policies to the masses, and as constitutive of the world. Jackson (2007), for instance, in his analyses of the development and public justification of torture by political elites, takes language as mainly constitutive of the world, but also instrumental and descriptive. Blakeley (2009; see also Maher and Thomson 2015), working from a CR methodology and drawing on HM to study the use of state terror by the global north, presumes that language primarily functions as a mirror. In short, then, depending on whether a CR methodology is combined with CDA or HM or some other set of methods and theoretical resources, the conceptualized function of language and discourse will vary.

Data and the process of data gathering are potentially problematized for CR compared to neo-positivism. Depending on what methods of analysis and theoretical supplements are used, CR can treat data as if it were lying about waiting to be found or CR can conceptualize data in a much more sensitive and problematic way. CR combined with HM treats data as if it had an *a priori* existence. Stokes (2006), for instance, argues that the United States promotes state terror in Colombia in the post-Cold War context, and the data he uses to make the argument are treated unproblematically. A CR perspective using CDA, however, problematizes the relationship between data and the researcher. Jackson, for instance, has discussed the politics of terrorism knowledge. It is "historically situated" and the researcher is embedded "within an existing set of power structures and cultural values," which means that knowledge generation is social and a "highly political" process that serves certain actors, purposes, and interests (R. Jackson 2011: 118–119). In short, a CR methodology approaches data in a variety of ways, from existing *a priori* to being politically and situationally created. This opens up the possibility of increased confusion and obliges researchers to make an effort to clarify where they stand.

Along the same lines as my discussion of CR's treatment of discourse and data, how terrorists and terrorism are conceptualized is also dependent. Researchers that combine a CR perspective with HM and methods of process tracing might, for example, conceptualize terrorism as a tactic of state domination targeting the poor (Maher and Thomson 2015) or as a set of "coercive tools" employed by liberal democracies (Blakeley 2009). Terrorism, in this sense, is less an independently existing thing (*a la* neo-positivism) and more a calculated strategy used by the powerful against the weak. In contrast, a CR perspective combined with CDA is less clear in its conceptualization of terrorism. Terrorists and terrorism are not simply descriptions of things or tactics, but a complex combination of discursive categories *and* material things. "Terrorism is a social relation that is overdetermined by both material and discursive practices," as Joseph put it (2011: 34); or, in Sluka's words (2008: 181), "'terrorism' is both an objective reality and a cultural construct" composed by elites, governments, academics, and mass media.

Relational methodology

Whereas neo-positivists and critical realists wager on a dualist ontology that starts from a subject-object distinction, a relational methodology dissolves or rejects dualism altogether. A relational approach adopts a monist ontology that presumes the world and knowledge of the world are complexly intertwined; indeed, "it maintains a fundamental continuity of knowledge with the world" (Jackson 2008: 133). Instead of subjective observers of objective things, "people are seen as animals 'suspended in webs of significance' that they themselves are actively and visibly spinning, or as 'nodes' in a 'causal network which binds' them 'together with' their 'environment'" (Stump and Dixit 2011: 202). Wagering on a relational methodology, in other words, enables the researcher to view acting persons (instead of agency) and their constitutive social ties (rather than structure) as two dimensions of a single overarching process of constitutive interdependency.

A relational methodology works from the position that knowledge is based on experience and empirically observable happenings. Unlike neo-positivism, relationalism does not claim that experience and empirically observable happenings are reflections of independently existing features of world politics that should be hypothesized, tested, and measured. At the same time, relationalism is distinct from CR because of its emphasis on observability and experience, which means that relational explanations avoid the logical need for an indispensability claim. Whereas CR explains manifest behavior and action by reference to underlying material relations, relationalism does not. A relational methodology argues that an act of violence categorized as "terrorism" is validated not by reference to a set of regularly occurring and historically contingent material characteristics that are interpreted by researchers; rather, it is validated by the practical and successful designation of that act as "terrorism" and the ensuing response that that designation justifies. From a relational methodology, then, knowledge is grounded on practical activities and not a material and mind-independent world.

A practice-centered approach to terrorism has a number of implications on the issue of "talking to terrorists." One notable point is that official prohibitions against speaking with people labelled terrorist functions to stabilize the self/other, state/terrorist boundaries that in turn legitimate counterterrorist violence. Furthermore, a relational understanding of terrorism entails that, political speaking, a researcher should not echo and affirm the official designation. Indeed, a relational and certainly a reflexive approach to the study of terrorism should challenge these commonplace distinctions, either by explaining how they were historically formed, how they are discursively sustained in the present, or by finding ways around the prohibition all together.

Epistemologically, a relational methodology deploys a set of analytical tools to make a "disciplined ordering" (P. T. Jackson 2011: 114) of episodes of observable and experiential processes that have been selected by the researcher as warranting explanation. The politics of this methodology are less about emancipation and more about explanation, specifically, the politics of systematically clarifying complex worldly matters and depicting the likely consequences of one course of action over another (Jackson and Kaufman 2007). The tools used to make experiences legible and the explanations themselves are seen as ideal-typical, meaning they make no claim to accurately represent a mind-independent world. The accounts made from a relational perspective are more or less useful, and always provisional, attempts at clarifying and comprehending observed and experienced events. The evaluation of a relational explanation is done pragmatically. A useful ideal-typical account "is efficacious in revealing intriguing and useful things" (P. T. Jackson 2011: 146) about terrorists and terrorism and their relations to the state and other significant agencies in world politics.

Given the monist philosophical ontology on which a relational methodology operates, neither the neo-positivist conception of language (as a mirror) nor the CR conceptualization of discourse (as having multiple possible functions) is adequate. CR moves in a logically appropriate direction by shifting away from the assumed mirror function of language, "but it stops short" (Herring and Stokes 2011: 10) of a relational approach to discourse because of its dualist ontology. If CR stops short, a relational methodology pushes through. This means that ongoing discursive processes are conceptualized as completely constitutive of objects, subjects, states, the economy, terrorists, citizens, and all other meaningful features of world politics. Data thus includes, but also goes well beyond, spoken words, texts, and images, which has been the focus of much research (see, for example, Shepherd 2008; Kolas 2010; Erlenbusch 2015). It also comprises nonverbal gestures and body language, from interpersonal movements between combinations of speakers to international military maneuvers between combinations of states (Hansen 2006: 23). Also, in contrast to the CR concern for external constraints or extradiscursive limitations, from a relational perspective these limitations are themselves not "situated outside of discourse but situated within, or products of, older and competing discourses" (Hansen 2006: 30). A relational conceptualization of discourse, in other words, is completely constructivist (Stump and Dixit 2011), which contrasts somewhat sharply with CR and very sharply with neo-positivism.

From a relational perspective, because there is a dissolving of the subject-object distinction, data are not simply seen as lying about waiting to be collected by a researcher. All data gathered by researchers to produce terrorism knowledge are historically situated and informed by cultural values and power relations. More specifically, a relational approach denies that evidence has an existence as data outside of the framework of a research project. Data are second- and third-order interpretations that are noted and taped by the researcher (Geertz 1973: 15). They are not outside of the framework of analysis; rather, data, the framework, and all knowledge generated by the researcher therein are in a relation of fundamental continuity. For a relational perspective, in other words, "the research question is what renders objects, acts, and language as evidence." Data are not given in certain circumstances, in other words, but "created" (Schwartz-Shea and Yanow 2012: 79). This means that researchers collecting data "should explicitly describe how they play an active role in producing their data" (Stump and Dixit 2011: 209). This emphasis on data creation and the researcher's role in its production makes a relational methodology significantly more reflexivist than neo-positivists or CR.

A relational conceptualization of terrorists and terrorism shifts dramatically away from the neo-positivist and CR conceptualization. Both neo-positivist and CR perspectives entail an ongoing effort to offer up a proper definition of terrorism, either for measurement and hypothesis testing or for disciplinary agreement and purposes of policymaking. A relational methodology, however, does not entail a definition of terrorists and terrorism in order to carry out empirical research. It does not deny that an analytical definition of terrorism cannot be fruitfully used, but only says that it is not necessary to offer essential or even contingent definitions of terrorism in order to investigate the practice of terrorism (Stump and Dixit 2013: 8).

From a relational perspective, then, terrorists and terrorism are conceptualized as ideal-typical interpretive practices – sensitizing practices employed by researchers to make certain experiences or observable happenings legible, and practices employed by various actors in various venues that are deemed important by researchers. Dixit's (2015) recent book on the Nepalise and British states' respective uses of the "terrorist" label to identify dissident groups operating inside their territories and to legitimate violence against them is one example. Another illustration of a relational methodology is Stump's (2009) investigation of the Washington Metro in the American capitol, especially the practical ways that the danger of terrorism is embodied in peoples' mundane use of the public transit system. Dixit's work primarily focuses on texts, while Stump's research also includes fieldwork and participant observations.

Conceptualizing terrorists and terrorism as interpretive practices entails that, on one hand, a researcher should reflexively acknowledge that these practices are instruments used to produce knowledge relating to the discourses of terrorism and security. On the other hand, it entails that researchers should study "how articulations of terrorism . . . are concretely used by interpretive communities to produce some effect, especially in terms of boundary-making," identity formation, and policy legitimation (Stump and Dixit 2011: 209, 211). In this way, the state and the terrorist are not simply pre-given actors existing and acting more or less independently in the world, but are seen as ongoing processes produced and reproduced through practically sustained relations of constitutive interdependency.

Reflexivism

A reflexivist perspective is committed to a monistic ontology that transcends both objectivism and subjectivism (Hamati-Ataya 2014: 155). It posits that there is a fundamental continuity between the world and our study and constitution of that world, between self and context. In contrast to the neo-positivist and relational position that knowledge is only experiential and empirical, a reflexivist methodology is more akin to CR insofar as knowledge is seen as transcending experience. This creates a tension, however, which CR resolves by seeking to explain and critique a mind independent world. But because knowledge for a philosophical monist must stem from ongoing practices and not a mind independent world, then a reflexivist methodology's warrant for knowledge "would have to be some measure of self-awareness" of the researcher's own practices and the broader contexts in which the researcher operates (P. T. Jackson 2011: 157). A reflexivist perspective is geared toward disclosing the "concrete practical involvements of the researcher" in "sets of social relations that are through and through imbued with and marked by race, class, gender, and other logics of distinction" (P. T. Jackson 2011: 157, 159). Knowledge production, in other words, is a political "device for increasing awareness" (P. T. Jackson 2011: 198), for critiquing the self, and for extending that critique into broader social contexts and arrangements that are beyond the individual researcher's experience.

A reflexivist perspective posits that discourse is constitutive of the world under study and critique, and not instrumental or merely descriptive. Indeed, a strong reflexive stance is intolerant of the neo-positivist wager that claims language is merely descriptive and functions as a mirror, particularly because it is seen as ethically and politically "biased in favor of dominant power positions and interests" (Hamati-Ataya 2014: 155), and because it fictively distances from the "I" actually doing the writing up of a research narrative. Further, because reflexive methodology is explicitly situated and political, with an emphasis on challenging logics of distinction (including the subject-object distinction), it "entails a strategy of confrontation" with, and a reclaiming of, "the cognitive, social, and ethical values of social science" from neo-positivist methodology (Hamati-Ataya 2014: 155). Relational and reflexivist methodologies are similar in this regard, with an emphasis on explicitly highlighting the value commitments that inform their research.

Data, along with methods of gathering and analyzing it, vary widely for reflexivist approaches. But following the monist philosophical ontology, data are not seen as having some prior existence to the researcher. Data are created through the framing of a research question and those actions in the specific setting that act on the framing, including the broader scholarly field and historical patterns in which the researcher and her research are implicated. Memories, fieldnotes, and other texts, along with observations and participatory experience, all count as data created by the researcher, while ethnography, autoethnography, and autobiography have been some of the methods used to interrogate, critique, and explain terrorism.

From a reflexivist perspective, then, terrorism is conceptualized as neither an independently existing feature of world politics nor a complex mixture of material and discursive relations. Similar to a relational methodology, terrorism is seen as a *practice*. Abufarha's *The Making of a Human Bomb* (2009) is perhaps one of the best examples of reflexive scholarship at work. An ethnography, it explores violent practices of Palestinian resistance against the Israeli occupation. It focuses in particular on the social processes through which martyrdom operations became a significant and legitimate mode of conduct. A reflexivist methodology conceptualizes terrorists and terrorism as practical sites of critique and emancipatory potential that are part of broader social arrangements and contexts. Abufarha, for instance, hopes "to open doors and possibilities for an alternative mediation of the social processes that are now being mediated through acts of violence" (2009: 7).

More specifically, reflexivist knowledge related to terrorism works to challenge distinctions of race, class, gender, religion, nationality, and so on. Research and writing function as a device for increasing the awareness of some audience to the political, economic, and social domination of their selves or others. Locating the experience of violent events deemed terrorism within the broader contexts of imperial political struggle, for example, draws our attention to the ways that racial domination and religious exclusion inform terrorism as a cultural practice of enduring inequality (Sangarasivam 2015). By drawing our attention to the racial and religious distinctions sustained by terrorism in the present, a reflexive knowledge aims to contribute to the reorganization of social and political relations in the future. By locating the silenced voices and experiences of Palestinian women who are caught up in the conflict with Israel in the present, a reflexive methodology aims to make visible the gendered and nationalistic inequalities that inform the Israeli war against Palestinians – and thus those distinctions can be potentially reorganized by international audiences in the future (Ryan 2015).

A post-foundational future for CTS that is more reflexive, creative, and explicit

There is no Archimedean point for studying terrorism – critically or not – and so the quest for unchallengeable foundations can fruitfully be abandoned. Instead, studies of terrorism can and should be more explicit about the presumptions that inform their methodological perspectives. Even more significantly, the politics those methodologies constitute should be a matter of consideration. That neo-positivist methodology utterly fails to consider the political life that they constituted in studies of terrorism – such as state centrism, national logics of distinction, and the missing human dimension, to name just a few concerns – combined with the sizable chunk of space that they occupy in the leading CTS journal, is potentially troubling. What makes neo-positivism critical, I wonder, especially since it is so often seen as contributing to status quo habits of mind?

Similarly, studies of terrorism that adopt a CR methodology have been, in more or less clear ways, the centerpiece of the development of CTS since the earliest gestures toward its institutionalization in the mid-2000s. Pushing CR toward greater clarity and reflexivity – especially in terms of its relationship to discourse, treatment of data, and conceptualizations of terrorism – can only serve to sharpen the methodological stance. Relational and reflexivist studies have been comparatively limited in the critical study of terrorism. Because of their philosophical ontology and the kinds of knowledge they generate about terrorism, relational and reflexivist methodologies are potentially the most radical perspectives currently working in CTS. More work in their vein is warranted.

References

Abufarha, N., 2009. *The Making of a Human Bomb: An Ethnography of Palestinian Resistance (The Cultures and Practice of Violence)*, Durham and London: Duke University Press.
Bartolucci, V., 2010. "Analyzing Elite Discourse on Terrorism and Its Implications: The Case of Morocco," *Critical Studies on Terrorism*, 3: 119–135.
Blakeley, R., 2009. *State Terrorism and Neoliberalism*, New York: Routledge.

Dixit, P., 2015. *States and 'Terrorists' in Nepal and Northern Ireland*, Manchester: Manchester University Press.

Erlenbusch, V., 2015. "Terrorism: Knowledge, Power, Subjectivity," in Dixit, P., and Stump, L., eds., *Critical Studies on Terrorism*, New York: Routledge.

Geertz, C., 1973. *The Interpretation of Cultures*, New York: Basic.

Hamati-Ataya, I., 2014. "Transcending Objectivism, Subjectivism, and the Knowledge In-Between: The Subject In/Of 'Strong Reflexivity'," *Review of International Studies*, 40: 153–175.

Hansen, L., 2006. *Security as Practice*, New York: Routledge.

Hawkesworth, M., 2006. "Contending Conceptions of Science and Politics: Methodology and the Constitution of the Political," in Yanow, D., and Schwartz-Shea, P., eds., *Interpretation and Method*, Armonk: M. E. Sharpe.

Herring, E., and Stokes, D., 2011. "Critical Realism and Historical Materialism as Resources for Critical Terrorism Studies," *Critical Studies on Terrorism*, 4: 5–21.

Jackson, P. T., 2008. "Foregrounding Ontology: Dualism, Monism and IR Theory", *Review of International Studies*, 34: 129–153.

Jackson, P. T., 2011. *The Conduct of Inquiry in International Relations*, New York: Routledge.

Jackson, P. T., and Kaufman, S., 2007. "Security Scholars for a Sensible Foreign Policy: A Study in Weberian Activism," *Perspectives on Politics*, 5: 95–103.

Jackson, R., 2007. "Language, Policy and the Construction of a Torture Culture in the War on Terrorism," *Review of International Studies*, 33: 353–371.

Jackson, R., 2011. "In Defence of 'Terrorism': Finding a Way Through a Forest of Misconceptions," *Behavioral Sciences of Terrorism and Political Aggression*, 3: 116–130.

Jackson, R., 2015. "Critical Discourse Analysis," in Dixit, P., and Stump, J., eds., *Critical Studies on Terrorism*, New York: Routledge.

Joseph, J., 2009. "Critical of What? Terrorism and its Study," *International Relations*, 23: 93–98.

Joseph, J., 2011. "Terrorism as a Social Relation within Capitalism: Theoretical and Emancipatory Implications," *Critical Studies on Terrorism*, 4: 23–37.

Joseph, J., 2015. "Reading Documents in their Wider Context: Foucauldian and Realist Approaches to Terrorism Discourse," in Dixit, P., and Stump, J., eds., *Critical Studies on Terrorism*, New York: Routledge.

Kolas, A., 2010. "The 2008 Mumbai Terror Attacks: (Re-)Constructing Indian Counter-Terrorism," *Critical Studies on Terrorism*, 3: 83–98.

Maher, D., and Thomson, A., 2015. "Applying Marxism to Critical Terrorism Studies: Analysis through a Historical Materialist Lens," in Dixit, P., and Stump, J., eds., *Critical Studies on Terrorism*, New York: Routledge.

Monteiro, N., and Ruby, N., 2009. "IR and the False Promise of Philosophical Foundations," *International Theory*, 1: 15–48.

Pettit, P., 2006. "Why and How Philosophy Matters," in Goodin, R., and Tilly, C., eds., *The Oxford Handbook of Contextual Political Analysis*, Oxford: Oxford University Press.

Rorty, R., 1979. *Philosophy and the Mirror of Nature*, Princeton: Princeton University Press.

Ryan, C., 2015. "'Why Does the World Think We Are The Terrorists? We Are Not the Terrorists!' Using a Reflexive Postcolonial Methodology in the West Bank of the Palestinian Territories," in Dixit, P., and Stump, J., eds., *Critical Studies on Terrorism*, New York: Routledge.

Rykka, L., Laegreid, P., and Fimreite, A., 2011. "Attitudes Towards Anti-Terror Measures: The Role of Trust, Political Orientation and Civil Liberties Support," *Critical Studies on Terrorism*, 4: 219–237.

Sangarasivam, Y., 2015. "Ecologizing 'Terrorism': Attending to Emergent Pathways of Ethnographic Fieldwork, Writing and Analysis," in Dixit, P., and Stump, J., eds., *Critical Studies on Terrorism*, New York: Routledge.

Schwartz-Shea, P., and Yanow, D., 2012. *Interpretive Research Design*, New York: Routledge.

Shepherd, L., 2008. "Visualizing Violence: Legitimacy and Authority in the 'War on Terror'," *Critical Studies on Terrorism*, 1: 213–226.

Sluka, J., 2008. "Terrorism and Taboo: An Anthropological Perspective on Political Violence Against Civilians," *Critical Studies on Terrorism*, 1: 167–183.

Stohl, M., 2008. "Old Myths, New Fantasies and the Enduring Realities of Terrorism," *Critical Studies on Terrorism*, 1: 5–16.

Stokes, D., 2006. "Why the End of the Cold War Doesn't Matter: The US War of Terror in Colombia," *Review of International Studies*, 29: 569–585.

Stump, J., 2009. "The Risk of 'Terrorism' and the Washington Metro," in Viteri, M. A., and Tobler, A., eds., *Shifting Positionalities: The Geopolitics of Surveillance and Policing*, Cambridge: Cambridge Scholars Publishing.

Stump, J., and Dixit, P., 2011. "Toward a Completely Constructivist Critical Terrorism Studies," *International Relations*, 26: 199–217.
Stump, J., and Dixit, P., eds., 2013. *Critical Terrorism Studies*, New York: Routledge.
Woods, J., 2011. "Framing Terror: An Experimental Framing Effects Study of the Perceived Threat of Terrorism," *Critical Studies on Terrorism*, 4(3): 199–217.
Yanow, D., 2006. "Neither Rigorous Nor Objective? Interrogating Criteria for Knowledge Claims in Interpretive Science," in Yanow, D., and Schwartz-Shea, P., eds., *Interpretation and Methods: Empirical Research Methods and the Interpretive Turn*, Armonk, NY: M. E. Sharpe.
Yanow, D., and Schwartz-Shea, P., 2006. "Doing Social Science in a Humanistic Manner," in Yanow, D., and Schwartz-Shea, P., eds., *Interpretation and Methods: Empirical Research Methods and the Interpretive Turn*, Armonk, NY: M. E. Sharpe.

PART II

The nature and causes of terrorism

10
THE DEFINITION OF TERRORISM

Timothy Shanahan

Introduction

On 1 March 2014, in an event some immediately dubbed "China's 9/11," eight black-clad assailants wielding daggers, machetes, and meat-cleavers killed 29 people and wounded more than 140 more in a crowded Kunming train station in southwestern China. Chinese police blamed the carnage on Uighur separatists from Xinjiang province. When the US embassy in China issued a statement calling the attack "a horrible and totally meaningless act of violence," Chinese state media immediately lashed out, accusing the US of a "persistent double standard in the global fight against terrorism." Whereas the US's strong moral condemnation of the attack formerly might have been interpreted as an appropriate expression of outrage at senseless killing, post-9/11 it was apparently not outraged enough. Chastened, a US spokesperson later declared that the Kunming massacre was indeed "an act of terrorism" (*Time Magazine*, 17 March 2014: 10).

Episodes like the Kunming massacre and its political aftermath invite some interesting questions. Did the US government carefully reexamined the incident in light of the Chinese complaint and determine that it was *in fact* an act of terrorism after all? *Could* it have done so? Is there some objective fact about whether an act *really* constitutes terrorism, or is the appellation of the word "terrorism" merely a matter of subjective preference and/or political expediency? Answers to such questions are deeply intertwined with the definitional status of "terrorism." (I use "terrorism" to refer to the *word* or *concept*, and terrorism [without quotation marks] to refer to its objective correlate, if any.)

Yet, despite decades of efforts by scholars in diverse academic fields, defining "terrorism" to everyone's satisfaction has so far proven elusive. In this chapter, the problems of and prospects for achieving a consensus definition of "terrorism" consistent with the fundamental commitments of critical terrorism studies (CTS) are considered. In agreement with a number of scholars, I contend that formulating a satisfactory definition is important for CTS research, as well as for policy issues. After clarifying the purpose and nature of such a definition, I critically examine a number of distinct elements that have been thought by some to be essential to "terrorism" and on that basis propose a novel definition that embodies the insights thereby gained. The final section of the chapter concludes by identifying directions for future CTS research on this issue.

Epistemological and ontological issues

The possibility of a consensus definition of "terrorism" depends on the cogency of more basic views concerning the ontological status of terrorism (see Zulaika, this volume; Stump, this volume). Opinions are sharply divided on this matter. On one side, objectivists typically assume that terrorism is a real, distinctive form of political violence characterized by epistemologically identifiable objective features. Ganor (2002: 288) provides a characteristic expression of this view and its significance:

> An objective definition of terrorism is not only possible; it is also indispensable to any serious attempt to combat terrorism. Lacking such a definition, no coordinated fight against international terrorism can ever really get anywhere.

Subjectivists, by contrast, take the view that "terrorism" is entirely in the eye of the beholder or is a term cynically co-opted to advance personal or political agendas. Witbeck (2004) provides a hyperbolic expression of this view:

> It is no accident that there is no agreed definition of terrorism, since the word is so subjective as to be devoid of any inherent meaning. Perhaps the only honest and globally workable definition of terrorism is an explicitly subjective one – violence I don't support.

In light of the term's ready appropriation by governments and others to vilify their perceived enemies, some scholars (see, for example, Bryan et al. 2011) conclude that the quest to define "terrorism" should be abandoned as inherently confused and ill-conceived.

Unfortunately, the clarity of the opposing views just described comes at the cost of plausibility. Surely "terrorism" means something more specific than "violence I don't support." Yet, treating "terrorism" as if the word describes an ontologically-real natural kind that exists independently of our particular ways of conceptualizing aspects of our experience ignores the fundamental fact that "terrorism," like all descriptive terms, represents one of indefinitely many ways of imposing order on aspects of our experience. "Terrorism" is a social construct rather than a brute fact, but it would be a fallacy to conclude from this observation that the term "terrorism" cannot identify objective features of the world. A "kilometer" is a standard unit of length that exists solely by virtue of social convention. Yet, it is an objective fact that Paris and London are separated by 343.93 kilometers. That is both an objective fact about the world *and* a social construct. Constructivist approaches that assume that terrorism is a purely subjective phenomenon having no basis in objective reality, no less than many orthodox approaches that naïvely assume the ontological independence of terrorism, fail to be sufficiently critical about the complex relationships between thoughts, words, and the world.

In this spirit, some CTS scholars (see Jackson 2010) seek a *via media* that permits an objective definition of "terrorism" while acknowledging the ontological instability of the phenomena that the term describes. In agreement with objectivists, they point out that there are real, objective events having empirically identifiable properties about which there can be widespread agreement. It is an objective fact, for example, that two commercial airliners were highjacked and deliberately flown into the twin towers of the World Trade Center on 11 September 2001. In agreement with subjectivists, they acknowledge that the label "terrorism" is a social construct, rather than a "brute fact" that exists independently of our practices of categorization. Describing the 9/11 attacks as "acts of terrorism" goes *beyond* a bare description of the objective facts to situate them within a system of meaning that confers upon them a particular significance. Important consequences follow. As Richards (2014: 219) observes,

> while "terrorism" may be socially constructed, this does not mean to say that there cannot be a universally agreed definition of the concept, even if we acknowledge that such a definition would not be the "truth" but the culmination of an agreed-on understanding at a given time in a contemporary context.

Methodological issues

An objective definition of "terrorism" in this view would be an agreed-upon set of criteria that distinguish a particular class of events from other such classes. To assert that terrorism is *real* is just to say that the events are objectively real and correspond to the elements of the definition. Definitions of "terrorism" in this sense are easy to come by; Easson and Schmid (2011) list over 250. Achieving a standard, consensus definition of "terrorism," however, requires *agreement* on a definition, and such agreement has been difficult to achieve. This is due to many factors, one of which is that the majority of definitions are put forth without any explicit articulation or defense of the methodology used to underwrite them. A notable exception is Schmid (2011: 40), who writes that "we have to realize that there is no intrinsic essence to the concept of terrorism – it is a man-made construct and as such tends to reflect the interests of those doing the defining." In this view, there is nothing more to "terrorism" than how the word is *in fact* used.

Accordingly, Schmid asked 91 terrorism experts to identify the definition of "terrorism" they use and to indicate what they agree and disagree with in several well-known formulations. He then distilled and combined the most common elements from these responses into what he calls "The Revised Academic Consensus Definition of Terrorism" (2011: 86–87). The result is an impressive 580-word description, consisting of 12 clauses spanning two pages. By eschewing the misconceived question of what "terrorism" *really is* in favor of analyzing what a range of terrorism experts *take it to be*, his definition promises to exhaust what we do and can mean by the term "terrorism."

Despite the ingenuity of this approach, Schmid's *expert consensus approach* can be faulted in at least five ways. First, the description that emerges does not necessarily represent a consensus among *all* terrorism experts. At best, it represents a consensus only among the 91 academics he contacted. Second, his characterization of "terrorism" may not even represent a *consensus* among the experts who responded. It is unclear how many of them would agree to Schmid's creative synthesis of the data. Third, Schmid's "revised academic consensus definition" is not quite a *definition*, that is, a set of necessary and sufficient conditions, insofar as it contains many explicit exceptions and qualifications. Fourth, at 580 words, it is far too long to be of direct *practical* use. Finally, the characterization of "terrorism" achieved in this way at best represents the *status quo* within current terrorism studies, and thereby fails to advance or reform our understanding of it.

A second methodology proceeds by assembling and then repeatedly testing a provisional definition of "terrorism" through comparison with a range of events that are widely considered to be paradigmatic cases of terrorism. As inadequacies of the provisional definition are exposed – for example, by being too broad or too narrow – definitional elements are added and subtracted. This back-and-forth process of seeking consistency between intensional and extensional factors continues until the elements of a clear, consistent, and empirically adequate set of necessary and sufficient conditions have been identified. A definition generated using this methodology of *reflective equilibrium* should be governed by at least three basic principles. First, it should identify paradigmatic instances of terrorism as such. A definition that failed to classify the 9/11 attacks as acts of terrorism, for example, arguably would fail this condition. Call this "the inclusion principle."

Second, the definition should exclude features that reasonably can be regarded as peculiar to specific incidents of terrorism. A definition specifying that acts of terrorism are always committed by Islamist extremists, for example, would be manifestly unsatisfactory. Call this "the exclusion principle." Third, the definition should be capable of functioning as an analytic tool for potential reclassifications, for example, by classifying some acts undertaken by governments as "terrorism," despite the fact that many existing state-centric definitions necessarily preclude this possibility. Such a definition can thereby become a tool for political reform rather than merely validating the status quo. To remain relevant, the definition itself should be subject to ongoing critical reevaluation. Call this "the revision principle."

Of course, this methodology is vulnerable to criticism as well. Antecedent to the formulation of a definition there may be disagreement about paradigmatic instances of terrorism. Likewise, there remains scope for disagreement about essential versus inessential elements of "terrorism." Finally, some may feel unease at the idea of a definition of "terrorism" that may reconfigure our (hard-won) understanding of the phenomena that the term is intended to describe. These are all substantial concerns that must be taken seriously. Nonetheless, they can be largely mitigated through careful selection of relatively uncontroversial cases, explicit arguments for why a given element does or does not deserve a place in a definition of "terrorism," and by a demonstration of the benefits to be gained by a definition that permits us to challenge common (for example, state-centric) conceptions of "terrorism." Most importantly, the methodology of reflective equilibrium holds out the best hope for *advancing* this important issue in CTS and is therefore deployed in the following sections.

Conceptual issues

Definitions of "terrorism" in the scholarly literature and elsewhere differ with respect to the range of features they include and exclude and that thereby affect their potential to be cogent consensus definitions. In the present context, an exhaustive survey of such features is obviously impossible. Rather, in this section some of the most important features are identified, in each case making a case for whether a proposed definitional element should be rejected, retained, or reformulated.

Violence, harm, and threats

Many definitions take for granted that terrorism necessarily involves the use of *violence* or *force*. Narveson (1991: 119), for example, defines "terrorism" as: "A political action or sequence of actions . . . to inspire the 'target' population with terror, by means of random acts of violence." Against this requirement, it is worth noting that whereas acts identified as "terrorism" are typically intended to *harm* their victims, not all harm-intending actions involve *violence*. In November 2001, letters containing anthrax spores were mailed to select US news outlets and members of the US Senate. Five people died and 17 people fell ill as a result. Following the US government's lead, news media described this as "a terrorist act." Similarly, acts described as "ecoterrorism" and "cyberterrorism" involve harm ultimately directed against individuals, but not necessarily violence.

Requiring *harm* may still be too restrictive, however, inasmuch as some *threats* that involve no actual harm also may qualify as acts of terrorism. On 21 October 2008, the Associated Press reported that more than 30 letters containing a suspicious white powder had been delivered to Chase Bank branches and federal banking regulators' offices in nine US cities, apparently in response to the US financial crisis at the time. The letters included a threatening communication implying that the recipients were going to die. Tests subsequently identified the powder as harmless calcium. Although none of the recipients was in any danger, the letters nevertheless communicated a credible *threat* of harm, and accordingly were described as part of a terrorist plot – suggesting that *harm or threatened harm*, rather than violence, is a key element of "terrorism."

Randomness

Some definitions require that acts of terrorism must be *random*. According to Walzer (2004: 136), for example, "Terrorism is the deliberate killing of innocent people, at random, in order to spread fear through a whole population and force the hand of its political leaders." But no act of terrorism is ever truly random in the sense that any given individual, regardless of location or group affiliation, is as likely as any other to be targeted. What "random" *can* plausibly mean in this context is that *within a group* selected for attack, *specific individuals* are not singled out because of their unique personal characteristics. Accordingly, Goodwin (2006: 2031) defines "categorical terrorism" as "directed against anonymous individuals by virtue of their belonging (or seeming to belong) to a specific ethnic or religious group, nationality, social class or some other collectivity." Such terrorism is "random" only insofar as it does not discriminate among individuals *within* the targeted category in question. Elsewhere, I have described terrorism as being "strategically indiscriminate" in this sense (Shanahan 2010).

This feature of terrorist acts is integral to achieving their intended aims. Scheffler (2006: 7) insightfully explains the intended psychological effect of such strategic indiscriminateness:

> It is to maximize (within the relevant parameters) the numbers of people who identify with the victims, thus subverting the defensive ingenuity with which people seize on any feature that distinguishes them from the victims of misfortune to preserve their own sense of invulnerability.

It is true that some acts of terrorism are directed against uniquely symbolic targets, such as the World Trade Center or the Pentagon. Even here, however, such attacks can be understood as intended to convey a credible threat against public safety more generally by providing compelling evidence that no place, not even the nerve center of the US military, is truly safe.

Terror, fear, and intimidation

Some scholars insist that acts of terrorism always involve the actual or intended generation of *terror*. According to Goodin (2006: 45), for example, "it would be etymologically odd (to say the least) for the analysis of 'terrorism' to lose track of its root, and fail to analyze 'terrorism' first and foremost in terms of 'terror'." Accordingly, he says, "any sensible definition of 'terrorism' simply must include, as a central feature, the fact that it involves the strategic use of terror" (2006: 1). Etymologically odd or not, it seems perfectly conceivable that an act of terrorism might not have incited terror, or even fear, among its actual or intended consequences. Acts of terrorism may be intended to produce feelings of revulsion, disgust, moral outrage, a desire for revenge, or even satisfaction (Rapin 2009).

As Jackson (2010: 5) points out, it is "the instrumentalisation of the victims as a means of communicating with an audience that characterizes terrorist violence." Such communication is intended to alter the audience's *behavior* in ways believed by the agents of a terrorist act to be conducive to the realization of their agenda. Terror and fear can be used for this purpose, but depending on the specific behavior desired, so can a range of other psychological effects. This is perhaps the most important way in which terrorism differs from conventional military operations. Whereas advantageous psychological effects on others may *accompany* the pursuit of military objectives, they are integral to terrorism as a strategy.

Psychological coercion

Some definitions require that terrorism involve *coercion* intended to force a target audience to comply with explicitly stated demands. According to Chomsky (2001: 57), for example, terrorism is "the use of coercive means aimed at civilian populations in an effort to achieve political, religious, or other aims." Some acts of terrorism, of course, do fit this description, but not all do. For over three years after the 9/11 attacks, no group (credibly) claimed responsibility for those attacks, and no conditional demands were issued. Finally, on 30 October 2004, Osama bin Laden publicly claimed responsibility for the attacks and issued a demand (withdrawal of infidel troops from the holy land of Saudi Arabia). But presumably the 9/11 attacks did not *become* acts of terrorism for the first time more than three years after the Twin Towers fell. All terrorist acts are undertaken to influence others' behavior in ways believed by the agents to be conducive to the realization of their agenda. Achieving this goal need not involve coercion or explicit demands. Some terrorist acts may have as their most important aim to publicize the terrorists' cause, to inspire sympathetic observers to join their ranks, to improve morale among supporters, or any number of other motivations (Kapitan and Schulte 2002: 181–182).

Political motivation

Common to many definitions of "terrorism" is the assumption that acts of terrorism must have *political* motivations and goals. According to Richardson (2006: 4), for example, "terrorism simply means deliberately and violently targeting civilians for political purposes." Guaranteeing that all acts of terrorism must have political purposes can be accomplished in two ways. The first is to narrowly *define* "terrorism" as a form of politically motivated action, as Richardson does. The second way is to expand the scope of "the political" to include a broad range of motivations that might otherwise be described in different terms. For example, on 16 November 2008, the Associated Press ran an article titled "Italy Fights Mob Terror Near Naples." The Camorra crime family was identified as responsible for "extorting 'protection' money from a terrorized citizenry" by committing a number of murders. As a police official in the provincial capital of Caserta explained the rationale for the murders, "You kill one to teach a lesson to 100." *Prima facie*, the motivation appears to be financial.

Yet, so deeply entrenched is the assumption that all terrorism *must* be "political" that some scholars, while acknowledging that "organized crime has turned to using tactics associated with terrorism," nonetheless insist that "the violence carried out by a criminal organization such as the Camorra acquires a political nature" (Toros and Mavelli 2013: 77, 74). The danger here is that the domain of "the political" may be expanded until it includes everything, and hence becomes devoid of any distinctive content. The solution is not to *deny* that many acts can have political dimensions, but rather to recognize that "terrorism" can stem from a range of primary motivations. In this view, political terrorism is but one species of terrorism, along with ecoterrorism, cyberterrorism, narcoterrorism, religious terrorism, and the like.

Unlawful violence by non-state actors

For reasons that are easy to fathom, governmental agencies often characterize "terrorism" as *unlawful* activity committed by *non-state actors*. For example, the US Federal Bureau of Investigation defines "terrorism" as "the unlawful use of force or violence against persons or property to intimidate or coerce a government, the civilian population, or any segment thereof, in furtherance of political or social objectives." Likewise, according to the US Department of State, "the term 'terrorism' means premeditated, politically motivated violence perpetrated against noncombatant targets . . . by sub-national groups or clandestine agents, usually intended to influence an audience" (Shanahan 2010). Remarkably, some scholars accept these stipulations whole-heartedly. Richardson (2006: 50) insists that, "*by definition*, terrorism is the behavior of sub-state groups" (emphasis added). Bittner (2005: 207) is especially adamant on this point: "States do not use terrorist means – mind you, not thanks to their virtue, but thanks to [the] concept: state terrorism is, on my understanding of the words, a square circle."

It is hard to understand the justification for acquiescing to these stipulations. As Blakeley (2007) cogently argues, defining "terrorism" to preclude state terrorism implies the legitimacy of prevailing power relationships and institutions. It hardly needs stating that this is a very large assumption (see also Blakeley and Raphael, this volume). Goodin (2006: 56) is right when he argues that if what states do is otherwise indistinguishable from others' acts of "terrorism," then those acts of states should likewise be considered to be terrorism. Generalizing this important insight, terrorism is best understood as a *strategy* rather than in terms of any specific *actors*.

Civilians, non-combatants, and innocents

Many definitions limit acts of terrorism to attacks upon civilians, non-combatants, or innocents. For example, Kapitan (2005: 22) defines "terrorism" as "deliberately subjecting civilians to violence, or to the threat of violence, in order to achieve political objectives." Coady (2004: 39) defines "terrorism" as "the organized use of violence to attack non-combatants ('innocents' in a special sense) or their property for political purposes." It is understandable why emphasis might be placed on attacks against civilian, non-combatant, or innocent victims. Nonetheless, there are at least three powerful arguments against codifying this restriction in a definition of "terrorism." First, some attacks on active-duty military personnel routinely are considered acts of terrorism – for example, the al Qaeda suicide attack on the *USS Cole* in the port of Aden (Yemen) on 12 October 2000, and again in 2008, when a jury convicted five Muslim immigrants of conspiring to kill US soldiers at Fort Dix, New Jersey.

Second, insisting that acts of terrorism are always directed exclusively at civilians entails some highly counterintuitive consequences. For example, whereas the 9/11 attacks on the World Trade Center may have been acts of terrorism, the attack an hour later on the Pentagon by the same cohort of hijackers necessarily *could not* have been. Third, the needed distinctions are notoriously difficult to sustain. Military activity typically requires an enormous support system that blurs the line between military and civilians, combatants and non-combatants. Insofar as civilians often create the policies that direct military operations, they seem no less responsible for combat operations. Finally, restricting acts of terrorism to attacks on "innocents" is presumably intended to differentiate morally illegitimate targets from potentially morally legitimate targets of violence (see Goodin 2006). However, attempts to distinguish "the innocent" as a distinct class of individuals proves difficult to accomplish in some contexts, as the tragic conscription of child soldiers in some parts of the world tragically demonstrates.

Moral issues

Finally, some definitions of "terrorism" entail that terrorism is *necessarily* morally wrong. For example, Rodin (2004: 752–753) characterizes "terrorism" as "[the use of] force against those who *should not* have force used against them," with the logical consequence that "wrongness is part of the *meaning* of terrorism" (emphases added). Agreeing that terrorism is morally wrong, however, does not require that it be *defined* as morally wrong. Keller (2005: 64) cogently argues that we can imagine exceptional situations in which the use of terrorism *may be* morally justified, and concludes that "someone who says that she doesn't disapprove of terrorism in all instances – that something's being an act of terrorism is not enough to establish its wrongness – need not . . . be suffering from a conceptual confusion" (2005: 58). Allied "terror bombing" during World War II may satisfy a reasonable definition of "terrorism."

Such bombing *may* have been morally wrong, but the truth of that assessment is not self-evident (Kapitan and Schulte 2002: 182). Moreover, *defining* "terrorism" as morally wrong can have the unfortunate consequence of rendering some acts of terrorism invisible. If acts of terrorism are defined as morally wrong, then any acts that are not deemed morally wrong *cannot* be acts of terrorism – even if they are similar in all other respects to acts that are considered terrorism. In such cases, an antecedent *moral judgment* determines a judgment about the *ontological status* of a given act. For those who think that moral judgments should be based on judgments about reality, this is backwards. The solution is to treat "terrorism" as a specific strategy whose moral status in any particular context must be determined by the application of moral theories in conjunction with the act's specific features. The wrongness of terrorism in this view stems from its violation of the principles of one or more *moral theories* rather than intrinsically from the nature of terrorism itself (Shanahan 2008, 2009).

A definition of "terrorism"

The foregoing litany of problems with common definitions of "terrorism" might be interpreted by some as conclusive evidence of the utter hopelessness of the definitional project (Bryan et al. 2011). Reflecting on this evidence, one might conclude that "in both the scholarly literature and the broader political discussions, it is simply impossible to find any agreement over the meaning of 'terrorism'" (Jackson et al. 2011: 100). Both responses would be overreactions. It is hard to imagine a satisfactory definition of "terrorism" that does not, in some fashion, include mention of its indiscriminateness, harm, psychological effects, and the aim of advancing an agenda.

Given these core insights, it would be fainthearted now to shrink from attempting a synthesis. Here, then, is a provisional definition of "terrorism" intended to embody these basic elements:

> "Terrorism" is the strategically indiscriminate harming or threat of harming members of a target group in order to influence the psychological states of an audience group in ways the perpetrators anticipate may be beneficial to the advancement of their agenda.

Understood in this sense, "terrorism" is the genus under which particular species of terrorism can be described. "Political terrorism," in this view, becomes a species of terrorism along with cyberterrorism, ecoterrorism, narcoterrorism, state terrorism, and so on. (For a contrary view, see Sorenson, this volume, who challenges the legitimacy of the term "ecoterrorism."). "Cyberterrorism," for example, then becomes the strategically indiscriminate harming or threat of harming computer systems in order to influence the psychological states of an audience group in ways the perpetrators anticipate may be beneficial to the advancement of their agenda.

Importantly, the proposed definition of "terrorism" does not indicate that it is morally wrong, *thereby expanding the geography of CTS to include analysis of acts that are currently not identified as "terrorism" because they are conventionally considered to be morally legitimate*. At the same time, the definition places limits on the extension of the term. So-called "patriarchal terrorism" (Johnson 1995), "family terrorism" (Hammer 2002), "*terrorismo machista*" (Ortbals and Poloni-Staudinger 2014), and "everyday terrorism" (Pain 2014) are misnomers insofar as the acts in question are directed toward specific persons because of their unique relationships with the perpetrators and do not instrumentalize these individuals for the sake of influencing others. Contrary to some feminist analyses (see Gentry and Sjoberg, this volume), individuals can use *terror* as a tool of intimidation without this amounting to *terrorism*. Domestic violence is reprehensible. But as Lutz (2010: 37) observes, "it needs to be recognized that not every form of violence that is evil or reprehensible . . . constitutes terrorism." The proposed definition of "terrorism" permits us to make this important distinction.

Conclusions

Convincing researchers and others to adopt a new definition of "terrorism" requires more than simply exposing the deficits of common definitions and displaying the virtues of the new definition. Definitions exercise power over how aspects of experience are conceptualized and negotiated. Antecedent political commitments are likely to exercise a disproportionately important influence with respect to the definition of "terrorism" one accepts. States (and scholars who benefit from their associations with them) may have an interest in resisting any definition that threatens to weaken an absolute moral distinction between terrorists and those who combat them. On a different front, CTS scholars whose research presupposes a narrower conception of "terrorism" may worry that by defining "terrorism" in the expansive terms proposed here, their field of study may lose rather than gain much-needed focus. I believe that such "losses" are illusory, and that increased clarity and consistency are more likely, but confirmation of that belief depends on demonstrating how the deployment of a specific definition can help to advance understanding and research aims.

Regardless of the specific definition of "terrorism" one adopts, clarification of its meaning is essential to the integration of CTS research by providing a common understanding of its central organizing concept. At the same time, the adoption of a definition of "terrorism" does not negate the value of research directed at understanding how and why the "terrorism" label is applied in ways that serve particular political interests. Indeed, having on hand an objective definition of "terrorism," in the sense explicated here, provides a neutral backdrop against which the forces behind particular politically motivated uses of the term can be more easily identified and understood. As Joseph (2009: 96) argues, a commitment to objectivity does not entail positing a "real truth of terrorism," but merely accepting the more modest claim "that what we are trying to understand has a real and meaningful existence that is open to investigation (although its social basis is obscured by mainstream theory)." By self-consciously adopting a skeptical attitude that challenges widely held assumptions about (the possibility of defining) "terrorism" *and* taking the constructive step of trying to do better, CTS research is aided in advancing to the next level.

In particular, the foregoing discussion suggests three main directions for future CTS research. First, although I think that the definition of "terrorism" proposed in this chapter improves upon previous definitions, the definitional project should never be considered ontologically secure. As Jackson (2010: 3–4) notes,

> the fact that all research is historically situated and exists within an existing set of power structures and cultural values means that scholars must remain sensitive to the ways in which their own values and ideologies – their subjectivity – impacts upon the research process.

With respect to defining "terrorism," the ways in which we classify aspects of the world need to keep pace through a self-critique of our existing tools of conceptualization.

Second, if terrorism in its most general sense is much more diverse and hence common than many existing analyses assume, reevaluation of databases of terrorist incidents is merited. For example, the analysis offered here would render moot the assertion by Jarvis and Macdonald (2014: 58) that "the idea of cyber-terrorism would seem to be an oxymoron, as it involves no *direct violence* against individuals" (emphasis added). It could turn out that most terrorist incidents are actions that *indirectly* target individuals, *without violence*, by directly attacking computer systems. Likewise, it could turn out that, in a historical sense, actions legally carried out by governments self-authorized to commit acts of harm – acts that are not usually recognized as acts of terrorism – are those that have imposed the greatest net costs on human well-being.

Third, if terrorism is both more common and more precisely defined than is often supposed, it becomes even more important to understand how and why the "terrorism" label is used in the severely restricted *and* promiscuous ways that it is. Which political or other factors influence whether an incident is described by governments or in the media as "terrorism"? How do existing power relationships entrench certain understandings of "terrorism" and prevent or impede alternative understandings of that concept? Social, political, and indeed even scholarly resistance to a revised understanding of "terrorism" is itself worthy of investigation insofar as it may reveal something significant about the interests vested in retaining existing understandings of that term.

References

Bittner, R., 2005. "Morals in terrorist times," in Meggle, G., ed., *Ethics of terrorism and counter-terrorism*, Frankfurt: Ontos/Verlag, pp. 207–213.
Blakeley, R., 2007. "Bringing the state back into terrorism studies," *European Political Science*, 6(3): 228–235.
Bryan, D., Kelly, L., and Templer, S., 2011. "The failed paradigm of 'terrorism'," *Behavioral Sciences of Terrorism and Political Aggression*, 3(2): 80–96.
Chomsky, N., 2001. *9/11*, New York: Seven Stories Press.
Coady, C. A. J., 2004. "Terrorism and innocence," *The Journal of Ethics*, 8: 37–58.
Easson, J. J., and Schmid, A., 2011. "250-plus academic, governmental and intergovernmental definitions of terrorism," in Schmid, A., ed., *The Routledge handbook of terrorism research*, London and New York: Routledge, pp. 99–200.
Ganor, B., 2002. "Defining terrorism: Is one man's terrorist another man's freedom fighter?," *Policy Practice and Research*, 3(4): 287–304.
Goodin, R., 2006. *What's wrong with terrorism?* Cambridge: Polity Press.
Goodwin, J., 2006. "A theory of categorical terrorism," *Social Forces*, 84(4): 2027–2046.
Hammer, R., 2002. *Antifeminism and family terrorism: A critical feminist perspective*, Lanham, MD: Rowman and Littlefield.
Jackson, R., 2010. "In defence of 'terrorism': Finding a way through a forest of misconceptions," *Behavioral Sciences of Terrorism and Political Aggression*, 3(2): 116–130. iFirst Article, DOI: 10.1080/19434472.2010.512148.
Jackson, R., Jarvis, L., Gunning, J., and Breen Smyth, M., 2011. *Terrorism: A critical introduction*, Houndmills: Palgrave Macmillan.
Jarvis, L., and Macdonald, S., 2014. "Locating cyber-terrorism: How terrorism researchers use and view the cyber lexicon," *Perspectives on Terrorism*, 8(2): 52–65.
Johnson, M., 1995. "Patriarchal terrorism and common couple violence: Two forms of violence against women," *Journal of Marriage and Family*, 57(2): 283–294.
Joseph, J., 2009. "Critical of what? Terrorism and its study," *International Relations*, 23(1): 93–98.
Kapitan, T., 2005. "'Terrorism' as a method of terrorism," in Meggle, G., ed., *Ethics of terrorism & counter-terrorism*, Frankfurt: Ontos/Verlag, pp. 21–37.
Kapitan, T., and Schulte, E., 2002. "The rhetoric of 'terrorism' and its consequences," *Journal of Political and Military Sociology*, 30(1): 172–196.
Keller, S., 2005. "On what is the war on terror?," in Shanahan, T., ed., *Philosophy 9/11: Thinking about the war on terrorism*, Chicago: Open Court Publishing, pp. 53–68.
Lutz, J., 2010. "A critical view of critical terrorism studies," *Perspectives on Terrorism*, 4(6): 31–40.
Narveson, J., 1991. "Terrorism and morality," in Frey, R., and Morris, C., eds., *Violence, terrorism, and justice*, Cambridge: Cambridge University Press, pp. 116–169.

Ortbals, C., and Poloni-Staudinger, L., 2014. "Women defining terrorism: Ethnonationalist, state, and machista terrorism," *Critical Studies on Terrorism*, 7(3): 336–356.

Pain, R., 2014. "Everyday terrorism: Connecting domestic violence and global terrorism," *Progress in Human Geography*, 38(4): 531–550.

Rapin, A., 2009. "Does terrorism create terror?," *Critical Studies on Terrorism*, 2: 165–179.

Richards, A., 2014. "Conceptualizing terrorism," *Studies in Conflict & Terrorism*, 37(3): 213–236.

Richardson, L., 2006. *What terrorists want*, New York: Random House.

Rodin, D., 2004. "Terrorism without intention," *Ethics*, 114: 752–771.

Scheffler, S., 2006. "Is terrorism morally distinctive?," *Journal of Political Philosophy*, 14(1): 1–17.

Schmid, A., 2011. "The definition of terrorism," in Schmid, A., ed., *The Routledge handbook of terrorism research*, London and New York: Routledge, pp. 39–98.

Shanahan, T., 2008. "The morality of Palestinian terrorism," in Law. S., ed., *Israel, Palestine, and terror*, London and New York: Continuum, pp. 34–46.

Shanahan, T., 2009. *The provisional Irish republican army and the morality of terrorism*, Edinburgh: Edinburgh University Press.

Shanahan, T., 2010. "Betraying a certain corruption of mind: How (and how not) to define 'terrorism'," *Critical Studies on Terrorism*, 3(2): 173–190.

Time Magazine, 2014. "A shocked China restores order after a deadly rampage," 17 March 2014: 10.

Toros, H., and Mavelli, L., 2013. "Terrorism, organized crime and the biopolitics of violence," *Critical Studies on Terrorism*, 6(1): 73–91.

Walzer, M., 2004. *Arguing about war*, New Haven, CT: Yale University Press.

Witbeck, J., 2004. "Terrorism: A world ensnared by a word," *The New York Times*, 18 February 2004.

11

THE NARRATIVE OF TERRORISM AS AN EXISTENTIAL THREAT[1]

Jessica Wolfendale

Introduction: the existential threat narrative of terrorism

Since the terrorist attacks of September 11, 2001, the narrative of terrorism as an existential threat has dominated the political, media, and academic discourse on terrorism. For example, in 2004, the Australian Minister for Foreign Affairs stated that Australia was involved in "a struggle to the death over values" against Islamic terrorists who sought to "destroy our society by waging a version of total war" (Michaelson 2012: 431); in 2001, US President George W. Bush claimed that "no civilized nation can be secure in a world threatened by terror" (De Castella & McGarty 2011: 185); and in 2002, UK Prime Minister Tony Blair warned: "If we do not deal with the threat from this international outlaw [Osama Bin Laden] and his barbaric regimes, it may not erupt and engulf us this month or next; perhaps not even this year or next. But it will at some point" (De Castella & McGarty 2011: 186). President Barack Obama has retreated from the more extreme language used by the Bush Administration (officially dropping the term "war on terrorism", for example (McCrisken 2011: 782), but the Obama Administration is still committed to the view that the fight against terrorism is a global war and has not questioned the portrayal of the threat of terrorism as an existential threat that must be defeated (McCrisken 2011: 784, 786; Jackson et al. 2011: 271–272; Mueller & Stewart 2012: 81)).

A number of terrorism scholars have also adopted this narrative (Cohen 2003), particularly in relation to the possibility of terrorists groups using weapons of mass destruction (WMDs). Some have argued that the threat of a terrorist attack with a nuclear weapon is "not negligible", and that terrorists could "destroy our society" (Goldstein 2004: 179) and "threaten the ascendancy of the modern state" (Ignatieff 2004: 16). A 2009 report from the US think tank Partnership for a Secure America claimed that "a nuclear, chemical, or biological weapon in the hands of terrorists remains the single greatest threat to our nation" (quoted in Enemark 2011: 384). The hypothetical possibility of terrorists destroying whole cities with WMDs has also played an important role in justifying the resort to torture, appearing in many academic and popular works defending the use of torture against terrorism suspects (Dershowitz 2003; Gross 2004; Ip 2009).[2]

Many scholars in critical terrorism studies have critiqued the existential threat narrative of terrorism (see, for example, Jackson 2005; Jackson et al. 2011; Michaelson 2012; Mueller 2006; Wolfendale 2007). The aim of this chapter is to offer an overview of these criticisms, in particular, critiques that focus on the role that the existential threat narrative has played in legitimizing political, legal, military, and academic responses to terrorism that have had serious long-term consequences on the lives and wellbeing of thousands of individuals and communities.

In the final section of this chapter, I offer some suggestions for future research on terrorism studies in light of these critiques. In particular, I propose that terrorism scholars should develop a broader critique of narratives of state and individual security. Developing more nuanced analyses of the concept of security will, I suggest, lead to a richer understanding not only of the effects of terrorism on individual and state security, but also of the role that state policies and institutions can play in undermining the security of individuals and communities.

Before I continue, a quick word on the definition of terrorism. Following Jackson et al. (2011) and others (Coady 2001: 1697; Primoratz 2013: 24), I define terrorism as a strategy in which violence is used against persons (typically but not exclusively noncombatants) and/or property for political or ideological ends.[3] So defined, terrorism is a tactic that can and has been used by states, non-state groups, and individuals.

Components of the existential threat narrative

Modern terrorism as "new" terrorism

Contemporary terrorism is portrayed as both an existential threat and a new kind of threat (Neumann 2009). As will become apparent, the "newness" of modern terrorism has played a crucial role in justifying not only the resort to war, but also exceptions to long-standing prohibitions in international law, such as the prohibition against torture and cruel, inhuman, and degrading treatment (Ip 2009: 39). According to Jackson et al. (2011), modern terrorism is claimed to be different from pre-1990s terrorism in several ways: it is characterized by international networks; the members of terrorist groups are driven by "a fanatical and absolutist interpretation of religion, characterized by a blind hatred and a disregard for concrete political aims"; and terrorist attacks are more indiscriminate and deadly than ever before (Jackson et al. 2011: 165). According to this view, since modern terrorist groups aim for the destruction of Western society rather than the achievement of specific political goals (such as the removal of US troops from a particular country, for example), modern terrorists will seek ever more inventive ways of causing mass casualties, particularly through the use of WMDs (Michaelson 2012: 439). This is what supposedly makes modern terrorists far more dangerous than earlier terrorist groups such as the Irish Republican Army, the Red Brigades in Italy, and ETA in Spain, each of which had specific political aims and none of which aimed to cause maximum civilian casualties in their use of terrorism.

Given the portrayal of modern terrorists such as Osama bin Laden and al Qaeda as religious fanatics (Jackson et al. 2011; Michaelson 2012), terrorism is depicted as being caused by "a pathological outcome of religiosity" (Mustapha 2011: 495) rather than resulting from factors such as poverty, disenfranchisement, political oppression, and local cultural and social conflicts. This view is exemplified in the 2006 American National Security Strategy report, which states categorically that terrorism is *not* caused by poverty, hostility toward US policies, or the Israel-Palestine conflict. Instead, the report claims that terrorism is caused by "blaming others for problems . . . keeping old wounds fresh and raw and religious ideologies that justify murder" (quoted in Mustapha 2011: 494). Likewise, the Australian Government's 2010 Counterterrorism White Paper claimed that "the main source of international terrorism today comes from people who follow a distorted and militant interpretation of Islam that calls for violence as the answer to perceived grievances" (quoted in Michaelson 2012: 432).

In summary, the existential threat narrative of terrorism is characterized by the belief that modern terrorists are part of a global network, are motivated by extremist religious beliefs that call for the destruction of Western civilization, and are likely to attempt to use WMDs to inflict maximum casualties. Therefore, modern terrorists pose a far more dangerous threat to Western states than previous terrorist movements – a threat that will require unprecedented and drastic counterterrorism measures.

New strategies for fighting the "new" terrorism

Since the threat posed by terrorists is claimed to be existential, a "rhetoric of necessity" (Heller 2006) dictates that extreme measures might be necessary to prevent such a threat from materializing. The need for extreme measures is justified in two ways. First, because the terrorist threat is existential, the mere *possibility* (however statistically remote) of a terrorist attack with WMDs might be sufficient to warrant the use of extreme preventive measures – a view sustained by the adoption of an "extreme precautionary dogmatism in which the 'unknown' is reflexively governed through preemptive action" (Jackson 2015: 35).

Secondly, if terrorists are barbarian extremists, then strategies such as negotiation and compromise will be ineffective (Jackson 2005: 139): one cannot reason with religious fanatics. Furthermore, given the terrorists' supposed dedication to destroying Western civilization, it is unlikely that they will be deterred by the threat of ordinary criminal prosecution (Luban 2002: 12). Thus, it follows that in order to stop terrorism, modern terrorists must be eradicated, a process that might require extreme measures.

Criticisms of the existential threat narrative

The previous discussion illustrates how the logic of the existential threat narrative leads to the conclusion that modern terrorism is a new and existential threat that will require unprecedented counterterrorism measures. A number of critiques have been leveled at this narrative by CTS scholars and others. As there is not space to discuss all such criticisms, in what follows, I summarize two of the most compelling critiques.

Is terrorism really an existential threat?

A number of scholars (Jackson et al. 2011, Chapter 6; Michaelson 2012; Mueller 2006; Wolfendale 2007) have pointed out that the existential threat narrative of terrorism is based on a false portrayal of the risks posed by modern terrorism. Simply put, there is no compelling evidence that non-state terrorism poses a significant risk to the physical security, economic stability, and continuing functioning of democratic states or to the lives of citizens of those states. Even in 2001, when nearly 3,000 people died in the 9/11 attacks, "three times as many [US citizens] died from malnutrition and almost 40 times as many people died in car accidents" as were killed in those attacks (Michaelson 2012: 436). In fact, non-state terrorism has *never* seriously undermined or threatened the political, economic, or physical survival of democratic states – a fact that holds true even for states such as Israel that have been the target of long-standing and ongoing terrorist attacks.

The adoption of the existential threat narrative of terrorism is not only based on a false assessment of the threat posed by non-state terrorism, but it has also sidelined and obscured other serious threats to individuals and communities. For example, the narrative ignores the fact that *state* terrorism and other forms of state violence have always posed a far greater threat to individuals and communities than non-state terrorism (Jackson et al. 2011: 193–194; Primoratz 2013). Second, serious nonviolent threats are neglected or ignored. For example, the threat posed by climate change has not received anything like the attention given by politicians, academics, and the media to the threat of terrorism. Yet, the predicted effects of climate change (such as the effect of just a 2° F increase in global temperature) include "5–15% reductions in the yields of crops grown . . . 3–10% increases in the amount of rain falling during the heaviest precipitation events, which can increase flooding risks . . . 200%–400% increases in the area burned by wildfire in parts of the western United States" (EPA 2014). These effects are likely to have a devastating impact on states' economies, environments, and infrastructure, not to mention on the lives of millions of individuals. However, despite the extremely serious and growing threat posed by climate change (Mooney 2014) and the global reach of this threat, the funding, research, and political capital spent on meeting this threat pales in comparison to that devoted to fighting terrorism.

The destructive effects of the existential threat narrative

A second set of criticisms focuses on the destructive impact of the existential threat narrative on communities, individuals, and states. As will become apparent, counterterrorism policies and practices driven by the existential threat narrative have in some cases caused a greater threat to the lives and security of individuals than terrorism itself.

In many countries, the most immediate consequence of the adoption of the existential threat narrative is the creation of new counterterrorism legislation. In the US, the UK, and Australia, components of the existential threat narrative were used to justify legislation that drastically broadened the powers of police and intelligence services to detain individuals suspected of terrorist activity or of having information relevant to terrorism investigations (Jackson et al. 2011: 229–231; Kostakopoulou 2008: 5–6; Wolfendale 2007: 75). For example, the 2005 UK Prevention of Terrorism Act permitted the home secretary to impose significant restrictions on individuals suspected of being involved in terrorism for an initial 12-month period, including restrictions on their "liberty, . . . movement, residence, occupational activity, association and communications" (Kostakopoulou 2008: 7). In September 2014, in response to a threat from the militant group Islamic State (IS), Australia passed legislation that expanded the powers of security forces to detain terrorism suspects without charge and to monitor phone and internet activity, and lowered the threshold required to execute control orders (Griffiths 2015).

The law enforcement and intelligence powers typical of such counterterrorism legislation lower the evidentiary standards required to arrest and detain persons suspected of terrorism and extend the powers of organizations such as the National Security Agency (NSA) to collect personal information from individuals by accessing email accounts, phone records, and other personal information without a warrant (Sledge 2014). These new forms of legislation have, not surprisingly, led to the arrest, investigation, and detention without charge of many individuals who had no information about terrorism (Friedersdorf 2013),[4] not to mention the violation of privacy of thousands of individuals whose phone records and email correspondence were monitored and collected by intelligence agencies.

If these consequences seem minor relative to the lives potentially threatened by terrorism, the following two examples illustrate how destructive counterterrorism strategies can be. First, consider the toll of the numerous military operations initiated by the US and its allies in the so-called war on terror (see Rogers, this volume). In the first 18 months of the Iraq war (a war justified by the claim that Saddam Hussein possessed WMDs and was connected to al Qaeda), over 100,000 Iraqis died (Michaelson 2012: 436). The civilian death toll of that conflict exceeds 140,000. If combatants are included, the death toll is nearly 200,000 (Iraq Body Count 2014).

Second, the case of Israel and Palestine is arguably another example of how a state's counterterrorism polices can threaten a community to a greater extent than vice-versa. Israeli counterterrorism strategies have included attacks on Palestinian communities that have killed and wounded hundreds of civilians (Human Rights Watch 2014; United Nations 2007),[5] the use of tactics such as torture (PCATI 2014), and the construction of illegal housing settlements in Palestinian territory (Human Rights Watch 2014). I am not claiming that such tactics rise to the level of an existential threat to the Palestinian community, or that they justify or excuse Palestinian terrorism. Instead, the point is that, in some cases, state counterterrorism measures can cause greater harm to a community than the harm caused by the non-state terrorism to which the measures are responding.

In addition, the existential threat narrative of terrorism has been used to justify massive funding increases for military operations and for security agencies such as the CIA and the NSA (Mueller & Stewart 2011). In the US, it led to the creation of the Department of Homeland Security, whose yearly budget is over $50 billion (Michaelson 2012: 442). In total, the expenditure of US domestic homeland security in the first ten years after 9/11 exceeded $1 trillion (Mueller & Stewart 2011: 1). One consequence of such massive spending is that government money is *not* being spent on other crucial areas such as health and education. A further consequence of this spending on security has been the acquisition by US police forces of military equipment, including tanks, mine-resistant ambush protected vehicles (MRAPs), and military-grade weapons on the grounds that such equipment might be necessary to prevent a terrorist attack (ACLU 2014: 3).[6] One of the effects of this militarization of the police has been the increasing use of SWAT teams for minor police operations such as executing search warrants, which in turn has led to the injury and death of several innocent individuals, including a 19-month old baby (Pow 2014).

Other, harder to quantify, effects of the adoption of the existential threat narrative of terrorism include the continuing damage to the environment, economy, and basic infrastructure of those countries that are targeted by the war against terrorism, such as Iraq, Afghanistan, and Pakistan. In addition, the destabilization of political power and social stability in those countries has led to continuing turmoil and unrest and contributed to the rise of militant groups such as IS (Collins 2014).

This political and social destabilization is compounded by the portrayal of terrorists as religiously motivated fanatics that are part of a "global network" governed by al Qaeda (Bergen et al. 2011). This portrayal has led to non-state groups (such as Jema'ah Islamiyah in Indonesia and Kumpulan Mujahideen Malaysia) being "lumped together" because of their identification with Islam, even if they are distinct from each other and from al Qaeda in terms of their origins, structure, aims, and uses of violence. Ironically, the view that these groups are part of an international al Qaeda network has "granted such groups more currency in their ability to evoke fear. This is despite the fact that the basic concerns and tactics of these groups did not necessarily undergo any substantive change after 9/11" (Mustapha 2011: 493).

The flip side of this portrayal of Islamic groups is that *legitimate* political groups and nonviolent movements have been demonized as "terrorist" merely on the basis of their identification with Islam, even when such groups have consistently opposed the use of terrorism (Mustapha 2011: 495). For example, the Indonesian Islamist organization Nadhatul Ulama (which has 30 million followers) has actively supported the Indonesian government's anti-terrorism efforts, yet has been portrayed as a terrorist organization purely because it is a Muslim organization (Gershman 2002: 64; Mustapha 2011). Once a group is labeled "terrorist" by states such as the US, this not only undermines the ability of those groups to effectively fight terrorism in their own countries, but it also makes it extremely difficult for the governments of those countries to work with those groups. In addition, such nonviolent groups can become the targets of governments who decide to use the war on terror as a justification for harsh repression of perceived enemies, as occurred in a number of Southeast Asian states (Mustapha 2011: 499–500).

Finally, since the existential threat narrative drastically restricts the range of possible counterterrorism strategies, nonviolent counterterrorism methods, such as the infiltration of dangerous organizations and negotiation with the leaders of non-state groups, are "off the table" from the beginning. Yet, historically, such methods have consistently proven to be more effective in preventing terrorism than military force and tactics such as torture (Arrigo 2004: 562–563; Jackson et al. 2011). A 2006 study of evaluations of the effectiveness of post-9/11 counterterrorism strategies (such as increased airport security, military interventions, and political regime change) found that most of these strategies were not only ineffective in reducing incidents of terrorism, but some were also linked to an *increase* in terrorism (Lum et al. 2006). However, this should not be surprising; the inefficacy of methods such as torture and "no concessions or negotiation" policies on terrorism was known well before 9/11. For example, the author of a 1998 article on terrorism criticized the US's "no concessions" policy on the grounds that it proved ineffective in deterring several high-profile terrorist attacks (Tucker 1998: 104–105).

The inefficacy of many counterterrorism strategies is a result of a number of factors. For example, the demonizing of nonviolent Islamic organizations (discussed earlier) has made it more difficult for those organizations and the governments who support them to counteract the radical versions of Islam utilized by more extreme groups (Mustapha 2011: 495). Another contributing factor is that states that adopt the existential threat narrative typically refuse to consider the possibility that terrorist groups might have legitimate grievances against their targets. Such grievances thus continue to go unaddressed, which can in turn fuel the anger and resentment of these groups (see Toros, this volume). This is not meant as an excuse for terrorism. Rather, the point is that if states are genuinely committed to reducing the possibility of non-state terrorism, they should be willing to address and, if possible, rectify any injustices that have resulted from their own current or past policies.

In summary, the critiques of the existential threat narrative of terrorism discussed here undermine its legitimacy in three ways. First, scholars have demonstrated that the claim that terrorists are religious extremists who pose an unprecedented threat to democratic states is largely false. Contemporary non-state terrorism does not seriously threaten (and never has threatened) the political and territorial integrity of the US and other liberal democracies (Michaelson 2012: 438; Mueller 2006; Mueller & Stewart 2012: 103). Nor does terrorism pose a serious threat to the lives of citizens of those states.

Second, states have used the existential threat narrative of terrorism and the portrayal of terrorists as irrational fanatics as the basis for executing counterterrorism policies that have had extremely serious and long-term consequences on the lives and wellbeings of thousands of individuals, as well as on the economic, political, and social structures of many countries. Such consequences include wars involving hundreds of thousands of casualties, the use of torture and indefinite detention, as well as other complex economic, political, environmental, and social repercussions. Finally, the counterterrorism policies supported by the existential threat narrative of terrorism have not only been ineffective in minimizing terrorism, but they have also arguably increased the threat of non-state terrorism.

What next for terrorism research?

I have argued that the existential threat narrative of terrorism is both false and implicated in harmful, ineffective, and counterproductive counterterrorism policies and practices. If we reject the existential threat narrative in debates about terrorism, how should scholars address the issue of terrorism?

Understanding security and threats to security

The existential threat narrative of terrorism is compelling because it seems to capture a truth about today's world – that there exist numerous dangerous groups with global reach whose principle desire is to attack and destroy the United States and other liberal democracies. That seems, on the face of it, an undeniable fact. Yet, not only does the existential threat narrative greatly exaggerate the nature and scope of the threat posed by these groups, it draws on a highly simplistic conception of individual and state security. It is true that terrorist acts have killed and maimed thousands of people over the last ten years and that non-state terrorism continues to threaten the basic physical security of individuals. Nothing in what I have said so far is intended to suggest that terrorism is not a threat or that nothing should be done to fight terrorism. However, as we have seen, current counterterrorism practices have themselves posed a very serious threat to individuals and communities. In addition, other serious threats to individual lives and state functioning have not been judged to warrant anything like the funding, research, and energy that have been devoted to fighting terrorism.

The dominance of the existential threat narrative in political, academic, and media discussions of terrorism is not just the result of the construal of the threat of terrorism as existential, it is also a product of the construal of the threat of terrorism as an attack on the *identity* of liberal democracies – hence the many references to the threat that terrorism poses to "values" made by leaders such as President Bush (Jackson 2005; Jackson et al. 2011). As we have seen, CTS scholars have argued convincingly that this construal of terrorism is false. But, it is also important that CTS scholars critique the basic concepts of security that underlie the existential threat narrative of terrorism – concepts that involve beliefs about security of identity, as well as physical safety. It would be extremely valuable for terrorism scholars to develop positive accounts of both individual and national security that can be used to assess the existence and nature of threats to security and thus to locate the debate about terrorism in the context of a broader debate about the meaning of security and insecurity (see Lindahl, this volume).

This process requires rejecting the belief that security and threats to security can be assessed independently from the ways in which national identity is defined and created. As has been argued by scholars in security studies (Campbell 1998; Husymans 1998; Williams 2003), those factors that states construe as threats and the goods and values that they see as being threatened (safety, sovereignty, freedom, and so forth) do not reflect objective or universal truths about risks, threats, and security. Instead, the concepts of security, insecurity, and threat are culturally produced and constructed within a society through political, academic, and popular discourse (Jackson 2005). How the concepts of security, insecurity, and threat are understood within a community reflect and shape that community's beliefs regarding its culture, identity, and status (Weldes et al. 1998: 9–17). Security is thus best understood as what Jeff Huysmans (1998: 228) calls a "thick concept": "the meaning of security does not just depend on the specific analytical questions it raises, it also articulates particular understandings of our relation to nature, other human beings, and the self". For example, the frequent claim that terrorism poses a threat to American "values" can be understood as arising from the long-standing belief that the US is the moral leader of the Western world – an aspect of US national identity that has a long history, particularly during the Cold War (Weldes 1998: 36–63). Likewise, the portrayal of terrorists as savage fanatics allows the US to position itself (by contrast) as a beacon of civilization and reason (Jackson 2005: 59–91).

If questions of national and individual security, identity, and threat construction became more central to research in terrorism, this would allow terrorism scholars to continue to critique current counterterrorism policies and rhetoric (an extremely important task) and would allow a deeper exploration of the relationship between the concepts of national and individual security and other domestic and foreign concerns. For example, in an earlier work (Wolfendale 2012), I argued that a plausible understanding of individual security should refer to the specific features of human persons that are relevant to a minimally decent life for a human being. Thus, I proposed that individual security should be understood as comprising moral security – security in a basic sense of moral worth – as well as basic physical safety (Wolfendale 2012: 104).

A consequence of my view of security is that states' duties to protect and promote citizens' security needs to be reevaluated, as does the construal of threats to security. One need not agree with my account of security to see how a more nuanced understanding of individual and national security could lead to certain issues being reframed as issues of security, a process that in turn would have implications for our understanding of national security and individual security and how we think about responses to threats to security in both senses.

To illustrate how this process of reframing might work in the context of individual security, consider the case of systemic discrimination. Systematic racial and sexual discrimination can create conditions of deep insecurity in members of discriminated groups. Members of such groups can be more vulnerable to physical assaults as well as economic insecurity, and they are also deeply vulnerable to attacks on their moral self-worth. Yet, as far as I am aware, academic and political discussions of discrimination have typically framed the issue as one of equality and justice rather than as an issue of security. However, framing discrimination as a security issue (at least in part) would have important implications for how seriously the question is addressed at the level of domestic and even foreign policy and how we construe states' duties in relation to dealing with the effects of systematic discrimination. For instance, if states have a duty to protect the security of citizens, and discrimination is a security issue, then it would follow that states have a security-based duty to respond to and eradicate the effects of discrimination and not only a duty based on ensuring equality or justice.

Regardless of whether one agrees with my suggestion that racial and sexual discrimination can be construed as a security issue, this example illustrates the rich theoretical and practical implications of extending research on security beyond the issue of terrorism. Thus, I propose that researchers of terrorism engage critically with the underlying theories of individual and state security that support and reinforce the existential threat narrative of terrorism, continue to expose the dangerous consequences of that narrative, and explore positive theories of security and its connection to individual and national identity and flourishing.

Notes

1 This chapter was written while I was a Resident Fellow at the Stockdale Center on Ethical Leadership at the United States Naval Academy. I thank the staff and members of the Stockdale Center for their continuing support of my research.
2 For example, the "torture memos" that were written for the Bush Administration regarding the definition of torture and legality of its use refer to the possibility of terrorists using WMDs in arguments justifying the use of torture (Ip 2009: 44).
3 I include reference to noncombatants in the definition of terrorism because definitions that do not include the targeting of noncombatants fail to adequately capture the moral status of terrorism (see Valls 2000 for one such definition). Also, I include reference to an ideological goal, because a definition that did not include a reference to an ideological goal would be unable to distinguish acts of terrorism from criminal acts such as mass murder.
4 A former senior state department official in the Bush administration claimed that the majority of prisoners detained at Guantanamo Bay were innocent of any involvement in terrorism (Friedersdorf 2013).
5 According to a 2007 report from the United Nations Office for the Coordination of Humanitarian Reports, in every year since 2000, the numbers of Palestinians killed has exceeded (sometimes by several hundred) the number of Israelis killed, and over half the deaths have been civilians.

6 In one New Hampshire town, the local police department claimed that they needed an armored truck to protect "the town's annual pumpkin festival" from potential terrorist attacks (Levitz 2014).

References

American Civil Liberties Union, 2014. *War comes home: the excessive militarization of American policing*, New York: ACLU Foundation.

Arrigo, J., 2004. "A utilitarian argument against the torture interrogation of terrorism suspects", *Science and Engineering Ethics*, 10(3): 543–572.

Bergen, P., Hoffman, B., and Tiedemann, K., 2011. "Assessing the Jihadist threat to America and American interests", *Studies in Conflict and Terrorism*, 34: 65–101.

Campbell, D., 1998. *Writing security: United States foreign policy and the politics of identity*, Minneapolis, MN: University of Minnesota Press.

Coady, C. A. J., 2001. "Terrorism", in Becker, L., and Becker, C., eds., *Encyclopedia of ethics*, 2nd ed., New York and London: Routledge, pp. 1696–99.

Cohen, A., 2003. "Promoting freedom and democracy: fighting the war of ideas against Islamic terrorism", *Comparative Strategy*, 22(3): 207–221.

Collins, R., 2014. "Inside the rise of ISIS", *Frontline*, 7 August 2014. Available online at: www.pbs.org/wgbh/pages/frontline/iraq-war-on-terror/losing-iraq/inside-the-rise-of-isis/. [Accessed 10 January 2015].

De Castella, K., and McGarty, C., 2011. "Two leaders, two wars: a psychological analysis of fear and anger content in political rhetoric about terrorism", *Analyses of Social Issues and Public Policy*, 11(1): 180–200.

Dershowitz, A., 2003. *Why terrorism works*, New Haven, CT: Yale University Press.

Enemark, C., 2011. "Farewell to WMD: the language and science of mass destruction", *Contemporary Security Policy*, 32(2): 382–400.

Environmental Protection Agency, 2014. *Climate change facts: answers to common questions*, 14 March 2014. Available online at: www.epa.gov/climatechange/basics/facts.html. [Accessed October 27, 2014].

Friedersdorf, C., 2013. "Former State Department official: team Bush knew many at Gitmo were innocent", *The Atlantic*, 26 April 2013. Available online at: www.theatlantic.com/politics/archive/2013/04/former-state-department-official-team-bush-knew-many-at-gitmo-were-innocent/275327/. [Accessed 26 January 2015].

Gershman, J., 2002. "Is Southeast Asia the second front?", *Foreign Affairs*, 81(4): 60–74.

Goldstein, J., 2004. *The real price of war: how you pay for the war on terror*, New York: New York University Press.

Griffiths, E., 2015. "Explainer: what do the new anti-terrorism laws involve and how will they be rolled out?", *ABC News*, 17 February 2015. Available online at: www.abc.net.au/news/2014-09-22/new-anti-terrorism-laws-explained/5761516. [Accessed 26 March, 2015].

Gross, O., 2004. "The prohibition on torture and the limits of the law", in Levinson, S., ed., *Torture: a collection*, New York: Oxford University Press, pp. 229–256.

Heller, J., 2006. "The rhetoric of necessity (or, Sanford Levinson's pinteresque conversation)", *George Law Review*, 40: 779–806.

Human Rights Watch, 2014. *World Report 2014: Israel and Palestine*. Available online at: www.hrw.org/world-report/2014/country-chapters/israel-and-palestine?page=1. [Accessed 10 January 2015].

Huysmans, J., 1998. "Security! What do you mean? From concept to thick signifier", *European Journal of International Relations*, 4(2): 226–255.

Ignatieff, M., 2004. *The lesser evil: political ethics in an age of terror*, Princeton: Princeton University Press.

Ip, J., 2009. "Two narratives of torture", *Northwestern Journal of International Human Rights*, 7(1): 35–77.

Iraq Body Count, 2014. Iraq Body Count. Available online at: www.iraqbodycount.org/ [Accessed 14 October 2014].

Jackson, R., 2005. *Writing the war on terrorism: language, politics, and counterterrorism*, Manchester: Manchester University Press.

Jackson, R., 2015. "The epistemological crisis of counterterrorism", *Critical Studies on Terrorism*, 8(1): 33–54.

Jackson, R., Jarvis, L., Gunning, J., and Breen Smyth, M., 2011. *Terrorism: a critical introduction*, Basingstoke, UK: Palgrave-Macmillan.

Kostakopoulou, D., 2008. "How to do things with security post 9/11", *Oxford Journal of Legal Studies*, 28(2): 317–344.

Levitz, J., 2014. "Towns say 'no tanks' to militarized police: growing unease over departments' use of vehicles and gear designed for battle", *The Wall Street Journal*, 7 February 2014. Available online at: http://online.wsj.com/articles/SB10001424052702304450904579366963588434656. [Accessed 4 November, 2014].

Luban, D., 2002. "The war on terrorism and the end of human rights", *Philosophy & Public Policy Quarterly*, 22(3): 9–14.

Lum, C., Kennedy, L., and Sherley, A., 2006. "Are counter-terrorism strategies effective? The results of the Campbell systematic review on counter-terrorism evaluation research", *Journal of Experimental Criminology*, 2(4): 489–516.

McCrisken, T., 2011. "Ten years on: Obama's war on terrorism in rhetoric and practice", *International Affairs*, 87(4): 781–801.

Michaelson, C., 2012. "The triviality of terrorism", *Australian Journal of International Affairs*, 66(4): 431–449.

Mooney, C., 2014. "Effects of climate change 'irreversible', U.N. panel warns in report", *The Washington Post*, 2 November 2014. Available online at: www.washingtonpost.com/national/health-science/effects-of-climate-change-irreversible-un-panel-warns-in-report/2014/11/01/2d49aeec-6142-11e4-8b9e-2ccdac31a031_story.html. [Accessed 3 November, 2014].

Mueller, J., 2006. *Overblown: how politicians and the terrorism industry inflate national security threats, and why we believe them*, New York: Simon & Schuster.

Mueller, J., and Stewart, M., 2011. "Balancing the risks, benefits, and costs of Homeland Security", *Homeland Security Affairs*, 7(16): 1–26.

Mueller, J., and Stewart, M., 2012. "The terrorism delusion: American's overwrought response to September 11", *International Security*, 37(1): 81–110.

Mustapha, J., 2011. "Threat construction in the Bush administration's post-9/11 foreign policy: (critical) security implications for Southeast Asia", *The Pacific Review*, 24(4): 487–504.

Neumann, P., 2009. *Old and new terrorism*, Cambridge, UK: Polity Press.

Pow, H., 2014. "SWAT team throws a stun grenade into a toddler's CRIB during drugs raid leaving him in a coma with severe burns", *The Daily Mail*, 29 May 2014. Available online at: www.dailymail.co.uk/news/article-2643344/Horror-SWAT-team-throw-stun-grenade-toddlers-CRIB-drugs-raid-leaving-coma-severe-burns.html. [Accessed October 25, 2014].

Primoratz, I., 2013. *Terrorism: a philosophical investigation*, Cambridge, UK: Polity Press.

Public Committee Against Torture in Israel (PCATI), 2014. *Israel – briefing to the human rights committee: for the committee's review of the fourth periodic report on Israel*, 14 September 2014. Available online at: www.stoptorture.org.il/en/node/2022. [Accessed 10 January, 2015].

Sledge, M., 2014. "Government privacy board says controversial NSA surveillance program is constitutional", *Huffington Post*, 2 July 2014. Available online at: www.huffingtonpost.com/2014/07/02/pclob-section-702_n_5550010.html. [Accessed October 14, 2014].

Tucker, D., 1998. "Responding to terrorism", *The Washington Quarterly*, 21(1): 103–117.

United Nations Office for the Coordination of Humanitarian Affairs, 2007. *OCHA special focus: occupied Palestinian territory*. Available online at: http://unispal.un.org/UNISPAL.NSF/0/BE07C80CDA4579468525734800500272. [Accessed 10 January 2015].

Valls, A., 2000. "Can terrorism be justified?", in Valls, A., ed., *Ethics in international affairs: theories and cases*, Lanham, MD: Rowman & Littlefield, pp. 65–79.

Weldes, J., 1998. "The cultural production of crises: U.S. identity and missiles in Cuba", in Weldes, J., Laffey, M., Gusterson, H., and Duvall, R., eds., *Cultures of insecurity: states, communities, and the production of danger*, Minneapolis: University of Minnesota Press, pp. 1–35.

Williams, M., 2003. "Words, images, enemies: securitization and international politics", *International Studies Quarterly*, 47: 511–531.

Wolfendale, J., 2007. "Terrorism, security, and the threat of counterterrorism", *Studies in Conflict and Terrorism*, 30(1): 75–92.

Wolfendale, J., 2012. "The concept of security in political violence", in Breen-Smyth, M., ed., *The Ashgate research companion to political violence*, Farnham, UK: Ashgate, pp. 99–118.

12
NEW VERSUS OLD TERRORISM

Alexander Spencer

Introduction

Since the early 1990s, a number of prominent scholars in traditional terrorism research have gone to great efforts to argue that "old terrorism" in the form of, for example, the Irish Republican Army (IRA), Euskadi Ta Askatasuna (ETA), or the Red Army Faction (RAF), is fundamentally different to the "new terrorism" predominantly perpetrated by radical Islamist groups such as al Qaeda (see Hoffman 1998; Laqueur 1999; Simon and Benjamin 2000; Neumann 2009; Kurtulus 2011). While scholars previously considered the difference between various types of "old terrorists", such as ethno-nationalist, separatist, as well as right- and left-wing groups, to be of importance, the trend in traditional terrorism research went in the direction of saying that these different old terrorist groups had some general common characteristics which were fundamentally different to the phenomenon of "new terrorism". In particular, this was said to involve very distinct motivations, behaviour, and organization.

However, this has been met with scepticism by a number of more critical scholars (see Copeland 2001; Tucker 2001; Crenshaw 2003; Duyvesteyn 2004; Spencer 2006, 2011; Field 2009). They criticized the notion of "new terrorism" by not only questioning the truthfulness of the newness claims based on historical real world examples, but also by questioning the accuracy of the category altogether due to the inability of objectively categorising the phenomenon of terrorism in one category rather than the other. In particular, they were concerned that some of the attributed "new" characteristics, such as an emphasis on the fanatical religious motivations, would function politically and ideologically to dehumanize and de-politicise the grievances of such groups as well as to legitimize the use of counterviolence (see Gunning and Jackson 2011).

Apart from the controversies surrounding questions of the definition of terrorism (see Shanahan, this volume), its causes, and appropriate countermeasures (see Lindahl, this volume), the debate about whether new terrorism can really be considered *new* or not has become one of the central disagreements in terrorism research. In fact, this question is very much part of the early development of critical terrorism studies (CTS) at a time when such a label was still nonexistent. This chapter will retrace this development by focusing on three distinct aspects which are said to be fundamentally different between new and old terrorism, including the *motivation* for terrorism, the *behaviour* and use of violence by the terrorist organization, as well as their structure and *organization*. Each of the following sections will examine one of these aspects by first noting the suggested differences between old and new terrorism in this regard, and then turning to the criticism of this distinction. In the conclusion, the chapter emphasizes that the importance of this debate does not so much lie in the establishment of whether new terrorism is really new or not, but in the realization that language and small, seemingly trivial words play an important role in our conceptualization of contemporary terrorism – and importantly, that the use of certain language enables highly questionable counterterrorism practices, such as targeted killings and the use of torture.

Motivations

Many proponents of old and new terrorism argue that one of the fundamental differences between the two types lies in their different motivations. First, old terrorist groups are classed as having predominantly secular motivations and rational political reasons for their violence. For example, left-wing terrorist groups used violence to politicize the working-class masses and convince them to rise up against the capitalist system. Similarly, ethno-nationalist terrorists wanted independence for their ethnic group in the form of a separation of their territory from that of another country, the creation of their own sovereign nation-state, or merger with another state. In either case, their specific demands were often said to be rationally negotiable, such as when they demanded the release of certain jailed comrades or payment in exchange for the release of hostages in a hijacking. Even when demands were difficult to meet, such as in the reunification of a divided country, the creation of an ethno-national homeland, or the abolishment of the existing capitalist system, in many circumstances there appeared to be room for dialogue or negotiation (Ramakrishna and Tan 2002: 6; Neumann 2009).

In contrast, new terrorism is said to be motivated predominantly by religion. Hoffman (1998: 87), for example, asserts that "the religious imperative for terrorism is the most important defining characteristic of terrorist activity today". Whereas old terrorism was primarily secular in its orientation and inspiration, terrorism linked to religious fanaticism is said to be on the rise. According to Nadine Gurr and Benjamin Cole (2000: 28–29), in 1980 only two out of sixty-four identifiable international terrorist organizations could be classified as religious, a figure that rose sharply to twenty-five out of fifty-eight by 1995. New terrorism is therefore often portrayed as terrorism that rejects all other political methods and promotes an uncompromising view of the world in accordance with the belief of the religion. In contrast to old terrorism, new terrorism is said to lack a political agenda or precise political demands. Hoffman believes this religious motivation is the defining characteristic of the new terrorism, producing "radically different value systems, mechanisms of legitimization and justification, concepts of morality and, Manichean world view" (1995: 272; see also Juergensmeyer 2000).

In response to the supposedly new characteristic of the religious motivations of new terrorism, critics have been quick to point out that, historically, religious terrorism is by no means a new phenomenon. According to David Rapoport, religiously motivated terrorism aimed at killing nonbelievers has existed for thousands of years. From the first-century Zealots to the thirteenth-century Assassins, and even up to the nineteenth century and the emergence of political motives such as nationalism, anarchism, and Marxism, "religion provided the only acceptable justification for terror" (Rapoport 1984: 659). Others hold that religious motivation is not so much a new characteristic as it is a cyclic return to earlier motivations for terrorism. Audrey Kurth Cronin (2002/2003: 38), for example, suggests that "the forces of history seem to be driving international terrorism back to a much earlier time, with echoes of the behavior of 'sacred' terrorists such as the Zealots-Sicarii clearly apparent in the terrorist activities of organizations such as al-Qaeda and its associated groups".

In addition, a number of scholars hold that many old terrorist organizations also had close links with and were at least partly motivated by religion (Gunning and Jackson 2011). The most prominent examples of this are the IRA with its predominantly Catholic membership, the Protestant Ulster Freedom Fighters or Ulster Volunteer Force, the primarily Muslim National Liberation Front (FLN) in Algeria, the Jewish terrorist group Irgun, and the National Organization of Cypriote Fighters (EOKA) in Cyprus, which was influenced by the Greek Orthodox Church. As Richard Jackson et al. (2011: 169) point out,

> many "secular" groups displayed "religious" characteristics. For example, both the German RAF and the Italian Red Brigades pursued a radically different world order, painted their conflict in terms comparable to "cosmic war", and described their enemies in similar eschatological terms to Al-Qaeda. Much of their violence was "symbolic" or "redemptive" rather than "strategic", and the level of loyalty demanded from members was as total as that of the most exacting religious cults.

Proponents of the new terrorism idea have responded to this by rightfully arguing that the underlying rhetoric and language used by terrorist organizations is different with regard to old and new terrorist groups (Kurtulus 2011). Very few would refute that the RAF used a more secular line of argumentation, while al Qaeda makes more references to religious themes in their public statements. Similarly, no one would disagree that most old terrorists, such as the RAF, came from the West, while most new terrorists come from the Middle East. It remains, however, open to debate as to whether this would justify the term *new terrorism,* especially considering that the motivation of new terrorists is fundamentally political as well.

As critics point out, it is important to recognize that although the actions of new terrorist groups may be clad in religious language, they still have specific political agendas. An examination of the demands and goals of al Qaeda (Lawrence 2005) or other new terrorists associated with them reveals that many are based on clear political goals and targets – for example, the spread of political Islam, the withdrawal of foreign influence from the holy lands, the overthrow of the existing governments in Saudi Arabia and Egypt, the creation of a worldwide pan-Islamic Caliphate, and the elimination of Israel. In reality, it is often extremely difficult, if not impossible, to distinguish between religious and political motivations. "Were the Jewish terrorists in British Palestine fighting for religion or against colonialism? Do the Tamil tigers want their own homeland because they are Hindus in a Muslim nation or because they are Tamils in a Sinhalese country?" (Quillen 2002: 288). The answer is probably a bit of both. Assigning religious motivations to individual terrorist attacks is subjective and open to interpretation. Quillen cites the example of the 1995 Oklahoma City bombing, which one might interpret as an act motivated by Timothy McVeigh's devotion to the Christian Identity movement or as the reaction of a political terrorist to gun control measures and the bloody federal raids at Ruby Ridge and Waco (Quillen 2002).

Behaviour

Second, the behaviour of old terrorists is said to be different, as violence by these groups in general is "targeted and proportionate in scope and intensity to the practical political objectives being pursued" (Simon and Benjamin 2000: 65). Old terrorism is viewed as discriminate, as they carefully select and attack well defined, highly symbolic targets of the authority they oppose, including politicians, government officials, members of the aristocracy, military or banking sectors as well as other symbolic targets such as government buildings. Rather than killing civilians, old terrorists have tried to maximise publicity and spread their ideological message. Attacks are considered "propaganda by deed" in order to increase popular support and are commonly followed by a communiqué taking credit for the act, laying out demands, or explaining why it was carried out against that particular target. In order to increase the impact of their action, attacks are often choreographed for the media to the extent that Brian Jenkins considered terrorism to be theatre (Jenkins 1975: 16).

In other words, old terrorists do not want to use excessive indiscriminate violence because it reduces their claims to legitimacy and alienates them from supporters, thereby reducing their access to new recruits and funding. The targeted violence is generally perpetrated with conventional tactics such as hand-held guns and machine guns, as well as bombs. Old terrorists have showed little interest in new tactics and nonconventional weapons, such as weapons of mass destruction (WMDs). They have tried not to kill innocent bystanders, because such casualties alienate the population and go against their aim of inciting a popular uprising (Laqueur 2003). Thus, by keeping the level of casualties low, old terrorists have "preserved their eligibility for a place at the bargaining table and, ultimately, a role in successor governments" (Laqueur 2003: 66).

In contrast, the behaviour of new terrorists is said to include, partly due to its religious motivations, an increased willingness to use excessive, indiscriminate violence. Laqueur (1999: 81), for example, argues that "the new terrorism is different in character, aiming not at clearly defined political demands but at the destruction of society and the elimination of large sections of the population". These religious-based new terrorists are believed to see their struggle as good against evil, thereby dehumanizing their victims and considering all nonmembers of their group to be infidels or apostates. Religious terrorists are often their own constituency, unconcerned about alienating their supporters with their acts of destruction and holding themselves accountable only to God. As a result, indiscriminate violence may be not only morally acceptable, but also a righteous and necessary advancement of their religious cause. Whereas old terrorists tended to strike only selected targets, new terrorists have become increasingly indiscriminate and try to produce as many casualties as possible. They are consequently not interested in any sort of negotiation; according to Matthew Morgan (2004: 30–31), "today's terrorists don't want a seat at the table, they want to destroy the table and everyone sitting at it".

Moreover, new terrorists are deemed far more willing to engage in risky, complex, and seemingly irrational acts. Whereas most actions by old terrorists involved an escape plan, new terrorists are more willing to give their own lives while orchestrating a terrorist act; martyrdom is viewed as a way of reaching heaven (Enders and Sandler 2000: 310). Furthermore, many scholars believe that because new terrorists are motivated to use extreme violence, they are more likely to obtain and use nuclear, biological, chemical, and radiological weapons. Hoffman (1998: 197) warns that with the rise of the new terrorism, "many of the constraints (both self-imposed and technical) which previously inhibited terrorist use of WMD are eroding". And with the collapse of the Soviet Union, acquiring material that could be used for WMDs has become easier and no longer requires the cooperation of a state sponsor.

However, critics of the new terrorism idea are not only sceptical of the difference between old and new terrorists with regard to motivation, but they are also doubtful of a fundamental difference in their behaviour and their specific use of suicide tactics and the potential use of WMD and general use of excessive and indiscriminate violence. With regards to the suicide tactics commonly attributed to new terrorism, critics point out that suicide bombing has been used extensively by the separatist Tamil Tigers in Sri Lanka since 1983. For example, Robert Pape (2003: 343) argues that the Tamil Tigers carried out 75 of 186 suicide terrorist attacks between 1980 and 2000. Even before this, during the Middle Ages, the Assassins' use of daggers at close range showed their "willingness to die in pursuit of their mission", while the Anarchists of nineteenth-century Europe regularly died in the process of attacking their targets (Gearson 2002: 14).

Similarly, others point out that the use of WMDs, including chemical, biological, and nuclear weapons as a characteristic of the new terrorism, is also problematic. The example of the 1995 sarin gas attack on the Tokyo subway by Aum Shinrikyo is frequently cited to make the connection between the new terrorism and WMDs. However, terrorists have planned and attempted to use WMDs for many decades. In 1972, members of the right-wing group Order of the Rising Sun were arrested and found to be in possession of 30 to 40 kilograms of epidemic typhus pathogens; they were seeking to poison the water supply of Chicago, St. Louis, and other Midwestern cities in order to create a new master race. In 1984, members of the Bhagwan Shree Rajneesh's group contaminated salad bars with salmonella, thereby poisoning 750 people in Oregon. In the 1980s, European authorities discovered botulinal toxin and considerable quantities of organophosphorous compounds, used to make nerve gas, in RAF safe houses in France and Germany. In addition, the Kurdistan Workers' Party (PKK) and the Tamil Tigers, both examples of old terrorists, have used chemical weapons. In 1992, the PKK poisoned water tanks of the Turkish air force near Istanbul with lethal doses of cyanide, and in 1990, the Tamil Tigers attacked a Sri Lankan military camp with chlorine gas. The PKK and Tamil attacks are significant because they seem to disprove the idea that all "traditional terrorist groups would avoid using nuclear, chemical or biological weapons under any circumstances" (Cameron 2004: 81).

Despite the speculation, no terrorist organization has used nuclear weapons in an attack. While no nuclear bombs have been exploded, old terrorists committed numerous attacks on nuclear power stations in the 1970s and 1980s. One of the first occurred in 1973 when a commando from a left-wing Argentinean group entered the construction site of the Atucha atomic power station north of Buenos Aires. During the years that followed, the separatist group Basque Fatherland and Liberty (ETA) conducted several attacks against the Lemoniz nuclear power station near Bilbao, Spain. Other attacks were directed against plants near San Sebastian, Pamplona, Tafalla, Beriz, and other sites in northern Spain. In 1982, the terrorist wing of the African National Congress (ANC) sabotaged two South African nuclear power plants. Both of their reactors were substantially damaged, but because they were not in operation at the time, there was no release of radiation (Laqueur 1999: 72). Although it was not proven that any of these groups was seeking to cause a nuclear explosion or contamination, these incidents prove that even old terrorists were clearly willing to cross the nuclear line.

Apart from the specific behaviour of employing suicide tactics and potentially using WMDs, proponents of the new terrorism idea have been vocal in their point that new terrorists have become more lethal and willing to resort to unlimited violence to cause large numbers of casualties indiscriminately. In their view, the old terrorists were more restrained in their use of violence and the number of casualties they intended. However, even within traditional terrorism research, some scholars refute the claim that the religious motivation of terrorist automatically leads to more violence and instead argue that "Islamist groups are no more likely than non-Islamist groups to commit higher casualty attacks" (Piazza 2009: 71). Others argue that indiscriminate mass-casualty attacks have long been a characteristic of terrorism. Examples of the mass fatalities produced by the old terrorists are the simultaneous truck bombings of the US and French barracks in Lebanon in 1983, which killed 367; the downing of Pan Am Flight 103 over Lockerbie, Scotland, which took the lives of 270; and the bombing of an Air India flight in 1985 by Sikh separatists, with 329 fatalities. It is easy to forget that one of the most violent incidents of terrorism prior to September 11, 2001, was the 1979 attack on an Abadan movie theatre in Iran that killed about 500 people (Pettiford and Harding 2003: 106–146). And, as Rapoport (1984) points out, evidence indicates that the Thugs of South Asia were by far the longest-lasting and most murderous terrorist organization in history, killing around half a million people over a period of roughly 400 years.

Even if the indiscriminate targeting of innocent people, such as the children in the attack on a school in Beslan, Russia, in 2004, is considered to be a characteristic of the new terrorism, one finds examples of old terrorists who did the same. For example, members of the Democratic Front for the Liberation of Palestine machine-gunned children in an Israeli school in 1974, killing twenty-seven and injuring seventy. And, even if one disregards the numbers and argues that the gruesome violence of the new terrorism, such as the beheading of reporters in Iraq in 2014, is more excessive than before, the old terrorists could be just as ruthless. For example, Martin Miller (1995: 45) describes how in 1884 "a Viennese banker and his eleven-year-old son were hacked to death with an axe in front of his other son" by anarchists.

It is true that none of these examples can be likened to the casualties caused by the 9/11 attacks. However, the term new terrorism appeared long before 2001. Marie Breen Smyth (2007: 260) points out that "the scale of atrocity at the World Trade Center was unprecedented in the practice of modern terror; however, the emphasis on the scale of the attack has tended to negate the value of previous scholarship and experience of 'terrorism'". In fact, examination of the data on international terrorism incidences reveals that although the number of events has generally declined since the mid-1980s, the number of fatalities per incident has steadily increased over the same period. Considering that the new terrorism is supposed to have started in the 1990s, this increase in fatalities might not be directly linked to the phenomenon of new terrorism. An equally plausible argument is that the increase in casualties is due at least in part to advanced technology. Explosives, timing, and remote-control devices have substantially improved in recent decades, with a corresponding effect on the numbers of casualties.

Furthermore, since the 1980s, governments have adapted to terrorist techniques such as kidnapping, hostage taking, hijacking, assassination, and sabotage by increasing security at airports, securing embassies, guarding likely kidnap targets, training specialist commando troops, and sharing intelligence with other states. In response, terrorists have adjusted their tactics by placing more emphasis on coordinated bombings, "soft" civilian targets, and hit-and-run tactics (Duyvesteyn 2004). Although it has become increasingly difficult for terrorists to get close to their traditional targets, they continue to find other ways of capturing the public's attention. The use of more spectacular coordinated violent tactics is one way of gaining greater media coverage. One may therefore argue that the use of terrorist violence as theatre has not faded with the emergence of the new terrorism. It is hard to think of a more symbolic and dramatically theatrical set of attacks than those of 9/11. Targeting the World Trade Center (a symbol of Western capitalism), the Pentagon (the heart of the US defence establishment), and the US Capitol seems too much even for a Hollywood film. Terrorists still want a big audience, and the larger, more coordinated, and more dramatic the attack, the bigger the audience will be. Therefore, the rising level of fatalities can be viewed as an ongoing process which does not necessarily represent a unique feature qualifying the concept of the new terrorism.

Beyond the historical example of indiscriminate and excessive violence by old terrorists, other critics hold that our understanding of what can be considered discriminate and indiscriminate is a subjective one. What one considers to be a "legitimate" or select target is not something established by nature. What we consider indiscriminate attacks on the Pentagon and the World Trade Center others may believe to be selective strikes on the military and financial heart of the United States. New terrorists are still very selective in their targeting. They generally do not go about randomly killing everybody, but continue to carefully plan their attacks and consciously select their targets for maximum effect. Just because the selected target group is considered wider and now includes Western civilians does not make it indiscriminate. Al Qaeda is probably not interested in killing a native villager in the middle of the rainforest. So selectivity and its influence on public opinion are still very important to new terrorists; it is only because wider selection includes categories such as "Western civilians" that we consider it an indication of the indiscriminate nature of new terrorism.

Scholars such as Ray Takeyh (2001) make a compelling case that public opinion plays as vital a role in the new terrorism as in old terrorism. One example is the 1997 al-Gama'a al-Islamiyya attack on the Temple of Hatshepsut in Luxor, Egypt. The attack, which killed fifty-eight tourists and four Egyptians, was widely condemned not only by Western governments but also by many radical Islamists, who believed the attack damaged their cause. Takeyh points out that support for al-Gama'a al-Islamiyya fell dramatically in Egypt as a result of the attack. Although the group remained active, its attack alienated the people to whom it most wanted to appeal, and over time, this development gravely hindered the group's efforts. The importance of public opinion is particularly true when one considers terrorists' political agendas. These political goals, such as the establishment of an Islamic state, will restrain terrorists. Public support will be required for the establishment of a new state, and therefore terrorists must be careful not to alienate their supporters and sympathizers by using excessive violence against the wrong people.

Organization

Third, the old terrorism is said to be organized in a hierarchical manner, including fairly well-defined command and control structures (Kurtulus 2011: 489–411). Although it is impossible to clearly demarcate the different layers, old terrorism is argued to be organized like a pyramid, with the leadership, who decide on the overall policy and plans, at the top. Underneath is a larger layer of active terrorists who carry out the attacks and are often specialized in certain activities such as bomb-making, assassination, or surveillance. At the next level are the active supporters who supply intelligence, weapons, supplies, communications, transportation, and safe houses. At the bottom are the passive supporters who agree with the goals of the terrorist organization and spread their ideas and express their emotional support (Henderson 2001: 17).

In contrast, one of the most emphasized aspects of the new terrorism is its loose network and less hierarchical organizational structure, aided by the emergence of new communications technology. As Rohan Gunaratna (2003) points out, each group within this network becomes relatively autonomous, but all are still linked by advanced communications and their common purpose. They therefore become much more flexible and can adapt and react more easily to different situations. Although members do communicate with their leadership, groups can also operate self-sufficiently. Steven Simon and Daniel Benjamin (2000: 70) refer to this as a combination of "a 'hub and spoke' structure (where nodes communicate with the centre) with a 'wheel' structure (where nodes in the network communicate with each other without reference to the centre)". This type of integrated structure is much more difficult to identify and penetrate than a traditional hierarchical structure. It is said to be far more resilient because each cell can still operate even if the leadership of the organization is lost.

Similar to the question of motivation and behaviour, critics of new terrorism are also sceptical of the idea that old terrorism was organized along hierarchical lines with a clear command structure, while the new terrorism is a loose, stateless network that is more weakly organized and has no strong command structure. Interestingly, even supporters of the new terrorism concept, such as Hoffman, admit that the newness of the loose network structure associated with the new terrorism is debatable, as it is visible in many old terrorist organizations (2001: 426). For example, over a century ago, the anarchist movement, responsible for a number of high-profile attacks against heads of state in Russia and across Europe, pursued a similar strategy of violence carried out by loosely networked, largely unconnected cells of like-minded radicals.

Other examples of network structures in old terrorists include the Palestine Liberation Organization (PLO), which served as an umbrella group in which the dominant faction, Fatah, did not have a monopoly of power. For decades, the different factions within the PLO were fairly independent and had different policies and strategies. Hezbollah is an umbrella organization of radical Shiite groups in which the relationship among members is unpredictable and does not follow strict lines of control. Network structures also existed in left-wing revolutionary groups such as the RAF, in which second-, third-, and fourth-generation terrorists did not really form a hierarchical organization, but rather a loose confederation with similar common goals (Tucker 2001:4).

In the same way in which there are network structures in old terrorist groups, there are clear signs of hierarchical command structures in the new terrorist organizations such as al Qaeda. They possess a clear leadership structure and operative subunits responsible for conducting attacks as well as "specialized units directly below the top leadership level" that are responsible for certain tasks such as recruitment, finances, procurement, and public relations (Mayntz 2004: 11–12). At the same time, today's terrorist organizations, including al Qaeda, have many different types of members, including core members or professional terrorists, part-time terrorists, or amateurs, who also lead normal lives outside of the organization, as well as less closely associated supporters. These different types of members exist in both old terrorism and new terrorism to an equally fluctuating degree.

Concluding implications and the importance of language

Why was, and is, this debate important? Why does it really matter what we call current terrorism? Is this not simply an example of academic bickering which has no relevance for the real world? It is important to stress that this debate is not so much about which side of the debate is right or wrong. The main purpose is not to prove that terrorism today is old and that terrorism has not changed, but that the category of "new terrorism" is contestable and not as unproblematic, as some may suggest. The aim is to question the dominant interpretations and thereby show the inherently contested nature of the new terrorism category. The concept of new terrorism is not simply an objective description of reality but a subjective choice. While at the beginning the debate was focused on the historical truthfulness of the new terrorism label and whether it was really new or not, the debate, together with the rise of CTS, has shifted from how terrorism really is to how terrorism is constructed to be and, importantly, what consequences this construction has for counterterrorism policies and strategies.

There are a number of avenues for continued research on the issue of new terrorism, both on ontological and epistemological levels. For example, the questioning of the ontological accuracy of new terrorism allows us to ask questions previously considered absurd due to the established fanatical, uncompromising, and apolitical nature of new terrorism. Here, there is a need to contemplate in detail alternative, previously marginalized means of dealing with terrorism, such as engagement and reconciliation (Renner and Spencer 2012; Tellidis and Toros 2015). This would include the question of what peace studies, conflict resolution, and transitional justice have to offer the analysis of contemporary terrorism.

A further avenue of research could potentially turn to the epistemological question of why the new terrorism concept was/is so successful at establishing itself as "truth" and how it became dominant in large parts of the discourse on terrorism. Why are certain discursive linkages in combination with terrorism more successful than others in establishing themselves in discourse? Why did the story of new terrorism become dominant? Possible research could here engage with literary studies and narratology to investigate the reasons for narrative dominance and the marginalization of alternative stories (Baker 2010; Spencer 2014). Possible investigations into the dominance of the new terrorism story could focus on the level of: (1) the narrator (the role of particularly powerful scholars, epistemic communities, or political actors); (2) the story (the way and structure of how the story is told, including the interplay of different narrative elements, such as setting, characterization, and plot); and (3) the audience (the necessity of preexisting dominant cultural understandings, such as orientalism, which stories on new terrorism have to link themselves to in order to be accepted as viable).

The debate on the ontological level about the accuracy of the predicate *new* has opened up space for the more important epistemological debate on the role of language and discourse in the constitution of terrorism (see Jackson 2005; Hülsse and Spencer 2008; Spencer 2010). Here, language is understood not only as a means of describing the real world out there, but also as a way or means of actively constituting it. The debate on new terrorism has set the stage for constructivist and post-structuralist perspectives on the role of language for the construction of the political world. That is, the concept of newness and the predicate *new* actively take part in the constitution of the world in general, and terrorism in particular.

By describing terrorism as new terrorism, our understanding of what is considered appropriate in response is already framed in a particular way. In particular, the concept of new terrorism makes only "new" *counterterrorism* seem appropriate in response. It is easier to gain political support for intrusive, violent, and expensive counterpolicies if the phenomenon which they are aimed at already linguistically includes the means of legitimizing them. Even proponents of the new terrorism idea seem to agree: "It is true that these politicians sometimes refer to a new terrorist threat in their speeches, most probably to justify new measures, increase their rating among the electors or simply to mobilize support for their policies" (Kurtulus 2011: 491). Therefore, small words have big implications for the study of terrorism. As one of the early critical voices in the field, Martha Crenshaw (1995: 7) pointed out, "what one calls things matters. There are few neutral terms in politics, because political language affects the perceptions of protagonists and audiences, and such effects acquire a greater urgency in the drama of terrorism".

References

Baker, M., 2010. "Narratives of Terrorism and Security: Accurate Translations, Suspicious Frames", *Critical Studies on Terrorism*, 3(3): 347–364.
Breen Smyth, M., 2007. "A Critical Research Agenda for the Study of Political Terror", *European Political Science*, 6(3): 260–267.
Cameron, G., 2004. "Weapons of Mass Destruction Terrorism Research: Past and Future", in Silke, A., ed., *Research on Terrorism-Trends, Achievement and Failures*, London: Frank Cass, pp. 72–90.
Copeland, T., 2001. "Is the New Terrorism Really New?", *Journal of Conflict Studies*, 21: 91–105.
Crenshaw, M., 1995. "Thoughts on Relating Terrorism to Historical Context", in Crenshaw, M., ed., *Terrorism in Context*, University Park: Pennsylvania State University Press, pp. 3–24.
Crenshaw, M., 2003. "'New' Versus 'Old' Terrorism", *Palestine-Israel Journal of Politics, Economics and Culture*, 10(1): 48–53.
Duyvesteyn, I., 2004. "How New Is the New Terrorism?", *Studies in Conflict and Terrorism*, 27(5): 439–454.
Enders, W., and Sandler, T., 2000. "Is Transnational Terrorism Becoming More Threatening? A Time-Series Investigation", *Journal of Conflict Resolution*, 44(3): 307–332.
Field, A., 2009. "The 'New Terrorism': Revolution or Evolution", *Political Studies Review*, 7(2): 195–207.
Gearson, J., 2002. "The Nature of Modern Terrorism", in Freedman, L., ed., *Superterrorism – Policy Responses*, Oxford: Blackwell Publishing, pp. 7–24.
Gunaratna, R., 2003. *Inside Al Qaeda: Global Network of Terror*, 3rd ed., New York: Berkley Books.
Gunning, J., and Jackson, R., 2011. "What Is So 'Religious' about 'Religious Terrorism'", *Critical Studies on Terrorism*, 4(3): 369–388.
Gurr, N., and Cole, B., 2000. *The New Face of Terrorism: Threats from Weapons of Mass Destruction*, London: I. B. Tauris.

Henderson, H., 2001. *Global Terrorism – The Complete Reference Guide*, New York: Checkmark Books.
Hoffman, B., 1995. "'Holy Terror': The Implications of Terrorism Motivated by a Religious Imperative", *Studies in Conflict and Terrorism*, 18(4): 271–284.
Hoffman, B., 1998. *Inside Terrorism*, London: Indigo.
Hoffman, B., 2001. "Change and Continuity in Terrorism", *Studies in Conflict and Terrorism*, 24(5): 417–428.
Hülsse, R., and Spencer, A., 2008. "The Metaphor of Terror: Terrorism Studies and the Constructivist Turn", *Security Dialogue*, 39(6): 571–592.
Jackson, R., 2005. *Writing the War on Terrorism: Language, Politics and Counter-Terrorism*, Manchester: Manchester University Press.
Jackson, R., Jarvis, L., Gunning, J., and Breen Smyth, M., 2011. *Terrorism: A Critical Introduction*, Basingstoke: Palgrave.
Jenkins, B., 1975. "International Terrorism: A New Mode of Conflict", in Carlton, D., and Schaerf, C., eds., *International Terrorism: Fanaticism and the Arms of Mass Destruction*, London: Croom Helm, pp. 13–49.
Juergensmeyer, M., 2000. *Terror in the Mind of God. The Global Rise of Religious Violence*, Berkley: University of California Press.
Kurth Cronin, A., 2002/2003. "Behind the Curve: Globalization and International Terrorism", *International Security*, 27: 30–58.
Kurtulus, E., 2011. "The 'New Terrorism' and Its Critics", *Studies in Conflict and Terrorism*, 34(6): 476–500.
Laqueur, W., 1999. *The New Terrorism: Fanaticism and the Arms of Mass Destruction*, London: Oxford University Press.
Laqueur, W., 2003. *No End to War: Terrorism in the Twenty-First Century*, New York: Continuum.
Lawrence, B., ed., 2005. *Messages to the World: The Statements of Osama Bin Laden*, New York: Verso.
Mayntz, R., 2004. "Organizational Forms of Terrorism – Hierarchy, Network, or a Type sui generis?", *MPIfG Discussion Paper* 04/04, Max Planck Institute for the Study of Societies, Cologne.
Miller, M., 1995. "The Intellectual Origin of Modern Terrorism in Europe", in Crenshaw, M., ed., *Terrorism in Context*, University Park: Pennsylvania State University Press, pp. 27–62.
Morgan, M., 2004. "The Origin of the New Terrorism", *Parameters*, 34(1): 29–43.
Neumann, P., 2009. *Old and New Terrorism*, Cambridge: Polity Press.
Pape, R., 2003. "The Strategic Logic of Suicide Terrorism", *American Political Science Review*, 97(3): 343–361.
Pettiford, L., and Harding, D., 2003. *Terrorism – The New World War*, London: Arcturus Publishing.
Piazza, J., 2009. "Is Islamist Terrorism More Lethal? An Empirical Study of Group Ideology, Organization and Goal Structure", *Terrorism and Political Violence*, 21(1): 62–88.
Quillen, C., 2002. "A Historical Analysis of Mass Casualty Bombers", *Studies in Conflict and Terrorism*, 25(5): 279–292.
Ramakrishna, K., and Tan, A., 2002. "The New Terrorism: Diagnosis and Prescriptions", in Ramakrishna, K., and Tan, A., eds., *The New Terrorism – Anatomy, Trends and Counter-Strategies*, Singapore: Eastern Universities Press, pp. 3–29.
Rapoport, D., 1984. "Fear and Trembling: Terrorism in Three Religious Traditions", *American Political Science Review*, 78(3): 658–677.
Renner, J., and Spencer, A., eds., 2012. *Reconciliation after Terrorism. Strategy, Possibility or Absurdity?*, London: Routledge.
Simon, S., and Benjamin, D., 2000. "America and the New Terrorism", *Survival*, 42(1): 59–75.
Spencer, A., 2006. "Questioning the Concept of New Terrorism", *Peace, Conflict and Development*, 8: 1–33.
Spencer, A., 2010. *The Tabloid Terrorist. The Predicative Construction of New Terrorism in the Media*, Basingstoke: Palgrave.
Spencer, A., 2011. "Sic[k] of the 'New Terrorism' Debate? A Response to Our Critics", *Critical Studies on Terrorism*, 4(3): 459–467.
Spencer, A., 2014. "Romantic Stories of the Pirate in IARRRH: The Failure of Linking Piracy and Terrorism Narratives in Germany", *International Studies Perspectives*, 15(3): 297–312.
Takeyh, R., 2001. "Islamism: R.I.P.", *National Interest*, 63: 97–102.
Tellidis, I., and Toros, H., eds., 2015. *Researching Terrorism, Peace and Conflict Studies. Interaction, Synthesis and Opposition*, London: Routledge.
Tucker, D., 2001. "What's New about the New Terrorism and How Dangerous Is It?", *Terrorism and Political Violence*, 15(3): 1–14.

13
RELIGION AND TERRORISM

Ioannis Tellidis

Introduction

Although the relationship between religion and terrorism had been examined before 11 September 2001 (Rapoport 1984; Hoffman 1995; Ranstorp 1996; Lesser et al. 1999), the attacks generated a new impetus for research, particularly on "Islamist" and/or "Islamic" terrorism. These terms, along with "jihadist", "Salafist", "Wahhabi", and "fundamentalist terrorism", are used interchangeably by the media, policymakers, and academics in a manner that presents the Muslim world and Islamic culture as monolithic and homogeneous (Antúnez and Tellidis 2013; Hellmich 2014). Despite the fact that numerous studies have shown the fallacy of causally linking terrorism and religion (see Crenshaw 2000; Wilkinson 2001, Bloom 2005; Pape 2005; Funk 2007; Jackson 2007; Cavanaugh 2009; Gunning and Jackson 2011), extreme Islamist organisations dominate research attention, with almost 40 per cent of articles devoted to such groups (Silke 2009: 43). As Silke (2007: 85) put it, "in the history of terrorism research no single category of terrorist group has enjoyed so much attention in this way". This dominant focus in terrorism studies is partially reflective of public and academic perceptions of (and attitudes towards) Islam being the primary cause of terrorist violence. Such generalisations are not entirely unjustifiable, since a number of terrorist and extremist groups project and invoke religion (and Islam in particular) in order to justify their actions, rally support, and attract more recruits.

Herein, however, is where the problem lies: unquestionably accepting a group's claims that its actions follow a religious doctrine is bound to lead security agencies and policy circles to misconceptions, misinformation, and ultimately, policy decisions and behaviours that alienate core segments of the broader – and most importantly, nonviolent – religious community. While it has already been shown that an uncritical adoption of such terminology is "counter-productive" and "intellectually contestable" (Jackson 2007: 395), it also contributes to augmenting the cultural gap between different ethno-religious communities (Jackson 2007) and reinforcing the correlation between Islamophobia and radicalisation (Runnymede Trust 1997; Abbas 2012). The post-9/11 discrimination and overall suspicion against persons of particular appearance or (presumed) identity by security agencies and the general public alike has contributed to the already well-rooted disaffection and alienation experienced by Muslim communities in the West. As shown recently (Goodman 2014; see also Maher 2014), the failure of integrating these communities (and the obstacles posed to their integration; see Runnymede Trust 1997) is more significant a factor when it comes to extremism than religion or immigration.

More concretely, it has been shown that the (perceived or actual) hate and fear of non-Muslims leads some members of the Muslim community to raise a defensive posture within their societies and a combative climate based on militant rhetoric that locates, and then blames, outside conspiracies (Ahmed 1999). In other words, terrorist attacks perpetrated by members of a particular religion are not the product of the religion itself. The conflict is not the result of the religious beliefs alone (Funk 2007); rather, it is the combination of grievances (perceived or actual) with a concrete translation of religious values that motivates the terrorists (Schmid 2010: 48). The opposite, of course, is also true: "the absence of widespread religious conviction [does not] guarantee the reign of political sense" (Ryan 2012: 987).

This chapter aims to explain the scepticism with which critical and mainstream scholarship has responded to the dominant approaches that highlight terrorism's religious motives. In order to do so, the next section conceptualises "religion" and its ontological relationship with the political. This will set the foundations for the exploration of how terrorism – an inherently political phenomenon – consolidated in the minds of international relations (IR) academics, policymakers, and the general public as a religiously motivated activity. As it will become apparent later in the chapter, calls to avoid linking religion with terrorism were made long before the emergence of critical terrorism studies (CTS), but they have gone unheeded in the aftermath of 9/11. As such, it has fallen to critical scholarship on terrorism to problematise, question, and critique this perception once again.

Conceptualising religion

A cursory look into writings on religion and violence shows that the definition of *religion* (Laitin 1978: 570; Thomas 2005: 21, 23; Cavanaugh 2009: 57; Toft 2012: 133) is not only as elusive as that of *terrorism*, but that it is also accompanied by statements of caution (Philpott 2002: 67) similar to those linked with the definition of terrorism. For instance, as Cavanaugh argues (2009: 16), while most scholars recognise the difficulty or the complexity of defining religion, they also "give some version of the assertion that 'everybody knows what we mean when we say "religion"'". The examination of the role of religion in IR has been somewhat inconsistent (Desch 2013: 15), since it is seen both as an increasingly irrelevant historical relic, as well as an increasing source of violence and conflict. The reasons for this inconsistency lie in the secularist normative assumptions that characterise the IR field as a whole. Such assumptions include the thesis that the secular sphere can be differentiated from the religious one (Casanova 2012: 25); the laicist belief that religion has lost much of its political significance because it has been resituated in the private sphere (Hurd 2007: 650); and the acceptance that the "privatization of religion [is] a precondition of modern democratic politics" (Casanova 2012: 25).

These predominantly modernist assumptions are perhaps the underlying cause of not only the contemporary, but also earlier, conflations of religion with terrorism, war, and violence more broadly, because they view religion "either as a backlash against modernization and globalization or as a harbinger of cultural conflict" (Hurd 2007: 661). Such views are what Esposito terms "secular fundamentalism" (1999: 259). A critical analysis of the ways in which scholars examined the Wars of Religion in medieval Europe (1550–1648), culminating in the Treaty of Westphalia, for example, has shown that the application of the concept of religion was retrospective and therefore misleading (Thomas 2003: 25). Instead, as Thomas explains, a social definition of religion has since been favoured – one that points to "a community of believers rather than a body of doctrines or beliefs". The implications of this are significant because what was being safeguarded and defended in the Wars of Religion was a sacred notion of the community defined by religion, as each community fought to define, redefine, or defend the boundaries between the sacred and the profane as a whole.

(Thomas 2003: 25)

Approached as such, it becomes increasingly difficult to disassociate religious ideas, agendas, and motives from political, economic, social, and other motives. In that regard, "what counts as religion . . . depends on who has the power and authority to define religion at any given time and place" (Cavanaugh 2009: 59). Two significant implications emerge from this observation. The first, similar to the study of terrorism, is that knowledge is also power in the study of religion (Hurd 2004; Salvatore 2006; McCutcheon 2007). The "strategic operationalization of religion" (Hurd 2012) involves the distinction between "peaceful" and "violent" religion. This distinction, in turn, allows states, institutionalised religions, and international governmental and nongovernmental organisations to marginalise violent manifestations of religion while simultaneously empowering the more peaceful ones, both domestically as well as globally (Hurd 2012).

The second implication of the relationship between knowledge and power is that the aforementioned distinction between "good" and "bad" religion, as well as the overall administration of religion, is overseen, dictated, and managed by predominantly secular actors, such as Western liberal states and international organisations (Hurd 2012). Indeed, as Casanova (2012: 31) notes,

> even the French state, the only self-defined secularist state in Western Europe . . . frequently regulates religious affairs, has established institutional relations with the Catholic Church . . . and has tried at different times to organise the other religious communities . . . into churchlike ecclesiastical institutions, which the state can use as interlocutor and institutional partner.

The significance of this implication lies in these actors' secularist normative assumptions[1] of what religion is, how it is defined, and how it should be practised in a way that does not become a risk to global governance. These constructed assumptions have become so well established and internalised that they "often prejudice and distort understanding and judgement" (Esposito 1999: 257). As McCutcheon (2007: 197–198) puts it,

> such distinctions as church/state, private/public, and sacred/secular [are] socio-rhetorical devices that have stayed on our minds because they continue to prove so useful to a variety of groups . . . , all of which have tried to regulate – to divide and rule – their highly competitive economies of signification.

When a religion, like Islam (in which politics, religion, and society are indivisible – see Ranstorp 1996: 42; Esposito 1999: 257), is viewed through the Western secularist construct of the privatisation of religion, it is perceived of as "'abnormal' insofar as it departs from an accepted 'modern' secular norm, and nonsensical. Thus Islam becomes incomprehensible, irrational, extremist, threatening" (Esposito 1999: 257–258). This perceived abnormality, as Salvatore (2006: 557–558) observes, is aggravating because "the Islamic Other evokes ghosts of a European past when the proliferation of untamed religious sectarianism unleashed the catastrophe of religious wars".

Yet, even though modern and contemporary references to those medieval wars continue to highlight their religious dimension, the same narratives and analyses tend to neglect their essentially political nature: the wars were the *statebuilding* tool that ruling elites used in order to consolidate their power vis-à-vis that of the church (Cavanaugh 2009: 162; emphasis added). As such, the creation of the state was not so much the solution to these wars, but rather its cause (Cavanaugh 2009). From the moment the religious was separated from, and subordinated to, the political in Western Europe, religion was securitised and its construction as an existential threat served "as a tool of legitimation of state-centric accounts of security" (Mavelli 2011: 193). This is of particular significance because, as Mavelli argues, a genealogy of security shows that "the emergence of insecurity as a political object – as the object of political strategies of power and knowledge – may be linked to the process of secularization" (2011: 180). Hence, Mavelli continues, "rather than solving the problem of religious insecurity, secularization makes the question of fear and the politics of exceptionalism central to the state-centric project of modernity and its related vision of security" (2011: 180).

The aforementioned is by no means an exhaustive exploration of the relationship between religion and politics, or the ways in which religion was constructed as a threat to the political, or indeed, how this construct became a naturalisation in the Western world before it was imposed on (or was expected to be adopted by) non-Western regions. Nevertheless, this brief discussion of the construction of religion and secularisation in the West may explain the Western political world's anxiety about the manifestation of violence that self-proclaims to be linked to religion. More concretely, it makes evident the reasons why such anxiety is disproportionately heightened when compared to more prominent and tangible threats to human security (rather than state security or that of its elites), like the spread of small arms (in the case of the United States), the ascendance of neo-fascism (in the case of Europe), poverty and inequality, and environmental degradation.

Furthermore, it also indicates how terrorism and violence more broadly generate distinct attention and security reflexes when linked to religion. Particularly when it comes to Islam following the events of 9/11, such reflexes reached levels that have not been witnessed in other conflicts where religion was also present (Cyprus, Kurdistan, Northern Ireland, and Sri Lanka, to name but a few). The following section will explore the perceptions and attitudes that seemingly verify a "clash of civilisations" (Huntington 1993) and will showcase the responses that critical research and scholarship have brought forward when examining terrorism and its relationship with religion. Such responses, it must be stressed, have been voiced by earlier scholars (for example, Crenshaw in 2000 and Wilkinson in 2001). The events of 9/11, however, provided a distinct momentum in the field of terrorism studies that generated an avalanche of research in which such cautionary and critical voices were lost.

Terrorism and religion

Although "terrorism motivated by religious fanaticism has been perpetrated throughout history" (Wilkinson 2001: 34), it declined throughout the twentieth century and was superseded by violence motivated by secular and/or ideological imperatives (Hoffman 1998). Yet, its reappearance in the 1990s gave prominence to the notion of "religious terrorism" as a distinct category of political violence. The emergence of the concept is closely related to the distinction between "old" and "new" wars (Kaldor 2007), which brings to the fore a historical transition from interstate conflict to an increasingly intrastate one, as well as a change from role to identity politics (Gilbert 2003: 13). According to scholars, increased lethality, unclear motives, and lack of ideology are the three main characteristics that differentiate "new" from "old" terrorism (Ranstorp 1996: 44; Hoffman 1998: 93–94; Laqueur 1999; Juergensmeyer 2000; Spencer, this volume). Secular terrorist violence, as Hoffman (1998) informs, was more discriminating and less lethal because of the desire to appeal to a tacitly supportive or uncommitted constituency. The general aim of religious groups, however, is "not installing a new political regime, pursuing limited political reforms or even fostering changes in the state's allocation of political and economic resources" (Weinberg et al. 2009: 32); rather, it is an "all-out war against their enemies" (Ranstorp 1996: 44) and "the total obliteration of the 'dark forces'" (Weinberg et al. 2009: 32) – that is, "anyone who is not a member of the terrorists' religion or religious sect" (Hoffman 1998: 95).

Such analyses entail two significant implications, the first of which is that there is nothing political in "religious terrorist" acts, as a result of which, the second implication is that there is no room for negotiation or prevention. Tools, policies, and strategies that have proved to be successful in states' counterterrorist dealings with secular terrorist organisations "would not only be irrelevant but also impractical, given both the religious terrorists' fundamentally alienated world-views and often extreme, resolutely uncompromising demands" (Hoffman 1998: 128). Their violence is often designed to be "symbolic", "dramatic", and "theatrical", which does not equate them to tactics but rather "performance violence" whose aim is "to have an impact on the several audiences they affect" (Juergensmeyer 2000: 160). As the former Director of the Central Intelligence Agency (CIA), James Woolsey, famously put it, "today's terrorists don't want a seat at the table, they want to destroy the table and everyone sitting at it" (National Commission on Terrorism 2000: 2).

These claims, however, are more sensationalist than they are epistemologically valid, and so they end up being misguiding. First, because they cannot explain, for example, the US administration's change of policy towards Afghanistan: the realisation that a military solution is not achievable led the White House to instigate talks with the Taliban (MacAskill and Tisdall 2010). How can one hold political negotiations with a religious group that is so driven by its dogmatic beliefs?

Second, and insofar as symbolism, theatricality, and performance are concerned, secular groups have been just as symbolic and dramatic in their attacks. Euskadi Ta Askatasuna's (ETA) assassination of Admiral Carrero Blanco (Spain's Prime Minister and General Franco's right-hand man) in 1973 involved a remote controlled bomb that targeted his passing car. According to the BBC's account (2008), "[the] explosion sent the car . . . over the roof of the San Francisco de Borga Church. . . . The vehicle landed on the second floor terrace of a building on the other side of the church". Similarly, the Irish Republican Army's (IRA) attack in Manchester city centre in 1996 involved the explosion of a 1.5 ton bomb (Payne 2014) that left a landscape not too different from the ones we currently see in the Middle East. A similar case could be made about the Oklahoma bombing a year earlier, or the more recent Oslo attacks by Anders Behring Breivik. Even if one were to include suicide bombing's symbolism and performance, Pape (2005) has shown that there is no direct link between religion and suicide bombing, while Bloom (2005: 3) has confirmed that many groups engaging this type of attack are "decidedly secular".

With regards to lethality, Piazza's study confirms that "Islamist groups are not more prone to launching high casualty attacks than other ideological types of groups" (2009: 71). This, as Gunning and Jackson argue, is due to the fact that "the statistics are skewed by a few exceptionally lethal attacks and by vast discrepancies between groups" (2011: 379). Furthermore, with regard to lack of clarity of motives or the absence of a concrete ideology, many groups that are labelled religious have engaged in political and terrorist activity that is closer to the secular character and strategies of old terrorists: Hamas, Hizballah, and the Christian Identity are three such examples (Gunning and Jackson 2011: 376). "For all their messianic semitones", as Townshend (2002: 107) put it, such organisations "are very real political forces engaged in an earthly power struggle".

Conversely, as mentioned above, old secular terrorist groups like the IRA in Northern Ireland, EOKA in Cyprus, and the LTTE in Sri Lanka were present in conflicts where their "enemies" were of a different religion or religious confession, yet religion did not feature in academic analyses and/or counterterrorist discourses in the same way as it does presently. What is more, even when the "enemy" did not belong to a different religious group, religion often played a significant role and provided the foundation for the organisation's emergence and survival. This was the case with ETA in Spain, whose triptych of "action-vocation-community" derived from the dogmas and staunch religious beliefs of Basque nationalism's father, Sabino Arana (Tellidis 2010: 420; Tellidis 2011). In all, it is at least arguable to claim that current trends in terrorist violence are driven by new terrorism's characteristics. According to Masters (2008), all manifestations of terrorism today are more violent, particularly its ethno-nationalist variants.

These arguments point to two significant implications for the persistent correlation between religion and terrorism. The first is that such linkages and causalities are at best problematic. This is because, albeit without a universally agreed definition, terrorist objectives serve a strategic function (Goodin 2006: 1; Neumann and Smith 2008; English 2009: 43), and their political nature is widely accepted by researchers (Schmid 2011: 99–157). Even the US Army has conceded that "in a sense, terrorist goals are *always* political, as extremists driven by religious or ideological beliefs usually seek political power to compel society to conform to their views" (quoted in Whittaker 2001: 17; emphasis added), while the United Nations Security Council recently emphasised that "terrorism cannot and should not be associated with any religion, nationality or civilization" (UNSC 2014: 1).

The second implication for the persistent correlation between religion and terrorism is that it is at worst sinister. As Goodwin argues (2012: 130), the term serves no other use but the advancement of "partisan interests of some of the key actors in many contemporary conflicts", or, as Hurd put it, "religion is often wielded most powerfully by those *in* power" (2012: 946).

Considering numerous other calls for the attention that should be paid to the political aims of organisations projecting a religious nature, the persistence of discourses and narratives seeking to link religion with terrorism is unfortunate, despite early research indicating the political background of religious terrorism. Schmid and Jongman's (2008: 45) seminal study of political terrorism, for instance, refers to a number of authors whose typologies incorporate religious terrorism under the category of "political terrorism". Schmid himself readjusted his original typology to reflect this too (2011: 171). In "Terrorism in the Name of Religion", Ranstorp agrees that although "largely motivated by religion, [religious groups] are also driven by day-to-day practical political considerations within their context-specific environment" (1996: 42). This leads Crenshaw to argue that "researchers should be cautious about . . . constructing general categories of terrorist actors that lump together dissimilar motivations, organizations, resources and contexts" (2000: 417).

In the same vein, the late Paul Wilkinson considered it "a serious error to assume that fanatical groups are uniquely capable of the fanatical belief in their cause and hatred of their enemies which enable them to carry out acts of great carnage and destruction" (2001: 62). Wilkinson, in fact, went one step further than this chapter's characterisation of the persistent attempt to link religion with terrorism: "It is *foolish*", he wrote, "to exaggerate [Islamic fundamentalism's] novelty or its religious significance. . . . What appears at first sight to be a purely religious phenomenon is in fact in large part about political control and socioeconomic demands" (Wilkinson 2001: 61; emphasis added). Related to this, Quinton's (1990: 35) exploration of how apolitical violence can still be considered terrorist led him to note that

> a member of a politically motivated group who takes part merely because he likes killing people or blowing things up is still a terrorist, because his violent action is part of the declared and, for the most part sincerely, politically motivated violent activity of the group.

This statement could perhaps be paraphrased to indicate the same categorisation when it comes to the relationship between the religious motivations of certain individuals and the political motivations of a religious group: a member of a politically motivated religious group who takes part merely because he believes that his religion dictates him to is still a terrorist, because his violent action is part of the declared and, for the most part sincerely, politically motivated violent activity of the religious group.

Even when religion is examined as a source of broader conflict, rather than solely terrorism, studies have shown the existence of other factors that supersede religion as its cause (Hasenclever and Rittberger 2000: 673; Canetti et al. 2010; IEP 2014: 7). A recent statistical survey conducted by the Institute for Economics and Peace has found that "there is no clear statistical relationship between either the presence or the absence of religious belief and conflict. Even at the extremes, the least peaceful countries are not necessarily religious, and vice versa" (IEP 2014: 2). The implications of this, following Hurd's (2007: 648) logic, are that the epistemological assumptions of secularist IR and terrorism theories reveal more about the two fields (and the latter's enduring problems – see Crenshaw 2000; Silke 2004; Ranstorp 2009) than they do about religion itself.

Conclusion

Following the events of 9/11, a general trend emerged that targeted Islam as an intolerant and violent religion. This trend was (and still is) particularly prevalent among the general public and some policy circles and is fed by media organisations. As of late, this trend may have begun to subside, with scholars and pundits increasingly differentiating mainstream Islam from "extremist", "radical", and "fundamentalist" circles. This may have happened because of their realisation that labelling a religion as intolerant and violent was incongruent with the fact that the vast majority of its adherents are neither violent nor intolerant. That, however, only verifies Hurd's aforementioned claim of religion's strategic operationalization by Western secular institutions, and it does little to dispel social and political perceptions that terrorism can be directly causally linked to religion.

With regards to Islam-related terrorism in particular and religious terrorism more broadly, the secular tradition of the Western world has led to research and policymaking that lack reflexivity. Knee-jerk reactions (Kilcullen 2006: 5) like those that followed the events of 9/11 and are still quite prevalent today, have led to acontextual and/or culturally insensitive "brandings" (CRCL 2008; Gelvin 2010), which have made the integration of Muslim communities in Western societies difficult and have undermined antiradicalisation efforts by security agencies and civil society organisations alike (Antúnez and Tellidis 2013), rendering them counterproductive (Mythen et al. 2009; Pantazis and Pemberton 2009; Schiffauer 2009).

Moreover, the predominantly sociopsychological and ideological focus of counterterrorist authorities on religious terrorism tends to ignore political factors, thus leading to the demonisation of entire communities and their construction as "suspect" – something that could well be termed "state radicalisation" (see Lindekilde, this volume). The claims of intellectual leaders of violent groups (Islamic or other, state or non-state) have not been sufficiently problematized as "the manifestation of ideas and practices of a contemporary community rather than a set of traditional beliefs or doctrines clearly identifiable in the ancient religious texts" (Hellmich 2014: 242). Such political attitudes could have allowed a more effective realignment of public policy with the research findings that recruitment and radicalisation are more a consequence of social bonds than religion itself (Sageman 2004).

A further problem that emerges from the privileging of the religious dimension is that "the term may downplay the wider context within which movements and actors operate" (Gunning and Jackson 2011: 381). It also leads to counterproductive counterterrorist strategies and policies which "create new sources of resentment" and "legitimise extraordinary measures", such as some of the prisoner interrogation techniques at Guantanamo and Abu Ghraib focusing on religious humiliation (Gunning and Jackson 2011: 382). Such morally dubious and strategically inefficient tactics "have enlarged the intercultural gap, undermined the moral and practical legitimacy of the 'War on Terror', and have alienated a large sector of the global populace (atheist and religious alike) by provoking repugnance" (Antúnez and Tellidis 2013: 122).

Perhaps secularisation, and the dogmatic and fundamentalist (Esposito 1999: 257) manner with which Western political societies perceive its usefulness and applicability, had a more significant role to play in the deployment of such tactics than has been realised or accounted for. This might be because of what Bossy calls "the migration of the holy" (Bossy in Cavanaugh 2009: 11) – that is, the appropriation of the holy by the state, making the latter a new religion in its own right. Viewed in this light, it is not paradoxical to claim that such strict (almost religious, ironically) adherence to secular assumptions have progressively categorised "Islam as the most 'religious' religion – that is, the religion most incompatible with the dictates of political liberalism" (Salomon and Walton 2012: 417). A greater degree of reflexivity and problematisation, such as the one aspired by CTS, with regard to the constructed concept of secularisation and its relationship to the politics of power and knowledge, may yield more insightful research on how research and politics are conducted, for "religion and politics overlap and intersect, composing enduring political settlements that wax and wane in their influence" (Hurd 2007: 661).

As Silke (2009: 48) put it, "it is understandable that the field would show heavy biases in focus in the immediate aftermath of 9/11 and the war on terror". It is only natural to expect such trends to continue, especially if one takes into account the emergence of the Islamic State (IS) and its inconceivable barbarity that made al Qaeda seem parochial almost overnight. Yet, just like al Qaeda, and despite its brutality, even IS possesses a political agenda that comprises issues of territoriality, governability, representation, and – more crucially – power. The overlapping of religion and politics, in the case of groups like IS, should not be missed by contemporary researchers. Problematizing and critically analysing its narrative(s), as well as the way the West has responded to such threats through the war on terror, may provide more insightful analyses of the wider context(s) of the emergence of such groups. What is more, a re-skewed focus on the intersection of religion and politics may lead to the formation and implementation of counterterrorist strategies that are more than antagonising the violence and brutality of such groups.

Note

1 On the differences between the Protestant and the French-Latin-Catholic path to secularization, see Casanova (2012: 28).

References

Abbas, T., 2012. "The symbiotic relationship between islamophobia and radicalisation", *Critical Studies on Terrorism*, 5(3): 345–358.
Ahmed, A., 1999. *Islam Today: A Short Introduction to the Muslim World*, London, New York: I.B. Tauris.
Antúnez, J., and Tellidis, I., 2013. "The power of words: The deficient terminology surrounding Islam-related terrorism", *Critical Studies on Terrorism*, 6(1): 118–139.
BBC, 2008. "1973: Spanish prime minister assassinated", 20 December, available online at: http://news.bbc.co.uk/onthisday/hi/dates/stories/december/20/newsid_2539000/2539129.stm (accessed 15 November 2014).
Bloom, M., 2005. *Dying to Kill: The Allure of Suicide Terror*, New York: Columbia University Press.

Canetti, D., Hobfoll, S. E., Pedahzur, A., and Zaidise, E., 2010. "Much ado about religion: Religiosity, resource loss and support for political violence", *Journal of Peace Research*, 47(5): 575–587.
Casanova, J., 2012. "Rethinking public religions", in Shah, T., Stepan, A., and Toft, M., eds., *Rethinking Religion and World Affairs*, Oxford: Oxford University Press, pp. 25–35.
Cavanaugh, W., 2009. *The Myth of Religious Violence: Secular Ideology and the Roots of Modern Conflict*, Oxford: Oxford University Press.
CRCL (Office for Civil Rights and Civil Liberties), 2008. *Terminology to Define the Terrorists: Recommendations from American Muslims*, January, Washington, DC: US Department of Homeland Security, available online at: www.dhs.gov/xlibrary/assets/dhs_crcl_terminology_08-1-08_accessible.pdf (accessed 16 November 2014).
Crenshaw, M., 2000. "The psychology of terrorism: An agenda for the 21st century", *Political Psychology*, 21(2): 405–420.
Desch, M., 2013. "The coming reformation of religion in international affairs? The demise of the secularization thesis and the rise of new thinking about Religion", in Desch, M., and Philpott, D., eds., *Religion and International Relations: A Primer for Research*, Unpublished report, University of Notre Dame: Mellon Initiative on Religion across Disciplines, pp. 14–55.
English, R., 2009. *Terrorism: How to Respond*, Oxford: Oxford University Press.
Esposito, J., 1999. *The Islamic Threat: Myth or Reality?*, 3rd ed., Oxford: Oxford University Press.
Funk, N., 2007. "Religious and cultural dimensions of peacebuilding", *Journal of Religion, Conflict and Peace*, 1(1), available online at: http://religionconflictpeace.org/volume-1-issue-1-fall-2007/religious-and-cultural-dimensions-peacebuilding (accessed 2 November 2014).
Gelvin, J., 2010. "Nationalism, anarchism, reform: Political Islam from the inside out", *Middle East Policy*, 13(3): 118–133.
Gilbert, P., 2003. *New Terror, New Wars*, Edinburgh: Edinburgh University Press.
Goodin, R., 2006. *What's Wrong with Terrorism?*, Cambridge: Polity.
Goodman, S., 2014. "The root problem of Muslim integration in Britain is alienation", *The Washington Post*, 6 October, available online at: www.washingtonpost.com/blogs/monkey-cage/wp/2014/10/06/the-root-problem-of-muslim-integration-in-britain-is-alienation/ (accessed 2 November 2014).
Goodwin, J., 2012. "'Religious terrorism' as ideology", in Jackson, R., and Sinclair, J., eds., *Contemporary Debates on Terrorism*, Abingdon: Routledge, pp. 127–134.
Gunning, J., and Jackson, R., 2011. "What's so 'religious' about 'religious terrorism'?", *Critical Studies on Terrorism*, 4(3): 369–388.
Hasenclever, A., and Rittberger, V., 2000. "Does religion make a difference? Theoretical approaches to the impact of faith on political conflict", *Millennium: Journal of International Studies*, 29(3): 641–674.
Hellmich, C., 2014. "How Islamic is al-Qaeda? The politics of Pan-Islam and the challenge of modernisation", *Critical Studies on Terrorism*, 7(2): 241–256.
Hoffman, B., 1995. "'Holy terror': The implications of terrorism motivated by a religious imperative", *Studies in Conflict and Terrorism*, 18(4): 271–284.
Hoffman, B., 1998. *Inside Terrorism*, London: Victor Gollancz.
Huntington, S., 1993. "The clash of civilizations?", *Foreign Affairs*, 72(3): 22–49.
Hurd, E., 2004. "The political authority of secularism in international relations", *European Journal of International Relations*, 10(2): 235–262.
Hurd, E., 2007. "Theorizing religious resurgence", *International Politics*, 44(6): 647–665.
Hurd, E., 2012. "International politics after secularism", *Review of International Studies*, 38(5): 943–961.
IEP (Institute for Economics and Peace), 2014. *Five Key Questions Answered on the Link between Peace and Religion*, Sydney; New York; Oxford: Institute for Economics and Peace.
Jackson, R., 2007. "Constructing enemies: 'Islamic terrorism' in political and academic discourse", *Government and Opposition*, 42(3): 394–426.
Juergensmeyer, M., 2000. "Understanding the new terrorism", *Current History*, 99(636): 158–163.
Kaldor, M., 2007. *New and Old Wars: Organized Violence in a Global Era*, 2nd ed., Stanford, CA: Stanford University Press.
Kilcullen, D., 2006. "Twenty eight articles: Fundamentals of company-level insurgency", *Small Wars Journal*, 1–11 March. Available online at: http://smallwarsjournal.com/documents/28articles.pdf (accessed 12 December 2012).
Laitin, D., 1978. "Review: Religion, political culture and the weberian tradition", *World Politics*, 30(4): 563–592.
Laqueur, W., 1999. *The New Terrorism: Fanaticism and the Arms of Mass Destruction*, New York: Oxford University Press.

Lesser, I., Hoffman, B., Arquilla, J., Ronfeldt, D., and Zanini, M., 1999. *Countering the New Terrorism*. Santa Monica, CA: Rand Corporation.

MacAskill, E., and Tisdall, S., 2010. "White House shifts Afghanistan strategy towards talks with Taliban", *The Guardian*, 19 July, available online at: www.theguardian.com/world/2010/jul/19/obama-afghanistan-strategy-taliban-negotiate (accessed 10 November 2014).

Maher, S., 2014. "From Portsmouth to Kobane: The British jihadis fighting for Isis", *New Statesman*, 6 November, available online at: www.newstatesman.com/2014/10/portsmouth-kobane (accessed 7 November 2014).

Masters, D., 2008. "The origins of terrorist threats: Religious, separatist or something else?", *Terrorism and Political Violence*, 20(3): 396–414.

Mavelli, L., 2011. "Security and secularization in international relations", *European Journal of International Relations*, 18(1): 177–199.

McCutcheon, R., 2007. "'They licked the platter clean': On the co-dependency of the religious and the secular", *Method and Theory in the Study of Religion*, 19: 173–199.

Mythen, G., Walklate, S., and Khan, F., 2009. "I'm a Muslim, but I'm not a terrorist: Victimization, risky identities and the performance of safety", *British Journal of Criminology*, 49: 736–754.

National Commission on Terrorism, 2000. *Countering the Changing Threat of International Terrorism: Report of the National Commission on Terrorism*, Washington: Government Printing Office.

Neumann, P., and Smith, M.L.R., 2008. *The Strategy of Terrorism: How It Works and Why It Fails*, London: Routledge.

Pantazis, C., and Pemberton, S., 2009. "From the 'old' to the 'new' suspect community: Examining the impacts of recent UK counter-terrorist legislation", *British Journal of Criminology*, 49: 646–666.

Pape, R., 2005. *Dying to Win: The Strategic Logic of Suicide Terrorism*, New York: Random House.

Payne, T., 2014. "Unseen photographs capture the devastating and emotional aftermath of the 1996 IRA bomb in Manchester city centre", *The Independent*, 15 June, available online at: www.independent.co.uk/news/uk/unseen-photographs-capture-the-devastating-and-emotional-aftermath-of-the-1996-ira-bomb-in-manchester-city-centre-9538378.html (accessed 15 November 2014).

Philpott, D., 2002. "The challenge of September 11 to secularism in international relations", *World Politics*, 55(1): 66–95.

Piazza, J., 2009. "Is Islamist terrorism more dangerous?: An empirical study of group ideology, organization and group structure", *Terrorism and Political Violence*, 21(1): 62–88.

Quinton, A., 1990. "Reflections on violence and terrorism", in Warner, M., and Crisp, R., eds., *Terrorism, Protest and Power*, Aldershot: Edward Elgar, pp. 35–43.

Ranstorp, M., 1996. "Terrorism in the name of religion", *Journal of International Affairs*, 50(1): 41–62.

Ranstorp, M., 2009. "Mapping terrorism studies after 9/11: An academic field of old problems and new prospects", in Jackson, R., Breen Smyth, M., and Gunning, J., eds., *Critical Terrorism Studies: A New Research Agenda*, Abingdon: Routledge, pp. 13–33.

Rapoport, D., 1984. "Fear and trembling: Terrorism in three religious traditions", *American Political Science Review*, 78(3): 658–677.

Runnymede Trust, 1997. *Islamophobia: A Challenge for Us All – Report of the Runnymede Trust Commission on British Muslims and Islamophobia*, London: Runnymede Trust.

Ryan, A., 2012. *On Politics: A History of Political Thought from Herodotus to the Present*, London: Penguin.

Sageman, M., 2004. *Understanding Terror Networks*, Philadelphia, PA: University of Pennsylvania Press.

Salomon, N., and Walton, J., 2012. "Religious criticism, secular critique and the 'critical study of religion': Lessons from the study of Islam", in Orsi, R., ed., *The Cambridge Companion to Religious Studies*, New York: Cambridge University Press, pp. 403–420.

Salvatore, A., 2006. "Power and authority within European secularity: From the enlightenment critique of religion to the contemporary presence of Islam", *The Muslim World*, 96(5): 543–561.

Schiffauer, W., 2009. "Suspect subjects: Muslim migrants and the security agencies in Germany", in Eckert, J., ed., *The Social Life of Anti-Terrorism Laws*, Bielefeld: Transcript Verlag, pp. 55–79.

Schmid, A., 2010. "The Importance of countering Al Qaeda's 'single narrative'", in The Netherlands National Coordinator for Counterterrorism, ed., *Countering Violent Extremist Narratives*, The Hague: The Netherlands National Coordinator for Counterterrorism, pp. 46–57.

Schmid, A., 2011. *The Routledge Handbook of Terrorism Research*, Abingdon: Routledge.

Schmid, A., and Jongman, A., 2008. *Political Terrorism: A New Guide to Actors, Authors, Concepts, Data Bases, Theories and Literature*, 3rd ed., New Brunswick, NJ: Transaction Publishers.

Silke, A., 2004. *Research on Terrorism: Trends, Achievements and Failures*, London: Frank Cass.

Silke, A., 2007. "The Impact of 9/11 on research on terrorism", in Ranstorp, M., ed., *Mapping Terrorism Research: State of the Art, Gaps and Future Direction*, Abingdon: Routledge, pp. 76–93.

Silke, A., 2009. "Contemporary Terrorism Studies: Issues in Research," in Jackson, R., Breen Smyth, M., and Gunning, J., eds., *Critical Terrorism Studies: A New Research Agenda*, Abingdon: Routledge, pp. 34–48.

Tellidis, I., 2010. "Terrorist conflict vs. civil peace in the Basque Country", in Richmond, O., ed., *Palgrave Advances in Peacebuilding: Critical Developments and Approaches*, London: Palgrave, pp. 415–438.

Tellidis, I., 2011. "Orthodox, criticals and the missing context: Basque civil society's reaction(s) to terrorism", *Critical Studies on Terrorism*, 4(2): 181–197.

Thomas, S. M., 2003. "Taking Religious and Cultural Pluralism Seriously", in Petito, F., and Hatzopoulos, P., eds., *Religion in International Relations: The Return from Exile*, London: Palgrave, pp. 21–53.

Thomas, S., 2005. *The Global Resurgence of Religion and the Transformation of International Relations: The Struggle for the Soul of the Twenty-First Century*, New York: Palgrave Macmillan.

Toft, M. D., 2012. "Religion, Terrorism and Civil Wars", in Shah, T. S., Stepan, A. C., and Toft, M. D., eds., *Rethinking Religion and World Affairs*, Oxford: Oxford University Press, pp. 127–148.

Townshend, C., 2002. *Terrorism: A Very Short Introduction*, Oxford: Oxford University Press.

UNSC, 2014. Resolution 2178 (24 September), UN Doc S/Res/2178, available online at: www.un.org/en/ga/search/view_doc.asp?symbol=S/RES/2178%20%282014%29 (accessed 16 November 2014).

Weinberg, L., Pedahzur, A., and Perliger, A., 2009. *Political Parties and Terrorist Groups*, 2nd ed., Abingdon: Routledge.

Whittaker, D., 2001. *The Terrorism Reader*, Abingdon: Routledge.

Wilkinson, P., 2001. *Terrorism versus Democracy: The Liberal State Response*, London: Franc Cass.

14
FEMALE TERRORISM AND MILITANCY

Caron Gentry and Laura Sjoberg

Introduction

A *New York Daily News* story on October 5, 2013, declared that "the world's most-wanted woman is raising a houseful of tiny terrorists" (McShane 2013). The reference to the world's most-wanted woman was to Samantha Lewthwaite, commonly called the "white widow," who has been linked to a number of terrorist attacks, most recently a firefight and hostage situation at a Nairobi mall in September 2013. The story in the *New York Daily News* focused on Lewthwaite's children, recounting a conversation where her husband "asked them what do you want to be when you are older? Both had many answers but both agreed to one of wanting to be a mujahid (fighter)" (McShane 2013).

Interest in Lewthwaite's children can be found in a surprising number of the news articles covering her story. ABCNews reported that she "wanted her young children to grow up as terrorists and die like their father" (Ross et al. 2013). Several stories speculate about who fathered her younger children, and others discuss the stories she read to her children, her choice of playmates for them, and the similarities between her relationship with her British parents and her relationship with her children. While the stories repeat a number of Lewthwaite's statements about the honor in terrorizing infidels, we did not find a single mainstream news story directly addressing the political motivations for her engagement in what most news outlets and governmental agencies characterize as terrorism. What we did find was that a disproportionate number of the stories on the attacks that she was allegedly involved in focused on Lewthwaite's personal life, and particularly on the fact that she was a widowed woman.

For scholars who have studied female terrorism and militancy for a number of years now, this sensationalistic, narrow, and gendered coverage was no surprise. Instead, it is characteristic of media, scholarly, and policy world reactions to women's participation in violence classified as terrorism. In these reactions, as we have chronicled before (see Sjoberg and Gentry 2007), women's terrorism is treated as not terrorism but *women's terrorism*, and women terrorists are at once characterized as aberrant, personally motivated, and beyond the agency of the *female* perpetrator. This chapter looks briefly at the existence and prevalence of female terrorists, before turning to the question of how those women are represented and understood. It discusses the advancement of feminist research on female militants, gender dynamics, and terrorism before concluding with some suggestions for future research.

Women's involvement in terrorism

As many of the chapters of this book demonstrate (see Shanahan, Chapter 10), the definition of terrorism is anything but agreed-upon, and all approaches to the study of terrorism choose certain foci at the expense of others. A significant amount of work, especially in critical terrorism studies (CTS), has noted that, whatever the focus, the word *terrorism* has normative connotations and is often used to delegitimize people that it labels (Jackson 2005; Hoffman 2006; Richardson 2006; Schmid and Jongman 2006; English 2009; Gentry and Sjoberg 2014). While various elements of the definition of terrorism describe it as the use of violence, force, and/or fear at civilian targets for political ends to get psychological reactions and/or enact coercion (Schmid and Jongman 2006), controversies over defining terrorism are related to controversies about the politics of terrorism. As a result, understandings of what counts as terrorism are subjective (see Jackson 2005), context-based (see Hoffman 2006), and tangled up in the politics of those doing the defining (see Jackson et al. 2009).

Feminist scholarship has suggested that, in addition, most definitions and characterizations of what counts as terrorism can be considered gendered. It has made the argument that the word *terrorism* is used to feminize politically violent actors, perpetuating the notion that masculinized states are (by definition) legitimate actors and feminized non-state actors are (by definition) less legitimate. Feminist scholarship (see Tickner 1992; Peterson and Runyan 2009) has argued that gendered power dynamics in these dichotomies reproduce themselves across interactions in the security arena. This is especially visible, as we have discussed, in the "new terrorism" literature (Gentry and Sjoberg 2014, citing Hoffman 1999, 2002; Laqueur 1996, 2000). That literature associates a new generation of terrorism with conservative, Islamic politics and a vicious circle of abuse of women,[1] and, in so doing, makes a number of racist and sexist assumptions about an imagined, unified Muslim culture that feminist and postcolonialist scholars have characterized as Orientalist (Said 1978; Akram 2000; Nayak 2006; Gentry and Whitworth 2011; Gentry 2011a).

Equally importantly, a number of feminist scholars have demonstrated that most technical definitions of terrorism would include a number of acts of violence that traditional scholars of terrorism would generally place outside of the category, for example, violence perpetrated by states against their own citizens (Hoffman 2006; Richardson 2006). Particular to a feminist argument are "the parallels between domestic violence and terrorism," where those on whom domestic violence is perpetrated "face violence or the threat of violence to inculcate fear and to coerce and intimidate them into compliance" (Sjoberg 2009a: 71). That is why feminist scholars have thought about domestic violence as the *terrorist* enforcement of a *politics* of gender subordination both within individual households and as a wider (though often unspoken) societal norm. They have labeled this sort of enforcement of existing, gender-subordinating social orders "patriarchal terrorism" (Gentry 2013, citing Johnson 1995; Dobash and Dobash 2004). Lisa Sharlach (2007) made this argument with reference to what she identified as a "state of terror" in Pakistan, where state rape, honor crimes, high rates of sexual and gender-based violence, and gender bias in justice systems perpetrate a system of stigma and fear.[2] For these reasons, Sharlach (2007: 95) has contended that "the understanding of terrorism should be expanded to encompass the types of violence most often experienced by women."

Similarly, using the definitions of terrorism provided by various women in the Basque regions of Spain and France, Candice Ortbals and Lori Poloni-Staudinger (2014: 336) identify three types of terrorism present there: ethnonationalist terrorism of ETA, state terrorism against ETA and its supporters, and intimate terrorism/gender violence (see also, for example, Pain 2014). These feminist studies suggest that terrorism in intimate spheres is an important dimension of the concept of terrorism.

These two critiques mean that the scope of "involvement in terrorism" is significantly broader than most traditional readings of the idea when conventional concepts and definitions are examined through gender lenses. Through gender lenses, the idea of terrorism, if it applies at all, applies as much to state actors as to non-state actors and to all perpetrators of fear and terror for the promotion or enforcement of a political cause, whether that political cause is one for which the label "terrorist" is commonly used (for example, nationalist secession or religious promotion) or one for which the label "terrorist" would be considered nonsensical in the status quo (for example, enforcement of existing national laws or enforcement of existing gender orders).

Gender analysis has also begun to question seriously the idea of "involvement" in terrorism. Much of the literature on the causes and logic of terrorism treats terrorists as if they are independent decision-makers acting rationally without constraints (see Pape 2005), which contrasts with the radicalization literature that emphasizes social context, psychological issues, and political extremism (Taylor and Horgan 2006; Bloom 2011; McCauley and Moskalenko 2011). Yet these two approaches are not integrated well, leaving scholars and students with a binary between rational automatons and emotionally driven extremists. This binary translates to our argument that understandings of the level of agency of "participants" in terrorism is *gendered* – that is, accounts of men's terrorism are significantly more likely to see them as active, rational participants than accounts of women's emotionally driven terrorism (Sjoberg and Gentry 2007). Arguing that women who commit extralegal political violence are "captured in storied fantasies which deny women's agency and reify gender stereotypes and subordination," we proposed a framework for analyzing people's decision-making in that violence that took account of *both* the existing of individual choice and the social constraints in which people make decisions (Sjoberg and Gentry 2007: 5, 13; citing Hirschmann 1989, 2004). Work since then has looked at the complex constitution of the subject of terrorism using gender as a category of analysis (see Åhäll 2012; Auchter 2012; Brown 2011; Gentry and Sjoberg 2011), which we will discuss in more detail later in this chapter.

For now, our point is that there are at least two very different ways to begin to address the question of the participation of women in terrorism. The first is to take for granted traditional definitions of women and terrorism and to treat the idea of participation as if it accounts for varied levels of agency unproblematically. The second is to problematize the ideas of women, participation, and terrorism. The remainder of this section takes the first approach as a prelude to our advocacy for the second approach in the rest of the chapter.

Many mainstream accounts of "terrorism" as traditionally understood either implicitly or explicitly make the assumption that anyone who is a terrorist is also a man. Previous work on women, gender, and terrorism has suggested that this assumption is overdetermined by prevalent gender stereotypes, including but not limited to the idea that women are more peaceful than men, that women are wars' innocent victims, and that extralegal violence requires a level of (both physical and decision-making) strength that women just do not have (see Sjoberg and Gentry 2007, 2008).

Like these underlying stereotypes, however, the assumption that women do not engage in terrorism as traditionally defined is historically inaccurate. While women constitute a minority of terrorists, however the word is defined, they are a significant and growing minority. Women have engaged in self-martyrdom or suicide terrorism in most conflicts in which that has been used as a tactic – including, but not limited to, the conflicts in Pakistan, India, Sri Lanka, Chechnya, Afghanistan, Palestine, Syria, Iraq, Yemen, and Kenya. Women have committed acts easily classified as terrorist for a very diverse group of organizations all across the world – from leftist organizations like the Shining Path (Peru), the FARC (Colombia), and the Liberation Tamil Tigers of Elam (LTTE), to rightist organizations like the Taliban (Afghanistan) and al Qaeda (globally).

When scholars do gender analysis of militant and/or terrorist groups, they find that women play multiple roles in those organizations, from support staff to militant attackers (see MacDonald 1988; Tétreault 1994; Alison 2008, 2011; Ness 2008; Parashar 2009, 2011a; MacKenzie 2009, 2012; McEvoy 2009; Sjoberg and Gentry 2011; Gentry 2011b).

Stories of *how* women commit acts of terrorism are as varied as the women who commit those acts and the organizations that they do so within. As we mentioned at the outset of this chapter, recent fascination in the media and among policymakers about women terrorists has focused on Samantha Lewthwaite, the so-called white widow of one of the London 7/7 bombers, a British woman who is by all accounts committed to a version of militant Islamism that involves terrorist attacks on non-Muslims in particular social and political contexts. A convert to Islam in her teenage years, and a self-described fighter, Lewthwaite has declared her commitment to a lifestyle of political violence in her diaries (see discussion, for example, in Kilpatrick 2013).

Across the world, stories of women's participation in terrorism in Kashmir have both similarities and differences. In Swati Parashar's (2011a: 102) account, Asiya Andrabi, a female militant in the Kashmiri independence movement, justified her participation in the movement by the justice of the political cause, arguing that "we have been victimized by India . . . the women have the same role. We believe in the anti-India movement. We believe that Kashmir should gain independence." At the same time, Andrabi described the organization that she participated in to Parashar (2011a: 105) in very gendered terms: "I, through the newspapers, told the women that they should not participate in the militancy. If you participate, our social setup will be destabilized . . . Allah has given the responsibility of Jihad on men."

In Chechnya, women terrorists are so numerous that the Russian government has a name for them – the "black widows" (see discussions in Eke 2003; Sjoberg and Gentry 2007) – a name on which British coverage of Samantha Lewthwaite has played to come up with the idea of the "white widow" (though the Chechen women terrorists are not, to our knowledge, ethnically black). The women terrorists in Chechnya are between 20 and 25 years of age, and characterizations of their organization describe a large degree of involuntariness, including being sold into terrorism and having their bombs operated by remote control (see, for example, *Argumenty y Fakty* 2003; Bruce 2003; Shermatova and Teit 2003). This coverage is significantly more prevalent than coverage of involuntary involvement in most terrorist organizations (see discussions in Sjoberg and Gentry 2007; Stack-O'Connor 2011), but the lack of first-hand accounts leaves observers to wonder whether a heightened level of involuntary participation exists or whether existent (or invented) involuntariness is more dramatized in this conflict than in other conflicts.

Samantha Lewthwaite's story, Aysia Andrabi's almost-unheard story, and the stories of nameless Chechen women fighters are just a few of literally thousands of accounts (and potential accounts) of women militants, insurgents, rebels, and terrorists. Even if these accounts are partial and perspectival, they tell parts of very complicated stories. Often, both in media representations and policy-world reactions, and even in scholarly examinations, these very complicated stories get simplified to fit inherited narratives and assumptions and/or particular political agendas. That is why a significant amount of work on female terrorism and militancy has (we argue appropriately) focused on the constitution of the subject of the female terrorist and the representation of her actions in public discourses. The next section discusses the dynamics involved in those processes.

The constitution of the subject of the female terrorist

Looking at a wide variety of media coverage of women's engagement in acts of terrorism across different times, places, cultures, and conflicts, we found commonalities in the ways that women who committed political violence were portrayed (Sjoberg and Gentry 2007, 2008, 2015). The first commonality that we found was that the sex of women who committed acts of terrorism was emphasized in discussions of their behavior significantly more than in discussions of the behavior of men who committed similar acts of political violence. In stories of women terrorists, the perpetrators are often described as women first and as terrorists second.

Another commonality that we found was the deployment of particular narratives about women who commit political violence that simultaneously focus on the violent women's *womanhood*, distinguish that (by definition broken) form of femininity from femininity's normalized manifestations, and imply that even women who commit political violence do not actively participate in the decision-making process that results in their violent acts. Our initial research related this to two related gender stereotypes: the idea that appropriate, or idealized, femininity is by definition passive, peaceful, and in need of help and protection, and the idea that femininity gone astray is somehow irrational and should be a source of fear. Within these two paired assumptions, we found three narratives, which we called the mother, monster, and whore narratives (Sjoberg and Gentry 2007). The mother narratives blame women's violence on a vengeful rage associated with harm to the woman's family, particularly her husband or sons. In this account, the "instincts" that usually bring about the tenderness of motherhood, gone awry, bring out the most heinous violence. The descriptions of Samantha Lewthwaite cohere with the mother narrative, as do Andrabi's statements to Parashar.

The monster narratives suggest that, since women are by nature more peaceful than men, women who engage in the same sort of terrorist violence as men do must be, *by definition*, psychologically disturbed. Women described by the monster narratives are described as crazy, irrational, and unpredictable – the worst manifestations of emotional femininity. The "black widow" label attempts to build upon this assumption of agency-less psychopathology.

The whore narratives blame women's violence on their sexuality. Founded in the assumptions that women's sexuality combines heterosexual impulse, chastity, and submissiveness, two versions of whore narratives associate pathologies in female sexuality with women's violence. The first associates excesses in women's violence with excesses in women's sexuality – characterizing violent women as seduced by the "demon lover," the male terrorist (Morgan 1989). In this understanding, the same loss of control that allows women to have unfettered sexual urges inspires violence, and there is no logical end to that desire. The second strand of the whore narratives associates women's violence with their inability or unwillingness to please men – the idea that deviant sexual urges and deviant violent behavior go together, especially when women are "lesbians" or "butch" or otherwise looking to emulate masculinities.

We argued that these narratives have two main functions. The first is to construct and reify a gendered personal/political divide in understanding people's motivations for engaging in terrorist acts. These narratives, situated in broader discussions of individual commission of terrorism, implicitly (see Pape 2005) or explicitly (see Bloom 2011) characterize "terrorists" as politically motivated and "women terrorists" as motivated by psychological disturbance, if they have a choice at all. "Terrorists" are often assumed to be deciding rationally, while "women terrorists" are more frequently characterized as emotional, out of control, or both. It leads, as Miranda Alison accounts, to the characterization of women terrorists as not only psychologically unstable and easily manipulated, but gender defiant, sexually deviant, and even unnatural (2008).

These characterizations are complicated by chains of gossip and misinformation about women terrorists, many of which are impossible to fully correct. There are untruths and biases in self-reporting of women's violence, some of which deploy the same gender stereotypes that feminists critique (see, for example, the discussion of Pauline Nyiramasuhuko in Sjoberg 2015). Different tellings of the stories of different women in different conflicts have different personal and political investments in the contextualization and signification of those stories. Those with a vested interest in a particular political order, including a particular gender order, often attribute particular motivations to (women) terrorists as they analyze their stories.

For example, Russia has a vested interest in portraying Chechens as ruthless, both externally in their bombings in Moscow or greater Russia but also internally in how Chechen men treat (control) Chechen women. As feminists we certainly are not above demonstrating where our own interests lie – we tend to look *for* the political motivations' role in women's decision to engage in political violence and to look *for* evidence of the deconstruction of the personal/political binary in both men's and women's engagement in terrorism. We look *for* that in part because it is neglected in most traditional work on women's terrorism, but also because we have a political interest in understanding women as agents of violence.

It is in that context that one of the major contributions from the work on the representation of female terrorism and militancy is that all knowledge *about* women's participation in those activities is both *perspectival* (related to the person and context producing the knowledge) and *political* (with investments in particular means and ends) – like all knowledge about terrorism more broadly. It has urged attention to the "political context of 'terrorist' actors, their interdependence, the role of emotion in triggering and reacting to their behavior" (Gentry and Sjoberg 2014). This interest has led to more sophisticated research on the representation of female terrorism and militancy.

Particularly after research in the field pointed out that it is important to think about both the politics of representation and the existence of women's agency, subsequent research has suggested that those questions have a greater level of depth to them than initial discussions revealed. The earlier discussions usefully pointed out that both self and other representations of women militants are always and everywhere draped with a political purposes and that portrayals that understood men as agents and women as without agency were both gendered and problematic. They suggested rethinking the ways that we think about terrorism in order to take account of these realizations (see Sjoberg and Gentry 2007).

At the same time, those discussions spent more effort thinking about the relationality of agency than deconstructing what others (see Åhäll 2012) have appropriately characterized as a masculinized understanding of measuring what political action is and who counts as political actors. Jessica Auchter (2012: 121) has argued that "agency remains the attribute which marks entrance into the legitimate political community," despite problems with the concept in theory and in practice. While it is a key contribution of gender analysis about terrorism that women can have *agency* in their political violence, feminists have critiqued notions of agency that characterize people as independent, rational actors with an unlimited number of choices available to them (Butler 1990; Hirschmann 2004). These critiques have focused on the recognition of incomplete independence, constrained choices, relational decision-making, and the social production of political subjects. Feminist critiques of traditional understandings of *how terrorist decisions are made* have led to exploring relationality and social context. Feminist critiques of the *social production of female terrorists as political subjects* have led to interrogating the utility of agent-based frameworks for understanding terrorism. We will discuss both briefly.

Research on women terrorists has paid attention to the social context in which acts of terrorism occur, particularly to race, class, and gender dynamics (see Parashar 2010; Gentry and Whitworth 2011; Qazi 2011; Gentry 2011a). It has done so motivated by the idea that (women) terrorists are not *only* personal actors or *only* political actors, or even actors who can properly be examined without attention to the opportunities, constraints, and experiences that they have as they decide to, and then do, engage in political violence. Using Nancy Hirschmann's (1989) understanding of people as relationally autonomous, we have argued that female terrorists, like male terrorists, and, indeed, like all political actors, do engage in decision-making, but do so inside a matrix of constraints, social expectations, and political pressures which are a part of the constitution of their decision-making process, rather than just an influence on it (Sjoberg and Gentry 2007, 2015). This inspires, using gender analysis, an understanding of terrorism (whether women are participating in it or not) as a *gendered* phenomenon that takes place in a *gendered* international arena (Sjoberg 2009a). This work builds on existing gender analysis in international relations (IR) (see Enloe 1990; Peterson and Runyan 1992; Tickner 1992) to suggest that, like other people in global politics, violent women's lives are structured by gender and structure gender relations (Sjoberg and Gentry 2007).

It is precisely this realization, though, that has inspired recent research on female terrorism and militancy to reach beyond discussions of representation and agency to try to understand the constitution of the subject of the female terrorist or female militant (see, for example, Åhäll 2012; Auchter 2012). This work looks to see "the effect of the operations of discursive power through which subjects are produced" (Åhäll 2012: 106). In other words, while it is important to look at what people decide and the contexts in which they decide it, it is equally important to look at the conditions of possibility for seeing them (or failing to see them) as decision-makers in those contexts. Without slipping into a new way to frame women militants as passive and acted upon, it is crucial to understand the discursive frames that make them visible when they are visible, invisible when they are invisible, and always filtered through comparisons of expectations of idealized feminine behavior and their actual behavior.

For these reasons, as Katherine Moon (1997: 52) once argued, "without jumping back from two opposite poles of self-agency and victimhood, a middle ground must be found." We suggest that this middle ground might be the basis for future research not only on female terrorism and militancy, but also on its meanings and significations in the larger context of understanding (gendered) political violence in the (gendered) international arena. The next section discusses current research and future directions analyzing women's participation, gender, and terrorism.

Thinking about women's participation, gender, and terrorism

Work on representation of women's political violence (see Sjoberg and Gentry 2007, 2008; Brown 2011; Gentry 2011a; Åhäll 2012; Auchter 2012) has been paired usefully with work that discusses those issues and pairs it with fieldwork trying to understand how women experience participation in conflict, militancy, and terrorism (see Alison 2008, 2011; MacKenzie 2009, 2012; McEvoy 2009; Parashar 2009, 2010, 2011b). This work has made a number of important contributions to analyzing female terrorism and militancy. The first major contribution is drawing attention to the existence of women who commit political violence. This serves as a corrective to the assumption that women are either less capable of violence than men or inherently more peaceful than men.

The second major contribution that the work has made is to put serious consideration into the type of attention that women's violence in global politics gets, when it gets attention. It has pointed out the sensationalistic, fetishizing reaction to some women's violence, next to the trivializing distancing of some violent women from any choice they might have had in their action. It has demonstrated that women's violence has been read, received, and even *deployed* and *denied* in gendered ways. This leads to the third major contribution that this work has offered – that women's terrorism and militancy take place in a context where gender structures the militant organizations in which they participate, the conflicts in which those organizations engage, the political contexts by which those conflicts are produced, and the international arena in which those conflicts are perpetuated or mediated.

Along these lines, then, the fourth major contribution of the existing research program on female militancy and terrorism is work that helps to rethink the ways we understand people's participation in political violence. As we argued in *Mothers, Monsters, Whores*, seeing that women participate in political violence not only inspires thinking about *why* women commit political violence and how it comes to be possible to see them as violent political subjects, but also more broadly why *people* commit political violence and how it becomes possible to see them as violent political subjects (Sjoberg and Gentry 2007). This is because it also reveals the partiality of accounts of *men's* participation in political violence – particularly as they leave out the traits associated with femininity that are so easily invoked in accounts of women's participation in political violence. It is not only important to recognize the elements of masculinity in women's terrorism and militancy, but the aspects of femininity in men's, and therefore the problematic nature of the masculine/feminine dichotomy in understanding individual political violence in global politics.

The masculine/feminine dichotomy, though, is not only present in explanations of why men and women commit acts of political violence but also, as we discussed earlier in this chapter, in understandings of what counts as terrorism and militancy and what does not. We have previously argued that there is a "you know it when you see it"[3] sense to defining terrorism in the policy practice of global politics (Gentry and Sjoberg 2014; see also Richardson 2006: 19). As we suggested, that sense of knowing terrorism (or of knowing what is not terrorism) leads some things that technically meet available definitions of terrorism to be excluded from common-sense notions. Normally, the things that are excluded are terrorisms that happen to women – the security of men bought at the price of the domestic abuse of women in their households or the security of states bought at the price of the insecurity of women within them. The omission of women and gender from many of the books and journal articles that are understood to be the "state of the art" in terrorism studies, from policymaking that constitutes terrorism and counterterrorism policy, and from the ranks of terrorists as traditionally understood has both a *representational effect* (the omission itself) and a substantive effect (which shapes the definition of what counts as terrorism).

The fifth major contribution of the existing research program on female terrorism and militants, then, is to critique, interrogate, and reconstruct the deployment of the word *terrorism* and its meanings in both popular and scholarly discourses. Firmly rooted in Cynthia Enloe's (1990) argument that "the personal is international and the international is personal," this work has suggested that the politics of terrorism reaches both into the bedroom and into the statehouse, rather remaining settled in the limited scope of sub-state actors that engage in political violence.

It is in the reconstruction of the notions of terrorism, militancy, political violence, and even womanhood that we think research on female terrorism and militancy is best suited to contribute to terrorism studies generally, and to critical terrorism studies specifically. It is well-suited to pair increasingly broad and increasingly sophisticated field research on *what women do* and *what men do* and what *happens to women* and what *happens to men*, with analysis of the gender dynamics, gender expectations, gendered subjectivity, and gendered power that constitutes not only their lives but the politics of the representations of those lives. It is well-positioned to understand the gendered nature of the CTS assertion that "in the twenty-first century, terrorism, it seems, is everywhere" (Jackson et al. 2011: 1) by providing a broad definition of terrorism that understands it as involving the violent enforcement of gender norms, whether it is the terrorism of domestic violence, the terrorism of martyrdom, or the ecoterrorism of property destruction. It is nuanced enough to back up the CTS claim that it is problematic to make "claims to objectivity which ignore the subjective baggage which shapes our understanding" (Jackson et al. 2011: 112) and to enrich that claim by understanding gender politics as part of the way that the use and deployment of the word *terrorism,* as well as acts that are often classified as "terrorist," are not only "inherently political" (Jackson et al. 2011: 112) but also inherently gendered (Sjoberg 2009a).

Perhaps more than each of these potential contributions, though, the research program on female militants and terrorists is well-suited to engage in a project of rethinking what terrorism is, for its self-identified and other-identified perpetrators, and for its victims, not only in terms of the scope of the phenomena, the politics of the deployment of the word, the analysis of the gendered dimensions of it, and the interrogation of what it really means to "participate" in political violence. Above and beyond those interventions, feminist work in terrorism studies, following feminist work in war theorizing and security studies (see Shepherd 2008; Sjoberg 2009b, 2013; Wibben 2011; Alexander 2012; Cohn 2012; Sylvester 2013; Wilcox 2015), can engage with the question of the roles of emotion, feeling, and embodiment in both the commission and constitution of the existence of the idea of terrorism. Those themes have run through existing work on female militants, gender, and terrorism and could provide a useful springboard both for future research in feminist terrorism studies and for critical terrorism studies more broadly.

Notes

1 See the related discussion about the "Arab Spring" in Sjoberg and Whooley (2015).
2 A situation that is by no means unique to Pakistan.
3 Louise Richardson (2006) makes this point too, linking it to USSC porn ruling.

References

Åhäll, L., 2012. "Motherhood, Myth, and Gendered Agency in Political Violence," *International Feminist Journal of Politics*, 14(1): 103–120.
Akram, S., 2000. "Orientalism Revisited in Asylum and Refugee Cases," *International Journal of Refugee Law*, 12(1): 7–40.
Alexander, R., 2012. "Remembering Hiroshima: Bio-Politics, Popoki, and Sensual Expressions of War," *International Feminist Journal of Politics*, 14(2): 202–222.
Alison, M., 2008. *Women and Political Violence: Female Combatants in Ethno-National Conflict*. Abingdon: Routledge.
Alison, M., 2011. "'In the War Front We Never Think We are Women': Women, Gender, and the Liberation Tamil Tigers of Elam," in Sjoberg, L., and Gentry, C., eds. *Women, Gender, and Terrorism*. Athens: University of Georgia Press, 131–155.
Argumenty y Fakty, 2003. "How Many More Suicide Bombers?," 9–16 July, What the Papers Say, available online at: www.lexisnexis.com/uk/nexis/docview/getDocForCuiReq?lni=491Y-6660–00K3-G4WX&csi=172571&oc=00240&perma=true
Auchter, J., 2012. "Gendering Terror," *International Feminist Journal of Politics*, 14(1): 121–139.
Bloom, M., 2011. *Bombshell*. New York: Viking Press.
Brown, K., 2011. "Blinded by the Explosion? Security and Resistance in Muslim Women's Suicide Terrorism," in Sjoberg, L., and Gentry, C., eds. *Women, Gender, and Terrorism*. Athens: University of Georgia Press, pp. 194–226.
Bruce, I., 2003. "Attacks Blamed on Black Widows," *The Herald*, 7 July 2003, available online at: www.heraldscotland.com/sport/spl/aberdeen/attacks-blamed-on-black-widows-1.114201. [Accessed 5 January 2014]
Butler, J., 1990. *Bodies that Matter*. New York: Routledge.
Cohn, C., ed., 2012. *Women and Wars*. London: Polity.
Dobash, R., and Dobash, R., 2004. "Women's Violence to Men in Intimate Relationships: Working on a Puzzle," *British Journal of Criminology*, 44(3): 324–349.
Eke, S., 2003. "Chechnya's Female Suicide Bombers," *BBC News*, 7 July 2003, available online at: http://news.bbc.co.uk/2/hi/europe/3052934.stm. [Accessed 5 January 2014]
English, R., 2009. *Terrorism: How to Respond*. Oxford: Oxford University Press.
Enloe, C., 1990. *The Morning After: Sexual Politics at the End of the Cold War*. Berkeley: University of California Press.
Gentry, C., 2011a. "The Neo-Orientalist Narratives of Women's Involvement in al-Qaeda," in Sjoberg, L., and Gentry, C., eds. *Women, Gender, and Terrorism*. Athens: University of Georgia Press, pp. 176–193.

Gentry, C., 2011b. "The Committed Revolutionary: Reflections on a Conversation with Leila Khaled," in Sjoberg, L., and Gentry, C., eds. *Women, Gender, and Terrorism*. Athens: University of Georgia Press, pp. 120–130.

Gentry, C., 2013. "Patriarchal Terrorism," *International Feminist Journal of Politics Annual Conference*, Brighton, UK.

Gentry, C., and Sjoberg, L., 2011. "The Gendering of Women's Terrorism," in Sjoberg, L., and Gentry, C., eds. *Women, Gender, and Terrorism*. Athens: University of Georgia Press, pp. 57–80.

Gentry, C., and Sjoberg, L., 2014. "Terrorism and Political Violence," in Shepherd, L., ed., *Gender Matters in Global Politics*, London: Routledge.

Gentry, C., and Whitworth, K., 2011. "The Discourse of Desperation: The Intersections of Neo-Orientalism, Gender and Islam in the Chechen Struggle," *Critical Studies on Terrorism*, 4(2): 145–161.

Hirschmann, N., 1989. "Freedom, Recognition, and Obligation: A Feminist Approach to Political Theory," *American Political Science Review*, 83(4): 1227–1244.

Hirschmann, N., 2004. *The Subject of Liberty: Towards a Feminist Theory of Freedom*. Princeton, NJ: Princeton University Press.

Hoffman, B., 1999. "Terrorism Trends and Prospects," in Lesser, I., Arquilla, J., Hoffman, B., Ronfeldt, D., and Zanini, M., eds. *Countering the New Terrorism*. Santa Monica, CA: RAND Corporation, pp. 7–38.

Hoffman, B., 2002. "Rethinking Terrorism and Counterterrorism Since 9/11," *Studies in Conflict and Terrorism*, 25(5): 303–316.

Hoffman, B., 2006. *Inside Terrorism*. New York: Columbia University Press.

Jackson, R., 2005. *Writing the War on Terrorism: Language, Politics, and Counter-terrorism*. Manchester: Manchester University Press.

Jackson, R., Jarvis, L., Gunning, J., and Breen Smyth, M., 2011. *Terrorism: A Critical Introduction*. London: Palgrave MacMillan.

Jackson, R., Breen Smyth, M., and Gunning, J., 2009. *Critical Terrorism Studies: A New Research Agenda*. London: Routledge.

Johnson, M., 1995. "Patriarchal Terrorism and Common Couple Violence: Two Forms of Violence against Women," *Journal of Marriage and Therapy*, 57(2): 283–294.

Kilpatrick, C., 2013. "White Widow Lewthwaite Fomenting Jihad in Somalia on Back of A Camel," *Belfast Telegraph*, 27 December 2013, available online at: www.belfasttelegraph.co.uk/news/local-national/northern-ireland/white-widow-lewthwaite-fomenting-jihad-in-somalia-on-back-of-a-camel-29868792.html. [Accessed 5 January 2014]

Laqueur, W., 1996. "Postmodern terrorism," *Foreign Affairs*, 75(5): 24–36.

Laqueur, W., 2000. *The New Terrorism: Fanaticism and the Arms of Mass Destruction*. London: Oxford University Press.

MacDonald, E., 1988. *Shoot the Women First*. London: Arrow Books.

MacKenzie, M., 2009. "Securitization and Desecuritization: Female Soldiers and the Reconstruction of Women in Post-Conflict Sierra Leone," *Security Studies*, 18(2): 241–261.

MacKenzie, M., 2012. *Female Soldiers in Sierra Leone: Sex, Security, and Post-Conflict Development*. New York: New York University Press.

McCauley, C., and Moskalenko, S., 2011. *Friction: How Radicalization Happens to Them and Us*. London: Oxford University Press.

McEvoy, S., 2009. "Loyalist Women Paramilitaries in Northern Ireland: Beginning a Feminist Conversation about Conflict Resolution," *Security Studies*, 18(2): 262–286.

McShane, L., 2013. "'White Widow' Samantha Lewthwaite Leaves 'Manifesto' Raising Kids as Terrorists: Report," *New York Daily News*, 5 October 2013, available online at: www.nydailynews.com/news/world/white-widow-raising-kids-terrorists-report-article-1.1477157. [Accessed 4 January 2014]

Moon, K., 1997. *Sex Among Allies: Military Prostitution in U.S.-Korea Relations*. New York: Columbia University Press.

Morgan, R., 1989. *The Demon Lover: The Roots of Terrorism*. New York: Washington Square Press.

Nayak, M., 2006. "Orientalism and 'Saving' U.S. State Identity after 9/11," *International Feminist Journal of Politics*, 8(1): 42–61.

Ness, C., ed., 2008. *Female Terrorism and Militancy: Agency, Utility, and Organization*. Abingdon: Routledge.

Ortbals, C., and Poloni-Staudinger, L., 2014. "Women Defining Terrorism: Ethnonationalist, State, and Machista Terrorism," *Critical Studies on Terrorism*, 7(3): 336–356.

Pain, R., 2014. "Everyday Terrorism: Connecting Domestic Violence and Global Terrorism," *Progress in Human Geography*, 38(4): 531–550.

Pape, R., 2005. *Dying to Win: The Strategic Logic of Suicide Terrorism.* New York, NY: Random House.

Parashar, S., 2009. "Feminist International Relations and Women Militants: Case Studies from Sri Lanka and Kashmir," *Cambridge Review of International Affairs,* 22(2): 235–256.

Parashar, S., 2010. "Women, Militancy, and Security: The South Asian Conundrum," in Sjoberg, L., ed. *Gender and International Security: Feminist Perspectives.* London: Routledge, pp. 168–188.

Parashar, S., 2011a. "Aatish-e-Chinar: In Kashmir, Where Women Keep Resistance Alive," in Sjoberg, L., and Gentry, C., eds. *Women, Gender, and Terrorism.* Athens: University of Georgia Press, pp. 94–119.

Parashar, S. 2011b. "Gender, Jihad, and Jingoism: Women as Perpetrators, Planners, and Patrons of Militancy in Kashmir." *Studies in Conflict and Terrorism* 34(4): 295-317.

Peterson, V., and Runyan, A., 1992. *Global Gender Issues.* Boulder, CO: Westview Press.

Peterson, V., and Runyan, A., 2009. *Global Gender Issues in a New Millennium.* Boulder, CO: Westview Press.

Qazi, F., 2011. "The *Mujahidaat:* Tracing the Early Female Warriors of Islam," in Sjoberg, L., and Gentry, C., eds. *Women, Gender, and Terrorism.* Athens: University of Georgia Press, pp. 29–56.

Richardson, L., 2006. *What Terrorists Want: Understanding the Terrorist Threat.* John Murray: London.

Ross, B., Margolin, J., Ferran, L., and Churchmarch, M., 2013. "Officials: Brits Seek 'White Widow' DNA for Kenya Investigation," *ABCNews.com,* 26 September 2013, available online at: http://abcnews.go.com/Blotter/brits-seek-white-widow-samantha-lewthwaite-dna-kenya/story?id=20382794. [Accessed 3 January 2014]

Said, E., 1978. *Orientalism.* London: Vintage.

Schmid, A., and Jongman, A., 2006. *Political Terrorism.* London: Transaction.

Sharlach, L., 2007. "Veil and Four Walls: A State of Terror in Pakistan," *Critical Studies on Terrorism,* 1(1): 95–110.

Shepherd, L., 2008. *Gender, Violence, and Security.* London: Zed Books.

Shermatova, S., and Teit, A., 2003. "Masterminds Unknown", *Moscow News,* 16 July 2003, available online at: www.lexisnexis.com/uk/nexis/docview/getDocForCuiReq?lni=4931-DV80-0061-K0FF&csi=10966&oc=00240&perma=true

Sjoberg, L., 2009a. "Feminist Interrogations of Terrorism/Terrorism Studies," *International Relations,* 23(1): 69–74.

Sjoberg, L., 2009b. "Introduction to Security Studies: Feminist Contributions," *Security Studies,* 18(2): 183–213.

Sjoberg, L., 2013. *Gendering Global Conflict: Toward a Feminist Theory of War.* New York: Columbia University Press.

Sjoberg, L., 2015. *Rape Among Women.* New York: New York University Press.

Sjoberg, L., and Gentry, C., 2007. *Mothers, Monsters, Whores: Women's Violence in Global Politics.* London: Zed Books.

Sjoberg, L., and Gentry, C., 2008. "Reduced to Bad Sex: Narratives of Violent Women from the Bible to the War on Terror," *International Relations,* 22(1): 5–23.

Sjoberg, L., and Gentry, C., eds., 2011. *Women, Gender, and Terrorism.* Athens: University of Georgia Press.

Sjoberg, L., and Gentry, C., 2015. *Beyond Mothers, Monsters, Whores.* London: Zed Books.

Sjoberg, L., and Whooley, J., 2015. "The Arab Spring for Women? Representations of Women in Middle East Politics in 2011," *Journal of Women, Politics, and Policy,* 36(3): 261–284.

Stack-O'Connor, A., 2011. "Zombies Versus Black Widows: Women as Propaganda in the Chechen Conflict," in Sjoberg, L., and Gentry, C., eds. *Women, Gender, and Terrorism.* Athens: University of Georgia Press, pp. 83–95.

Sylvester, C., 2013. *War as Experience; Contributions from International Relations and Feminist Analysis.* New York: Routledge.

Taylor, M., and Horgan, J., 2006. "A Conceptual Framework for Addressing Psychological Process in the Development of the Terrorist," *Terrorism and Political Violence,* 18(4): 585–601.

Tétreault, M., ed., 1994. *Women and Revolution in Africa, Asia, and the New World.* Columbia, SC: University of South Carolina Press.

Tickner, J., 1992. *Gender in International Relations: Feminist Perspectives on Global Security.* New York: Columbia University Press.

Wibben, A., 2011. *Feminist Security Studies: A Narrative Approach.* London: Routledge.

Wilcox, L., 2015. *Bodies of Violence: Theorizing Embodied Subjects in International Relations.* Oxford: Oxford University Press.

PART III

State terrorism

15
UNDERSTANDING WESTERN STATE TERRORISM

Ruth Blakeley and Sam Raphael

Introduction

Throughout history, a significant proportion of state violence has been used to coerce populations into complying with the agendas of political and economic elites by using such violence to instil fear in an audience beyond the direct victim. State violence of this kind is intended to achieve certain political objectives, particularly curtailing political dissent. This is state terrorism. As we have argued elsewhere (Blakeley 2009a; Raphael 2009b), the academic literature on terrorism pays relatively little attention to terrorism perpetrated by states. This is the case even though state terrorism results in far more deaths than non-state terrorism: an estimated 170–200 million deaths were caused by state-instigated mass murder, forcible starvations, and genocide in the twentieth century (Rummel 2011), while in the last two decades of the twentieth century alone, 300,000 people were "disappeared" by state agents worldwide (Sluka 2000).

Where state terrorism is discussed, the focus tends to be on totalitarian regimes, with far less attention paid to the use of state terrorism by now liberal democratic states. Certainly, the regimes of Stalin, Hitler, and Pol Pot were responsible for state violence on an industrial scale, perpetrating genocide but also terrorising populations into submission to the regime. Yet, European colonial powers also used terrorism widely to establish and maintain their empires and to try to thwart independence movements in their colonies. The allies during World War II bombed civilians in German cities to try and incite the public to turn against Hitler. The Latin American national security states during the Cold War, with significant support from the US, also deployed violence, including disappearances and torture, to try and curtail support for political movements that would threaten US and local elite interests. Liberal democratic states have continued to use and sponsor terrorism during the last two decades of the twentieth century and into the twenty-first century as part of a process of guaranteeing access to resources and markets across the globe. As we show in Chapter 17 of this volume, US- and allied-sponsored state terrorism has been used in particular against many suspects in the "war on terror".

A handful of scholars have undertaken excellent work which examines state terrorism by powerful liberal democratic states. The emphasis has been predominantly US or Western state-sponsored terrorism during the Cold War (Chomsky and Herman 1979a, 1979b; Gareau 2004; George 1991b; Herman 1985). Chomsky and Herman paved the way in developing an argument that US support for, and use of, state terrorism during the Cold War was part of a process of organising under US sponsorship "a neo-colonial system of client states ruled mainly by terror and serving the interests of a small local and foreign business and military elite" (Chomsky and Herman 1979b: ix). Their work provided a fine framework for this type of analysis. Curtis (2003) and Cobain (2013) have followed up with contributions that have similarly documented the use of terror as a central component of UK foreign policy during the twentieth century, while Stokes (2005) has examined how state terrorism has been hardwired into US counterinsurgency doctrine for decades.

Our own work has further developed such analyses along these lines. Blakeley (2009b) has provided a comprehensive update of Chomsky and Herman's earlier work by tracing the historical use of state terrorism as part of the European, and then American, imperial projects. In particular, she argues that state terrorism has been central to processes of neoliberalisation, documenting how efforts to roll out neoliberalism across the globe have often been accompanied by considerable violence and terrorism by states and state-sponsored paramilitaries. At the core of this neo-imperial project by leading capitalist states is an objective to secure unfettered access to key markets and strategic resources, such as oil. In this light, Stokes and Raphael (2010) have documented the use of US-sponsored state terror within oil-rich regions specifically to "armour" processes of neoliberal globalisation, to insulate local elites from popular discontent, and to stabilise the production of oil that underpins American hegemony. In a further update to critical work published during the Cold War (George 1991a; Herman and O'Sullivan 1989), Raphael (2009b) has also explored the role that terrorism experts, including in the academy, have played in diverting attention from US and allied use and sponsorship of state terrorism.

Our work seeks not only to provide an empirical account of the use of state terror by Western states, but it also aims to situate this longstanding practice within an explanatory framework which emphasises the economic interests of the ruling capitalist class. Such an understanding is the subject of considerable debate and has led a number of critical scholars to further explore the interrelation between state power, capitalist elite interest, and the use of disciplinary terrorist violence "from above". Some of these scholars have made significant theoretical contributions to the debate (for example, Herring and Stokes 2011; Jarvis and Lister 2014; Joseph 2011; McKeown 2011), whilst others have offered detailed empirical analyses of particular cases of state terrorism in the name of neoliberalism (Maher and Thomson 2011; Raphael 2009a). Together, these works are beginning to address the substantial gap in the literature by bringing the inconvenient truth of the use of terrorism by powerful democratic states to the fore.

Our aim in this chapter is to outline our understanding of the nature and purposes of Western state terrorism. With reference to specific examples, we show that state terrorism involves the illegal use of force against persons that the state has a duty to protect. The purpose of this violence is not simply to cause harm, but to send a message to a wider target audience. We then offer an account of the historical uses and underlying purpose of Western state terrorism. State terrorism in the contemporary era is not simply an instrument used to curtail political dissent by repressive regimes; it is also one of a number of coercive tools that have been used by powerful states as part of a process of securing and maintaining access to resources and markets.

The nature of state terrorism

State terrorism is no different from non-state terrorism in terms of its constituent features. Common to most definitions of terrorism are three key elements. First, it involves threatened or perpetrated violence directed at some "protected victim". Second, the violent actor intends the violence to induce terror in some witness who is generally distinct from the victim. Third, the violent actor intends or expects that the terrorised witness to the violence will alter their behaviour in some way (Walter 1969). The only difference between terrorism by state and non-state actors is the agent perpetrating the act. Therefore, for an act to constitute state terrorism, a fourth element is present: the act is perpetrated by agents on behalf of or in conjunction with the state, including paramilitary and private security agents, against individuals that the state has a duty to protect.

It is worth noting that the use of paramilitaries and private security forces is a strategy which has often been employed by states wishing to hide their hand in the violence. The use of paramilitaries can also increase the degree of terror experienced by target audiences beyond that resulting from military violence. As Michael Stohl (2006: 10) points out, fear is maximised through the use of "notoriously vicious vigilante groups who are widely recognised in society to act as agents of the state but who are not 'legally' constrained in ways that official organs might be felt to be". Specifically,

> such extensive use of groups who appear to be virtually "uncontrolled" and who are notoriously unrestrained in their use of vicious methods is not a strategy designed primarily to effectuate the physical elimination of the adversary; that can be accomplished easily by efficient, technologically-sophisticated police organs. Rather, it is a strategy designed primarily to induce extreme fear in a target population. It is a strategy of terrorism and is understood as such by the populations of targeted societies.

Whether state terrorism is conducted by official state agents or affiliated paramilitary groups, the target audience is central. While states often go to great lengths to conceal their complicity in terrorism against their own or an external population, there is nevertheless always an audience for these acts. For example, while occasionally an individual may be tortured in complete secret, this is only rarely the case. Rather, torture is intended to send a message to a much wider population about the risks individuals face if they are not compliant with the wishes of the regime. Populations governed by torturing regimes often know where the torture chambers are, who the torturers are, and what types of activities (such as political organising) must be avoided in order to stay safe. Torture was used to send a message to a wider audience in this way by the Guatemalan state during the counterinsurgency war of the 1970s and 1980s, during which time newspapers were permitted to publish photographs of dead torture victims:

> Guatemalan counterinsurgency operations in the early 1980s . . . included the terrorisation of targeted rural populations in an effort to ensure that they did not provide support for guerrillas. Tortured, dying villagers were displayed to relatives and neighbours who were prevented from helping them. Newspapers in urban areas during this period were allowed to publish photographs of mutilated bodies, ostensibly as an aid to families seeking their missing relatives, but also as a warning to all citizens not to oppose the government.
>
> *(Amnesty International 1976)*

Overall, state terrorism takes on two forms. The first involves small-scale operations aimed at specific targets, which we refer to as *limited state terrorism*. This includes one-off events and small-scale terror directed at one group or sector or a series of small operations. For example, assassination attempts may be made on leading political figures, particularly opposition leaders, or, in the case of international state terrorism, against the leaders of other states. In such cases, the target audience is the allies of those political leaders who are being warned of the risks of their continued political opposition and activities.

Examples of this include the initial use of disappearances, illegal and arbitrary detentions, and torture by the Latin American national security states during the Cold War. In states such as Chile under Pinochet and Argentina under the military junta, initially specific political opponents, critical journalists, and trade union leaders were disappeared, with their bodies never returned. The specific aim was to instil fear among groups that were critical of the regime. But these acts were not simply carried out within the state. In some cases, those states were able to target citizens who were in exile overseas. This occurred through programmes such as Operation Condor, in which the intelligence agencies of Argentina, Brazil, Uruguay, Paraguay, and Chile all collaborated in the interdiction, detention, torture, and sometimes assassination of individuals from one of the partner states living abroad in one of the other partner states (Dinges 2004; McSherry 2002). Likewise, the many assassination attempts made by the CIA against the Cuban leader Fidel Castro can be considered "limited state terrorism" (McClintock 1992, Chapter 5).

The second form of state terrorism is that which is intended to instil fear among large sections of the population. This might be termed *generalised, governance,* or *wholesale state terrorism,* referring to its use as a tool for controlling entire populations or for use during war time. Examples include aerial bombardments, mass detention, interrogation, and torture. Specific programmes have been implemented for these purposes by states in the past. Military planners argue that aerial bombardment is aimed at attacking strategically significant targets. This can include the targeting of the civilian population with the intention of terrorising the population to provoke a political response. In 1942, Directive 22, issued to the British Bomber Command, called for the deliberate targeting of residential neighbourhoods in Dresden. The designated targets were "the morale of the enemy and civilian population, in particular industrial workers" and the points to be aimed at were "built-up areas, not for instance, the dockyards or aircraft factories" (Grosscup 2006: 64). "Bomber" Harris was clear in his memoirs of his conviction that "air power alone could win the war if the RAF were allowed to bomb the working class into open revolt against the Nazis" (Grosscup 2006: 65).

It is worth noting that campaigns of limited state terrorism often broaden into more generalised efforts to terrorise entire populations. Indeed, as Amnesty International (2006) noted, of all the decades they have researched torture, they have found that it always expands from a few targeted individuals aimed at intimidating the immediate circle of that group to a much more widespread and indiscriminate policy involving disappearances and extrajudicial executions, not simply of supposed political opponents but anyone assumed to have even loose associations with them. In the case of Chile, over 2,000 people were killed or disappeared in the years following the 1973 coup, according to the National Commission for Truth and Reconciliation (CNCTR 1991). In the case of Argentina, some 10,000 disappearances were documented by the US Embassy in the first three years of the dictatorship alone (US Embassy 1979).

Whether state terrorism involves acts limited to a small number of victims and a limited audience, or whether it is targeted at a much wider section of the population, the methods used always involve the deliberate targeting of persons protected by international law. Such methods include kidnap, disappearances, arbitrary or secret detentions, torture, and other cruel, inhumane, and degrading treatment and punishment, assassinations, and mass murder. All of these acts are prohibited under international law, both in peacetime under International Human Rights Law (IHRL) – for example, the Convention Against Torture (CAT) and the International Covenant on Civil and Political Rights (ICCPR) – or during war under International Humanitarian Law (IHL), specifically the Geneva Conventions. Even combatants are protected: while it is legitimate to target armed enemy combatants directly participating in hostilities, assassination, torture, rape, and other inhumane treatment are always prohibited.

We will now provide a brief account of the history of, and purposes of, Western state terrorism. Our focus is specifically on the functionality of state terror for the imperial projects of powerful states, undertaken in collaboration with co-opted local elites in regions considered by Western planners to be strategically important.

Understanding Western state terrorism

As outlined in our introduction, state terrorism has been widely used by repressive regimes as a tool to curtail political opposition. Rarely acknowledged and far less well understood is the use of terrorism by states now considered to be world leaders in terms of their democratic and human rights credentials, both in the past and currently. Our main argument here is that the use of terrorism by these states is best understood in relation to their broader foreign policy objectives. Following a historical materialist tradition (for an excellent overview, see Herring 2010), we argue that there is an important continuity in the foreign policies of now powerful liberal democratic states that can be traced back to the European colonial era. Specifically, there has been a consistent drive by these states to ensure access to, and dominance of, resources in states in the south. Where necessary, coercion, including state terrorism, has underpinned efforts to achieve these goals, especially where more consensual means of achieving them are deemed likely to fail. To elaborate on our argument, we trace this continuity in the foreign policy objectives of the European colonial era up to the end of the twentieth century. We offer several illustrative examples of how these policies played out in practice, but these are indicative rather than exhaustive (for a much more comprehensive account, see Blakeley 2009b).

Coercion dominated the colonial practices of the European powers, both during the process of colonisation and as part of efforts to maintain control over conquered territories, as well as early American imperialism (for detailed accounts, see Arendt 1966; Beckett 2001; Elkins 2005; Fanon [1961] 1967). Empire, as practised by the European post-feudal state, was aimed at dominating trade and extracting resources through the exploitation of indigenous labour and, in some cases, through shipping slave labour from one conquered territory to another region of the empire. The colonisers often terrorised the indigenous populations to achieve their goals. For example, the colonisation of Brazil by Portugal involved the genocide of 2 million indigenous people (80% of the population), while in territories occupied by the Spanish, an initial wave of extreme violence was meted out against the indigenous people that refused to hand over foodstuffs. This violence had a deliberate terrorising effect, with surrounding populations witnessing the violence and being terrorised into supplying resources lest they meet the same fate (Bethell 1984: 8–10).

The British, Belgians, Germans, and French were involved in very similar practices in their own colonies in the 1800s, relying on terror to achieve their objectives (Killingray 1973, 1986; Porter 1968; Suret-Canale 1971 [1964]). In numerous African colonies, for example, houses and even whole villages would be razed to the ground if labour and taxes were insufficiently forthcoming or if resistance emerged (Bush and Maltby 2004). By the early twentieth century, British powers proved willing to have the same effect using aerial bombing campaigns. In response to a rebellion in Iraq in 1920, 4,008 missions were flown to drop 97 tonnes of bombs on the supposed rebels, referred to as night "terror" raids, with one official writing that it should be "relentless and unremitting and carried on continuously by day and night, on houses, inhabitant, crops and cattle" (Glancey 2003).

In the post-war era, several European powers used widespread state terrorism in an attempt to resist movements for national independence in their surviving colonies. Indiscriminate detention and torture were used on a massive scale in British-ruled Kenya in the 1950s and in French

Algeria during the war of the 1960s (Blakeley 2009b: 84–85). To illustrate with the case of Kenya, in 1952, the British declared a state of emergency in Kenya in response to the rebellion of the Mau Mau movement. The Mau Mau largely comprised Kikuyu people, the poorest and most exploited group under British rule. Independence was not secured until 1963, and for a ten-year period, mainly Kikuyu were subjected to extreme violence, mass incarceration, and torture. Official figures of the numbers detained are around 78,000. However, research involving detailed analysis of the now declassified documents suggest the figure to be at least two, and more likely four times higher (Beckett 2001: 125; Elkins 2005: xi). As Elkins shows, many of those detained had not only had their livestock seized and been forced into slave labour, but they were also subject to torture, including simulated drowning, food and water deprivations, and beatings, as well as threats of further violence. She also found many that women lived under siege and were subjected to violence and rape (Elkins 2005: 214, 33–74, 327–8).

As European powers were declining through the nineteenth and into the early twentieth centuries, the US was on the rise. It had already shown its hand in the 1901–02 war aimed at bringing the Philippines under US control, a war that saw US forces engage in the use of torture, rape, shootings, hangings, and the systematic burning of homes and villages, all aimed at quelling support for the insurgency (Welch 1974). This was just a glimpse of the methods that would be used to further US interests and entrench the US as a global hegemon in the latter half of the twentieth century. Throughout the Cold War, US intervention around the world was publically justified as necessary to contain communism. Yet, our analysis shows that there was frequently an underlying material imperative, with coercive interventions aimed at shoring up an emerging US-led global order: one based on universal free trade underpinned by American strategic primacy (see, for example, Layne 2006; Williams 1988). Officials explicitly pointed to the economic threats posed to the US when left-wing governments were elected and frequently stated that interventions to support repressive regimes would serve US capitalist interests.

This was the case in Guatemala in 1954, where the CIA was involved in the coup which ousted the Arbenz government after its economic reform agenda included the expropriation of lands previously occupied by the US-based United Fruit Company. Similarly, declassified memos relating to the military coup in Chile show that the CIA was complicit in its organisation and that the US state continued to support the ensuing campaign of state terror. This campaign took place alongside a period of intense neoliberal economic restructuring which directly served US interests. Indeed, the threat to US investments posed by Allende's relatively mild economic reforms was a key driver for overthrowing his government, as outlined in a memo from Henry Kissinger to President Nixon:

> The consolidation of Allende in power in Chile would pose some very serious threats to our interests and position in the hemisphere, and would affect developments and our relations to them elsewhere in the world: US investments (totalling some one billion dollars) may be lost. . . . Chile would probably become a leader of the opposition to us in the inter-American system, a source of disruption in the hemisphere and a focal point of support for subversion in the rest of Latin America.
>
> *(Kissinger 1970)*

Counterinsurgency (CI) campaigns undertaken by local military and paramilitary groups with generous support from Washington have been a hallmark of US sponsorship of state terrorism throughout the post-war era. US security assistance to its allies in unstable regions has aimed to reorient security forces away from external defence and towards internal security, policing their own populations in order to combat signs of political unrest or subversion.

CI forms a bedrock of US assistance, with tens of thousands of officers from foreign security forces receiving training throughout the Cold War and beyond (Blakeley 2006; Priest 1998; Shafer 1989). US training in counterinsurgency focuses not only on defeating armed groups, but also on controlling the populations within which they move and policing those populations for signs of "subversive" activity.

As one Cold War training manual published by the US Army made clear, so-called Insurgent Activity Indicators include the operation of political organisations that push for "immediate social, political or economic reform". In particular, CI forces need to be on the lookout for:

> Refusal of peasants to pay rent, taxes, or loan payments or unusual difficulty in their collection. Increase in the number of entertainers with a political message. Discrediting the judicial system and police organizations. Characterization of the armed forces as the enemy of the people. Appearance of questionable doctrine in the educational system. Appearance of many new members in established organizations such as labour organizations. Increased unrest among labourers. Increased student activity against the government and its police, or against minority groups, foreigners and the like. An increased number of articles or advertisements in newspapers criticizing the government. Strikes or work stoppages called to protest government actions. Increase of petitions demanding government redress of grievances. Proliferation of slogans pinpointing specific grievances. Initiation of letter-writing campaigns to newspapers and government officials deploring undesirable conditions and blaming individuals in power.
>
> (DoD 1970)

A politicised civil society was characterised as a threat to stability, and therefore as a legitimate target of CI campaigns (Stokes and Raphael 2010: 64–72). In US terms, "psychological operations" ("psyops") are seen to be a central plank of this effort, targeting the "local civilian population", including the deployment of programmes "designed to instil doubt and fear." However, if psyops fail, "it may become necessary to take more aggressive action in the form of harsh treatment or even abductions. The abduction and harsh treatment of key enemy civilians can weaken the collaborators' belief in the strength and power of their military forces" (DoD 1962).

An important example of counterinsurgency campaigns as state terrorism is Operation Phoenix, a CIA-led programme established in Vietnam aimed at improving intelligence with a view to wiping out the Vietcong infrastructure and leadership. In reality, it involved the widespread use of torture and killings intended to instil fear in citizens suspected of supporting the insurgency. Under Phoenix, the torture was brutal, as Douglas Valentine has documented, with the use of rape, electric shock torture, and other forms of extreme violence (Valentine 2000: 85). Numbers of those killed as part of the Phoenix programme according to the CIA are some 20,000. The South Vietnam government placed the number at over 40,000 (Blum 2003: 131; Chomsky and Herman 1979b: 324).

The Phoenix programme was an important precursor to the methods used by numerous US-backed Latin American national security states during the Cold War, as reformist regimes were overthrown and forces friendly to US material interests were bolstered through massive levels of CI training. Declassified documents show that the US military was complicit in the campaign of state terrorism unleashed in Guatemala after the coup, in the form of extensive military training and material support, despite the US state knowing of widespread human rights abuses committed against sectors of the population (Vaky 1968, 1978). Indeed, 20,000 people were disappeared or murdered by the US-backed regime between 1966 and 1976 alone, with US military assistance having a significant bearing on the human rights violations that occurred (Tomuschat et al. 1999). Similar campaigns of state terror characterised the strategies of numerous US-backed regimes during the 1970s and 1980s, alongside the entrenchment of economic reform that would allow greater penetration by US and other Western capital.

Indeed, this "Chilean model" would become the blueprint for the US-led initiative to roll out neoliberalisation across the Southern hemisphere in the succeeding decades (Robinson 1996: 165–6), with receptive local elites often provided with significant political and material assistance by the US in order to insulate their reform agenda from popular forms of resistance. Coercion, often with a strategy of terror at its heart, was the dominant means by which the US established control of resources and markets overseas during the Cold War, and it has continued to underpin US strategy where it seems unlikely that the roll-out of neoliberalism can occur without resistance.

This can be seen clearly in the case of Colombia, which has been the recipient of massive amounts of US military support as it wages a campaign of state terror to insulate capitalist social relations from resistance (Stokes 2005). Although justified variously as an anti-communist, counter-narcotics, or counterterrorism campaign, US assistance is primarily designed to secure processes of neoliberalisation, particularly in the oil sector. As Lieutenant Colonel Francisco Javier Cruz, head of an elite CI unit and responsible for protecting part of Colombia's oil operations, made clear, his units were able to use "helicopters, troops and training provided in large part by [the US]. . . . Security is the most important thing to me. Oil companies need to work without worrying and international investors need to feel calm" (Stokes and Raphael 2010: 193). Units receiving direct US training and funding have, for decades, embarked on a sustained campaign of state terror, targeting politicians, trade unionists, church leaders, human rights workers, and community activists. Torture and disappearances have been endemic and are specifically designed to create fear amongst wider populations (for further details, see HRW 2001; Raphael 2009a).

Conclusion

The practice of terrorism is traditionally associated with non-state actors, or, in some limited cases, with the acts of so-called "rogue states" such as Iran and Syria. However, a close examination of the historical record shows that Western states have long employed strategies of terrorism to further their foreign policy interests. Whether used to secure territories for colonial expansion, defending colonial interests from national liberation movements, or working to entrench neoliberal forms of globalisation, the use of state terror by some Western states can be seen to have long formed a central plank in efforts to secure domination over strategically important and resource-rich regions of the world. The fact that this is a history often overlooked by those writing on the subject of terrorism cannot be accounted for by an absence of empirical data documenting Western state terror. Rather, it is a reflection of the poor state of most terrorism research, which has a myopic focus on "anti-Western" terror and a seeming inability to engage with the uncomfortable truths borne witness by the full historical record.

There has also been a strong tendency among more critical scholars to focus predominantly on analysing the discourses that enable and constrain specific policy decisions in relation to state violence and responses to terrorism (see Jarvis, this volume; Holland, this volume). While this work is extremely valuable, providing as it does a lens through which to view the counterterrorism strategies of powerful liberal states, such work has tended to overshadow careful empirical studies of state terrorism, as well as the materialist agendas that underpin the extensive use of terrorism by those states (see Herring 2008 for an excellent argument along these lines). Such empirically driven, and materialist-minded endeavours add flesh to the bones of critical work that tends to focus on the ideational aspects of the counterterrorism strategies of powerful states by providing an account of how the policies, infused by certain discourses and ideas, play out on the ground.

Particular areas for investigation in this regard include the use and sponsorship of terror in on-going efforts to further entrench neoliberal economic models of resource extraction and appropriation across the global south (see Lasslett 2014 for an excellent example). Much work also remains to be done in fully assessing the extent to which the US and its allies have used terrorism as part of their efforts to deal with the threats presented by al Qaeda-inspired terrorism and its successors. In our own work, explained in more detail in Chapter 17 of this volume, we have focused on mapping the global system for the rendition, detention, and interrogation of terror suspects and providing extensive evidence of the extent to which victims were subjected to a range of human rights abuses, all of which are underpinned by the intent to terrorise.

There are also many other unexplored avenues. For example, a full analysis is needed of the terrorising effects of the US-led programme of targeted killings, both by drone strikes (see Calhoun, this volume) and by elite special forces units operating under deep cover in targeted regions of the world. Another productive avenue for research would be to examine the various ways in which terroristic practices such as arbitrary detention, kidnap, and torture (see Brecher, this volume), as used by the US in its "war on terror", have been adopted and integrated by the domestic and external security agencies of a whole range of states, including many liberal democratic ones. Overall, we would argue that further research into historical and contemporary forms of Western state terrorism remains crucial, not least because it provides a grounded alternative to dominant narratives of Western foreign policy as an undisputed force for good.

References

Amnesty International, 1976. "Guatemala", London: Amnesty International Briefing Papers, No. 8.
Amnesty International, 2006. "Torture and Ill-Treatment: The Arguments". Available online at: <http://web.amnesty.org/pages/stoptorture-arguments-eng>, [accessed 21 June 2006.]
Arendt, H., 1966. *The Origins of Totalitarianism*, New York: Harcourt, Brace and World.
Beckett, I., 2001. *Modern Insurgencies and Counter-Insurgencies: Guerrillas and their Opponents Since 1750*, London: Routledge.
Bethell, L., 1984. *The Cambridge History of Latin America*, vol II, Cambridge: Cambridge University Press.
Blakeley, R., 2006. "Still Training to Torture? US Training of Military Forces from Latin America", *Third World Quarterly*, 27(8): 1439–61.
Blakeley, R., 2009a. "State Terrorism in the Social Sciences: Theories, Methods and Concepts", in Murphy, E., Poynting, S., and Jackson, R., eds., *Contemporary State Terrorism: Theory and Cases*, Routledge Critical Terrorism Studies; London: Routledge, pp. 12–27.
Blakeley, R., 2009b. *State Terrorism and Neoliberalism: The North in the South*, London: Routledge.
Blum, W., 2003. *Killing Hope: US Military and CIA interventions since World War II*, London: Zed Books.
Bush, B., and Maltby, J., 2004. "Taxation in West Africa: Transforming the Colonial Subject into the 'Governable Person'", *Critical Perspectives on Accounting*, 15, 5–34.
Chomsky, N., and Herman, E., 1979a. *After the Cataclysm: Postwar Indochina and the Reconstruction of Imperial Ideology*. The Political Economy of Human Rights, vol II, Nottingham: Spokesman.
Chomsky, N., and Herman, E., 1979b. *The Washington Connection and Third World Fascism: The Political Economy of Human Rights*, vol I, Boston: South End Press.
CNCTR, 1991. "Report of the Chilean National Commission on Truth and Reconciliation". Available online at: <www.usip.org/files/resources/collections/truth_commissions/Chile90-Report/Chile90-Report.pdf>, [accessed 22 November 2010.]
Cobain, I., 2013. *Cruel Britannia: A Secret History of Torture*, London: Portobello Books.
Curtis, M., 2003. *Web of Deceit: Britain's Real Role in the World*, London: Vintage.
Dinges, J., 2004. *The Condor Years*, New York: The New Press.
DoD, 1962. *Field Manual 33–5: Psychological Operations*, Washington, DC: US Department of Defense.

DoD, 1970. *Field Manual 30–21: Stability Operations – Intelligence,* Washington, DC: US Department of Defense: Army.
Elkins, C., 2005. *Britain's Gulag: The Brutal End of Empire in Kenya,* London: Jonathan Cape.
Fanon, F., [1961] 1967. *The Wretched of the Earth,* London: Penguin.
Gareau, F., 2004. *State Terrorism and the United States: From Counterinsurgency to the War on Terrorism,* London: Zed Books.
George, A., 1991a. "The Discipline of Terrorology", in George, A., ed., *Western State Terrorism,* Cambridge: Polity Press, pp. 76–101.
George, A., 1991b. *Western State Terrorism,* Cambridge: Polity Press.
Glancey, J., 2003. "Our Last Occupation: Gas, Chemicals, Bombs: Britain has used them all before in Iraq", *The Guardian,* 19 April, 2003. Available online at: <www.guardian.co.uk/world/2003/apr/19/iraq.arts>, [accessed 6 February 2010.]
Grosscup, B., 2006. *Strategic Terror: The Politics and Ethics of Aerial Bombardment,* London: Zed Books.
Herman, E., 1985. *The Real Terror Network,* 2nd ed., Montreal: Black Rose Books.
Herman, E., and O'Sullivan, G., 1989. *The "Terrorism" Industry: The Experts and Institutions that Shape Our View of Terror,* New York: Pantheon.
Herring, E., 2008. "Critical Terrorism Studies: An Activist Scholar Perspective", *Critical Studies on Terrorism,* 1(2): 197–211.
Herring, E., 2010. "Historical Materialism", in Collins, A., ed., *Contemporary Security Studies,* 2nd ed., Oxford: Oxford University Press, pp. 152–66.
Herring, E., and Stokes, D., 2011. "Critical Realism and Historical Materialism as Resources for Critical Terrorism Studies", *Critical Studies on Terrorism,* 4(1): 5–21.
HRW, 2001. *The 'Sixth Division': Military-Paramilitary Ties and US Policy in Colombia,* New York: Human Rights Watch.
Jarvis, L., and Lister, M., 2014. "State Terrorism Research and Critical Terrorism Studies: An Assessment", *Critical Studies on Terrorism,* 7(1): 43–61.
Joseph, J., 2011. "Terrorism as a Social Relation within Capitalism: Theoretical and Emancipatory Implications", *Critical Studies on Terrorism,* 4(1): 23–37.
Killingray, D., 1973. *A Plague of Europeans: Westerners in Africa Since the Fifteenth Century,* London: Penguin.
Killingray, D., 1986. "The Maintenance of Law and Order in British Colonial Africa", *African Affairs,* 85(340): 411–27.
Kissinger, H., 1970. "Memorandum for the President, from National Security Council Meeting, 6 November, Chile (National Security Archive, George Washington University, Washington DC, Document 2 of NSA Electronic Briefing Book 110)", (6 November). Available online at: <www.gwu.edu/~nsarchiv/NSAEBB/NSAEBB110/chile02.pdf>, [accessed 6 February 2010.]
Lasslett, K., 2014. *State Crime on the Margins of Empire,* London: Pluto Press.
Layne, C., 2006. *The Peace of Illusions: American Grand Strategy from 1940 to the Present,* New York: Cornell University Press.
Maher, D., and Thomson, A., 2011. "The Terror that Underpins the 'Peace': The Political Economy of Colombia's Paramilitary Demobilisation Process", *Critical Studies on Terrorism,* 4(1): 95–113.
McClintock, M., 1992. *Instruments of Statecraft,* New York: Pantheon Books.
McKeown, A., 2011. "The Structural Production of State Terrorism: Capitalism, Imperialism and International Class Dynamics", *Critical Studies on Terrorism,* 4(1): 75–93.
McSherry, J., 2002. "Tracking the Origins of a State Terror Network: Operation Condor", *Latin American Perspectives,* 29(1): 38–60.
Porter, B., 1968. *Critics of Empire: British Radical Attitudes to Colonialism in Africa, 1895–1914,* London: Macmillan.
Priest, D., 1998. "US Military Trains Foreign Troops", *Washington Post,* 12 July, p. A01.
Raphael, S., 2009a. "Paramilitarism and State Terror in Colombia", in Murphy, E., Poynting, S., and Jackson, R., eds., *Contemporary State Terrorism: Theory and Cases,* London: Routledge, pp. 163–80.
Raphael, S., 2009b. "In the Service of Power: Terrorism Studies and US Intervention in the Global South", in Jackson, R., Breen Smyth, M., and Gunning, J., eds., *Critical Terrorism Studies: A New Research Agenda,* Abingdon: Routledge, pp. 49–65.
Robinson, W., 1996. *Promoting Polyarchy: Globalisation, US Intervention, and Hegemony,* Cambridge: Cambridge University Press.
Rummel, R., 2011. *Death by Government,* New Brunswick, NJ: Transaction Publishers.
Shafer, M., 1989. *Deadly Paradigms: The Failure of US Counterinsurgency Policy,* New Jersey: Princeton University Press.

Sluka, J., 2000. "Introduction: State Terror and Anthropology", in Sluka, J., ed., *Death Squad: The Anthropology of State Terror*, Philadelphia: University of Pennsylvania Press, pp. 1–45.

Stohl, M., 2006. "The State as Terrorist: Insights and Implications", *Democracy and Security*, 2: 1–25.

Stokes, D., 2005. *America's Other War*, London: Zed Books.

Stokes, D., and Raphael, S., 2010. *Global Energy Security and American Hegemony*, Baltimore: Johns Hopkins University Press.

Suret-Canale, J., 1971 [1964]. *French Colonialism in Tropical Africa 1900–1945*, trans. Till Gottheiner, London: C Hurst and Company.

Tomuschat, C., Lux-de-Cotí, O., and Balsells-Tojo, A., 1999. "Guatemala: Memory of Silence, Report of the Commission for Historical Clarification", *CEH*, (26 February). Available online at: <http://shr.aaas.org/guatemala/ceh/report/english/toc.html>, [accessed 30 March 2010.]

US Embassy, 1979. "Airgram from US Embassy in Argentina to the US Department of State: Human Rights Case Reports (National Security Archive, George Washington University, Washington DC, Document 8 of NSA Electronic Briefing Book 73, Part One)", (19 June). Available online at: <www.gwu.edu/~nsarchiv/NSAEBB/NSAEBB73/790619dos1.pdf>, [accessed 8 February 2006.]

Vaky, V., 1968. "Memorandum. Subject: Guatemala and Counter-Terror, Sent to Covey Oliver, Assistant Secretary of State for Inter-American Affairs (National Security Archive, George Washington University, Washington DC, and document 5 of 32 compiled for the Guatemala Documentation Project, in NSA Electronic Briefing Book no. 11)". Available online at: <www.gwu.edu/~nsarchiv/NSAEBB/NSAEBB11/docs/05-01.htm>, [accessed 24 January 2006.]

Vaky, V., 1978. "Memorandum to State Department: Evolution of US Human Rights Policy in Argentina (National Security Archive, George Washington University, Washington DC, Document 13 of NSA Electronic Briefing Book 73, Part Two)", (11 September). Available online at: <www.gwu.edu/~nsarchiv/NSAEBB/NSAEBB73/780911.pdf>, [accessed 8 February 2006.]

Valentine, D., 2000. *The Phoenix Program*, 2nd ed., Lincoln: Authors Guild BackinPrint.Com.

Walter, E., 1969. *Terror and Resistance*, Oxford: Oxford University Press.

Welch, R., 1974. "American Atrocities in the Philippines: The Indictment and the Response", *The Pacific Historical Review*, 43(2): 233–53.

Williams, W., 1988. *The Tragedy of American Diplomacy*, New York: Norton.

16
TORTURE

Bob Brecher

Introduction

Although the widespread use of torture to terrorise people predates the so-called war on terror (see Cobain 2012 for the British story), "the gloves came off" (Rothschild 2005) in September 2001. Since then, torturing people has been normalised (Shue 2014), both empirically and morally. This is of fundamental importance for critical scholars of terrorism. First because it is in relation to so-called terrorism that the normalisation of the worst we do to each other has taken place and purportedly been justified. Consider the response to the CIA Torture Report in late 2014: no surprise, and no prosecutions, whether of the perpetrators, politicians or lawyers involved, whether in the United States or elsewhere (*Independent* 2015).

Second, while nobody tries justifying any other uses of torture, not even the strongest critiques of interrogational torture have actually persuaded too many academics, let alone the public at large. The argument is settled, but its conclusions remain unaccepted. It is as if even the best critics (see Ginbar 2008; Luban 2014; Rejali 2009; Shue 2014) had written in vain. I shall return to this. For the moment, let me just note that the position of critical terrorism studies (CTS) scholars seems exactly parallel: consider, for example, the lack of impact our arguments have on people's responses to acts of terror such as the *Charlie Hebdo* and kosher supermarket murders of 2015 (*Economist* 2015).

I shall focus on the "ticking bomb" scenario as both creation and furtherance of the fantasy of "interrogational torture", itself a response to the September 2001 attacks. I shall do so, first, to dispose of its purported justifications (Brecher 2007; Ginbar 2008) and thus of torture's least implausible defence; and, second, to help stimulate a similar approach to the phenomenon of "terrorism". Hence, the structure of this chapter: what torture is; the "ticking bomb" fantasy and its consequences; some examples of the careless thinking that permits the debate to continue as it does; and finally, some comments on lessons to be learnt.

What torture is

Torture cannot be defined, but only described. This is not because "torture" is particularly recalcitrant, but because it is impossible to define *any* real things, such as tables, rivers or friendship, since, being part of the real world, they can change without becoming something else. For instance, you cannot specify exactly what makes this a book: it remains a book even if you tear out a couple of pages or make some notes in it. Only our inventions, our ideas, can be defined: a metre, a triangle, legal guilt. For – unlike real things – these become something else if you take anything away or add anything to them.

But would not a definition of torture help stop it? No: trying to define torture is not just a mistake; it is counterproductive. Consider the infamous Bybee Memorandum which allows those who advocate the use of torture by other names to manipulate definitions so as (perhaps) to pretend to themselves, and certainly to persuade others, that torture is not torture. Bybee (2002: 120) states that inflicting severe pain does not amount to torture unless it attains a "level that would ordinarily be associated with a sufficiently serious physical condition or injury such as death, organ failure, or serious impairment of body functions" – while "Goss, the CIA director, defended waterboarding in March 2005 testimony before the Senate as a 'professional interrogation technique'" (Roth 2005: 94). It is all too easy to think that "harsh interrogation", or "torture lite" (Wolfendale 2009), is not torture because, as with white noise or certain drugs some decades ago, it does not fall within a particular definition of torture. But, as Jeremy Waldron argues, a soldier accused of torture should not be able to say: "I am shocked – shocked! – to find that 'waterboarding' or squeezing prisoners' genitals or setting dogs on them is regarded as torture" (Waldron 2005: 1700).

The United Nations' Convention Against Torture (1984) illustrates the problem. It defines torture as the intentional infliction of "severe pain or suffering, whether physical or mental . . . by or at the instigation or with the consent or acquiescence of a public official or other person acting in an official capacity" and explicitly excludes any "pain or suffering arising only from, inherent in or incidental to lawful sanction" (UN 1984). So, on this definition, if interrogational torture were accepted as lawful it would no longer count as torture!

As a *description* of torture, however, Christopher Tindale's is the best I know:

> any [systematic] act by which severe pain or suffering, whether physical or mental, is intentionally inflicted on a person for such purposes as obtaining from that person or a third person information or confession, punishing that person for an act committed or suspected to have been committed, or intimidating or dehumanizing that person or other persons.
>
> *(Tindale 1996: 355)*

I add "systematic" to stress that torture is purposeful, structured and not just any gratuitously inflicted pain. That seems to me adequately to describe torture: any act like that is *sufficient* to count as torture, but we cannot specify in advance what is *necessary* for an act to count as torture. What sort of intention is it, then, that issues in the systematic infliction of "severe pain or suffering" on a person? What *sort* of act is the act of torture?

Central to institutional or political torture – as contrasted with, say, two youngsters torturing a classmate in what might, however tastelessly, be termed an amateurish way – is that it is the "deliberate infliction of pain in order to destroy the victim's normative world and capacity to create shared realities" (Cover 1986: 1602; for a detailed victim's account, see Slahi 2015). Pain itself is not the end; rather, it is a means of achieving an end and therefore has to be of specific sorts and intensities. Pain is used *to destroy the victim's normative relation to the torturer* and thereby to destroy their understanding and treatment of themselves as a person; to make the person tortured into something that is no longer a person, as Harold Pinter brilliantly shows (Pinter 1984, 1993). Alone with their torturers, the tortured "subject" ceases under torture to be a person.

Here is Jean Améry:

> Only in torture does the transformation of the person into flesh become complete. Frail in the face of violence, yelling out in pain, awaiting no help, capable of no resistance, the tortured person is only a body, and nothing else besides that.
>
> *(Améry 1980: 33)*

This is what the Nazis did to him:

> In the bunker there hung from the vaulted ceiling a chain that above ran into a roll. At its bottom end it bore a heavy, broadly curved iron hook. I was led to the instrument. The hook gripped into the shackle that held my hands together behind my back. Then I was raised with the chain until I hung about a meter over the floor. In such a position, or rather, when hanging this way, with your hands behind your back, for a short time you can hold at a half-oblique through muscular force. . . . But this cannot last long, even with people who have a strong physical constitution. As for me, I had to give up rather quickly. And now there was a crackling and splintering in my shoulders that my body has not forgotten until this hour. The balls sprang from their sockets. My own body weight caused luxation; I fell into a void and now hung by my dislocated arms, which had been torn high from behind and were now twisted over my head. Torture, from Latin *torquere*, to twist.
>
> *(Améry 1980: 32)*

"The pain," he goes on to say, "was what it was. Beyond that there is nothing to say. Qualities of feeling are as incomparable as they are indescribable. They mark the limit of the capacity of language to communicate" (33). No wonder he could not forget it: "It was over for a while. It still is not over. Twenty-two years later I am still dangling over the ground by dislocated arms, panting, and accusing myself" (36).

But, crucially, it is not a question *only* of physical pain. Even "the first blow brings home to the prisoner that he is helpless, and thus it already contains in the bud everything that is to come" (Améry 1980: 27). That, Améry tells us, is why "with the first blow from a policeman's fist, against which there can be no defense and which no helping hand will ward off, a part of our life ends and it can never again be revived" (29). That is why "whoever has succumbed to torture can no longer feel at home in the world. The shame of destruction cannot be erased. Trust in the world, which already collapsed in part at the first blow, but in the end, under torture, fully, will not be regained" (40).

Thirty-three years after being released from the site of the last of his tortures, on 17 October 1978, Jean Améry committed suicide. Note that Améry's torturers had to *start* by treating him as a person – as an embodied rational agent – for only *then* could they go on to break him by breaking his body. Améry's torturers, one might say, turned his personhood against him. Eventually, having bodily survived the torture, Améry's reaction (not his response) was to become someone else. That is how he survived, as someone else. Many others do not. It is also why he eventually killed himself. Torture really does delineate the limit point of personhood, which is why it delineates also the limit point of reason. That is why torture is the worst thing we do.

Torture and the "ticking bomb"

No one – yet – defends torture as punishment, intimidation, revenge or pleasure. The entire literature deals solely with torture as a means of obtaining information: the "ticking bomb" scenario. The argument is always utilitarian. Its chief exponent remains Alan Dershowitz:

> The classic hypothetical case involves the train engineer whose brakes become inoperative. There is no way he can stop his speeding vehicle of death. Either he can do nothing, in which case he will plow into a busload of schoolchildren, or he can swerve onto another track, where he sees a drunk lying on the rails. (Neither decision will endanger him or his passengers.) There is no third choice. What should he do?
>
> (Dershowitz 2002: 132)

Drawing on this classic "trolley problem" (Thompson 1985), Dershowitz reminds us that we are sometimes faced with an unavoidable moral dilemma: we have to choose, and the only question is what consequentialist criteria we should use – the number of people involved, who those people are, both, or what? Even leaving it to chance is a decision. However you decide, *someone* is going to suffer the consequences. And so with interrogational torture to prevent catastrophe: if the benefit of an action outweighs its costs, then that action is morally right.

Not everyone is a utilitarian, of course. For example, some people think that (broadly Kantian) considerations about not treating people merely as a means to an end, but always also as an end in themselves, are enough to show that *any* torture is *always* wrong. For what could instantiate using a person merely as a means more clearly than torturing them? That is why torture is *absolutely* forbidden by international human rights law: there are no exceptions. Others, however, think that it is pretty obvious that the ticking bomb scenario shows exactly why this sort of view is wrong; a moral theory which permits the death and maiming of hundreds, maybe thousands, of people, rather than torturing one person who has the information to prevent such carnage, exposes its own absurdity. So it is often said that it will not do "to play the student in Philosophy 101", as Sanford Levinson (2003) puts it, "where Kantian deontologists contend with utilitarians as to the propriety of lying to Nazis . . . [for] unless one *is* a Kantian, it is hard to understand why one would embrace this position".

Maybe so; maybe not. Certainly, there is more than one way of saying what is wrong with torture. What matters, however, is to persuade those who think interrogational torture is justified, and that requires addressing them in their own utilitarian terms. These may be *unstraightforwardly* utilitarian. Michael Walzer famously argues that supreme emergency justifies moving from deontology to utilitarianism (Walzer 1973) – just as democracy must be abandoned when anti-democrats threaten to win a democratic mandate – and then proceeds on that basis to justify interrogational torture (Walzer 2003). Responding to the questions, "What if it were necessary to torture the suspect's mother or children to get him to divulge the necessary information? What if it took threatening to kill his family, his friends, his entire village?", Dershowitz himself comments that this

> is morality by numbers, unless there are other constraints on what we can properly do. These other constraints can come from rule utilitarianisms or other principles of morality, such as the prohibition against deliberately punishing the innocent. Unless we

are prepared to impose some limits on the use of torture or other barbaric tactics that might be of some use in preventing terrorism, we risk hurtling down a slippery slope into the abyss of amorality and ultimately tyranny.

(Dershowitz 2002: 146)

Quite so. But the whole point of utilitarianism is that it claims *there are no other (valid) principles* (Brecher 2007: 49–52). Dershowitz's "limits" are nonsense. And Walzer's "dirty hands" approach doesn't fare much better (Walzer 1973). For even if he were right that it is sometimes right to do something morally wrong – and granting the thought is coherent – then *refusing* to (order) torture remains one way of dirtying your hands.

Why the "ticking bomb" argument fails in its own terms

The ticking bomb scenario is a deceptive fantasy. When unpacked, it disintegrates: its time and effectiveness constraints run against each other; the likelihood of accurate information is minimal; what looks like necessity is not; and what "we" would do is beside the point. Let me outline the arguments in brief.

Time and effectiveness

Dershowitz argues that "it is precisely because torture sometimes does work and can prevent major disasters that it still exists in many parts of the world and has been totally eliminated from none" (Dershowitz 2002: 138). Ignatieff asserts that "the argument that torture and coercion do not work is contradicted by the dire frequency with which both practices occur" (Ignatieff 2006). So why does the American *Field Manual* 34–52, like all others, prohibit "the use of coercive techniques because they produce low quality intelligence" (Rose 2004: 95)? Consider the specific circumstances of a ticking bomb. Such evidence as we have is inevitably anecdotal. While Levinson claims that "there is no known example of this actually occurring, in the sense of having someone in custody who knew of a bomb likely to go off within the hour" (Levinson 2003: n. 1), Dershowitz offers an unreferenced claim that in Israel "there is little doubt that some acts of terrorism – which would have killed many civilians – were prevented. There is also little doubt that the cost of saving these lives – measured in terms of basic human rights – was extraordinarily high" (Dershowitz 2002: 140).

Strikingly, while Dershowitz at least offers some evidence, it is entirely irrelevant: "Jordan apparently broke the most notorious terrorist of the 1980s, Abu Nidal, *by threatening his mother*. Philippine police reportedly helped crack the 1993 World Trade Center bombings by torturing a suspect" (Dershowitz 2002: 249, n. 11; emphasis added). The first case contradicts what he says about not availing himself of "raw" utilitarianism; and neither involves any ticking bomb. And it gets even odder:

> There are numerous instances in which torture has produced self-proving, truthful information that was necessary to prevent harm to civilians. The *Washington Post* has recounted a case from 1995 in which Philippine authorities tortured a terrorist into disclosing information that may have foiled plots to assassinate the pope and to crash eleven commercial airliners carrying approximately four thousand passengers into the Pacific ocean, as well as a plan to fly a private Cessna filled with explosives into CIA headquarters. For sixty-seven days, intelligence agents beat the suspect.
>
> *(Dershowitz 2002: 137)*

Sixty-seven days? So what on earth has this to do with anything *imminent*?

Still, let us generously suppose that the captive really does know where the bomb is. What will they do? Remember that only *interrogational* torture is allowed; theoretically, torture would have to stop while the authorities checked the captive's story. The captive's position, then – as Dershowitz recognizes – is that "the torturee [How *can* anyone use such a word?] will know that there are limits to the torture being inflicted" (Dershowitz 2002: 249, n. 11). First, they know that unless they reveal the bomb's location, they will be tortured; second, that the torture will stop *immediately* when they give the information; and third, that the torture – being interrogational *only* – will stop if the bomb explodes. The time for which they have to endure the torture is therefore comparatively short. Surely, they will simply lie, and repeatedly, to buy time – or out of desperation (the *Field Manual* again). The less time there is, the more likely lying, whether deliberately or desperately, would work. So, the more urgent the situation – and thus, the putatively more justified the torture – the smaller the chance of preventing the catastrophe.

The right captive?

Any competent bomb-planter will leave as little time as possible between planting and detonation. Unless they had already been under surveillance – so the authorities would already know the bomb's location – their being captured in the interval between planting and detonation must be extraordinarily unlikely. The chances of error are correspondingly high, as the real world attests: "In the two and a half years since September 11, 2001, five thousand foreign nationals suspected of being terrorists have been detained without access to counsel, only three of whom have ever eventually been charged with terrorism-related acts; two of those three have been acquitted" (Scarry 2004: 284).

Necessity?

The whole point of the fantasy is to create a sense of necessity: "the terrorist" *has* to be tortured to prevent thousands dying or being maimed. But what sort of necessity is this? How do we know torture is necessary? Of course, no empirical knowledge is certain: "necessity" is here to be understood in the ordinary, everyday sense, not as a technical philosophical term. Fair enough; but then, precisely because certainty is unavailable, the argument must be that interrogational torture is morally justifiable because it *might* avoid a catastrophe. If it is not *known* that time is (sufficiently) short, then it cannot be *known* that the case is a matter of necessity. So how *does* the interrogator know that time is (sufficiently) short?

The suspect is not going to tell them. Perhaps *someone else* might say they know that there is a ticking bomb somewhere, that they do not know where, but that they do know the suspect knows. But then what makes *that* information reliable? How can anyone have the knowledge that is a logical condition of invoking necessity? In short, the necessity of torture in any particular instance *cannot be known in advance*. So, there has to be a risk of torturing the wrong person, and the greater the so-called necessity, the greater the risk must be. No wonder that the best evidence Dershowitz can cite is that "the Israeli security services claimed that, as a result of the Supreme Court's decision, at least one preventable act of terrorism had been allowed to take place, one that killed several people when a bus was bombed". In fairness, he clearly recognises the shortcoming; he says that "whether this claim is true, false, or somewhere in between is difficult to assess" (Dershowitz 2002: 150). But, he cheerfully ignores the impact that has on his argument. At best, it can be claimed that torture *may be necessary*. But substitute that claim in the argument and any initial plausibility it may have had disappears.

Who tortures?

Here is Anthony Quinton, back in 1971, commenting on the British army's notorious "interrogation techniques" in the north of Ireland:

> I do not see on what basis anyone could argue that the prohibition of torture is an absolute moral principle. . . . Consider a man caught planting a bomb in a large hospital, which no one dare touch for fear of setting it off. It was this kind of extreme situation I had in mind when I said earlier that I thought torture could be justifiable.
>
> (Quinton 1971: 758)

He notices that "any but the most sparing recourse to [torture] will nourish a guild of professional torturers, a persisting danger to society much greater, even if more long-drawn-out, then anything their employment is likely to prevent" and that "if a society does not professionalise torture, then the limits of its efficiency make its application in any particular extreme situation that much more dubious" (Quinton 1971: 758). But, he misses the implications of what he notices. The inevitable limits of amateur torture's efficiency do not render its efficacy dubious; *they rule it out*, simply because the ticking bomb fantasy requires just that efficiency which the amateur torturer could not bring to it. "We" are not trained torturers. That is why those who order the use of torture have to employ professionally trained torturers, not psychopaths; torture is a skilled activity.

Summary

Not only is the ticking bomb scenario nonsense, and the necessity it is claimed to generate spurious, but it also blithely ignores the most important consequence of all – the impact of the institutionalised practice of torture on any society adopting it. For the fantasy's plausibility not to collapse at the outset, it requires professional torture.

A real case

But what about a real case? In 2002, the Frankfurt police genuinely knew that Magnus Gäfgen had kidnapped the 11-year-old son of a banker and had imprisoned him in circumstances where his lingering death was imminent. He refused to say where the boy was. So the police president "ordered his men to threaten Gäfgen with violence to force a statement" (Schroeder 2006: 188). The threat was enough to elicit what he knew. Unhappily, the boy was already dead. Would torture have been justified? A utilitarian view takes all the foreseeable consequences outlined above into account, and so, brutal though this is, they outweigh one child's life. If, however, such a conclusion is morally repugnant, then so much for utilitarianism. Not all moral disasters are avoidable in the real world; sometimes it is just too late. Perhaps it is the task of politics to fashion a world in which such disasters are minimised (MacIntyre 1999).

The state of the "torture debate"

The "torture debate" mirrors precisely both theoretical and policy debate about "terrorism": consider as just one example the recent response to Islamic State in Iraq and Syria. Just as that response is no advance on the response to 11 September 2001, so both the terms and conduct of the "torture debate" since Dershowitz's "modest proposal" (Gray 2003) are being recycled.

Here are just a few examples. Jeff McMahan (2008: 91) starts by referring to "those of us who oppose torture", but goes on to say that he "will argue that the moral justifiability of torture in principle is virtually irrelevant in practice". So what exactly does it mean to oppose torture, if you also think it is sometimes morally justifiable? This is Walzer's threshold deontology without even an attempted justification.

Or, consider Uwe Steinhoff's recent "Legalising Defensive Torture" (and notice the title's sleight of hand):

> Since people have a right even to *kill* a culpable aggressor if, in the circumstances, this is a proportionate and necessary means of self-defense (a term that is used here, as is common, to include other-defense) against an imminent or ongoing attack, and since most forms of torture are not as bad as killing, people must also have a right to torture a culpable aggressor if this, too, in the circumstances, is a proportionate and necessary means of self-defense against an imminent or ongoing attack.
>
> *(Steinhoff 2012: 19)*

Yet nowhere in the article does Steinhoff bother to defend the assumption he is making, namely that killing is worse than torture (compare Dershowitz [2002: 17, cf. 148]: "Pain is a lesser and more remediable harm than death").

Seumas Miller at least glances in the direction of giving reasons:

> It does not follow that torture is less preferable than being killed because the duration of the torture might be brief, one's will might not ultimately be broken, and one might go on to live a long and happy life; by contrast, being killed – theological considerations aside – is always "followed by" no life whatsoever.
>
> *(2005: 180; see also 2008)*

So was Améry wrong? Unlike killing, torture requires that a person be recognised as such precisely in order to undermine their personhood. That is why torture really is the bottom line of morality and why torturing a person is worse than killing them. It goes to the very basis of what we are: embodied rational agents, that is to say, persons. Consider, for example, the fact that it may in certain circumstances be an act of recognising someone's personhood to kill them. Even if you think that assisted voluntary euthanasia is never justified, then your reasons constitute a recognition of human beings as not merely biological beings, but as persons. That is why torture matters so much. Contrary to the ignorant or disingenuous views of some thinkers, torture is the worst thing we do to each other.

Even if you disagree with that, argument is nonetheless required; assumption is not enough. But, Miller's minimalist gesture apart, argument is conspicuously absent. And note that Miller's gesture happens also *exactly* to reflect what the Bush administration's lawyers notoriously "argued" in the infamous Bybee memorandum, where Yoo, on Bybee's behalf, claims that for a practice to constitute torture it has to result in "a sufficiently serious physical condition or injury such as death, organ failure, or serious impairment of body function" (Bybee 2002/2005: 120).

Finally, consider Fritz Allhoff, a leading defender of interrogational torture over the past few years. He asks us to

> return to the dictionary definitions, which held that severe treatment must be either "extreme" or "hard to sustain," depending on the selected definition. Now take hooding. Is this really either extreme or hard to sustain? Certainly, it is unpleasant, but I think

that it falls short of these other metrics. Stress positions are not hard to sustain so much as uncomfortable to sustain: if they were hard to sustain, they could not be sustained for hours (or indefinitely) as they sometimes are.

(2012: 65)

If "stress positions . . . were hard to sustain, they could not be sustained for hours". *Really?* So if marathon running were hard, running marathons would be impossible? It is; therefore, marathons are impossible. Admittedly this is a pretty extreme example of the genre. But notice its remarkable similarity to Rumsfeld's notorious "argument": at the bottom of a "memorandum authorizing interrogation techniques against detainees at Guantanamo that the current President of the United States, Barack Obama, has described as 'torture', Rumsfeld wrote, 'I stand for 8–10 hours a day. Why is standing limited to 4 hours?'" (Waas 2009). If it weren't overly cynical, and thus unthinkable, you might be forgiven for concluding that Allhoff actually learnt his lines from Rumsfeld. Arguing from dictionaries on the basis of an inadequate understanding of definition is bad enough. Offering conclusions which do not even follow from their erroneous premises is disgraceful.

Conclusion: academics as court jesters

In light of all that, the obvious question is this: how is it that this fantasy has achieved its status as a justification, not just in the public mind but also in the academy? There seems to be only one plausible answer: the so-called war on terror. First, fantasy is its central component: from Sadaam Hussein's nonexistent weapons of mass destruction, to the British government's "advice" to universities on how to combat "Islamic extremism", fantasy is the key element in feeding the required public fear (see Zulaika, this volume). Second, torture is the bottom line for "civilized values"; therefore, the prohibition on torture must go. And so, third, the ticking bomb scenario is wheeled in to justify torture.

Central in its ready acceptance is a refusal to distinguish between what you or I *might do* in that imagined case, what you or I *could do* in an actual case, and what *"someone" would be expected to do* in an actual case. But this is unconscionable. You or I can imaginatively put ourselves in the position of Dershowitz's train driver, at least to the extent of knowing how to operate the controls so as to "swerve onto another track". But, we cannot put ourselves in the position of a torturer. First, there is the nature and precision of the skills required; second, and crucially, there is the question of the depths to which the acquisition and practice of such skills requires the torturer to sink. You need only read Ronald Crelinsten's (1995) discussion of how torturers are recruited and trained to realise the absurdity of asking the question, "What would *you* do in a 'ticking bomb' case?" Even if "you" were there when the person "you" knew to know where the bomb was, "you" would not know what to do. The train driver example and the ticking bomb fantasy are radically different. The latter requires us not to imagine what *we* would do, but to imagine what we would require *someone else* – a professional torturer – to do on our behalf, and not, furthermore, as an act of supererogation or altruism, but as the practice of their profession.

Beware thought experiments. They may illuminate moral and political theory, but they have no place in shaping public policy. To confuse inviting people to think through the implications of their own beliefs with advocating policy is, at best, intellectually irresponsible.

What else? What sort of scholarship is needed to upset the apparent settlement I noted earlier? The ticking bomb argument of course needs repeated refutation; originality is not the sole virtue of scholarship. But there is something else. What is needed actually to shift people's attitudes is not just philosophical, political and moral argument, but remorselessly bringing facts into the public domain to jolt *all* of us out of our roles as court jesters or public bystanders. We need more empirical work like Crelinsten's (1995) and Cobain's (2012) and more testimony, as particularly painfully and brilliantly instantiated by Slahi (2015).

Finally, and obviously, people who write about serious subjects such as torture are under a particular obligation to do so responsibly. What may be thought in some areas to be merely unfortunate – nonsequiturs, assuming one's conclusion, failing to take into account the obvious – is far more damaging in this context. Here, there is no clear line between intellectual and public responsibility. Nor between an academic readership and public impact: *24* and suchlike are bad enough in the context of popular culture; their inanities should not be embraced. Otherwise we become not critical irritants, let alone speakers of truth to power, but simply court jesters; court jesters who perform for their masters by helping to make people think whatever those masters want them to.

Further reading

Brecher, B., 2011. "Torture: a touchstone for global social justice", in Widdows, H., and Smith, N., eds., *Global Social Justice*. London: Routledge, pp. 90–101.

Dershowitz, A., 2004. "The torture warrant: a response to Professor Strauss", *New York Law School Legal Review*, 48: 275–294.

Elshtain, J., 2004. "Reflection on the problem of 'dirty hands'", in Levinson, S., ed., *Torture: A Collection*. Oxford: Oxford University Press, pp. 77–89.

Levinson, S., ed., 2004. *Torture: A Collection*. Oxford: Oxford University Press.

Luban, D., 2009. "Unthinking the ticking bomb", in Beitz, C., and Goodin, R., eds., *Global Basic Rights*, Oxford: Oxford University Press, pp. 181–206.

References

Allhoff, F., 2012. *Terrorism, Ticking Time-Bombs, and Torture*. Chicago: Chicago University Press.

Améry, J., 1980. *At the Mind's Limit*, trans. S. and S. Rosenfeld. Bloomington: Indiana University Press.

Brecher, B., 2007. *Torture and the Ticking Bomb*. London: Wiley-Blackwell.

Bybee, J., 2002/2005. "Memorandum for Alberto R. Gonzales, counsel to the President, re: standards of conduct for interrogation under 18 U.S.C. (1 August)", in Danner, M., ed., *Torture and Truth: America, Abu Ghraib, and the War on Terror*. New York: New York Review of Books, pp. 115–166.

Cobain, I., 2012. *Cruel Britannia*. London: Portobello Books.

Cover, R., 1986. "Violence and the word", *Yale Law Journal*, 95: 1601–1628.

Crelinsten, R., 1995. "In their own words: the world of the torturer", in Crelinsten, R., and Schmid, A., eds., *The Politics of Pain: Torturers and their Masters*. Boulder: Westview Press, pp. 65–97.

Dershowitz, A., 2002. *Why Terrorism Works*. London: Yale University Press.

Economist Briefing, 2015. "After the atrocities", available online at: www.economist.com/news/briefing/21639540-attacks-charlie-hebdo-and-kosher-supermarket-brought-french-together-unity. [Accessed 24 January 2015.]

Ginbar, Y., 2008. *Why Not Torture Terrorists?* Oxford: Oxford University Press.

Gray, J., 2003. "A modest proposal for preventing torturers in liberal democracies from being abused, and for recognising their benefit to the public", *New Statesman*, 17 February, 22–25. Available online at: www.newstatesman.com/node/144806 [Accessed 4 July 2014.]

Ignatieff, M., 2006. "If torture works", *Prospect*, unpaginated, available online at: www.prospectmagazine.co.uk/features/iftortureworks. [Accessed 4 July 2014.]

Independent, 2015. "CIA 'torture report' in full: Read the Senate Intelligence Committee's damning findings", available online at: www.independent.co.uk/news/world/americas/cia-torture-report-read-the-senate-intelligence-committees-damning-findings-in-full-9913648.html. [Accessed 24 January 2015.]

Levinson, S., 2003. "The debate on torture", *Dissent*, Summer, unpaginated, available online at: www.dissentmagazine.org/article/?article=490. [Accessed 5 July 2014.]

Luban, D., 2014. *Torture, Power, and Law*. Cambridge: Cambridge University Press.

MacIntyre, A., 1999. "Social structures and their threat to moral agency", *Philosophy*, 74: 311–329.

McMahan, J., 2008. "Torture in principle and in practice", *Public Affairs Quarterly*, 22: 91–108.
Miller, S., 2005. "Is torture ever morally justified?", *International Journal of Applied Philosophy*, 19: 179–92.
Miller, S., 2008. *Terrorism and Counter-Terrorism*. London: Wiley.
Pinter, H., 1984. *One for the Road*. London: Methuen.
Pinter, H., 1993. *Party Time* and *New World Order*. London: Grove Press.
Quinton, A. 1971. Views. *The Listener*, 2 December, 757–8.
Rejali, D., 2009. *Torture and Democracy*. Princeton: Princeton University Press.
Rose, D., 2004. *Guantanamo: America's War on Human Rights*. London: Faber and Faber.
Roth, K., 2005. "Justifying torture", in Roth, K., and Worden, W., eds., *Torture*. New York: Press and Human Rights Watch, pp. 184–202.
Rothschild, M., 2005. "Stripping Rumsfeld and Bush of Impunity", *The Progressive*, 1 July, available online at: www.progressive.org/mag_impunity. [Accessed 12 September 2014.]
Scarry, E., 2004. "Five errors in the reasoning of Alan Dershowitz", in Levinson, S., ed., *Torture: A Collection*. Oxford: Oxford University Press, pp. 281–299.
Schroeder, D., 2006. "A child's life or a 'little bit of torture'? State-sanctioned violence and dignity", *Cambridge Quarterly of Healthcare Ethics*, 15: 188–201.
Shue, H., 2014. "Torture", in Moellendorf, D., and Widdows, H., eds., *Routledge Handbook of Global Ethics*. London: Routledge.
Slahi, M., 2015. *Guantánamo Diary*. Edinburgh: Canongate.
Steinhoff, U., 2012. "Legalizing Defensive Torture", *Public Affairs Quarterly*, 26: 19–32.
Thompson, J., 1985. "The trolley problem", *Yale Law Journal*, 94: 1395–1415.
Tindale, C., 1996. "The logic of torture", *Social Theory and Practice*, 22: 349–374.
United Nations' Convention Against Torture, 1984. Available online at: www.un.org/documents/ga/res/39/a39r046.htm. [Accessed 28 July 2014.]
Waas, M., 2009. "Rumsfeld on detainees: 'I stand for 8–10 hours a day. Why is standing limited to 4 hours?'", *Huffington Post*, 22 April, available online at: www.huffingtonpost.com/murray-waas/rumsfeld-on-detainees-i-s_b_189833.html. [Accessed 28 July 2014.]
Waldron, J., 2005. "Torture and positive law: jurisprudence for the White House". *Columbia Law Review*, 105: 1681–1750.
Walzer, M., 1973. "Political action: the problem of dirty hands". *Philosophy and Public Affairs*, 2: 160–180.
Walzer, M., 2003. "Interview, *Imprints 7*", available online at: http://eis.bris.ac.uk/~plcdib/imprints/michaelwalzerinterview.html. [Accessed 23 July 2014.]
Wolfendale, J., 2009. "The Myth of 'Torture Lite'". *Ethics and International Affairs*, 23: 47–61.

17
RENDITION IN THE "WAR ON TERROR"

Sam Raphael and Ruth Blakeley

Introduction

In the years after the declaration of the "war on terror" in September 2001, the United States government led the way in constructing a global system of detention outside the law, illegal prisoner transfers between states (rendition), and interrogation and detainee treatment practices that were cruel, inhuman, and degrading and that, in some cases, involved torture. This was, we will argue, the latest manifestation of the use by Western states of state terror in pursuit of their strategic goals, in this case the elimination of the threat posed to Western interests by radical Islamist groups with global reach. (See Chapter 15 for a fuller discussion of Western state terrorism.)

Our aim in this chapter is to outline the findings from our ongoing work to uncover, map, and understand the establishment and evolution of the CIA's rendition, detention, and interrogation (RDI) programme. This is based on our work on *The Rendition Project* (www. therenditionproject.org.uk), established in 2011 with the aim of developing an understanding of the scope, reach, and workings of the RDI programme. Working closely with a range of NGOs, lawyers, and investigators, we have gathered an enormous amount of data which has enabled us to identify which countries were involved in the programme, what their roles were, and how the programme evolved. We have been able to provide convincing evidence of the ill treatment to which prisoners were subjected and show the terrorising effects this has had. Here, we will set out the main features of the global torture programme, as well as examine the roles played by specific states. We illustrate this with a more detailed look at the involvement of the United Kingdom.

As well as making an important contribution to understandings of rendition, our work challenges arguments made by some terrorism experts that while undesirable, sometimes human rights violations, including torture, are necessary for curtailing the terrorist threat (see also Brecher, this volume). We show that the evidence from the RDI programme presents a strong challenge to this assumption. Finally, we offer some insights into how critical work into secret programmes involving state terrorism might be undertaken, specifically through collaboration with nonacademics working to investigate human rights abuses and litigate on behalf of victims. This may provide a model for other critical scholars seeking to carry out research on various forms of state terrorism.

The contours of the CIA's torture programme

The decision by the United States government to operate outside the law in the "war on terror" was deliberate, and almost immediate. Less than a week after the 9/11 terrorist attacks, on 17 September 2001, President Bush authorised the Director of the CIA to engage in "clandestine intelligence activity" as part of the counterterrorism campaign, including the formation of a "terrorist detention and interrogation program". Less than two months later, on 13 November 2001, President Bush issued an Executive Order on the Detention, Treatment, and Trial of Certain Non-Citizens in the War Against Terrorism (Bush 2001), providing the Pentagon with the authority to detain indefinitely any non-American in the world, in any place in the world, considered to pose a terrorist threat to US interests.

Furthermore, within just three months of the second Executive Order, on 7 February 2002, President Bush issued a memo to his senior staff declaring that members of al Qaeda and the Taliban were "unlawful combatants" (Bush 2002), and as such, did not qualify as "prisoners of war" under the Geneva Conventions when detained. As well as denying prisoner of war status to the war on terror detainees, Bush determined that Common Article 3 of the Geneva Conventions did not apply to al Qaeda or Taliban detainees, thus denying their protection under International Humanitarian Law (IHL).

This policy laid the foundations of the CIA torture programme, as well as the official military detentions in Afghanistan and Guantánamo Bay, Cuba. In turn, the CIA programme provided the overarching framework for the establishment and operation of a secret prison network which operated at numerous locations across four continents and encompassed the detention of at least 119 terror suspects between 2001 and 2008 (SSCI 2014). The secret detention of terror suspects took place within a complex "network" of prisons. At its core was a set of US-run facilities overseen by the Pentagon and CIA. These existed in several locations around the globe, including Iraq, Afghanistan, Thailand, Poland, Romania, Lithuania, and Cuba (alongside the official prison at Guantánamo Bay). Supplementing these was a series of preexisting detention sites, centred in North Africa and the Middle East, which were run by foreign security forces known to regularly use torture, but to which the CIA had direct access.

The CIA's torture programme was made possible by using a number of small, private aircraft to transfer terror suspects around the world so that they could be held undetected for the purposes of interrogation using torture. The use of multiple aircraft and dozens of prison sites was deliberately intended to keep the programme under wraps. The use of these aircraft, though, would eventually result in the unravelling of the entire programme. As details of the RDI programme began to emerge in 2004 and 2005, the importance of these aircraft became clearer, and investigators began to track their movements (Grey 2004; AI 2006). At the heart of the programme was a complex contracting network involving a number of companies which either did not exist or else had been hired to facilitate rendition operations.

For example, some aircraft were owned by the CIA via a shifting array of shell companies, such as Stevens Express, Premier Executive Transport, Rapid Air Transport, Path Corporation, and Aviation Specialties. These companies were the registered owners of the aircraft, but they only existed on paper as a front for the CIA. They were regularly dissolved, with the aircraft "sold" to other shell companies and often re-registered with new tail numbers along the way to cover their tracks. Meanwhile, the aircraft themselves were operated by a set of real companies that were responsible for maintenance, providing hangers, and arranging the logistical details for each flight circuit. Many of these operating companies, such as Aero Contractors, Pegasus Technologies, and Tepper Aviation, have been reported as having very close links to, or even working exclusively for, the CIA (Shane et al. 2005; Weissman 2012). Other companies appearing in the data strings, such as Jeppesen International Trip Planning/Jeppesen Dataplan and Universal Weather and Aviation, were companies providing so-called trip planning services to a range of corporate and government clients. These companies were responsible for ensuring that the required flight plans were filed, overflight and landing authorisations were received, and hotel reservations were booked.

Meanwhile, corporate documents analysed by the authors reveal a parallel contracting network. At the top was the "prime contractor", first DynCorp Systems and Solutions, LLC, and later, Computer Sciences Corporation. These companies undertook to organise flight operations on behalf of the US government. They subcontracted to two brokering companies – Capital Aviation and SportsFlight – which in turn contracted with more than a dozen aircraft-operating companies to secure the services of particular aircraft and the logistics required to mount global, multiday trips (for more details on the contribution that our work has made to the uncovering of the programme, see Raphael et al. 2016).

The programme was deliberately intended as an instrument for secretly extracting intelligence from prisoners, as well as holding them incommunicado for months or years on end. While the primary aim of the rendition programme was to extract intelligence, the entire process was underpinned by a strategy to terrorise and dehumanise the prisoners, and in so doing, intimidate others connected to them, whether within or outside the CIA's secret prison network. CIA torture was, to a certain extent, authorised through a set of official memoranda drawn up by the US Department of Justice. These memos were couched in the language of "enhanced interrogation techniques" (EITs) – a euphemism for what was in fact, a series of aggressive techniques which most experts consider fall within the definition of torture. The CIA was authorised to subject prisoners to beatings, nudity, sleep deprivation, sensory overload and deprivation, water dousing, confinement in extremely small boxes, and simulated drowning (waterboarding). Official investigations by the CIA's Inspector General and by the Senate Select Committee on Intelligence have revealed that a whole set of unauthorised torture techniques were also used, including mock executions, ice baths to induce hypothermia, power drills, and rape through rectal feeding without medical necessity (OIG 2004; SSCI 2014).

Many other states were directly involved, or indirectly complicit in, the RDI programme. There is evidence, for example, that states which hosted US-run secret prisons – such as Poland, Romania, and Lithuania – knew about what was going on and provided key logistical assistance and diplomatic cover to facilitate operations. The Polish site consisted of two buildings within a military intelligence training base located in the woods outside the village of Stare Kiejkuty in the lakes region of north-eastern Poland. Recent reports suggest that the CIA paid its Polish counterparts $15 million in cash for the use of the site and at least $300,000 for improvements at the site (including the installation of security cameras and the conversion of the two-storey villa and adjacent shed) (Goldman 2014).

The location and layout of the Romanian site, code-named "Bright Light", were revealed in December 2011 by journalists working for the Associated Press and the German ARD news programme *Panorama*. The team confirmed that they had spoken to "former US intelligence officials familiar with the location and inner working of the prison" and that the site was located in the basement of a building in northern Bucharest used by the National Registry Office for Classified Information (ORNISS) to store sensitive EU and NATO files. The basement was, according to one senior ORNISS official, "one of the most secure rooms in all of Romania" (Goldman 2014).

Lithuania, meanwhile, hosted two sites on behalf of the CIA: Project No. 1, a single-storied detached building in the centre of Vilnius, and Project No. 2, a larger facility housed at a former horse riding school in the village of Antaviliai, on the edge of woodland 15 miles from Vilnius (CSND 2009). According to *ABC News*, citing unnamed Lithuanian and US officials, the CIA

> built a thick concrete wall inside the riding area. Behind the wall, it built what one Lithuanian source called "a building within a building." On a series of thick concrete pads, it installed what a source called "prefabricated pods" to house prisoners, each separated from the other by five or six feet. Each pod included a shower, a bed, and a toilet. Separate cells were constructed for interrogations.
>
> *(Cole and Ross 2009)*

In each case, preexisting buildings were adapted to provide bespoke detention facilities suitable for housing a relatively small number of prisoners, and local security forces and private contractors were involved in the construction of the sites (Johnston and Mazzetti 2009; Day 2012).

Other states played a key role in the capture of individual detainees and their transfer to US forces for rendition, secret detention, and abuse. These states included Canada, Italy, Macedonia, Sweden, Kenya, Tanzania, Malawi, Zambia, Sudan, Mauritania, Gambia, Djibouti, Dubai, Yemen, Indonesia, Thailand, and, most importantly, Pakistan. States across the Middle East and North Africa – including Jordan, Syria, Egypt, Libya, and Morocco – have received, detained, and interrogated suspects on behalf of the US. Some Western states have also played a key role, albeit often from an "arms-length" position. Dozens of states have been used as refuelling and logistical stop-off points for aircraft undertaking rendition operations, turning a blind eye as torture flights criss-crossed the globe. Security forces from Canada, Sweden, and Italy have facilitated the capture and transfer of terror suspects into the system of secret detention and torture. This has been either through involvement in the initial "arrest" and handover to US forces or through the passing of intelligence to friendly security forces to locate suspects and facilitate their capture.

Canadian intelligence agencies, along with their German and Australian counterparts, have also been accused of direct involvement in the interrogation of suspects in secret prisons, or else being complicit in their mistreatment through sending questions for interrogators and receiving intelligence derived from torture (PACE 2006; EP 2007; UN 2010). It was the UK intelligence agencies, however, which appear more than any others to have been working hand-in-hand with the CIA as it operated outside the law. As such, we will outline the involvement of the UK in some more detail in the next section.

The UK's role in the CIA's RDI programme

UK authorities were not formally confronted with allegations of complicity in the CIA's global torture programme until 2005, when evidence first emerged that UK airports had been stop-off points for a series of rendition operations. UK Foreign Secretary Jack Straw appeared before the Commons Foreign Affairs Select Committee on 13 December 2005 and stated, "We know of no occasion where there has been a rendition through UK territory, or indeed over UK territory, nor do we have any reason to believe that such flights have taken place without our knowledge" (UK House of Commons Select Committee on Foreign Affairs 2005). He further stated,

> Unless we all start to believe in conspiracy theories and that the officials are lying, that I am lying, that behind this there is some kind of secret state which is in league with some dark forces in the United States, and also let me say, we believe that Secretary Rice is lying, there simply is no truth in the claims that the United Kingdom has been involved in rendition full stop, because we have not been.

Yet, through the dogged investigative work of a small number of NGOS, journalists, legal teams, and academics, it has since been revealed that the UK had quietly been providing crucial logistical support to the RDI programme from the beginning.

The UK intelligence and security agencies played a key role in ensuring that individuals considered a threat to national security were identified, located, and apprehended by the CIA and disappeared into the network of secret prisons. In one example, Bisher al-Rawi and Jamil el-Banna were held and tortured within the CIA secret detention programme after MI5 provided details to the CIA of their whereabouts and travel plans. In another example, MI6 provided the intelligence necessary to locate, capture, and render Libyan dissidents and their families to Gaddafi's Libya, where they were subsequently tortured. Abdel Hakim Belhadj (also known as Abu Abdullah al-Sadiq) and his pregnant wife, Fatima Bouchar, were rendered to Libya in early March 2004. Documents found in Tripoli after the fall of Gaddafi outline the role played by MI6, which first located Belhadj and arranged with the Libyan and American intelligence services to render Belhadj and Bouchar back to Libya. Among the documents found was a fax by MI6 to the Head of Libyan International Relations Department, informing them of Belhadj's detention (MI6 2004a).

Whilst the CIA took the lead in carrying out the rendition, the key role played by the British was summed up after the event, in a memo from Mark Allen, then Director of Counterterrorism at MI6, to his counterpart in Libya, Musa Kusa. Dated 18 March, ten days after the operation, it explicitly congratulates Kusa on the "safe arrival" of Belhadj and discusses securing direct British access to the detainee's interrogations:

> Most importantly, I congratulate you on the safe arrival of Abu Abd Allah Sadiq [Belhadj]. This was the least we could do for you and for Libya to demonstrate the remarkable relationship we have built over the years. I am so glad. I was grateful to you for helping the officer we sent out last week. Abu 'Abd Allah's information on the situation in this country is of urgent importance to us. Amusingly, we got a request from the Americans to channel requests for information from Abu 'Abd Allah through the Americans. I have no intention of doing any such thing. The intelligence on Abu 'Abd Allah was British. I know I did not pay for the air cargo. But I feel I have the right to deal with you direct on this and am very grateful for the help you are giving us.
>
> (MI6 2004b)

This involvement was clearly not an exception: still-classified documents gathered by the Detainee Inquiry make clear that UK involvement in rendition was widespread. Although the inquiry was closed before it was able to examine any case in detail, there were clearly numerous operations where ministerial approval had been received, as well as "some instances of US renditions or post-rendition liaison where the appropriateness of such involvement [by UK intelligence] may be open to question and/or where the involvement may have lacked ministerial approval" (Detainee Inquiry 2013: 34).

We now also know a great deal more about the direct role UK intelligence agents played in sharing intelligence with the CIA and the extent to which they were aware of the abuse of specific prisoners. The Detainee Inquiry identified around 200 cases in which UK involvement in, or knowledge of, mistreatment of detainees had been reported, either in documents received from the government or from other information in the public domain (Detainee Inquiry 2013: 7). The inquiry was clear that the material shows that UK intelligence officers were aware in numerous cases of "a range of treatment issues" by liaison partners. These "issues" included the use of hooding, stress positions, sleep deprivation, physical assaults, poor detention facilities, and "questionable methods of transfer between detention sites". And not only were officers aware of the mistreatment that prisoners were subjected to, but it also appears that the torture was at times "supported by locally deployed officers" (Detainee Inquiry 2013: 23).

In one case which well illustrates the collusion, an MI5 officer was granted access to the British resident, Binyam Mohamed, in May 2002, during his period of secret detention and torture in Pakistan. Mohamed was detained in Pakistan in April 2002 and subjected to severe mistreatment while held incommunicado in an ISI interrogation centre. Interrogations were conducted by US agents, while the torture came from the Pakistanis. He was "hung up for a week by a leather strap around the wrists so he could only just stand" and beaten with a leather strap. At one point, a Pakistani agent loaded a semi-automatic gun in front of Mohamed: "He pressed it against my chest. He just stood there. I knew I was going to die. He stood like that for five minutes. I looked into his eyes, and I saw my own fear reflected there. I had time to think about it. Maybe he will pull the trigger and I will not die, but be paralyzed. There was enough time to think the possibilities through" (Reprieve 2008: 6).

Before Mohamed was rendered for 18 months of further secret detention and torture in Morocco in July 2002, the MI5 officer travelled to Pakistan to conduct his own interrogation. Crucially, before he left London, the agency was clearly briefed on his mistreatment at the hands of the CIA. In a subsequent court case (*Binyam Mohamed v Secretary of State for Foreign and Commonwealth Affairs*), it was revealed that the CIA had passed at least 42 documents to MI5 before its officer travelled to Pakistan. These documents made it clear that Mohamed had been interrogated by US authorities while in Pakistani custody, during which time he had been subjected to continuous sleep deprivation, shackling, and threats of being "disappeared". The documents also made clear that this mistreatment was "having a marked effect upon him and causing him significant mental stress and suffering", and that as a consequence, he was being kept under self-harm observation. The UK High Court, having reviewed the documents, concluded that "the reports provided to [MI5] made clear to anyone reading them that BM was being subjected to the treatment that we have described and the effect upon him of that intentional treatment" and that this treatment "could readily be contended to be at the very least cruel, inhuman and degrading treatment by the United States authorities". Indeed, the court concluded, the mistreatment reported by the CIA to MI5, if it "had been administered on behalf of the United Kingdom, would clearly have been in breach of the undertakings given by the United Kingdom in 1972" (UK Royal Courts of Justice 2010).

Torture, terror, and intelligence

Within the orthodox literature on terrorism, there are those who share the view that sometimes torture, while objectionable on many levels, may nevertheless be a necessary evil (Dershowitz 2001, 2004a, 2004b; Ramsey 2006). The so-called ticking bomb scenario (see Brecher, this volume) is often deployed to argue the case from a utilitarian perspective: there may well be instances, the argument goes, where the use of torture can prevent more harm than it causes. Where a prisoner is within custody of an authority and is refusing to divulge what they know about other suspects or forthcoming plots, it may be that the use of torture will produce actionable intelligence that otherwise would not be gained through more restrained methods.

This was, indeed, the argument put forward by the CIA as it sought to both legitimise and justify its use of torture. The use of the "enhanced interrogation techniques" was saving lives, and anyone feeling queasy about the use of torture on these bad men should simply remember the carnage of 9/11. The intelligence value of torture in the war on terror has consistently been called into question, both by critical scholars (Blakeley 2011) and by official investigations. The CIA Inspector General, for example, found that interrogators frequently deviated from the guidelines set down by the Department of Justice, using methods that had not been sanctioned and using those that had been sanctioned in more prolonged and harsher ways than had been permitted. He also raised serious doubts over the use of these techniques as methods for securing accurate intelligence, concluding that there was very little evidence of useful intelligence having been secured that had any bearing on any imminent terrorism plots (OIG 2004).

The Senate investigation concurred with this assessment, finding that "the CIA's use of its enhanced interrogation techniques was not an effective means of acquiring intelligence or gaining cooperation from detainees" and that claims to the contrary "rested on inaccurate claims of their effectiveness" (SSCI 2014: 2). In fact, many prisoners were incarcerated, incommunicado, for years on end, and tortured repeatedly, simply because they were in the wrong place at the wrong time, were victims of erroneous so-called intelligence, or were sold for bounties by corrupt agents of third-party states. Others may have in reality posed a threat to US interests, but nonetheless did not produce accurate intelligence under torture, instead telling interrogators what they thought they wanted to hear.

Indeed, an analysis of how suspects were treated whilst in secret detention demonstrates that acquiring intelligence was not the only driver for the torture programme. Time and again, prisoners were treated to a regime of abuse unconnected to any attempts to secure intelligence. Instilling a sense of fear and helplessness in those held by the CIA was an explicit objective of the programme, as achieved through a relentless control over prisoners' bodies, environment, and treatment. The secret nature of the detention was itself a form of torture, designed to instil fear amongst those held within it and those on the outside who were witness to the enforced disappearances of their family and friends. It was, overall, a system of terror, perpetrated by the world's most powerful state acting in conjunction with other governments from around the world.

Conclusion

As evidence that the US had condoned torture as part of the war on terror emerged, a number of scholars that take a more critical approach to terrorism have paid close attention to the use of torture and its justifications (see, for example, Bellamy 2006; Blakeley 2007, 2011; Brecher, this volume; MacMaster 2004). A number of critical scholars have also offered detailed analyses of the ways in which certain discourses around terror suspects have served to dehumanise specific individuals, thereby opening up the possibility that treating them inhumanely can be justified (see Devetak 2005; Jackson 2005, 2007a, 2007b). This literature is extremely instructive for understanding how elites constructed particular discourses that lent themselves to both the overt and covert ways in which the human rights of terror suspects were being eroded.

Our work has developed in parallel with these critiques and has begun to scope out an alternative, complementary research agenda. Through *The Rendition Project* we have begun to map the CIA's rendition programme in granular detail, building large, robust datasets and utilising a range of investigative techniques to uncover the precise nature of the torture programme. Working closely with a range of investigators, we have been able to build a much more comprehensive picture of the workings of a major campaign of contemporary state terror. In short, we have been able to advance understanding of the RDI programme by mapping many of the human rights violations which took place. This is important, as we have been able to provide evidentiary support for those seeking redress through the international justice system (for example, ECtHR 2012, para 156–165; 2014, para 405–15).

This research effort points a way to potential future directions for scholars working within critical terrorism studies (CTS) which will complement the valuable focus on critiquing discursive representations. Detailed empirical research, necessitating the use of innovative investigative methods and collaboration with those outside the academy, can help us to understand how states and allied forces employ terrorism as a central policy tool, albeit whilst simultaneously parading their actions as legitimate counterterrorism efforts. This will be an important focus moving forward and will help the field develop its role in uncovering and understanding how state terrorism manifests in the contemporary world.

References

Amnesty International (AI), 2006. *Below the Radar: Secret Flights to Torture and "Disappearance"*. Available online at: <www.therenditionproject.org.uk/pdf/PDF%2030%20[AI-2006–04-REP%20Below%20the%20Radar].pdf>.

Bellamy, A., 2006. "No Pain, No Gain? Torture and Ethics in the War on Terror", *International Affairs,* 82(1): 121–48.

Blakeley, R., 2007. "Why Torture?", *Review of International Studies,* 33(3): 373–94.

Blakeley, R., 2011. "Dirty Hands, Clean Conscience? The CIA Inspector General's Investigation of 'Enhanced Interrogation Techniques' in the 'War on Terror' and the Torture Debate", *Journal of Human Rights,* 10(4): 544–61.

Bush, G., 2001. The White House, Executive Order: Detention, Treatment, and Trial of Certain Non-Citizens in the War Against Terrorism, *Federal Register,* 66(2): 57831–36.

Bush, G., 2002. The White House: Memorandum for the Vice President, The Secretary of State, the Secretary of Defense, The Attorney General, Chief of Staff to the President, Director of Central Intelligence, Assistant to the President for National Security Affairs, and Chairman of the Joint Chiefs of Staff: *Humane Treatment of Al Qaeda and Taliban Detainees,* 7 February. Available online at: <www.torturingdemocracy.org/documents/20020207–2.pdf>.

Cole, M., and Ross, B., 2009. "Exclusive: CIA Secret 'Torture' Prison Found at Fancy Horseback Riding Academy", *ABC News,* 18 November.

CSND, 2009. *Findings of the Parliamentary Investigation by the Seimas Committee on National Security and Defence Concerning the Alleged Transportation and Confinement of Persons Detained by the Central Intelligence Agency of the United States of America in the Territory of the Republic of Lithuania,* Annex to the Resolution of the Seimas of the Republic of Lithuania, 22 December. Available online at: <www.therenditionproject.org.uk/documents/RDI/091222-CNSD- Findings_Rendition_and_Detention_in_Lithuania.pdf>.

Day, M., 2012. "CIA 'Ordered Cage to Hold Prisoners in Poland'", *The Telegraph,* 20 June.

Dershowitz, A., 2001. "Is There a Torturous Road to Justice?", *Los Angeles Times,* 8 November, sec. Part 2 p. 19.

Dershowitz, A., 2004a. "Tortured Reasoning", in Levinson, S., ed., *Torture, A Collection,* Oxford: Oxford University Press, pp. 257–80.

Dershowitz, A., 2004b. "The Torture Warrant: A Response to Professor Strauss", *New York Law School Law Review,* 48(1–2): 275–94.

Detainee Inquiry, 2013. *The Report of the Detainee Inquiry*, London: HMSO.

Devetak, R., 2005. "The Gothic Sense of International Relations: Ghosts, Monsters, Terror and the Sublime after September 11", *Review of International Studies,* 31(4): 621–43.

European Court of Human Rights (ECtHR), 2012. *Judgement: Case of el-Masri v. The Former Yugoslav Republic of Macedonia,* Application no. 39630/09, Strasbourg, 13 December.

European Court of Human Rights (ECtHR), 2014. *Judgment: Case of Husayn (Abu Zubaydah) v. Poland,* Application no. 7511/13, Strasbourg, 24 July.

European Parliament (EP), 2007. *European Parliament Report on the Alleged Use of European Countries by the CIA for the Transportation and Illegal Detention of Prisoners,* Document No: 2006/2200(INI) [A-0020/2007], 30 January. Available online at: <www.europarl.europa.eu/sides/getDoc.do?pubRef=-//EP//NONSGML+REPORT+A6-2007–0020+0+DOC+PDF+V0//EN>.

Goldman, A., 2014. "The Hidden History of the CIA's Prison in Poland", *The Washington Post,* 23 January. Available online at: <www.washingtonpost.com/world/national-security/the-hidden-history-of-the-cias-prison-in-poland/2014/01/23/b77f6ea2=7c6f-11e3-95c6-0a7aa80874bc_story.html>.

Grey, S., 2004. "US Accused of 'Torture Flights'", *Sunday Times,* 14 November.

Jackson, R., 2005. *Writing the War on Terrorism. Language, Politics and Counter-Terrorism*, Manchester: Manchester University Press.

Jackson, R., 2007a. "Language, Policy, and the Construction of a Torture Culture in the War on Terrorism", *Review of International Studies,* 33(3): 353–71.

Jackson, R., 2007b. "Constructing Enemies: 'Islamic Terrorism' in Political and Academic Discourse", *Government and Opposition,* 42(3): 394–426.

Johnston, D., and Mazzetti, M., 2009. "A Window into CIA's Embrace of Secret Jails", *New York Times,* 12 August.

MacMaster, N., 2004. "Torture: From Algiers to Abu Ghraib", *Race and Class,* 46(2): 1–21.

MI6, 2004a. "'Abdullah Sadeq', Memo to al-Sadiq Karima, Head of Libyan International Relations Department", 1 March.

MI6, 2004b. "'For the Urgent Personal Attention of Musa Kusa, Department of International Relations and Collaboration', Memo", 18 March 2004.

Office of the Inspector General of the CIA (OIG), 2004. *Special Review: Counterterrorism Detention and Interrogation Activities (September 2001–October 2003)*, 7 May. Available online at: <www.therenditionproject.org.uk/pdf/PDF%2020%20[CIA%20IG%20Investigation%20EITs%202004].pdf>.

Parliamentary Assembly of the Council of Europe (PACE), 2006. *Alleged Secret Detentions and Unlawful Inter-State Transfers Involving Council of Europe Member States*, 12 June. Available online at: <www.therendition-project.org.uk/pdf/PDF%2068%20[EP-MEM-2006–06%20Alleged%20Secret%20Detentions].pdf>.

Ramsey, M., 2006. "Can the Torture of Terrorist Suspects be Justified?", *The International Journal of Human Rights,* 10(2): 103–19.

Raphael, S., Black, C., Blakeley, R., and Kostas, S., 2016. "Tracking Rendition Aircraft as a Way to Understand CIA Secret Detention and Torture in Europe", *International Journal of Human Rights,* 20(1): 78–103.

Reprieve, 2008. *"Human Cargo": Binyam Mohamed and the Rendition Frequent Flier Programme,* 10 June.

Shane, S., Grey, S., and Williams, M., 2005. "CIA Expanding Terror Battle Under Guise of Charter Flights", *New York Times,* 31 May. Available online at: <www.nytimes.com/2005/05/31/national/31planes.html?pagewanted=all&_r=2&>.

Senate Select Committee for Intelligence (SSCI), 2014. *Committee Study of the Central Intelligence Agency's Detention and Interrogation Program,* Declassified Executive Summary, 3 December.

UK House of Commons Select Committee on Foreign Affairs, 2005. *Examination of Witnesses* (Questions 20–51), 13 December. Available online at: <www.publications.parliament.uk/pa/cm200506/cmselect/cmfaff/uc768-i/uc76802.htm>.

UK Royal Courts of Justice, 2010. *R(b Mohamed) v Foreign Secretary,* Court of Appeal Judgement, (Case No: T1/2009/2331), London, 26 February. Available online at: <www.5rb.com/wp-content/uploads/2013/10/R-Mohamed-v-Secretary-of-State-No-2-2010-EWCA-Civ-158.pdf>.

UN, 2010. "Joint Study on Global Practices in Relation to Secret Detention in the Context of Countering Terrorism", A/HRC/13/42, New York, 20 May. Available online at: <www.unhcr.org/refworld/pdfid/4d8720092.pdf>.

Weissman, D., 2012. *The North Carolina Connection to Extraordinary Rendition and Torture,* University of North Carolina School of Law, January 2012. Available online at: <www.therenditionproject.org.uk/documents/RDI/120100-UNC-North_Carolina_Connection.pdf>.

18
TARGETED KILLING AND DRONE WARFARE

Laurie Calhoun

The question of legality and human rights in drone warfare

The controversy surrounding the use of unmanned combat aerial vehicles (UCAVs), or lethal drones, stems in large part from fundamental disagreements over the very nature of remote-control killing, which is new in human history. Never before was it possible for soldiers to fight wars without themselves facing the prospect of personal sacrifice. Those who believe that remote-control killing is a perfectly legitimate act of war and an important counterterrorism tactic praise the practice for preserving innocent life and minimizing collateral damage, while sparing allied soldiers the risk of physical harm. The most vocal advocates of drone warfare have maintained that targeted killing is the best – or even the only – available means for fighting the number one enemy in the twenty-first century: shadowy and fluid terrorist groups such as al Qaeda, Al-Shabaab, and ISIS (Porter 2010; Bowden 2013; Byman 2013).

The governments of both the United States and Israel have openly used lethal drones in combating their perceived enemies, and other states now in the process of acquiring this technology can be expected to follow suit, under the assumption that lethal drones merely extend the warrior's arm and therefore pose no new or special legal challenges. According to Article 51 of the *Charter of the United Nations* (1945), states have a right to use military force in self-defense, and this has been the primary line of justification offered by those who insist that drone warfare is legitimate and legal under international law (Carvin 2012: 172). Some authors have gone so far as to claim that a moratorium on targeted killing would entail a commitment to pacifism – the abolition of war, *tout court* (Statman 2005). The sense that remote-control killers differ only in distance, not in kind, from conventional combat pilots or snipers on the battlefield appears to be widely shared by military supporters. *If a soldier can fire a missile from a plane flying above a territory, then why not from a trailer in Nevada?*

One notable distinction between a drone operator killing by remote control from thousands of miles away and a combat pilot dropping bombs onto enemy soldiers located thousands of feet below his aircraft is that the drone operator cannot be said to be defending his life through launching a missile, since his target could not possibly harm him, having no idea who or where he is. Critics have observed that removing risk from one side of the war equation fundamentally transforms the act of homicide, for drone operators are not faced with the choice *kill or be killed*. They cannot, therefore, be said to be engaged in *literal* self-defense when they direct Hellfire missiles to destroy human targets located on the other side of the world (Riza 2013).

The "self-defense" pretext for remote-control killing in places where there are no soldiers on the ground to protect is said by drone advocates to apply to the nation from which the killers hail, not the killers themselves – at least not immediately so. In this view, advanced in the Obama administration's White Paper, the danger posed by targeted suspects is still "imminent" but not necessarily "immediate" (US Department of Justice 2010). However, drone killing as currently practiced aims at the death of human beings, not merely the neutralization of an imminent threat, as becomes evident in the grisly "double tap" strikes wherein already wounded persons are fired on a second time to ensure their annihilation. In the most disturbing of these cases, first-responders attempting to help wounded victims have been killed in the follow-up strikes, raising concerns that the actions may constitute full-fledged war crimes (Shane 2012).

Antiwar activists who oppose the targeted killing of suspects in places such as Pakistan and Yemen have traveled to drone strike sites and reported on civilian casualties and effects on communities to bolster their critiques, but they reject the practice first and foremost on deontological grounds: that the positive intention to destroy a human being marks this form of homicide as equivalent to murder (Benjamin 2013). "Double tap" strike evidence suggests that in lands where there are no US soldiers on the ground for the targets to harm, the fact that they cannot easily be taken prisoner is paradoxically regarded as a reason to liquidate even wounded suspects. A number of scholars have expressed concern that drone strikes may violate the *jus in bello* requirements of just war theory (Enemark 2013).

The most basic rules of engagement (ROE) of uniformed soldiers on the ground appear to be altogether ignored in remote-control killing, for the persons targeted are often unarmed and not directly threatening anyone with harm. US administrators have persisted in claiming that they kill targets only when capture is "infeasible", but the unarmed Osama bin Laden was shot to death rather than taken prisoner on May 2, 2011. US citizen Anwar al-Awlaki was released from prison – having been held without charges in Yemen at the US government's request – before being hunted down and slain on September 30, 2011 (Gardner 2013; Scahill 2013).

Given this quest to terminate lives, rather than simply neutralize threats, the letter of international law alone as it stands today may not be quite enough for advocates of targeted killing. Further linguistic maneuvering is needed, for the persons obliterated by drone strikes are neither warned that they have been deemed combatants on a battlefield nor provided with the opportunity to lay down their arms, as would be required in a war governed by the Geneva Conventions. Some scholars, pointing out that international agreements and protocols must take into consideration current realities, have argued for a revision of "the rules" so as to accommodate remote-control killing (Brunstetter and Braun 2011; Mallette-Piasecki 2012/2013; Strawser 2013). Others maintain that drone warfare is not incompatible with protocols grounded in the just war tradition (Orr 2011).

The Bush administration construed al Qaeda members as *unlawful combatants* who do not enjoy the protections of international protocols, which were forged by states and therefore apply only to regular soldiers. The Obama administration followed suit, insisting that its drone campaigns comply fully with the requirements of law. The White Paper reiterated the Bush stance on the preemptive use of deadly force and inverted the burden of proof on suspects as follows: "The US government may not be aware of all al-Qa'ida plots as they are developing and thus cannot be confident that none is about to occur" (US Department of Justice 2010). But the fact that the US government refused for years to acknowledge the very existence of its Predator drone program suggests that remote-control killing was initially conceived of as covert action, not warfare.

Under Obama, the CIA, a civilian (nonmilitary) organization, assisted by a number of associated private contractors, was given free rein to designate persons to be dispatched as a part of the ongoing war against violent extremists. Before the advent of remote-control technology, the hunting down and killing of individual persons far from formally declared battlefields was carried out in covert black ops by deniable agents acting under assumed names precisely because the practice – *assassination* or *extrajudicial execution* – was understood to be illegal, prohibited by both domestic and international law, including Article 23b of the Hague Regulations (Alston 2010; Fisher 2010; O'Connell 2010; Heyns 2013). When spies who had been enlisted to eliminate enemies in other parts of the world were apprehended by the government of the country in which they killed, they were charged with murder (Weiner 2007; Geraghty 2009, 2010). The question, then, arises: how can merely switching the implement of death from a gun or poison or a strangulation wire to a UCAV change the legality of an act of premeditated homicide?

Some defenders of drone warfare insist that targeted killing on a battlefield is not tantamount to assassination in a peacetime setting. Others regard the two labels as interchangeable but then proceed to argue that the ban on assassination should be formally lifted, or that it simply does not apply when "we are at war" (Kaufman 2007; White 2012:97–8). Treachery is said by some to mark the distinction between assassination and targeted killing (Yoo 2011/12; Vlasic 2012). However, it is unclear whether *treachery* differs intrinsically from *secrecy* when the objective in question is the annihilation of a person rather than the neutralization of a threat. "State Secrets Privilege" is often cited as essential to the protection of intelligence assets working in the field and to ensure that missions in the planning stages will not be undermined by leaking out crucial information in advance of strikes. Perhaps it is supposed to be conceptually impossible to act treacherously in the case of terrorist suspects, against whom administrators appear to believe that "everything is permitted."

The Obama administration, like its predecessor, has traded on ambiguities between military missions and fighting crime, painting alleged terrorists or militants as combatants in some contexts and criminals in others, while withholding the evidential basis for execution even after the target's death has been acknowledged, as in the case of Anwar Al-Awlaki (Addicott 2012; Savage 2014). The perpetrators cannot, however, have it both ways. If the persons being targeted are suspected of crimes, then Article 11, the "innocent until proven guilty" clause of the Universal Declaration of Human Rights (1948) applies, and the suspects should be provided with the opportunity to defend themselves in a court of law. If the targets are truly combatants, then they must be actively engaged in hostilities in order to be lawfully killed. Instead, the persons slain – both the innocent and the guilty – have been systematically stripped of all rights under both international and domestic law. US officials have decreed drone zones to be battlefields in order to broaden their license to kill dangerous terrorists, but they have in the process waged a frontal assault on universal human rights. The designation of civilian-inhabited areas as "battlefields" is presumed to transform what would be manslaughter into innocuous "collateral damage" whenever innocent bystanders or suspects targeted on the basis of faulty intelligence are destroyed.

Moral problems unique to drone warfare

State security-focused theorists, who are generally of a hawkish bent, unsurprisingly tend to support remote-control killing, which they deem to be a legitimate military tool. Human security-focused theorists, human rights activists and civil libertarians have been far more critical of the practice. All of the moral wrongs and injustices which arise in warfare more generally arise in the case of drone warfare in particular, including the tragic plight of collateral damage victims, who are essentially punished for other people's crimes whenever they are killed by military munitions (Calhoun 2013: 87–103).

A technology capable of taking soldiers completely out of harm's way while making "surgical strikes" against "evil enemies" may sound like a military dream come true. In reality, the diminished risk to drone operators of their lethal actions (relative to the soldiers of centuries past) is fully paid for by an increase in risk – both physical and psychological – to the people on the ground, most of whom are not terrorists but merely live where they happen to live. The physical risks formerly assumed by warriors are effectively transferred to the innocent persons unfortunate enough to inhabit what have been identified as "hostile" territories or "battlefields" by analysts. Advocates of remote-control killing claim that drones keep collateral damage to a minimum. However, the practice has dramatically widened the *domain* for collateral damage because the killers have asserted the right to target terrorists wherever they may be said to hide. The drone strikes in Pakistan began under George W. Bush as an effort to track down and kill insurgents fleeing from Afghanistan, but eventually the northwestern part of Pakistan came to be regarded as a battlefield unto itself, with the Federally Administered Tribal Areas (FATA), the homeland of hundreds of thousands of civilians, being a primary CIA targeting site (Amnesty International 2013).

Following in the longstanding just war tradition according to which collateral damage is both unavoidable and morally permitted, US officials generally omit the deaths of innocent victims in reports of "successful" strikes against "militants", "insurgents", and their "associates". These reports have been uncritically digested, replicated, and disseminated by mainstream journalists and other authors who fail to process the significance of the fact that the persons who provide the actionable intelligence on the ground used to finger targets also report back after the strikes (see Williams 2013 for one example of this replication of "the official story" in what is claimed to be "knowledge"). In a "successful" strike, a person identified by an informant as perilous has been slain, but this is then depicted by the media as the death of a terrorist or militant, not a suspect. In this way, the secretive use of lethal drones to summarily execute suspects has arguably abraded some of the most cherished and fundamental principles of Western democratic states: due process and transparency. The persons intentionally slain are effectively "convicted" in the public eye through state execution.

Anti-drone activists have cried foul in many cases where the CIA reportedly destroyed enclaves of terrorists with nefarious schemes in the works, but later fact-finding missions revealed death tolls including significant numbers of obviously innocent women and children, in addition to men with no ties to terrorist groups (CIVIC 2010; Amnesty International 2013; Human Rights Watch 2013). Despite Obama's vociferous opposition to the 2003 invasion of Iraq as a "stupid war", his targeted killing campaigns in unoccupied lands can be understood as micro-preemptive war with reflections in Iraq. Lethal habits formed in that vexed postwar context were transferred to other places where war had never been waged, not even on dubious grounds. Under George W. Bush, thousands of terrorist suspects were either herded away to secret prisons and subjected to torture or else "met a different fate", as the president exultantly described extrajudicial execution during his 2003 State of the Union Address (BBC News 2003). The rallying call to deploy drones in what might be termed "battlefields without borders" was reiterated by President Obama during his public address in support of military action against ISIL (the Islamic State in Iraq and the Levant, also known as ISIS) in Syria: "I have made it clear that we will hunt down terrorists who threaten our country, wherever they are" (Obama 2014).

The steady stream of disturbing reports on the harm caused by drones to civilians on the ground has not deterred those in charge of the CIA's targeted killing operations, including the director appointed in 2013, John Brennan, from doggedly insisting that collateral damage is next to nonexistent in these actions. A key reason for the disparity in the number of civilian casualties reported by the killers and their critics emerged in 2012: military-age males (between 16 and 50) located in areas designated hostile were defined by drone program administrators as unlawful combatants and therefore suitable targets (Becker and Shane 2012). One illuminating study by the UK human rights group Reprieve analyzes the number of people killed in multiple strikes intended to eliminate 41 suspected terrorists but which culminated in the deaths of 1,147 persons, most of whom were unnamed (Ackerman 2014).

Concern has been aired that drone killing is "unreal" or "surreal" and becomes even trivial to the killers, as it is empirically indistinguishable from playing a video game using a computer and joystick to fire at icons on a screen (Cole, Dobbing, and Hailwood 2010). One surprise in the Drone Age is that the operators, who are sequestered far away from the bloody fray, may nonetheless develop post-traumatic stress disorder (PTSD) and abandon the lucrative profession (Martin 2011). This development suggests that, more than fear of death, guilt for wrongful killing weighs heavily upon the consciences of some of the persons enlisted to execute suspects by remote control (Abé 2012; Engel 2013).

Operators and analysts troubled by what they have done renounce their positions, leaving only enthusiasts behind to rise in the ranks and perpetuate the practice in which they have already participated. Such dynamics of institutional conservatism were arguably in play during the transfer of power from Bush to Obama, when resident advisers naturally sought to promote to the new president the use of lethal drones, touted by former CIA director Leon Panetta as "the only game in town" for dealing with al Qaeda (Porter 2010). With such directors in charge, no one opposed to drone warfare will find employment with the agency, ensuring that the proverbial range of "options on the table" remains focused on lethality to the exclusion of other approaches to conflict resolution.

Structurally speaking, targeted killing bears some similarities to paid contract killing by hitmen, who, like drone operators, stalk and observe their targets over a period of time before striking without warning. In both drone strikes and contract killing, the victim is denied any right to surrender or appeal and poses no direct physical threat to his killer. In both drone strikes and contract killing, the person wielding deadly force is financially compensated for his willingness to dispatch another human being at the request of somebody else, for reasons which the killer is not permitted to second guess. The distinction between a Mafia boss and the president of a nation calling for the death of a human being, as Obama did in the case of US citizen Anwar al-Awlaki, begins to fade when the political leader declines to make use of the robust institutions available to him for the apprehension and indictment of citizens suspected of crimes (Calhoun 2015: Chapter 3).

Civil rights advocates and libertarians balked when Obama ordered the summary execution of a US citizen, observing that, if suspected of treason, then Al-Awlaki should have been indicted and made to stand trial (Titus and Olson 2013). The burden of proof enshrined in both US criminal law and Article 11 of the Universal Declaration of Human Rights (1948) is inverted in drone strikes, with suspects presumed guilty until proven innocent. Yet the persons targeted are systematically denied even the right to demonstrate their innocence, for they are neither indicted nor warned of their imminent demise. Many Americans nonetheless accepted the administration's characterization of Al-Awlaki as a traitor and have been largely supportive of any initiative which can be said to "take the battle to the enemy", whoever he may be and wherever he may reside.

In considering the harm done to innocent persons by lethal drones, focusing only on noncombatant death tolls obscures the more fundamental moral question whether any human being should ever be subjected to the specter of terrifying "death machines" hovering above in the sky, a concern pressed by anti-drone and human rights groups. In areas where informants on the ground select targets for execution, entire communities come under siege, as inhabitants avoid interacting with one another or assembling for fear of being mistaken as terrorists or their associates. Exacerbating the already deplorable security conditions in drone zones, in the aftermath of strikes, angry militants have tortured and executed persons suspected of being informants (Rohde and Mulvihill 2010).

Rival views of drone warfare efficacy

There is no question that lethal drones are extraordinarily effective at slaughtering human beings. Critics of this tactical means of dealing with violent extremists, facetiously termed by some a "whack-a-mole" approach, have observed that the incidence of global terrorism increased markedly in the years following the 2003 invasion of Iraq and that groups such as ISIS did not even exist until the US government began targeting Muslims in their own lands (Bergen and Cruickshank 2007). These developments suggest that remote-control killing may inspire more angry locals to take up jihad than it stops plots already underway (Johnsen 2013:143). Factions critical of what they characterize as US military hegemony can be expected to continue to follow Osama bin Laden's lead, garnering support by pointing to what they regard as US war crimes (BBC News 2001).

The efficacy of lethal measures in contending with terrorist groups is impugned by a 2008 RAND study according to which only 7 percent of the 648 terrorist groups studied were neutralized through the use of military force (Jones and Libicki 2008). The strategic efficacy of drone warfare, in particular, has been called into question by The Stimson Report (2014), issued by a US government-commissioned task force, which concludes that without proper transparency regarding outcomes and procedures used in drone strikes, the targeted killing program risks undermining US security (Stimson Task Force 2014).

One of the major recommendations of the Stimson Report is to remove lethal drones from CIA control, on the grounds that they are military weapons and should be wielded by military personnel, not civilian intelligence agents, who in this capacity look not unlike the asymmetrical, irregular, "unlawful combatants" they are targeting. Staunch opponents to remote-control killing in territories christened "battlefields" by the killers themselves argue that the CIA's drone campaigns, like its discredited program of rendition and torture (see Blakeley and Raphael, this volume), are both intrinsically wrong and strategically counterproductive, ultimately imperiling the very citizens who pay for it, though this will emerge only later, in blowback (Shane 2014; The Guardian 2014).

An oft-rehearsed rhetorical refrain by US officials is that drone strikes have saved lives. But there is no hard data to support this claim, for the details of these cases – the plots supposedly foiled – are not shared with the public. Furthermore, empirical studies have found in various historical contexts (including the Palestinians in Israel, the IRA in Ireland, and the ETA in Spain) that the tactical use of targeted killing has not decreased the number of terrorist attacks by the groups under fire (Silke 2012: 179). Even a more simplistic measure of success, such as the "dead terrorist tally", needs to be scrutinized, given that reports of "successful strikes" are based on the confirmation by paid informants on the ground that terrorists have been slain with "surgical" precision. When it emerged that in early 2015 two Western hostages had been taken out by Predator drone along with persons presumed to be terrorists because they were located in what was considered to be a place frequented by terrorists, the world was made acutely aware of just how far the drone program administrators are from knowing the identities of the targets being killed in the name of national defense (Lewis, Ackerman, and Boone 2015).

Further cause for skepticism about the effectiveness of drone warfare is that the very same sorts of "actionable intelligence" (often acquired through bribery) used in drone strikes were used in the Bush administration's rendering of suspects to secret prisons in torture-friendly countries. A sizable percentage of those detainees are now acknowledged to have been entirely innocent (Shane 2014). Most of the prisoners in Guantánamo Bay, too, were eventually cleared for release, having been swept up and spirited away for being in the wrong place at the wrong time. It therefore seems reasonable to infer that approximately the same percentage of the men intentionally destroyed by Hellfire missiles have been innocent of any wrongdoing, above all in "crowd killing" and "signature strikes", where unnamed persons are executed on the basis of their apparent association with other suspects and their "pattern of life movements" said to reflect a "disposition matrix" of typical terrorist behavior (Miller 2012).

All sources of "actionable intelligence" in these cases, HUMINT (from paid informants on the ground) and SIGINT (from video footage transmitted by drones or from cellphone SIM card analysis), are both fallible and corruptible. Drone operators have no means by which to assess the value of the intelligence provided to them and furthermore labor under a confirmation bias, having been told that the areas which they monitor are sites of suspicious activity. Tragically, analysts and operators may misinterpret civilian events such as jirgas, weddings, and even funerals as terrorist gatherings, as has happened on a disturbing number of occasions, with the slaughter of sometimes dozens of innocent people and the devastation of entire communities (Engelhardt 2013).

Politicians and the populace alike remain oblivious to the fact that the longer-range effects of short-term tactics may be much worse than having done nothing at all. Throughout his two-term presidency, Obama has repeatedly recited the "no boots on the ground" slogan as a way of drumming up support for a variety of lethal missions abroad in which drones have played key roles. When those missions have failed, as in Iraq, Afghanistan, Libya, Somalia (where the US government supported the 2006 Ethiopian invasion), and Yemen, the postwar anomie has been written off to other causes and ascribed vaguely to "the evil enemy", whose existence is then, in turn, adduced as a pretext for further military engagement abroad.

Political implications and future areas of research

The very first publicly acknowledged drone strike by the CIA, in Yemen on November 3, 2002, was permitted by President Saleh on the condition that a cover story be used to mask the US application of lethal force on sovereign Yemen soil (Johnsen 2013: 123; Scahill 2013: 17). Praised as the November 2002 action in Yemen was by pundits and politicians, and largely unquestioned by a citizenry traumatized by the terrorist attacks of September 11, 2001, the strike proved to be both a technological and a public relations success in the United States. Thereafter, drone killing became more and more frequent, although the practice was not publicly acknowledged again until 2012, by President Barack Obama himself, who upon assuming office in 2009 had authorized a wide-ranging and secretive drone campaign conducted by the CIA (Hastings 2012).

A combination of factors no doubt contributed to Obama's decision to expand the targeted killing program in what some have termed a policy of "kill don't capture". In addition to having to contend with the political difficulty of housing detainees and mounting criminal trials in US voting jurisdictions, Obama was said to favor a "light footprint" approach to foreign policy, having promised voters that he would avoid embroiling the nation in full-scale military invasions such as Bush's war on Iraq (Klaidman 2012).

To date, the drone killing of suspects has been carried out not in Western democratic states (at least not overtly), but primarily in places where either the central government authority has granted permission to the US government to operate (as in Yemen, Pakistan, and postwar Afghanistan and

Iraq), or in anomic contexts such as Somalia and post-Gaddafi Libya. Notably, when the *Charlie Hebdo* newspaper office in Paris was attacked by a group of Islamist militants on January 7, 2015, the French government, which had used drones in Mali, did not respond by sending lethal drones out to strike Paris banlieues known to house Muslim males from the ages of 16 to 50.

Journalists in "hostile" areas are often males of military age and become fair game for attack according to the same sweeping criterion, underscoring how fundamental the issues raised by the US government's use of weaponized drones really are. Simply getting the facts on casualties straight has been a daunting task given the omnipresent danger of drones ready to prey on adult males in remote regions. Tyrants are well known for suppressing dissent by stamping out critics, but freedom of speech is championed, at least nominally, by the US government. "The victors write history" is an age-old war-time cliché, but in the Drone Age, it takes on a new and frightening meaning, when the killers act as the police, the judges, the jurors, the executioners, and the historians of their own acts of homicide perpetrated far from the homeland of the people presumably being protected.

By arming despotic leaders, the US government has suppressed calls for democratic reform in the process of rooting out insurgents who may or may not ever have set their sights on the United States (Ahmed 2013). In Yemen, the central government authority continued to collaborate with the US drone warriors until President Abdu Rabu Mansour Hadi was deposed by a coup mounted by angry dissidents in 2015 (McDonnell and Bulos 2015). This development raises the question whether the use of drones does not in fact destabilize lands by galvanizing support for groups opposed to petty despots willing to bow to US demands in exchange for military aid. The seemingly intractable conflict in Israel, where targeted killing has gained favor as a means of contending with suspected Palestinian terrorists, offers another cause for pause. Figures such as Osama bin Laden and his associates have been depicted by officials and pundits as larger-than-life bogeymen akin to Adolf Hitler, but factional terrorism is not new to the twenty-first century. The "new enemies" are not really so new, only the technology being used to deal with them.

Critical counterterrorism scholars are apt to reject the Manichean division of allies and enemies into absolute categories of good and evil, having appreciated the force of the adage "one man's terrorist is another man's freedom fighter" (Jackson 2014). Insurgents, partisans, and violent dissenters – who of necessity deploy innovative tactics, including terrorism, to combat their adversaries, lacking as they do standard military means – have emerged in many historical contexts. Before the Drone Age, dissidents who acted in violation of domestic law were primarily dealt with using methods of criminal investigation and prosecution. When in rare instances segregationist movements have succeeded in securing political aims, as in Ireland, Kosovo, and South Sudan, new nations came into being.

Twenty-first century "terrorists" – lumped together into a monolithic category and vehemently denounced by state officials as incorrigibly evil and worthy of annihilation – have in some cases been not so different from the partisans in Vichy France under German occupation. Most notably, many of the insurgents in Iraq, a country invaded by a foreign aggressor in 2003, may have viewed themselves as acting in self-defense when they rose up against the illegal occupiers of their land (BBC News 2004). The widespread and concerted use of drone killing to dispatch "militants" broadly construed would cement political reality as it stands, making it impossible for smaller factions to rise up against oppressive regimes, as has happened throughout history when new nations, including the United States, were formed.

Great champions of peace such as Nelson Mandela, who was imprisoned as a young man while protesting in a "hostile" territory, might have been wiped out by a drone, had the technology existed at the time. Societies have progressed over the course of history only as a result of the willingness of courageous dissidents to stand up to the powers that be. The current drone program perpetrated by the US government threatens the very possibility of fundamental political change. No less troubling is that most of the persons being annihilated in tribal regions are of Arab origin. "Signature strikes", which destroy groups of unnamed persons pegged as suspicious by paid analysts, bear similarities to racial profiling. Extended to its logical limit, the use of such profiling in selecting targets for elimination could culminate in genocide under some political leaders (Calhoun 2015: Chapter 6).

Even if one accepts that rigorous standards (albeit opaque) are in place, little if any attention appears to have been given to the potential for remote-control killing capacity in the hands of government leaders less scrupulous than those of the United States. The global impact of the precedent set by Presidents Bush and Obama in promoting and spreading the use of targeted killing as a way of contending with political conflict will emerge only later on down the line. By 2015, the exportation of lethal drones to current allies by US manufacturers was well underway (Dickinson 2015).

References

Abé, N., 2012. "Dreams in Infrared: The Woes of an American Drone Operator," *Spiegel Online International*, December 14.
Ackerman, S., 2014. "41 Men Targeted but 1147 Killed: US Drone Strikes – the Facts on the Ground," *The Guardian*, November 24.
Addicott, J., 2012. "Rightly Dividing the Domestic Jihadist from the Enemy Combatant in the 'War Against al Qaeda' – Why It Matters in Rendition and Targeted Killing," *Case Western Reserve Journal of International Law*, 45: 259–302.
Ahmed, A., 2013. *The Thistle and the Drone: How America's War on Terror Became a Global War on Tribal Islam*. Washington, DC: The Brookings Institute Press.
Alston, P., 2010. "Report of the Special Rapporteur on Extrajudicial, Summary or Arbitrary Executions," United Nations General Assembly Human Rights Council, May 28.
Amnesty International, 2013. "*Will I Be Next?' US Drone Strikes in Pakistan*," October report. London: Amnesty International Publications.
BBC News, 2001. "Bin Laden's Warning: Full Text," October 7.
BBC News, 2003. "State of the Union Address: Full Text," January 29.
BBC News, 2004. "Iraq War Illegal, Says Annan," September 16.
Becker, J., and Shane, S., 2012. "Secret 'Kill List' Proves a Test of Obama's Principles and Will," *New York Times*, May 29.
Benjamin, M., 2013. *Drone Warfare: Killing by Remote Control*. New York: Verso.
Bergen, P., and Cruickshank, P., 2007. "The Iraq Effect: War Has Increased Terrorism Sevenfold Worldwide," *Mother Jones*, March/April 2007.
Bowden, M., 2013. "The Killing Machines: How to Think About Drones," *The Atlantic*, September: 58–70.
Brunstetter, D., and Braun, M., 2011. "The Implications of Drones on the Just War Tradition," *Ethics & International Affairs*, 25(3): 337–358.
Byman, D., 2013. "Why Drones Work: The Case for Washington's Weapon of Choice," *Foreign Affairs*, July/August: 32–43.
Calhoun, L., 2013. *War and Delusion: A Critical Examination*. New York: Palgrave Macmillan.
Calhoun, L., 2015. *We Kill Because We Can: From Soldiering to Assassination in the Drone Age*. London: Zed Books.
Carvin, S., 2012. "Is the Targeted Assassination of Terrorist Suspects an Effective Response to Terrorism? Yes: A Viable and Vital Policy Option," in Jackson, R., and Sinclair, S., eds., *Contemporary Debates on Terrorism*, London and New York: Routledge, pp. 166–173.
Center for Civilians in Conflict (CIVIC), 2010. "Civilians in Armed Conflict: Civilian Harm and Conflict in Northwest Pakistan," October report.
Cole, C., Dobbing, M., and Hailwood, A., 2010. "Convenient Killing: Armed Drones and the 'Playstation' Mentality," Report, The Fellowship of Reconciliation (Oxford).
Dickinson, E., 2015. "Business Is Booming at Abu Dhabi's Great Arms Bazaar," *Foreign Policy*, March 5.
Enemark, C., 2013. "Unmanned Drones and the Ethics of War," in Allhoff, F., Evans, N., and Henschke, A., eds., *Routledge Handbook of Ethics and War: Just War Theory in the Twenty-first Century*, London and New York: Routledge, pp. 327–337.

Engel, R., 2013. "Former Drone Operator Says He's Haunted by His Part in More Than 1,600 Deaths," *NBC News*, June 6.

Engelhardt, T., 2013. "Tomgram: Engelhardt, Washington's Wedding Album from Hell," TomDispatch.com. December 20. Available online at: www.tomdispatch.com/blog/175787/tomgram%3A_engelhardt,_washington's_wedding_album_from_hell/

Fisher, William 2010. "UN Expert Calls on US to Halt CIA Targeted Killings," IPS (Inter Press Service) News Agency, June 2.

Gardner, L., 2013. *Killing Machine: The American Presidency in the Age of Drone Warfare*. New York: New Press.

Geraghty, T., 2009. *Soldiers of Fortune: A History of the Mercenary in Modern Warfare*. New York: Pegasus Books.

Geraghty, T., 2010. *Black Ops: The Rise of Special Forces in the C.I.A., the S.A.S., and Mossad*. New York: Pegasus Books.

The Guardian, 2014. "The Senate Intelligence Committee's Torture Report: Full Text," December 9.

Hastings, M., 2012. "The Rise of the Killer Drones: How America Goes to War in Secret," *Rolling Stone*, April 16.

Heyns, C., 2013. "Report of the Special Rapporteur on Extrajudicial, Summary or Arbitrary Executions," United Nations General Assembly Human Rights Council, September 13.

Human Rights Watch. 2013. "Between a Drone and Al Qaeda: The Civilian Cost of US Targeted Killings in Yemen," October report.

Jackson, R., 2014. *Confessions of a Terrorist: A Novel*. London: Zed Books.

Johnsen, G., 2013. *The Last Refuge: Yemen, Al-Qaeda, and America's War in Arabia*. New York: W. W. Norton & Company.

Jones, S., and Libicki, M., 2008. "How Terrorist Groups End: Lessons for Countering al-Qa'ida," RAND Corporation Report. Available online at: www.rand.org/pubs/monographs/MG741-1.html

Kaufman, W., 2007. "Rethinking the Ban on Assassination: Just War Principles in the Age of Terror," in Brough, M., Lango, J., and Van Der Linden, H., eds., *Rethinking the Just War Tradition*, New York: State University of New York Press, pp. 171–182.

Klaidman, D., 2012. *Kill or Capture: The War on Terror and the Soul of the Obama Presidency*. New York: Houghton Mifflin Harcourt.

Lewis, P., Ackerman, S., and Boone, J., 2015. "Obama Regrets Drone Strikes that Killed Hostages but Hails US for Transparency," *The Guardian*, April 23.

Mallette-Piasecki, M., 2012/2013. "Missing the Target: Where the Geneva Conventions Fall Short in the Context of Targeted Killing," *Albany Law Journal*, 76(1): 263–297.

Martin, R., 2011. "High Levels of 'Burnout' in US Drone Pilots," *NPR News*, December 18.

McDonnell, P., and Bulos, N., 2015. "Yemeni President Flees Houthi-controlled Capital, Denounces 'Coup'," *Los Angeles Times*, February 21.

Miller, G., 2012. "Plan for Hunting Terrorists Signals US Intends to Keep Adding Names to Kill Lists," *Washington Post*, October 23.

Obama, B., 2014. "Statement by the President on ISIL," September 10. The White House Office of the Press Secretary.

O'Connell, M., 2010. "Rise of the Drones II: Examining the Legality of Unmanned Targeting," US Congress, House of Representatives, Committee on Oversight and Government Reform. Hearing before the Subcommittee on National Security and Foreign Affairs, 111th Congress, 2nd session, April 28.

Orr, A., 2011. "Unmanned, Unprecedented, and Unresolved: The Status of American Drone Strikes in Pakistan Under International Law," *Cornell International Law Journal*, 44: 729–752.

Porter, G., 2010. "CIA Drone Operators Oppose Strikes as Helping al Qaeda," IPS (Inter Press News Service) Agency, June 3.

Riza, M. S., 2013. *Killing Without Heart*. Washington, DC: Potomac Books.

Rohde, D., and Mulvihill, K., 2010. *A Rope and a Prayer: A Kidnapping from Two Sides*. New York: Viking.

Savage, C., 2014. "Court Releases Large Parts of Memo Approving Killing of American in Yemen," *New York Times*, June 23.

Scahill, J., 2013. *Dirty Wars: The World Is a Battlefield*. New York: Nation Books.

Shane, S., 2012. "US Said to Target Rescuers at Drone Strike Sites," *New York Times*, February 5.

Shane, S., 2014. "Amid Details on Torture, Data on 26 Who Were Held in Error," *New York Times*, December 12.

Silke, A., 2012. "Is the Targeted Assassination of Terrorist Suspects an Effective Response to Terrorism? No: The Case Against Targeted Assassination," in Jackson, R., and Sinclair, S., eds., *Contemporary Debates on Terrorism*, London and New York: Routledge, pp. 173–180.

Statman, D., 2005. "Targeted Killing," in Shanahan, T., ed., *Philosophy 9/11: Thinking about the War on Terrorism*, Peru, IL: Carus Publishing Company.

Stimson Task Force, 2014. The Stimson Report. Available online at: www.stimson.org/books-reports/recommendations-and-report-of-the-stimson-task-force-on-us-drone-policy/

Strawser, B., ed., 2013. *Killing by Remote Control: The Ethics of an Unmanned Military*. New York: Oxford University Press.

Titus, H., and Olson, W., 2013. "Assassin in Chief?" *American Thinker*, February 7.

Universal Declaration of Human Rights, 1948. Available online at: www.un.org/en/documents/udhr/

US Department of Justice, 2010. "Department of Justice White Paper: Lawfulness of a Lethal Operation Directed Against a U.S. Citizen Who Is a Senior Operational Leader of Al-Qa'ida or An Associated Force," June.

Vlasic, M., 2012. "Assassination & Targeted Killing – A Historical and Post-Bin Laden Legal Analysis," *Georgetown Journal of International Law*, 43(2): 259–333.

Weiner, T., 2007. *Legacy of Ashes: The History of the CIA*. New York: Doubleday.

White, J., ed., 2012. *War, Terrorism, Torture and Assassination*, 4 ed. Boston, MA: Wadsworth.

Williams, B., 2013. *Predators: The CIA's Drone War on al Qaeda*. Washington, DC: Potomac Books.

Yoo, J., 2011/12. "Assassination or Targeted Killings after 9/11," *New York Law School Review*, 56: 57–79.

PART IV

Contemporary responses to terrorism

19
THE LANGUAGE OF COUNTERTERRORISM

Jack Holland

Introduction

Orthodox approaches have traditionally divided counterterrorism efforts into three forms – socioeconomic, policing, and military – all of which are conducted by the state. This focus enables, for example, counterterrorism efforts in Northern Ireland to be understood with reference to anti-discrimination legislation, enhanced police powers, and the deployment of the British armed forces. More recently, it enables an analysis of post 9/11 counterterrorism policies with reference to efforts to promote greater integration, extensive surveillance programmes, and prolonged wars in Afghanistan and Iraq.

On the one hand, such an approach is to be welcomed: it enables a fuller conceptualisation of the range of efforts that comprise counterterrorism than taking any one element in isolation. Such an approach also highlights the tensions between different forms of counterterrorism and reminds us that military (and policing) solutions often struggle to achieve their aims, especially if underlying socioeconomic conditions are not addressed. On the other hand, such an approach risks ignoring the processes through which terrorism and counterterrorism arise, take shape, and prosper. It ignores how the context and conditions of terrorism and counterterrorism are created. This is important because counterterrorism policies are rendered a possibility through significant instrumental and cultural processes. These "conditions of emergence" – the contexts within which terrorism and counterterrorism are enabled, constrained, and formed – are the focus of many scholars of critical terrorism studies (CTS). This chapter begins by assessing the reasons for this particular focus, exploring what it means for how CTS scholars research terrorism and counterterrorism.

CTS research exploring how terrorism and counterterrorism are enabled has focused on a number of key and uniting features. First, CTS approaches terrorism and counterterrorism as symbiotic social constructions. That is to say that they are social (rather than natural) phenomena which are related and actually help to promote and sustain each other, despite claims of desiring the other's destruction. Second, CTS research has often highlighted the role of culture, language, and discourse. More specifically, counterterrorism is seen to be both cultural and discursive. The chapter's second section, therefore, traces some of the best known research in CTS analysing dominant discourses of terrorism and counterterrorism. Third, in the chapter's final section, I trace some of the more recent and novel additions to CTS approaches, highlighting exciting future avenues for enquiry centred around concepts such as affect, emotion, resonance, and memory.

Why so much critical discourse analysis?

In the early twentieth century, Ludwig Wittgenstein famously remarked that "the limits of my language are the limits of my world" (Ogden 1999: section 5.6). This is a claim that many CTS scholars have seized upon and developed. Like many of the social sciences, politics and international relations, outside of North America at least, have embraced the insights of continental philosophy. Foucault and Bourdieu are the two most cited scholars of all time, and their ideas are hugely important for a large number of critical approaches across the social sciences. Foucault's work, in particular, stands out for its influence in shaping European alternatives to North American orthodoxies. And, his ideas have been central to the development of CTS, which has made use of his central arguments and methodological insights in order to interrogate the assumptions of (orthodox) terrorism studies, as well as the very notion of "terrorism" itself.

While Foucault's approach evolved in important ways throughout his career, one unifying theme throughout his work was the importance of focusing on the analysis of discourse. To understand the concept of "discourse", it is useful to begin by acknowledging that we – as humans – would struggle to engage with the world without thinking about it in some way. The point here is that ideas matter, which is a mantra that lies at the heart of constructivist thinking within international relations. These ideas very rarely emerge or remain purely at the level of the individual; rather, they are expressed and shared. They go from being subjective to intersubjective (and back again). And, one of the principal mediums through which this process occurs is language. By talking and writing about the world, we actually script, create, and construct that world; we do not just (in)accurately describe it. Everything from a table, to a tank, to a terrorist emerges out of the words that help to build up that "thing" into what we understand it to be. A discourse occurs where language produces the meaning of things in a fairly systematic, regular, and predictable way. Consider, for example, dominant discourses in early 2003 which suggested Saddam Hussein was mad, evil, or both. Arguing otherwise was difficult, because the language used to talk about the Iraqi leader was so pervasive, resonant, and dominant (see Holland 2013a, 2013b).

A focus on language and discourse has been a consistent theme of CTS research since its emergence as a subdiscipline. This is because CTS has often adopted a discursive ontology and a linked (sceptical) epistemology.[1] To say that CTS has adopted a discursive ontology is to acknowledge that very many scholars working within the subdiscipline view the world as discursively constructed. Most immediately, the result of this position is that terrorism is understood and studied as a "social fact", rather than a "brute fact" (Jackson et al. 2011: 35). This is to suggest that there is nothing inherent or objective about terrorism at all (see Zulaika, this volume).

Consider, for example, that violence is a frequent occurrence in various myriad forms. However, the label "terrorism" is reserved for specific types of violence conducted by particular actors in certain circumstances, but the label is applied in an inconsistent way, which usually serves a broader political or policy agenda. In the context of an ongoing "war on terrorism", several media commentators have noted that the label is more likely to be used when the perpetrators of violence are Muslims (see Friedersdorf 2014) and that the label actively excludes violence conducted in the name of Western states' foreign policies (which may even be labelled as counterterrorism). The point here is that terrorism becomes what it *is* through the words of those whose voices are heard and accepted. This is why Glen Greenwald (2010) has referred to the term as "meaningless" and "manipulated", in the sense that terrorism is not an objective category, but rather one that is discursively constructed, often by those seeking to enable and legitimise certain policies in the name of counterterrorism.

Coupled to a discursive ontology, CTS has largely adopted a linked (sceptical) epistemology. This is to acknowledge that studying discourse brings inevitable (inter)subjective biases into the research process and that it is impossible to step outside of discourse altogether in order to attempt to uncover ultimate truths which might accurately and objectively explain the way the world works (see Fitzgerald, this volume). Epistemologically, then, CTS scholars recognise that the pervasiveness of language and (the ontological) production of meaning through discourse limits the claims that can be made. This is why CTS scholars are so unlikely to suggest that there are clearly identifiable root causes of terrorism (such as poverty or ideology); a claim such as this would rely on a different epistemology derived from an alternative ontological view of the world. Instead, CTS scholars focus on analysing discourse and the impact that particular discourses have. A strong normative commitment runs through the heart of much of this work, as CTS scholars have focused on analysing dominant discourses in order to challenge and resist their effects.

For many CTS scholars, dominant discourses surrounding terrorism and counterterrorism are troubling and dangerous. There are three principal components of CTS's normative approach. First, CTS scholars have revealed the impacts of dominant discourses of terrorism and counterterrorism (Cole 2003; Jackson 2007b; and Jarvis and Lister 2013 offer good accounts of some of these impacts). For example, if Saddam Hussein is constructed as evil, it is very difficult to justify dialogue and conflict resolution efforts.

Second, CTS scholars have considered which voices might be silenced by dominant discourses. For instance, those labelled as "terrorists" often articulate clear political agendas, which are largely ignored (see Jackson 2014b). Likewise, those "on the receiving end" of counterterrorism efforts are rarely afforded the platform to have their voices and opinions heard (see, for example, Breen Smyth 2014; Toros 2012). Third, therefore, CTS has asked if alternative discourses might be preferable and less dangerous. For instance, would it be possible to speak of 9/11 as an international crime, rather than an act of war, in the hope of inspiring an international policing response rather than initiating and sustaining military interventions?

This normative desire to challenge dominant discourses is reflected in the dominance of one of CTS's preferred methodological approaches: critical discourse analysis (CDA). Drawing on Foucault, Derrida, and other continental philosophers, but most associated with Norman Fairclough's (1995, 2003) extensive work, CDA has been referred to as "discourse analysis with an attitude" (van Dijk 2001: 96). This means that CDA, like CTS, is self-consciously "critical"; it tends to side with the interests of dominated groups who suffer as the result of dominant discourses. While CDA, as a broad methodological approach, can take many forms and be applied to many issues, CTS focuses on the discursive construction of terrorism and counterterrorism with a view to revealing, for example, the patriarchy, Eurocentrism, orientalism, or racism which might underpin it (see, for example, Shepherd 2006, on the construction of gender within the language of counterterrorism).

Methodologically, then, CTS scholars are committed to deconstructing dominant discourses, through a critical discourse analysis approach, in two senses. First, CTS attempts to denaturalise dominant discourses, in a more general sense, by revealing them to be cultural not natural. Second, and in a more specifically Derridean vein, CTS attempts to reveal the binaries (such as good and evil, for example) upon which broader discourses are built. Both of these related "moves" are evident in CTS's most influential works to date. And, they are both designed to reveal the construction of terrorism and counterterrorism in order to challenge and resist their oppressive effects, with a view to realising a space to think and speak in less dangerous and oppressive ways.

Dominant discourses

To a considerable extent, CTS has emerged as a subdiscipline motivated by the policies of the war on terror and the perception of its inadequate orthodox analysis. It is no surprise, therefore, that CTS research analysing the language of counterterrorism has predominantly, if not exclusively, focused on dominant post-9/11 (Western) foreign and security discourses.[2] Here, this broad and diverse field of research is divided into three parts for analytical, chronological, and heuristic reasons. First, CTS research is renowned for its analyses of US foreign policy discourse and the language of counterterrorism espoused by American policymakers and practitioners. It is important to begin here, as this is both where the war on terror started and where CTS first took aim in pursuing its normative agenda to challenge dominant and dangerous language. Second, CTS research has also highlighted the diversity of the language of counterterrorism during the war on terror, both within and outside the Coalitions of the Willing that led military interventions in Afghanistan and Iraq. Third, CTS research has begun to show the important role played by the media and popular culture in perpetuating and reworking the discourse(s) of the war on terror.

If one work has become synonymous with critical terrorism studies it is Richard Jackson's (2005a) *Writing the War on Terrorism*. This book remains the best-known and fullest deconstruction of the language of counterterrorism after 9/11. Jackson's (2005a) work builds on Campbell (1998), as well as Foucault, Derrida, and Fairclough, taking insights from critical constructivism and post-structuralism. Substantively, it builds on Silberstein (2002), as well as Collins and Glover (2002). Using "a Constructivist approach . . . rooted in an explicitly normative Critical Theory framework", Jackson's (2005a) work is an attempt to "challenge the lies and obfuscations of those in power, and to work for positive social change" (Jackson 2005b). Using critical discourse analysis, Jackson denaturalises and disrupts the hegemonic official discourses undergirding the "war on terror" precisely because "the *practice* of counterterrorism is predicated on and determined by the *language* of counterterrorism . . . [and] the language of the 'war on terrorism'. . . is a carefully constructed *discourse*" (Jackson 2005a: 8).

Jackson (2005a: 8–18) denaturalises the dominant discourses of the "war on terror", arguing that a new social reality was created for the American public through the creation of a whole new language. These efforts commence with the interpretation of 9/11 as an act of war (Jackson 2005b: 38–40). A response to 9/11 which prioritised military interventions overseas, Jackson (2005a) shows, required the events of 11 September 2001 to be framed as simultaneously new and unique, and yet like Pearl Harbor, despite the obvious contradictions such a framing entailed.[3]

More specifically, this framing wrote 9/11 as an act of war, perpetrated by an enemy posing a continued existential threat to the United States who could not be eradicated through the dialogue and negotiation of diplomatic efforts (Jackson 2005a: 58–76). Having interrogated the framing of 9/11 as an "act of war", Jackson goes on to trace the considerable discursive work which was invested in attempts to construct the war on terror as good, moral, and just (2005a: 121–152). These efforts, Jackson (2005a: 59–91) reveals, are in part a quest for resonance and legitimacy by politicians (see also Barnett 1999), an insight which has been particularly important for CTS research analysing the language of counterterrorism after 9/11.

For CTS scholars, language matters for two overriding reasons. First, the interplay of competing discourses establishes the possibility and likelihood of particular policies. That is to say that language is a prerequisite for policy (in democracies at least), and politics takes place within a particular discursive context. Military intervention, for example, is much more likely (perhaps even inevitable) if 9/11 is framed as an act of war in the first place. Second, language enables politicians to garner support for policy by packaging it in particular ways. Again, in Western democracies, it is not possible for politicians to do anything they like; rather, it is necessary to sell policies – including counterterrorism – to the public. This insight, and its assumption of strategic agency on the part of elected officials, has underpinned research into divergent discourses of counterterrorism as the language of the war on terror is indigenised and contextualized in different states with distinct political cultures. As Holland (2013b) argues, elected elites can increase the political possibility of foreign policy by constructing a language that is not only conceivable and communicable, but also coercive.

Holland's (2013a, 2013b) three-part framework emphasises, first, that politicians and policymakers use language to paint a particular picture of the world; they spatialise world politics by giving friends and enemies geographic addresses, locating threats and opportunities on the world map. The identities of states and the nature of regions are written in this first analytical moment of the foreign policy process. In this first step, certain policies will become increasingly conceivable, as others readily appear illogical or even unthinkable. Consider, for example, the discursive effort undertaken by state leaders in denigrating their enemies as they seek to set the ground for military intervention.

Second, in democracies, politicians cannot map out any geopolitical globe that they choose; rather, they must draw upon and plug into the preexisting cultural knowledge of their target audience. This may include mobilising widely understood national mythology or speaking in terms that resonate with core constituencies. Consider, for example, those moments when politicians instrumentally employ folksy, populist terms in their quest to render foreign policy communicable and to achieve a necessary degree of resonance for their chosen course of action. Articulating communicable and resonant foreign policy is an important second step, as rarely is sufficient political capital retained from electoral victories alone for significant foreign policy initiatives without attempts to appeal to core domestic audiences.

Third, the war on terror has been a good example of the impact that the articulation of a coercive foreign policy can have. Silencing potential critics by winning a discursive war of position can force potential opponents into a position of reluctant acquiescence. Speaking in the language of the national interest and the national identity can make speaking out in favour of alternative stances a challenging task. Consider, for example, the period from September 2001 through January 2002. The three states at the forefront of the Coalition of the Willing in Afghanistan were the United States, the United Kingdom, and Australia. The language of counterterrorism in these three states converged around two key ideas: that 9–11 was "an attack on all of us" and "a moment of temporal rupture"[4] and that the Taliban in Afghanistan were "harbouring" al Qaeda (Holland 2013b; see also Jarvis 2009 on time/rupture and the language of counterterrorism).

Despite this convergence, however, leaders in all three states also relied upon distinct and divergent framings in order to garner support from key electoral constituencies and silence potential domestic opponents (Holland 2010, 2012, 2013a; Krebs and Lobasz 2007; Krebs and Jackson 2007). In the United States, President Bush "relied upon a proclivity for Manichean binaries within a language of frontier justice" (Holland 2013b: 104). In the United Kingdom, Blair's language "was characterised by an emphasis on rationality and British leadership" (on the British war on terror, see also Bulley 2008 and Croft 2007). Whereas in Australia, Prime Minister Howard's language of counterterrorism "was distinct in: the conflation of overtly emotional and practical solidarity; an emphasis on the defence of shared values through mutual sacrifice in war; and a particularly exclusionary language tied to the issue of immigration" (Holland 2013b: 8). These themes continued, despite evolving, throughout the war on terror, due to the culturally embedded nature of the language of counterterrorism and the need for politicians to sell policy at home (Holland 2013a). The language of counterterrorism therefore says as much about its articulator as it does its chosen subject or topic of focus. To paraphrase Anais Nin, we do not see or speak about things as they are; we see and speak about them as we are.

Finally, in all three states, but particularly the US and Australia, foreign policy was also constructed in terms that made it difficult to speak out in opposition. In the US, for example, opponents risked being labelled as failing to defend freedom or as simply being un-American. Some were even noted as constituting a threat to the United States through their sympathising with the cause of America's enemies.

Jackson's project, then, is a seminal text for CTS and the joint project to denaturalize the dominant discourses of the war on terror. It reveals, for example, the process of writing a new post-9/11 era filled with new and omnipresent dangers which require new approaches to counterterrorism (see also Mueller 2006).

However, while particular linguistic strategies operated across the Coalition of the Willing, such as Manichean binaries, for example, it is imperative to note that the language of counterterrorism looks and sounds different in different states, regardless of their participation in mutual military interventions. American emphasis on freedom (Jackson 2005a; Silberstein 2002), UK notions of continued British leadership on the world stage (Holland 2012), and Australian appeals to the mutual sacrificial defence of values shared by culturally similar "mates" (Burke 2001; Dyrenfurth 2007; Gleeson 2014; Holland 2010; McDonald 2005; McDonald and Merefield 2010) were essential in the process of enabling the war on terror. Such processes were also, of course, evident outside of the Coalition of the Willing, where, again, the language of counterterrorism was reworked to meet the demands of domestic audiences, cultures, and imperatives (see Baker-Beall 2009 and Jackson 2007a on the EU; Campana 2014 on Russia).

For Jackson (2005a) and Holland (2013b), the dominant discourses of the war on terror were primarily constructed in a top-down fashion, led by elected representatives. This is not to deny the importance of the media and popular culture, which served to amplify, reproduce, modify, and resist the official language of counterterrorism. Most frequently, however, the media and popular culture contributed to a process of co-production, looping, and communicating official language in a manner that maximized its dissemination, reach, and resonance. This extended from news anchors struggling initially to find their own frames of reference for the events of September 11th and repeating the words of officials (Holland 2009; Holmes and Sullivan 2014) via looped images of the events on television screens (Hoskins 2006), to Hollywood movies (Hammond 2011), novels, video games (Robinson 2012), candlelight vigils, websites (Jarvis 2011), acts of remembrance (Holland and Jarvis 2014), and even tattoos (Croft 2006). While much excellent work exists on the role of news and popular media for the language of counterterrorism, the single most important work to date remains Stuart Croft's (2006) *Culture, Crisis and America's War on Terror*.

Like Jackson (2005a) and Holland (2013b), Croft (2006) notes that for a war on terror to follow, 9/11 had to first be constructed in a particular and contingent way. This construction centred upon the framing of 9/11 as a moment of crisis, out of which the war on terror would emerge as a necessary solution. Croft (2006: 57, 79) notes that "crises are pivotal points in understanding the development of policy", and "the war on terror emerged as the dominant discourse through the crisis of 2001". Viewed in this way, the chronology of the language of counterterrorism after 9/11 first saw meaning disrupted as Americans struggled to comprehend and articulate events (Holland 2009; see also Edkins 2002, 2003, 2004; Nabers 2009). Second, state officials filled this void through authorized statements which rapidly coalesced into the undergirding discourse(s) of the war on terror – a discursive framework that enabled the war on terror to be prosecuted. Third, this new language of counterterrorism filtered through, and was reproduced by, news and popular media. It is this third focus that preoccupies Croft's (2006) study.

Croft traces the (re)production of the war on terror in and through cultural sources, as dominant discourses are amplified, disseminated, and defended in film, in television shows, and through myriad other forms of cultural expression normally excluded from political science and international relations explorations of terrorism. By seeking out the political in the cultural (Croft 2006: 8), Croft is able to show the role played by *Wonder Woman* and *Fahrenheit 9/11*, as well as Jay Leno and David Letterman, in the co-constitution of a crisis narrative (see also Faludi 2008). Importantly, Croft's analysis also considers popular culture as a real and potential site of resistance to dominant and oppressive discourses (see also Robinson 2012).

However, as with much work on the language of counterterrorism, the realization arrived at is one of concern at the hegemony achieved by official discourses of war on terror, which have proven to be pervasive, enduring (Bentley and Holland 2014), and forcefully defended (Holland and Jarvis 2014). Croft (2006), then, shares the concerns of Jackson (2005a, 2014a) and many other CTS scholars: the dominant discourses of the war on terror were, and remain, normalized and institutionalized in many Western states; they now serve as a background context, structuring how people think and directing the kinds of policies that can realistically be pursued.

Future directions

The previous section sketched the landscape of CTS work on the language of counterterrorism with a distinct focus on the seminal research at the core of the field, in particular, that which focuses on the subdiscipline's dominant topic of enquiry – the war on terror. In recent times, language has evolved, if not been overhauled, as Western leaders have, for example, come to realise the political and electoral toxicity of the phrase "war on terror". Western states now fight "overseas contingency operations"; we have seen drawdown in Afghanistan and Iraq, along with new "limited interventions" in Libya and elsewhere. The first point to note, then, in a section discussing future directions is that much excellent work is ongoing as a second generation of CTS scholars (many of whom studied under the supervision of CTS's original founders) has helped to lead in the analysis of today's language of counterterrorism.

Research on Obama's language of counterterrorism has revealed his (prevalent) continuities and (more limited) evolutions in language as he has opted (see McCrisken 2014) or been structurally coerced (see the majority of Bentley and Holland 2014) into retaining the core discursive framework of the war on terror (Bentley 2014; Jackson 2014a). When faced with new instances of terrorism or political violence, state officials have tended to reproduce rather than challenge dominant discourses (see, for example, Jarvis and Holland 2014 on the killing of Osama bin Laden; see Holland and Aaronson 2014 on Libya). Similarly, the media has retained much of the discursive framework introduced following 9/11, albeit with adaptations as drawdown in Afghanistan and Iraq has been planned and realised (see, for example, King 2014). Likewise, popular culture frequently remains within a post-9/11 moment (Hammond 2011), albeit with important sites of resistance (Alford 2011). Plenty of excellent work is emerging in this area (see Grayson 2013), including exciting new research into social media (see al-Lami et al. 2012).

Two areas of analysis which are already proving fruitful for CTS will hopefully attract further study in the near future. First, having deconstructed and denaturalised the official post-9/11 language of counterterrorism, CTS scholars have not only created a space to hear and amplify marginalised and silenced voices, but are also actively seeking to incorporate these views into analyses (see Breen-Smyth 2014; Toros 2012). Ensuring that CTS is geographically and socially diverse and that it provides a platform for marginalised actors to be heard will be central to the ongoing normative agenda of the subdiscipline. Second, similarly to security studies, as Croft (2008) notes, CTS can perhaps more accurately and usefully be thought of as a subfield, rather than a subdiscipline. Numerous cognate disciplines dilute the dominance of political science and international relations scholars, helping to create a subfield which is greater than the sum of its parts due to the synergies of cross-, multi-, and interdisciplinary research. Anthropology, geography, sociology, history, and psychology, to name only five disciplines, all have important insights for CTS research (see, for example, Gregory 2004 in geography).

A number of research avenues have recently also highlighted the benefits of thinking of CTS as an interdisciplinary subfield. First, research into the role of affect, emotion, and memory, partly inspired by work in neuroscience, has added a rich vein of analysis to discourse analytic studies. Influenced by the likes of (social theorist) Brian Massumi, (political theorist) William Connolly, and (neuroscientist) Antonio Damasio, both memory studies and the turn to affect/emotion are producing a burgeoning literature across the social sciences (see Bleiker and Hutchison 2008; Crawford 2000; Holland and Solomon 2014; Mercer 2010; Ross 2006; Solomon 2012; Zehfuss 2009; see also Heath-Kelly, this volume). This body of work has acknowledged "the role of biology" and the fact that humans do "not stand outside nature" but rather are, in fact, "full of all kinds of impulses which are outside its comprehension" (Thrift 2008: 25). It therefore offers hugely important insights for efforts to overcome a focus on elite-led discourses of terrorism and counterterrorism, with a view to better connecting and understanding the relationship of elites to ordinary citizens (see, for example, Lundborg 2012). In short, if we are to understand *resonance* and how and why some language "sticks" and "sells" (whereas other language falls and fails), interdisciplinary research insights such as these will be key.

Conclusion

This chapter has attempted three things. First, I have outlined why CTS has focused on the study of language and discourse, explaining what this means and entails. In short, a discursive ontology, far from being a flaw, as some critics would suggest, is a necessary starting point for scholars who believe the relatively simple (and arguably irrefutable) claim that meaning is created through language. CTS marries this ontological starting point with an epistemological scepticism, an emancipatory normative drive (akin to the Welsh School in security studies; see Lindahl, this volume), and frequently, a methodology focused on critical discourse analysis, which is well suited to these attributes and aspirations (see Booth 1991, 2007 on emancipation in security studies).

Second, the chapter sketched some of the major claims of CTS research on the language of counterterrorism, with a deliberate focus on the seminal work in this area, namely Jackson (2005a) and Croft (2006). Here, we saw that work in CTS has helped to reveal the constructed nature of the language of the war on terror, denaturalising dominant discourses that sustain and enable dangerous policies with a view to opening a space for resistance and alternative approaches to world politics. Third, the chapter noted ongoing efforts to better understand the relationship between elite discourse and its resonance or otherwise for ordinary citizens. This work will be crucial in better understanding how and why, for example, military intervention was rendered a necessity in Iraq but not Syria. And, it will help us to understand why unpicking the dominant official language of counterterrorism since 9/11 has been so challenging.

Notes

1 These terms are often used but rarely explained in plain language. *Ontology* refers to the "nature of being" but alludes, more simply, to what exists; for example, ontological questions pertain to what is out there for us to study and, more bluntly still, what "stuff" we consider to make up the world. *Epistemology* refers to theories of knowledge, which can be thought of as: What can we know about the stuff that makes up the world? (see Jarvis and Holland 2015).
2 While the language of counterterrorism has risen to prominence since September 11, 2001, such discourses do of course have longer histories (see, for example, Kuei-Tsui 2014).

3 On the "exceptional" nature of 9/11, see Jackson 2005a: pp. 31–38; on comparisons to Pearl Harbor, see pp. 41–44; and on the Cold War, see pp. 45–47.
4 In turn, this idea relied upon the framing of 9/11 "as: an act of war; the dawn of new and dangerous times; a moment of unity; and a moment of crisis or opportunity" (Holland 2013a: 104).

References

Alford, M., 2011. "Why Not a Propaganda Model for Hollywood?", in Hammond, P., ed., *Screens of Terror: Representations of War and Terrorism in Film and Television since 9/11*, Suffolk: Arima Publishing.
Al-Lami, M., O'Loughlin, B., Cahdwock, A., 2012. "Mobilisation and Violence in the New Media Ecology: The Dua Khalil Aswad and Camilia Shehata Cases", *Critical Studies on Terrorism*, 5(2): 70–84.
Baker-Beall, C., 2009. "The Discursive Construction of EU Counter-Terrorism Policy: Writing the Migrant 'Other', Securitisation and Control", *Journal of Contemporary European Research*, 5(2): 188–206.
Barnett, M., 1999. "Culture, Strategy and Foreign Policy Change: Israel's Road to Oslo", *European Journal of International Relations*, 5(1): 5–36.
Bentley, M., 2014. "Continuity We Can Believe in: Escaping the War on Terror", in Bentley, M., & Holland, J., eds., *Obama's Foreign Policy: Ending the War on Terror*, London: Routledge.
Bentley, M., and Holland, J., eds., 2014. *Obama's Foreign Policy: Ending the War on Terror*, London: Routledge.
Bleiker, R., and Hutchison, E., 2008. "Fear No More: Emotions in World Politics", *Review of International Studies*, 34(1): 115–135.
Booth, K., 1991. "Security and Emancipation", *Review of International Studies*, 17: 313–326.
Booth, K., 2007. *Theory of World Security*, Cambridge: Cambridge University Press.
Breen-Smyth, M., 2014. "On the Receiving End", Conference at the University of Surrey, 16–17 June 2014.
Bulley, D., 2008. "'Foreign' Terror? London Bombings, Resistance and the Failing State", *British Journal of Politics and International Relations*, 10(3): 378–394.
Burke, A., 2001. *In Fear of Security: Australia's Invasion Anxiety*, Annandale: Pluto Press Australia.
Campana, A., 2014. "The Multiple Contexts of Russian Counterterrorism Frames: Framing Process and Discursive Field", in Pisoiu, D., ed., *Arguing Counter-Terrorism: New Perspectives*, Abingdon: Routledge.
Campbell, D., 1998. *Writing Security: United States Foreign Policy and the Politics of Identity*, Revised Edition, Manchester: Manchester University Press.
Cole, D., 2003. *Enemy Aliens: Double Standards and Constitutional Freedoms*, New York: New Press.
Collins, J., and Glover, R., 2002. *Collateral Language: A User's Guide to America's New War*, New York: New York Press.
Crawford, N., 2000. "The Passion of World Politics: Propositions on Emotions and Emotional Relationships", *International Security*, 24(4): 116–156.
Croft, S., 2006. *Culture, Crisis and America's War on Terror*, Cambridge: Cambridge University Press.
Croft, S., 2007. "British Jihadis and the British War on Terror", *Defence Studies*, 7(3): 317–337.
Croft, S., 2008. "What Future for Security Studies", in Williams, P., ed., *Security Studies: An Introduction*, London: Routledge.
Dyrenfurth, N., 2007. "John Howard's Hegemony of Values: The Politics of Mateship in the Howard Decade", *Australian Journal of Political Science*, 42(2): 211–230.
Edkins, J., 2002. "Forget Trauma? Responses to September 11", *International Relations*, 16(2): 243–256.
Edkins, J., 2003. *Trauma and the Memory of Politics*, Cambridge: Cambridge University Press.
Edkins, J., 2004. "Ground Zero: Reflections on Trauma, In/Distinction and Response", *Cultural Research*, 8(3): 247–270.
Fairclough, N., 1995. *Critical Discourse Analysis*, Boston: Addison Welsey.
Fairclough, N., 2003. *Analysing Discourse: Textual Analysis for Social Research*, Abingdon: Routledge.
Faludi, S., 2008. *The Terror Dream: What 9–11 Revealed About America*, Cornwall: MPG Books.
Friedersdorf, 2014. Available online at: www.theatlantic.com/politics/archive/2014/06/if-these-killers-were-muslims-wed-call-them-terrorists/372472/
Gleeson, K., 2014. *Australia's War on Terror Discourse*, Farnham: Ashgate.
Grayson, K., 2013. "Encounters Through the Cooking Glass: Geopolitics and Aesthetic Subjects in Breaking Bad", Paper Presented at the International Studies Association (ISA) Annual Conference, San Francisco, April 2013.
Greenwald, G., 2010. "Terrorism: The Most Meaningless and Manipulated Word", *Salon*, 19 February, available online at: www.salon.com/2010/02/19/terrorism_19/
Gregory, D., 2004. *The Colonial Present: Afghanistan, Palestine, and Iraq*, Malden: Blackwell Publishing.

Hammond, P., ed., 2011. *Screens of Terror: Representations of War and Terrorism in Film and Television since 9/11*, Suffolk: Arima Publishing.
Holland, J., 2009. "From September 11th 2001 to 9/11: From Void to Crisis", *International Political Sociology*, 3(3): 275–292.
Holland, J., 2010. "Howard's War on Terror: A Conceivable, Communicable and Coercive Foreign Policy Discourse", *Australian Journal of Political Science*, 45(4): 643–661.
Holland, J., 2012. "Blair's War on Terror: Selling Intervention to Middle England", *British Journal of Politics and International Relations*, 14(1): 74–95.
Holland, J., 2013a. "Foreign Policy and Political Possibility", *British Journal of Politics and International Relations*, 19(1): 48–67.
Holland, J., 2013b. *Selling the War on Terror: Foreign Policy Discourses after 9/11*, London: Routledge.
Holland, J., and Aaronson, M., 2014. "Dominance through Coercion: Strategic Rhetorical Balancing and the Tactics of Justification in Afghanistan and Libya", *Journal of Intervention and Statebuilding*, 8(1): 1–20.
Holland, J., and Jarvis, L., 2014. "'Night Fell on a Different World': Experiencing, Constructing and Remembering 9/11", *Critical Studies on Terrorism*, 7(2): 187–204.
Holland, J., and Solomon, T., 2014. "Affect is What States Make of it", *Critical Studies on Security*, 2(3): 262–277.
Holmes, D., and Sullivan, R., 2014. "Plenty of Oxygen: Terrorism, News Media and the Politics of the Australian Security State", in Pisoiu, D., ed., *Arguing Counter-Terrorism: New Perspectives*, Abingdon: Routledge.
Hoskins, A., 2006. "Temporality, Proximity and Security: Terror in a Media-Drenched Age", *International Relations*, 20(4): 453–466.
Jackson, R., 2005a. *Writing the War on Terrorism: Language, Politics, and Counter-terrorism*, Manchester: Manchester University Press.
Jackson, R., 2005b. "A Reply to Jonathon Rodwell", *49th Parallel*, 15, available online at: https://fortyninthparalleljournal.files.wordpress.com/2014/07/3-jackson-reply-to-jonathan-rodwell.pdf
Jackson, R., 2007a. "An Analysis of EU Counter-terrorism Discourse Post 9/11", *Review of International Affairs*, 20(2): 233–247.
Jackson, R., 2007b. "Language, Policy and the Construction of a Torture Culture in the War on Terror", *Review of International Studies*, 33(3): 353–371.
Jackson, R., 2014a. "The War on Terror as Hegemonic Discourse: Institutionalisation, Interests and the Sedimentation of Counterterrorism Ideology", in Bentley, M., & Holland, J., eds., *Obama's Foreign Policy: Ending the War on Terror*, London: Routledge.
Jackson, R., 2014b. *Confessions of a Terrorist*, London: Zed Books.
Jackson, R., Jarvis, L., Gunning, J., and Breen Smyth, M., 2011. *Terrorism: A Critical Introduction*, Basingstoke: Palgrave.
Jarvis, L., 2009. *Times of Terror: Discourse, Temporality and the War on Terror*, Basingstoke: Palgrave.
Jarvis, L., 2011. "9/11 Digitally Remastered? Internet Archives, Vernacular Memories and WhereWereYou.org", *Journal of American Studies*, 45(4): 793–814.
Jarvis, L., and Holland, J., 2014. "'We (For)got Him': Remembering and Forgetting in the Narration of bin Laden's Death", *Millennium Journal of International Studies*, 42(2): 425–447.
Jarvis, L., and Holland, J., 2015. *Security: A Critical Introduction*, Basingstoke: Palgrave Macmillan.
Jarvis, L., and Lister, M., 2013. "Disconnected Citizenship?: The Impacts of Anti-terrorism Policy on Citizenship in the UK", *Political Studies*, 61(3): 656–675.
King, E., 2014. *Obama, the Media, and Framing the U.S. Exit from Iraq and Afghanistan*, Farnham: Ashgate.
Krebs, R., and Jackson, P., 2007. "Twisting Tongues and Twisting Arms: The Power of Political Rhetoric", *European Journal of International Relations*, 13(1): 35–66.
Krebs, R., and Lobasz, J., 2007. "Fixing the Meaning of 9/11: Hegemony, Coercion, and the Road to War in Iraq", *Security Studies*, 16(3): 409–451.
Kuei-Tsui, C., 2014. "Tracing the Discursive Origins of the War on Terror: Clinton and the Construction of the Terrorist Threat in the Post-Cold War Era", Paper Presented at the International Studies Association (ISA) Annual Conference March 2014, Toronto.
Lundborg, T., 2012. *Politics of the Event: Time, Movement, Becoming*, London: Routledge.
McCrisken, T., 2014. "Obama's War on Terrorism in Rhetoric and Practice", in Bentley, M., & Holland, J., eds., *Obama's Foreign Policy: Ending the War on Terror*, London: Routledge.
McDonald, M., 2005. "Constructing Insecurity: Australian Security Discourse and Policy Post-2001", *International Relations*, 19(3): 297–320.
McDonald, M., and Merefield, M., 2010. "How was Howard's War Possible? Winning the War of Position over Iraq", *Australian Journal of International Affairs*, 64(2): 186–204.

Mercer, J., 2010. "Emotional Beliefs", *International Organization*, 64: 1–31.
Mueller, J., 2006. *Overblown: How Politicians and the Terrorism Industry Inflate National Security Threats, and Why We Believe Them*, New York: Simon and Schuster.
Nabers, D., 2009. "Filling the Void of Meaning: Identity Construction in US Foreign Policy After 9/11", *Foreign Policy Analysis*, 5(2): 191–204.
Ogden, C., 1999. Translation of Wiggenstein, L., 1921. *Tractatus Logico-Philosophicus*, Mineola, New York: Dover. Available online at: www.kfs.org/jonathan/witt/tlph.html [accessed 1/12/2014].
Robinson, N., 2012. "Videogames, Persuasion and the War on Terror: Escaping or Embedding the Military-Entertainment Complex?", *Political Studies*, 60(3): 504–22.
Ross, A., 2006. "Coming in from the Cold: Constructivism and Emotions", *European Journal of International Relations*, 12(2): 197–222.
Shepherd, L., 2006. "Veiled References: Constructions of Gender in the Bush Administration Discourse on the Attacks on Afghanistan post-9/11", *International Feminist Journal of Politics*, 8(1): 19–41.
Silberstein, S., 2002. *War of Words: Language, Politics, and 9/11*, London: Routledge.
Solomon, T., 2012. "'I wasn't Angry, Because I couldn't Believe it was Happening': Affect and Discourse in Responses to 9/11", *Review of International Studies*, 38(4): 907–928.
Thrift, N., 2008. *Non-Representational Theory: Space, Politics, Affect*, London: Routledge.
Toros, H., 2012. *Terrorism, Talking and Transformation: A Critical Approach. Routledge Critical Terrorism Studies*, Abingdon: Routledge.
van Dijk, T., 2001. "Multidisciplinary CDA: A Plea for Diversity", in Wodak, R., & Meyer, M., eds., *Methods of Critical Discourse Analysis*, London: Sage.
Zehfuss, M., 2009. "Hierarchies of Grief and the Possibility of War: Remembering UK Fatalities in Iraq", *Millennium: Journal of International Studies*, 38(2): 419–440.

20
CRITICAL EVALUATION OF COUNTERTERRORISM

Sondre Lindahl

Introduction

> Countering terrorism is intimately related to understanding the nature of the terrorist phenomenon and how it fits into the wider security environment. How we conceive of terrorism determines to a great extent how we go about countering it and what resources – money, manpower, institutional framework time horizon – we devote to the effort.
>
> *(Crelinsten 2009: 39)*

This quote is at the heart of a CTS approach to counterterrorism. It highlights that terrorism is a social fact, meaning that the term is open to different conceptualizations and wholly dependent on human agreement (see Shanahan, this volume). Defining terrorism is of the utmost importance, and given the wide array of different definitions, counterterrorism can take on a great many different shapes and forms. A separation is sometimes made between counterterrorism and anti-terrorism, where counterterrorism is understood to comprise the policies that seek to eliminate terrorist environments and groups, while the latter refers to target hardening and other defensive measures that can deter or prevent attacks (Martin 2003: 345). However, these terms are often conflated, and because they both aim to save lives by preventing or decreasing the number of attacks, this chapter will use the term *counterterrorism* to describe any efforts taken to deal with terrorism.

Furthermore, the range of possible counterterrorism approaches can broadly be summarized under four headings: the use of force, intelligence and policing, homeland security, and conciliation and dialogue (Jackson et al. 2011: 225–229). *The use of force* views terrorism as a special kind of warfare that emphasizes military force to destroy, disrupt, deter, or prevent terrorism. *Intelligence and policing* views terrorism as a criminal activity and a security threat that can be countered via the state's security services. *Homeland security* views terrorism as a manageable security threat that can be mitigated by enhancing the state's resilience to, and protection from, terrorism. *Conciliation and dialogue* views terrorism as the expression of sociopolitical grievances and conflicts that can be addressed with nonviolent efforts. This is a brief summary of the main types of counterterrorism, but it sums up the traditional understanding and approach to counterterrorism in the field of terrorism studies, as well as the counterterrorism policies of Western states.

The remainder of this chapter will provide an overview of the key arguments made by CTS of current counterterrorism, suggest research areas that scholars should explore, and finally argue that CTS needs to focus on providing alternatives to orthodox counterterrorism in order to move the research agenda forward.

CTS critique of counterterrorism

As Crelinsten (2009) put it, how we conceive of terrorism necessarily determines how we go about countering it. Critiquing the terrorism discourse in general has therefore been an important feature of CTS, especially how discourse has been used to "write" the war on terror (Appleby 2010; Kolås 2010; McCrisken 2011; Zalman and Clarke 2009). Jackson (2005) is important in this respect because he utilized critical discourse analysis to show how language had been deployed to justify and normalize a global campaign of counterterrorism after 9/11 (see Holland, this volume). Even though he was not the first to argue for the importance of language when studying counterterrorism, his book did to a large extent solidify discourse analysis as an important part of a CTS research agenda.

Other scholars have critiqued the connection between the "new" terrorism discourse and consequently the apparent need for new counterterrorism measures, even though the newness of the concept of terrorism is found to be questionable and more likely to obfuscate our understanding of terrorism (Duyvesteyn and Malkki 2012; Lynch and Ryder 2012; Spencer 2010, this volume; Stohl 2008). In an attempt to give coherence to this critique, Daniela Pisoiu's (2014) edited volume, *Arguing Counterterrorism: New Perspectives,* provides a collection of articles which on the one hand seeks to address and demystify some of the rigidified concepts and assumptions of counterterrorism discourse and, on the other, to open up the counterterrorism argumentation to historical and cultural contexts.

At this point it is worth mentioning the work of Joseba Zulaika. Although not exclusively a CTS scholar as such, his anthropological and ethnographical approach encapsulates in many ways the CTS research agenda's aim of a much more holistic approach to studies of terrorism and counterterrorism. Zulaika (2009) advances a sophisticated argument for counterterrorism as "a self-fulfilling prophecy" because its discourse creates and perpetuates the very thing it seeks to control. This is because counterterrorism's ignorance of the languages, cultures, and histories of the context in which terrorism emerges is marked by a knowledge crisis which is based on an unwillingness to engage seriously with the subjectivity, or the will and desire, of the terrorists. Because of the taboo that surrounds terrorism, the counterterrorist cannot allow herself to take the terrorist's subjectivity literally, and as such, it prevents any real understanding of how acts of terrorism become possible. Zulaika describes what some CTS scholars refer to as "the epistemological crisis of counterterrorism" (Heath-Kelly 2012; Jackson 2015; Stampnitzky 2013). Instead of taking into consideration the existing empirical evidence, governments and orthodox scholars and experts resort to *imagining* what could possibly happen. As our fantasies and imagination know no boundaries, bizarre and ever-expanding counterterrorism practices become normal. Indeed, one could argue that such practices are inevitable in this framework.

Although orthodox terrorism studies have conceptualized terrorism as an ontologically stable fact that can be identified, isolated, and eliminated (see Fitzgerald, this volume), counterterrorism has spread beyond merely the technical aspects of fighting terrorism. Indeed, our lives are to an ever-increasing degree shaped by counterterrorism policies and measures as they have spread into immigration (Hickman et al. 2012; Oriola 2009), counter-radicalization (Baker-Beall et al. 2015; Heath-Kelly 2013; Lynch 2013, Lindekilde, this volume), banking (Napoleoni 2010; Warde and Humphrey 2008), and urban planning (Coaffee 2010; Geoghegan and Casciani 2007), among others. The Department of Homeland Security has even expanded into raiding lingerie shops for selling copyrighted baseball-inspired panties (Fox News 2014). This proliferation arguably takes its toll on civil liberties and rights (Davidson 2014; Donohue 2008; Toivanen 2010), and CTS importantly rejects the argument that a trade-off between liberty and security is necessary. In fact, it can be argued that it represents a false dichotomy (Jackson et al. 2011: 233). This critique is intimately related to the CTS's affiliation with critical theory (see Toros, this volume), where the individual, not the state, is the primary referent to be secured. As such, the emphasis is not on how the state can be made more secure, but how the rights and liberties of individuals can be preserved.

Although terrorism is considered to be one of the biggest security threats, CTS has critiqued what it perceives to be an exaggeration of the terrorist threat (see Wolfendale, this volume). Mueller and Stewart have led that critique, and their research suggests that the terrorist threat has been overblown, and concomitantly, the amount of resources allocated to counterterrorism measures has not been based on rigorous risk assessment (Mueller 2006; Mueller and Stewart 2014; Stewart and Mueller 2013).

The critique of force-based counterterrorism

The utility of repressive force as a central component of counterterrorism has been a major point of criticism for CTS as scholars question the effectiveness of current counterterrorism policies and measures. The question of how we might evaluate the effectiveness of different counterterrorism policies is essential because there is little empirical evidence that evaluates in a convincing manner what actually works (Chowdhury and Fitzsimmons 2013; De Graaf and de Graaff 2010; Um and Pisoiu 2011).

Targeted assassination (see Calhoun, this volume), a much favored strategy under both the Bush and Obama administrations, has, for instance, been found to be counterproductive and plagued by questions regarding its legality and legitimacy (Morehouse 2014; Mucha 2013; Silke 2012). Moreover, assassinating leaders of particular groups can be counterproductive in ending conflicts because when trying to negotiate an end to a conflict, if the politically minded cadre is eliminated, there is no one left to talk to (Mac Ginty 2010). Thus, groups can be driven underground and forced away from a moderate path (Pedahzur and Perliger 2006: 1988). Consequently, it would be hard for a group to convene in order to pursue a political path, and moderate members of the group would find it hard to pursue a strategy of accommodation when faced with a brutal force-based counterterrorism approach (Mac Ginty 2010: 220). Gunning (2009) likewise claims that Israel's policy of targeted assassinations delayed Hamas's ceasefire declaration in 2003 and eventually became a contributing factor in the ceasefire's breakdown. A recent study also points to the negative effect of violent counterterrorism in Israel as compared to conciliatory measures (Sharvit et al. 2013).

The use of torture (see Brecher, this volume) is another practice that has become normalized in the global war on terror (GWOT), with images and stories from Abu Ghraib and Guantánamo Bay providing evidence of extensive use of torture or so-called enhanced interrogation methods. These practices have been defended by noted scholars like Alan Dershowitz, who argues for its legalization as a counterterrorism tool (Dershowitz 2010). The use of torture by Western states and their allies as a tool of counterterrorism has been substantially reported, and the critique has centered on torture as a unique kind of moral wrong, how torture does not yield useful information for countering terrorism, and how there is now a torture-supporting culture in several Western countries.

The critique of current counterterrorism practices is also closely related to CTS's attempt to bring the state back into the study of terrorism. The concept of state terrorism is a cornerstone in the CTS research agenda, and much attention has been focused on highlighting how states can be perpetrators of terrorism through their counterterrorism efforts. Of particular significance is the Rendition Project (see Blakeley and Raphael, this volume) which aims to analyze the emergence, development, and operation of the global system of rendition and secret detention in the years since 9/11 (www.therenditionproject.org.uk). The project sheds light on dubious counterterrorism practices deployed in the war on terror and provides an important perspective, as well as broadening the counterterrorism debate.

In sum, CTS makes a compelling critique of the use of repressive force in counterterrorism and how it more often than not is counterproductive. Indeed, little or no empirical research exists to date that supports the argument that the use of force is effective and efficient in countering terrorism or in dealing with its roots in the long term. This situation has led Rogers to argue that:

> the notable failure of the current counter-terrorism framework based on suppression and military force may prove to be an encouragement in the search for a new security paradigm that focuses on sustainable security rooted in emancipation and justice, not the maintenance of the status quo.
>
> *(2012: 150)*

CTS has pointed out and critiqued the failures of the current counterterrorism paradigm, but there are at least four areas that should be explored to further advance the CTS research agenda: counterterrorism in the global south, the empirical evaluation and critique of counterterrorism, nonviolent and peaceful forms of counterterrorism, and a broader evaluation and conceptualization of counterterrorism which brings politics back into counterterrorism.

Counterterrorism in the global south

Most of the research that has been conducted on counterterrorism in the global south has focused on the involvement of Western states, mostly the United States, in other countries as part of their worldwide global efforts to counter terrorism (see Keenan 2010; Qureshi 2010; Smith 2010). The journal, *Critical Studies on Terrorism*, dedicated a special issue in 2010 to the views from "the Others" of the war on terror, and most of the articles in the special issue also focused on the implications and effects the GWOT has had in some countries outside the "West". Research and narratives on "terrorism" from the global south are important to broaden our understanding of the concept. What does counterterrorism, for instance, look like in Uganda or Madagascar, and are there elements in their dealings with terrorism we can learn from? What are examples of counter-radicalization programs in the global south? What are the effects of counterterrorism expenditure in the global south, and have they affected domestic spending on education, health care, and so forth? Have the responses to separatist insurgencies and armed groups which utilize terrorist tactics changed after the declaration of the GWOT? For instance, Richmond and Franks suggest that conflicts which get overlaid with a discourse of terrorism find it much harder to negotiate and settle matters peacefully (Richmond and Franks 2009).

The point is that researchers should not be afraid to look outside the lines. It seems reasonable to assume that a Eurocentric focus necessarily will skew the research output, and this silence in research should be addressed to potentially add different perspectives and broaden the debate. In addition, moving beyond a Eurocentric focus may illuminate how Western counterterrorism fits within broader structures of imperial domination of the current international system.

Empirical evaluation

By now it has become routine for CTS scholars to point to the review conducted by Lum, Kennedy, and Sherley in 2006 which found that only a small percentage of empirical studies on counterterrorism exists, and only seven studies evaluated the effectiveness of counterterrorism programs in a moderately rigorous way (Lum et al. 2006: 510). Um and Pisoiu have continued that exercise to see whether there have been more engaged and systematic efforts in researching the effectiveness of counterterrorism after 2006 (Um & Pisoiu 2015). Despite an increase in studies on counterterrorism effectiveness, the authors found that our knowledge of whether or not it works remains limited. This is, on the one hand, due to case and data selection biases and, on the other hand, to the use of different indicators and differing definitions of what effectiveness is, which in turn leads to contradictory results.

The lack of empirical studies is obviously not a problem exclusive to CTS, but empirical research plays a crucial role in destabilizing and debunking prevailing myths regarding counterterrorism practices. In this respect, Mueller and Stewart are perhaps the two scholars that have devoted the most attention to the empirical evaluation of counterterrorism measures (see Mueller and Stewart 2014; Stewart and Mueller 2013). After 9/11, Western intelligence communities have shown an insatiable appetite for information, not only about potential terrorists abroad, but also their own citizens. Based on an assumption that more intelligence is the key to prevent future attacks, the US now spends $68 billion annually on seventeen different intelligence outfits and a National Security Agency (NSA) that stores its data in zettabytes. More ominously, the NSA states that for the good of the nation the center was built "with future expansion in mind and the ultimate capacity will definitely be 'alottabytes'!" (NSA 2014). Thus, there is a need not only for more research on the effectiveness and efficiency of specific counterterrorism practices, but also on how effective the increase in intelligence gathering really is in countering terrorism.

Besides highlighting some of the technical issues and difficulties when attempting to measure the effectiveness of counterterrorism, Um and Pisoiu also claim that a major source of confusion is the lack of any standard or notion of what an effective counterterrorism policy is supposed to bring about. That is an essential point which researchers should answer prior to any studies of effectiveness, and this chapter will discuss this point later. For now, suffice it to say that the notion of emancipation may provide an answer.

Nonviolent and peaceful forms of counterterrorism

If force-based counterterrorism is found to be counterproductive, often morally wrong, and usually very expensive, there is a need for research that illuminates how terrorism can be countered nonviolently. Nonviolent responses are often mentioned in the counterterrorism literature, but often as something that can be done only after the initial threat has been dealt with through force. It is counterterrorism's sidekick. This notion of nonviolent responses as something that comes secondary to force-based counterterrorism needs to be challenged. In the last few years, excellent research has been conducted on talking and negotiating with terrorists, and the importance of reconciliation and the renunciation of violence (see Goerzig 2010; Toros 2012). Research so far points to clear advantages of nonviolent responses as compared to force-based ones. The great challenge for the nonviolent argument is to counter the mimetic quality of violence; we see violence and we respond with violence. The commitment to nonviolence is important because it runs counter to the prevalent belief that "bad" violence can be countered successfully with "good" violence. Essential to a CTS approach to counterterrorism is an acceptance of the means-ends connection which suggests that using violence as a means to counterviolence is untenable.

This connection is ultimately tied to the notion of emancipation which will be discussed later on in this chapter (see also Booth 2007: 112).

The situation in 2014 with ISIL in Iraq and Syria is case in point. To remove the "cancer" that is ISIL (Payne 2014), a US-led coalition is now attacking the group with missiles, fighter jets, and drones. There simply is no other way to stop an organization which is hell-bent on destruction. Or so the argument goes. The situation is thus akin to the one in western movies, where a town needs a gunslinger to get rid of the evil despot that rules it. The violent solution is portrayed as the effective one while the nonviolent inhabitants are passive bystanders incapable of coping with the situation. As such, the gunslinger prepares the ground for peace by removing the "bad guys", much like the US hoped the invasion of Iraq would prepare the ground for democracy there.

Holism: bringing politics back into counterterrorism

Most of the critique that has been leveled at orthodox counterterrorism is that counterterrorism is approached through a narrow problem-solving perspective which in large part ignores the context, the complexity, and the unstable nature of the phenomenon of terrorism in the first place. As Zulaika has shown, counterterrorism creates and constitutes its own discourses, practices, and in part, its own reality, whereby it constantly reproduces the threat it seeks to fight (Zulaika 2009). This is a clear impetus for CTS scholars to localize counterterrorism in the broader context of politics and work toward reconceptualizing counterterrorism as remaking the broader dysfunctional international system that in large part is conducive to terrorism in the first place. This commitment to social change is essential because Abu Ghraib, or the flirtation with legalizing torture, is only possible if terrorism is construed in such a way that fundamental human rights no longer apply in order to counter the threat. In sum, what the CTS critique boils down to is a different ontological, epistemological, and ethical-normative position that approaches counterterrorism in a radically different manner than its orthodox counterpart.

As such, there is a need to focus on the root causes of terrorism, not just the symptoms. This is not a call for finding *the* root cause of terrorism; rather, it is to critically identify and examine the conditions that are conducive to terrorism. Here one might find that the foreign policy of a country (Eland 1998), or perhaps the exploitation of oil resources in countries like Algeria, are conditions that increase the likelihood of acts of terrorism. The point is to locate acts of terrorism in a broader context and study how, for instance, Western foreign policy creates and constitutes both terrorism and counterterrorism. How the US acts will necessitate a response, and it is this link that is often forgotten by Western governments and orthodox scholars (Eland 1998). If acts of terrorism are the direct response to a country's policies, then clearly a reconfiguration of those policies is in order if ending terrorism is the real objective. This is the argument put forward by Booth and Dunne, that successful counterterrorism is not just a question of better models of counterterrorism; instead, it is a call for reducing the pathologies of the world order and striving for greater human security (Booth and Dunne 2012: 181–184). The question then becomes, what is all this critique good for, or perhaps *who* is it good for?

CTS, emancipation, and counterterrorism

The core values of CTS, such as a focus on root causes, prioritizing nonviolence, and eschewing state centrism for the freedom and security of the individual can arguably be summed up by the notion of "emancipation". The first articulation of the CTS research agenda identified emancipation as a guiding principle for research (Jackson 2009a: 223–224; McDonald 2009; Toros and Gunning 2009), and Toros has advanced the case for emancipation further in this volume. The emancipatory commitment has been understood as a "normative commitment to both ending the use of terrorist tactics (whether by state or non-state actors), and to addressing the conditions that can be seen to impel actors to resort to terrorist tactics" (Jackson 2009a: 224).

However, it does not make matters easier that Booth's definition of emancipation, the one adopted by CTS, stops short of providing a clear idea of what emancipation looks like in practice, or "how it might inform our analyses of empirical contexts" (McDonald 2009: 112). Instead, it is argued that emancipation is better conceived of as a continuous process to "secure people from those oppressions that stop them from carrying out what they would freely choose to do, compatible with the freedoms of others" (Booth 2007: 112). As a strategic process it can realize concrete utopias, promote emancipatory ideas, and work toward the betterment of human life. Here, realizing concrete utopias means that critical scholars must avoid suggesting a blueprint for an emancipated order that is unrelated to the possibilities inherent in the present (Wyn-Jones 2005: 230). The incorporation of emancipation has profound implications for a CTS research agenda as the individual, not the state, is the primary referent to be secured, and the focus is on locating possibilities for emancipatory change within particular contexts.

However, as Heath-Kelly has pointed out, there were some shortcomings in the appropriation of the emancipatory commitment by CTS (Heath-Kelly 2010). As orthodox terrorism studies is understood to be rooted in positivism and favoring a problem-solving approach, CTS by its connection to critical theory may enjoy ontological and epistemological supremacy in terms of the *content* of reason – that is, understanding knowledge as a social process that is for someone and for some purpose (Cox 1981: 128). But, CTS fails to account from where it obtains the necessary justificatory force to assert its normative *function* as preferable to the function of instrumental reason. This is important because the appropriation of critical theory and a minimal foundationalist approach leads to skepticism about the secure foundations of knowledge. Critical theory itself may not be able to generate normative force, but Heath-Kelly claims that CTS could retain its normative project by describing the existence of contemporary human suffering, delineating why this is bad and why it necessitates counteraction, and finally by "legitimating itself within academic terrain by exposing the non-objectivity and contextual constitution of the traditional academic project, and introducing its own legitimacy, which stems from conceptualization of the emancipatory project as a solution to suffering in the world" (Heath-Kelly 2010: 252).

This is of great importance when we seek to move beyond critique and offer clear alternatives to current counterterrorism practices. Similarly to how critical theory can salvage the *content* of reason but struggles to justify its normative *function*, so too does CTS struggle to justify its normative *function*. CTS can critique counterterrorism practices, and so far it has done so in a compelling manner, but that in itself does not necessarily provide strong grounds for why CTS counterterrorism is preferable to orthodox approaches. To transcend the realm of critique and offer alternative counterterrorism policies and approaches, CTS scholars need to come to terms with, and clearly articulate how to incorporate, an emancipatory commitment. Without one, it is hard to conceive of any substantial and coherent CTS critique of counterterrorism that also contains positive visions of what CTS counterterrorism could look like, or in the language of critical theory, identify and realize concrete utopias. Um and Pisoiu (2015) have documented the current limitations of empirical research and identified the lack of a notion of what effective counterterrorism should bring about. Jackson et al. have claimed that the maximal test of counterterrorism is whether it improves human security and well-being (Jackson et al. 2011: 245). It seems to me that emancipation can provide that principle on which to measure the effectiveness of counterterrorism.

How can we know if counterterrorism policies are effective? It starts with an old enlightenment principle: dare to know. First, we need to destabilize the taboo that surrounds terrorism so that we can engage seriously and critically with terrorist subjectivity. Second, there is a need to critically examine our own policies as enabling conditions for terrorism. Addressing these two points would go quite some way toward mitigating the epistemological crisis of counterterrorism. Finally, when we understand that our policies can be directly responsible for acts of terrorism, and that violence only breeds more violence, it should be clear that the best way to counter terrorism is to provide security for individuals everywhere, with them and not at their expense.

Glimmers of a new paradigm?

It is the contention of this chapter that going forward, CTS scholars should focus on providing alternatives to orthodox counterterrorism with an emancipatory commitment at its core. A lot has been said about emancipation, and I have argued for its importance in a CTS research agenda. Yet, there is a considerable gap in the CTS counterterrorism literature regarding examples of what emancipation could look like in practice. CTS has emancipation as a guiding principle, but besides a commitment to ending avoidable human suffering (Jackson et al. 2009: 224), there has not been enough attention devoted to research on what realizing concrete utopias would look like.

An intrinsic element of emancipation is to open up discursive space and amplify the voices that have been silenced by dominating discourses. According to McDonald, who has formulated what emancipation could look like in a CTS research agenda, emancipation is best advanced through "the freeing up of space to think, speak, and write differently about what 'terrorism' means, how it might be studied, and how to make sense of effective responses to it" (McDonald 2009: 121). This is closely linked to the concept of immanent critique which Jackson notes is not about establishing the "correct" or "real truth", but highlighting contradictions or alternative explanations from the same sources (Jackson 2009b: 68). This means questioning who defines terrorism and who defines the counterterrorism approaches. Given that knowledge is always *for* someone and *for* some purpose, these questions are imperative in identifying how dominant groups or elites can narrow the discursive space and thus the room for dissent. On the other hand, immanent critique can engage with the core arguments of the dominant discourses and destabilize them by laying bare the flaws and inherent shortcomings of the discourse. Giving voice to the voiceless, therefore, through counterhegemonic discourse and narratives, has great emancipatory potential.

Another way scholars could incorporate emancipation into a research agenda is to construct a CTS framework of counterterrorism. Based on the research produced so far, it should be possible for CTS scholars to construct a counterterrorism approach that is fundamentally different in terms of its ontology, epistemology, and ethical-normative commitment guided by emancipation. Taken together, much of the critique produced by CTS argues for the need to contextualize acts of terrorism, or understand them in their own cultural grammar. A CTS approach to counterterrorism would have several advantages compared to orthodox approaches. It would understand terrorism as an ontologically unstable fact; that it is context-dependent; that most acts of terrorism are the result of conflicts; that countering violence with more violence will only lead to a self-fulfilling prophecy in which counterterrorism constantly creates and re-creates the enemy it is sworn to defeat; that narratives play a huge part in maintaining the status quo but also have the potential to be counterhegemonic; and finally, an emancipatory commitment would truly set it apart from its orthodox counterparts due to its unfaltering commitment to enhance the security of all people with them and not at someone's expense.

Importantly, a CTS framework of counterterrorism does not aim to provide solutions to terrorism in a problem-solving manner. If acts of terrorism are dependent upon their context and not just incarnations of an extraordinary menace that threatens civilization, we then see how terrorism derives from deeper conceptions of politics. At that point, it is clear that emancipation needs to be at the foundation of CTS approach to counterterrorism, as terrorism in many ways is just another symptom of a world gone wrong for a vast number of people.

References

Appleby, N., 2010. "Labelling the Innocent: How Government Counter-Terrorism Advice Creates Labels That Contribute to the Problem." *Critical Studies on Terrorism* 3(3): 421–36.
Baker-Beall, C., Heath-Kelly, C., and Jarvis, J., eds., 2015. *Counter-Radicalization: Critical Perspectives*. Abingdon, UK: Routledge.
Booth, K., 2007. *Theory of World Security*. Cambridge: Cambridge University Press.
Booth, K., and Dunne, T., 2012. *Terror in Our Time*. Abingdon: Routledge.
Chowdhury, A., and Fitzsimmons, S., 2013. "Effective but Inefficient: Understanding the Costs of Counterterrorism." *Critical Studies on Terrorism* 6(3): 447–56.
Coaffee, J., 2010. "Protecting the Urban: The Dangers of Planning for Terrorism." *Theory, Culture & Society* 26(7–8): 343–55.
Cox, R. W., 1981. "Social Forces, States and World Orders: Beyond International Relations Theory." *Millennium – Journal of International Studies* 10(2): 126–55.
Crelinsten, R., 2009. *Counterterrorism*. Cambridge: Polity Press.
Davidson, H., 2014. "Counter-Terrorism Proposals 'Greatly Concerning', Say Civil Liberties Groups." *The Guardian*. Available online at: www.theguardian.com/world/2014/aug/18/counter-terrorism-proposals-greatly-concerning-say-civil-liberties-groups.
De Graaf, B., and de Graaff, B., 2010. "Bringing Politics Back in: The Introduction of the 'Performative Power' of Counterterrorism." *Critical Studies on Terrorism* 3(2): 261–75.
Dershowitz, A., 2010. "There Is a Need to Bring an Unfortunate Practice within the Bounds of Law," in Gottlieb, S., ed., *Debating Terrorism and Counterterrorism: Conflicting Perspectives on Causes, Contexts, and Responses*. Washington, DC: CQ Press, pp. 320–35.
Donohue, L., 2008. *The Cost of Counterterrorism*. Cambridge: Cambridge University Press.
Duyvesteyn, I., and Malkki, L., 2012. "The Fallacy of the New Terrorism Thesis," in Jackson, R., and Sinclair, S., eds., *Contemporary Debates on Terrorism*. Abingdon: Routledge, pp. 35–42.
Eland, I., 1998. "Does U.S. Intervention Overseas Breed Terrorism?" *Cato Institute Foreign Policy Briefing* (50): 1–24.
Fox News. 2014. "Kansas City Lingerie Shopowners in a Twist after Homeland Security's Panty Raid." Available online at: www.foxnews.com/politics/2014/10/23/kansas-city-lingerie-shopowners-in-twist-after-homeland-security-panty-raid/.
Geoghegan, T., and Casciani, D., 2007. "How to Terror-Proof Shopping Centres and Other Buildings." *BBC*. Available online at: http://news.bbc.co.uk/2/hi/uk_news/magazine/7095884.stm.
Goerzig, C., 2010. *Talking to Terrorists: Concessions and the Renunciation of Violence*. Abingdon: Routledge.
Gunning, J., 2009. *Hamas in Politics: Democracy, Religion, Violence*. New York: Columbia University Press.
Heath-Kelly, C., 2010. "Critical Terrorism Studies, Critical Theory and the 'Naturalistic Fallacy.'" *Security Dialogue* 41(3): 235–54.
Heath-Kelly, C., 2012. "Can We Laugh Yet? Reading Post-9/11 Counterterrorism Policy as Magical Realism and Opening a Third-Space of Resistance." *European Journal on Criminal Policy and Research* 18(4): 343–60.
Heath-Kelly, C., 2013. "Counter-Terrorism and the Counterfactual: Producing the 'Radicalisation' Discourse and the UK PREVENT Strategy." *The British Journal of Politics & International Relations* 15(3): 394–415.
Hickman, M., Thomas, L., Nickels, H., and Silvestri, S., 2012. "Social Cohesion and the Notion of 'Suspect Communities': A Study of the Experiences and Impacts of Being 'Suspect' for Irish Communities and Muslim Communities in Britain." *Critical Studies on Terrorism* 5(1): 89–106.
Jackson, R., 2005. *Writing the War on Terrorism*. Manchester: Manchester University Press.
Jackson, R., 2009a. "Critical Terrorism Studies: Framing a New Research Agenda," in Jackson, R., Breen Smyth, M., and Gunning, J., eds., *Critical Terrorism Studies: A New Research Agenda*. Abingdon: Routledge, pp. 216–36.
Jackson, R., 2009b. "Knowledge, Power and Politics in the Study of Political Terrorism," in Jackson, R., Breen Smyth, M., and Gunning, J., eds., *Critical Terrorism Studies: A New Research Agenda*. Abingdon: Routledge, pp. 66–83.

Jackson, R., 2015. "Bin Laden's Ghost and the Epistemological Crises of Counter-Terrorism," in Susan Jeffords and Fahed al-Sumait, eds., *After bin Laden: Global Media and the Representation of Terrorism*. Urbana, IL: University of Illinois Press, pp. 3–19.

Jackson, R., Breen Smyth, M., and Gunning, J., eds., 2009. *Critical Terrorism Studies: A New Research Agenda*. Abingdon: Routledge.

Jackson, R., Jarvis, L., Gunning, J., and Breen Smyth, M., 2011. *Terrorism: A Critical Introduction*. New York: Palgrave Macmillan.

Keenan, J., 2010. "Africa Unsecured? The Role of the Global War on Terror (GWOT) in Securing US Imperial Interests in Africa." *Critical Studies on Terrorism* 3(1): 27–47.

Kolås, Å., 2010. "The 2008 Mumbai Terror Attacks: (Re-)constructing Indian (Counter-)Terrorism." *Critical Studies on Terrorism* 3(1): 83–98.

Lum, C., Kennedy, L., and Sherley, A., 2006. "The Effectiveness of Counter-Terrorism Strategies." *Campbell Systematic Reviews* 2: 1–51. Available online at: www.campbellcollaboration.org/lib/download/53/1010_R2.pdf.

Lynch, O., 2013. "British Muslim Youth: Radicalisation, Terrorism and the Construction of the 'Other.'" *Critical Studies on Terrorism* 6(2): 241–61.

Lynch, O., and Ryder, C., 2012. "Deadliness, Organisational Change and Suicide Attacks: Understanding the Assumptions Inherent in the Use of the Term ' New Terrorism.'" *Critical Studies on Terrorism* 5(2): 257–75.

Mac Ginty, R., 2010. "Social Network Analysis and Counterinsurgency: A Counterproductive Strategy?" *Critical Studies on Terrorism* 3(2): 209–26.

Martin, G., 2003. *Understanding Terrorism: Challenges, Perspectives, and Issues*. London: SAGE Publications Ltd.

McCrisken, T., 2011. "Ten Years on : Obama's War on Terrorism in Rhetoric and Practice." *International Affairs* 87(4): 781–801.

McDonald, M., 2009. "Emancipation and Critical Terrorism Studies", in Jackson, R., Breen Smyth, M., and Gunning, J., eds., *Critical Terrorism Studies. A New Research Agenda*. Abingdon: Routledge, pp. 109–23.

Morehouse, M., 2014. "It's Easier to Decapitate a Snake than It Is a Hydra: An Analysis of Colombia's Targeted Killing Program." *Studies in Conflict & Terrorism* 37(7): 541–66.

Mucha, W., 2013. "Does Counterinsurgency Fuel Civil War? Peru and Syria Compared." *Critical Studies on Terrorism* 6(1): 140–66.

Mueller, J., 2006. *Overblown: How Politicians and the Terrorism Industry Inflate National Security Threats, and Why We Believe Them*. New York: Free Press.

Mueller, J., and Stewart, M., 2014. "Terrorism and Counterterrorism in the US: The Question of Responsible Policy-Making." *The International Journal of Human Rights* 18(2): 228–40.

Napoleoni, L., 2010. *Terrorism and the Economy: How the War on Terror Is Bankrupting the World*. New York: Seven Stories Press.

NSA, 2014. "NSA: Utah Data Center." Available online at: http://nsa.gov1.info/utah-data-center/.

Oriola, T., 2009. "Counter-Terrorism and Alien Justice: The Case of Security Certificates in Canada." *Critical Studies on Terrorism* 2(2): 257–74.

Payne, E., 2014. "Kerry: 'The Cancer of ISIS Will Not Be Allowed to Spread.'" *CNN*. Available online at: http://edition.cnn.com/2014/08/30/us/kerry-isis/.

Pedahzur, A., and Perliger, A., 2006. "The Changing Nature of Suicide Attacks: A Social Network Perspective." *Social Forces* 84(4): 1987–2008.

Pisoiu, D., ed., 2014. *Arguing Counterterrorism: New Perspectives*. Abingdon: Routledge.

Qureshi, A., 2010. "'War on Terror': The African Front." *Critical Studies on Terrorism* 3(1): 49–61.

Richmond, O., and Franks, J., 2009. "The Impact of Orthodox Terrorism Discourses on the Liberal Peace: Internalisation, Resistance, or Hybridisation?" *Critical Studies on Terrorism* 2(2): 201–18.

Rogers, P., 2012. "Wars of Terror – Learning the Lessons of Failure," in Jackson, R., and Sinclair, S., eds., *Contemporary Debates on Terrorism*. Abingdon: Routledge, pp. 143–51.

Sharvit, K., Kruglanski, A. W., Mo Wang, Xiaoyan Chen, Boyatzi, L. M., Ganor, B. and Azani, E., 2013. "The Effects of Israeli Use of Coercive and Conciliatory Tactics on Palestinian's Use of Terrorist Tactics: 2000–2006." *Dynamics of Asymmetric Conflict* 6(1–3): 22–44.

Silke, A., 2012. "The Case against Targeted Assassination," in Jackson, R., and Sinclair, S., eds., *Contemporary Debates on Terrorism*. Abingdon: Routledge, pp. 173–80.

Smith, M., 2010. *Securing Africa: Post-9/11 Discourses on Terrorism*. Farnham: Ashgate.

Spencer, A., 2010. *The Tabloid Terrorist: The Predicative Construction of New Terrorism in the Media*. New York: Palgrave Macmillan.
Stampnitzky, L., 2013. *Disciplining Terrorism, How Experts Invented "Terrorism."* Cambridge: Cambridge University Press.
Stampnitzky, L., 2015. "Problematic Knowledge: How Terrorism Resists Expertise," in Berling, T., and Bueger, C., eds., *Capturing Security Expertise: Practice, Power and Responsibility*. Abingdon: Routledge, pp. 1–13.
Stewart, M., and Mueller, J., 2013. "Terrorism Risks and Cost-Benefit Analysis of Aviation Security." *Risk Analysis: An Official Publication of the Society for Risk Analysis* 33(5): 893–908.
Stohl, M., 2008. "Old Myths, New Fantasies and the Enduring Realities of Terrorism." *Critical Studies on Terrorism* 1(1): 5–16.
Toivanen, R., 2010. "Counterterrorism and Expert Regimes: Some Human Rights Concerns." *Critical Studies on Terrorism* 3(2): 277–94.
Toros, H., 2012. *Terrorism, Talking, and Transformation: A Critical Approach*. Abingdon: Routledge.
Toros, H., and Gunning, J., 2009. "Exploring a Critical Theory Approach to Terrorism Studies," in Jackson, R., Breen Smyth, M., and Gunning, J., eds., *Critical Terrorism Studies. A New Research Agenda*. Abingdon: Routledge, pp. 87–108.
Um, E., and Pisoiu, D., 2011. *Economics of Security, Effective Counterterrorism: What Have We Learned so Far?* Berlin. Available online at: www.diw.de/documents/publikationen/73/diw_01.c.386651.de/diw_econsec0055.pdf
Um, E., and Pisoiu, D., 2015. "Dealing with Uncertainty: The Illusion of Knowledge in the Study of Counterterrorism Effectiveness." *Critical Studies on Terrorism* 8(2): 229–45. Available online at: www.tandfonline.com/doi/full/10.1080/17539153.2014.981400.
Warde, I., and Humphrey, C., 2008. *The Price of Fear: The Truth behind the Financial War On Terror*. London: I.B. Tauris & Co. Ltd.
Wyn-Jones, R., 2005. "On Emancipation: Necessity, Capacity and Concrete Utopias", in Booth, K., ed., *Critical Security Studies and World Politics*. Boulder: Lynne Rienner, pp. 215–35.
Zalman, A., and Clarke, J., 2009. "The Global War on Terror: A Narrative in Need of a Rewrite." *Ethics & International Affairs* 23(2): 101–13.
Zulaika, J., 2009. *Terrorism. The Self-Fulfilling Prophecy*. Chicago: The University of Chicago Press.

21
A CRITICAL PERSPECTIVE ON THE GLOBAL WAR ON TERROR

Paul Rogers

Introduction

On the night of 22 September 2014, just under thirteen years after the start of the US operation to terminate the Taliban regime and destroy the key centre of the al Qaida movement in Afghanistan, US cruise missiles and strike aircraft were launched in a coordinated series of attacks on the Islamic State (IS) movement in northern Syria. This followed seven weeks of air attacks on IS in Iraq, a response to the rapid gains that IS had made across northern Iraq earlier in the year, including the taking of Mosul on 10 June. President Barack Obama and other Western politicians warned that operations against IS would be long and difficult, preparing their electorates for what some were calling the Third Gulf War and what others saw as an extension of the global war on terror.

This was in contrast to the optimism that had been evident when the Taliban regime had been terminated in late 2001 within three months of the 9/11 attacks. Indeed, in his first State of the Union Address in January 2002, President George W. Bush was able to report great progress in the global war on terror and to extend it beyond al Qaida and the Taliban to an "axis of evil" centred on Iraq, Iran, and North Korea. It was also in contrast to his "Mission Accomplished" address of 1 May 2003 after the collapse of the Saddam Hussein regime in Iraq within three weeks of the start of US-led coalition military operations. The political attitude in early 2015 also contrasted with the view of the Obama administration at the start of its first period in office in 2009, when plans were afoot to withdraw US troops from Iraq and negotiate with the Taliban in Afghanistan from a position of strength. At that time, it was also believed that the wider global Islamist threat was much diminished, a view supported by the killing of Osama bin Laden in May 2011.

The expectation of a long new war against the Islamic State is a reflection of the changing attitude to the problem of Islamist political violence and a reflection of the development of a number of potent movements linked to the original al Qaida outlook. While the most significant of these, at the time of writing (June 2015) is the Islamic State in Iraq and Syria, there is also concern over Boko Haram in Nigeria; a number of movements in Mali, Niger, and Libya; continuing Islamist paramilitary actions in Somalia and Yemen; the Caucasus Emirate in Russia; the reemergence of the Taliban in Afghanistan; and a complex of Islamist movements in Pakistan (Khalil 2015).

Put together, there is a sense that a struggle of almost Manichean proportions is once more under way, a struggle shown by the rapid growth of the Western involvement in Iraq and Syria to encompass a force of strike aircraft from the UK, Australia, Canada, Denmark, Belgium, and France, together with several regional states. While there are not plans to put substantial numbers of troops on the ground, the repeated inference of Western politicians is that the war on terror has entered a new and substantial phase. Indeed, military analysts are already arguing that IS cannot be countered except by the direct use of Western troops, the Iraqi Army being incapable of doing so without years of training and re-equipping.

Furthermore, the experience of the wars against al Qaida, Islamic State, and other Islamist movements has extended well beyond direct warfare and has permeated many other aspects of society in the countries opposing extreme Islamist movements, not least in terms of a hardening of public attitudes, a considerable expansion in domestic counterterrorism activity and expenditure, and greatly increased levels of surveillance. These developments may be incremental in states that have a long experience of extreme Islamist movements, such as Russia with the Caucasus Emirate (International Institute for Strategic Studies 2012) and those facing unexpected opposition such as China (Holdstock 2015), but they constitute much more sudden changes in policing, legal procedures, public order control, and other aspects of governance in Western states such as the UK and Australia.

It is the contrast between optimistic expectations of success following the 9/11 attacks with the reality of two appallingly costly wars and a sustaining of the al Qaida idea that is the concern of this chapter. In particular, it seeks to examine the reasons for the persistent view that al Qaida and the axis of evil presented threats to the West that verged on the existential, and that the large-scale use of military force was the appropriate – indeed the only – response (see Lindahl, this volume). It also attempts to throw light on the paucity of critical analysis of this approach from the terrorism studies community in the years immediately after 9/11 and the reasons why even the development of more critical analysis in the more recent past has not resulted in substantial changes in policy.

The chapter is structured to commence with a history of the fourteen years of the war on terror with an emphasis on expectations and outcomes of the different phases. It then explores the main reasons for the series of decisions to respond with considerable force, including the subtle change over the past decade from "boots on the ground" to "remote control". The latter is a convenient term for an approach that embraces the increased use of Special Forces, armed drones (see Calhoun, this volume), privatised military corporations, prompt global strike, and other means of distant control as it becomes central to Western military thinking. Finally, it contributes to explaining the academic context, although this is covered in much greater depth elsewhere in this volume.

Phase 1: 9/11 to the State of the Union Address

The al Qaida movement developed initially in southeastern Afghanistan in the late 1980s within the vigorous mujahidin insurgency that was in the process of expelling Soviet forces from the country. Centred on the young Saudi logistician, Osama bin Laden, and his intellectual mentor, Ayman al-Zawahiri, and influenced much by the writings of Islamist scholars such as Sayidd Qutb, the group conceived of a movement to renew Islam in a rigorous and puritanical interpretation. The success of the anti-Soviet uprising showed that a determined movement could defeat a superpower and even bring it to its knees, and even though the insurgency had been primarily nationalistic and ethnic in its motivation and had been supported by the Pakistani Inter-Service Intelligence agency and the Central Intelligence Agency, the religious element was seen by the core leadership of al Qaida as the key motivation for the future (Lawrence 2005).

By the late 1990s, the movement had been much dispersed, with bin Laden based successively in Saudi Arabia and Sudan before returning to Afghanistan to aid the new Islamist Taliban movement in its determination to unify the country as a theocratic state, fighting the warlords of the Northern Alliance in order to do so. By 2000, al Qaida could be described as a revolutionary movement determined to bring down unacceptable regimes across the Middle East, especially the House of Saud, replacing these "near enemies" with true theocracies. While centred still in Afghanistan, it was already taking the form of a loose network across many countries and also had a clear intention of taking the war to the "far enemy" of the United States and Western Europe, their alliance with the Zionist entity of Israel, with its control of the Third Holy Place, being a key motivation. What was hugely significant, and distinguished the al Qaida movement from most revolutionary groups, was its eschatological dimension, looking beyond earthly life and therefore operating to a timescale to be measured in decades, if not centuries.

In this context, the attack on the United States planned by the Frankfurt cell had a particular place in that it would demonstrate to the *Umma*, the wider Moslem community, the power of the new movement and would also ensure a massive reaction from the United States. Indeed, there was the strong possibility that US forces would be ordered to occupy Afghanistan, terminate the Taliban regime in Kabul, and seek to kill the al Qaida leadership and destroy the movement. An attack by the US in early autumn had the specific advantage that it would take many months for US troops to move into Afghanistan in force, given winter conditions on the long supply routes, so that a guerrilla war could be developed that might ultimately wear down the United States and its allies, even if this might take a decade or more.

The 9/11 attacks in New York and Washington killed some 3,000 people and had a devastating effect on the US political system, especially under the Republican administration of Bush. But support for a strong military response stretched well beyond the United States, not least to the Blair administration in the UK. Terminating the Taliban regime and destroying the al Qaida movement was indeed an immediate requirement, but the US military chose to achieve this not by a major invasion of Afghanistan, but by a combination of intensive air attacks, use of Special Forces, and immediate support for the militias of the Northern Alliance warlords.

The success of this unexpected strategy was little short of spectacular, with the Taliban melting away within two months. Most of the al Qaida supporters retreated out of Afghanistan, principally to northwest Pakistan, and neither bin Laden nor Zawahiri, nor the Taliban leader Mullah Omar, was killed or captured. By December 2001, the Berlin conference of allied states agreed to oversee the transition of Afghanistan to democracy, promising much support in the process. Some UN officials and Afghan leaders warned that the Taliban had not been comprehensively defeated in the conventional sense and that they could reassert themselves if a security vacuum was allowed to develop. Some spoke of the need for an international peacekeeping and stabilisation force of 30,000 personnel being required, but this was not forthcoming; the eventually established International Security Assistance Force (ISAF) numbered no more than 5,000 people.

As might reasonably have been expected, the remarkable success of the US-led global war on terror boosted the popularity of the Bush administration and allowed the president to deliver a singularly upbeat State of the Union Address to both Houses of Congress on 29 January 2002 (Bush 2002). In this notable speech, Bush extended the war to encompass a much wider "axis of evil" of states that supported terrorism and were seeking weapons of mass destruction. The primary elements were Iraq, Iran, and North Korea, with Syria, Libya, and Cuba forming part of a wider threat. By March 2002, the Bush administration was beginning to form a coalition aimed at regime termination in Iraq, with this seen as a prelude to the remaking of Middle Eastern politics to usher in an era of liberal free-market democracies with close affinity to the United States and willing to accept Israel as a legitimate state.

Phase 2: a mission accomplished?

Over the twelve months from March 2002 to February 2003, a primarily Western coalition of states was assembled for the action against the Saddam Hussein regime. Support came from Italy and Spain, and especially from the UK, but some other states in Western Europe were far more cautious, especially France and Germany. And in the region, the Turkish government was sufficiently concerned to block US attempts to move an Army Division into Iraq through southeast Turkey. A UN mandate was sought for the planned operation, but this was not forthcoming at the level required to ensure full international legitimacy; yet, by February of 2003, a war was clearly imminent.

One of the main arguments used was that Iraq was close to achieving a significant capability to deliver weapons of mass destruction, particularly chemical weapons, in spite of the substantial work of the UN inspection teams that had been active for a decade. Evidence for this was far from clear and was one of the factors that led to a singularly vigorous anti-war movement developing in a number of Western countries, not least the UK.

In the event, regime termination commenced on 20 March 2003 with a substantial air assault. This was followed immediately by a ground invasion, principally into southern Iraq from Kuwait. The main forces were drawn from the US Army and Marine Corps but with other states contributing, especially the UK. Progress appeared to be rapid, with troops moving up the Euphrates and Tigris valleys to the outskirts of Baghdad in little more than two weeks. Opposition forces were poorly organised and hugely susceptible to the use of area-impact munitions, although irregular attacks on the advancing forces, including suicide attacks, commenced almost at once. Even so, after three weeks, US forces were in Baghdad, the felling of a Saddam Hussein statue was seen across the world, the regime collapsed, and the war appeared won.

On 1 May 2002, President Bush made his "Mission Accomplished" speech from the flight deck of the *USS Abraham Lincoln* off the California coast reporting success in the war, if warning that more had to be done. By this time, there was considerable satisfaction in Washington that the impact of the 9/11 atrocities had been countered, with the added advantage that the transition that could now be effected by the newly established Coalition Provisional Authority in Baghdad would also limit Iran's power and influence in the region. With US forces stationed in Afghanistan to the east and Iraq to the west, with close allies in Saudi Arabia, Kuwait, Bahrain, the United Arab Emirates, and Oman, and with the US Navy's augmented Fifth Fleet in control of the Arabian Sea and the Persian Gulf, Iran would scarcely be problematic. Given the view from the Bush administration of Iran as the greatest threat to the region, if not the world, this explains a phrase popular in Republican circles in the Spring of 2002 that "the road to Tehran runs through Baghdad".

Phase 3: not according to plan

During the course of May to December 2003, the security situation for occupying forces in Iraq worsened steadily. The bombing of the UN Mission Headquarters and the Jordanian diplomatic mission in Baghdad were visible signs of this, but across much of central Iraq the coalition ground forces found themselves facing a determined urban insurgency, at the centre of which were elite Iraqi groups drawn principally from Saddam Hussein's Special Republican Guard, a force of some four brigades. These had avoided conflict with heavily armed US forces in the approach to Baghdad, going to ground in order to provide opposition to the subsequent occupation.

For most US military, their training and equipment was not suited to such a conflict. Casualties grew rapidly and were actually made worse in terms of morale because so many terribly wounded soldiers survived due to improvements in battlefield wound treatment and rapid casualty evacuation. Given that the prevailing outlook was that the war in Iraq was responding to the 9/11 attacks and that the Iraqis were viewed as terrorists, one consequence was the frequent use of overwhelming firepower against them, causing substantial civilian casualties. There were many examples during 2003 and 2004 of overt reprisal raids, one notable instance being the destruction of part of the city of Fallujah following an attack on a Marines convoy (Constable 2004). An inevitable effect was to harden opposition to the coalition, made worse by the CPA decision to disband the Iraqi Army, throwing well over 100,000 young men into unemployment.

Furthermore, the many instances of prisoner abuse, especially in the Abu Ghraib prison west of Baghdad, were widely known in Iraq before they caused controversy in the United States and among its coalition partners. Similarly, the practice of rendition of prisoners to third countries for extreme interrogation and the treatment of prisoners en route to and at the Guantanamo detention centre in Cuba were also widely known (see Blakeley and Raphael 2014, this volume).

Two particular factors were to have an effect across the region, enabling Islamist propagandists to make much of what they presented as an assault on Islam. One was the coverage of the war by new regional TV news channels such as Al Jazeera, with the impact on civilians shown in much more graphic detail than in Western media outlets. Even though the war later morphed into a bitter interconfessional Sunni-Shi'a conflict that caused even more deaths, it was the impact of Western states killing thousands of Moslems that was of greatest help to radical Islamists.

The second was that the United States military inevitably turned to the one ally in the region with considerable experience of urban counter-insurgency – Israel. During the course of 2004–2005, the preexisting collaboration was greatly strengthened, with Israeli advisers and military trainers, as well as Israeli equipment, being drafted in to aid the troubled military operations (Opall-Rome 2003). This may have been fully understandable from a US perspective, but it provided Islamist propagandists with an opportunity to portray the entire war as a Crusader/Zionist assault on the Moslem world, with only the radical Islamist movements offering resistance. If one purpose of the al Qaida attacks on New York and Washington was to provoke the "far enemy" into occupying Afghanistan, what happened, at least initially, was the occupation of a state far more significant in Islamic history, Iraq – the centre of the remarkable Abbasid Caliphate of a thousand years ago.

The deterioration of security in Iraq in 2004–2005 had been paralleled by other evolving problems in the war on terror, three being significant. One was the development of many al Qaida offshoots, some comprising just a few individuals, others being larger groups. They were responsible for numerous attacks across Europe and Asia, most of them directed at Western targets and including bombings and shootings in Morocco, Tunisia, Egypt, Jordan, Saudi Arabia, Yemen, Pakistan, Turkey, India, Indonesia, London, and Madrid. Few if any were directed by the al Qaida leadership, making counterterrorism endeavours singularly difficult.

A second problem was the evolution of larger radical movements, not least in Yemen and Somalia, and the third was the reemergence of the Taliban in Afghanistan, especially in Kandahar and Helmand Provinces. By early 2006, security across much of Afghanistan was deteriorating rapidly leading to a massive expansion in NATO's ISAF forces, primarily American but with major British, Canadian, Dutch, and German contingents. In spite of this, the Taliban made considerable progress in taking territory, and even the much-vaunted Western aim of controlling cultivation of the opium poppy failed.

Phase 4: withdrawal

By late 2007, a combination of three developments resulted in some easing of the level of opposition in Iraq. One was an extremely violent shadow war in which four Special Forces units, collectively and most commonly termed TF (Task Force) 145, were formed by the Joint Special Operations Command (JSOC) to work in concert with intelligence and reconnaissance assets to identify and kill or capture presumed insurgents. Over a three-year period from 2004 to 2007, and reaching its peak with Operation Arcadia in 2006, the units drawn from SEAL Team 6, the Rangers, Delta Force, and a UK SAS squadron had considerable freedom to seek out insurgents, the peak intensity involving some 300 raids per month (Niva 2013; Urban 2010).

Detainees in raids would frequently be subject to intense physical interrogation to gain further information that would form the basis of further raids, sometimes conducted within hours. Such was the independence and intensity of these operations that there were reports that barely half of those killed or detained were actually integral to the insurgency. The numbers killed are not known with any confidence, but they probably ran into the thousands, with tens of thousands detained, including more than 20,000 in Camp Bucca near Basra alone. During this period, the leader of the most extreme of the opposition group, al Qaida in Mesopotamia (AQIM), Abu Musab al Zarqawi, was killed, and his eventual successor, Abu Bakr al Baghdadi, was detained.

The second development was the gathering of some Sunni clan militias to form auxiliaries to the US forces and those of the Iraqi government, this being possible by a combination of clan opposition to the extreme violence of what was then known as al Qaida in Iraq (AQI) and also substantial payments from US sources. Finally, the Bush administration surged troops into Iraq to capitalise on the improving situation. Even so, by the start of the 2008 presidential election in the United States, domestic support for the war had declined sufficiently such that the Democratic contender, Barack Obama, campaigned on the basis of withdrawing US forces from Iraq but continuing the war in Afghanistan, as this related more closely to the original 9/11 attacks.

During his first term, Obama fulfilled his pledge and all US combat troops left Iraq by the end of 2011, although some thousands of trainers, support staff, and private military contractors remained in the country. After much consideration, Obama surged an additional 30,000 troops into Afghanistan with the aim of gaining sufficient military advantage over the Taliban to negotiate a partial withdrawal in the knowledge that the Taliban would be too weakened to have more than a peripheral role in future Afghan governance. With other coalition forces involved, this brought the total number of foreign troops in the country to 130,000, but it did not succeed, and by 2013, the Obama administration had decided on a fixed timetable for withdrawal of all but 10,000 troops by the end of 2014. Coalition partners such as Britain followed suit.

Phase 5: remote control

By mid-2011, the end result of a decade of the global war on terror was radically different from that anticipated in Bush's (2002) State of the Union Address and his 2003 "Mission Accomplished" speech. A report from Brown University published in June 2011 was summarised by Rogers (2014):

- At a conservative estimate the overall death toll in Iraq, Afghanistan and elsewhere, including civilians, uniformed personnel and contractors, was at least 225,000.[1]
- There were 7.8 million refugees created among Iraqis, Afghans, and Pakistanis.
- The wars will cost close to $4 trillion dollars and are being funded substantially by borrowing, with $185 billion in interest already paid and another $1 trillion likely by 2020.

In terms of Western domestic politics and military thinking, the huge civilian casualties were less important than their own military casualties. For the United States, the deaths were well over 6,000, with at least 25,000 seriously injured, many of them maimed for life. Casualties for many of the coalition partners such as the UK were also significant, and the constant reports of deaths and serious injuries had a cumulative effect on public opinion. In terms of military posture, the failure of the "boots on the ground" model appears to have accelerated the move to what has been termed "remote control", a rather different approach to handling distant threats. Some elements of this were hardly new, including the use of Special Forces as in TF 145, but these underwent a substantial expansion in numbers and capabilities and were joined by two other developments: the greatly expanded deployment of private military company personnel and the development of unarmed and armed drones (Donnellan and Kersley 2014; see also Calhoun, this volume).

From 2008 to 2012, the extensive use of these approaches, especially armed drones in Pakistan and Afghanistan and Special Force night raids in Afghanistan, led to the view that this was far more appropriate and less costly (in financial and human terms), a view boosted both by the killing of bin Laden by a US Special Forces unit and the widespread if controversial armed drone attacks on the al Qaida leadership and other Islamist groups in Pakistan. Even the extensive NATO operation in Libya during 2011 was seen as a success in this context, with air power and limited Special Forces operations acting to support rebels as the Gaddafi regime was terminated, even if it was a six-month-long process.

By the time of Obama's second election campaign, there was some satisfaction to be taken from the apparent transition to stability in Iraq, the diminishing of the al Qaida movement in Pakistan, and the decrease in attacks on Western targets. Overall, and much as in early 2002 and mid-2003, there was a view that the global war on terror was at last diminishing as a project. The term began to be dropped from use as the troops came home and the al Qaida movement began to be seen as ephemeral rather than enduring. That may have been true of the movement but certainly not of the idea, and in the following two years, there was a radical rethinking towards the view that had previously been held by a small minority of analysts, namely that this might be a decades-long conflict (Rogers 2006).

Phase 6: the renewed global war on terror

During the early months of 2011, a political upheaval across the Arab Middle East started with the sudden and popular overthrow of the Ben Ali regime in Tunisia, followed by the astonishing fall of the Mubarak regime in Egypt. The prospect of improved governance across much of the region could have presented a great threat to revolutionary Islamist movements that sought the violent overthrow of regimes and their replacement by theocracies, but progress in this direction was limited. In Tunisia, there was certainly a slow if positive move towards democratic governance, and there were significant reforms in Morocco. But the Egyptian experiment led to a short-lived Moslem Brotherhood regime that failed to be sufficiently inclusive and was replaced by the markedly anti-Islamist al-Sisi administration. Most western Gulf States responded with concessions backed up by repression of dissent, but in Syria an initially nonviolent movement was put down with extreme force by the Assad regime, leading to armed rebellions which the regime claimed to be Islamist and terroristic. Dominated initially by secular if disunited opposition movements, the rebellion was increasingly led by Islamist paramilitaries.

As significant as this was, the failure of the Nouri al-Malaki government in Iraq to reach out to the Sunni minority led to bitter political opposition, the reemergence of Baathist elements, and increasing support from Sunni clan militias, especially in Anbar Province (Dodge 2012). Most important of all was the emergence of an entity eventually termed Islamic State and comprising elements of the original al Qaida in Mesopotamia, including a paramilitary core of Iraqis who had survived the TF 145 era and Operation Arcadia. Under its leader, Abu Bakr al-Baghdadi, this operated across Iraq and Syria; gained support from Baathists and Sunni clans; overran much of northwest Iraq, including the country's second city of Mosul; and declared the formation of a new Caliphate.

The growth of Islamic State has been aided through having a core of hardened combat-trained paramilitaries, experienced technocrats able to manage towns and cities, an ability to raise funding through numerous means, a highly practised media operation using numerous social media outlets (Atwan 2015), and an ability to latch on to the deep resentments across the Middle East over the substantial failure of the anticipated democratic transition (Barnett 2014). It gains from the persistent economic marginalisation of educated young people at a time when the region has not yet experienced a full demographic transition, and it also gains from a perception of marginalisation among young Moslems in Western countries. Finally, the movement receives added boosts when the Israeli-Palestinian conflict becomes intense, the copious media coverage of Israel's Operation Protective Edge, killing well over 2,000 in Gaza during August 2014, being an example.

More generally, by 2015, Western attitudes to Islamist paramilitarism had undergone a transformation away from a belief that it was a receding threat to a renewed conflict with global dimensions. While this was centred on Islamic State and its progress in Syria and Iraq (Barnett 2014; Cockburn 2014), the sense of a global challenge was also heightened by the rise of Islamist elements in Libya; continuing violence in Yemen and Somalia; radicalisation in Mali, Niger, and other countries of the Sahel; and, above all, the growth of the Boko Haram movement in Nigeria (Yourish et al. 2015).

Although the development of Islamist movements in countries such as Nigeria, Mali, and across North Africa in the past decade have their own contexts, part of the sense of potential within the movements came from seeing themselves as part of a transnational struggle against Western forces. This stems in part from the vigour of the pursuit of al Qaida in the years immediately after 9/11 by the Western coalition and the consequent belief that Islam was under systematic attack.

Thus, fourteen years after the 9/11 attacks and the onset of the global war on terror, the prospect was for a long, drawn-out war, although this would be fought avoiding the commitment of tens of thousands of troops abroad and, instead, would involve a much heavier reliance on the components of remote control. Given that the Taliban was surging in Afghanistan, that Islamic State paramilitaries had survived and learnt from Task Force 145, and that there was evidence that even the much vaunted era of the armed drones could have unexpected consequences (Aslam 2014), there was a strong case for arguing for a fundamental reappraisal of policy; yet, there was little sign of this forthcoming.

Explanations

Given the failure of Western states to succeed in their war on terror, it is appropriate to seek possible explanations. In part, this is quite straightforward in relation to the early years. The 9/11 attack was a visceral shock to the United States, given the loss of life, the iconic status of the New York World Trade Center, and the ability of apparently amateur terrorists to attack the headquarters of the world's strongest military force. An administration of almost any political complexion would have reacted with considerable force, but the George W. Bush administration was particularly tough in its approach and readily willing to extend the war to an axis of evil stretching across the world.

This was largely down to the development of a particularly vigorous foreign and military outlook embodied in the highly influential Project for a New American Century, which saw the United States having a near-Messianic mission to show the world the path to a global system based on free market liberal democracy. Prior to 9/11, the first seven months of the Bush administration had made much progress down the path towards such a uni-polar world, not least in its attitude to arms control, trade agreements, and international law. Multilateral action was sometimes acceptable but rarely desirable given America's unique global role, a role succinctly stated by Krauthammer (2001):

> Multipolarity, yes, when there is no alternative. But not when there is. Not when we have the unique imbalance of power that we enjoy today – and that has given the international system a stability and essential tranquillity it had not known for at least a century. The international environment is far more likely to enjoy peace under a single hegemon. Moreover, we are not just any hegemon. We run a uniquely benign imperium.

This outlook persisted throughout the two administrations of George W. Bush, although the Department of Defense was moving toward the methods and technologies of remote control by 2008. It was also fuelled by the need for the armed forces as a whole to enhance the defence budget, given the relative drawdown of the Clinton era following the end of the Cold War. An added element was the profitability of the global war on terror for the defence industrial complex (*Defense News* 2015), especially as the problems arising in Iraq and Afghanistan required immediate solutions, often at considerable cost. The nature of the wars in Iraq and Afghanistan was such that the greatest demands were made on the US Army and the Marine Corps, with the Air Force and Navy relatively less relevant. This might be expected to aid defence companies specifically relevant to these branches of the armed forces, but such is the consolidation of the US defence industrial complex into a handful of large corporations that versatility of production capabilities is almost guaranteed.

The unexpected problems arising in both wars had two other outcomes, one being the rapid growth in the use of Private Military and Security Companies (PMSCs), which themselves developed a sophisticated lobbying presence in Washington (McFate 2014). The other was the surge in funding for think tanks and universities engaged in security analysis. With very few exceptions, these accepted as the basis for their work the validity of the war on terror and, in broad terms, the manner in which it was being fought.[2] Critical independent analysis was in short supply.

The academic complex

By 2015, and after fourteen years of the global war on terror, there was no prospect of it ending soon, even though there had been three clear periods – late 2001, mid 2003, and 2009–2010 – when there was a broad consensus among mainstream analysts that the war was being won. This was clearly not the case, and there were certainly exceptions to the general acceptance of the rightness of the policies, even in the immediate aftermath of the 9/11 attacks (Bello 2001; Rogers and Elworthy 2001). More recently, there has been a notable increase in independent analysis (Jackson et al. 2011; Jackson and Sinclair 2012), especially with the publication over the past decade of *Critical Studies on Terrorism*. While much of this has been concerned with the conduct of the war on terror (Blakeley and Raphael 2014), there has been renewed interest in state terrorism (Blakeley 2009), as well as particular concern with the significance of the language embodied in the war on terror (Jackson 2005).

Even so, these represent a minority activity within international relations in general, and international security studies in particular, and it is appropriate to conclude with some suggestions as to why this is the case and an indication of areas requiring more study. Why has the academy largely failed to challenge the "control paradigm" (Rogers 2010) which focuses on maintaining control in the face of threats in preference to seeking the underlying circumstances from which threats arise?

Some explanations are relatively straightforward. Research funding, for example, can be heavily dependent on defence departments and ministries, and Western states commonly have their own military think tanks. Further funding is frequently available from the defence industrial sector, whereas funding for seriously critical analysis is mainly dependent on a few charitable trusts and foundations, especially in the US and UK. While some researchers funded from defence ministries and the corporate sector may seek to be independent, this is difficult because prospects for future funding may be affected if research results are negative towards governments or industries. Given that most research on international security can be described as mainstream, it follows that peer review of more radical proposals through research councils may tend towards those proposals that fit the current paradigm. This may also apply at the other end of the pipeline when publication is being sought, one effect being that critical independent scholarship may limit the potential for academic promotion, particularly if that scholarship leads to controversy extending to the political arena. A further element is that undertaking research on many military topics can be particularly difficult because of the classification of information. This leads to a dilemma for some researchers who may need security clearance to access material while wanting to maintain complete independence of analysis, yet that very independence may militate against preserving security clearance.

Research priorities

In addition to the extensive work in progress within critical terrorism studies, not least in terms of exploring the manifest problems of the contemporary military pursuit of Islamic State and similar movements, the concern with language and presentation of Western policies, issues of control of information, and analysis of state terrorism, there is a specific need for high quality analysis of those diverse elements of current military conduct that are shrouded in secrecy. These include the use of armed drones, Special Forces, privatised military personnel, rendition, and interrogation.

There is, more generally, a need to analyse the relevance of the experience of the war on terror for wider issues of international security. There is a common assumption that Islamic State and allied movements are specific problems with regional and religious underpinnings, but an alternative view is that they are likely to be markers for the kinds of security challenges facing the global community as new drivers of conflict emerge. These include rapidly developing problems of climate disruption that are likely to have a particularly disastrous effect on the global south, including much of northern Africa and the Middle East.

Such problems will add to instabilities in precisely those regions where extreme movements have been developing, but a second issue may transcend this. It is the evident failure of the neoliberal economic model to deliver equity (Mason 2015). This, combined with welcome improvements in education and communications, means that the majority margin – the 80% of the world's population that is sharing far less in the fruits of economic growth – is progressively more likely to gestate extreme movements, of which Islamic State may be little more than an early example. The growth of such movements is far more likely if it proves impossible to move to a global economic model rooted in an ultra-low carbon and emancipated approach (Rogers 2016).

Such responsive movement may not be peculiar to any one religious outlook, an analysis that was pointed to nearly two decades ago:

> What should be expected is that new social movements will develop that are essentially anti-elite in nature and draw their support from people on the margins. In different contexts and circumstances they may have the roots in political ideologies, religious beliefs, ethnic, nationalist or cultural identities, or a complex combination of several of these. They may be focussed on individuals or groups but the most common feature is an opposition to existing centres of power. They may be sub-state groups directed at the elites in their own state or foreign interests, or they may hold power in states in the South, and will no doubt be labelled as rogue states as they direct their responses towards the North. What can be said is that, on present trends, anti-elite action will be a core feature of the next 30 years – not so much a clash of civilisations, more an age of insurgencies.
>
> (Rogers 2000)

Conclusion

In the fourteenth year of conflict in the wake of the 9/11 attacks, a consensus was developing among Western academics that there were many more years of conflict ahead; yet the prevailing view was that there was no alternative to the use of force, even if it was advisable to avoid the commitment of large numbers of ground troops. This was in spite of the persistent failure of such force to achieve the anticipated outcomes. Whether there will be a radical reassessment of these failures is far from clear and may be considered unlikely, given the considerable political and financial capital invested in the control paradigm. It is possible that more critical independent research may have an effect, but there is little cause for optimism before many more tens of thousands of people have died in what may once again come to be termed the global war on terror.

Notes

1 The Brown University study relies on direct casualty-counting methods used by Iraq Body Count and others. Estimates made by surveys may indicate a larger number of casualties. The advantages of direct counting are that more reliable indications of the causes of casualties can be gained (for example, air strikes, improvised explosive devices, or light arms) and comparisons can be made over time. Iraq Body Count figures, for example, indicate that civilian casualties in Iraq in 2014 were about double those of the previous year.
2 In the UK, the Ministry of Defence, the Foreign and Commonwealth Office, the Home Office, the Department for International Development, and private contractors such as Qinetiq all put funding into universities and think tanks for work on terrorism and related subjects.

References

Aslam, W., 2014. "Terrorist Relocation and the Societal Consequences of US Drone Strikes in Pakistan", London: Remote Control Project. Available online at: http://remotecontrolproject.org/terrorist-relocation-and-the-societal-consequences-of-us-drone-strikes-in-pakistan/.
Atwan, A., 2015. *Islamic State: the Digital Caliphate,* London: Saqi Books.
Barnett, R., 2014. *The Islamic State,* New York: The Soufan Group.
Bello, W., 2001. "Endless War", Manila: Focus on the Global South, September 2001. Available online at: www.focusweb.org/publications/2001/endless_war.html.
Blakeley, R., 2009. *State Terrorism and Neoliberalism: The North in the South,* Abingdon, UK: Routledge.

Blakeley, R., and Raphael, S., 2014. "Dirty Little Secrets: State and Corporate Complicity in Rendition, Secret Detention and Torture", paper presented at the British International Studies Association Annual Conference, June 2013, Birmingham.

Bush, G., 2002. "State of the Union Address", January, 2002, Available online at: www.whitehouse.gov/stateoftheunion/2002/.

Cockburn, P., 2014. "War against Isis: US Strategy in Tatters as Militants March on", *The Independent on Sunday,* 12 October.

Constable, P., 2004. "A Wrong Turn, Chaos and a Rescue", *Washington Post,* 15 April.

Defense News, 2015. "Surge in Jet Purchases Reshuffles Fighter Market", 11 May. Available online at: www.defensenews.com/story/defense/air-space/strike/2015/05/10/fighter-surge-kuwait-qatar-egypt-india-rafale-hornet/26977289/.

Dodge, T., 2012. *Iraq: From War to a New Authoritarianism,* Abingdon, UK: IISS/Routledge.

Donnellan, C., and Kersley, E., eds., 2014. *New Way of War: Is Remote Control Warfare Effective?* London: Remote Control Project. Available online at: http://remotecontrolproject.org/.

Holdstock, N., 2015. *China's Forgotten People: Xinjiang, Terror and the Chinese State,* London: I B Tauris.

International Institute for Strategic Studies, 2012. "Jihad in Russia: The Caucasus Emirate", *Strategic Comments,* 45. Available online at: www.iiss.org/en/publications/strategic%20comments/sections/2012-bb59/jihad-in-russia- the-caucasus-emirate-2-345b.

Jackson, R., 2005. *Writing the War on Terrorism: Language, Politics and Counter-terrorism,* Manchester, UK: Manchester University Press.

Jackson, R., Jarvis, L., Gunning, J., & Breen Smyth, M., 2011. *Terrorism: A Critical Introduction,* Basingstoke, UK: Palgrave Macmillan.

Jackson, R., & Sinclair, S. J., eds., 2012. *Contemporary Debates on Terrorism,* Abingdon, UK: Routledge.

Khalil, E., 2015. "Expansive Year: Islamic State Approaches its First Anniversary", *Jane's Intelligence Review,* 27(7): 20–23.

Krauthammer, C., 2001. "The Bush Doctrine: ABM, Kyoto and the New American Unilateralism", *The Weekly Standard,* 6(36), 4 June.

Lawrence, B., ed., 2005. *Messages to the World: The Statements of Osama bin Laden,* London: Verso.

Mason, P., 2015. *PostCapitalism: A Guide to Our Future,* London: Allen Lane.

McFate, S., 2014. *The Modern Mercenary: Private Armies and What They Mean for World Order,* Oxford: Oxford University Press.

Niva, S., 2013. "Disappearing Violence: JSOC and the Pentagon's New Cartography of Networked Warfare", *Security Dialogue,* 44(3): 185–202.

Opall-Rome, B., 2003. *Defense News,* 15 December.

Rogers, P., 2000. *Losing Control: Global Security in the 21st Century,* 1st edition, London: Pluto Press.

Rogers, P., 2006. *A War too Far: Iraq, Iran and the New American Century,* London: Pluto Press.

Rogers, P., 2010. *Losing Control: Global Security in the 21st Century,* 3rd edition, London: Pluto Press.

Rogers, P., 2014. "States of War – Afghanistan in Context", in Houen, A., ed., *States of War since 9/11: Terrorism, Sovereignty and the War on Terror,* London: Routledge.

Rogers, P., 2016. *Irregular War: ISIS and New Threats from the Margins,* London: I B Tauris.

Rogers, P., & Elworthy, S., 2001. "The United States, Europe and the Majority World after 11 September", *Briefing Paper,* October, Oxford: Oxford Research Group.

Urban, M., 2010. *Task Force Black,* London: Abacus Books.

Yourish, K., Watkins, D., and Giratikanon, T., 2015. "Where ISIS Has Directed and Inspired Attacks Around the World", *New York Times,* 17 June. Available online at: www.nytimes.com/interactive/2015/06/17/world/middleeast/map-isis-attacks-around-the-world.html?src=mv&_r=0.

22
THE GOVERNMENTALITY OF TERRORISM
Uncertainty, risk management, and surveillance

Luca Mavelli

Introduction

Since 1968, the average number of deaths caused every year by terrorism in nonconflict zones is about 300–700, whereas the number of people who, just in the US, lose their lives drowning in their baths is estimated at 320, and the number of those who die of influenza worldwide is about 4 million (Booth and Dunne 2011: 33–34). Similarly, the probability of being killed in a terrorist attack is 1 in 80,000, whereas the chance of death from "falling down" is 1 in 236 (Booth and Dunne 2011: 33–34; see also Wolfendale, this volume). Hence, if the statistical risk of terrorism is so low, why has terrorism acquired such a centrality in the political debate and our lives?

In order to answer this question, this chapter will provide an overview of the current state of research on the governmentality of terrorism – with a particular focus on uncertainty, risk management, and surveillance – and will advance two main arguments. First, terrorism or, more precisely, terrorist threats, have contributed to disrupt a fundamental aspect of modernity, namely, the idea that states would be capable of coping with risk and uncertainty through technological, political, and social developments. Second, terrorism combines the seemingly egalitarianism of the threat with the particularism of the response, in the sense that although everyone may be a target of a terrorist attack, it is also the case that counterterrorism measures have disproportionately targeted certain groups (Muslims, minorities, immigrants) and specific nations (Afghanistan, Iraq, Palestine).

The combined outcome of these two elements is that terrorism has had both *subtractive* and *productive* effects on our lives. The subtractive effect concerns the adoption of exceptional measures – such as "preemptive arrest, detention and deportation of migrant terror suspects, monitoring library records, the analysis of telephone and other communications data, and the mining of financial data for suspicious transactions" (De Goede 2008a: 162) – which have compressed our freedom and liberties in the name of security. The productive effect, on the other hand, has encompassed the incorporation of the terrorist threat into politics through the active cultivation of a politics of fear. This has resulted in new forms of governmentality, that is, new frameworks of meaning and power actively deployed to govern populations. The outcome has been not governing despite terrorism, but "governing through terrorism" (Mythen and Walklate 2008). From this perspective, terrorism is not a hard fact, but a socially constructed phenomenon (see Shanahan, this volume) whose danger and relevance is the product of regimes of power and knowledge.

In order to illustrate these arguments, I will proceed in four steps. First, I will discuss how terrorism has captured the current political imagination by considering how a distinctive feature of modern societies has been the attempt to reduce risk in the face of uncertainty. Following a brief discussion of Ulrich Beck's theory of risk society and François Ewald's philosophy of precaution, I will dwell on the seeming irrationality of certain counterterrorism preventative measures which claim to control a potential threat, "even if one does not know whether it exists" (Beck 2006: 335).

However, in the second section, I will argue that these measures should not be understood as irrational, but as part of a rational endeavour to establish new governmental practices. Hence, following a discussion of the Foucauldian concept of governmentality, I will consider how the terrorist threat has further reinforced the biopolitical turn of modern politics, with its focus on bodies and populations as objects of management and intervention.

In the third section, I will look at how modern biopolitical governmentality is enacted through forms of precautionary and preemptive risk management which no longer rest on the calculation of possible scenarios, but on the "creative imagination of disaster and catastrophe" (De Goede 2008b: 157; see also Jackson 2014) that is grounded not in what we know, but in "what we do not know" (Aradau and Van Munster 2007: 102). This approach, I will argue, has resulted in the adoption of exceptional extrajudicial measures, the targeting of specific groups, and practices of disruption rather than prosecution.

In the fourth section, I will look at surveillance as a specific instantiation of the logic of risk management. Moving from the case of the NSA scandal, I will question the top-down idea of surveillance ("the government is doing it to us") by considering our complicity and participation in practices of "lateral surveillance", and how surveillance is only apparently egalitarian ("we are all spied on") as it reproduces logics of inequality and class. In the conclusion, I will consider how the governmentality of terrorism contributes to a politics of fear which reinforces the multiplication and penetration of sovereign power and the construction of docile and compliant subjects.

The modern attempt to reduce risk in the face of uncertainty

According to Ulrich Beck (1992, 2006), the history of mankind is characterised by a distinctive attempt to rationalise and reduce risk in the face of uncertainty. For Beck (2006), this attempt has unfolded through three macro-historical phases: pre-modernity, first modernity, and second modernity. Pre-modernity revolved around the idea that human beings lived in a God-given order where they had no control over tragic events such as droughts, famines, diseases, epidemics, or wars. It is with first modernity, that is, with the death of God and the development of modern science, that human beings begin to believe that they live in a world of their own making where they can exercise agency and thus actively intervene to reduce risk and uncertainty. First modernity was thus characterised by a fundamental belief in science as a tool of intervention and manipulation of the outside world, as well as by a conceptualisation of risk as localised, calculable, and compensable (Beck 2006: 334).

This belief, however, has been shattered by the arrival of the second modernity, where science has proven increasingly unable to assist human beings in providing answers, let alone effectively controlling risks that they have actively created, such as climate change, global financial crises, or the dangers associated with genetic manipulations, global terrorism, and new forms of war. These risks are global in character, unforeseeable in their consequences, and, most of all, noncompensable. Hence, in the current "second modernity", the logic of nonambiguity has been replaced by a logic of ambiguity "in which the realms of the social, religious and political are governed by something like an Uncertainty principle" (Beck 2010: 67). This transformation has had important implications for our social, political, and individual attitudes towards risk.

According to François Ewald, the most fundamental transformation has been a shift from a logic of prevention to one of precaution. In the first modernity, which Ewald (2002) calls "the paradigm of solidarity", a rational and scientific approach could be used to prevent the occurrence of a dangerous event through mechanisms such as mass vaccination, social insurance, increased road safety, and so on. In this phase, uncertainty could be reduced to calculable risk.

However, in the second modernity, which Ewald calls "the paradigm of precaution", a new generation of risks emerge. Transnational terrorism, climate change, and global pandemics confront us with "the possibility of serious and irreversible damage" and the incapacity of science and technology to provide answers (Ewald 2002: 284). Accordingly, uncertainty can no longer be reduced to risk, because we simply do not know what the risk is. Since now damage concerns "the irreparable, the irremediable, the incompensable", we are now "concerned with preventing, forbidding, sanctioning and punishing" not just what could be reasonably expected or anticipated, but "what one can only imagine, suspect, presume or fear" (Ewald 2002: 284–286). This has resulted in a general climate of "doubt, suspicion, . . . mistrust, fear, and anxiety" (Ewald 2002: 294). This climate, Beck (2006: 335–36) contends, has contributed to blurring "the boundary between rationality and hysteria" and has resulted in the expansion of the authoritarian state and the related compression of individual freedoms. For Beck, this outcome is a potentially "irrational" and "inefficient" response of governments under pressure from a concerned and distraught public opinion which demands a security that governments cannot deliver.

In the remainder of this chapter, I will challenge this interpretation by suggesting that the growing hold of sovereign power is not the product of irrational, inefficient, or misguided assumptions, but part of a rational strategy of governments to incorporate the terrorist threat and use it to establish new governmental practices.

Governmentality

For Michel Foucault (1991: 102–3), governmentality is the ensemble of "institutions, procedures, analyses and reflections, . . . calculations and tactics that allow the exercise of . . . power, which has as its target population, as its principal form of knowledge of political economy, and as its essential technical means apparatuses of security". Governmentality can also be described as a way of governing populations through the production of discourses and frameworks of meaning in which certain statements, practices, narratives, and actions, however controversial they may appear to the critical mind, are "recognized to be true" (Foucault 1970: 158). For instance, some of the controversial measures adopted in the war on terror – such as torture, indefinite detention, or the surveillance of entire populations – are highly questionable, not just morally, but also scientifically.

In fact, there is no evidence that torture used in the war on terror may have contributed to produce better or vital intelligence (Welch 2009), or that the exceptional measures (such as administrative arrest and indefinite detention) targeting Muslims in the US in the aftermath of 9/11 may have resulted in the identification and trial of terrorist suspects (Cole 2006). And yet, these measures have been generally accepted in the discursive framework of a war in which "the terrorists want to destroy our way of life" and thus we need to adopt whatever measure is needed, however extreme, in order to stop them (Jackson 2005). How does governmentality make possible the widespread acceptance and normalization of these undemocratic and extreme measures?

The key feature of governmentality, Foucault argues, is that it transcends traditional 19th century notions of sovereign power based on the principle of punishment for the transgression of the law. The modern idea of sovereignty focuses primarily on the population as a subject of management and intervention. Accordingly, sovereign power no longer manifests itself solely as a "power of deduction" (the power to take life), but becomes also a power of production, whose main goal is to "incite, reinforce, control, monitor, optimise, and organise the forces under it" (Foucault 1978: 136). This power no longer expresses itself exclusively through the law, but through a series of disciplinary and regulatory apparatuses such as the police, schools, workshops, health insurance systems, patterns of consumption, reproduction, and education (Foucault 2003: 250–251). These regimes are not directly enacted through a direct exercise of sovereign power, but through processes of internalisation of norms, codes, and models of behaviour which directly invest life.

In this politics-turned-biopolitics, these regimes "are designed to maximize and extract forces" (Foucault 2003: 246) and to inscribe a specific order onto the body which may enable the "increase of its usefulness and its docility, [and] its integration into systems of efficient and economic controls" (Foucault 1978: 139). This transformation, to be sure, does not mean that sovereign power as a power of deduction is "replaced" by sovereign power as a power of production. Sovereign power retains its right to kill, but exercises it against those bodies or – to use Foucault's terminology – those "body-species" which endanger the ability of the "body-species" under its control to produce, grow, and proliferate (Foucault 2003: 239–263).

The discourse of the war on terror as propagated by governments and their disciplinary apparatuses (the police, surveillance agencies, security experts) has crucially rested on the narrative of the terrorist "other" as an existential threat which menaces "our way of life" and thus our capacity to live, produce, circulate, and expand. Functional to this narrative has been, for instance, the revelation of a number of terrorist plots by Islamic terrorists which have been successfully thwarted by the state security apparatuses, "including the crashing of a plane into Canary Wharf Tower, the launching of surface-to-air missiles at Heathrow" in the UK, or the 2006 al Qaeda plan to "fly a plane into . . . the 73-storey Library Tower in Los Angeles" (Mythen and Walklate 2008: 227). As there is no way to prove the authenticity of these claims, it can be argued that they have nurtured a politics of fear which has long been "an integral component of the governance of terrorism" (Mythen and Walklate 2008: 228; see also Furedi 2005). These claims can thus be considered part of a disciplining regime that, exploiting our vulnerability in a second modernity of scientific uncertainty, has normalised a number of "exceptional practices" such as torture, rendition, target killing, indefinite detention, administrative arrest, forms of domestic surveillance, "tighter control of aviation, collection of personal and biometric data, . . . and the creation of enormous online databases for police and government departments" (Kessler and Werner 2008: 295).

As Claudia Aradau and Rens Van Munster (2007: 91) observe, the war on terror transcends the fight against terrorism and concerns a broader governmental logic which encompasses a rationale for the wars that have been fought in the aftermath of 9/11, a justification for increasingly pervasive strategies of surveillance, the securitization of integration of minorities and immigrants, and "drastic policies against anti-social behaviour". Hence, apart from a general climate of de-politicization and normalization of the exception, a second implication of the emergence of terrorism as a new form of governmentality has been a selective targeting of certain populations – or "body species", in Foucault's jargon – considered to be at a higher risk of generating potential terrorists wanting to destroy "our way of life". This has resulted in governmental practices of precautionary risk management where individual responsibility for criminal acts has been replaced by collective responsibility for potential threats to come through a process of identification, measurement, and attribution of risk to different social, ethnic, and religious groups.

Risk management

Precautionary risk management has been a primary tool of implementation of logics of biopolitical governmentality. Moving from the impossibility of reducing uncertainty to risk in the absence of knowledge and exploiting the fear and anxiety of this condition, precautionary risk management has replaced science with imagination and delved into all possible potential scenarios of disaster and catastrophe. Hence, the 9/11 Commission ascribed the incapacity to anticipate and prevent the attacks to a "failure of imagination" and recommended "routinizing, even bureaucratizing, the exercise of imagination" as a way to prevent similar tragedies in the future (cited in De Goede 2008b: 155). Similarly, the British Intelligence and Security Committee enquiry into the 2005 London bombings stated that future prevention will require security officials to "get into 'the unknowns' – to find ways of broadening coverage to pick up currently unknown terrorist activity or plots" (cited in De Goede 2008b: 156). For Richard Jackson (2014: 3), these instances are an indication of the "epistemological crisis of counterterrorism", which has resulted in the "legitimization and institutionalization of imagination and fantasy as a necessary counterterrorist tool".

One consequence of this logic has been the implementation of exceptional measures such as torture carried out in the Abu Ghraib and Guantanamo prisons, and extraordinary rendition, namely, the US government practice of abducting individuals (often with the support of European states) and bringing them to countries such as Egypt or Jordan where they could be tortured (so that the US and Europe would not be formally violating the Convention against Torture) (see Blakeley and Raphael, this volume). The primary aim of torture in the war on terror has not been that of extracting confessions, but of harvesting actionable intelligence which could contribute to saving lives (Welch 2009; see also Brecher, this volume). However, suspicion has been growing on the value the information obtained by coercive means, fuelled by the fact that the vast majority of the thousands who have been tortured have been released or cleared for release without charges.

This case highlights four crucial features of precautionary risk management practices. First, suspicion replaces evidence. As Ron Suskind (2006: 166) argues, the war on terror has been guided by a new paradigm of security, namely, "the principle of actionable suspicion" which holds that "not having hard evidence shouldn't hold you back", and thus, even though there is only a one percent chance that a particular threat may materialise, the US should act. Second, disruption replaces prosecution. In the absence of hard evidence, and given that every possible suspicion (or imagination) needs to be actioned upon, legal prosecution is no longer possible. Accordingly, new counterterrorism measures have been developed in order to circumvent the problem of insufficient evidence "that might not stand up in court". These measures include asset freezing, which lowers the "threshold of evidence" and casts "the net wider" because funds are not seized (former US Treasury Secretary Paul O'Neill, cited in De Goede 2008a: 166) and, of course, rendition and "enhanced interrogations techniques".

Another measure is the US "no-fly list". Managed and updated by the US Terrorist Screening Center, this is a list of people who are banned from boarding any commercial flight entering, leaving, or flying within the United States. It is reported that, during the Obama administration, the names on the list almost doubled, reaching 21,000 in February 2013 (Lennard 2013). Yet, almost all those on the list have never been charged, let alone convicted, for any criminal offense. The list has been criticised for being arbitrary and lacking in transparency. As Jennifer Abel

(2010) observes, "Nobody knows how names get on the list, and there's no way to get names off. There's no due process, or seeing the evidence against you. All it takes is some anonymous bureaucrat who thinks you're a threat . . . [and] you won't even know it until you try boarding an aeroplane and learn you can't". Moreover, the list has been accused of being ineffective, with names "not linked to a physical description, birth date, or other unique identifier" (ACLU 2005), thus often generating false positives. Famous are the cases of Senator Ted Kennedy and eight-year-old Mikey Hicks, who have been repeatedly stopped, searched, and questioned at airports, most likely because some alleged terrorist shared or had used their same name.

The no-fly list case raises a third crucial dimension of precautionary risk management: the expansion of sovereign power through its multiplication, fragmentation, and heterogeneous reproduction. Judith Butler uses the term "petty sovereigns" to describe "bureaucrats and mid-level officials [lacking legitimate authority and legal and democratic accountability] who are newly authorized to make security decisions in the extra-legal spaces of detention and freezing" (Butler 2004: 56; De Goede 2008a: 176). In a similar vein, Didier Bigo (2002: 65) uses the term "managers of unease" for those security professionals (police, customs, immigration controls, intelligence experts) actively engaged in the management of risk. For Bigo (2008: 12), these experts are an essential component of the biopolitical governmentality of security as they do not simply identify threats, but construct "regimes of truth" aimed at establishing "what constitutes security" and "the 'legitimate' causes of fear, of unease, of doubt and uncertainty". Their power rests on their status as experts who can rely on dedicated knowledge and skills, "numerical data and statistics, technologies of biometrics and sociological profiles of potential dangerous behaviour" (Bigo 2008: 12).

Hence, we get to the fourth and possibly even more paradoxical dimension of precautionary risk management. The latter, it was argued, emerged precisely because science and, more generally, technical knowledge are no longer able to develop an effective policy of prevention, reduce uncertainty to risk, and quantify possible outcomes. And yet, precautionary risk management crucially rests on the expertise of security experts who employ sophisticated techniques of biometric profiling and surveillance. Biometrics rests on a series of "dividing practices in which the subject is broken up into calculable risk factors, both within herself (such as, for example, 'student' and 'muslim' and 'woman'), and necessarily also in relation to others (as, for example, 'alien', 'immigrant' or 'illegal')" (Amoore 2006: 339). Biometrics enables the possibility of circulation, growth, and expansion of the "legitimate subjects" and the securitization, exclusion, and confinement of the "threatening others".

According to Louise Amoore (2006: 342), "the allure of biometrics derives from the human body being seen . . . as a source of absolute identification". However, the objectification of identities and subjectivities via the body, rather than producing accurate and sophisticated screenings, has resulted in more basic forms of racism targeting entire groups, such as immigrants, minorities, and Muslims. Thus, for instance, in the weeks following the tragic events of 9/11, a massive campaign of racial profiling was launched in the US. This resulted in more than 5,000 foreign nationals, the overwhelming majority of which were of Arab and Muslim descent, being rounded up and detained for up to two years in violation of the most basic legal protections, including presumption of innocence, bond, and public and speedy trial (Cole 2006). Revealingly, five years later, none of these 5,000 foreign nationals had been convicted for a terrorist crime (Cole 2006: 430).

Similarly, in the UK, "the number of Asians stopped and searched by police jumped by 41% between 2000/01 and 2001/02, and among black people by 30%, compared to 8% for whites in the same period", and overall, "the spectre of surveillance that hangs over the Muslim community' seems to far exceed that hanging over other ethnic and religious groups" (Mythen and

Walklate 2008: 229). This raises an interesting question: Is surveillance (as a specific instantiation of the logic of risk management) targeting specific groups or the whole population, as the recent National Security Agency scandal seems to suggest?

Surveillance

The existence of a global system of mass surveillance dates back at least to 1971, with the creation of a network of surveillance among the so-called Five-Eyes, namely, the United States, Canada, the United Kingdom, Australia, and New Zealand. Hence, it long predates the 2013 National Security Agency (NSA) scandal, when the leaking of documents from a former contractor, Edward Snowden, revealed how the NSA had undertaken mass surveillance of entire populations, including heads of state, public and political figures, and ordinary people, through phone hacking and location tracking by violating networks and commercial data centres and, most of all, by collecting metadata and often the content of billions of phone calls and emails of US and foreign citizens. According to one of Snowden's leaked documents, and as reported by the *Washington Post*, on a single day in 2012, the NSA collected "444,743 e-mail address books from Yahoo, 105,068 from Hotmail, 82,857 from Facebook, 33,697 from Gmail and 22,881 from unspecified other providers" (Gellman and Soltani 2013). These figures correspond to an average of 250 million address books collected every year. Moreover, every day "the NSA collects contacts from an estimated 500,000 buddy lists on live-chat services as well as from the inbox displays of Web-based e-mail accounts" (Gellman and Soltani 2013). The value of these data is huge, as through one person's contacts, connections, and exchanges it is possible to draw a full "personal, professional, political and religious" profile (Gellman and Soltani 2013).

Following the scandal, an inquiry was launched, including the creation of a White House review panel on NSA surveillance. Contra the agency's claim that the collection of data had contributed to increased national security by preventing several terrorist attacks, the review panel concluded that there was no evidence that the data had provided time-sensitive information which had contributed to thwart an imminent threat (Isikoff 2013). Indeed, as observed by Glenn Greenwald (2014: 202, 195) (the journalist contacted by Snowden to leak the classified documents), "much of the data collection conducted by the NSA has manifestly nothing to do with terrorism or national security", but concerns the exercise of power: the power to obtain political, economic, and financial gains by spying on foreign political leaders; the power to monitor protestors and dissidents; and the power to invite "passivity, obedience and conformity" among ordinary people by suggesting that, as long as you remain "quiet, unthreatening and compliant", you will have "nothing to worry about" from the mass system of global surveillance.

Unlike the direct power aimed at obtaining economic/political advantage or quelling dissent, the power of surveillance of ordinary people squarely fits within a biopolitical governmental logic. Its purpose is to create the framework of truth and meaning in which subjects can govern themselves. It is thus a disciplining power whose manifestations go beyond the NSA and concerns a broader governmental framework in which we have been progressively educated to relinquish our privacy (personal data, list of contacts, pages viewed, geo-location, and the like) as a currency to obtain seemingly "free" services on the Internet, such as apps, email accounts, or participation in social networks. As Facebook founder and CEO Mark Zuckerberg declared in a 2010 interview, "people have really gotten comfortable . . . sharing more information . . . more openly and with more people", hence suggesting that privacy should no longer be considered a "social norm" (cited in Greenwald 2014: 170). This statement should not appear surprising from the CEO of a company whose business is personal information and which, together with Google, Yahoo!, and other major internet companies, gave the NSA access to their databases (Greenwald 2014).

Indeed, the collapse of the private/public distinction in the logic of surveillance epitomises the neoliberal goal of economic liberty and homeland security, with private companies collecting personal data for profit and passing them on to the NSA for security, thus reducing citizens to a source of surplus value and objects of control, management, and intervention. It is not surprising, then, that Google CEO Eric Schmidt's response to a question concerning Google's policy of retention of personal data – "If you have something that you don't want anyone to know, maybe you shouldn't be doing it in the first place" (cited in Greenwald 2014: 170) – echoes the same idea championed by the US government that "only those who have something to hide should fear surveillance from the state". At the heart of this idea is an underlying logic of normalisation and racism that reinforces the dichotomy of "good citizens" versus "threatening others".

This logic, however, pre-exists the attempt to build a global system of surveillance and is not purely a top-down exercise of sovereign power or a product of "petty sovereigns", but a disciplining power that we have contributed to produce and condone. As has been observed:

> Power . . . needs docile bodies to normalize in the service of imperialism, racism and capitalism. We've been developing a culture of surveillance for decades in the United States. People of color [and now Muslims] have long been the subject of massive police surveillance without a massive outrage from the mainstream media . . . [it is] racism that justifies this surveillance.
>
> *(Wolters 2013)*

The inscription of racism into logics of governmentality enacted through forms of risk management has resulted in programs and practices of "lateral surveillance" (Andrejevic 2002), where citizens have been actively encouraged to spy on other citizens and report anything suspicious that may affect security. These programs have included the "Be Alert, Not Alarmed" 2003 campaign in Australia, which "emphasised the need for individual vigilance and the right to suspicion" (Chan 2008: 225); the "Preparing for Emergencies: What You Need to Know" 2004 campaign in the UK, which focused on "what you can do to protect yourself and your community against risk" (Mythen and Walklate 2006: 134); the "If You See Something, Say Something" 2010 campaign in the US, which through a series of sixty-second video broadcasts in stadiums, hotels, airports, and WalMarts encouraged citizens to report anything suspicious "such as leaving one's backpack unattended, talking nervously on a cell phone, using cash, or repeatedly checking one's wristwatch" (Reeves 2012: 235); and the cooptation of "teachers into monitoring students and their immigration credentials" in the UK (Kampmark 2014).

As a specific instantiation of the precautionary logic that informs the governmentality of terrorism, surveillance thus combines the particularism of the consequence – as it will be the marginalised, the dissidents, the "others" who will be targeted – with the universalism of the technology, which makes us all objects of scrutiny and investigation; and yet, this latter discourse is seemingly neutralised by the normalising idea that "good ordinary citizens have nothing to fear". However, the categories of good citizens and bad citizens are more mobile than one may expect, and as Glenn Greenwald (2014: 197) observes, "yesterday's cheerleaders [of surveillance] can quickly become today's dissenters". Perhaps, then, we should all remind ourselves of the words of Martin Niemöller, the German Lutheran pastor who was an outspoken critic of Nazism:

> First they came for the Socialists, and I did not speak out –
> Because I was not a Socialist.

Then they came for the Trade Unionists, and I did not speak out –
Because I was not a Trade Unionist.
Then they came for the Jews, and I did not speak out –
Because I was not a Jew.
Then they came for me – and there was no one left to speak for me.

Conclusion

This chapter analysed counterterrorism as a form of biopolitical governmentality made possible by the crisis of uncertainty of the modern condition. It argued that precautionary risk management has been a key tool for the implementation of governmental practices, and it discussed surveillance as a specific instantiation of the logic of risk management. At the heart of these developments, it was suggested, lies an underlying tension between universalism and particularism whereby, although we may be all equal in the face of the terrorist threat, we are not equal when it comes to counterterrorism measures. Precautionary risk management was shown to rest on practices of identification, measurement, and attribution of risk to different social, ethnic, and religious groups that ultimately (re)produce hierarchies, exclusion, inequalities, and logics of class.

The multiplication, fragmentation, and heterogeneous reproduction of sovereign power that come with this process perform disciplinary functions geared towards the production of docile subjects compliant with the neoliberal biopolitical order and the parallel production of "threatening others", which justifies the adoption of exceptional measures and universal practices of surveillance in a narrative in which "good people have nothing to fear". The combined outcome of this governmental apparatus which has incorporated counterterrorism as a tool of governance is a process of de-politicization, of normalization of the exception, of compression of democratic freedoms, of exclusion, and, ultimately, of distraction, through the promotion of "an inward-looking and fearful [attitude]" where "the cultural fixation with risk detracts attention from more severe and deep-rooted global problems of poverty, malnutrition and disease" (Mythen and Walklate 2008: 227, discussing Frank Furedi 2005).

These reflections suggest that future research on the governmentality of terrorism should increasingly focus on its "productive" aspects and, in particular, on how the incorporation of terrorism into logics of governmentality is deeply affecting the constitution of ourselves as subjects and communities. In particular, future critical research cannot ignore how the dominant narratives surrounding terrorism may also represent a projection of our fear and anxieties, our incapacity to cope with uncertainty, and thus, ultimately, the expression of a crisis of our modern condition. This raises important questions about the transformation of the notion of sovereignty which go well beyond the traditional national/supranational framework of traditional international relations scholarship. The penetration of vertical sovereignty and multiplication of horizontal sovereignty is also a response to our quest for reassurance, yet one which entails an overall expansion of sovereign power which has yet to be fully grasped, as it is often carried out by agents and institutions, such as bureaucracies and the market, not traditionally associated with sovereign power. Combined with the crisis of uncertainty of the modern condition, the pervasive dissemination and multiplication of sovereign power has conjured up a situation in which the compression of our freedom may not have made us more secure, but only more fearful. And here probably lies the most challenging task for future research: moving beyond the security/freedom trade-off and challenging the politics of fear as an inescapable condition of our times.

References

Abel, J., 2010. "Exiled on the no-fly list", *The Guardian*, 18 June, available online at: www.theguardian.com/commentisfree/cifamerica/2010/jun/17/no-fly-list-american-muslim-egypt [accessed 12 September 2014].

ACLU (American Civil Liberties Union), 2005. " FAQs about the 'No Fly List'", available online at: www.aclu.org/national-security/frequently-asked-questions-about-no-fly-list [accessed 17 September 2014].

Amoore, L., 2006. "Biometric borders: Governing mobilities in the war on terror", *Political Geography*, 25(3): 336–351.

Andrejevic, M., 2002. "The work of watching one another: Lateral surveillance, risk, and governance", *Surveillance & Society*, 2(4): 479–497.

Aradau, C., and Van Munster, R., 2007. "Governing terrorism through risk: Taking precautions, (un)knowing the future", *European Journal of International Relations*, 13(1): 89–115.

Beck, U., 1992. *Risk society: Towards a New Modernity*. London: Sage.

Beck, U., 2006. "Living in the world risk society", *Economy and Society*, 35(3): 329–345.

Beck, U., 2010. *A God of One's Own: Religion's Capacity for Peace and Potential for Violence*. Cambridge: Polity.

Bigo, D., 2002. "Security and immigration: Towards a critique of the governmentality of unease", *Alternatives*, 27 (Special Issue): 63–92.

Bigo, D., 2008. "Globalized (In)Security: The Field and the Ban-Opticon", in Bigo, D., and Tsoukala, A., eds., *Terror, Insecurity and Liberty: Illiberal Practices of Liberal Regimes*, London: Routledge.

Booth, K., and Dunne, T., 2011. *Terror in Our Time*. London: Routledge.

Butler, J., 2004. *Precarious Life: The Powers of Mourning and Violence*. London: Verso.

Chan, J., 2008. "The new lateral surveillance and a culture of suspicion", *Sociology of Crime, Law and Deviance*, 10: 223–239.

Cole, D., 2006. "Double standards, democracy, and Human Rights", *Peace Review*, 18(4): 427–437.

De Goede, M., 2008a. "The politics of preemption and the war on terror in Europe", *European Journal of International Relations*, 14(1): 161–185.

De Goede, M., 2008b. "Beyond risk: Premediation and the post-9/11 security imagination", *Security Dialogue*, 39(2–3): 155–176.

Ewald, F., 2002. "The Return of Descartes's Malicious Demon: An Outline of a Philosophy of Precaution", in Baker, T., and Simon, J., eds., *Embracing Risk*, Chicago: Chicago University Press, pp. 273–301.

Foucault, M., 1970. *The Order of Things: An Archaeology of the Human Sciences*. London: Tavistock Publications.

Foucault, M., 1978. *The History of Sexuality: Volume 1*. New York: Pantheon Books.

Foucault, M., 1991. "Governmentality", in Burchell, G., Gordon, C., and Miller, P., eds., *The Foucault Effect: Studies in Governmentality*, Chicago: University of Chicago Press, pp. 87–104.

Foucault, M., 2003. *Society Must Be Defended: Lectures at the Collège De France, 1975–76*. New York: Picador.

Furedi, F., 2005. "Terrorism and the Politics of Fear", in Hale, C., Hayward, K., Wahidin, A., and Wincup, E., eds., *Criminology*, Oxford: Oxford University Press, pp. 307–322.

Gellman, B., and Soltani, A., 2013. "NSA collects millions of e-mail address books globally", *The Washington Post*, 14 October, available online at: www.washingtonpost.com/world/national-security/nsa-collects-millions-of-e-mail-address-books-globally/2013/10/14/8e58b5be-34f9-11e3-80c6-7e6dd8d22d8f_story.html [accessed 17 September 2014].

Greenwald, G., 2014. *No Place to Hide: Edward Snowden, the NSA and the Surveillance State*. New York: Penguin Books.

Isikoff, M., 2013. "NSA program stopped no terror attacks, says White House panel member", NBC News, 20 December, available online at: www.nbcnews.com/news/other/nsa-program-stopped-no-terror-attacks-says-white-house-panel-f2D11783588 [accessed 21 September 2014].

Jackson, R., 2005. *Writing the War on Terrorism: Language, Politics and Counter-terrorism*. Manchester: Manchester University Press.

Jackson, R., 2014. "The epistemological crisis of counterterrorism", paper presented at the 2014 BISA Critical Studies on Terrorism Working Group Conference, Nottingham, 15–16 September 2014.

Kampmark, B., 2014. "Britain, students, and immigration extending the surveillance state", *Dissident Voice*, 4 March, available online at: http://dissidentvoice.org/2014/03/britain-students-and-immigration/ [accessed 21 September 2014].

Kessler, O., and Werner, W., 2008. "Extrajudicial killing as risk management", *Security Dialogue*, 39(2–3): 289–308.

Lennard, N., 2013. "No-fly lists: A new tactic of exile?" *Salon*, available online at: www.salon.com/2013/02/05/no_fly_lists_a_new_tactic_of_exile/ [accessed 21 September 2014].

Mythen, G., and Walklate, S., 2006. "Communicating the terrorist risk: Harnessing a culture of fear?" *Crime, Media, Culture,* 2(2): 123–142.

Mythen, G., and Walklate, S., 2008. "Terrorism, risk and international security: The perils of asking 'what if?'", *Security Dialogue,* 39(2–3), 221–242.

Reeves, J., 2012. "If you see something, say something: Lateral surveillance and the uses of responsibility", *Surveillance & Society,* 10 (3/4): 235–248.

Suskind, R., 2006. *The One Percent Doctrine: Deep Inside America's Pursuit of Its Enemies Since 9/11.* New York: Simon & Schuster.

Welch, M., 2009. "American 'Pain-ology' in the war on terror: A critique of 'scientific' torture", *Theoretical Criminology,* 13(4): 451–474.

Wolters, E., 2013. "The mainstream media just discovered Foucault and they're all wrong", 30 July, *Verso Books,* available online at: www.versobooks.com/blogs/1366-the-mainstream-media-just-discovered-foucault-and-they-re-all-wrong [accessed 21 September 2014].

23
RADICALIZATION, DE-RADICALIZATION, AND COUNTER-RADICALIZATION

Lasse Lindekilde

Introduction

Radicalization and derivations such as *de-radicalization* and *counter-radicalization* have become central terms in terrorism studies and counterterrorism policymaking. These terms have received enormous attention in policymaking and academic circles, leading to an avalanche of writings, research centers, policies, and funding opportunities. Particularly after the 2004 Madrid and 2005 London bombings, "radicalization" became a convenient term for European policymakers, and soon academics, to describe "home grown terrorism" (Schmid 2013: 2).

Briefly described, the radicalization perspective on terrorism is a renewed search for the root causes of terrorism and answers to the question: Why do people come to accept terrorism as a course of action? As pointed out by Peter Neumann:

> Following the attacks against the United States on 11 September 2001, it suddenly became very difficult to talk about the "roots of terrorism", which some commentators claimed was an effort to excuse and justify the killing of innocent civilians. Even so, it seemed obvious that some discussion about the underlying factors that had given rise to this seemingly new phenomenon was urgent and necessary, and so experts and officials started referring to the idea of "radicalization" wherever they wanted to talk about "what goes on before the bomb goes off"... it was through the notion of radicalization that a discussion about the political, economic, social and psychological forces that underpin terrorism and political violence became possible again.
>
> *(Neumann 2008: 4)*

However, the radicalization perspective on terrorism has yet to fulfill this potential and actually shed new light on the "causes of causes" of terrorism. In fact, there is a remarkable gap between the term's popularity and its conceptual and analytical precision. One explanation offered by critical scholars on terrorism is that the radicalization perspective, despite (or possibly because of) its imprecision, is functional to policymakers and counterterrorism practitioners because it provides a framework which renders the path to terrorism recognizable, understandable, and, not least, actionable (Heath-Kelly 2013; Heath-Kelly, Jarvis, & Baker-Beall 2014).

In a critical review of the radicalization perspective on terrorism and counterterrorism, this chapter discusses the conceptualization and definition of radicalization and examines the current state of research on the causes and mechanisms of radicalization. It highlights conceptual, explanatory, and predictive weaknesses in the radicalization perspective on terrorism and counterterrorism, in particular, its inadequacy in dealing with the emergence of radicalism (the causes of the causes); its tendency to focus on sociopsychological and ideological mechanisms and ignore political factors, including the fact that state authorities also at times radicalize; and the way the radicalization discourse and counter-radicalization policies construct "suspect communities" and potential counterproductive reactions. The chapter makes a plea for a more context-sensitive, relational, and critical perspective on radicalization and counter-radicalization which takes seriously the performative and potentially counterproductive nature of the radicalization discourse (see also Sedgwick 2010: 481–482; Kundani 2012).

Defining radicalization, de-radicalization, and counter-radicalization

As pointed out in review articles on the concept of radicalization, there is no standard or even broadly accepted definition of radicalization and, as a consequence, de-radicalization (Borum 2011; Bouhana & Wikström 2011; Schmid 2013). This is damaging to any research program, as it makes attempts at cumulative science impossible at worst and shaky at best. However, the radicalization perspective on terrorism is by no means the only field haunted by conceptual vagueness and imprecision. This is not the place to resolve the definitional issues of the radicalization concept (for a thoughtful attempt, see Schmid 2013). The number of applied definitions of radicalization in grey literature and academic writings is vast and beyond the scope of this chapter. Instead, we shall discuss some overall trends in the conceptualization of radicalization and propose a couple of academic definitions that represent different positions in the field.

Traditionally, the term *radical* has primarily been defined in terms of political desires and ends: a "radical" was a revolutionary who wanted to change society fundamentally. This change could be achieved through nonviolent and democratic means, or through violent and nondemocratic means (Kundani 2012). Thus, a radical could be a democrat. This is rarely the case in recent conceptualizations. In the late 19th to early 20th centuries, radical meant progressive and pro-democratic; today, it mostly means the opposite, as radical and the process of radicalization are most often defined in terms of violent or undemocratic means. A central perception in many recent definitions is that radicals use illegal political violence to reach political goals, progressive or regressive, and radicalization is, thus, the process of coming to accept violence as an appropriate strategy of action (Dalgaard-Nielsen 2010). However, it is useful to bear in mind that the close connection between radicalism and violence is a very recent invention.

Following the tendency to define radicalization in terms of means rather than ends, recent conceptualizations also favor absolute over relative definitions. As argued by Mark Sedgwick, one weakness in contemporary conceptualizations of radicalization is the quest to define the term without reference to any particular context or situation. He argues that radicalization is best understood in relation to mainstream political activities and what is considered "moderate" in a particular context at a given point in time (Sedgwick 2010). From this perspective, radicalization becomes the process that leads individuals from moderate, mainstream beliefs toward radical ones, whatever that may be in a given context. If spelled out, modern conceptions of radicalization typically refer to core Western liberal values as the benchmark of radicalization.

For example, the Danish government in 2009 defined radicalization as a process that gradually

> brings individuals or groups to use violent or undemocratic methods as a tool to reaching a specific political objective, or they may seek to undermine the democratic social

order or make threats or carry out demeaning harassment against groups of people based on e.g. their skin colour, sexuality or beliefs.

(Danish Government 2009: 8)

Being radical is here the opposite of being democratic, peaceful, pro-equality, tolerant, and respectful of law and order. In fact, one sometimes gets the impression that radicalism is used to denote everything liberal democrats dislike. Scholars have pointed out that the term radicalization in contemporary conceptualizations marks the boundaries of tolerance in democratic states and, at the same time, fortifies consensus around core liberal values and principles in ways that render these values and principles "post-political" and, thus, nondebatable (Lindekilde & Kühle 2012).

It is implicit to all official and most academic definitions of radicalization that the process applies to non-state actors only. In fact, most often, radicalization is reserved for individuals and smaller groups. However, a growing number of researchers and subject matter experts in the area are arguing that just like we have to consider the possibility of "state terrorism", we need to consider the possibility that state actors radicalize (Schmid 2013: 14). To grasp radicalization in a society, we need to be able to research and understand tactics and repertoires of actions on both sides – state and non-state. McCauley and Moskalenko (2011) have underlined the necessity of bringing in state and political actors to the study of radicalization, not just as actors of de-radicalization initiatives, but highlighting how the relational dynamic – the "friction" as they call it – between non-state actors and state actors is central to understanding radicalization in many situations.

It is clear that any definition of radicalization that addresses all the distinctions discussed here (ends/means, relative/absolute, state/non-state) will be complex and lengthy. That is, indeed, the case with the definition proposed by Alex P. Schmid in his attempt to reconceptualize radicalization as

> an individual or collective (group) process whereby, usually in a situation of political polarization, normal practices of dialogue, compromise and tolerance between political actors and groups with diverging interests are abandoned by one or both sides in a conflict dyad in favour of a growing commitment to engage in confrontational tactics of conflict-waging. These can include either (i) the use of (non-violent) pressure and coercion, (ii) various forms of political violence other than terrorism or (iii) acts of violent extremism in the form of terrorism and war crimes. The process is, on the side of rebel factions, generally accompanied by an ideological socialization away from mainstream or status quo-oriented positions towards more radical or extremist positions involving a dichotomous world view and the acceptance of an alternative focal point of political mobilization outside the dominant political order as the existing system is no longer recognized as appropriate or legitimate.
>
> *(Schmid 2013: 18)*

This definition has many advantages. However, critics may argue that, despite its many defining properties, it denotes a large set of empirical phenomena which would in practice make it difficult to sort cases of radicalization from cases of, for example, normal, but confrontational and contentious, political activism in politically charged situations.

A more common strategy today is, as suggested, to reserve the label of radicalization to cover the move toward using political violence, and often specifically terrorism, as an action repertoire. This strategy has the advantage of providing much more parsimonious definitions and apparent better conditions for sorting cases of illegal violence and legal political activism. Bouhana and Wikström define radicalization as "the developmental process by which a person comes to see an act of terrorism as an action alternative and comes to choose to carry it out" (2011: 4). Inspired by situational action theory in criminology, they argue that to be radicalized is to acquire a morality that supports and encourages acts of terrorism, and that to explain radicalization, we must explain this process of acquisition. It is obvious that by focusing narrowly on the acquisition of a terrorism propensity by individuals, Bouhana and Wikström's definition denotes a much smaller set of cases than Schmid's. It is also clear that in order to use the definition in practice, one would have to define terrorism, for example, by reference to terrorism laws in the relevant country or countries.

The span and trends in definitions of radicalization discussed create a gap between the popularity of the concept and its analytical precision. This gap becomes no less apparent if we turn to the derivations *de-radicalization* and *counter-radicalization*. Often, de-radicalization is simply defined as the reverse process of radicalization, however defined. But there is growing consensus in the field that, as a minimum, we have to distinguish between de-radicalization and *disengagement*, where de-radicalization refers to an ideological change and renouncement of radical beliefs and tactics, while disengagement involves a behavioral change away from radical activities. As pointed out in a number of studies, de-radicalization and disengagement do not necessarily happen simultaneously; in fact, disengagement often happens without de-radicalization (Bjørgo & Horgan 2009; Horgan 2009).

One conclusion drawn from the imprecision and blurriness of the concept of radicalization and its derivations is to abandon the concepts altogether (Kundani 2012; Goodwin unpublished). This chapter takes a less drastic position, namely, that the radicalization perspective on terrorism is here to stay and that the best way forward is to critically engage with the perspective, point out its flaws, and suggest improvements and new directions of research. This is not just a pragmatic position, it also reflects the conviction that although research on radicalization started out with very "clear", but awfully simplistic and preconceived, notions of radicalization, it has gradually developed toward more complex and nuanced understandings that may offer important insights to terrorism studies.

Causes and mechanisms of radicalization: what we think we know

We now turn to the large body of research and grey literature on the causes and mechanisms of radicalization. The impression one gets from reading this literature is that the conceptual imprecision of the radicalization perspective translates into analytical fuzziness in the attempt to explain why, how, and when radicalization happens. The literature suggests various causes and mechanisms of radicalization, but appears inconclusive as to their relative importance and generalizability. One literature review states that "the causes of radicalization are as diverse as they are abundant" (COT 2011: 11).

Perhaps the many and diverse apparent causes described in the literature simply reflect that radicalization is a very complex process that is not easily modeled and put into a formula. Randy Borum points out that radicalization seems to be characterized by both equifinality (the same outcome [terrorism] can be caused by different factors and combinations of factors) and multifinality (the same factors can lead to several different outcomes [terrorism and nonviolent political activism]) (Borum 2011: 57). Because of this, some early explanatory models of radicalization (see Precht 2007; Silber & Bhatt 2007), claiming to be more or less universal, have been criticized. Much literature in the field now suggests that radicalization does not unfold in a linear manner through fixed phases whenever certain factors are at play (McCauley & Moskalenko 2011).

The search for robust causes and mechanisms of radicalization has proven difficult, and the gradual shift from simplistic linear models of radicalization and a narrow focus on individual profiles and predispositions toward more nuanced pathway models has been a major achievement (Horgan 2009). Despite a continuing, fundamental debate about the appropriate levels of analysis, a number of findings are generally considered important to explaining radicalization. These findings can be organized according to the level of analysis – individual (micro level), group (meso level), or society (macro level). In the radicalization-inspired literature, the vast majority of findings and research focus on individual vulnerability (micro level) and/or exposure and mobilization to radical settings (meso level). Much less attention has been paid to factors at larger societal and political levels (macro level).

Individual vulnerability

It is a repeated claim in the field that a clear profile of the typical radical does not exist (Schmid 2013). However, many studies point toward some types of individual vulnerability as key risk factors: people who have been radicalized show signs of self-uncertainty (who am I and where do I belong?) and an inability to cope with stress, challenging situations, or complex worldviews and nonrecognition of others' perspectives (Wiktorowicz 2005; Bouhana & Wikström 2011; Hogg 2012). Faced with particular life events (starting college, migration, death in family, losing job, and the like) or having experienced social, cultural, or political grievances (bullying, discrimination, foreign policy, and the like), individuals with these characteristics can be prone to seek out answers and increased certainty by self-selecting to radical milieus. This propensity is found to increase if the individual has social ties to radical milieus through friends or family (social selection); a disposition for certain milieus through, for example, religious upbringing (preferences); or radical milieus are present in the immediate surroundings (Sageman 2004).

Some studies use the concept of "cognitive openings" to refer to a situation in which an individual, for different reasons, is experiencing decreased attachment to formerly held beliefs and searches for a new position, outlook, and answers to fundamental life questions (Silber & Bhatt 2007). Obviously, not everybody who experiences "cognitive openings" will radicalize; most deal with life tensions in more productive ways. However, in this situation, the individual is seen as vulnerable to self-selection or outreach from radical milieus. A number of studies suggest that radical groups deliberately recruit among such vulnerable and searching youngsters (Wiktorowicz 2005; Olsen 2009). Radical ideology may resonate with "cognitively open" individuals, as it provides black-and-white answers to complex issues and easily digestible action prescriptions (Bouhana & Wikström 2011).

However, not all pathways to radicalism entail ideology (McCauley & Moskalenko 2011: 206–210). Radicalized individuals may be ideologically motivated, but often ideology enters at a later stage and functions as a retrospective justification for violence (Olsen 2009). Instead, the initial drivers of radicalization are seen to be individuals searching for belonging, identity, comradeship, security, excitement, and the like (McCauley & Moskalenko 2008).

Exposure to radicalizing settings

Many studies with a radicalization perspective on terrorism argue that for radicalization to happen, the individual demand for radical answers has to meet a relevant supply (Borum 2011). In other words, the individual must be exposed to radicalizing settings through self-selection, social selection, or recruitment outreach. Exposure may entail talking to radicalizing agents or reading radical material (offline or online). Studies of exposure to radicalizing settings, several of them drawing upon elements of social movement theory, have stressed how opportunities for exposure are consciously created by radical groups by providing, for example, language training, study circles, and the like (Wiktorowicz 2005; Olsen 2009). In this way, "front organizations" are created that fertilize recruitment. In the recruitment process, framing activities by radicalizing agents are seen as important in constructing "resonance" between individual grievances and experiences and the ideological outlook and goals of the group (della Porta 1995).

As far as individuals searching for certainty, research has shown how radicalizing settings have specific characteristics that render them superior to many other milieus in terms of reducing individual self-uncertainty (Hogg 2012). Radical groups often offer intense interaction and comradeship, clear boundaries between in-group/out-group, and through socialization and cultivation, radical ideologies are dispersed that provide clear answers to difficult questions and prescribe actions.

For good reasons, few studies have investigated the actual small-group dynamics of radical groups. Nevertheless, such dynamics are often highlighted as important factors in driving radicalization forward after an individual has been exposed to radical settings. In a number of studies, Cass Sunstein and colleagues argue that radicalization is the product of deliberation among likeminded people in bordered enclaves (Sunstein 2000; Schkade, Sunstein, and Hastie 2010). By providing a limited pool of arguments, which all point in the same direction, enclave deliberation leads to group polarization, understood as individual and group movement in the direction of more extreme positions vis-à-vis the predeliberation starting point. By coming into contact with likeminded people in a radicalizing setting, the individual will become more convinced that initial beliefs are correct and more willing to take risks in terms of acting upon those beliefs (see also Myers 1975; Baron, Hoppe, Kao, & Brunsman 1996). Likewise, such deliberation in closed radical groups has been found to entail "moral detachment" and "dehumanization" of the enemy, and thereby help to dissolve normative bonds on the use of violence (della Porta 1995).

The emergence of radicalizing settings

As already stated, most research on radicalization to terrorism has focused on individual vulnerability and/or exposure to radicalizing settings. The emergence of radicalizing settings and the mechanisms that sustain them over time have received much less attention, including the role played by radical state actions in the field of counterterrorism (drone killings, torture, renditions, and the like). Put differently, the radicalization perspective on terrorism has so far been relatively quiet about the "causes of the causes" of radicalization, not being able to explain the timing and differences in location and survival of radicalizing settings.

There are exceptions. For example, Peter Waldmann and Stefan Malthaner suggest that the concept of "radical milieus" better grasps the links between violent groups and their social constituencies (Malthaner 2011; Malthaner & Waldmann 2014). For a violence-endorsing setting to emerge and be sustained, the broader moral context has to be supportive of it. Violent groups are dependent on moral support and resources from constituencies to continue their campaigns in the longer run and must therefore engage in resonance building with these constituencies.

Exploring the social and political context of emerging violent groups, some older studies have highlighted the importance of the limited availability of legitimate, nonviolent forms of political participation as factors in the emergence of radicalizing settings. Donatella della Porta (1995) has shown from a social movement theory perspective how the formation of left-wing terrorist groups in Italy and Germany in the 1970s and 1980s was connected to closing "political opportunity structures", including increased repression of normal political activism. In this atmosphere, the organizational splintering of student organizations and the internal positioning of groups as the "avant-garde" led to the creation of underground violent groups.

Likewise, Ehud Sprinzak has pointed out how the emergence of the Weather Underground terrorist group in the US in the late 1960s was a product of the Vietnam war, which created a "crisis of legitimacy" among many students vis-à-vis political authorities, which in turn was fueled by the hard repression of student anti-war protests on university campuses (Sprinzak 1990). At a more general level, the emergence of radicalizing settings has been connected to state repression and shows how repression may "backfire" (for a summary discussion, see Lindekilde 2013a).

Focusing on the emergence of radical Islamist settings in Western Europe, some accounts, and many political observers, have pointed to the importance of failed government policies of integration and multiculturalism (see Bouhana & Wikström 2011). Out of misunderstood political correctness, Muslim communities have been left to themselves, leading to ineffectively monitored settings where radical entrepreneurs have been free to spread radical Islamist ideology and gather the necessary moral support of violent groups (Wiktorowicz 2005).

Finally, the Internet has been cited as an important background factor in explaining the emergence of radical settings today (Conway 2012). The easy access, high speed, and anonymity of the Internet have fertilized the creation of radicalizing settings – online and offline. Through the Internet, it is argued, likeminded people can come together, avoid surveillance, and let radical ideas grow.

Limitations to current knowledge on the causes of radicalization

The fact that only a few studies have systematically investigated the emergence of radical settings limits our knowledge on the causes of radicalization. The strong focus in the literature on individual vulnerability and exposure to radical settings, emphasizing psychological, social psychological, and ideological factors, portrays radicalization as a virus that spreads through social networks and small-group interactions. Whether this is true or not, we have learned very little about why the virus has appeared and where it originated. Political grievances exist in all societies, but only under certain sociopolitical conditions where certain political narratives exist may violence come to be seen as legitimate (Kundani 2012: 18). If we want to advance the radicalization perspective on terrorism, we must explore these conditions and look at political, contextual factors such as political opportunities, repression, discrimination, foreign policy, and counter-radicalization policies. For example, we need to pay more attention to the "where-question" of radicalization, that is, why radicalizing settings develop in some contexts and not in others under similar conditions.

We also have a limited understanding of when and why some, but not all, carriers of certain (radical) attitudes and grievances choose violence over other means. Much of the literature on individual vulnerability and exposure to radical settings describes mechanisms that explain why people become aggrieved and what they do in order to reduce such feelings, but not why they would favor violence as a tactical choice (Goodwin unpublished: 12). The problem is that many of the mechanisms and causes of radicalization seem too general and produce many "false positives" when used as predictors of radicalization. There is a lack of attention to the rationales of violence – that is, choosing violence as a reasoned decision. Too much research has been obsessed with the question of which individuals and groups are more vulnerable to radicalization, instead of asking under what circumstances these individuals and groups become more likely to take up violence as an action alternative.

In addition, the question of causality, and what that really means in the context of radicalization, is normally left untouched (Kundani 2012: 10). The problem here is that not enough studies actively distinguish between the predictors/correlates and the casual mechanisms of radicalization. For example, factors such as age, certain ideological traits, felt uncertainty, and so on are correlates of radicalization rather than causes. Aggregated risk factors alone make poor predictions of vulnerability and radicalization. There is an urgent need to realize that individual and group risk factors could suggest the presence of causal mechanisms and pathways to radicalization, but that they in themselves are not explanations hereof. It is the dynamic interaction of risk factors and contextual factors that causes radicalization.

Finally, our knowledge, even about individual vulnerability and exposure, is most often based on thin empirical evidence. There is a severe lack of systematic empirical studies in the field. One reason is obviously the notorious problem of limited data access and data quality. Another reason is that there seems to be more academic prestige involved in providing conceptual critiques and writing literature assessments than in conducting empirical research on the causes of radicalization. Regardless of the reasons, the problem is that the robustness of empirical findings is rarely checked, as very few studies indulge in comparative research of radicalization or make use of control groups (nonviolent individuals who share central characteristics with violent radicals). This means that both the internal and external validity of many studies, normally based on small-N case studies, is low.

Counter-radicalization: policies and critique

It should be clear by now that the radicalization perspective on terrorism in many ways is ill-suited to prescribe policy recommendations. Nevertheless, the growth of the radicalization research field has happened simultaneously with an upsurge in counter-radicalization policies across the world. Academic knowledge about radicalization is used extensively to legitimate counter-radicalization efforts, often in ways that obscure the limitations of this knowledge (Sedgwick 2010). As mentioned, some critical scholars of terrorism have argued, through Foucauldian governmentality analysis of counter-radicalization programs, that the modeling/conceptualization of radicalization that focuses on individual and group risk factors makes the future actionable and preemptively governable. In other words, knowledge about radicalization, despite its limitations, provides authorities with a map for action and intervention (Heath-Kelly 2013). In this perspective, knowledge about radicalization is seen as performative and productive in constructing particular individuals and communities as potential threats and thereby legitimating governmental interventions (Githens-Mazer & Lambert 2010; Heath-Kelly 2013; Kundani 2012; Heath-Kelly et al. 2014).

Specifically, knowledge about radicalization has led to the formulation of policies that differ widely in terms of aims, targets, and involved actors. One set of initiatives focuses on preventing radicalization by engaging with supposed vulnerable communities, most often Muslim communities, through resilience-building activities and community partnerships (Van Dongen 2010). In the area of counter-radicalization, "community resilience" has become a key perspective and refers to efforts taken to strengthen protective resources and reduce opportunities of radicalization in communities through, for example, targeted information campaigns, school workshops, funding for leisure activities, partnership with local civic organizations, and the like (Alya, Taylor, & Karnovsky 2014). Another set of initiatives focuses on interdicting unfolding radicalization through individualized interventions. Examples here are the British Channel Programme and the Danish mentoring scheme (see Lindekilde 2014), which involve schools, local police, youth clubs, and the like in spotting "signs of radicalization" and making referrals.

Critics of current counter-radicalization policies have argued that they serve to construct "vulnerable individuals" and "suspect communities" by highlighting particular risk factors (Thomas 2010; Heath-Kelly et al. 2014). Put differently, risk factors become "performative" in that they produce the effects they name. Our knowledge about radicalization suggests that risk factors (self-uncertainty, exposure to radical ideology, poor integration, and the like) indicate a future risk. Those "at risk" become "risky" as vulnerability implies potential future riskiness (Heath-Kelly 2013). Through this policy lens, particularly Muslim communities are seen as problematic borderlands within society, liable to produce violence. Thus, lack of integration and community cohesion/resilience comes to signify a risk of becoming risky and legitimates the use of community cohesion and integration programs as elements of counter-radicalization. A number of studies emphasize how labeling entire communities as suspect may have counterproductive effects in terms of radicalization prevention (Mythen, Walklate, & Khan 2009; Lindekilde 2012).

In recent years, some of the criticism of counter-radicalization policies, for example in the UK and Denmark, has contributed to a development and learning process within the counter-radicalization nexus, which has led to policy changes. In 2011, a revised PREVENT strategy was released in Britain, which among other things, meant a decoupling, at least institutionally, of citizenship and social cohesion agendas from counter-radicalization efforts (Home Office 2011). Likewise, the current Danish government has worked toward separating the goals of counter-radicalization from social cohesion building and integration agendas, narrowing policies to individual interventions aimed at interdicting radicalization underway (Lindekilde 2014).

We have still to see reliable evaluations that tell us which counter-radicalization strategies work and which do not (cf. Lindekilde 2013b). As pointed out by Tore Bjørgo and John Horgan:

> We need to be frank in admitting that we have limited data and knowledge to illuminate the processes at an individual and group level of disengagement and de-radicalization. Furthermore, we lack the necessary data to test whether the various programmes are actually effective (and if so, why?) as most governments and organizations running such programmes are only releasing the data they consider convenient to make public.
>
> *(2009: 245)*

Systematic evaluations of counter-radicalization efforts are sorely needed and should be a part of future research.

Future research

This chapter has pointed out a number of shortcomings in the radicalization perspective on terrorism and counterterrorism. I will emphasize three avenues for future research that would advance the field. The first concerns the relationship between particular conceptualizations and models of radicalization and the way counter-radicalization programs are designed. Building on insights by critical scholars, we need to address, accept, and foreground that the way we define how radicalization creates vulnerable individuals and suspect communities in particular ways, which again calls for particular counter-measures. Definitions and conceptualizations need to be relative and context sensitive, and counter-radicalization efforts should be viewed as contingent and not as universally given. Only by acknowledging how the knowledge of radicalization and the policies that it informs are tools of power that draw boundaries of tolerance can future research avoid stigmatizing communities and individuals as problematic (Heath-Kelly 2013; Lindekilde & Kühle 2012).

The second avenue of future research concerns the incorporation of relevant insights from neighboring problem areas into radicalization studies. The potential of more interdisciplinary research on radicalization has yet to be exploited. In criminology, for example, the turn to violence and the propensity acquisition vis-à-vis immoral behavior have been studied for years (Bouhana & Wikström 2011). Gang studies, to mention one area, deal intensively with the development of rationales for violence over other forms of behavior. Working often with large datasets, criminologists have been able to identify better correlates and causes of violent behavior, which are insights that could function as starting points for future studies of radicalization. In addition, scripting technology used to produce crime scripts seems a promising methodology for future studies of radicalization and counter-radicalization (Brayley, Cockbain, & Laycock 2011).

Likewise, radicalization studies could learn from social movement studies, especially on the emergence of radicalizing settings and the relational and political sides of radicalization. Social movement scholars have long been preoccupied with the relational dynamic between state actions and social movement mobilization (see, for example, Davenport, Johnston, & Mueller 2005). Following the cue from this literature would entail studying how particular social movements, groups, or states become constituted in conflicts with each other and how the interaction between these different political actors produces a context in which violence becomes acceptable. This would also mean studying the role of, for example, targeted assassinations, drone attacks, torture, and renditions carried out by authorities in response to terrorism in causing further radicalization.

The third and final proposed avenue for future research concerns the need for more systematic empirical studies of the causes and mechanisms of radicalization. Future investigations should build on research designs that allow more integrated theories of radicalization to be tested (that is, the combination of micro-, meso-, and macro-level factors). This would be challenging in terms of data collection and methodology, but not impossible. One way forward would be more mixed designs that combine qualitative and quantitative studies. More rigid methodologies, such as survey experiments and group deliberation experiments, are promising avenues in radicalization studies, as they would implicate a focus on internal and external validity of causal findings, which could boost the confidence in what we know about radicalization.

References

Alya, A., Taylor, E., and Karnovsky, S., 2014. "Moral Disengagement and Building Resilience to Violent Extremism: An Education Intervention", *Studies in Conflict & Terrorism*, 37(4): 369–385.

Baron, R. S., Hoppe, S. I., Kao, C. F., and Brunsman, B., 1996. "Social Corroboration and Opinion Extremity", *Journal of Experiential Social Psychology*, 32: 537–560.

Bjørgo, T., and Horgan, J., eds., 2009. *Leaving Terrorism Behind. Individual and Collective Disengagement*. London: Routledge.

Borum, R., 2011. "Radicalization into Violent Extremism II: A Review of Conceptual Models and Empirical Research", *Journal of Strategic Security* 4(4): 37–62.

Bouhana, N., and Wikström, P., 2011. *Al Qai'da-Influenced Radicalisation: A Rapid Evidence Assessment Guided by Situational Action Theory*. RDS Occasional Paper 97. London: Home Office Research, Development and Statistics Directorate.

Brayley, H., Cockbain, E., and Laycock, G., 2011. "The Value of Crime Scripting: Deconstructing Internal Child Sex Trafficking", *Policing*, 5(2): 132–143.

Conway, M., 2012. "From al-Zarqawi to al-Awlaki: The Emergence of the Internet as a New Form of Violent Radical Milieu", s. 1–17. Available online at: www.isodarco.it/courses/andalo12/doc/Zarqawi%20to%20 Awlaki_V2.pdf.

COT – Institute for Safety, Security and Crisis Management, 2011. *Radicalisation, Recruitment and the EU Counter-radicalisation Strategy*. The Hague: COT.

Dalgaard-Nielsen, A., 2010. "Violent Radicalisation in Europe: What We Know and What We Do Not Know", *Studies in Conflict and Terrorism*, 33(9): 797–814.

Danish Government, 2009. *A Common and Safe Future. An Action Plan to Prevent Extremist Views and Radicalisation among Young People*. Available online in English at: www.nyidanmark.dk/NR/rdonlyres/ 58D048E7-0482-4AE8-99EB-928753EFC1F8/0/a_common_and_safe_future_danish_action_plan_ to_prevent_extremism.pdf.

Davenport, C., Johnston, H., and Mueller C., eds., 2005. *Repression and Mobilization*. Minneapolis: University of Minnesota Press.

della Porta, D., 1995. *Social Movements, Political Violence and the State. A Comparative Analysis of Italy and Germany*. Cambridge: Cambridge University Press.

Githens-Mazer, J., and Lambert, R., 2010. "Why Conventional Wisdom on Radicalization Fails: The Persistence of a Failed Discourse", *International Affairs*, 86(4): 889–901.

Goodwin, J., unpublished. "A Radical Critique of the Radicalization Perspective on Political Violence", Unpublished paper.

Heath-Kelly, C., 2013. "Counter-terrorism and the Counterfactual: Producing the 'Radicalisation' Discourse and the UK PREVENT strategy", *British Journal of Politics and International Relations*, 15(3): 394–415.

Heath-Kelly, C., Jarvis, L., and Baker-Beall, C., eds., 2014. *Counter-Radicalisation: Critical Perspectives*. London: Routledge.

Hogg, M., 2012. "Self-Uncertainty, Social Identity and the Solace of Extremism", in Hogg, M., and Blaylock, D., eds., *Extremism and the Psychology of Uncertainty*. Blackwell Publishing, pp. 19–35.

Home Office, 2011. Prevent strategy. Presented to Parliament in June 2011. Available online at: www.homeoffice.gov.uk/publications/counter-terrorism/prevent/prevent-strategy/prevent-strategy-review?view0Binary.

Horgan, J., 2009. *Walking Away from Terrorism: Accounts of Disengagement from Radical and Extremist Movements*. Abingdon: Routledge.

Kundani, A., 2012. "Radicalisation: The Journey of a Concept", *Race & Class*, 54(2): 3–25.

Lindekilde, L., 2012. "Neo-liberal Governing of 'Radicals': Danish Radicalization Prevention Policies and Potential Iatrogenic Effects", *International Journal of Conflict and Violence*, 5(2): 109–125.

Lindekilde, L., 2013a. "A Typology of Backfire Mechanisms: How Soft and Hard Forms of State Repression can have Perverse Effects in the Field of Counterterrorism", in Bosi, L., Demetriou, C., & Malthaner, S., eds., *Dynamics of Political Violence: A Process-Oriented Perspective on Radicalization and the Escalation of Political Conflict*. Farnham: Ashgate, pp. 51–71.

Lindekilde, L., 2013b. "Assessing the Impact of Counter-Radicalisation Prevention Policies on End Target Groups: The Case of Denmark", *European Journal of Criminal Policy and Research*, 18(4): 385–402.

Lindekilde, L., 2014. "Refocusing Danish Counter-radicalisation Efforts: Zooming in on the (Problematic) Logic and Practice of Individual De-radicalisation Interventions", in Heath-Kelly, C., Jarvis, L., & Baker-Beall, C., eds., *Counter-Radicalisation? Critically Rethinking Community-based Counter-Terrorism Agendas in Europe, Australia and the United States*. Abingdon: Routledge, pp. 223–242.

Lindekilde, L., and Kühle, L., 2012. "Radicalization and the Limits of Tolerance," *Journal of Ethnic and Migration Studies*, 38(10): 1607–1623.

Malthaner, S., 2011. *Mobilizing the Faithful: Militant Islamist Groups and Their Constituencies*. Frankfurt: Campus Verlag.

Malthaner, S., and Waldmann, P., 2014. "The Radical Milieu: Conceptualizing the Supportive Social Environment of Terrorist Groups", *Studies in Conflict and Terrorism*, 37(12): 979–998.

McCauley, C., and Moskalenko, S., 2008. "Mechanisms of Political Radicalization: Pathways towards Terrorism", *Terrorism and Political Violence*, 20(3): 415–433.

McCauley, C., and Moskalenko, S., 2011. *Friction: How Radicalisation Happens to Them and Us*. Oxford: Oxford University Press.

Myers, D., 1975. "Discussion-induced Attitude Polarization", *Human Relations*, 28: 699–714.

Mythen, G., Walklate, S., and Khan, F., 2009. "'I'm a Muslim, but I'm Not a Terrorist': Victimization, Risky Identities and the Performance of Safety", *British Journal of Criminology*, 49(6): 736–754.

Neumann, P., 2008. *Perspectives on Radicalisation and Political Violence: Papers from the First International Conference on Radicalisation and Political Violence, London, 17–18 January 2008*, London, International Centre for the Study of Radicalisation and Political Violence.

Olsen, J., 2009. *Roads to Militant Radicalisation – Interviews with Five Former Perpetrators of Politically Motivated Organized Violence*, DIIS Report 2009, 12: 21–40.

Precht, T., 2007. *Home Grown Terrorism and Islamist Radicalization in Europe: From Conversion to Terrorism*. Danish Ministry of Defense, December 2007.

Sageman, M., 2004. *Understanding Terror Networks*. Philadelphia: University of Pennsylvania Press.

Schkade, D., Sunstein, C., and Hastie, R., 2010. "When Deliberation Produces Extremism", *Critical Review*, 22 (2–3): 227–252.

Schmid, A., 2013. *Radicalisation, De-radicalisation and Counter-radicalisation: A Conceptual Discussion and Literature Review*. International Centre for Counter-Terrorism – The Hague, ICCT Research Paper.

Sedgwick, M., 2010. "The Concept of Radicalization as a Source of Confusion", *Terrorism and Political Violence*, 22 (4): 479–494.

Silber, M., and Bhatt, A., 2007. *Radicalization in the West: The Homegrown Threat*. New York: New York Police Department, NYPD Intelligence Department.

Sprinzak, E., 1990. "The Psychopolitical Formation of Extreme Left Terrorism in a Democracy: The Case of the Weathermen", in Reich, W., ed., *Origins of Terrorism: Psychologies, Ideologies, Theologies, States of Mind*. Washington, DC: Woodrow Wilson Center Press, pp. 65–86.

Sunstein, C., 2000. "Deliberative Trouble? Why Groups Go to Extremes", *The Yale Law Journal*, 110(1): 71–119.

Thomas, P., 2010. "Failed and Friendless: The UK's 'Preventing Violent Extremism' Programme", *The British Journal of Politics and International Relations*, 12(3): 442–458.

Van Dongen, T., 2010. "Mapping Counterterrorism: A Categorisation of Policies and the Promise of Empirically Based, Systematic Comparisons", *Critical Studies on Terrorism*, 3(2): 227–241.

Wiktorowicz, Q., 2005. *Radical Islam Rising: Muslim Extremism in the West*. Lanham, MD: Rowman & Littlefield.

PART V
Emerging debates

24
ECOTERRORISM AND EXPANSIONARY COUNTERTERRORISM

John Sorenson

Inventing ecoterrorism

The invention of "eco-terrorism" illustrates how the concept of terrorism has been expanded beyond sensible limits and how counterterrorism discourse operates to serve the interests of powerful corporations, manipulating social anxieties and fear in order to marginalize and undermine radical dissent. The term *ecoterrorism* can describe institutionalized and systemic violence against nonhuman animals and the environment, exemplified by the destructive impact of corporate oil and mining operations globally (Nocella II 2014: 181). Typically, however, it is used to describe those who oppose such violence and protect other animals and the environment.

Powerful corporations with investments in agribusiness, biotechnology, pesticides, pharmaceuticals, vivisection, and resource extraction want to ensure that their highly destructive practices are normalized and that other perspectives, especially those of animal rights and environmental activists who challenge their profits, are marginalized. This is achieved not only in the rhetoric and practices of these industries themselves, but in those of the public relations corporations they hire to promote them and demonize their enemies. The discourse of ecoterrorism finds ready acceptance in the counterterrorism industry, which needs a steady supply of terrorists to counter. Thus, there is a vast constellation of institutions and personnel with direct material interests in the social construction of ecoterrorism. As Jackson (2011: 395) notes, the threat narrative in terrorism discourse is essential to the functioning of "a materially grounded, self-perpetuating structure."

Faced with growing undercover investigations exposing institutionalized animal abuse and fearful of new ideas about relationships with other animals and the spread of veganism, industry groups repeat constant warnings of danger from animal activists and demand strategies to defeat them. Media uncritically reproduce these exaggerated dangers, and mainstream academic studies take it as their mission to "curb . . . the plague of eco-terrorism which currently threatens environmentally-involved research and production" (Nilson and Burke 2002).

The term *ecoterrorism* was coined by Ron Arnold of the Center for the Defense of Free Enterprise in a 1983 article for the right-wing magazine *Reason* and a book denouncing activists who commit crimes to save nature (Smith 2008: 545–546). A paid propagandist for oil, mining, ranching, and logging industries, Arnold was instrumental in promoting commercial "wise use" of public wilderness areas by private corporations. Arnold's approach toward environmentalists is widely quoted: "We're out to kill the fuckers. We're simply trying to eliminate them. Our goal is to destroy environmentalism once and for all" (Helvarg 2004: 7). The ecoterrorism industry developed to pursue that strategy.

The ecoterrorism industry

The "ecoterrorism industry" provides intellectual-ideological services to corporate interests that profit from the exploitation of nonhuman animals and the environment. Just as a counterterrorism industry promotes the agenda of powerful states that practice terrorism (see Blakeley and Raphael, this volume), the ecoterrorism industry involves a set of opinion-makers who participate in conferences and produce books, articles, and statements for mass media and who "reiterate the official line as in an echo chamber" (Herman and O'Sullivan 1989: 9). Groups such as the US-based Animal Agriculture Alliance (AAA) advise on how to counter animal advocacy campaigns and strategies and produce propaganda for animal-exploitation industries. For example, in Canada, the Alberta Farm Animal Care (AFAC), "the collective voice of the livestock industry" (AFAC n.d.) sells its services as "a highly specialized information bureau" to oppose animal activists and "special interest groups" that pose a "threat . . . from ideologically driven intrusions into how producers, processors, retailers, food service, and supply input companies conduct their business. Profitability and prosperity is being compromised" (AFAC 2013). Warning that activists are influencing policies and forcing businesses to respond to public concerns about the treatment of animals sparked by undercover investigations, it advises that farmers must manage perceptions of animal welfare issues because these will affect their profits.

Similarly, the AAA works for agribusiness, pharmaceutical corporations, feed companies, slaughterhouses, and retail companies, defending various institutions that exploit and kill animals on a massive scale. Reporting on the 2011 Conference to End Factory Farming in Arlington, Virginia, the AAA (2011) described this as a gathering of "extremist organizations" that included "Farm Sanctuary, . . . the ASPCA, . . . the Humane Society of the United States, Mercy for Animals, Compassion Over Killing, A Well Fed World, Compassion in World Farming, *E: The Environmental Magazine*, Discovery's TreeHugger, and Whole Foods Market." The AAA depicted these groups as dedicated to veganism, to "intimidating farmers and ranchers," and to "eliminating animal agriculture in entirety." In reality, rather than supporting abolitionist vegan campaigns, these organizations partnered with industry and endorsed what they call improved welfare standards of corporate meat retailers (Francione 2014).

While defending the institutionalized animal use and endorsing every cruelty inflicted upon them in the normal course of business, the AAA lobbied for "Ag-gag" laws to prevent activists from obtaining information about exploitation. Like other industry lobby groups, the AAA denounces undercover investigations that expose the normalized atrocities conducted in factory farms and slaughterhouses. For example, the AAA's Communications Director, Emily Meredith, characterizes undercover investigations as an attack on the farming industry in order to promote a "vegan agenda" and claims that undercover videos are "edited and manipulated" to make legal practices seem cruel (Caigle 2013). The fact that practices might be both cruel and legal is ignored.

Exaggerating ecoterrorist violence

Lobbyists for corporations that profit from exploitation of the environment and nonhuman animals deploy the term "ecoterrorism" to demonize activists. In *Forbes* magazine, Byme and Miller (2013) reject the FBI's description of such acts as eco-sabotage as "too tepid." To exemplify ecoterror, they cite Greenpeace's 1995 interception of a package of genetically modified seeds. They use a typical rhetorical strategy, acknowledging that Greenpeace's actions were nonviolent, but nonetheless link them to the New York and Washington, DC, 9/11 attacks in order to present them as murderous:

> The theft of the rice seeds was non-violent, but dating back to the mid-1990's [sic] and through the time of the September 11, 2001 attacks, eco-terror acts targeting research on GE plants had become all too common.

Corporate propaganda consistently uses this strategy to link legal and peaceful animal and environmental advocacy with the extreme violence of the 9/11 attacks.

Wealthy ecoterrorists

Industry propaganda characterizes animal advocates as wealthy organizations that undermine working people's livelihoods. For example, Byme and Miller (2013) state that domestic ecoterrorist groups opposed to biotechnology are funded by the organic food industry. In fact, most advocacy groups have miniscule budgets, while groups promoting environmental and animal exploitation are supported by huge corporations. Corporations such as Exxon Mobil, as well as individual right-wing funders such as the Koch brothers and Donors Trust, have provided $120 million to support hundreds of anti-environmental and climate change-denial groups (Goldenberg 2013a). Groups such as the Heartland Institute received millions from wealthy donors and channeled this to hundreds of anti-science "experts" and bloggers (Goldenberg 2013b).

For example, the anti-environmental group Committee for a Constructive Tomorrow (CFACT) was "funded by at least $542,000 from ExxonMobil, $60,500 from Chevron, and $1,280,000 from Scaife family foundations, which are rooted in wealth from Gulf Oil and steel interests" and is "part of a climate change denialist network funded by the ExxonMobil-financed Competitive Enterprise Institute" (People for the American Way 2011). Similarly, in the UK, Lord Lawson's Global Warming Policy Foundation was funded by wealthy right-wing donors to deny climate change (Ward 2013). As well as denying climate change, groups such as CFACT (2004) denounce environmentalist and animal advocacy groups' "dark world of violence and terrorism."

Exaggerating ecoterrorist danger

On its website, the NABR (n.d.) warns that the animal rights movement has "successfully manufactured a climate of public opposition to research involving animals." Yet the NABR claims that, despite having manipulated public opinion, the movement still employs widespread violence:

> According to the Federal Bureau of Investigation (FBI), the Earth Liberation Front (ELF) and . . . the Animal Liberation Front (ALF), were responsible for the vast majority of terrorist acts committed in the United States in the 1990s.

Industry groups consistently link animal advocacy with Islamist terrorism, although no actual connections exist. For example, in 2006 the Animal Agriculture Alliance announced its "anti-terrorism training course," citing imminent danger: "documents recovered from al-Qaeda training camps indicate that the USA's food supply is a high-priority target." The Alliance links al Qaeda with domestic "terrorists/activists" who have "declared war on modern food and agriculture" (Slebaugh 2006). It insinuates that "terrorists/activists" are motivated by atavistic hatred of modernity, comparable to the primitive fanaticism of Islamist suicide bombers. The Alliance cites Dr. Bob Norton, Professor of Veterinary Microbiology and Biosecurity in the Department of Poultry Science at Auburn University, who suggests:

> Our nation is now a target from [sic] adversaries, both foreign and domestic, who would like to destroy the American way of life and devastate our people. . . . Anyone responsible for securing food and agriculture facilities from internal and external threats along with protecting their workforce and the public should get training that will help them effectively execute this task.
>
> (Pork Magazine *2006*)

The Alliance warns of great danger, citing FBI estimates of "damage from eco- and animal rights-extremists at over $200 million" and an "increasing number of incidents of violence at farms, processing plants, research centers, and other business locations." No details or evidence are provided. The fact that sensible concerns exist about industrial agriculture, such as animal abuse, environmental degradation, misuse of antibiotics, pesticide poisoning, and so on, is disregarded.

The 9/11 attacks provided corporations with an opportunity to exploit a climate of fear and exaggerate ecoterrorist dangers. However, the threat is less significant than suggested. Mueller (2009: 2–3) notes that "international terrorism generally kills a few hundred people a year worldwide – not much more, usually, than the number who drown yearly in bathtubs in the United States", and finds the statistical chances of being killed by terrorists to be "microscopic." While the danger of terrorism generally is exaggerated (see Wolfendale, this volume), any ecoterrorist threat is even smaller. Nevertheless, Mueller's colleague at the right-wing Cato Institute, Doug Bandow (2005), emphasizes the danger of international terrorism and links this inflated threat with animal activists and environmentalists: "international terrorism, exemplified by the September 11 attacks and most recently in London, may pose the greatest security threat facing America but domestic terrorists also lurk among us, mostly in the guise of animal-rights and environmental activists."

Corporate media and industry propaganda use terms such as *terrorists* and *extremists* to suggest that activists typically use violence to achieve their ends. For example, Britten (2006) conjures a "contrary world of animal rights extremists . . . where every prison sentence moves you up the ladder; where the more extreme violence you use, the higher you are regarded."

Bandow (2005) depicts animal activists as dangerous fanatics who "see themselves in a war against the entire government and industrial democracy itself." He quotes Frankie Trull, of the Foundation for Biomedical Research: "these are unbelievably mean-spirited people [who] operate in a classic terrorist organization mode." Bandow says animal activists have committed hundreds of criminal acts, that the ALF has caused extensive damage and "threatened" employees at the University of Iowa, and that even the mainstream group PETA "has accosted Kentucky Fried Chicken executives, intimidated company advertising pitchmen and breached KFC events." This sounds alarming, but Bandow does not explain the "criminal acts," which doubtless include many cases of rescuing animals from situations in which they are to be harmed – actions normally considered compassionate and praiseworthy.

Similarly, the nature of the "threats" is unexplained, as are the PETA actions that so "intimidated company advertising pitchmen." Typical PETA actions consist of distributing leaflets or dressing in lettuce bikinis, and none of PETA's (n.d.) Activism Tips suggest particularly threatening actions (for example, holding a vegan bake sale, buying nonleather shoes, volunteering at an animal shelter, and the like). The "breach[ing]" of a KFC event may have involved peaceful and legal demonstrations. To emphasize the threat, Bandow quotes FBI Deputy assistant director John E. Lewis at government hearings on ecoterrorism: "there is nothing else going on in this country over the last several years that is racking up the high number of violent crimes and terrorist actions." Lewis may have said more than he intended: with "nothing else . . . going on" in terms of terrorism, the FBI and the huge counterterrorism apparatus created after the 9/11 attacks must produce other "threats" to justify their own existence, with ecoterrorism providing a convenient target.

Bandow concludes:

> PETA doesn't look much like al Qaeda, and the groups are very different. But the danger of animal-rights and environmental terrorism is exacerbated by the enabling role of supposedly more mainstream groups such as PETA. We shouldn't wait until people die to combat this threat.

This is standard rhetorical practice, constructing a double message, seeming to acknowledge the absurdity of comparing PETA to al Qaeda while actually making that very comparison and warning of imminent danger.

Industry lobbyists denounce even conservative welfarist groups as terrorists, such as Animals Australia, which campaigns against the live export industry, for cage-free hens, and against factory farm-style puppy mills. Its website contains no information about veganism and the only mention of vegetarianism is on the FAQ page of its website which states that "Animals Australia's position has always been that animals should be processed onshore, under Australian laws and regulations, with their meat exported" – hardly an extremist view, and one which many activists would find much too limited. Nevertheless, New South Wales Primary Industries Minister, Katrina Hodgkinson, attacked the group at the NSW Farmers' Association's 2013 annual conference in Sydney:

> We have to keep putting it up to city people that don't, may not necessarily understand our farming practices and how important they are, that they cannot support these groups such as Animals Australia and cannot support what they're doing. These people are vandals. These people are akin to terrorists.
> *(Australian Broadcasting Corporation 2013)*

While most animal advocates use legal, nonviolent activities, the ecoterrorism industry represents them as dangerous and violent. The Animal Liberation Front (ALF), founded in England in 1976, has used arson and small explosives. But ALF guidelines reject harming any animals, including humans, and the ALF has never killed anyone. The ELF, which began operations in 1996, based its own guidelines upon those of the ALF and, likewise, has never killed or injured a human. Much of the ALF's activity has involved rescuing animals from situations in which they were to be tortured in experiments or killed for their flesh or fur. Where "violence" has been used, both the ALF and ELF have only committed property damage.

Entrapment, informants, and provocateurs

A few individuals have used violence against humans. In 1988, Fran Trutt was charged with attempted murder for trying to place a bomb near a parking spot used by Leon Hirsch, CEO of US Surgical Corporation, a biomedical tools company. Trutt was manipulated by Mary Lou

Sapone, an undercover agent for Perceptions International, a security firm specializing in actions against the animal rights movement. Hirsh hired Sapone and others to infiltrate animal rights groups and prod them to commit illegal activities. The plot to entrap Trutt was discussed at a meeting that included representatives of the federal Bureau of Alcohol, Tobacco and Firearms; the Connecticut States Attorney's office; the US Surgical Corporation's security director; and Perceptions International (Berlet 1991). Sapone had attempted to involve numerous other activists, but all rejected her incitements. Perceptions International agents pretended to befriend Trutt, suggested the bombing, paid for the equipment, and drove her to the parking lot. When Trutt expressed reluctance to continue, another undercover agent persuaded her to carry out the operation.

In 2001, David Blenkinsop received a three-year sentence for assaulting Huntingdon Life Sciences Managing Director Brian Cass (Blenkinsop was also sentenced for possessing incendiary devices and for rescuing pigs, for a total of nearly ten years). In 2006, Donald Currie pleaded guilty to arson and planting explosives at the home of a director of a courier business associated with Huntingdon Life Sciences, Britain's largest vivisection company. These are acts of political violence intended to intimidate, but even these can be distinguished from what is generally understood as terrorism, since they are not intended as mass killings or random killings of civilians to create fear in whole communities (Guelke 2008). Although not all activists consider such tactics acceptable and some vociferously condemn them, the "ecoterrorist" label is applied indiscriminately to all.

The use of informants and agents provocateurs is standard police practice. For example, an FBI informant identified as "Anna" was central to the 2006 arrest of three so-called ecoterrorists, Zachary Jenson, Eric McDavid, and Lauren Weiner, in California for conspiracy to blow up a dam, fish hatchery, cell phone towers, power stations, and a forestry research center. Anna was ideologically motivated, holding strong right-wing views (Todd 2008), and was paid at least $65,000 by the FBI. In 2005, she attended protests and meetings across the US to make contacts with anarchists and animal and environmental activists. Working for the FBI, Anna was involved in numerous other prosecutions of anarchists, and she brought Jensen, McDavid, and Weiner together, encouraged them to undertake direct action, pushed them to select targets, provided them with transportation across the country, paid for their living expenses, gave them a place to live and work, supplied them with bomb-making recipes, purchased the bomb-making materials, and shouted at them when they expressed unwillingness to carry out the plans she advocated.

After their arrest, Jenson and Weiner made a deal with the FBI for probation, in return for testifying against McDavid. McDavid himself was in love with Anna and adopted an increasingly radical demeanor to impress her and to meet her demands for direct action, although he characterized the plan to blow up the Nimbus Dam as "silly" (Kuipers 2012). These practices of police spies cultivating intimate relationships with activists are widespread. For example, police spies from the Special Demonstration Squad in the UK "routinely formed sexual relationships" with activists. London Metropolitan University criminologist Robert Lambert (2014) defends such practices, not surprisingly, as he faced calls for his dismissal after being exposed in 2011 as a police spy who fathered a child with an activist as part of his cover when he infiltrated the ALF in the 1980s. However, as Loadenthal (2014) illustrates, the effects of such tactics are pernicious and are designed to produce an atmosphere of totalized surveillance and to undermine progressive social movements.

The fact that ALF/ELF activists take care not to harm people presents a problem for those who depict them as violent terrorists. The usual strategy of industry lobbyists is to warn that "it is only a matter of time" before activists start assassinating corporate executives, farmers, and vivisectionists. In some cases, these accusations have been exposed as propaganda. For example, the *Observer* published an article by Mark Townsend and Nick Denning (2008) that accepted at face value warnings from the National Extremism Tactical Co-ordination Unit (NETCU) that Earth First!-inspired ecoterrorists were poised "to kill large numbers of Britons to help reduce Earth's population by 80 per cent." NETCU's stated aim was to support the business community, and it endorsed provivisection groups (*SchNews* 2008). Townsend and Denning (2008) quoted an anonymous NETCU "senior source" who said police were "monitoring blogs and internet traffic connected to a network of UK climate camps and radical environmental movements under the umbrella of Earth First!" and had found evidence of an imminent terrorist strike:

> We have found statements that four-fifths of the human population has to die for other species in the world to survive. There are a number of very dedicated individuals out there and they could be dangerous to other people.

Townsend and Denning published NETCU's statements without investigating, and Townsend admitted that they had not actually seen a statement about reducing the human population but simply accepted NETCU's assertion that it had appeared on someone's blog (*SchNews* 2008). After receiving many complaints, the *Observer* retracted the article, acknowledging there was "no evidence whatsoever" for NETCU's claims (Corporate Watch 2008). Townsend and Denning's article itself suggests why police would spread such unfounded fears:

> The rise of eco-extremism coincides with the fall of the animal rights activist movement. Police said the animal rights movement was in "disarray" and that its ringleaders had either been prosecuted or were awaiting prosecution, adding that its "critical mass" of hardcore extremists was sufficiently depleted to have halted its effectiveness.

With the animal rights movement in "disarray," the ecoterrorism industry needed new targets. Environmentalists were suitable. NETCU was rebranded in 2011 as the National Domestic Extremism Unit and focused its surveillance on environmentalists, amassing a secret database on almost 9,000 "domestic extremists" (Lewis, Evans, and Dodd 2013).

The discourse of ecoterrorism is used to discredit, marginalize, and control groups whose messages threaten corporate interests and profit. The language of "ecoterrorism" is used to legitimize surveillance and the imposition of harsh prison sentences. Until recently, the animal rights movement was not a serious threat to industry; activists could be dismissed as sentimentalists and eccentrics. However, as activist campaigns began to have effects and corporations feared financial losses, they demanded legislation to silence critics and stifle their campaigns. Corporations are continuously engaged in manufacturing consent, attempting to shape public opinion in ways favorable to their interests, both through paid advertising that stimulates demand for their products and by shaping news so that ideas about workers' rights, public health, and the environment can be managed. The concerns and campaigns of animal and environmental activists constitute problems for corporations, because there is considerable public sympathy for them. Therefore, corporations find it necessary to pay for propaganda campaigns to discredit them and to undermine this sympathy and replace it with fear of ecoterrorists.

Repressive legislation

Industry lobby groups promote the use of animals in agribusiness, biomedical and pharmaceutical research, clothing, and entertainment and were instrumental in having repressive laws passed to target animal advocates, restrict their actions, and have them designated as terrorists. These industries exaggerated the ecoterrorism menace to lobby for legislation. They created the Green Scare (an analogy with the Red Scare – the prosecution of American left-wing activists or sympathizers in the 1950s): a corporate-driven propaganda campaign to counteract animal advocates; demonize them; make their ideas seem dangerous, extreme, and unthinkable; and to develop legal tools to criminalize their activities. Their broader goals are to send a message about political dissent itself and to maintain a culture of fear in which activism is identified with danger and irrational violence that goes against common sense understanding of the world. Corporations based upon animal exploitation – agribusiness, pharmaceuticals, retail food, fur, entertainment, the pet industry, and the like – seek to protect their particular interests, but also to oppose criticism of the system of neoliberal capitalism in which they all operate.

These industries found an ally in Senator James Inhofe, who chaired the 2005 Senate Committee on Environment and Public Works hearing on "Oversight on Eco-Terrorism Specifically Examining the Earth Liberation Front ('ELF') and the Animal Liberation Front ('ALF')." Inhofe called the ALF and ELF "terrorists by definition" who used "intimidation, threats, acts of violence, and property destruction to force their opinions . . . upon society," and he held them accountable for damages totally over $110 million in over a thousand "acts of terrorism." Inhofe considered the ALF and ELF as interchangeable, compared both to al Qaeda, and claimed that these "terrorist" groups draw money from "mainstream activists," including PETA. Admitting that ecoterrorists "have not killed anyone to date," Inhofe nonetheless asserted that "it is only a matter of time" before they do.

John Lewis, Deputy Assistant Director of the FBI's Counterterrorism Division, told the Committee that "the No. 1 domestic terrorism threat is the eco-terrorism animal rights movement," stated that the FBI "certainly shares your opinion that these individuals are most certainly domestic terrorists," and identified this as the FBI's top priority, calling for expanded federal laws to allow them to "dismantle these movements" (Lewis 2005: 18, 11, 13). Using the same rhetorical strategy as Inhofe, Lewis acknowledged that these "terrorists" had killed no one, but predicted it would happen, citing "escalation in violent rhetoric" (2005: 12). Lewis said that compared to anti-abortionists, the KKK, and right-wing extremists, the ALF and ELF "are way out in front in terms of the damage they are causing." Anti-abortionists had murdered at least nine people in the United States and wounded at least 12 others in shootings, arsons, acid attacks, and bombings prior to the 2005 hearings, and at least one other murder and several attacks followed.

Similarly, while the FBI characterized animal and environmentalist activists as the major domestic terrorist threat, right-wing groups are clearly more dangerous. For example, since the 9/11 attacks, right-wing extremists have killed 34 people in the US for political reasons, while those motivated by Islamist ideology have killed 21 people (Bergen and Sterman 2014). Rightwing terrorists have been arrested with biological and chemical weapons and radioactive material to build "dirty bombs" and have planned or conducted bombings of "government buildings, banks, refineries, utilities, clinics, synagogues mosques, memorials and bridges"; assassinations of "police officers, judges, politicians, civil rights figures and others"; robberies of "banks, armored cars and other criminals [and have] amass[ed] illegal machine guns, missiles, explosives, and biological and chemical weapons. . . . Most contemplated the deaths of large numbers of people – in one case as many as 30,000, or ten times the number murdered on Sept. 11, 2001" (Keller 2009: 13, 23). Moreover, right-wing extremists have repeatedly stated their intentions to kill as many people as possible.

Nevertheless, government, police, and media continue to focus more attention on ecoterrorists. For example, Fox News (2008) reported that the FBI still considered animal rights and environmentalist groups the number one domestic terrorism threat, noting 180 ecoterrorism ongoing investigations, but they mentioned nothing about right-wing terrorism. When attention has turned to the more serious threat of right-wing terrorism, conservative groups have issued sharp condemnations. For example, in 2009, a Department of Homeland Security intelligence report on right-wing terrorism created a huge political controversy.

The 2005 hearing was a prelude to establishing the 2006 Animal Enterprise Terrorism Act (AETA), which replaced the 1992 Animal Enterprise Protection Act (AEPA). The AEPA was crafted by the National Association for Biomedical Research (NABR), and they created the term *animal enterprise terrorism*. AETA instigators included NABR and influential agribusiness and biomedical industry lobby groups, such as the Animal Enterprise Protection Coalition, American Legislative Exchange Council, the Foundation for Biomedical Research, and the Fur Commission. Scores of other animal exploitation groups endorsed the act, which essentially transformed into terrorists those who interfered with their profits. Animal-exploitation industries guided the legislation through to its passage, assisted by politicians whose services they had purchased through financial contributions and who had personal investments in industries the legislation would affect.

For example, Inhofe had considerable personal investments in oil and gas industries, and he received significant funding from the chemical and forestry industries, the oil and gas companies, the nuclear energy industry, and their political action committees. He consistently voted against environmental and public health safety regulations that would affect these industries. Inhofe denounced climate change as a "hoax" perpetrated by the UN and "the Hollywood elite" and opposed the international consensus of scientific experts at the UN Climate Change Conference in Copenhagen (O'Brien 2009; Roug 2009). In his 2010 Minority Report, Inhofe denounced leading scientists associated with the Intergovernmental Panel on Climate Change and the United States Global Change Research Program as "key players" in an international conspiracy and demanded their prosecution by the US Justice Department (United States Senate Committee on Environment and Public Works 2010). As the public sought corporate accountability after the 2010 BP oil spill, Inhofe blocked a bill to increase liability of oil companies responsible for such environmental disasters. He also attempted to keep the Environmental Protection Agency from regulating power plant and refinery emissions and rolled back rules on increased fuel efficiency for automobiles manufactured from 2012 to 2016. Inhofe also defended the cruel practices of factory farming.

In turn, these industries lauded Inhofe's services to them: "in 2008, the Oklahoma Independent Petroleum Association honored Inhofe for 'voting consistently in the 110th Congress to protect the interests of the oil and gas industry,'" and in 2004, the National Association of Chemical Distributors named him legislator of the year, while the American Farm Bureau designated him as an official Friend of Farm Bureau, the Oklahoma Farm Bureau gave him a Lifetime Achievement Award, and the Oklahoma Pork Council recognized his efforts on their behalf with a Distinguished Service Award (Lovitz 2010: 85–86).

Senator Dianne Feinstein co-sponsored the bill. Although she was not directly funded by animal exploitation industries, her husband, Richard Blum, was Chairman of the Board of CB Richard Ellis Group, a real estate firm that serves the vivisection industry and associated major pharmaceutical companies such as American Pharmaceutical Partners, Astra Zeneca, Bayer Pharmaceuticals, Chiron, DuPont, Eli Lilly and Company, Johnson and Johnson, Merck, Novartis, Pfizer, Schering Plough, and Wyeth (Lovitz 2010: 85). Other co-sponsors of the AETA also had financial interests in industries served by the legislation. Representative Tom Petri was funded by the dairy industry and headed the Badger Fund, a political action committee funded by American Foods Group, owner of slaughterhouses; and Representative Robert Scott had investments in Johnson and Johnson, Procter & Gamble, and Yum! Brands (Lovitz 2010: 86).

In 2006, the AETA received support from the Chair of the Committee on the Judiciary, Representative James Sensenbrenner, who owns stock in major pharmaceutical, chemical, petroleum, and defense industries. Sensenbrenner opposed the Animal Fighting Prohibition Act and intended to increase penalties for such activities, despite the fact it had unanimously passed the Senate and had hundreds of co-sponsors. Like Inhofe, Sensenbrenner is a climate change denier, claiming climate change scientists were engaged in "massive international scientific fraud" and "scientific fascism" (Sundt 2009). He vigorously advocated for the AETA, saying existing laws were inadequate and that activists had committed over a thousand terrorist actions, causing millions in damages.

While animal exploitation industries cheered the legislation they had created, animal activists and civil rights advocates said the AETA was too broad and vague, in part because it did not define "animal enterprise," meaning that it could be applied to any business that involves animals in some way. Penalties imposed by the AETA are disproportional to actions covered, imposing longer sentences for nonviolent actions that cause profit losses to animal enterprises than for actions that directly harm people. Opponents said the AETA would have a chilling effect on legal protest in general, because activists would fear being charged as terrorists.

Although the AETA's defenders claimed it would not constrain legally protected political expression, it is clear that police and prosecutors see the legislation as a weapon against dissidents. For example, in 2009, four activists were charged under the AETA for protesting at University of California vivisectors' homes in 2007 and 2008. Police said they wore bandanas and wrote "Stop the Torture," "Bird Killer," and "Murder for Scientific Lies" on the pavement with chalk. In July 2010, a federal judge dismissed the indictment because it was too vague and because prosecutors could not specify how the activists had broken any laws. Individual activists challenged the AETA's legitimacy, but in 2014, the First Circuit Court rejected their case on the grounds that they lacked standing. Some scholars and activists are taking a more critical approach to the constructed menace of ecoterrorism, challenging the AETA as an unconstitutional effort to undermine activism itself (Lovitz 2010; Potter 2011; Del Gandio and Nocella II 2014).

Conclusion

Future research on ecoterrorism must place this in the context of destruction of Earth's ecosystems, to the point where species are disappearing at a thousand times the natural rate of extinction, where air and water are dangerously polluted, forests are being decimated, and global warming may soon make the planet uninhabitable for our own species. A significant aspect of this dysfunctional system is the growing global production of animals for food. In this system, billions of nonhuman animals are raised in horrifying factory-farm conditions which makes their short existence a nightmare for them.

The discourse of ecoterrorism characterizes this institutionalized abuse as normal and acceptable and focuses on those who criticize these practices, depicting them as misguided, misanthropic, and violent. The rhetoric of ecoterrorism serves corporate interests by characterizing activists who challenge the ethical legitimacy of animal exploitation and of unrestrained resource extraction and endanger corporate profits as extremists. It also provides the counterterrorism industry with a supply of dangers that must be vanquished and a set of easily achievable victories. Critical scholars can work to expose the discursive and material structures of ecoterrorism by tracing the rhetorical strategies employed and the particular interests involved. They can advance this agenda by changing the narrative of public/political discourse on ecoterrorism to, first, focus not on minor acts of property damage by activists, but on the actions of corporations that are responsible for environmental degradation and animal exploitation. They can also work to increase recognition that ecoterrorism is a discursive construction that serves both the interests of those corporations and the counterterrorism industry itself.

As Herman (1982:13) observed in relation to state terrorism, we are "in an age of Orwell, where words are managed and propaganda and scholarship are organized so that terror *means* the lesser terror – the greater terror is defined out of existence and given little attention." These observations are equally applicable to the creation of ecoterrorism by the animal-industrial complex. As Paul Watson (2011) of Sea Shepherd suggests, the discourse of terrorism operates to marginalize dissent: "today, calling someone a terrorist is simply a way of attempting to demonize someone you disagree with. The word itself is beginning to lose its meaning." While some activists engage in unlawful actions, these have been limited to property damage and sabotage rather than murderous acts against the public. To describe these actions as terrorism is to distort the meaning of that term. Critical scholarship should not perpetuate such distortions, but instead focus on institutionalized, normalized ecoterrorism as described previously (Nocella II 2014).

References

Alberta Farm Animal Care (AFAC), n.d. "Membership Information Package." Available online at: http://afac.ab.ca/application/files/9814/4797/6263/2015_New_Membership_Information_Package.pdf.

Alberta Farm Animal Care (AFAC), 2013. "Annual Report." Available online at: www.afac.ab.ca/documents/2013_AFAC_AnnualReport.pdf.

Animal Agriculture Alliance, 2006. "Alliance Announces First Midwest Anti-Terrorism Training Course Protect Yourself from Agro-Terrorism." Press Release. Available online at: http://animalagalliance.org/current/home.cfm?Category=Press_Releases&Section=2006_0810_Midwest.

Animal Agriculture Alliance (AAA), 2011. "Myths Promoted at 'End Factory Farming' Conference." *Dairy Business*. November 7. Available online at: http://dairybusiness.com/seo/headline.php?title=myths-promoted-at-end-factory-farming-confere&date=2011-11-17&table=headlines#ixzz38DUMjbLg.

Australian Broadcasting Corporation, 2013. "Animal Rights Activists 'Akin to Terrorists', says NSW Minister Katrina Hodgkinson." July 18. Available online at: www.abc.net.au/news/2013-07-18/animal-rights-activists-27terrorists272c-says-nsw-minister/4828556.

Bandow, D., 2005. "Animal Terrorism." *Washington Times*, August 22. Available online at: www.washtimes.com/functions/print.php?StoryID=20050821-103902-4686r.

Bergen, P., and Sterman, D., 2014. "U.S. Right Wing Extremists More Deadly Than Jihadists." *CNN Opinion*, April 15. Available online at: www.cnn.com/2014/04/14/opinion/bergen-sterman-kansas-shooting/.

Berlet, C., 1991. "Attacks on Greenpeace and Other Ecology Groups." Somerville: Political Research Associates, August 22. Available online at: www.publiceye.org/liberty/greenspy.html.

Britten, N., 2006. "Peace and Love From the Vegan Who Chose Violence." *The Telegraph*, April 12. Available online at: www.telegraph.co.uk/news/uknews/1515452/Peace-and-love-from-the-vegan-who-chose-violence.html.

Byme, J., and Miller, H., 2013. "Domestic Eco-Terrorism Has Deep Pockets, and Many Enablers." *Forbes*. July 10. Available online at: www.forbes.com/sites/henrymiller/2013/07/10/domestic-eco-terrorism-has-deep-pockets-and-many-enablers/.

Caigle, S., 2013. "Two Views on Ag-Gag: the Investigator and the Farm Advocate." *Grist*, April 25. Available online at: http://grist.org/food/two-views-on-ag-gags/.

CFACT, 2004. "Crucial Difference in Animal Welfare and Rights." May 7. Available online at: www.cfact.org/2004/05/07/crucial-difference-in-animal-welfare-and-rights/.

Corporate Watch, 2008. "Whose Agenda Do Reports of Eco-Terrorism Serve?", November 30. Available online at: www.corporatewatch.org/?q=node/3179%3f.

Del Gandio, J., and Nocella II, A., eds., 2014. *The Terrorization of Dissent*. New York: Lantern.

Fox News, 2008. "FBI: Eco-Terrorism Remains No. 1 Domestic Terror Threat." March 31. Available online at: www.foxnews.com/story/2008/03/31/fbi-eco-terrorism-remains-no-1-domestic-terror-threat/.

Francione, G., 2014. "The Animal Confusion Movement." *Animal Rights: The Abolitionist Approach*, July 22. Available online at: http://abolitionistapproach.com/author/gary/.

Goldenberg, S., 2013a. "Secret Funding Helped Build Vast Network of Climate Denial Thinktanks." *Guardian*, February 14. Available online at: www.theguardian.com/environment/2013/feb/14/funding-climate-change-denial-thinktanks-network.

Goldenberg, S., 2013b. "Leak Exposes How Heartland Institute Works to Undermine Climate Science." *Guardian*, February 15. Available online at: www.theguardian.com/environment/2012/feb/15/leak-exposes-heartland-institute-climate.

Guelke, A., 2008. "Great Whites, Paedophiles and Terrorists: The Need for Critical Thinking in a New Age of Fear." *Critical Studies on Terrorism*, 1(1): 17–25.

Helvarg, D., 2004. *The War Against the Greens*. Boulder: Johnson.

Herman, E. S., 1982. *The Real Terror Network*. Montreal: Black Rose.

Herman, E., and O'Sullivan, G., 1989. *The 'Terrorism' Industry: The Experts and Institutions that Shape Our View of Terror*. New York: Pantheon Books.

Jackson, R., 2011. "Culture, Identity and Hegemony: Continuity and (the Lack of) Change in US Counterterrorism Policy from Bush to Obama." *International Politics*, 48(2/3): 390–411.

Keller, L., 2009. "The Second Wave. Return of the Militias." *Southern Poverty Law Center*, Montgomery. Available online at: www.splcenter.org/sites/default/files/downloads/The_Second_Wave.pdf.

Kuipers, D., 2012. "Judge Orders Testing of Evidence in Judi Bari Bombing." *Los Angeles Times*, April 2. Available online at: http://articles.latimes.com/2012/apr/02/local/la-me-gs-judge-orders-testing-of-evidence-in-judi-bari-bombing-20120402.

Lambert, R., 2014. "Researching Counterterrorism: A Personal Perspective from a Former Undercover Police Officer." *Critical Studies on Terrorism*, 7(1): 165–181.

Lewis, J., 2005. "Hearing Statement to the United States Senate Committee on Environment and Public Works." Available online at: http://epw.senate.gov/hearing_statements.cfm?id=237817.

Lewis, P., Evans, R., and Dodd, V., 2013. "National Police Unit Monitors 9,000 'Domestic Extremists'." *Guardian*, June 26. Available online at: www.theguardian.com/uk/2013/jun/25/undercover-police-domestic-extremism-unit.

Loadenthal, M., 2014. "When Cops 'Go Native': Policing Revolution Through Sexual Infiltration and Panopticonism." *Critical Studies on Terrorism*, 7(1): 24–42.

Lovitz, D., 2010. *Muzzling A Movement*. New York: Lantern.

Mueller, J., 2009. *Overblown: How Politicians and the Terrorism Industry Inflate National Security Threats and Why We Believe Them*. New York: The Free Press.

NABR, n.d. "Animal Rights Extremism." Available online at: www.nabr.org/Animal_Activism/Animal_Rights_Extremism.aspx.

Nilson, C., and Burke, T., 2002. "Environmental Extremists and the Eco-Terrorism Movement." *ACJS [Academy of Criminal Justice Sciences] Today*. January/February. Available online at: www.unl.edu/eskridge/ecoterrorism.html.

Nocella II, A., 2014. "A Green Criminologist Perspective on Eco-Terrorism", in Del Gandio, J., & Nocella II, A., eds., *The Terrorization of Dissent*, New York: Lantern, pp. 177–202.

O'Brien, M., 2009. "Inhofe to Travel to Climate Summit as 'One-man Truth Squad'." September 9. Available online at: http://thehill.com/blogs/blog-briefing-room/news/59979-inhofe-to-travel-to-climate-summit-as-one-man-truth-squad.

People for the American Way, 2011. "The Green Dragon Slayers." Available online at: www.pfaw.org/sites/default/files/rww-in-focus-green-dragon-final.pdf.

People for the Ethical Treatment of Animals, n.d. "PETA's Activism Tips." Available online at: www.peta.org/action/activism-guide/your-animal-saving-style-quiz/activism-tips/.

Pork Magazine, 2006. "Alliance Announces First West Coast Anti-Terrorism Training Course." Available online at: www.ocm.auburn.edu/clippings/2006/062306.html.

Potter, W., 2011. *Green Is the New Red*. San Francisco: City Lights.

Roug, L., 2009. "Jim Inhofe Gets Cool Reception in Denmark." December 19. Available online at: www.politico.com/news/stories/1209/30769.html.

SchNews, 2008. "Fifth Columnist." November 14. Available online at: www.schnews.org.uk/archive/news655.htm.

Slebaugh, S., 2006. "State Helps Turn Up Heat Over CAFO Public Relations." *Star Press*, September 6. Available online at: www.thestarpress.com/apps/pbcs.dll/article?AID=/20060907/NEWS01/609070345/1002.

Smith, R., 2008. "Vilification of Environmental Activists." *Environmental Law*, 38(2): 537–576.

Sundt, N., 2009. "WWF Climate Blog In Congressional Hearing, Administration Officials Respond to E-Mail Controversy." January 7. Available online at: www.wwfblogs.org/climate/content/congressional-hearing-administration-officials-respond-e-mail-controversy.

Todd, A., 2008. "The Believers." *Elle*. April: 266–272, 373–375.

Townsend, M., and Denning, N., 2008. "UK Police Warn of Growing Threat from Eco-terrorists." *Observer*. November 9. (Retracted)

United States Senate Committee on Environment and Public Works, 2010. "'Consensus Exposed'. The CRU Controversy." Available online at: www.epw.senate.gov/public/_cache/files/7db3fbd8-f1b4-4fdf-bd15-12b7df1a0b63/crufinal.pdf.

Ward, B., 2013. "Secret Funding of Climate Sceptics is Not Restricted to the US." *Guardian*, February 15. Available online at: www.theguardian.com/environment/2013/feb/15/secret-funding-climate-sceptics-not-restricted-us.

Watson, P., 2011. "The Terrible, Troubling Tribulations of Being Called An Eco-Terrorist." *Huffington Post*, March 4. Available online at: www.huffingtonpost.com/paul-watson/sea-shepherd-whaling_b_831638.html.

25
MEDIA COVERAGE OF TERRORISM

Ben O'Loughlin

Introduction

In January 2015, Tarik Kafala, the head of BBC Arabic, announced that his news reports would not describe as 'terrorists' the attackers who killed 12 people at the *Charlie Hebdo* magazine in Paris earlier that month. He told *The Independent* newspaper:

> We try to avoid describing anyone as a terrorist or an act as being terrorist. What we try to do is to say that 'two men killed 12 people in an attack on the office of a satirical magazine'. That's enough, we know what that means and what it is.
>
> *(Kafala, cited in Sherwin, 2015)*

Since terrorist is such a 'loaded word', he continued, it was better to use language that was factual and value-free. This episode encapsulates many of the problems in media coverage of terrorism. How does Kafala know this choice will best serve his audience? With a factual description, he says, 'we know what that means and what it is'. But who is the 'we' here? The BBC, BBC Arabic, all journalists, or Kafala and all those who consume BBC Arabic news? Does his audience really all know that the factual description is referring to? Would it not be quicker and easier to describe the event as a terrorist attack? Furthermore, even such neutral language offended the values of those who call a spade a spade and want to call a terrorist a terrorist. Conservative groups immediately raised objections. In the UK, the *Daily Mail* news site found various politicians willing to say the BBC's policy meant obscuring the nature of the attacks and attackers being reported (Greenhill, 2015). The US *Newsbusters* site accused the BBC of 'bias' and 'leftism' by refusing to use language that condemns violence (Graham, 2015). These critics argued that the BBC's choice of non-value-laden, descriptive language was a value-laden decision resulting in *less* accurate and *less* informative reporting to its audiences. This dispute indicates there is something at stake in media coverage of terrorism. It *makes a difference* in politics and is worth arguing about. It makes a difference to public understandings of political and religious violence; it therefore makes a difference to what counterterror policies those publics will find legitimate and desirable, and it makes a difference to the role journalists should play in signifying the moral nature of incidents they report upon.

Terrorism is an act of communication (Schmid, 1989; Devji, 2005; Carr, 2006; Nacos, 2007). This is why these arguments matter. Violence is committed in order to make a political point: we want our country back; stop committing atrocities against us; you may have a stronger military but your people are still not safe. This poses a series of dilemmas for news media. In most countries journalists are bound to inform and to exercise their rights as free press. Terrorism is newsworthy because it is immediate, visual, dramatic and – despite occurring regularly – unexpected. It may indicate local political tensions or appear to be part of a global chain of attacks; either way, the public should be informed. Audiences will also want to know the personalities of the perpetrators, victims and those leading the response: terrorism as human interest. There are therefore reasons of commerce, professional ethics and democratic duty driving the reporting of terrorism. However, in reporting an act of terrorism, journalists make that act real. They do not just represent or cover terrorism, they are part of the very act of terrorism. News images are not what follow a terrorist attack, they are integral to the attack. News media and violent actors are co-creators of terrorism. Acts of terrorism are carefully planned to ensure media amplify alarm by disseminating news of the attack to a wider public. Does this make them complicit, handing 'victory' to terrorists and encouraging further copycat attacks (see Nacos, 2003)?

Here, it is important to be precise about how we define media and media coverage. Traditionally, broadcast media such as radio, television and the press were 'one-to-many' mediums. News was distributed from a central point in a standardised format to a large audience. Those committing terrorism would seek to exploit this distribution system by getting those core journalists to spread coverage of their acts to large audiences in order to have effects on public opinion. Most media and terrorism studies were conducted in the broadcast era. There were three basic theoretical models of how power and control of news agendas worked (Cottle, 2006). Marxists argued that economic power gave elites control of news, such that they could 'manufacture consent' among the masses. Liberals argued that no single group can dominate in pluralist, democratic political-media systems and that the likelihood of consent or dissent towards power was not predetermined by power structures. Cultural studies scholars took a middle path. They argued that elites may control media production but not its reception and interpretation. News media are everywhere, the very cultural milieu or ecology all actors exist within, like water to fish. Government does not dominate communication about security through winning 'frames' or 'messages', but by creating a general climate of unease or anxiety.

Digital media and a post-broadcast era has forced researchers to reconsider how media power and control function. The interactivity of digital media promised a diffusion of communication power. Instead of watching the media, people can *do* media (Merrin, 2014). The capacity to produce and disseminate was no longer centralised. The computer absorbed all previous forms of the production, communication and storage of information, knowledge and news; television, radio, the press and film were all digitised (Manovich, 2001). Accounting for the Internet was not an *addition* to studying terrorism and communication through traditional media. Rather, from the 2000s, the Internet had changed the basis of *all* media and communication. Having an 'and the Internet' final chapter in a textbook on terrorism or security was simply not good enough (Merrin, 2014: 40).

The media-political system became hybrid (Chadwick, 2013). It was both broadcast *and* post-broadcast at once; elite control could be disrupted or enhanced by citizen-users' use of social media. Traditional concepts for explaining media power, such as gatekeeping and framing, still described important functions, but how these functions worked and what these concepts described were changing. For example, if, traditionally, news editors acted as gatekeepers of information flows, deciding what news audiences did and did not receive, in a digital media ecology gatekeeping is networked. Users can choose what they receive from multiple sources and feeds; they can act as gatekeepers for what their friends or followers see on their social media feeds; and they can promote content on mainstream news sites by 'liking' it or sharing it so it gets more clicks and becomes a trending story. Boundaries between professional and amateur news producers remain in terms of pay and legal accountability, but the tasks each perform have blurred. Through the hybrid interactions of mainstream and margin, journalist and audience, the determination of media coverage of terrorism operates in ways marked simultaneously by continuity and change.

Granular and hybrid media are not new, however. Whether pamphlets and the telephone during the broadcast era, or members-only websites or social media groups today, we can ask how terrorist groups build their numbers, their ideological cohesiveness and their finances through 'some-to-some' or 'one-to-one' mediums (e.g. Weimann, 2006, 2015; Conway, 2012). Interactive, 'many-to-many' platforms, such as an open Facebook group, Twitter account or YouTube comments section, can allow numerous people who could never meet face-to-face to discuss an act of terrorism, and this provides another opportunity for those ready to use terrorism to justify and seek to legitimise their acts.

Current research of media coverage of terrorism is very poor (Archetti, 2013). This is symptomatic of a peculiar and longstanding unwillingness of security researchers and practitioners to seriously engage with research findings from media and communication (Schlesinger, 1991: 25). Many make claims about 'the power of media' or 'information effects' while ignoring a century of research that has identified the conditions under which media and communication might have effects on certain audiences at certain times. In the security and counterterrorism world, military force is serious; communication is fluffy; the public gullible and easily brainwashed. Those working in or researching security and terrorism ask whether the state or terrorists' narratives are covered in mainstream media and are circulated on the Internet, but few if any can explain the effect this media coverage has and what difference it makes to policy, public opinion or the course of conflict.

Researchers who study a single medium – 'how terrorists use Twitter' or 'newspaper coverage of counterterrorism policy' – contribute little to our knowledge of media and terrorism (Hoskins, 2013). To explain power and influence, researchers must trace these relations across different media, mainstream and marginal, and across a range of actors taking part in the production and consumption of information about terrorism. Researchers must use different methods to identify the impact of communication about terrorism on different social groups, government departments and terrorist groups themselves.

The aim of this chapter is to help researchers achieve those goals. The chapter begins by introducing four standard questions asked within what Philip Schlesinger (1991: 21) called a quarter century ago the 'orthodox consensus': the view that assumes the state is rational and creates security, terrorists are irrational and threaten security, news media are exploited by terrorists to keep publics in fear, and publics must remain grateful to the state and dutifully seek information on potential threats. I then introduce five critical questions asked by those suspicious of the way state and media power are currently organized and used. These are followed by three more nuanced questions that have emerged in the past decade concerning how the time, space and trajectory of terrorism events are generated and experienced through media. Finally, the chapter sets out empirical, theoretical and normative questions that will guide research in the coming years.

Standard, critical and emerging questions about media coverage of terrorism

There is a set of standard questions that emerge from dilemmas about media coverage of terrorism. These concern the actions of those using terrorist violence, journalists reporting it, states responding to it and publics exposed to it. First, how do those using terrorist tactics exploit different media? Media can be used for publicity to intimidate public opinion and undermine government confidence, but it can also be used to recruit new supporters, mobilise existing supporters, glorify past acts and achieve numerous other objectives. The focus in this chapter is the former. To use a common analogy, how do media create the theatre for terrorists to stage attacks? How do media create understandings of the scripts that terrorists, victims and authorities are expected to follow and the roles they should play during and after attacks? Before attacks occur, how do authorities use media to deter or "de-radicalise" potentially violent actors, and how do those committed to a terrorist attack use media to record their final testimony in martyrdom videos? To record a martyrdom video is a promise to die for a cause in a violent, symbolic act. Once the record button is pressed, that person is effectively dead; digital media then provide a strange afterlife in which the communication continues (Straub, forthcoming). Should mainstream news broadcast such videos to inform audiences, or is this likely to increase terror?

Second, how do journalists cover this violence? News organisations worry that they are providing terrorists with the oxygen of publicity. If journalists refused to report an act of terrorism, that act would not be communicated. The ability of those committing the terrorist act to make a political point would be extinguished. By targeting symbolic locations, organisations or people, groups using acts of terrorism can make various points. An attack on a shopping centre, airport or train station shows members of the public are vulnerable. An attack on a government building shows the government cannot even look after its own security. An attack on an organisation expressing certain values expresses an attack on those values. The attack on the *Charlie Hebdo* magazine in Paris exemplifies this. News organisations report these incidents because the symbolic sites are familiar to audiences. Since they cannot ignore such attacks, the question is *how* journalists describe the attacks and attackers – hence the dispute about BBC Arabic using the term *terrorist*.

Third, how does the state respond? This question often takes the form of whether Goliath can quietly disarm David, or whether David has outmanoeuvred Goliath again. How does the weaker military actor exploit media to overpower the military giant? A key term here is *asymmetry*. Military leaders worry about asymmetric warfare, in which weaker actors use unconventional tactics such as clever public communications to undermine a stronger actor's legitimacy, for instance luring a state into a disproportionately violent response that leads to curtailed freedoms and civilian casualties. As stated previously, through the exploitation of a society's symbolic sites, a terror attack requiring little finance or military hardware can generate a disproportionate effect. A terrorist attack may even be motivated by the desire for presence and recognition; groups use violence to say, 'we exist and we are doing this to you.' For example, Israel's conflicts with its neighbours in recent decades have generated a body of research concerning the role of media coverage in generating understandings of the legitimacy, proportionality and consequences of actions of all parties involved (*Media, War and Conflict*, 2014). Given that many political campaigns using terrorist tactics continue for years and decades, journalists do not simply 'cover terrorism' or 'report asymmetric conflict': they play a key role here in managing public debate about norms and values.

Finally, how do publics respond to terrorism, to media coverage of terrorism and to state responses to terrorism? Do people feel more secure as a result of counterterrorism policy? Studies have examined public expectations of the degree of security government should provide and found this is related to the news they consume or their social or religious identities (Gillespie, 2007; Jarvis and Lister, 2015). Audience members look for media offering credible, accurate news about terrorism that leaves them able to act as informed citizens. But does the media provide platforms for publics to have their say about terrorism or counterterrorism policy and contribute to democratic deliberation? Do news media contribute to public anxiety or even trauma after terrorist attacks, or do they render attacks intelligible and help societies come to terms with violence and its effects?

These four standard questions begin to illuminate how power and influence operate between four core constituencies: perpetrators, media, state and publics. By analysing two or more of these questions together, researchers can begin to map relations between these four groups. Are those relations characterised by trust or suspicion, interdependence or ignorance? Who benefits from the status quo mode of media coverage of reporting of terrorism, and who or what is lost? In other words, the questions so far allow researchers to build explanations of power and influence between actors. Once these power relations are understood, some researchers ask how these relationships could be organised differently, to reflect a different set of values or interests. For critical researchers, whatever we research, the point is to change it.

A number of critical questions are asked by scholars studying media and terrorism. Media coverage of terrorism may produce sensational scenes of horror in places we know involving people whose lives seem close to our own. For those who suspect mainstream media are motivated by financial profit rather than creating an informed citizenry, do media continue to cover acts of terrorism because it increases their audiences and thus their advertising revenue? Policymakers can also use media-amplified threats of terrorism to urge citizen-consumers to demonstrate patriotism by shopping, as research indicates happened in the US following the 9/11 attacks (Altheide, 2004).

A second critical question is to ask why terrorism committed by states is ignored or framed as action other than terrorism. A state with far greater military power may seek to intimidate a smaller state through 'shock and awe' tactics, as the US did in Iraq in 2003 or the UK did in Dresden and other German cities during World War II. This was the use of violence against both military and nonmilitary targets in order to spread fear of total destruction and make the political point to publics and the enemy state: surrender or die. Since media organisations usually depend on their state for regular information and legal protection, editors and journalists may be reluctant to name the acts of violence their state commits as terrorism, even when those acts meet a definition of terrorism. Under what conditions could they have the confidence and security to do so? Christian Christensen (2008) has found, for instance, that US soldiers in Iraq have regularly uploaded self-recorded footage to YouTube of their violent and anti-social acts, which offer a very different lens on the conflict than that presented by mainstream news. Indeed, in 2007 soldiers in a US gunship in Iraq shot dead 23 civilians including those injured on the ground. Two were Reuters journalists. It was not until 2010, when Wikileaks released self-recorded footage, that debate about this was triggered (Christensen, 2014). The footage is visceral. The viewer watches from the perspective of the perpetrators in the helicopter, shooting a human being lying on the ground. One feels the imbalance of power – here is asymmetric war in reverse. No doubt there is further footage of state militaries creating terror and havoc, but under what conditions is it likely to be reported in mainstream news and receive wide public attention?

A third critical question is to ask why terrorism or the threat of terrorism in some parts of the world receives far greater media coverage than terrorism elsewhere. Nagdy and Roser (2015) describe the countries that have suffered the highest percentage of all terrorist attacks globally in two periods, before and after the 11 September 2001 attacks by al Qaeda on the United States. From 1970 until 9/11, Columbia, Peru and El Salvador suffered the most attacks. From then until 2008, Iraq, India and Afghanistan were the countries most frequently subject to attack. These figures suggest that if we live in a world of global media that features journalists reporting global terrorism, there should be very little coverage of threats or attacks in Western countries. Anyone living in a Western country knows the opposite is the case. Why are attacks on Western civilians more newsworthy than attacks on civilians elsewhere?

A fourth critical question concerns why media coverage of terrorism seems to overemphasise the culpability of certain identity groups and contribute to stereotyping against all members of that group. In the UK, decades of violent political struggle between those who believed Northern Ireland should be part of a united Irish state, led by the Irish Republican Army (IRA), and those who believed it should remain joined to the UK state, led by various 'loyalist' groups and the UK state, meant regular media coverage of the IRA's acts of violence both in Northern Ireland and on the English mainland. This led to stereotyping of people from Ireland and Northern Ireland as terrorists. When a peace settlement was reached in the 1990s, mainstream media were increasingly covering acts of terrorism that seemed linked to Islam. The 9/11 attackers and the rise to prominence of al Qaeda (and subsequently ISIS) meant that media coverage of terrorism became media coverage of Islam, leading to stereotyping of Muslims as terrorists (Richardson, 2004; Strabac and Listhaug, 2008). Here, the dilemma is how news media can report on terrorism in a proportionate way and in a way that can avoid indirectly or directly demonising a whole identity group or population. Journalists often rely on state sources for information, at times when state officials may feel themselves at war primarily with a single enemy (the IRA, al Qaeda, ISIS). This makes it difficult for journalists to situate that 'enemy' as one of many groups involved in violence and terrorism around the world at any one time.

A fifth and final critical question, building on the fourth, concerns whether media coverage of terrorism creates a moral panic. A moral panic refers to an exaggerated reaction to the behaviour or values of a person or group who becomes labelled a threat to society's moral order. It is a 'panic' because the threat is constructed by politicians, journalists and other opinion leaders in a way disproportionate from any actual threat. A political leader may say a single failed terrorist attack is symptomatic of a new and wide danger to society. A moral panic cannot exist without media, who amplify anxiety and visualise the faces that threaten society (Cohen, 1972). It is 'moral' because causal responsibility for threatening behaviour is attributed to the immoral intent of a person or group, or blame is attached to authorities who have failed to eliminate the threat. However, moral panics can stigmatise people or groups, and thus constitute immoral responses. Research is needed to identify how moral panics are triggered by specific events or emerge incrementally through continual reporting of a certain type of threat or risk (Garland, 2004). Researchers also need to identify the different interests the judiciary, policy, reporters, risk analysts and terrorism 'experts' have in creating and sustaining moral panics (Hall et al., 2013) and whether this explains whether terrorist threats receive disproportionate coverage relative to other behaviours that kill far more people, such as driving or smoking. Finally, this and the previous question suggest research should investigate ways in which news or entertainment media create certain stereotypes based on ethnicity and gender (Conway and McInerney, 2012). There are stereotypes about the nature of those watching illicit content on websites, for instance. In 2015, the Mayor of London, Boris Johnson, said that men who watch ISIS videos and then decide to fight for them 'typically will look at porn. They are literally wankers.' He continued: 'they are not making it with girls and so they turn to other forms of spiritual comfort – which of course is no comfort' (cited in Perraudin and Malik, 2015). Such generalisations may downplay more than panic, but they hardly contribute to informed democratic deliberation about terrorism.

While these standard and critical questions remain important, a number of more nuanced and urgent questions have been asked in recent years. This has been made possible by the assembly of interdisciplinary teams who approach media and security from very different perspectives, use different methods, and aim to answer different questions. Here I focus on questions about the time of terrorism, the space of terrorism and how terrorism becomes an event that stretches forward into space and time.

Emerging questions

Time has always been vital to those using terrorist tactics. A threatening message or one attack can create suspense and dread: publics and officials wait in fear of the promised attack. In 1984, the IRA bombed a hotel in which the conservative government was staying, missing the prime minister but killing others. The IRA put out a statement: 'today we were unlucky, but remember, we only have to be lucky once; you will have to be lucky always. Give Ireland peace and there will be no war' (BBC News, 2005). Such language – reported in mainstream media – creates a qualitative sense of expectation of further attacks and, for security services, a sense that they must be permanently on guard. This anxiety also feeds into democratic politics. Should counterterrorism policy be rushed through, or would more patient deliberation encourage public support and greater legitimacy? In short, terrorism triggers a series of overlapping political and security temporalities. These matter because they help explain how relations between media, policymakers and publics unfold. We must ask who dictates the pace and cycles of terrorism and counterterrorism.

Digital media change the temporality of terrorism. On the one hand, digital media enable an acceleration of terrorism and counterterrorism. A group mounting a terrorist attack can follow in real-time the tweets of those they are attacking to find out their movements and intentions, as happened in the Mumbai hotel attack of 2008. During the 2013 Westgate Mall hostage crisis, the Twitter account @HSMPress_ (now suspended) provided continuous updates supporting the actions of the terrorist organisation Al-Shabaab (Sullivan, 2014). It is possible to correspond with a terrorist group openly in real-time. In 2012, one of my university colleagues got into a debate on Twitter with Al-Shaabab about whether their posting of images of prisoners broke the Geneva conventions (tweets since deleted). Instant connectivity potentially transforms relations between terrorist groups and ordinary people. On the other hand, digital media slow things down. News media still keep terrorism on the public's horizon, on the edge of awareness, a vague and potentially threatening presence that the security services are supposed to deal with. But terrorism is now always there, one click away, on the Internet. Digital media have allowed numerous groups and individuals to produce terrorism-related videos, websites and other content. This content lies alongside mainstream news sites' pages on past attacks and profiles of former terrorist leaders. Being digital, this content is archived, can be found through search, shared and commented on. Despite the apparently ephemeral nature of digital communication, its permanence and accessibility mark a new feature in people's media environments on an everyday basis. As Archetti (2013: 33) writes, 'communication is not just relevant at times of terrorist attacks but at *all times*'.

The first set of emerging questions, then, concerns how these new digital temporalities feed into previous ones. Is a terrorist campaign stretched or warped in some way by digital permanence and accessibility? How do journalists incorporate the instaneity and openness of social media into traditional news cycles and responsibilities to inform and contextualise? Is it impossible to 'move on' from a terrorist attack if footage remains on YouTube? Should media remove content that may traumatise audiences? It is in this context that the European Union has introduced a 'right to be forgotten', such that victims of violence or those falsely implicated in terrorism can request that content depicting them is removed and not accessible by search.

A second set of questions concerns the space of terrorist events. Take the dispute about BBC Arabic's use of the term terrorist, with which we began this chapter. This dispute crossed borders and cultures: an attack in France; a news organisation broadcasting from London to anywhere that Arabic speakers listen or could access BBC Arabic digital content; instant outcry from within the UK but also the US. Tracing this event and media coverage of it opens out how global media and politics operate in the twenty-first century. As a public service broadcaster with a history of public diplomacy – portraying British life to the outside world and reporting that world back to Britain – the BBC is tasked by the British government to create a 'global conversation'. This suggests the possibility that news media can create and maintain a global public sphere in which information is shared and dialogue can proceed across borders.

The *Charlie Hebdo* example shows how difficult such dialogue is, however, and what leaps of imagination are needed. We imagine ourselves and all those concerned about the attack. We imagine others, the evil perpetrators, or those who did not hear about the attack. We imagine ourselves as part of a community that should have a perspective on the attacks, a perspective that may or may not fall within (imagined) mainstream opinion. And we imagine the world, and all the events taking place, communities and lives affected, and actors trying to steer history in certain ways. Concretely, French publics imagine how others are viewing their reaction and their society; BBC Arabic audiences are imagining how the *Charlie Hebdo* attacks compare to attacks in other countries. Western conservative critics compare the attacks to others on targets they hold dear and try to imagine, in fury, how anyone could see things differently. A terrorist attack, once covered by news media, sparks a collision of imaginations and imagined communities in different parts of the world. This is where much interesting conceptual thinking is happening (Christensen and Christensen, 2013; Cottle, 2014), but there is a need for multilingual, multimethod teams to design research projects that do justice to these dimensions.

Third, unifying the questions of time and space, is the question of how interactional trajectories form and unfold across local and global public spheres. What happens between the instant of the event and the instances that follow of the event being remembered? New relations are formed between survivors, witnesses, police and emergency services and a host of others touched directly or indirectly by the event. New policy measures are debated. New memorial practices are initiated. New facts and narratives emerge, become part of a record or records and intermingle with prior facts and narratives. In short, a series of 'interactional trajectories' are generated (Hoskins, 2011). These trajectories involve political argument and contestation and news media investigation, but they also involve textures, uncertainties and overlaps that give substance and meaning to those thinking about the attack or its aftermath (see, e.g. Allen, 2014).

Researchers can use a variety of methods to track the interactional trajectory of a terrorist event, whether it is a hostage video, a prominent speech calling for terrorism or an actual attack. What mixes of amateur camera phone and professional news photography are used the day after an attack and in an anniversary broadcast a year later? How do icons come to stand for a whole event? How quickly do mainstream media or officials settle on a stable narrative of the event, and is this later challenged? There is a pressing need for audience research to identify the extent to which publics were alarmed or afraid after an attack or by warnings of an attack, but also to follow the trajectory. When do news media report processes of grieving and caregiving that follow a violent attack, and when do they move quickly onto the next attack?

A final aspect of interactional trajectories concerns their origin or starting point. State policymakers often wish to ensure publics are prepared or alert to the likelihood of attack. Filmmakers, novelists and video game producers offer regular visions of possible terrorist scenarios. Richard Grusin's concept 'premediation' is a key concept here (Grusin, 2004, 2010; see also Awan et al., 2011). Premediation refers to the manner in which media or public authorities speculatively envision possible futures so that, should any disaster emerge, publics are not shocked and normal life is not disrupted, as in the US immediately after 9/11 (Grusin 2004). The logic of premediation is illustrated by the example of a major anthrax scare in the US in 2002, not long after 9/11, when it was believed that members of Congress were in danger from letters in the post laced with the deadly material. Terror seemed to be emerging from within the US homeland. Grusin writes:

> The anthrax scare became an obsession of the media not for the damage it had done but for the damage it could do in the future, for the threat it might become. In order that the news media would not be surprised as it had been by 9/11, it was imperative that the fullest extent of the national security threat from anthrax be premediated before it had ever happened, or *even if it never did*.
>
> (Grusin 2004: 23; emphasis added)

Another example occurred in the UK. The 7/7 London bombings of 2005 had been anticipated by the BBC's Panorama pre-construction in 2004, 'London under attack' (BBC News, 2004). Was the BBC's simulation just a sensible prediction, an extrapolation from intelligence and recent attacks in Spain? This is to ignore the strategic temporal looping that comes into play: by previewing the event, government and media can rehearse their strategic discourses for such eventualities and identify how publics respond to such an event (even if it never actually happens).

In short, the core concerns – media, policymakers and publics and terrorist groups – remain the basis for research that answers standard, critical and nuanced questions. What makes a difference is the researcher's approach and the imagination to devise appropriate methods to trace the time, space and trajectory of terrorism events. In concluding, I will highlight a number of empirical, theoretical and normative or political questions that will drive this research in the coming years.

Conclusion: future directions

This chapter has set out standard, critical and future questions for researchers of media coverage of terrorism. This topic will remain a fundamental area of research because the dilemmas facing journalists appear insurmountable. Terrorism is newsworthy, but terrorism only exists when covered by news. Cultural anxieties, economic systems and media technologies may change, but the interdependent relationships between those using terrorism, journalists, political leaders and publics will remain. It is important to close this chapter with a reminder that research is needed that is empirical, theoretical, and normative and political (see also Eder and Klonk, forthcoming). Good research addresses all three of these dimensions.

Empirically, we need to describe how media cover terrorism. What terrorist groups, threats or attacks are given coverage, and what counterterrorist responses? Do media cover the long-term effects of terrorism on survivors or society at large or only focus on immediate events? What visual, verbal and other materials are used to report terrorism, and does this change as media technologies transform? However, this leads to the theoretical task of identifying the factors that explain the form and content of media coverage of terrorism. Existing Marxist, liberal and cultural theories of media power and influence on public opinion and government policy must be continually tested as media become more digital and hybrid. We must also develop studies of how the symbiotic relation of media and terror functions in specific events or over years and decades and explain the roles that symbols, metaphors and narratives play in terrorist acts and counterterror responses.

Normative and political questions must drive any study. On what basis can media coverage of terrorism be criticised? What alternative forms of reporting are possible? How can research contribute to alternative forms of reporting? What media literacy, historical literacy and political literacy would be appropriate foundations for public debate about media coverage of terrorism?

With such knowledge, it is imperative scholars communicate publicly and use research to foster those literacies and those alternatives.

References

Allen, M. (2014). *The Labour of Memory: Memorial Culture and 7/7*. Basingstoke: Palgrave Macmillan.
Altheide, D. L. (2004). Consuming terrorism. *Symbolic Interaction*, 27(3), 289–308.
Archetti, C. (2013). *Understanding Terrorism in the Age of Global Media: A Communication Approach*. Basingstoke: Palgrave.
Awan, A. N., Hoskins, A., and O'Loughlin, B. (2011). *Radicalisation & Media: Connectivity and Terrorism in the New Media Ecology*. Routledge: London.
BBC News. (2004). 'London under Attack', 6 May. Available at: http://news.bbc.co.uk/2/hi/programmes/panorama/3686201.stm (accessed 20 February 2015).
BBC News. (2005). '1984: Tory Cabinet in Brighton bomb blast', 12 October. Available at: http://news.bbc.co.uk/onthisday/hi/dates/stories/october/12/newsid_2531000/2531583.stm (accessed 17 February 2015).
Carr, M. (2006). *Unknown Soldiers: How Terrorism Has Transformed the Modern World*. London: Profile Books.
Chadwick, A. (2013). *The Hybrid Media System: Politics and Power*. Oxford: Oxford University Press.
Christensen, C. (2008). Uploading dissonance: YouTube and the US occupation of Iraq. *Media, War & Conflict*, 1(2), 155–175.
Christensen, C. (2014). WikiLeaks and the afterlife of collateral murder. *International Journal of Communication*, 8(10), 2594–2602.
Christensen, M., and Christensen, C. (2013). The Arab Spring as meta-event and communicative spaces. *Television & New Media*, 14(4), 351–674.
Cohen, S. (1972). *Moral Panics and Folk Devils*. London: McGibbon and Kee.
Conway, M. (2012). What is Cyberterrorism and How Real Is the Threat? A Review of the Academic Literature, 1996–2009. In P. Reich, & E. Gelbstein (Eds.) *Law, Policy, and Technology: Cyberterrorism, Information Warfare, and Internet Immobilization*. Hershey, PA: IGI Global.
Conway, M., and McInerney, L. (2012). What's love got to do with it? Framing 'JihadJane' in the US press. *Media, War & Conflict*, 5(1), 6–21.
Cottle, S. (2006). *Mediatized Conflict: Developments in Media and Conflict Studies*. Maidenhead: Open University Press.
Cottle, S. (2014). Rethinking media and disasters in a global age: What's changed and why it matters. *Media, War & Conflict*, 7(1), 3–22.
Devji, F. (2005). *Landscapes of the Jihad: Militancy, Morality, and Modernity*. London: Hurst.
Eder, J., and Klonk, C. (eds.) (forthcoming). *Image Operations: Still and Moving Pictures in Political Conflicts*. Manchester: Manchester University Press.
Garland, D. (2004). *The Culture of Control*. Oxford: Oxford University Press.
Gillespie, M. (2007). Security, media and multicultural citizenship: A collaborative ethnography. *European Journal of Cultural Studies*, 10(3), 275–293.
Graham, T. (2015). Biased BBC avoids 'loaded' lingo like 'terrorism' to describe Charlie Hebdo massacre. *Newsbusters*, 1 February. Available at: http://newsbusters.org/blogs/tim-graham/2015/02/01/biased-bbc-avoids-loaded-lingo-terrorism-describe-charlie-hebdo-massacre (accessed 1 February 2015).
Greenhill, S. (2015). BBC branded 'mad' by critics after refusing to call Paris killers 'terrorists': Peers and MPs launch chorus of criticism over 'outrageous' decision to not use term. *The Daily Mail*, 27 January. Available at: www.dailymail.co.uk/news/article-2926375/Paris-Charlie-Hebdo-extremists-murdered-17-people-not-called-terrorists-says-BBC-executive.html#ixzz3Q1QtIRVR (accessed 1 February 2015).
Grusin, R. (2004). 'Remediation'. *Criticism*, 46(1), 17–39.
Grusin, R. (2010). *Premediation: Affect and Mediality in America after 9/11*. Basingstoke: Palgrave.
Hall, S., Critcher, C., Jefferson, T., Clarke, J., and Roberts, B. (2013). *Policing the Crisis: Mugging, the State and Law and Order*. Basingstoke: Palgrave Macmillan.
Hoskins, A. (2011). 7/7 and connective memory: Interactional trajectories of remembering in post-scarcity culture. *Memory Studies*, 4(3), 269–280.
Hoskins, A. (2013). Death of a single medium. *Media, War & Conflict*, 6(1), 3–6.
Jarvis, L., and Lister, M. (2015). *Anti-Terrorism, Citizenship and Security in the UK*. Manchester: Manchester University Press.

Manovich, L. (2001). *The Language of New Media*. London: MIT Press.
Media, War & Conflict. (2014). 'Media, Israel and Conflict, Virtual Special Issue', Available at: http://mwc.sagepub.com/cgi/collection/media_israel_conflict (accessed 11 May 2015).
Merrin, W. (2014). *Media Studies 2.0*. London: Routledge.
Nacos, B. L. (2003). The terrorist calculus behind 9–11: A model for future terrorism?. *Studies in Conflict and Terrorism*, 26(1), 1–16.
Nacos, B. L. (2007). *Mass-mediated Terrorism: The Central Role of the Media in Terrorism and Counterterrorism*. New York: Rowman & Littlefield.
Nagdy, M., and Roser, M. (2015). 'Terrorism', OurWorldInData.org. Available at: http://ourworldindata.org/data/war-peace/terrorism/ (accessed 19 November 2015).
Perraudin, F., and Malik, S. (2015). Boris Johnson: Jihadis are porn-watching 'wankers'. *The Guardian*, 30 January. Available at: www.theguardian.com/politics/2015/jan/30/boris-johnson-jihadis-are-porn-watching-wankers?CMP=share_btn_tw (accessed 1 February 2015).
Richardson, J. E. (2004). *(Mis)Representing Islam: The Racism and Rhetoric of British Broadsheet Newspapers*. Amsterdam and Philadelphia: John Benjamins Publishing.
Schlesinger, P. (1991). *Media, State and National: Political Violence and Collective Identities*. London: Sage.
Schmid, A. P. (1989). Terrorism and the media: The ethics of publicity. *Terrorism and Political Violence*, 1(4), 539–565.
Sherwin, A. (2015). Paris attacks: Do not call Charlie Hebdo killers 'terrorists', BBC says. *The Independent*, 25 January. Available at: www.independent.co.uk/news/media/tv-radio/paris-attacks-do-not-call-charlie-hebdo-killers-terrorists-says-head-of-bbc-arabic-tarik-kafala-10001739.html (accessed 30 January 2015).
Strabac, Z., and Listhaug, O. (2008). Anti-Muslim prejudice in Europe: A multilevel analysis of survey data from 30 countries. *Social Science Research*, 37(1), 268–286.
Straub, V. (forthcoming). The Making of a Martyr: Images of Female Suicide Bombers in Palestine. In J. Eder and C. Klonk (Eds.) *Image Operations: Still and Moving Pictures in Political Conflicts*. Manchester: Manchester University Press.
Sullivan, R. (2014). Live-tweeting terror: A rhetorical analysis of@ HSMPress_ Twitter updates during the 2013 Nairobi hostage crisis. *Critical Studies on Terrorism*, 7(3), 422–433.
Weimann, G. (2006). *Terror on the Internet: The New Arena, the New Challenges*. Washington: The United States Institute of Peace.
Weimann, G. (2015). *Terrorism in Cyberspace: The Next Generation*. New York: Columbia University Press.

26
COLLECTIVE MEMORY AND TERRORISM

Charlotte Heath-Kelly

Introduction

Collective memory is an important new area of research for critical terrorism studies (CTS), enabling scholarly reflection on the political functionality of memorials to terrorism and the formation of historical discourses after episodes of political violence. This chapter explores the multidirectional relationship between CTS and collective memory and the contributions each can make to the other. But what is collective memory?

The concept of collective memory was made prominent by Maurice Halbwachs in 1952.[1] As a protégé of the renowned Emile Durkheim, Halbwachs authored several sociologies of knowledge, the most famous of which was the posthumously published "Collective Memory". In this text, Halbwachs made a major contribution to the ways in which memory is understood. Rather than an individualised capacity to store information from the past, Halbwachs argued that the existence of a social framework for memory underpins our individual abilities to remember. Memory is social, and we cannot process our sensory experiences into memories without reliance upon social frameworks of language and political understanding. Halbwachs showed that we do not recollect objectively or impartially; rather, the things we remember are reliant upon the structures which make events meaningful or silent. He stated:

> It is in this sense that there exists a collective memory and social frameworks for memory; it is to the degree that our individual thought places itself within these frameworks and participates in this memory that it is capable of the act of recollection.
> *(Halbwachs 1992: 38)*

As such, we can understand that our memories are constituted through the matrixes of class, geography, race, sex, and language in which we are located. Our memories are shaped according to the tropes and narratives which construct reality. Memory is thus a product of discourse, shaped by structures of power.

These insights provided the stimulus for memory studies to emerge concurrently to the study of history. Whereas traditional approaches within the discipline of history are involved with the establishment of linear, objective chronology and explanation – even during revisionist critique of dominant narratives – memory studies is more aligned with the disciplines of oral and cultural history and the ways in which the past is diversely represented, experienced, and silenced. Work in memory studies is often careful to avoid the proposition of exclusive renderings of "how the past happened", given the multiple and diverse social constitution of experience and recollection. It also carefully explores how the past is constituted through the lens of the present. The past does not exist objectively, it is a social construction – and as a social construction, it is serving some purpose for somebody or something. It is political.

Memory studies is an incredibly broad "field" of research which stretches across the disciplines of anthropology, sociology, politics, literature, cultural studies, and beyond, and the insights of Halbwachs on collective memory provide particular leverage to interrogate the representation of terrorism from a critical perspective. His critical sociological insights into the politicality of memory, and its centrality to the maintenance of rule, are extremely relevant when one considers the "rush to memory" which follows every new terrorist attack or disaster. But the connection between CTS and collective memory is deeper and multidirectional and stems from the fixation of both upon political violence.

Violence is *everywhere* in memory studies, just like in the study of terrorism. One can observe the intimate connection between violence and memory by studying how the memory studies field relates to armed conflict and killing; it is constituted through literatures on war memorials (Inglis 1998; Rigney 2008; Wagner-Pacifici & Schwartz 1991), truth and reconciliation committees (Norval 1998; Wilson 2001), post-conflict memory (Conway 2003; Heath-Kelly 2014a; Lundy & McGovern 2001; Thomson 1994), counter-memorials which acknowledge state terrorism (Hite 2012; Williams 2004), the challenge of appropriately remembering genocide (Cooke 2000; Young 1989, 1993), and the contemporary era of memorialisation within the war on terror (Greenspan 2013; Heath-Kelly 2015; Lundborg 2012).

Indeed the centrality of violent episodes to memorial practices seems almost "given": memorials, for example, are *only built* to past glories and/or horrors. But why should this be? The insights of CTS regarding the discursive constitution and functionality of violence are well suited to exploring this phenomenon within collective memory, while memory studies research in turn enables CTS to explore the constitution of historical knowledge around political violence. This chapter is dedicated to probing the multidirectional relationship between the two fields, as they converge in nascent academic collaboration.

CTS fills the gaps in memory studies: memory of terrorism as political technique

As stated, there appears to be a particular connection between memorialising practices and violent conflict, given the proliferation of memorials around wars and terror attacks. However, very few scholars have addressed or problematized this connection. How can a critical reading of violence or terrorism begin to explain this tendency within the production of collective memory? To begin to address this, we should think about the distinction between what gets publicly memorialised (wars, civil conflicts, genocide, terrorism) and *what doesn't*: "normal", everyday violence like poverty and oppression.[2] A critical approach to violence and terrorism enables us to problematise the silence of public memory around everyday violence.

A recent study by Tyner et al. (2014) has paid particular attention to the links between memorialisation and types of violence. They show that certain types of violence are made memorable, and others non-memorable, dependent upon their articulation in discourse. Societies build memorials to wars and terrorist attacks, to that which is framed as exceptional and happened to "us" at the hands of the other, but the discursive constitution of other types of violence does not lead to memorial landscaping. The discursive constitution of what is "exceptional" sets the limits for what becomes memorable. Societies never, for example, build memorials to structural violence (Galtung's concept which signifies the harm caused to people by social structures). Similarly, if a violent event cannot be assimilated into a discursive category of attack by the externalised other (like terrorism or war), then it is not acted upon by memory technologies.

Tyner et al. discuss the specific example of the 1979 shooting of five left-wing activists in Greensboro, North Carolina, by the Ku Klux Klan, which was constituted by the authorities and media as the incursion of violence between outside agitators. These left-wing activists were not framed as part of the mainstream community, nor the perpetrators as outsiders. Despite the horror and outrage of the shootings, their discursive formulation does not assimilate the event within the frame of violence committed by an outsider which happened to *us* (war, terror), and, as a result, no memorialisation has occurred upon the site. The authors convincingly argue that memorialisation is inextricably connected to the discursive rendering of types of violence (Tyner et al. 2014). Memorialisation is not an automatic response to violence, then, only to certain framings of violence as "war" or "terrorist". As such, we should enquire into its functionality – and a CTS approach is extremely helpful in doing so.

In the Greensboro shooting, both victims and perpetrators were Americans. The event wasn't framed as exceptional in discourse, because the victims were not framed as representative of ordinary Americans (they were left-wing activists), and the perpetrators were not foreigners. It did not become framed as "terrorism". No memorialisation occurred because the event was not assimilated within the discursive category of an attack on America. In an interesting counterexample which supports the argument of Tyner et al. concerning the connection between memorialisation, types of violence, and attributed identities, Edward Linenthal has shown that the Oklahoma bombing of 1995 was (conversely) immediately discursively allocated to the category of terrorism – and has since been provided with a prominent memorial. The immediate assumption was that outside parties were responsible and thus the framing of terrorism was applied. However, problems with this discursive rendering and the path to memorialisation occurred when the true identities of the bombers were revealed.

The victims of the Alfred P. Murrah Federal Building bombing in Oklahoma were easily associated with mainstream American identity: employees of various federal agencies and their children. This fits with the discursive rendering of what is terrorism. Similarly, it was immediately reported in the media and public discourse (despite the circulation of images of two white suspects by police) that the perpetrators were "Middle Eastern" (Linenthal 2001: 20). Again, this provided a smooth framing within the terror discourse. However, upon the arrest of Timothy McVeigh and Terry Nichols, two American white men – one a war hero adorned with the Bronze star for his conduct in the Gulf War – the discursive rendering of the violence as terrorism hit a problem: the perpetrators fit the frame of mainstream American masculinity.

The shock that two Americans could attack their own federal building and massacre 168 people was widely felt. It simply *did not fit* the rendering of the bombing as terrorism and the immediate conviction of the country that external others must be to blame. Could Americans be terrorists? To resolve the antagonism between an enormous bomb attack upon the American state (which fit the discursive remit of terrorism) and the conviction of two white American males for the crime (which apparently did not), discourse went to work in intensive and fascinating ways. The conception of terrorism had to be protected from its internal contradictions. Linenthal's book details the extensive efforts made by media and public officials to separate McVeigh and Nichols from their identity as Americans and to safeguard the interpretation of the bombing as terrorism.

First, they were distinguished as "oddball paranoiac trailer-park terrorists" – different from the rest of the population; "domestic aliens", rather than Americans. They became nonrepresentative of the nation, and thus external. Then, to alleviate the antagonism between their crimes and their "heroic" military service, President Clinton signed special legislation to remove military burial privileges from McVeigh which had been afforded to him with the award of the Bronze Star (Linenthal 2001: 20). To complete the alienation of the perpetrators from American society such that an "externalised" other could be provided for the narration of the event as terrorism, public and academic discourse subsequently created a category of domestic right-wing extremist groups that could be juxtaposed against mainstream identity as the dangerous other. The antagonism resolved, the Oklahoma bombing was stabilised in discourse as an exceptional event, and it paved the way for an enormous public memorial on the site – one which has provided guidance for the memorialisation of the sites attacked on 9/11. A clear "us" and an external "they" had been articulated in discourse and could now be solidified into stone.

The examples of Greensboro and Oklahoma both point towards the connections between violence, the framing of terrorism, and subsequent memorialisation. For memorialisation to occur, the event must securely fit the criteria of terrorism. It must be pruned and framed so that is satisfies the discursive criteria of being an "attack upon the nation" by outsiders – or those who can be rendered as outsiders. How, then, should we understand the functionality of this connection? A CTS approach proves extremely useful in explaining this. If everyday, normalised violence is silenced within public memory, while war and terrorism are conversely proclaimed as important within collective memory and history, then we can interrogate the functionality of the "exceptional" event to the manufacture of identity and history in the same vein as constructivist analyses of the war on terror (Croft 2006; Jackson 2005). States utilise memory practices to assimilate and contain violent ruptures like terrorism, using them to service discourses of identity. Framing something as exceptional enables practices of memorialisation to take place, consolidating particular identity discourses and political effects.

As readers of this volume will no doubt be aware, terrorism is a discursive category applied to delegitimise certain types of violence. As research within critical terrorism studies has shown, the deployment of the "terrorism" signifier constitutes the identity of the state as the legitimate violent actor by contrast (Croft 2006; Jackson 2005). The performance of this discourse becomes solidified through repetition and, as time passes, through the instantiation of memory. The importance of Halbwachs's formulation of collective memory allows us to frame the ways in which this discourse about "the past" governs us as subjects, moulding us into a population which cannot think outside the confines of the given discourse.

It may seem strange to assert that memory is a political technique, especially with reference to your own individual recollections rather than through public edifices of stone. Yet, when you think back, you are not remembering things as you experienced them at the time; rather, you are recalling a narrativised version, framed through the present day.

This is the assertion which underwrites Halbwachs's theorisation of collective memory. Maja Zehfuss puts this well in her article "Forget September 11", when she asks what you are actually remembering when you recollect the events of 9/11. Looking back at that day, we inadvertently frame the planes crashing into the buildings through a context we did not possess at the time (Zehfuss 2003). We know that there is a second plane, a third, a fourth. We know, without realising that we are attributing present-day knowledge to the past, that this is not the outbreak of world war between Russia and the United States. Crucially, we also recollect the events of September 11 as the day "we" were attacked – inadvertently performing a discursive juxtaposition of "us" and "them" which was manufactured in the immediate aftermath of the attacks by political leaders. While this performance of "we" and "they" seems neutral, it elides the multiple conflicting details which would upset the politicised performance of identity. For example, it elides the education of the pilots of the hijacked planes in the West. The narrative of "their" attack upon "us" also elides the history of US/European invasions of the Middle East and South Asia and the co-option of these regions into neocolonial economies which service the West. Furthermore, "we" and "they" silences the objection of those populations within the West to the subsequent war on terror, carried out in their name (Zehfuss 2003).

The effect of these elisions is politically functional: by constituting "the past" as such, it makes the war on terror look like the natural consequence of September 11. September 11 looks like the root of the war on terror, rather than decades of exploitative foreign policy decisions which affected the Middle East. Given the embedding of this chronology in the loss of 3,000 lives, it also becomes unquestionable without disrespecting their legacy (Zehfuss 2003). Thus, it becomes very hard to think outside the war on terror narrative, given the production of a collective memory which frames 9/11 in particular ways and erases any traces of the changes it has made to our individual recollection of that day. By framing the past through the lens of the present, we are governed as subjects who then perform in accordance with the tropes of 9/11 – for example, believing that a military, rather than a legal, response was necessary to combat al Qaeda; that preemptive security technologies will protect us (rather than the consideration of foreign policy change); and that militants are inspired by religious extremism (rather than attaining political goals).

Given the formation of collective memory around the Oklahoma bombing and 9/11, a CTS approach to memory studies suggests that we should be highly suspicious of public memorialising processes. When a narrative is constructed around events, our attention is drawn to the details contained within. What is perhaps more important are the multiplicity of other factors which are left out. When visiting either memorial site, we imbibe the approved and settled story of "what happened" and how "terrorists attacked us". In both cases, the more inconvenient details are silenced within the constitution of collective memory, such as the role of American foreign policy in generating radical movements around the world and the failures in American governance which turned a war hero like Timothy McVeigh towards his bomb attack. The mainstream discourse of terrorism ("us", the honourable, versus "them") consumes and elides such inconvenient facts and contributes to the myopic historical framing of violent events.

Memory studies fills the gaps in CTS: remembering heroes, remembering villains

CTS has remained relatively quiet on issues of memory and history. However, a nascent literature has begun to open new research areas for CTS through engagement with questions of collective memory. Memory is essential to the discursive processes of the terrorism signifier, in more ways than one. This section explores the new literature on ex-militant memory which extends the CTS project towards a deeper engagement with the discursive constitution of terrorism, history, and reality.

The collective memory thesis allows us to gain a sophisticated purchase on how the discursive constitution of reality relies upon narratives of history, and vice versa. The present cannot be understood without its constitution through narratives of the past, and the past cannot be understood without its constitution through understandings of the present. This is particularly interesting when one considers the examples of societies which have experienced prolonged violence and civil war, where discourse has been severely divided between protagonists during the conflict period and even ruptured in the undertaking of a successful revolution. How is memory invoked in the response to such conflict? Simply put, the possession of political authority enables the labelling of certain actors as terrorist and others as heroes. If you win a revolutionary struggle, you can use memory and language to render your struggle as the heroic foundation of the new nation. If you lose, your struggle and its militants become terrorists. *The identity of "terrorist" is reserved for those who do not possess the discursive power to make meaning.* Terrorists are the losers, despite often using the same tactics as victorious revolutionary militants from other contexts who became heroes.

While those familiar with a critical approach to terrorism studies will be versed in the techniques of labelling which effect this discursive ordering, the collective memory thesis enables CTS researchers to probe the ways in which ex-militant memory *itself* shifts around the allocation of terrorist identity. We can trace the solidification of post-conflict discourse through the ways that ex-militants remember, or struggle to remember, their pasts. Ex-militant memory takes very different forms, dependent on the ending of revolutionary struggles. In a comparative study of ex-militant memory between the successful anti-colonial struggle of Cypriot fighters and the defeated left-wing Italian struggle against capitalism, it is possible to observe the intersection of political power, discourse, and memory – confirming much of Halbwachs's thesis that we can only recollect what is inscribed within political discourse (Heath-Kelly 2014a).

For example, when asking militants about their participation in militant movements, those who were victorious (such as the EOKA organisation which contested British imperial sovereignty on Cyprus in the 1950s) responded to interview questions with detailed chronology and certainty. However, those who were defeated in their revolutionary struggles, like the Italian leftists of the 1970s and 80s, struggled to impose any linearity on their recollections, endlessly circling and exploring tributaries of conflicting meaning, while complaining that defeat had left them stranded without the tools of language (Heath-Kelly 2014a).

This is very interesting for the exploration of collective memory, post-conflict societies, and political power. In the minds of the victorious EOKA fighters, the history of the struggle is objective and fixed. Indeed, the level of homogeneity displayed throughout the EOKA testimonies, and their resolute reliance upon chronological narratives of history was fascinating. For instance, it was remarkable how many times the question "why did you join EOKA?"[3] received a response that began by referencing the events of 1878 (when Britain took over the administration of Cyprus from the Ottoman Empire) and which then listed each historical disappointment to the nationalist cause, many of which occurred before interviewees were born.

An example of this can be seen in Sophoulis Karlettides's (who had been an assistant area leader of a guerrilla unit within the Troodos mountains) testimony. In response to the question "why did you join EOKA?" he stated:

> You must remember Cyprus is an island which, since the beginning of the world, has always been Greek. When there was the effort to liberate Hellenism from the Turkish yoke, Cyprus was excluded. The British took over from the Turks, which was a relaxing of the yoke – the transition from the Ottomans to the British. But the yoke was there – we were enslaved to a foreign power. Always the Greeks of Cyprus wanted their liberation in order to rejoin the national core, the national body. We were expecting that Britain would accept enosis through a peaceful way, through diplomacy and so forth. At some point, we realised that this was impossible when the foreign minister of England said some areas can never be independent, so the only way to achieve enosis was revolt. . . . I had this model as a paradigm, the 1821 Greek liberation struggle, and I believed that at some point we were going to do something like that.
>
> *(Karlettides quoted in Heath-Kelly 2014a)*

In this example of ex-militant testimony, and many others from Cyprus, the past was presented as chronological, secure, and objective because, confirming Halbwachs's thesis, it is constructed through the lens of the stable present. The militants expelled the British Empire and wrote their own national story. They obtained discursive power to represent the past and script collective memory. The situation for ex-militants from defeated struggles could not be more radically different.

Unlike the testimonies of EOKA fighters, defeated Italian ex-militants did not usually deploy chronological accounts. Instead, their testimonies recognised that every detail of their struggle is contested. Given their lack of political power and status, one might expect ex-militants to challenge the hegemonic narrative which classifies them as terrorists. They did, extensively. But what is extremely interesting is how they struggled to manage their individual recollections against the collective memory of "terrorism". Enormous tension was generated through the antagonism between these competing versions of the past. Such tensions were voiced by militants in various ways. Susanna Ronconi, a prominent militant in several organisations, highlighted the challenges of remembering against the grain of collective memory by commenting as follows:

> When you think back on it now you can give a rationalisation of everything and understand logically what happened, but when you're living in it and experiencing things of course it's not that easy to understand what is really going on. It's difficult to understand that time, because back at that time you would really think in revolutionary terms.
> *(Ronconi quoted in Heath-Kelly 2014a)*

The linear hegemonic narrative doesn't fit with their experience of the turbulence of the era – something that the current discourse wants to elide, to perform its neoliberalism as popular and naturalised. Marco Solimano, a prominent militant of the Prima Linea organisation now living in the port city of Livorno, echoed Susanna's feelings of alienation from the past. He problematised the potential of language to render a turbulent era that had long passed by saying that

> now it might be simplistic to speak in these ways, but in those days, you woke up in the morning and there was a train that had exploded somewhere, there was a bomb that exploded in a bank or in a square, so you couldn't escape from that – and while now we acknowledge that we might have been wrong, but in those days you couldn't escape from that taking place.
> *(Solimano quoted in Heath-Kelly 2014a)*

The phenomenological experience of the turbulent climate is not something fully expressible in present day language, given that politics and language have been reconsolidated since the conflict. To cope with this, Italian interviewees often introduced disconnections between themselves and their militant pasts, describing how their experience of the struggle has become impossible to adequately narrate and how the position of hindsight leads to the imposition of inappropriately linear structures upon memory. This "gap" between the narrator and the conflict could also appear in simple statements about the numerous futile efforts expended to understand personal histories.

The implications of this for the critical study of terrorism relate to ways in which political power, violence, and meaning are interconnected. Of course, it is obvious to CTS researchers that powerful elites will label those who contest them as terrorists to delegitimate them. But what the collective memory thesis offers to CTS is a way to explore the interconnection of power and the scripting of reality through the *impacts upon ex-militant memory itself*. If you lose your revolutionary struggle, you are not only called a terrorist but *you lose the ability to express the legitimacy of your struggle in language*. Language betrays you, if you lack political power.

For example, interviewees from the defeated Italian struggle made frequent problematisations of language and history which powerfully asserted not only the ability of institutions to discursively disconnect Italy from aspects of its past, *but also hindered ex-militants' own access to their histories*. Susanna Ronconi, a prominent militant from the Prima Linea organisation discussed the changes in cultural context that render the conflict inaccessible to memory and language. She stated:

> It's difficult to understand that time, because back at that time you would really think in revolutionary terms. . . . When now we talk about that period, we use terms that have no meaning. . . . We have to use words that nowadays have no sense anymore, no meaning, it's really difficult, sometimes it's difficult for me to talk about this – because in that time it was absolutely obvious to us the world revolution, the world to change in a drastic way, the society, the state, and so on. And it was something obvious, in the cultural context.
>
> *(Ronconi quoted in Heath-Kelly 2014a)*

So while Italian testimonies deployed a political challenge to official accounts of the 1970s and 1980s, these testimonies could not maintain authoritative speaking positions. Instead, ex-militants felt obliged to contextualise their resistant narratives with descriptions of a gap between their memories and that which is speakable.

This speaks to the original formulation of collective memory by Maurice Halbwachs. Halbwachs argued that the existence of a social framework for memory underpins our individual abilities to remember. Memory is social and we cannot process our sensory experiences into memories without reliance upon social frameworks of language and political understanding. The public discourse of the Italian conflict has excluded militants' own recollections of the struggle, and as a result, ex-militants struggle to verbalise their experiences – often commenting on the impossibility of speaking about the conflict effectively. In Susanna's words, "When now we talk about that period, we use terms that have no meaning. . . . We have to use words that nowadays have no sense anymore" (Ronconi quoted in Heath-Kelly 2014a). In complete contrast, the Cypriot militants who won their struggle against the British Empire gained control of discourse and thus of collective memory. A collective memory approach thus enables CTS to engage with militant memory and the deeper ramifications of the discursive relationship between terrorism, power, and meaning.

Memory studies fills the gaps in CTS: traumatic memory

As discussed previously, one way to consider the contribution made to CTS through collective memory is to explore the retrospective construction of memory, and national identity, in the aftermath of conflict. However, a different way to approach the question is to explore the ways in which violence impacts upon discourse, necessitating that subsequent retrospective fixing of memory and meaning. Is physical violence the method of terrorism because it is so functional at disrupting hegemonic discourse?

Poststructuralist and psychoanalytic theory are the disciplines which connect international politics with the study of traumatic memory. They open new research trajectories to CTS which have yet to be exploited (see Fitzgerald, this volume). These approaches point to the nonlinearity of traumatic memory, which bursts into the consciousness, repetitively, because its respective event was too horrific to be rendered in discourse (Edkins 2003; Žižek 1991: 272–3). The importance of traumatic memory (something more conventionally associated with the disciplines of psychology and psychiatry) for international politics stems from the connection with discourse and the capacity to remember. When a person's senses of security, safety, and stability have been so totally undermined, the associated memory will not fit within the collective construction of memory in discourse. We do not have a language for it. It cannot be processed because it is beyond words. Thus, the event returns and returns until it is either placed within linearity (during therapy) or until the subject affirms the contingency and unpredictability of all claims to security, removing the dissonance caused by the event. Trauma, as such, is the other side of the coin to Halbwachs's collective memory. It is the event which will not fit in language.

Jenny Edkins has explored the effects of spectacular violence – such as 9/11 – on state behaviour and noted the decisive and dedicated attempts of state actors to close down the unpredictable event through the reassertion of linear "memory" (Edkins 2003). She notes that traumatic events, such as famine, genocide, and war, provoke the deployment of memory technologies (memorials, truth commissions) because they undermine the symbolic order[4] presented to us. We assume that we are safe; indeed, it is our privilege that we often are. We are constantly told by the state that it will provide for our security, but the traumatic content of violence comes from the up-ending of this fundamental relationship between citizen and state. When we realise that anything can happen and that nothing will protect us, our place in the social order is radically disrupted and made contingent. Language and memory fail.

Subject positions are constituted by the state in relation to it (Edkins & Pin-Fat 1999). Indeed, the word *subject* hints at this relationship, indicating the relationship of subjection to authority in exchange for security. But when the state turns upon its people, or fails to protect them, the subject is radically displaced, and the effects of trauma begin. The event which terrified the subject dislodges her from the symbolic order and her relationship to authority (Edkins 2003). While this has extremely unpleasant effects for the subject, trauma also becomes an issue of consternation for the state. Its claims to authority and sovereignty have been exposed as foundationless. It could not protect its citizens nor perform the supposedly god-like omnipotence of sovereignty. Its foundational claim is thus made contingent. The "lack" of sovereignty, to use a psychoanalytic term invoking the imperfect mapping of language onto the world, is exposed.[5]

Attempts to conceal this aporia of sovereignty are then rapidly deployed. States deal directly with those who have experienced trauma by medicalising their conditions, often as post-traumatic stress disorder, aiming to reinsert them into structures of power from their position of liminality through therapy, narrativisation of the event, and recovery. Importantly, for this discussion of collective memory and violence, states also attempt to reassert the linear time upon which their rule relies through the assertion of collective memory (Edkins 2003). Memorials and hegemonic narratives constitute "the" past as singular, erasing the inconvenient details and legitimising the present state of affairs.

"Exceptional" violence (like terrorism and war) disrupt discourse and the mutually constitutive relationship between subjects and state in psychoanalytic readings of politics. The state's solution to the unmasking of its authority and sovereignty involves the retrospective manufacture of memory to reconstitute the integrity of political discourse. This explains why memory practices so often appear to be dedicated to events of exceptional violence, for it is the exceptional which exposes the deceit of sovereignty. The intention of terrorism violence can even be interpreted as the ripping apart of the discursive order of the hegemonic power to expose the contingency within (Heath-Kelly 2014a, 2014b). In response, the state must attempt to conceal that aporia and reconstitute its symbolic authority. It does this through the production of collective memory. As such, this field of memory research offers a wealth of potential for CTS scholars because it explains how, and why, memory work has become integral to the counterterrorist response. Post-terrorist sites cannot simply be left alone – instead, they are centralised within ceremonies, discourses of remembrance, and adorned with grand symbolic memorials which reassert the symbols of the nation (Heath-Kelly 2015). This area of research is definitively underexamined in both critical and traditional research into terrorism: a gift from memory studies currently left unwrapped.

Conclusion

In this brief exploration of memorialisation, post-conflict memory, and traumatic memory, this chapter has considered the critical approaches to terrorism studies made possible through Halbwachs's formulation of collective memory. Building upon his important realisation that memory is discursive and that individual recollection is constituted through social frameworks of memory, it becomes possible to interrogate the memorialisation of terrorism and unveil the political functionality of representations of the past. Inconvenient political details about events of terrorism can be silenced underneath a collective memory which consolidates representations of "us", the good, against "them", the bad.

Furthermore, this chapter explored the poststructuralist work on post-conflict memory and traumatic memory which digs deeper into Halbwachs's assertion that recollection is constituted through discourse. The memories of ex-militants were shown to reflect the allocation of power in the resolution of conflicts. Victory enabled militants to narrate secure stories about heroism and the birth of the nation, whereas defeat cast ex-militants into positions whereby their histories could not be expressed in language. The connections between power, speakability, and memory were then traced further through an introduction to psychoanalytical readings of politics, whereby traumatic memory offers a window onto the disruption of authoritative discourse by violence.

Each of these critical approaches highlights the social construction of reality, where the present rests upon an imagination of the past. In their application to terrorism, these uses of collective memory show the ways in which events and struggles are framed as exceptional – and then deployed to consolidate discursive boundaries between "us" and "them", the acceptable and the barbaric. Memory, in short, is an essential topic for the development of the CTS field.

Notes

1 Although for earlier traces of the concept in academic literature, and a re-reading of Halbwachs's prominence in memory studies as a reappropriation of the past in and of itself, see Olick and Robbins (1998).
2 Oppression within a state does become memorialised, however, once regime change has occurred; the functionality of memory in this case relates to the distancing of the new regime from the crimes of the old. But the state responsible for oppressing its people will not tolerate such memorials.
3 This was usually my second or third question to the EOKA fighters. It followed initial questions about the person's rank in the organisation and the details of how they joined.
4 A term referring to the ordering of discourse as it constructs reality.
5 See also Derrida (1990) for a deconstructionist reading of the aporia within law and sovereignty.

References

Conway, B., 2003. "Active Remembering, Selective Forgetting, and Collective Identity: The Case of Bloody Sunday", *Identity: An International Journal of Theory and Research*, 3(4): 305–23.
Cooke, S., 2000. "Negotiating Memory and Identity: The Hyde Park Holocaust Memorial, London", *Journal of Historical Geography*, 26(3): 449–65.
Croft, S., 2006. *Culture, Crisis and America's War on Terror*, Cambridge: Cambridge University Press.
Derrida, J., 1990. "Force of Law: The Mystical Foundation of Authority", *Cardozo Law Review*, 11(5–6): 919–1045.

Edkins, J., 2003. *Trauma and the Memory of Politics*, Cambridge: Cambridge University Press.
Edkins, J., & Pin-Fat, V., 1999. "The Subject as Political", in Edkins, J., Persram, N., & Pin-Fat, V., eds., *Sovereignty and Subjectivity*, Boulder, CO: Lynne Rienner, pp.1–18.
Greenspan, E., 2013. *Battle for Ground Zero: Inside the Struggle to Rebuild the World Trade Center*, New York: Palgrave Macmillan.
Halbwachs, M., 1992. *On Collective Memory*, trans. Coser, L., Chicago: University of Chicago Press.
Heath-Kelly, C., 2014a. *Politics of Violence: Militancy, International Politics, Killing in the Name*, Abingdon: Routledge.
Heath-Kelly, C., 2014b. "Counter-Terrorism: The Ends of a Secular Ministry", in edited by Jarvis, L., & Lister, M., eds., *Critical Perspectives on Counter-Terrorism*, Abingdon: Routledge, pp.41–55.
Heath-Kelly, C., 2015. "Securing through the Failure to Secure? The Ambiguity of Resilience at the Bombsite", *Security Dialogue*, 46(1): 69–85.
Hite, K., 2012. *Politics and the Art of Commemoration: Memorials to Struggle in Latin American and Spain*, Abingdon: Routledge.
Inglis, K., 1998. *Sacred Places: War Memorials in the Australian Landscape*, Melbourne: Melbourne University Publishing.
Jackson, R., 2005. *Writing the War on Terrorism: Language, Politics and Counter-Terrorism*, Manchester: Manchester University Press.
Linenthal, E., 2001. *The Unfinished Bombing: Oklahoma City in American Memory*, Oxford: Oxford University Press.
Lundborg, T., 2012. "The Folding of Trauma: Architecture and the Politics of Rebuilding Ground Zero", *Alternatives: Global, Local, Political*, 37(3): 240–52.
Lundy, P., & McGovern, M., 2001. "The Politics of Memory in Post-Conflict Northern Ireland", *Peace Review: A Journal of Social Justice*, 13(1): 27–33.
Norval, A., 1998. "Memory, Identity and the (Im)possibility of Reconciliation: The Work of the Truth and Reconciliation Commission in South Africa", *Constellations*, 5(2): 250–65.
Olick, J., & Robbins, J., 1998. "Social Memory Studies: From 'Collective Memory'" to the Historical Sociology of Mnemonic Practices", *Annual Review of Sociology*, 24: 105–40.
Rigney, A., 2008. "Divided Pasts: A Premature Memorial and the Dynamics of Collective Remembrance", *Memory Studies*, 1(1): 89–97.
Thomson, A., 1994. *ANZAC Memories: Living with the Legend*, Oxford: Oxford University Press.
Tyner, J., Inwood, J., & Alderman, D., 2014. "Theorizing Violence and the Dialectics of Landscape Memorialization: A Case Study of Greensboro, North Carolina", *Environment and Planning D: Society and Space*, 32(5): 902–914.
Wagner-Pacifici, R., & Schwartz, B., 1991. "The Vietnam Veterans Memorial: Commemorating a Difficult Past", *American Journal of Sociology*, 97(2): 376–420.
Williams, P., 2004. "Witnessing Genocide: Vigilance and Remembrance at Tuol Sleng and Choeung Ek", *Holocaust and Genocide Studies*, 18(2): 234–54.
Wilson, R., 2001. *The Politics of Truth and Reconciliation in South Africa: Legitimizing the Post-Apartheid State*, Cambridge: Cambridge University Press.
Young, J., 1989. "The Biography of a Memorial Icon: Nathan Rapoport's Warsaw Ghetto Monument", *Representations*, 26: 69–106.
Young, J., 1993. *The Texture of Memory: Holocaust Memorials and Meaning*, Yale: Yale University Press.
Zehfuss, M., 2003. "Forget September 11", *Third World Quarterly*, 24(3): 513–28.
Žižek, S., 1991. *For They Know Not What They Do: Enjoyment as a Political Factor*, London: Verso.

27
TERRORISM AND PEACE STUDIES[1]

Ioannis Tellidis

Introduction

It is an oft-repeated cliché that September 11, 2001, was a milestone, not only for international relations, but also for the study of terrorism. What is less often noted is that 9/11 also had a catalytic effect in the regeneration and reinvigoration of peace studies. The motivation and drive to understand what makes individuals commit such acts is shared by both fields (see Lindekilde, this volume), although their end objectives and the methodologies behind those are diametrically opposed. In the case of terrorism studies, security and preemption top the agenda, and they do so largely with the application of hard-power measures and policies. The vast array of research centres, think tanks, and policy institutions that sprang up throughout the world in the aftermath of the attacks has contributed to the "fetishization" (Wyn Jones 1999: 22) of certain parts of the phenomenon and the misconception that terrorism is somehow a special, more dangerous type of political violence (Mac Ginty 2014). The highlighting of the "evilness" and "irrationality" of terrorist violence by policy circles and a significant part of terrorism scholars (see Stampnitzky, this volume) has not only resulted in blocking and preventing detailed, accurate, and systematic research to take place, but it has also resulted in the villainisation and demonisation of researchers as "sympathisers" and "defenders" of terrorism (Stampnitzky 2013: 189). If terrorism is "evil" and we are the "good guys", then any effort to understand it means that one is crossing the line. Similarly, there is no rationality to be extracted from something "irrational" and "incomprehensible" (Stampnitzky 2013: 191), and thus, any such efforts must be inherently tainted as "sympathising".

The combination of such unproblematised conceptualisations of "terrorism" and "terrorists", on the one hand (what are often called "orthodox theories of terrorism"), and liberal peacebuilding frameworks, on the other hand, have often led to a situation where the state, and the system of states, is elevated to the position of the most important referent object that needs to be secured (Richmond 2003; Richmond and Franks 2009; Richmond and Tellidis 2012). This happens at the expense of human security, from which a more holistic, inclusive, and sustainable peace may emerge. The counterintuitive policies of proscription directed towards groups and individuals (NGOs, community leaders, and even diplomats) who are seeking to transform terrorist conflicts by engaging armed groups in peace processes (Haspeslagh 2013) are but one example where territorial integrity and institutional security are more important than the people they represent.

Despite governmental narratives and discourses of non-negotiation with terrorists, it has been shown that negotiations contribute to the end of a terrorist group more often than policing or military confrontation (Jones and Libicki 2008). It is through the critical analysis of such findings that the critical terrorism studies group emerged shortly after 9/11, while calls for the resuscitation of a more critical peace research agenda are growing (Jutila, Pehkonen, and Väyrynen 2008; Richmond 2008a; Shinko 2008; Jackson 2015).

Research on the potential synergy between the two fields (see Toros and Tellidis 2014; Tellidis and Toros 2015) has rested on the common factors between the two – among others, the conceptualisations of security, peace, and violence; the effect of terrorism's framing on the proceedings of peace; and the relationship between scholarship and political power (Jackson 2012). What became evident was that traditional understandings of security and peace dominated both fields until the end of the Cold War. More interestingly, although both fields saw the emergence of their more critical branches after that, it was critical peace research with its "local turn" (Mac Ginty and Richmond 2013) that saw at least some of its findings being adopted by the policy-making world. Terrorism studies, on the other hand, continued to be dominated by orthodox understandings of security and peace (Jackson 2007; see also Lindahl, this volume) and broke away from the broader study of conflict (Richmond 2003), which led to the insulation of much terrorism research from interdisciplinary debates.[2]

What this chapter aims to do is to sketch the relationship between the two fields and their interaction(s) in order to highlight mutually beneficial avenues. As such, the next section explores the academic and policy conceptualisations of terrorism, and this is followed by an analysis of how peace is understood (and misunderstood). The chapter concludes with the observation that there is much more to gain epistemologically and ontologically from an analysis of terrorism from a peace perspective rather than from the security perspective.

Terrorism without context

All serious scholarly research that has analysed terrorism confirms the complexity of the phenomenon – which partly explains the existence of definitional obstacles (see Shanahan, this volume). Terrorist attacks have been conducted by religious groups, but that does not explain the many more instances where secular groups and movements have also found refuge in terrorist violence (for example, European Marxist groups in the 1960s and 1970s, or self-determination movements throughout the globe). Psychological profiling has verified that terrorists are not psychologically abnormal, but that there may be common elements (for example, psychological impulses such as a feeling of revenge) between those who decide to join a terrorist group and partake in terrorist violence. Similarly, cultural approaches have also failed to adequately explain why some individuals of a particular cultural group partake in terrorism (or in a specific form of terrorism, like suicide bombings), whereas others from the same group do not (Bloom 2005). The only commonality between all manifestations of terrorism, as the vast majority of researchers concur, is the terrorists' perceptions that their strategic dimensions (Neumann and Smith 2008) will yield them political advantages (Goodin 2006: 1). In other words, terrorism is a type of war, "for, as with other kinds of warfare, terrorist violence does involve strategy" (English 2009: 43). As I have argued elsewhere by paraphrasing Clausewitz, terrorism, like war, is the continuation of politics through other means (Tellidis 2010: 425).

There are a plethora of cautionary statements from early scholars of terrorism (the educational background of virtually all of whom was Anglo-Saxon; see Ranstorp 2007) concerning the conduct, design, and delivery of research on terrorism. Before 9/11, many scholars critiqued the way in which research was conducted, funded, and disseminated, and these arguments are still being put forward today (Sageman 2015). Rather than 9/11 prompting us to familiarise ourselves with these early writings and the warnings they heeded when it came to counterterrorist policies, social and political attitudes and behaviours meant that this problem required immediate solutions.

Following 9/11, and despite the fact that there is no unanimous definition of the phenomenon, terrorism has turned into an autonomous field of study.[3] September 11's impact created an impetus for the prevention of such events in the future, and "terrorism studies" became virtually ubiquitous in university syllabi. Nevertheless, the exoticisation of terrorism (Breen-Smyth 2008) and the fascination with the sensationalist aspect of the phenomenon gained more attention than rigorous academic findings (Sageman 2015), while specific political agendas effectively shaped anti-terrorist policies and narratives (Sageman 2015). The latter, combined with the urgency to prevent future terrorist attacks, marginalised those voices that highlighted the need for understanding before implementation (Jackson 2007: 244–246) and "stimulated the emergence of a culture of fear" (Brzezinski 2007).

Despite its pejorative semantics and the hard security responses it generated, terrorism was conceptualised as a *method* and/or a *strategy* to conduct *conflict* well before, but also after, 9/11 (Walter 1969; Leach 1977; Groom 1978; Laqueur 1986; Wilkinson and Stewart 1987; Schmid and Jongman 2008; Hoffman 1992; Weinberg, Pedahzur, and Perliger 1992; Malik 2000; Wilkinson 2001; see also Bjørgo 2005; Goodin 2006; English 2009; Schmid 2011; Stampnitzky 2013). This ontological dimension may in part explain how and why individuals like Nelson Mandela, Gerry Adams, Martin McGuinness, Yasser Arafat, and others were transformed into accepted interlocutors and even peacebuilders by the very state actors that had originally branded them as terrorists.

In the post-9/11 environment, however, terrorism was reclassified (through speech and act) as the greatest existentialist threat (see Wolfendale, this volume). Counterterrorist measures were used to reinforce state security and institutions, as a result of which the terrorist label was misused and even abused (Loadenthal 2013). Exceptional threats required exceptional measures, and even though these were temporary at the time of implementation, they are still with us fourteen years later (Fisher 2013). Furthermore, the emergence of "homegrown terrorism"[4] and "lone-wolf terrorism" meant that the state is now as austere with its internal security as it was with its external security (if not more). Mass surveillance and other policies directly affecting civil liberties are a testament to Brzezinsky's aforementioned quote that the state's security is founded on fear (see Mavelli, this volume).

Aiming to widen the skewed, statist focus of so-called orthodox terrorism studies and to deepen the conceptualisations and understandings of the phenomenon, the emergence of critical terrorism studies (CTS) broadened the study of terrorism to include a more problematized role for the state and the instances in which it produces terror as part of its monopoly of violence (Jackson 2009). Even though CTS was received with scepticism (Horgan and Boyle 2008; Weinberg and Eubank 2008; Jackson 2012) and some scathing attacks that it constitutes radical jihadism's intellectual arsenal (Jones 2015), critical scholars brought about more reflexivity than the dominant positivist, problem-solving approaches; a degree of methodological pluralism; as well as the awareness that terrorism research will never be objective or neutral (Jackson 2007; Toros 2012).

A similar endeavour is currently unfolding in the field of peace studies. Also dominated until recently by positivist theories, problem-solving approaches, and hard security agendas (Jackson 2015), peace studies was more receptive of the critical frameworks that developed both before but also, crucially, after 9/11. The following section explores how various and diverse understandings about peace prevented it from being constructed.

Peace studies and terrorism

Within the field of international relations, peace has always been conceived of as either the absence of war or a utopian ideal that is impossible to achieve. The former relates to realist theories and their belief that human selfishness and aggression are two conditions that find their way into states' behaviour. The latter, on the other hand, is linked to liberalist theories according to which freedoms- and rights-based frameworks may constitute the foundations for governability schemes that may be universally applicable. In order for these frameworks to succeed in generating the necessary conditions of peace, liberal theories put forward the protection and guarantee of the institutions of sovereignty, governance, and the free market.

However, as it has been noted repeatedly during the last two decades of research into peacebuilding, the liberal paradigm is prone to ignoring or even sidelining the contextual particularities of conflicts, because it is applied in a one-size-fits-all fashion whereby policies are executed top-down and operate inside exclusionary normative frameworks (Lederach 1997; Bleiker 2000; Clark 2001; Duffield 2001; Paris 2004; Jabri 2007; Richmond 2007; Pugh, Cooper, and Turner 2008; Mac Ginty 2011; Richmond 2012). Peacebuilding efforts have often led to failure because they focus excessively on the security of the state, rather than on the security of communities and the roles they may hold for the transformation of conflict. Moreover, this type of top-down, state-security-oriented politics tend to make the liberal peace quite dysfunctional and contradictory when it encounters negative responses and reactions from local populations (Mac Ginty 2011), which it frames as counterproductive, rather than as inputs into processes of change and transformation (Kappler 2014a). Far from being voiceless, in other words, local demands and needs are marginalised or ignored by the "expertise" of powerful international and national actors. Even when these latter act in good faith (Lyotard 1988: xi), their conceptualisations of peace mean that peace can only emanate from a secure and strong state. As a result, said approaches are often geared towards "peacefulness" rather than "peace".

Such skewed focus is not entirely inexplicable. The field of international relations was always focused on security and the expectation of violence the term carries (Huysmans 1998), despite the fact that peace has been its main preoccupation ever since its inception. The example of the United Nations and its Security Council is quite indicative. Even though the UN was born with the explicit purpose "to maintain international peace and security" (United Nations 1945: 3), the Security Council (rather than the Peace Council, or the Peace and Security Council) is tasked with responding to war rather than (pro)actively seeking peace. This is significant ontologically and normatively speaking, for "the concept of peace emphasises both the international system as a whole, and individuals as its ultimate building blocks, at the expense of states, and emphasises the dynamic of harmony at the expense of that of conflict" (Buzan 1984: 110). The fact that we never thought of, wrote of, or talked about peace in the same way as we have done about violence and war (Jabri 1996; Richmond 2008a; Dower 2009) has had a significant effect on our attitudes and behaviours. Our students will readily identify Thucydides and Hobbes as the forefathers of realist politics, but are clueless about these writers' preoccupations with peace (Gittings 2012). Similarly, although Erasmus was writing at the same time as Machiavelli, it is the latter's writings that feature prominently in international relations course syllabi.

The first academic calls for a peace research agenda that would move beyond the established preoccupations with power preservation and maximisation that emerged in the late 1960s and early 1970s (Schmid 1968: 221; Caroll 1972: 605). These calls were virtually unheeded, however, until a more solid scholarly movement for the formation and establishment of a critical peace research (CPR) agenda began taking shape in the post-9/11 era (Jutila, Pehkonen, and Väyrynen 2008). Peace, according to critical scholars, is yet another essentially contested concept that is part of various discourses, narratives, and specific theories. As such, it is not much different from terrorism or the intention to frame it as a problem whose solution must be imposed. Of particular significance to terrorism, as it is understood, framed, and conceptualised by orthodox theories, is critical peace agenda's aim to do away with the dichotomies imposed by the liberal-realist paradigm. This allows for a reenvisioning of "peace as a cacophonic and cluttered terrain of political struggle, denoted by multi-layered and discontinuous sites of emergence" (Shinko 2008: 490). This will be possible by unearthing the role that the subaltern and the everyday could have in peace processes.

As such, it bridges earlier calls for research agendas that would focus on "the power and competence of the allegedly powerless" (Reid and Yanarella 1976: 326) or, as Caroll (1972: 605) would have put it, to move away from the blinding light and into the unexplored darkness. It reaffirms its duty to go beyond solving the problem of war and violence and to introduce more interdisciplinary understandings of the diverse concepts, perceptions, and dimensions of peace. It places a much needed emphasis on pluralist ontologies, epistemologies, and methodologies that "should be broadly representative of all actors at multiple levels, public and private, gendered and age, and of multiple identities" (Richmond 2008b: 462).

Considering the aforementioned, it is easy to see why researchers of terrorism – particularly those from fields like sociology, anthropology, and peace studies – have been branded "sympathisers" and/or "defenders" of terrorism by their orthodox counterparts. Nonetheless, if "valid inferences by the systematic use of well-established procedures of inquiry" have yielded "little practical knowledge" so far with regard to making peace (Bleiker 2001: 509), perhaps alternative methods that broaden our understanding may also be useful, without necessarily overthrowing or outcasting conventional scientific methodologies. This is not a call for war between academic fields (much to the disappointment of certain sectors of both terrorism and peace studies; see, in particular, Jones 2015 and Mac Ginty 2014). Instead, it is an effort whose aims are two-fold: on the one hand, to enhance our understandings of terrorism manifestation and, on the other, to better inform policy decisions whose implementations affect the lives of millions and can result in reinforcing the vicious cycle of violence.

Viewed from this perspective, an interconnection between the two fields can be mutually beneficial. On the one hand, terrorism studies may gain significant insights if it distances itself from the vilification of persons or groups that is prevalent among policy circles (Jackson 2007, 2015). Such a distance would offer the field a broader and deeper understanding of motives, structures, hierarchies, ideologies, and dynamics. Moreover, it would allow the ontological, epistemological, and methodological problematisation of the field itself – much like the direction CTS has brought in and now CPR aspires to establish. Doing away with the constructed rigidity of concepts such as "legitimacy", "sovereignty", and "security" may be of significant benefit to the field, particularly with regard to interventions by third parties in terrorist conflicts. Research on the potential of engagement and negotiations with terrorist groups has taken place both before (Zartman 1990) as well as in the immediate aftermath of 9/11 (Lederach 2001a, 2001b), and more recent analyses have shown that such talks do not lead to more violence (Goerzig 2010; Toros 2012; see also Hampson and Zartman 2011; Lederach 2011; Zartman and Faure 2011), as policy myths prescribe. Despite the application of conflict resolution and peacebuilding frameworks on terrorist violence, however, the conceptual and policy pillars of the current war on terror continue to alienate and vilify entire groups and communities (ethnic, religious, social, or other), thus resulting in the reinforcement of frictions and tensions and the perpetuation of violence (Richmond and Franks 2009).

On the other hand, peace studies also stands to gain significant insights from terrorism studies. As mentioned, the circumstances that lead to the splintering of armed groups could be one such area where expertise from terrorism studies can be of great benefit to scholars of peace and practitioners of conflict resolution alike. The same goes for the constant evolution of terrorist groups and the psychological mechanisms behind recruitment, radicalisation, and de-radicalisation (Horgan 2005, 2009): how do the internal dynamics of a terrorist group affect processes of engagement for peace and windows for negotiation? Addressing the issue of constituencies and civil society, social movement, and anthropological research on terrorism could have a catalytic effect on how peace is conceptualised by the networks of people that surround terrorist groups (Bosi and della Porta 2015). Perhaps most important, however, is the question of symmetry. Terrorist conflicts are asymmetrical by definition, yet the opposite is true for most frameworks of conflict transformation and resolution. Even critical peace research, as highlighted previously, seeks to be as inclusive and representative as possible, but there are serious questions as to how one can navigate through the power relations across all levels (group, local, national, and international) without creating false symmetries.

Conclusion

The previous discussion has made clear that a relationship between terrorism studies and peace studies has always existed, despite the former breaking away from conflict studies early on and skewing its findings in order to favour and facilitate hard security responses (Richmond 2003). Early traditional or orthodox understandings of what terrorist violence is also informed (and continues to do so in cases) understandings of what peace should be. The central core of traditionalist approaches in both fields concerns the security of the state through the elimination of actors and agendas that question and oppose its legitimacy. In many cases, such opposition is generated by the behaviour of the state itself and its dominance-seeking policies. This has been quite evident in instances where the "terrorist" label has been applied not only to extremist actors but also moderate, nonviolent groups that sought to rectify grievances caused by states' policies. This has been true in autocratic and totalitarian regimes as much as it has been in liberal democratic states like the United Kingdom, the United States, Spain, and elsewhere. If terrorism seeks to destroy the guarantor of security, stability, and prosperity that is the state, it then follows that peace will emerge when the state defeats terrorist organisations.

In too many cases, however, the state behaved no differently than the terrorists themselves, with extrajudicial killings, paramilitary organisations, fabrication of accusations, distortion, and/or prevention of justice and measures of general oppression. Peace, therefore, was synonymous with the absence of violence, and even the absence of opposition (see Loadenthal 2013 for an excellent analysis of how domestic anti-terrorist legislation was utilised and promoted by specific business interests).

The emergence of critical voices in both scholarly fields has reinvigorated the interconnection between terrorism and peace research. Just like CTS questioned the lack of epistemological reflexivity that led to terrorism being perceived ontologically as a brute fact or an ideology (Jackson et al. 2011), CPR is also questioning the concepts of peace, legitimacy, sovereignty, and security. One might claim that the two critical strands share the same links as their traditionalist counterparts, but this time in an inverted fashion: rather than seeing terrorism or violence as a problem that needs to be solved, critical approaches stress the need for a holistic understanding that moves beyond and outside the nexus between knowledge and power. Both fields, moreover, share the understanding that any type of violence – whether structural or direct, whether by state or non-state actors – is a manifestation of power. As such, it should not be condemned without prior understanding of the reasons, the issues, the dynamics, and the ideologies behind said manifestations. Furthermore, both CPR and CTS stress the importance of recognising subjectivity when analysing both the actors and the use(s) of the concepts. In fact, CTS scholars have explicitly called for more application of peace studies to terrorism studies (Jackson 2012) and for the exploration of nonviolent responses to terrorism (Jackson 2012; see also Martin 2002; Hastings 2004; Hampson and Zartman 2011; Lederach 2011).

At first glance, therefore, the trajectory of both fields seems complementary – perhaps even co-constitutive. Critical approaches to terrorism, with their focus on cosmopolitan solutions to conflict and their potential for a more effective peace at the everyday level, seem more appropriate for liberal peacebuilding approaches (Richmond and Tellidis 2012). Nevertheless, certain differentiations do exist between the two camps. For example, even though it is accepted that CTS scholars have widened and deepened the study of terrorism, their use (and therefore legitimation) of the very term has been criticised because it perpetuates the term's association with state projects of counterinsurgency and counterterrorism, and therefore human rights abuses (Mac Ginty 2014). Furthermore, despite its suitability for peacebuilding approaches, CTS cannot sufficiently distance itself from the normative role of the state, thus favouring state and formal actors at the expense of the local/everyday strata (Tellidis 2011; Richmond and Tellidis 2012). This point, of course, is not entirely irrelevant to peace studies. Peace scholars have also questioned the extent to which their research can go beyond the role of the state and what the possibilities are for post-state alternatives (Boege 2014; Kappler 2014b).

In other words, the commonalities between the two fields are not exhausted in the way(s) they tackle peace, conflict, and terrorism in conceptual, epistemological, ontological, and methodological terms. Rather, these commonalities include the obstacles and problems that both fields encounter and will continue to encounter in the future. Such obstacles involve the need for more inclusive and participatory forms of research between the global north and the global south in ways that do not "merely reconstitute an essentially neo-colonial relationship" (Richmond and Mac Ginty 2014: 13–14). The political economies of research in the global north, and the ways in which they often contradict and subvert the aims and objectives of research, are of equal importance (Richmond and Mac Ginty 2014: 14). With emancipation as their focus (see Lindahl, this volume), both CTS and CPR future research should explore further the questions raised by negotiations with armed actors. For example, how can one measure the effect they may have on peace movements and the extent to which these latter accept said negotiations as legitimate (Toros 2015)? Consequently, but equally significantly, could said negotiations be (or be seen to be) yet another tool of imposition of the global north's perceptions of a liberal peace?

More significantly, a key issue for research from both fields should concentrate on ways that can encourage positive peace as the reversal of structural violence, which, as Gleditsch et al. (2014) have shown, is not as popular a topic as it used to be. Research on nonviolence is a crucial step towards that, but it must go beyond the extent to which it simply reduces the likelihood of violence (Gleditsch et al. 2014) and interprets peace as non-war (Jabri 1996). Finally, and considering the advances and insights of feminist studies on the topics of conflict and violence, more gendered perspectives should also be sought if we are to enhance our understanding of how terrorism and peace affect and are perceived by a core segment of the local/everyday (see Gentry and Sjoberg, this volume).

While it is true that systematic research on the interconnection between terrorism and peace has only taken off after 9/11, the previous discussion indicates that we can afford to be pragmatically optimistic about developments in both fields. As described earlier, the obstacles and pitfalls for research in both terrorism studies and peace studies will be significant, but that is part and parcel of academic research, progress, and emancipation, particularly as envisaged by critical theories. The emergence of both fields was important, and their acute relevance has contributed to their establishment. Their evolution and development, however, will depend on the degree of commitment to self-reflection and perseverance to influence everyday-affecting policies. If not, both fields will risk becoming irrelevant, at best, or, at worst, nothing more than an exercise in debating and/or purposeless academic gatherings.

Notes

1 This chapter draws upon writings that first appeared in Tellidis 2015.
2 For anthropological studies, see Leach (1977), Zulaika and Douglass (1996), and Sluka (2009). For social movement studies, see della Porta (1995), Irvin (1999), and Gunning (2009). For peace studies, see Azar (1990), Burton (1990a, 1990b), Lederach (1997), Francis (2002), Richmond (2003), and Franks (2006).
3 It must be noted, however, that scholars have expressed their reservations about this observation. See Wilkinson in Schorkopf (2004), Silke (2004: 27), and Gordon (2005, 2007).
4 One could in fact argue that "homegrown terrorism" re-emerged, since it predated 9/11 but never attracted much anti-terrorist commitment until 9/11.

References

Azar, E., 1990. *The Management of Protracted Social Conflict: Theory and Cases*, Aldershot: Dartmouth.
Bjørgo, T., ed., 2005. *Root Causes of Terrorism*. Abingdon: Routledge.
Bleiker, R., 2000. *Popular Dissent, Human Agency and Global Politics*, Manchester: Cambridge University Press.
Bleiker, R., 2001. "The Aesthetic Turn in International Political Theory", *Millennium*, 30(3): 509–533.
Bloom, M., 2005. *Dying to Kill: The Allure of Suicide Terror*, New York: Columbia University Press.
Boege, V., 2014. "Roundtable: Building a Peaceful State – Desirable? Why? Possible? How?", 3rd Annual Conference, International Association of Peace and Conflict Studies, University of Manchester, 12 September.
Bosi, L., and della Porta, D., 2015. "Processes of Disengagement from Political Violence: A Multi-Level Relational Approach", in Tellidis, I., and Toros, H., eds., *Researching Terrorism, Peace and Conflict Studies: Interaction, Synthesis and Opposition*, London: Routledge, pp. 81–98.
Breen-Smyth, M., 2008. "Geographies of Conflict: Meanings and Effects of Political Violence", International Studies Association annual convention, San Francisco, March 28.
Brzezinski, Z., 2007. "Terrorized by 'War on Terror'", *Washington Post*, 25 March, available online at: www.washingtonpost.com/wp-dyn/content/article/2007/03/23/AR2007032301613.html [accessed 25 May 2014].
Burton, J., 1990a. *Conflict: Resolution and Prevention*, London: Macmillan.
Burton, J., ed., 1990b. *Conflict: Human Needs Theory*, London: Macmillan.
Buzan, B., 1984. "Peace, Power and Security: Contending Concepts in the Study of International Relations", *Journal of Peace Research*, 21(2): 109–125.
Caroll, B., 1972. "Peace Research: The Cult of Power", *Journal of Conflict Resolution*, 16(4): 585–616.
Clark, I., 2001. *The Post-Cold War Order: Spoils of Peace*, Oxford: Oxford University Press.
della Porta, D., 1995. *Social Movements, Political Violence and the State: A Comparative Analysis of Italy and Germany*, Cambridge: Cambridge University Press.
Dower, N., 2009. *The Ethics of War and Peace*, London: Polity Press.
Duffield, M., 2001. *Global Governance and the New Wars: The Merging of Development and Security*, London: Zed Books.
English, R., 2009. *Terrorism: How to Respond*, Oxford: Oxford University Press.
Fisher, K., 2013. "Exploring the Temporality in/of British Counterterrorism Law and Law Making", *Critical Studies on Terrorism*, 6(1): 50–72.
Francis, D., 2002. *People, Peace and Power: Conflict Transformation in Action*, London: Pluto Press.
Franks, J., 2006. *Rethinking the Roots of Terrorism*, London: Palgrave.
Gittings, J., 2012. *The Glorious Art of Peace: From the Iliad to Iraq*, Oxford: Oxford University Press.
Gleditsch, N. P., Jonas, N., and Håvard, S., 2014. "Peace Research – Just the Study of War?", *Journal of Peace Research*, 51(2): 145–158.
Goerzig, C., 2010. *Talking to Terrorists: Concessions and the Renunciation of Violence*, Abingdon: Routledge.
Goodin, R., 2006. *What's Wrong with Terrorism?*, Cambridge: Polity.

Gordon, A., 2005. "Terrorism as an Academic Subject after 9/11: Searching the Internet Reveals a Stockholm Syndrome Trend", *Studies in Conflict and Terrorism*, 28(1): 45–60.

Gordon, A., 2007. "Transient and Continuant Authors in a Research Field: The Case of Terrorism", *Scientometrics*, 72(2): 213–224.

Groom, A., 1978. "Coming to Terms with Terrorism", *British Journal of International Studies*, 4: 62–77.

Gunning, J., 2009. "Social Movement Theory and the Study of Terrorism", in Jackson, R., Breen Smyth, M., and Gunning, J., eds., *Critical Terrorism Studies: A New Research Agenda*, Abingdon: Routledge, pp. 156–177.

Hampson, F., and Zartman, I., 2011. *The Global Power of Talk: Negotiating America's Interests*, Boulder, CO: Paradigm Publishers.

Haspeslagh, S., 2013. "'Listing Terrorists': The Impact of Proscription on Third-Party Efforts to Engage Armed Groups in Peace Processes – a Practitioner's Perspective", *Critical Studies on Terrorism*, 6(1): 189–208.

Hastings, T., 2004. *Nonviolent Response to Terrorism*, Jefferson, NC: McFarland and Company.

Hoffman, B., 1992. "Low-intensity Conflict: Terrorism and Guerrilla Warfare in the Coming Decades", in Howard, L., ed., *Terrorism: Roots, Impact, Responses*, New York: Praeger, pp. 139–54.

Horgan, J., 2005. *The Psychology of Terrorism*, London: Routledge.

Horgan, J., 2009. *Walking Away from Terrorism: Accounts of Disengagement from Radical and Extremist Movements*, London: Routledge.

Horgan, J., and Boyle, M., 2008. "A Case Against 'Critical Terrorism Studies'", *Critical Studies on Terrorism*, 1(1): 51–64.

Huysmans, J., 1998. "Security! What do You Mean? From Concept to Thick Signifier", *European Journal of International Relations*, 4(2): 41–62.

Irvin, C., 1999. *Militant Nationalism: Between Movement and Party in Ireland and the Basque Country*, Minneapolis: University of Minnesota Press.

Jabri, V., 1996. *Discourses on Violence: Conflict Analysis Reconsidered*, Manchester: Manchester University Press.

Jabri, V., 2007. *War and the Transformation of Global Politics*, London: Palgrave.

Jackson, R., 2007. "The Core Commitments of Critical Terrorism Studies", *European Political Science*, 6(3): 244–251.

Jackson, R., 2009. "Knowledge, Power and Politics in the Study of Political Terrorism", in Jackson, R., Breen Smyth, M., and Gunning, J., eds., *Critical Terrorism Studies: A New Research Agenda*, Abingdon: Routledge, pp. 66–83.

Jackson, R., 2012. "Unknown Knowns: The Subjugated Knowledge of Terrorism Studies", *Critical Studies on Terrorism*, 5(1): 11–29.

Jackson, R., 2015. "Towards Critical Peace Research: Lessons from Critical Terrorism Studies" in Tellidis, I., and Toros, H., eds., *Researching Terrorism, Peace and Conflict Studies: Interaction, Synthesis and Opposition*, London: Routledge, pp. 19–37.

Jackson, R., Jarvis, L., Gunning, J., and Breen Smyth, M., 2011. *Terrorism: A Critical Introduction*, London: Palgrave.

Jones, D., 2015. "The Trouble with Empathising with Terrorists: Critical Theory and Terrorism", in Tellidis, I., and Toros, H., eds., *Researching Terrorism, Peace and Conflict Studies: Interaction, Synthesis and Opposition*, London: Routledge, pp. 38–63.

Jones, S., and Libicki, M., 2008. *How Terrorist Groups End: Lessons for Countering Al Qa'ida*, Santa Monica, CA: RAND Corporation.

Jutila, M., Pehkonen, S., and Väyrynen, T., 2008. "Resuscitating a Discipline: An Agenda for Critical Peace Research", *Millennium*, 36(3): 623–640.

Kappler, S., 2014a. *Local Agency and Peacebuilding: EU and International Engagement in Bosnia-Herzegovina, Cyprus and South Africa*, London: Palgrave.

Kappler, S., 2014b. "Roundtable: Building a Peaceful State – Desirable? Why? Possible? How?", 3rd Annual Conference, International Association of Peace and Conflict Studies, University of Manchester, 12 September.

Laqueur, W., 1986. "Reflections on Terrorism", *Foreign Affairs*, 65: 86–100.

Leach, E., 1977. *Custom, Law and Terrorist Violence*, Edinburgh: Edinburgh University Press.

Lederach, J., 1997. *Building Peace*, Washington, DC: United States Institute of Peace.

Lederach, J., 2001a. *The Challenge of Terror: A Traveling Essay*, available online at: www.emu.edu/cjp/publications/beyond-september-11th/2001/the-challenge-of-terror/ [accessed 7 December 2014].

Lederach, J., 2001b. *Quo vadis? Reframing terror from the perspective of conflict resolution*, available online at: www.mediate.com/articles/lederach2.cfm [accessed 7 December 2014].

Lederach, J., 2011. "Addressing Terrorism: A Theory of Change Approach", in Life and Peace Institute, ed., *Somalia: Creating Space for Fresh Approaches to Peacebuilding*, Uppsala: Life and Peace Institute, pp. 7–19.

Loadenthal, M., 2013. "Deconstructing 'Eco-Terrorism': Rhetoric, Framing and Statecraft as Seen Through the Insight Approach", *Critical Studies on Terrorism*, 6(1): 92–117.

Lyotard, J., 1988. *The Differend: Phrases in Dispute*, translated by Georges Van Den Abeele, Manchester: Manchester University Press.

Mac Ginty, R., 2011. *International Peacebuilding and Local Resistance: Hybrid Forms of Peace*, London: Palgrave.

Mac Ginty, R., 2014. "Against Critical Terrorism Studies: Don't give it the oxygen of publicity", unpublished manuscript.

Mac Ginty, R., and Richmond, O., 2013. "The Local Turn in Peacebuilding: A Critical Agenda for Peace", *Third World Quarterly*, 34(5): 763–783.

Malik, O., 2000. *Enough of the Definition of Terrorism*, London: Royal Institute of International Affairs.

Martin, B., 2002. "Nonviolence Versus Terrorism", *Social Alternatives*, 21(2): 6–9.

Neumann, P., and Smith, M., 2008. *The Strategy of Terrorism: How it Works and Why it Fails*, London: Routledge.

Paris, R., 2004. *At War's End*, Cambridge: Cambridge University Press.

Pugh, M., Cooper, N., and Turner, M., 2008. *Whose Peace? Critical Perspectives on the Political Economy of Peacebuilding*, London: Palgrave.

Ranstorp, M., 2007. *Mapping Terrorism Research. State of the Art, Gaps and Future Direction*. Abingdon: Routledge.

Reid, H., and Yanarella, E., 1976. "Toward a Theory of Critical Peace Research in the United States: The Search for an 'Intelligible Core'", *Journal of Peace Research*, 13(4): 315–341.

Richmond, O., 2003. "Realizing Hegemony? Symbolic Terrorism and the Roots of Conflict", *Studies in Conflict and Terrorism*, 26(4): 289–309.

Richmond, O., 2007. *The Transformation of Peace*, London: Palgrave.

Richmond, O., 2008a. *Peace in International Relations*, Abingdon: Routledge.

Richmond, O., 2008b. "Reclaiming Peace in International Relations", *Millennium*, 36(3): 439–470.

Richmond, O., 2012. *A Post-Liberal Peace*, London: Routledge.

Richmond, O., and Franks, J., 2009. "The Impact of Orthodox Terrorism Discourses on the Liberal Peace: Internalisation, Resistance or Hybridisation?", *Critical Studies on Terrorism*, 2(2): 201–218.

Richmond, O., and Mac Ginty, R., 2014. "Where now for the critique of the liberal peace?", *Cooperation and Conflict*, published online before print, 20 August, DOI: 10.1177/0010836714545691.

Richmond, O., and Tellidis, I., 2012. "The Complex Relationship between Peacebuilding and Terrorism Approaches: Towards Post-Terrorism and a Post-liberal Peace?", *Terrorism and Political Violence*, 24(1): 120–143.

Sageman, M., 2015. "The Stagnation in Terrorism Research", *Terrorism and Political Violence*, 26(4): 565–580.

Schmid, A., and Jongman, A., 2008. *Political Terrorism: A New Guide to Actors, Authors, Concepts, Data Bases, Theories and Literature*, [3rd ed.] New Brunswick, NJ: Transaction Publishers.

Schmid, A. P., 2011. *The Routledge Handbook of Terrorism Research*, Abingdon: Routledge.

Schmid, H., 1968. "Peace Research and Politics", *Journal of Peace Research*, 5(3): 217–232.

Schorkopf, F., 2004. "Behavioural and Social Science Perspectives on Political Violence", in Walter, C., Vöneky, S., Röben, V., and Schorkopf, F., eds., *Terrorism as a Challenge for National and International Law: Security versus Liberty?*, Berlin: Springer, pp. 3–22.

Shinko, R., 2008. "Agonistic Peace: A Postmodern Reading", *Millennium: Journal of International Studies*, 36(3): 473–491.

Silke, A., ed., 2004. *Research on Terrorism: Trends, Achievements, Failures*, London: Frank Cass.

Sluka, J., 2009. "The Contribution of Anthropology to Critical Terrorism Studies", in Jackson, R., Breen Smyth, M., and Gunning, J., eds., *Critical Terrorism Studies: A New Research Agenda*, Abingdon: Routledge, pp. 137–155.

Stampnitzky, L., 2013. *Disciplining Terror: How Experts Invented "Terrorism"*, Cambridge: Cambridge University Press.

Tellidis, I., 2010. "Terrorist Conflict vs. Civil Peace in the Basque Country", in Richmond, O., ed., *Palgrave Advances in Peacebuilding: Critical Developments and Approaches*, Basingstoke: Palgrave, pp. 415–38.

Tellidis, I., 2011. "Orthodox, Criticals and the Missing Context: Basque Civil Society Reaction(s) to Terrorism", *Critical Studies on Terrorism*, 4(2): 181–197.

Tellidis, I., 2015. "Researching Terrorism, Peace and Conflict: An Introduction", in Tellidis, I., and Toros, H., eds., *Researching Terrorism, Peace and Conflict Studies: Interaction, Synthesis and Opposition*, London: Routledge, pp. 1–15.

Tellidis, I., and Toros, H., eds., 2015. *Researching Terrorism, Peace and Conflict Studies: Interaction, Synthesis and Opposition*, London: Routledge.

Toros, H., 2012. *Terrorism, Talking and Transformation: A Critical Approach*, London: Routledge.

Toros, H., 2015. "Terrorism Studies, Critical Terrorism Studies and Peace Studies: A Vibrant Intersection of a Cul-de-sac?", in Tellidis, I., and Toros, H., eds., *Researching Terrorism, Peace and Conflict Studies: Interaction, Synthesis and Opposition*, London: Routledge, pp. 221–226.

Toros, H., and Tellidis, I., eds., 2014. *Terrorism, Peace and Conflict Studies: Investigating the Crossroad*, London: Routledge.

United Nations, 1945. *Charter of the United Nations*, 24 October 1945, 1 UNTS XVI, available online at: https://treaties.un.org/doc/publication/ctc/uncharter.pdf [accessed 30 July 2014].

Walter, E., 1969. *Terror and Resistance: A Study of Political Violence with Case Studies of Some Primitive African Communities*, New York; London: Oxford University Press.

Weinberg, L., and Eubank, W., 2008. "Problems with the Critical Studies Approach to the Study of Terrorism", *Critical Studies on Terrorism*, 1(2): 185–195.

Weinberg, L., Pedahzur, A., and Perliger, A., 1992. *Political Parties and Terrorist Groups*, London: Frank Cass.

Wilkinson, P., 2001. *Terrorism Versus Democracy: The Liberal State Response*, London: Franc Cass.

Wilkinson, P., and Stewart, A., eds., 1987. *Contemporary Research on Terrorism*, Aberdeen: Aberdeen University Press.

Wyn Jones, R., 1999. *Security, Strategy and Critical Theory*, Boulder, CO: Lynne Rienner.

Zartman, I., 1990. "Negotiating Effectively with Terrorists", in Rubin, B., ed., *The Politics of Counterterrorism: The Ordeal of Democratic States*, Washington: Foreign Policy Institute, pp. 163–188.

Zartman, I., and Faure, G., eds., 2011. *Engaging Extremists: Trade-offs, Timing and Diplomacy*, Washington DC: United States Institute of Peace.

Zulaika, J., and Douglass, W., 1996. *Terror and Taboo: The Follies, Fables and Faces of Terrorism*, London: Routledge.

INDEX

Aberystwyth School/Welsh School 55, 71, 74, 210
Abu Ghraib 1, 31, 141, 216, 219, 229, 241
Afghanistan 43, 118, 138, 147, 182, 193, 196, 203, 206–7, 209, 225–33, 237, 280
African National Congress (ANC) 128
Agamben, Giorgio 45, 64–5
Al-Awlaki, Anwar 191–2, 194
Al-Gama'a al-Islamiyya 130
Al-Qaeda 8, 43, 46, 73, 77, 109, 115, 117–18, 124–6, 129, 131, 141, 147, 167, 182, 190–1, 194, 207, 240, 265, 267, 270, 280–1, 291
Al Qaida in Mesopotamia (AQIM) 230, 232
Al Shabaab 35, 190, 282
Al-Zawahiri, Ayman 43, 226–7
Améry, Jean 172, 177
anarchists 125, 127, 129, 130, 268
Andrabi, Aysia 148–9
Animal Agriculture Alliance (AAA) 264–5
Animal Enterprise Terrorism Act (AETA) 271–2
Animal Liberation Front (ALF) 265, 267, 270
anthrax 106, 283–4
Arafat, Yassir 300
Argentina 162
assassins 125, 127
Aum Shinrikyo 128
Australia 7, 34, 114–17, 184, 207–8, 226, 243–4, 267
Automated Targeting System (ATS) 65–6

Baghdad 228–9
Bagram 64
bare life 64, 68
Basque 5, 39, 128, 139, 146
Beck, Ulrich 238–9
Belhadj, Abdel Hakim 185
Benjamin, Walter 64
Bergen, Peter 43

bin Laden, Osama 43, 108, 114–15, 191, 195, 197, 209, 225–7, 231
BISA 1, 3, 28
Blind Sheikh 42–3
Boko Haram 35, 225, 232
Booth, Ken 71, 74–6, 219–20
Breivik, Anders 138
Britain 230, 256, 268, 283, 292
Bush, George 28, 45, 61, 114, 120, 177, 182, 191, 193–4, 196, 198, 207, 216, 225, 227–8, 230, 232–3
Bybee Memorandum 171, 177

causes (of terrorism) 4–7, 21–2, 31–2, 67, 75, 124, 147, 205, 219, 248–9, 251–5, 257
Central Intelligence Agency (CIA) 43, 85, 118, 138, 162, 164–5, 170–1, 174, 181–7, 192–6, 226
Charlie Hebdo 41, 57, 170, 197, 276, 279, 283
Chechnya/Chechen 147–8, 150
Cheney doctrine 46
Chile 85, 162, 164, 166
China 103, 226
Chomsky, Noam 85, 108, 159, 160
clash of civilisations 137, 235
climate change 10, 117, 238–9, 265, 271–2
Cold War 3, 6, 8, 28, 44, 62, 81, 94, 120, 159–60, 162, 164–6, 211, 233, 299
collective intellectual 10
Colombia 32, 73, 86, 94, 147, 166
CONTEST 93
Contras 85
Convention Against Torture (CAT) 162, 171, 241
Cox, Robert 49
critical discourse analysis (CDA) 93–4, 204–6, 210, 215
critical security studies (CSS) 1, 33, 52, 56, 71, 74, 210

309

Critical Studies on Terrorism 1, 28, 34–5, 49, 52, 54–5, 217, 233
critical theory 2–4, 33, 54–5, 70–8, 206, 216, 220
CSTWG 1, 10
Cyprus 126, 137–8, 292

de Menezes, Jean Charles 65
Department of Homeland Security 65, 118, 215, 271
Derrida, Jacques 46, 63–4, 205–6, 296
Dershowitz, Alan 173–8, 186, 216
De Saussure, Ferdinand 60
Dev Sol 72
dialogue 8, 74–5, 77–8, 125, 205–6, 214, 250, 283

emancipation 4, 30, 33, 54, 70–1, 74–8, 95, 210, 217–22, 304
EOKA 126, 138, 292–3, 296
Euskadi Ta Askatasuna (ETA) 39, 72, 115, 124, 128, 138–9, 146, 195
Ewald, François 238–9
expertise 2–3, 10, 17–19, 21, 23–6, 30, 50, 242, 301, 303
extrajudicial killings 5, 45, 303

Fallujah 75, 229
FBI 39–41, 43, 47, 264–8, 270
fear 4, 8, 30, 41, 44–6, 53, 107, 118, 135, 137, 146–7, 149, 159, 161–2, 165–6, 176, 178, 186–7, 194–5, 237–42, 244–5, 263, 266, 268–70, 272, 278, 280, 282, 300
Federally Administered Tribal Areas (FATA) 193
Fort Dix 109
Foucault, Michel 63, 65, 204–6, 239–40
France 57, 128, 146, 197, 226, 228, 282
Frankfurt cell 227
Frankfurt School 33, 70–1, 74–5, 83
Front for the Liberation of Quebec (FLQ) 72

Gäfgen, Maguns 176
Galtung, Johan 76, 289
Global South 9, 31, 167, 217, 234, 304
governmentality 7, 65–6, 237–41, 243, 245, 255
Guantanamo Bay 45, 64, 121, 141, 178, 182, 196, 216, 229, 241
Guatemala 85, 161, 164–5

Halbwachs, Maurice 287–8, 290, 292, 294–6
hearts and minds 71, 74
Hezbollah 131
Hoffman, Bruce 25, 71, 125, 127, 130, 137
Holder, Eric 40
Home Office 57, 66, 235, 256
Horkheimer, Max 70, 75
human rights 6, 8, 32, 86, 118, 163, 165–7, 174, 181, 187, 192, 194, 219, 304
human security 137, 192, 219–20, 298
Hussein, Saddam 39–40, 73, 117, 204–5, 225, 228

immanent critique 54, 221
Indonesia 118, 184, 229
inequality 10, 21, 82, 98, 137, 238
International Human Rights Law (IHRL) 162, 173
International Security Assistance Force (ISAF) 227, 229
Inter-service Intelligence Agency (Pakistan) 226
interstitial space 23, 50
Iran 40, 128, 166, 225, 227–8
Iraq 39–40, 46, 64, 73, 117–18, 129, 147, 163, 176, 182, 193, 195–7, 203–4, 206, 209–10, 219, 225–6, 228–33, 235, 237, 280
Irish Republican Army (IRA) 115, 124, 126, 138, 195, 281–2
Islamic State/ISIS 1, 8, 41, 56–7, 117, 130, 141, 176, 190, 193, 195, 225–6, 232, 234, 281
Israel 7, 19, 34, 97–8, 115–16, 118, 121, 126, 129, 174–5, 190, 195, 197, 216, 227, 229, 232, 279
Israeli state terrorism 7

Jema'ah Islamiyah 118
Jenkins, Brian 25, 127

Kaczynski, Ted 41
Kunming massacre 103
Kurdistan Workers' Party (PKK) 128

Lebanon 128
Lewthwaite, Samantha 145, 148–9
Lithuania 182–4
Lockerbie 128
London 40, 65–6, 104, 148, 186, 229, 241, 248, 266, 281–2, 284
Lord's Resistance Army 35
Luxor 130

Marxism 82, 84, 86–7, 125, 277, 284, 299
Marx, Karl 74, 80–2, 84
Mau Mau 164
May, Theresa 40
Mayer, Arno 84–5
McVeigh, Timothy 54–6, 83
meta-theory 82
MI5 185–6
MI6 185
minimal foundationalism 54–6, 83
Mohamed, Binyam 186
moral panic 281

Nairobi 145
narrative 4–6, 10, 40, 44, 50, 54, 56, 62, 67, 71, 80, 85–6, 97, 114–21, 131–2, 136, 139, 141, 148–9, 167, 209, 217, 221, 239–40, 245, 254, 263, 272, 278, 283–4, 287, 290–5, 299–300, 302
National Security Agency (NSA) 117–18, 238, 243–4
naturalism 51, 53

Index

neoliberal(ism) 4, 7–8, 65–6, 81, 86, 160, 164, 166–7, 234, 244–5, 270, 293
new terrorism thesis 4, 53, 115, 124–32, 139, 146, 215
New York 39–40, 43, 47, 227, 229, 232, 265
9/11 1–4, 7, 9, 23, 25, 28, 32, 40, 42–3, 53, 62, 103–5, 108–9, 116, 118–19, 129, 135, 137, 140–1, 182, 186, 203, 205–6, 208–11, 217–18, 225–30, 232–3, 235, 239–42, 265–7, 270, 280–4, 290–1, 298–302, 304–5
no-fly list 241–2
nonviolence/nonviolent 8, 75–6, 116, 118–19, 134, 214, 217–19, 231, 249, 251, 253, 255, 265, 267, 272, 303–4
Northern Ireland 32, 137–8, 203, 281
Norway 34, 92

Obama, Barack 31–2, 114, 178, 191–4, 196, 198, 209, 216, 225, 230–1, 241
Oklahoma City bombing 126, 138, 289–91
orthodox terrorism studies 2, 6, 18, 29–30, 32, 49–50, 204, 215, 220, 300
Osman, Hussein 65

Pakistan 32, 34, 47, 118, 146–7, 153, 184, 186, 191, 193, 196, 225–7, 229–31
Palestine/Palestinian 7, 19, 97–8, 115, 118, 121, 126, 129, 147, 195, 232, 237
Palestine Liberation Organization (PLO) 131
Paris 41, 104, 197, 276, 279
Patriot Act 64
PETA 266–7, 270
Philippines 32, 34, 85, 164
political economy 28, 31, 86, 239
political violence 5, 9, 11, 19, 21–2, 24–6, 50, 52–3, 55–6, 75, 87, 104, 137, 139, 147–53, 209, 225, 248–50, 268, 287–8, 298
post-9/11 1, 8, 24, 39, 44, 51–2, 103, 119, 134, 206, 208–9, 300, 302
post-traumatic stress disorder (PTSD) 194, 295
PREVENT 57, 66, 68, 256
Prevention of Terrorism Act 117
privacy 8, 117, 243
private security companies/agents/forces 9, 161
problem-solving 28, 30, 49–50, 52–3, 219–21, 300

Rahman, Omar Abdul 42–3
Red Army Faction (RAF) 124, 126, 128, 131, 162
Red Brigades 115, 126
Rendition Project, The 6–7, 32, 181, 187, 217
resistance 5, 7, 8–10, 78, 86, 97, 112, 163, 166, 209, 210, 229
Revolutionary Armed Forces of Colombia (FARC) 86, 147
right-wing extremism/terrorism 68, 270–1, 290

ritual 41–2, 46
Robespierre, Maximilien 85

Sandinista National Liberation Front (SNFL) 85
Schmitt, Carl 64
7/7 148, 284
Shining Path 147
signature strikes 196, 198
signifier 3, 57, 60, 63, 290–1
Sikh 128
sovereign power 63, 65–6, 238–40, 242, 244–5
Spain 115, 128, 138–9, 146, 195, 228, 284, 303
Sri Lanka 72, 127–8, 137–8, 147
Stimson Report, The 195
structural violence 76–7, 289, 304
suspect communities 8, 54, 249, 255–6
Syria 1, 147, 166, 176, 184, 193, 210, 219, 225, 227, 231–2

taboo 2, 7, 17–18, 25, 29, 42, 46, 215, 220
Taliban 138, 147, 182, 207, 225, 227, 229–30, 232
Tamil Tigers (LTTE) 72, 126–8, 138, 147
terrorism industry 1, 3, 18, 30, 43, 85, 263, 272–3
trauma 46, 196, 279, 282, 294–6
Twitter 278, 282

Unabomber 41, 46
United Kingdom 34, 93, 181, 184, 186, 207, 243, 303
United Nations Security Council 139
United States 4, 10, 18, 34, 39, 43, 46, 53, 64, 72–3, 82, 85, 94, 117, 120–1, 129, 137, 170, 178, 181–2, 184, 186, 190, 196–8, 206–8, 217, 227, 229–33, 241, 243–4, 248, 264–6, 270–1, 280, 290, 303
USS Cole 109

Van Gogh, Theo 66

Walzer, Michael 107, 173–4, 177
waterboarding 171, 183
weapons of mass destruction (WMD) 39–40, 114–16, 121, 127–8, 178, 227–8
Weather Underground 72, 254
Wendt, Alexander 61
Western foreign policy 5, 167, 219
Westgate Mall hostage crisis 282
Wikileaks 280
Wilkinson, Paul 71–3, 139
World War II 62, 110, 159, 280

Xinjiang 103

Yemen 109, 147, 184, 191, 196–7, 225, 229, 232